Máire Devlin Quinn and Derval McGrath

DEUTSCH KOMPLETT

Access your eBook

Scratch to reveal your **eBook Licence Code**:

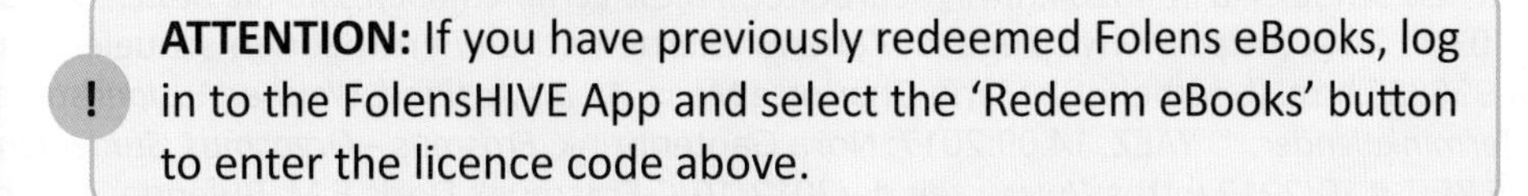

! **ATTENTION:** If you have previously redeemed Folens eBooks, log in to the FolensHIVE App and select the 'Redeem eBooks' button to enter the licence code above.

Follow these steps if it is your first time to redeem an eBook:

1. Go to www.folenshive.ie
2. Click on **Register as Student** and fill in the form
3. You will need your Parent/Legal Guardian's email address to register
4. Your Parent/Legal Guardian must grant permission before you can log in
5. Download the FolensHIVE app from the app store and log in
6. Select the 'Redeem eBooks' button to enter the licence code above

The listening activities to accompany this book are available as podcasts. Visit folensonline.ie/podcasts to access the podcast on your preferred device.

Leaving Certificate German Ordinary and Higher Levels

2nd Edition

First published in 2019 by Folens Publishers
Hibernian Industrial Estate, Greenhills Road, Tallaght, Dublin 24

© Máire Devlin Quinn and Derval McGrath, 2019

Illustrations: Illustrated by 081 Simon (KJA Artists) and Dusan Lakicevic (Beehive Illustration)

ISBN 978-1-78927-013-6

All rights reserved. No part of this publication may be reproduced, stored in a retrieval system or transmitted in any form or by any means, electronic, mechanical, photocopying, recording or otherwise, for whatever purpose, without the prior written permission of the publisher, or a licence permitting restricted copying in Ireland issued by the Irish Copyright Licensing Agency, 63 Patrick Street, Dún Laoghaire, Co. Dublin.

To the best of the publisher's knowledge, information in this book was correct at the time of going to press. No responsibility can be taken for any errors.

The FOLENS company name and associated logos are trademarks of Folens Publishers, registered in Ireland and other countries.

Acknowledgements

Karin Ernst, *Neue Nachbarn*, e-stories.de website; Elisabeth Schwiontek, *Ausgehen unter 18 – so feiern Jugendliche*, © www.pasch-net.de – die Website der Initiative „Schulen: Partner der Zukunft" (PASCH); *Mein Sohn schwänzt die Schule*, © Michael Felten, Kolumne „Schulfrage" bei ZEIT Online, 18.01.2018; *Wie bekomme ich Lust auf Lernen*, ABItipps.de website (https://abitipps.de/schriftliche-pruefungen/effektives-lernen/generelle-lerntipps/); Bernd Kramer, *Diese Fremdsprachen lernen Europas Schüler*, SPIEGEL ONLINE, 27.08.2015 (http://www.spiegel.de/lebenundlernen/schule/europa-diese-fremdsprachen-lernen-schueler-a-1046284.html (bearbeitet)); *Diese Lernmethoden sind die besten*, © Carola Padtberg, SPIEGEL ONLINE, 03.11.2014 (http://www.spiegel.de/lebenundlernen/schule/lerntheorien-schueler-lernen-vokabeln-im-experiment-a-996886.html (bearbeitet)); Marie-Charlotte Maas, *Ab ins Ausland: Welcher Auslandsaufenthalt passt am besten in deinen Terminkalender*, © YAEZ, 14.09.2017; Nora Gantenbrink, *Erasmus – Orgasmus: Studenten, lasst euch bloß nicht stressen!*, DIE ZEIT # 10/2012 (https://www.zeit.de/2012/10/C-Erasmus); Doris E.M. Bulenda, *Andorra – Spanien; an der Grenze*, e-stories.de website, 13.10.2017; Ruth Asan, *Was will ich werden?* die taz, 22.06.2014; Lena Greiner und Carola Padtberg, *Wer bin ich, was kann ich?*, SPIEGEL ONLINE, 14.01.2015 (http://www.spiegel.de/lebenundlernen/schule/berufsberatung-fuer-schueler-was-soll-ich-werden-a-1007911.html); *München feiert Saint Patrick's Day mit bunter Parade*, 12.03.2017, © dpa; Christine Bazalka, *St Patrick's Day in Wien*, www.meinbezirk.at, 16.03.2016; Marlene Schimanski, *15 Gap Year Möglichkeiten: Nach dem Abitur, Studium oder im Beruf ins Ausland*, Auslandskarriere.de, 06.04.2017; *Arbeitswelt im Wandel: Die Wirtschaft brummt bedrohlich*, © Bernadette Conrad für ZEIT ONLINE (www.zeit.de) vom: 27.12.2017; Nina Piatscheck, „Noch kein Abi, trotzdem Boss", ZEIT Campus # 1/2018 (https://www.zeit.de/campus/2018/01/marketing-tubeconnect-media-charles-bahr); *Alptraum*, © Gudrun Pausewang (https://kindergeschichten.wordpress.com/2014/02/28/1/), 2014; Wolfgang Dahlmann, *Lukas kämpft sich aus der virtuellen Welt zurück ins echte Leben*, T Online website, 03.11.2015, © dpa; *Wir sind keine Computer-Dummies!* (http://www.tipps-vom-experten.de/senioren-am-computer/); © Olaf Lüken, *Wer Kochsendungen sieht, kocht nicht* (https://www.e-stories.de/view-kurzgeschichten.phtml?43532), 04.02.2018; *Ich pumpe, also bin ich*, Maria Timtschenko, Spiegel ONLINE, 09.12.2013 (http://www.spiegel.de/lebenundlernen/schule/jugendliche-im-fitnessstudio-hobby-sport-oder-koerperwahn-a-919483.html); *075. Unfair – Eine Fußballgeschichte*, © Marco Wittler, www.366geschichten.de, 12.09.2014; *10 Tipps, wie wir die Umwelt schützen können*, Antenne Niedersachsen (https://www.antenne.com/tipps/service/verbraucher/10-tipps-wie-wir-die-umwelt-schuetzen-koennen-id54796.html), 08.08.2017; *Die Abenteuer eines Seefahrers 2 Vor Westafrika*, © Meinhard Pahlke (https://www.e-stories.de/view-kurzgeschichten.phtml?34930), 2012. Es handelt sich um wahre Geschichten. Der Autor hat über 80 Länder bereist und hat noch weitere Kurzgeschichten als Reiseberichte, Kindergeschichten und spannende Geschichten geschrieben. [These are based on true stories. The author has travelled to more than 80 countries and has written other short stories, travel accounts, children's stories and exciting stories.]

Photograph Acknowledgements

Alamy, Getty, iStock, State Examinations Commission, Shutterstock

The publisher has made every effort to contact all copyright holders but if any have been overlooked, we will be pleased to make any necessary arrangements.

Any links or references to external websites or third-party publications should not be construed as an endorsement by Folens of the content or views of these websites or publications.

Contents

Welcome to Your New *Deutsch Komplett*!

Your Second Edition of *Deutsch Komplett* is even easier to use than before! We have created a brand new design for you, with the following icons to help you find your way around easily:

- Learning outcomes
- Ordinary Level
- Higher Level
- Common Level
- Pair work
- Group work
- Listening
- Spoken production/interaction
- Writing
- Reading
- Grammar
- Vocabulary
- Culture
- Homework
- Solutions/documents online
- Tip
- Exam tip
- Exam focus
- Self-evaluation pages (OL/HL)
- Jump to another page in this book

Digital Resources with *Deutsch Komplett*

We have created a suite of exam-focused digital resources which are closely linked to your *Deutsch Komplett* textbook:

Resource	Details	Chapters
1. Mock oral exam videos	• Theme-based examiner-student mock oral exams, focusing on the most commonly examined oral topics • Higher Level and Ordinary Level versions	1–7
2. Video worksheets	• Linked to mock oral exam videos • Questions and exercises based on theme and/or mock oral exam videos	1–7
3. Video transcripts	• Available as PDF online	1–7
4. SEC role plays	• Official SEC role-play cards in German and English, with sample answers • Higher Level and Ordinary Level versions • Recorded and available as podcasts or audio downloads • To be updated for the new set of SEC role-play cards for the Leaving Certificate German oral 2021+	n/a
5. SEC picture sequences	• Official SEC picture sequences, with sample answers • Higher Level and Ordinary Level versions • Recorded and available as podcasts or audio downloads • To be updated for the new set of SEC picture sequences for the Leaving Certificate German oral 2021+	n/a
6. Solutions	• Solutions to exercises in the textbook, including reading, writing and grammar exercises • Available as PDF online	all

01 Meine Familie und ich

Learning Outcomes

- **Oral:** discussing family life
- **Reading:** reading and discussing three texts on family life
- **Writing:** writing an opinion (**Äußerung**), a picture description and a letter on family life
- **Aural:** listening to and answering questions on four extracts on family life

Grammar

- Regular verbs in the present and imperfect tenses
- Irregular verbs in the present tense

Vocabulary

- Family members
- Family relationships
- Personal characteristics

German Culture

- German films

Exam Tips

- Underline phrases in the texts that you can adapt for your oral and written work.
- Look out for useful idioms that will enrich your German expression.
- Complete the rapid revision checklist at the end of each chapter.

Mündliche Arbeit: Ihre Familie und Sie

Stellen Sie sich gegenseitig die Fragen unten.

Working in pairs, ask each other all of the questions below.

Wie heißen Sie?

Beschreiben Sie Ihre Familie.

Was macht Ihr Bruder/ Ihre Schwester?

Wie kommen Sie mit Ihren Eltern aus?

Haben Sie Geschwister?

Gibt es manchmal Streit zu Hause?

Was machen Ihre Geschwister/Ihre Eltern?

Lesen Sie die folgenden Sätze. Welche treffen auf Sie zu? Schreiben Sie sie um!

Read the following sentences. Which ones apply to you? Change them to suit you!

1. Ihre Familie *Your family*	
Zu meiner Familie gehören vier/fünf Personen.	*Four/five people belong to my family.*
Mein Bruder/**Meine** Schwester, **der/die** _____ heißt, ist _____ Jahre alt.	*My brother/sister, who is called _____ , is _____ years old.*
Er besucht die Grundschule/das Gymnasium.	*He attends primary school/secondary school.*
Sie geht auf die Universität/arbeitet im Ausland.	*She goes to university/works abroad.*
Ich bin Einzelkind/**der/die** Älteste/Jüngste/**das** Mittelkind.	*I'm an only child/the oldest/youngest/middle child.*
Weil ich **der/die** Älteste bin, sitze ich am längeren Hebel/habe ich viel Verantwortung.	*Because I'm the oldest, I have the advantage/I have a lot of responsibility.*
Ich bin gern **der/die** Jüngste, denn ich muss zugeben, dass ich ein bisschen verwöhnt bin.	*I like being the youngest, because I must admit that I'm a bit spoiled.*
Zum Glück sind meine Großeltern noch am Leben.	*Luckily my grandparents are still alive.*
Mein älterer Bruder beleidigt mich immer.	*My older brother always insults me.*
Das regt mich tierisch auf.	*That really infuriates me.*
Das finde ich gut, denn ich habe viel Freiheit.	*I find that good, because I have a lot of freedom.*

Schreiben Sie anhand der Sätze oben vier bis fünf Sätze über Ihre Familie in Ihr Heft. Üben Sie sie.

Now write **four to five** sentences about your family in your copy, using the model sentences above. Practise saying them out loud.

2. Ihre Eltern *Your parents*	
Glücklicherweise sind meine Eltern immer ermutigend.	*Luckily my parents are always encouraging.*
Ich habe wahnsinniges Glück mit meinen Eltern und ich kann mit ihnen über alles reden.	*I'm incredibly lucky with my parents and I can talk to them about everything.*
Meine Mutter schmeißt den Laden.	*My mother runs the show.*
Ich habe ein positives Verhältnis zu meinen Eltern.	*I have a positive relationship with my parents.*
Meine Eltern sind immer für mich da.	*My parents are always there for me.*
Wir lösen Probleme immer gemeinsam.	*We always solve problems together.*
Meine Eltern sind getrennt/geschieden und ich wohne bei **meiner** Mutter/**meinem** Vater.	*My parents are separated/divorced and I live with my mother/my father.*

3. Was passt zusammen? *What matches?*	
1. Wir kommen ziemlich gut aus.	**A** I can usually do what I want.
2. Meine Eltern behandeln mich nicht wie ein Erwachsener.	**B** My family is close to my heart.
3. Meine Eltern haben Vertrauen zu mir.	**C** My parents don't treat me like an adult.
4. Ich kann meistens machen was ich will.	**D** We get along quite well.
5. Meine Familie liegt mir am Herzen.	**E** My parents trust me.

Übersetzen Sie die folgenden Sätze. Translate the following sentences.

Ich kann es nicht leiden, ständig eingeschränkt zu werden.
Ich bin streng erzogen worden.
Manchmal erwarten meine Eltern zu viel von mir und deshalb stehe ich unter viel Druck.
Meine Mutter meckert immer über mein unordentliches Zimmer.
Mein Vater flippt aus, wenn ich spät nach Hause komme.
Meine Eltern sind mega sauer, wenn ich schlechte Noten bekomme.

4. Ihre Geschwister *Your brothers and sisters*	
Ich hätte gern Geschwister, denn es kann einsam sein, wenn man Einzelkind ist.	*I would like to have siblings, because it can be lonely when you are an only child.*
Meine Geschwister und ich quatschen über alles.	*My siblings and I chat about everything.*
Mit **meinem** Bruder/**meiner** Schwester/**meinen** Geschwistern unternehme ich viel.	*I do a lot with my brother/my sister/my siblings.*
Obwohl wir uns manchmal streiten, verstehen wir uns meistens richtig gut.	*Although we sometimes fight, we usually get on really well.*
Ich kann mich immer auf meine Geschwister verlassen.	*I can always rely on my siblings.*

5. Ihr Verhältnis zu Ihren Geschwistern *Your relationship with your brothers and sisters*	
Wir haben den gleichen Sinn für Humor.	*We have the same sense of humour.*
Wir haben bei Klamotten den gleichen Geschmack, deshalb gibt es manchmal Streit.	*We have the same taste in clothes, so sometimes there's fighting.*
Mein kleiner Bruder ist total verwöhnt und verlangt immer alles.	*My little brother is totally spoiled and always demands everything.*
Mit meiner Schwester gibt es immer Streit, denn sie benimmt sich immer schlecht.	*There is always fighting with my sister because she always behaves badly.*
Ich bin fuchsteufelswild wenn meine Schwester meine Klamotten klaut.	*I get hopping mad when my sister steals my clothes.*

Hausaufgaben

Use the sentences above to write a paragraph about your own family life. Practise saying these sentences out loud. Keep a file of these paragraphs for your oral examination.

Text 1: Wie kommst du mit den Eltern aus?

Bitte beantworten Sie die folgenden Fragen:

1. Was sieht man auf dem Bild?
2. Was feiert die Familie, Ihrer Meinung nach?
3. Was sieht man auf dem Tisch?
4. Gibt es eine gute oder schlechte Stimmung, Ihrer Meinung nach?

Vorarbeit *Preparation*

1. **Finden Sie diese Ausdrücke im folgenden Text.** Find these expressions in the text below.
   - **A** ... about relationships at home.
   - **B** At the weekend I meet my friends.
   - **C** I do a bit at home.
   - **D** ... I can't be bothered to study.
2. **Finden Sie das Deutsche für die Wörter unten!** Find the German for the words below.
   - **A** fights/results/untidy/complains
   - **B** family celebration/tidy up/responsibility
   - **C** bad/necessary/relaxed/dishwasher/mow
   - **D** clean/trouble/to dye/allow/mad

A Verena (16)

Wir haben eine Umfrage in der Schule gemacht. Wir wollten über die Verhältnisse zu Hause herausfinden. Die Ergebnisse? Bei den meisten Jugendlichen gibt es wenig Streit mit den Eltern. Meine Eltern sind tolerant, aber es gibt Streit, wenn mein Zimmer unordentlich ist. Meine Mutter klagt immer darüber, dass Kleidung auf dem Boden liegt. Für mich ist Ordnung nicht das Wichtigste! Ich koche oft das Abendessen.

B Annika (15)

Ich habe viel Freiheit aber auch viel Verantwortung. Das finde ich in Ordnung. Mein Bruder Karl und ich müssen viel zu Hause mithelfen, weil meine Mutter arbeitet. Wir arbeiten im Garten, räumen im Haus auf und manchmal kochen wir das Abendessen. Das ist alles geregelt. Am Wochenende treffe ich mich mit meinen Freunden. Das mag ich. Wenn es eine Familienfeier gibt, dann muss ich mitfahren. Das gefällt mir überhaupt nicht.

C Jens (16)

Ich verstehe mich mit meinen Eltern gut, und ich fühle mich in meiner Familie sehr wohl. Manchmal gibt es Streit wegen Hausaufgaben oder Fernsehen, aber nie was Schlimmes. Ich mache zu Hause einiges: Ich mähe den Rasen oder räume die Spülmaschine aus. Ich mache das, was nötig ist. Ich bin gern zu Hause, aber ich unternehme auch gern was mit Freunden. Bei uns ist alles ganz locker.

D Sebastian (14)

Es gibt öfters Ärger zu Hause, weil ich einfach keinen Bock zum Lernen habe. Es gibt manche Sachen, die meine Eltern nicht erlauben und dann gibt's Krach. Ich darf, zum Beispiel, mir die Haare nicht färben. Sie verbieten auch einen Nasenring. Es gibt auch Krach, wenn ich ausgehen will. Dann bin ich ziemlich sauer. Bei uns muss jeder aushelfen. Ich putze das Badezimmer und manchmal mache ich den Einkauf: das mache ich gern.

Prüfungstipp

Find at least five sentences in the text which you can use in your oral and written work. Keep these sentences in a folder organised into different topics.

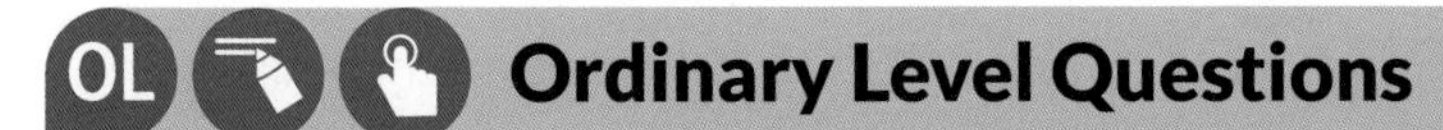

OL Ordinary Level Questions

1. a) Give **two** details about the survey recently carried out. (A)
   b) What were the results for most students?
2. Fill in the required information in the box below.

Name	Chores	One thing liked	One cause of arguments
Verena			
Annika			
Jens			
Sebastian			

3. Are the following statements true or false?
   a) Verena kocht immer das Abendessen.
   b) Annika hilft gar nicht im Haushalt.
   c) Es gibt Streit bei Jens wegen Hausarbeit.
   d) Jens wohnt nicht gern zu Hause.
   e) Sebastian lernt nicht gern.
4. Select the correct prepositions for the following sentences.
   a) Die Schüler/innen wollten **(von/über/mit/durch)** Verhältnisse zu Hause wissen.
   b) Annika arbeitet **(am/in/im/beim)** Garten.
   c) Jens versteht sich gut **(mit/von/an/für)** seinen Eltern.
   d) Sebastian hat keinen Bock **(ans/um/für/zum)** Lernen.

HL Higher Level Questions

1. Beantworten Sie folgende Fragen auf Deutsch!
   a) Wer hat neulich eine Umfrage durchgeführt? Geben Sie Details! (A)
   b) Wann gibt es bei Annika keine Ausrede? (B)
   c) Wie hilft Jens zu Hause aus? (C)
   d) Warum wird Sebastian manchmal sauer? (D)
2. Answer the following questions in English.
   a) What were the results of the survey? (A)
   b) How does Annika help out at home? (B)
   c) Why does Jens believe that things at home are relaxed? (C)
   d) Sebastian's parents forbid certain things. Give **three** examples of these things. (D)
3. Finden Sie **drei** Sätze im Text, die dieses Foto gut beschreiben!
4. **Was passt zusammen?** What matches?

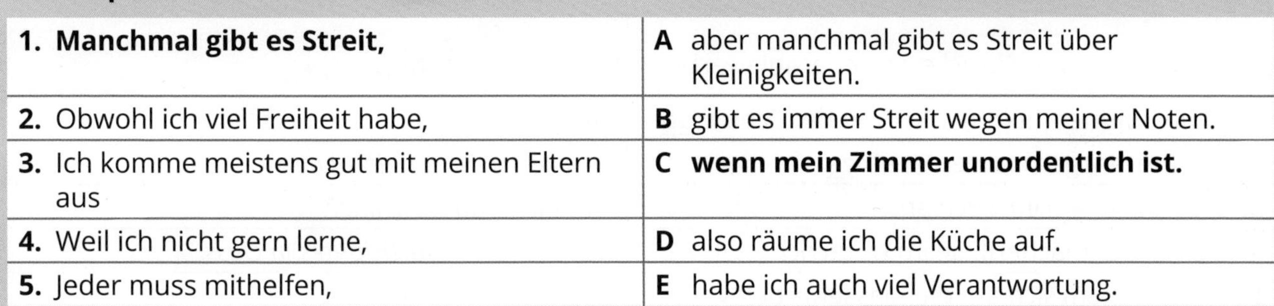

1. Manchmal gibt es Streit,	**A** aber manchmal gibt es Streit über Kleinigkeiten.
2. Obwohl ich viel Freiheit habe,	**B** gibt es immer Streit wegen meiner Noten.
3. Ich komme meistens gut mit meinen Eltern aus	**C** **wenn mein Zimmer unordentlich ist.**
4. Weil ich nicht gern lerne,	**D** also räume ich die Küche auf.
5. Jeder muss mithelfen,	**E** habe ich auch viel Verantwortung.

Grammatik: Zeitformen/Tenses

p. 20 (Übung macht den Meister)

Present Tense: Regular Verbs

There are two present tenses in English: **Ich spiele** can mean 'I play' *or* 'I am playing'.
In German there is only one present tense: you cannot say **Ich bin spielen**.

To form the **present tense** of regular verbs in German, take the infinitive form of the verb. Remove the **-en** and add the endings, as in the example of **spielen** below. Verbs such as **arbeiten** which end with **-ten** or **-den** include an **-e** in the **du**, **er/sie/es** and **ihr** forms:

ich spiel**e**	wir spiel**en**
du spiel**st**	ihr spiel**t**
er/sie/es/man spiel**t**	Sie/sie spiel**en**

ich arbeit**e**	wir arbeit**en**
du arbeit**est**	ihr arbeit**et**
er/sie/es arbeit**et**	Sie/sie arbeit**en**

Put the following bracketed verbs into the present tense.

1. Ich (absolvieren) nächstes Jahr das Abitur.	*I'm completing the Leaving Cert next year.*
2. (Freuen) du dich auf die Ferien?	*Are you* (singular) *looking forward to the holidays?*
3. Mein Vater (achten) auf seine Gesundheit.	*My father watches his health.*
4. Meine Mutter (akzeptieren) mich wie ich bin.	*My mother accepts me as I am.*
5. Das Kind (weinen) ständig.	*The child cries constantly.*
6. Man (brauchen) einen Tapetenwechsel.	*One needs a change of scenery.*
7. Wir (feiern) die ganze Nacht.	*We celebrate all night long.*
8. Ihr (brauchen) mehr Geduld.	*You* (plural) *need more patience.*
9. Herr Braun, Sie (stammen) aus Deutschland.	*Mr Braun, you* (polite) *come from Germany.*
10. Die Kinder (kaufen) die Ostereier.	*The children buy the Easter eggs.*

Present Tense: Regular Separable Verbs

Separable verbs are formed with a *prefix* and a **verb**: *ab***holen**, *an***rufen**, *auf***räumen**.

- The *prefix* can separate from the **verb**: Ich **räume** am Wochenende mein Zimmer *auf*.
- If the root verb is regular, the separable verb will also be regular.

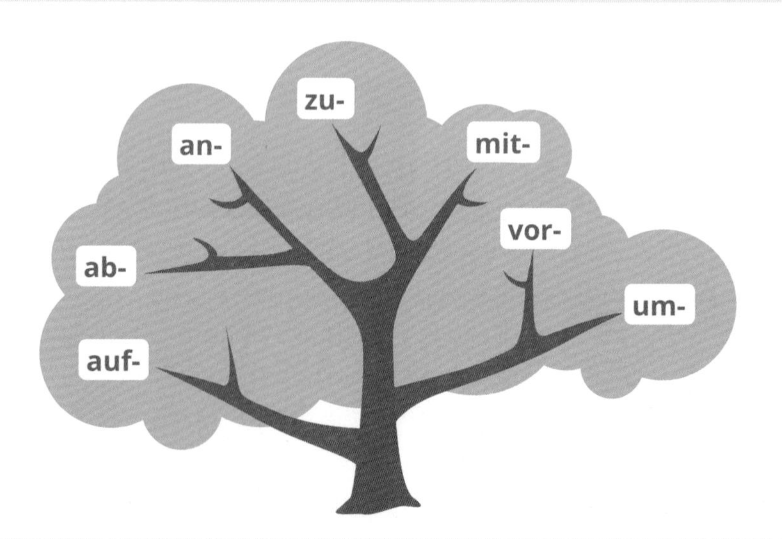

Put the following bracketed separable verbs into the present tense.

1. Meine Mutter (holen) mich von der Schule ab.	*My mother collects me from school.*
2. Wir (hören) gern lauter Musik zu.	*We like listening to loud music.*
3. Was (schauen) ihr euch an?	*What are you watching?*
4. Der Junge (machen) nie im Unterricht mit.	*The boy never participates in class.*
5. Sie (bereiten) sich auf die Klassenarbeit vor.	*She prepares for the test.*

Present Tense: Regular Inseparable Verbs

Inseparable verbs do not separate, because the prefix (**be-**, **emp-**, **ent-**, **er-**, **ge-**, **miss-**, **ver-**, **zer-**) is not a word in its own right and therefore cannot stand on its own. If the root verb is regular, the inseparable verb will also be regular.

Exceptions: some verbs beginning with **unter** and **über** are inseparable.

unterhalten: Wir unterhalten uns in der Pause. *We talk during the break.*

überleben: Wir überleben den Sturm. *We survive the storm.*

Put the following bracketed inseparable verbs into the present tense.

1. Was (bedeuten) das auf Englisch?	*What does that mean in English?*
2. Ich (benutzen) den Computer jeden Tag.	*I use the computer every day.*
3. Die Ärzte (entwickeln) neue Medikamente.	*The doctors develop new medicines.*
4. Meine Lehrerin (erklären) alles ganz deutlich.	*My teacher explains everything very clearly.*
5. Er (gewöhnen) sich an die Arbeit.	*He is getting used to the work.*

01.01 Hörverständnis Teil 1

Vorarbeit *Preparation*

Landwirt	*farmer*	**Bauernhof**	*farmyard*	**Verantwortung**	*responsibility*
Privatsphäre	*privacy*	**gut gelaunt**	*good-humoured*	**behandeln**	*to treat*
berufstätig	*working*	**füttern**	*to feed (animals)*	**beschäftigt**	*busy*
volljährig	*of age/adult*	**auf den Wecker gehen**	*to annoy*	**Vertrauen**	*trust*

Ordinary + Higher Level Questions

Note: O = Ordinary; H = Higher

1. Give **three (O)/five (H)** details about Klaus.
2. **a)** Name **two** disadvantages of being the eldest, according to Klaus.
   b) Name **two (O)/three (H)** advantages of being the eldest, according to Klaus.
3. **a)** How does Klaus get on with his brother? Give **two (O)/three (H)** details.
   b) How does Klaus get on with his sister? Give **two (O)/three (H)** details.
4. Mention **two (O)/three (H)** ways in which Klaus helps out at home.
5. **a)** When is Klaus's birthday, and what is special about this birthday?
   b) How does Klaus intend to celebrate his birthday? Give **two (O)/three (H)** details.

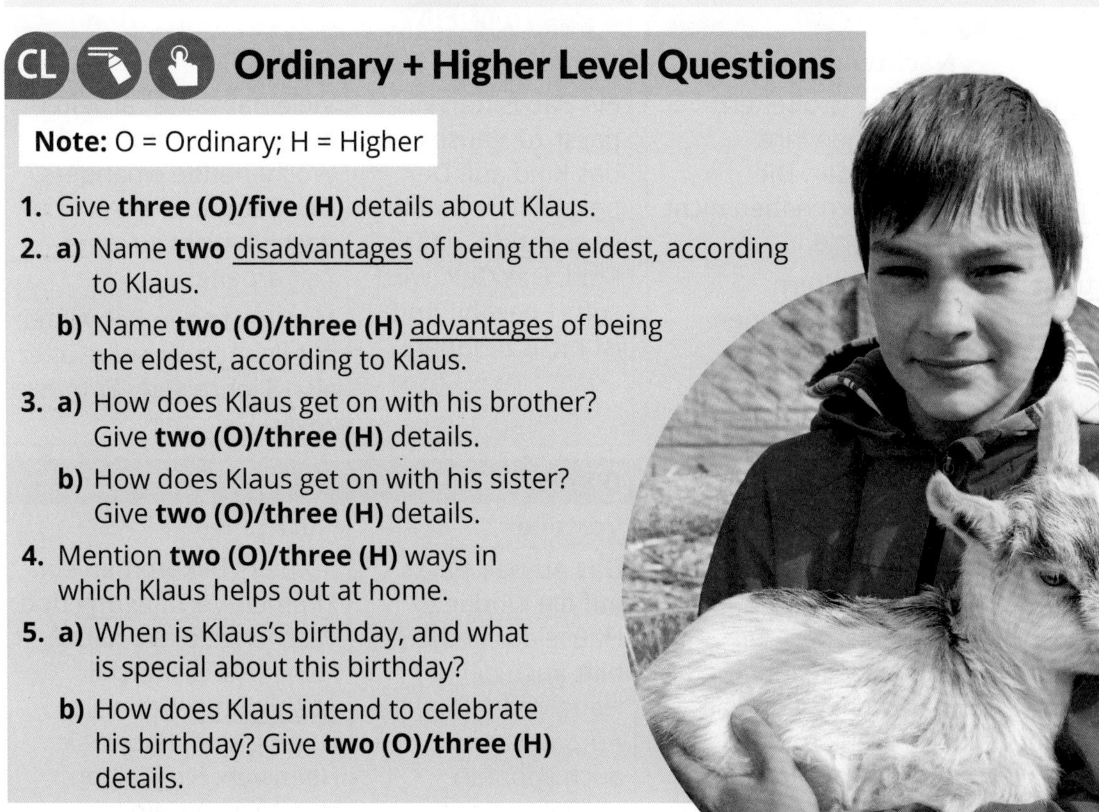

Text 2: Wer passt auf die Kinder auf?

Bild 1

Bild 2

Bitte beantworten Sie die folgenden Fragen:

Bild 1

1. Was machen die Großeltern und Enkelkinder?
2. Wo sind sie?
3. Was sieht man im Hintergrund?

Bild 2

1. Was macht die Babysitterin?
2. Sind die Kinder froh oder traurig?
3. Was werden die Kinder danach machen?

Vorarbeit *Preparation*

1. **Finden Sie diese Ausdrücke im folgenden Text!** Find these expressions in the text below.
   - **A** One can trust the grandparents.
   - **B** He must be reliable.
   - **C** Often young children are homesick.
   - **D** The au pair often becomes a part of the family.
2. **Finden Sie das Deutsche für die Wörter unten!** Find the German for the words below.
   - **A** to trust/to mind/grandchild/to spoil
   - **B** reliable/expensive/important/to know
   - **C** skills/looks after/nap/crèche
   - **D** board/to step in/to get used to/training

A Die Großeltern

Vorteile:	Nachteile:
Die Großeltern passen zu Hause auf das Kind auf. Sie verbringen gern Zeit mit dem Enkelkind. Man kann den Großeltern vertrauen und die Großeltern kosten kein Geld.	Manche Großeltern verwöhnen ihre Enkelkinder. Die Großeltern haben nicht viel Energie. Die Großeltern wollen ihre eigenen Freizeitsaktivitäten machen. Manche wohnen weit weg.

B Der Babysitter/Die Babysitterin

Vorteile:	Nachteile:
Ein Babysitter passt zu Hause auf das Kind auf. Der persönliche Kontakt ist wichtig für das Kind. Das Geld wird sofort bezahlt und ist nicht zu teuer.	Viele Babysitter arbeiten abends oder am Wochenende woanders. Der Babysitter kann deshalb nicht zu jeder Zeit arbeiten. Man muss den Babysitter gut kennen. Er sollte älter als 15 Jahre sein. Er muss zuverlässig sein.

C Die Kinderkrippe

Vorteile:	Nachteile:
Ein Erzieher betreut viele Kinder. Die Kinder lernen also soziale Kompetenz und schließen Freundschaften. Die Krippe ist jeden Tag geöffnet. Die Kinder essen dort und machen einen Mittagsschlaf.	Das Kind muss die neuen Menschen kennenlernen. Oft haben Kleinkinder Heimweh. Wenn das Kind krank ist, muss das Kind zu Hause bleiben. Für die Kinderkrippe muss man viel Geld bezahlen.

D Das Au-pair

Vorteile:	Nachteile:
Das Au-pair passt auf die Kinder zu Hause auf und hilft auch bei der Hausarbeit. Das Au-pair kann auch spontan als Babysitter einspringen. Das Au-pair wird oft Teil der Familie.	Au-pairs bekommen ein Zimmer, Verpflegung und Taschengeld. Sie haben keine professionelle Ausbildung. Wenn sie zu jung sind, haben sie Heimweh. Sie bleiben meistens nur ein Jahr. Das Kind muss sich dann an eine neue Person gewöhnen.

OL Ordinary Level Questions

1. Fill in advantages and disadvantages of the different forms of childcare (**three** examples each).

Who/Where?	Advantages	Disadvantages
Grandparents		
Babysitter		
Crèche		
Au pair		

2. True or false?
   a) Some grandparents live far away and cannot mind their grandchildren.
   b) A babysitter is available at all times.
   c) Children learn social skills and make friends at a crèche.
   d) Au pairs receive professional childcare training.

3. Choose the correct answer: **i)**, **ii)**, **iii)** or **iv)**.
   a) Großeltern können ______________ auf ihre Enkelkinder aufpassen.
   i) in der Schule **iii)** bei ihnen zu Hause
   ii) zu Hause **iv)** im Park
   b) Viele Babysitter arbeiten nur ______________ .
   i) am Sonntag **iii)** abends und am Wochenende
   ii) während der Woche **iv)** manchmal
   c) Wenn das Kind ______________ ist, bleibt es zu Hause.
   i) müde **iii)** verwöhnt
   ii) launisch **iv)** krank
   d) Ein Au-pair hilft bei ______________ .
   i) der Hausarbeit **iii)** dem Einkaufen
   ii) den Hausaufgaben **iv)** der Gartenarbeit

CL Ordinary + Higher Level Questions

Lückentext: Fill in the blanks with the correct missing words from the box.

und bei oft jedes aus

Meine Großeltern wohnen gleich um die Ecke und ich besuche sie **1** ______________ Wochenende. Ich helfe meinem Opa **2** ______________ der Gartenarbeit und meine Oma und ich gehen **3** ______________ einkaufen. Ich komme gut mit ihnen **4** ______________ , weil sie so lieb sind. Sie sind auch sehr selbstständig. Mein Opa spielt sehr gern Golf **5** ______________ meine Oma macht regelmäßig Yoga-Kurse.

HL Higher Level Questions

1. Beantworten Sie folgende Fragen auf Deutsch und in Ihren eigenen Worten!
   a) i) Wo passen die Großeltern auf die Kinder auf, und wie viel Geld bekommen sie dafür? A
   ii) Warum können manche Großeltern nicht auf ihre Enkelkinder aufpassen? (**3** Gründe) A
   b) i) Wann und wie viel wird der Babysitter bezahlt? B
   ii) Worauf muss man achten, bevor man einen Babysitter einstellt? (**3** Beispiele) B
   c) i) Was sind die Vorteile bei einer Kinderkrippe, laut Text? C
   ii) Was passiert bei einer Kinderkrippe, wenn ein Kind krank ist? C
   d) Was für Arbeit macht ein Au-pair, und was bekommt das Au-pair dafür? D

2. Answer the following questions in English.
   a) i) Name **three** advantages of grandparents looking after their grandchildren.
      ii) What can happen to some grandchildren if they are minded by their grandparents? A
   b) What can a babysitter give a child? What time constraints are involved for a babysitter? B
   c) When are the opening hours for crèches? Whom must the children first get to know? C
   d) What can the au pair do spontaneously? What happens when the au pair leaves? D
3. **Was passt zusammen?** What matches?

1. Manche Großeltern wohnen nicht in der Nähe	**A** und Kinder lernen neue Freunde kennen.
2. Ein Babysitter passt zu Hause auf das Kind auf	**B** wenn das Jahr zu Ende ist.
3. In einer Krippe werden viele Kinder betreut	**C und können nicht auf ihre Enkelkinder aufpassen.**
4. Kinder wollen mit ihren Eltern sein,	**D** und bekommt ein eigenes Zimmer.
5. Ein Au-pair wohnt bei der Familie	**E** und verbringt persönliche Zeit mit dem Kind.
6. Ein Au-pair wird vermisst,	**F** wenn sie Heimweh haben.

4. Put the regular bracketed verbs from Text 2 into the present tense.
   a) Ich (aufpassen) auf meinen kleinen Bruder.
   b) Meine Oma (verwöhnen) mich.
   c) Meine Eltern (arbeiten) in der Stadt.
   d) Wieviel Geld (kosten) das?
   e) Wieviel Geld (bezahlen) du?

01.02 Hörverständnis Teil 2

Vorarbeit *Preparation*

am Apparat	*on the line*	**sich Sorgen machen**	*to worry*
schuften	*to slog*	**übertreiben**	*to exaggerate*
überfordert	*overburdened*	**erschöpft**	*exhausted*
Druck	*pressure*	**ausrichten**	*to inform*
sich ausruhen	*to relax*	**bestehen auf**	*to insist upon*
reine Sklaverei	*pure slavery*		

OL Ordinary Level Questions

1. Whom does the caller want to speak to?
2. Whom is the caller worried about, and why?
3. When will the woman be contacted?
4. What is the **name** and **number** of the caller?
   Name: ______________________________
   Number: ____________________________

HL Higher Level Questions

1. Write down **in German** the key information from the conversation.
   Write ***key phrases***, not full sentences. The note should contain:
   - The name of the person **making** the call
   - The reason for the call
   - Details regarding further contact
   - The caller's phone number

Gesprächsnotiz

Anruf von: ______________________ Gesprächsanlass: ______________________

Die Anruferin

- erwartet am Abend einen Rückruf ☐
- wird in zwei Tagen noch einmal anrufen ☐
- bekommt innerhalb einer Stunde einen Rückruf ☐
- wird auf der Webseite einen Kommentar hinterlassen ☐

Kontaktnummer: *Vorwahl* ______ *Rufnummer* __________

2. In listening to the phone call for the ***third*** time, write down **three** examples of the language used (***expressions and phrases***) which show that the caller is **upset**.

Prüfungstipp: Higher Level

Build up a collection of frequently expressed emotions for Question 2. Here are some examples from Hörverständnis Teil 2:

Ich mache mir solche Sorgen   Das ist viel zu viel   reine Sklaverei   überfordert   Druck

OL Äußerung zum Thema: Ordinary Level

You are interviewing an au pair. Complete the au pair's dialogue based on the information given in Text 2.

Sie: Was für Arbeit machen Sie als Au-pair?
Au-pair: ______________________________
Sie: Sind Sie auch Teil der Familie?
Au-pair: ______________________________
Sie: Was bekommen Sie für Ihre Arbeit?
Au-pair: ______________________________
Sie: Haben Sie eine professionelle Ausbildung?
Au-pair: ______________________________
Sie: Wie lange bleiben Sie bei der Familie?
Au-pair: ______________________________

Prüfungstipp

Use the State Examinations Commission website to become more familiar with German. The marking schemes will help you to see what the examiners are looking for. You will find the transcripts at the end of the marking schemes. These are an invaluable resource for improving vocabulary.

HL Äußerung zum Thema: Higher Level

Write 13 to 15 sentences, answering the questions below.

- Beschreiben Sie das Foto rechts in **drei bis vier** Sätzen.
- Wer sollte, Ihrer Meinung nach, auf die Kinder aufpassen? Begründen Sie Ihre Meinung.
- Was für Probleme gibt es heutzutage in Familien? Geben Sie Beispiele. Wie könnte man diese Probleme lösen? Wie ist es bei Ihnen zu Hause?

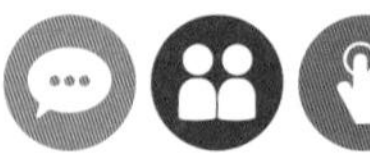

Nützliche Sätze/Useful Sentences

1. **Übersetzen Sie die folgenden Sätze.** Translate the following sentences.
   a) Ich passe auf die Kinder auf und helfe mit der Hausarbeit.
   b) Ich bekomme ein Zimmer, Verpflegung und Taschengeld.
   c) Ja, ich bin Teil der Familie und ich mag das.
   d) Nein, ich habe keine professionelle Ausbildung.
   e) Ich bleibe für ein Jahr bei der Familie.
   f) Meine Schwester ist ein Plappermaul und geht mir auf die Nerven.
   g) Man muss das Problem zusammen besprechen. Schreien schafft nichts.
   h) Wenn wir ein Problem haben, sitzen wir zusammen und finden eine Lösung.
   i) Das kommt in jeder Familie vor.
   j) Wenn ich schlechte Noten bekomme, kriege ich Hausarrest.
2. **Was passt zusammen?** What matches?

1. Man muss auch verständnisvoll sein.	**A** I never get enough pocket money.
2. Natürlich gibt es Streit über den Computer, das Fernsehen und das Ausgehen.	**B** One has to learn to make compromises.
3. Ich kriege nie genug Taschengeld.	**C** Of course there are fights about the computer, watching television and going out.
4. Man streitet über Hausaufgaben, Taschengeld und Hausarbeit.	**D** One must also be understanding.
5. Man muss lernen, Kompromisse zu machen.	**E** One fights about homework, pocket money and housework.

Prüfungstipp

Ordinary Level: Make sure that you answer every question in the **Äußerung**. Use the information and the vocabulary from Text 2. Remember to use full sentences.

Higher Level: Make sure that you answer every question in the **Äußerung**. It is generally useful to have five sentences in your picture description. Remember to rephrase sentences; do not copy sentences directly from the text. It is a good idea to build up a vocabulary of opinion: **Meiner Meinung nach ... /Ich bin davon fest überzeugt ...**

Grammatik: Zeitformen/Tenses

p. 20 (Übung macht den Meister)

Present Tense: Irregular Verbs

Irregular verbs often have a vowel change, but do follow certain rules. To form the **present tense of irregular verbs**, remove the **-en** from the infinitive and add the same endings as regular verbs. The irregularity is a vowel change in the middle of the **du**, **er**, **sie**, **es** and **man** forms of the verb:

fahren (to travel)	**helfen** (to help)	**sehen** (to see)	**nehmen** (to take)
ich fahre	ich helfe	ich sehe	ich nehme
du fährst	**du** hilfst	**du** siehst	**du** nimmst
er/sie/es/man fährt	**er/sie/es/man** hilft	**er/sie/es/man** sieht	**er/sie/es/man** nimmt
wir fahren	wir helfen	wir sehen	wir nehmen
ihr fahrt	ihr helft	ihr seht	ihr nehmt
Sie/sie fahren	Sie/sie helfen	Sie/sie sehen	Sie/sie nehmen

1. Put the following bracketed verbs into the present tense. Then translate each sentence.

a) Das Kind (schlafen) die ganze Nacht lang.
b) Ich (schlafen) samstags bis 11 Uhr.
c) Wir (tragen) eine Uniform.
d) Der Junge (tragen) keine Uniform.
e) Meine Mutter (geben) mir Taschengeld.
f) Meine Eltern (geben) mir kein Taschengeld.
g) Wir (sprechen) auf Deutsch im Unterricht.
h) Warum (sprechen) du so laut?
i) Was (lesen) der Junge?
j) Die Schüler (lesen) einen Text.

2. Put the following irregular separable verbs into the correct form.

a) Der Bus (fahren) um 8 Uhr los.
b) Die Männer (sehen) beschäftigt aus.
c) Das Mädchen (nehmen) Schulbücher mit.
d) Der Unterricht (fangen) um 9 Uhr an.
e) Der Direktor (sprechen) die ganze Schule an.

3. Put the following irregular inseparable verbs into the correct form.

a) Elke (besprechen) alles mit ihren Eltern.
b) Wir (erfahren) viel darüber.
c) Die Schüler (unterhalten) sich in der Pause.
d) Das Kind (benehmen) sich schlecht.
e) Der Mann (bewerben) sich um die Stelle.

4. Identify each type of verb (simple, separable, inseparable) in the balloons.

Text 3: Die Patchwork-Familie

Bitte beantworten Sie die folgenden Fragen:

1. Was machen die zwei Mädchen?
2. Was sieht man im Hintergrund?
3. Was sieht man im Vordergrund?
4. Wie sieht das Zimmer aus?
5. Beschreiben Sie die zwei Mädchen!

Vorarbeit *Preparation*

1. **Finden Sie diese Ausdrücke im Text!** Find these expressions in the text.
   - **A** Life was quiet.
   - **B** But Laura would prefer to have her own room.
   - **C** That annoys Laura.
   - **D** But he can't take a joke.
   - **E** But ... she likes her new life in her patchwork family.

2. **Finden Sie das Deutsche für die Wörter unten.** Find the German for the words below.
   - **A** married/joy/stepfather/trouble
   - **B** shelves/pale pink/share/bigger
   - **C** curly/cries/cute/in a good mood
   - **D** thinks/generous/romp/gets angry
   - **E** complains/responsibility/get on/tidy up

A Bei Lauras neuer Patchwork-Familie gibt es viel Freude, aber auch manchmal Ärger. Früher haben Mutti, Laura und ihr Bruder Franz in einer kleinen Wohnung gelebt. Das Leben war ruhig und Mutti hatte immer Zeit für Laura und Franz. Letzes Jahr hat Mutti ihren Freund Paul geheiratet. Paul hatte selber eine Tochter, Magda, und plötzlich hatte Laura nicht nur einen Bruder, sondern auch noch eine Schwester. Und vor drei Monaten wurde Lina geboren. Jetzt hat Laura eine große Familie: eine Mutter, einen Stiefvater, einen Bruder, eine Stiefschwester und eine Halbschwester.

B Die Familie wohnt jetzt in einer größeren Wohnung. Die neue Wohnung ist viel schöner als die alte und liegt ganz zentral. Laura und Magda teilen ein Zimmer. Sie haben das Zimmer selber dekoriert und es sieht sehr schön aus. Die Wände sind hellrosa gestrichen und es gibt Regale für die vielen Bücher. Laura kommt gut mit Magda aus, denn Magda ist nur ein Jahr jünger als sie und ist auch ganz freundlich. Aber Laura würde lieber ihr eigenes Zimmer haben.

C Das Baby Lina ist niedlich und lieb. Sie hat blonde, lockige Haare. Laura spielt gern mit Lina, wenn Lina gut gelaunt ist. Aber Lina bekommt Zähne und sie weint manchmal stundenlang. Das nervt Laura, wenn sie viele Hausaufgaben hat. Dann kann sie sich auf die Hausaufgaben nicht konzentrieren. Mutti ist im Moment sehr müde und hat keine Zeit, Laura bei den Hausaufgaben zu helfen. Manchmal hilft Paul Laura bei den Mathehausaufgaben, aber er kann ihr nicht mit Englisch helfen – er spricht kein Wort Englisch!

D Laura mag Paul, ihren neuen Stiefvater. Er ist hilfsbereit und großzügig. Er gibt Laura, Franz und Magda jede Woche Taschengeld und wenn sie etwas brauchen, bekommen sie es sofort. Aber er versteht keinen Spaß. Wenn die drei älteren Kinder im Wohnzimmer herumtoben, ärgert er sich. Er nimmt das Leben viel zu ernst. Er meint, die Kinder sollen entweder Schularbeit machen oder im Haushalt mithelfen.

E Meistens verstehen sich Laura und Franz. Sie interessieren sich für Fußball und spielen gern zusammen Fußball im Park. Aber Franz ist sehr unordentlich und will nie bei der Hausarbeit mithelfen. Wenn Laura darüber klagt, sagt Franz immer, dass er keine Zeit hat, Hausarbeit zu machen. Dann streiten sie sich. Laura mag es nicht, die Älteste zu sein, denn sie hat zu viel Verantwortung. Sie muss auf das Baby aufpassen und das Wohnzimmer aufräumen. Aber im Großen und Ganzen gefällt ihr das neue Leben in der Patchwork-Familie.

OL Ordinary Level Questions

1. a) Name the people in Laura's family. A
   b) With whom does Laura share a room? B
   c) Why can Paul not help Laura with her English homework? C
   d) How does Laura feel about Paul? D
   e) What do Laura and Franz like doing together? E

2. Choose a suitable heading for each paragraph and explain your choice in English.

   Laura hat viel Verantwortung | **Ein schönes Schlafzimmer** | **Laura und ihr Stiefvater** | **Das Baby weint stundenlang** | **Die neue Familie**

3. What belongs together?

1. **Seit Mutti Paul geheiratet hat,**	A und er ist sehr unordentlich.
2. Laura und Magda verstehen sich,	B aber Laura hätte lieber ein eigenes Zimmer.
3. Laura kann sich nicht konzentrieren,	C **hat Laura eine große Familie.**
4. Paul ist großzügig,	D wenn Lina weint.
5. Franz hilft nicht bei der Hausarbeit	E denn er gibt den Kindern Taschengeld.

4. Select the correct prepositions for the following sentences.
   a) Mutti, Laura und ihr Bruder Franz haben **(in/bei/an/am)** einer kleinen Wohnung gelebt.
   b) Es gibt Regale **(mit/vor/an/für)** die vielen Bücher.
   c) Laura kann sich nicht **(für/mit/auf/in)** die Hausaufgaben konzentrieren.
   d) Die Kinder müssen **(in/im/an/am)** Haushalt mithelfen.
   e) Franz und Laura interessieren sich **(in/an/ohne/für)** Fußball.

CL Ordinary + Higher Level

Lückentext: Fill in the blanks with the correct missing words from the box.

mich gestrichen bei eigenes nervt

Ich freue mich, dass ich ein **1** _______ Zimmer habe. Die Wände sind hellgrün **2** _______ und es gibt Regale für meine Bücher. Es **3** _______ mich, wenn ich zu viele Hausaufgaben bekomme. Ich finde es schwierig, **4** _______ auf die Hausaufgaben zu konzentrieren. Manchmal hilft mein Vater mir **5** _______ den Hausaufgaben.

HL Higher Level Questions

1. Beantworten Sie folgende Fragen auf Deutsch!
   a) **Wo** und **mit wem** hat Laura früher gewohnt? A
   b) Beschreiben Sie das Zimmer von Laura und Magda. B
   c) Warum kann Mutti bei den Hausaufgaben nicht helfen? C
   d) Warum ärgert sich Paul? D
   e) Wie muss Laura zu Hause mithelfen? E

2. Answer the following questions in English.
   a) Name **three** changes in Laura's life over the past year. A
   b) List **three** differences between the old apartment and the new apartment. B
   c) Why is it sometimes difficult for Laura to do her homework? Give **two** reasons. C
   d) What does Laura like **and** dislike about her stepfather? D
   e) Give **three** examples of Laura's mixed feelings about her new patchwork family.

3. Aus welchen Wörtern bestehen die zusammengesetzten Wörter, und was bedeuten sie auf Englisch?
   a) Stiefvater = _______ + _______ = _______
   b) hellrosa = _______ + _______ = _______
   c) stundenlang = _______ + _______ = _______

Select **five** phrases from Reading Text 3 that you can use or adapt in your oral and written work.

OL Schriftliche Produktion: Ordinary Level

Write a letter to your pen pal, Denis/Denise. Complete the first paragraph by inserting the correct phrases from the box. Then follow the instructions.

letzte Woche meinen Geburtstag gefeiert
dich besuchen **dir zu schreiben**
eine Flugkarte nach Berlin
eine Überraschung für

Liebe(r) Denis/Denise,

endlich habe ich die Zeit gefunden, ______________________________! Wie geht's? Mir geht's super. Ich habe ______________________________ dich. Wie du weißt, habe ich ______________________________. Meine Eltern haben mir ______________________________ geschenkt! Ich kann ______________________________! Ich kann es gar nicht glauben!

Now continue the letter.

- Say that you had a great party last week (where, who came to the party).
- Describe what you had to eat and drink.
- Say the present from your parents was a big surprise (when, for how long, where you are staying).
- Say that you are looking forward to visiting Berlin and seeing Denis/Denise during your stay.
- Ask Denis/Denise if he/she can suggest other things to do in Berlin.
- Write a suitable closing sentence.

HL Schriftliche Produktion: Higher Level

You have received the following letter from your pen pal. Reply in German. Ensure you answer all the questions he/she asks.

Liebe(r) ______________,

ich hoffe, dass es dir gut geht. Mir geht's gut, aber gestern hatte ich schlechte Laune. Ich habe einen riesigen Streit über etwas Doofes mit meiner Mutter gehabt. Ich streite jetzt immer mit ihr. Aber für meine kleine Schwester ist es ganz anders. Sie kann gar nichts Böses tun. Ich fühle mich gegenüber meiner jüngeren Schwester ungerecht behandelt. Ich wünsche mir, dass meine kleine Schwester nicht immer bevorzugt wird, nur weil sie jünger ist. Ich finde das total ungerecht. Was meinst du? Hast du ein gutes Verhältnis zu deinen Eltern? Streitest du oft mit deinen Geschwistern oder Eltern? Worüber?

Ich habe neulich einen Teilzeitjob im Supermarkt bekommen. Ich arbeite samstags von 9 Uhr bis 1 Uhr. Die Arbeit ist nicht zu anstrengend und wird relativ gut bezahlt. Ich freue mich darüber, denn mein Taschengeld reicht nie! Bekommst du Taschengeld? Wofür brauchst du eigentlich Geld? Hast du auch einen Job? Ist es leicht, einen Teilzeitjob in Irland zu finden?

Ich verbringe gern Zeit bei meinen Großeltern. Sie erzählen mir lustige Geschichten aus der Vergangenheit, was ich echt interessant finde. Sind deine Großeltern noch am Leben? Findest du es gut, wenn Jung und Alt Kontakt miteinander haben? Was können Jung und Alt voneinander lernen? Warum glaubst du das? Jetzt muss ich aber Schluss machen, denn ich habe noch Hausaufgaben zu erledigen. Lass bald von dir hören.

Dein(e) Denis/Denise

Prüfungstipp

Ensure you underline all of the questions when you first read the text. That way you won't miss anything.

Grammatik: Zeitformen/Tenses

p. 20 (Übung macht den Meister)

Imperfect Tense: Regular Verbs

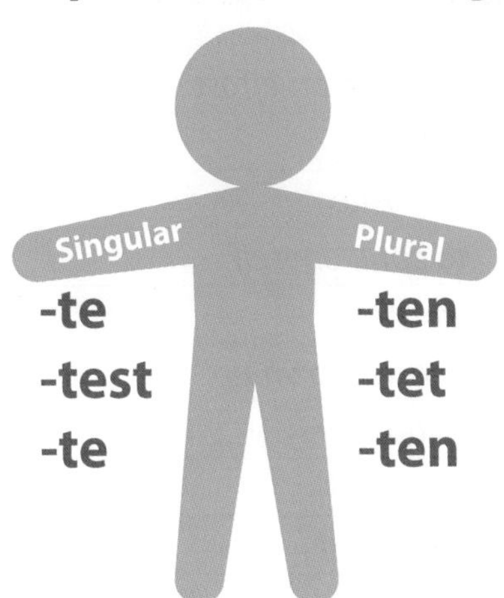

In German, the **imperfect tense** tends to be used in writing. **Ich wohnte** can be translated as 'I lived' *or* 'I have lived' *or* 'I did live'.

Weak (regular) verbs in the imperfect have the same verb endings as in the present tense. However, **-t** is put in front of the verb ending. The **-t**, which is like the English '-ed', indicates that the verb is regular.

ich wohn**te**	wir wohn**ten**
du wohn**test**	ihr wohn**tet**
er/sie/es/man wohn**te**	Sie/sie wohn**ten**

ich arbeit**ete**	wir arbeit**eten**
du arbeit**etest**	ihr arbeit**etet**
er/sie/es arbeit**ete**	Sie/sie arbeit**eten**

Put the bracketed verbs into the imperfect tense. Then translate the sentences.

1. Mein Vater (bauen) ein Vogelhaus.
2. Was (grillen) du am Wochenende?
3. Wir (lachen) viel bei der Party.
4. Die Kinder (lernen) fleißig für die Schule.
5. Warum (stricken) das Mädchen?
6. Ich (träumen) oft davon.
7. Wie (teilen) ihr die Arbeit?
8. Man (reden) über alles.
9. Meine Schwester (studieren) im Ausland.
10. Frau Meier, was (suchen) Sie?

Imperfect Tense: Regular Separable Verbs

Put the bracketed verbs into the imperfect tense, with the separable prefix at the end of the phrase. Then translate the sentences.

1. Ich (ablehnen) die Einladung.
2. Michael (zuhören) im Unterricht.
3. Das Kind (umdrehen) sich.
4. Wir (weiterspielen) auf dem Sportplatz.
5. Meine Mutter (aufwärmen) das Essen.

Imperfect Tense: Regular Inseparable Verbs

Put the bracketed verbs into the imperfect tense. Then translate the sentences.

1. Der Vater (besorgen) das Essen.
2. Die Kinder (verstecken) sich im Garten.
3. Ich (erleben) eine neue Kultur.
4. Das Buch (gehören) meinem Großvater.
5. Meine Eltern (behandeln) mich wie ein Kind.

Hausaufgaben

Turn the following sentences from Text 3 into the imperfect tense. The verbs are all regular.

1. Die Familie wohnt jetzt in einer größeren Wohnung.
2. Laura und Magda teilen ein Zimmer.
3. Laura spielt gern mit Lina.
4. Lina weint manchmal stundenlang.
5. Er ärgert sich, wenn die Kinder herumtoben.
6. Dann streiten sie sich.

Prüfungstipp

Practise tenses regularly by talking about everyday activities. First describe daily activities in the present tense and then use the same verbs in the imperfect tense to talk about what you used to do.

01.03 Hörverständnis Teil 3

Vorarbeit *Preparation*

sich anstrengen	*to make an effort*
stolz	*proud*
Gegenteil	*opposite*
sich verwöhnen	*to spoil oneself*
besorgt	*worried*
fast erwachsen	*nearly grown up*
scheinen	*to appear*
klingen	*to sound*
belohnt	*rewarded*
Wahrheit	*truth*
sich kümmern um	*to care about*
geteiltes Leid ist halbes Leid	*a problem shared is a problem halved*

CL Ordinary + Higher Level Questions

Hören Sie jetzt das Gespräch zwischen Georg und Ursula. Now listen to the conversation between Georg and Ursula.

1. **a)** The conversation is between:
   - **i)** two classmates ☐
   - **ii)** a parent and teenage child ☐
   - **iii)** a teacher and a parent ☐
   - **iv)** two parents of teenage children ☐

   b) Find **one (O)/two (H)** points from the conversation that support your choice.
2. **a)** Which word best describes the male speaker's attitude during the conversation?
   - **i)** worried ☐
   - **ii)** angry ☐
   - **iii)** embarrassed ☐
   - **iv)** shocked ☐

   b) Write down **one (O)/two (H)** details from the conversation that support your choice.
3. The female speaker has a different experience from the male speaker. Give **one (O)/two (H)** detail(s).
4. What do the speakers decide to do after the Leaving Certificate? Give **one (O)/two (H)** detail(s).

Prüfungstipp

If you find aural work difficult, try to read audio scripts while you listen to them. Hearing and seeing words at the same time will improve your listening skills. The transcripts at the end of the State Examinations Commission marking schemes are a useful resource.

A clever way to learn vocabulary is to learn synonyms.

sich Sorgen machen um = sich kümmern um
es geht mir auf den Wecker = es geht mir auf die Nerven
die jungen Leute = die Jugendlichen
Ärger = Krach
schlimm = schlecht

01.04 Hörverständnis Teil 4

Vorarbeit *Preparation*

ausgeben	*to spend*	**Beliebtheitsskala**	*popularity scale*	**ungewöhnlich**	*unusual*
Handgelenk	*wrist*	**ins Schleudern kommen**	*to skid*	**prallen**	*to crash*
Totalschaden	*write-off*	**gepflegt**	*groomed*	**Körper**	*body*
Laufen	*running*	**Auflockerung**	*clearing up*	**Schneeregen**	*sleet*

Beschreiben Sie das Bild in **vier bis fünf** Sätzen. Benützen Sie so viele Ausdrücke aus der Vokabelliste wie möglich.

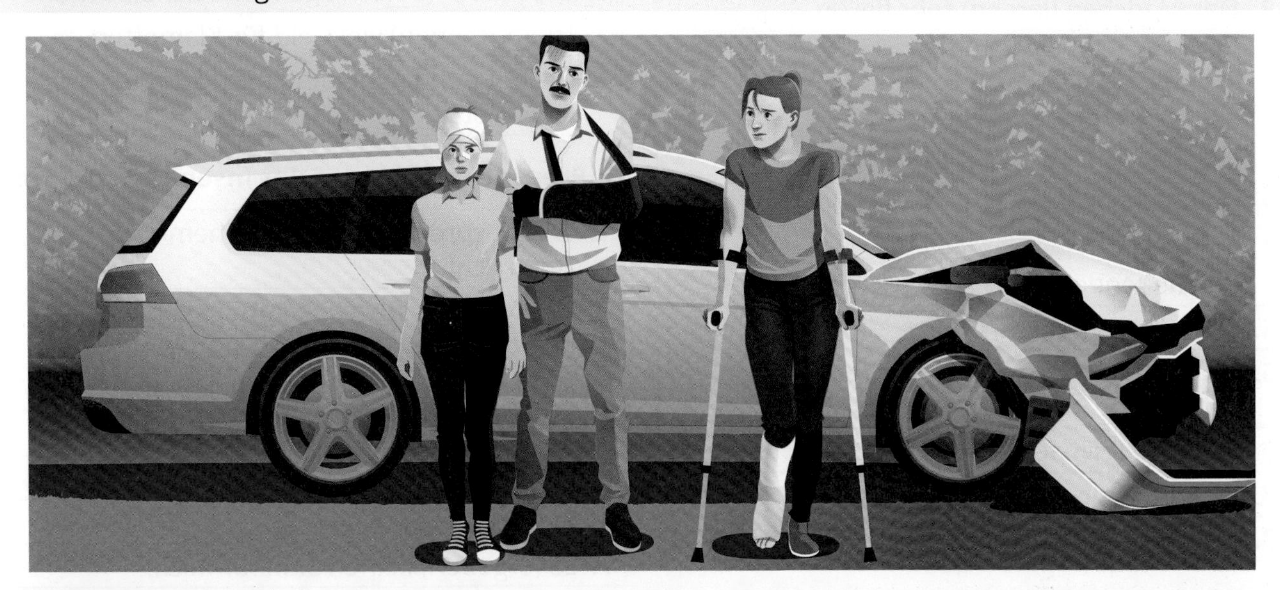

Ordinary + Higher Level Questions

1. **a)** The Germans consider themselves fond of animals. What details confirm this?
   b) Rank the popularity of different types of pets according to the text.
2. **a)** A family from Darmstadt had an unusual series of misfortunes. What happened to the daughter and father while they were on holiday?
   b) What happened to the family on the way home? Give **three** details.
3. **a)** What **two (O)/three (H)** things does the modern German man consider to be particularly important?
   b) What are the most popular types of sport according to the text?
4. **a)** What is the weather forecast for today? Give **three** details.
   b) What is the forecast for Friday? Give **two** details.

Kulturecke

You should speak and listen to as much German as possible. News sources such as *Deutsche Welle*, *Spiegel TV* and *Tagesschau* will familiarise you with spoken German. *Deutsche Welle* features vocabulary sheets and news, which is spoken slowly. The *Helles Koepfchen* and *News4Kids* websites are useful and contain news adapted for young people.

There are also lots of excellent German films available online, including many with subtitles. As well as being enjoyable, these films will give you a much better sense of German culture and history. Good films to watch include *Der Untergang*; *Das Leben der Anderen*; *Good Bye Lenin!*; *Die Welle*; *Wir sind die Nacht*.

Übung Macht den Meister!

Write the sentences in your copy, inserting the correct form of the verb. Then translate them.

A Present Tense: Regular Verbs

1. Ich (brauchen) gute Noten im Abitur.
2. Wann (feiern) du Geburtstag?
3. Wer (fehlen) heute?
4. Der Computer (funktionieren) nicht.
5. Wir (wohnen) gern auf dem Land.
6. In Irland (regnen) es fast jeden Tag.
7. Die Schüler (reisen) nach Deutschland.
8. Das Mädchen (lernen) sehr fleißig.

B Present Tense: Regular Separable Verbs

1. Ich (ausschalten) das Licht, um Strom zu sparen.
2. Die Kinder (einpacken) ihre Schulsachen.
3. Meine Eltern (ausruhen) sich am Wochenende.
4. Wann (wegräumen) du den Müll?
5. Er (vorbereiten) sich auf die mündliche Prüfung.
6. Man (weitermachen) mit der Arbeit.
7. Wann (anrufen) du mich?
8. Ich (auswandern) nach Deutschland.

C Present Tense: Regular Inseparable Verbs

1. Der Schüler (verbessern) seine Deutschnoten.
2. Wie (übersetzen) man das auf Deutsch?
3. Ich (gewöhnen) mich an die Arbeit.
4. Das Kind (entschuldigen) sich.
5. Morgens (beeilen) wir uns immer.
6. Wie viel Geld (verdienen) du?
7. Wir (verbessern) unsere Aussprache.
8. Die Lehrer (erwarten) zu viel von uns.

D Present Tense: Irregular Verbs

1. Der Junge (fahren) gern Auto.
2. Was (lesen) das Kind?
3. Mein Bruder (helfen) nie zu Hause mit.
4. Wir (essen) zu Mittag in der Kantine.
5. Die Katze (schlafen) dauernd.
6. Was (nehmen) du?
7. Der Junge (werfen) den Ball.
8. Wir (sprechen) oft auf Deutsch.

E Present Tense: Irregular Separable Verbs

1. Wer (teilnehmen) am Wettbewerb?
2. Am Wochenende (ausschlafen) meine Mutter.
3. Ich (fernsehen) jeden Tag eine Stunde.
4. Wie (aussehen) der Mann?
5. Mein Lehrer (aufgeben) zu viele Hausaufgaben.
6. Die Kinder (aufschlagen) ihre Schulbücher.
7. Ich (ausgeben) viel Geld für Klamotten.
8. Mein Freund (einladen) mich zum Geburtstag.

F Present Tense: Irregular Inseparable Verbs

1. Wir (besprechen) wichtige Themen im Unterricht.
2. Das Mädchen (bewerben) sich um ein Praktikum.
3. Die Kinder (erhalten) viele Trophäen.
4. Mein Bruder (unterbrechen) mich immer.
5. Was (empfehlen) du mir?
6. Er (versprechen) mir alles.
7. Es (ergeben) keinen Sinn für mich.
8. Das Essen (gefallen) uns sehr.

G Imperfect Tense: Regular Verbs

1. Die Zeiten (ändern) sich.
2. Wir (dekorieren) den Weihnachtsbaum.
3. Der Unterricht (dauern) vierzig Minuten.
4. Ich (fühlen) mich erschöpft.
5. Die Schülerin (hassen) Fremdsprachen.
6. Meine Mutter (kaufen) viele Geschenke.
7. Mein Vater (kochen) gern Eintopf.
8. Ich (hoffen) auf ein gutes Ergebnis.

H Imperfect Tense: Regular Separable Verbs

1. Wir (ausräumen) den Dachboden.
2. Ich (aussuchen) mir ein schönes Kleid.
3. Der Lehrer (fortsetzen) mit dem Unterricht.
4. Mein Bruder (mitmachen) begeistert.
5. Das (anhören) sich gut.
6. Wann (einkaufen) du?
7. Wann (aufräumen) ihr?
8. Warum (zurückkehren) Sie?

Für die Prüfung/Exam Focus

Prüfungstipp

The next two pages are a great opportunity to put what you have learned in this chapter into practice! Work on your own at first, and try to complete as many of the exercises as possible. Then, in pairs or small groups, compare your answers and correct any mistakes. Go over these sections often in preparation for your exams.

1. Was passt zusammen?

1. Am Wochenende sind wir alle müde,	**A** und wandern oft am Wochenende.
2. Da wir beschäftigt sind,	**B** und ist eine sehr gute Zuhörerin.
3. Wir sind ganz sportlich	**C** also gucken wir uns einen guten Film an.
4. Meine Großmutter gibt guten Rat	**D** ohne zu klopfen.
5. Meine Mutter/Mein Vater kommt in mein Zimmer	**E** haben wir wenig Freizeit zusammen.

2. Was passt zusammen?

1. Mein Bruder/Meine Schwester ist manchmal launisch und faul,	**A** denn er/sie ist egoistisch und rücksichtslos.
2. Er/Sie raubt mir den letzten Nerv,	**B** tragen wir alle Freizeitkleidung.
3. Weil es das Wochenende ist,	**C** verbringt man wenig Zeit zusammen.
4. Wenn beide Eltern berufstätig sind,	**D** und jeder guckt sich eine andere Sendung an.
5. Jetzt hat jeder sein eigenes Gerät	**E** aber wir haben eine Menge Spaß zusammen.

3. Select the correct prepositions for the following sentences.

a) Ich gehe gern **(um/mit/aus/an)** meiner Mutter einkaufen.
b) Meine Eltern haben Vertrauen **(zu/an/in/auf)** mir.
c) Ich passe **(für/in/auf/an)** meine Geschwister auf.
d) Großeltern können **(für/bei/an/durch)** der Kinderbetreuung mithelfen.
e) Wir lernen Höflichkeit und Geduld **(von/durch/vor/neben)** Älteren.
f) Mein Opa hat weiße Haare und geht **(in/auf/neben/mit)** einem Stock.
g) Wir streiten uns **(über/von/mit/in)** die kleinste Kleinigkeit, weil er mich ständig nervt.
h) Ich decke den Tisch, bringe den Müll raus und ich kümmere mich **(für/in/um/an)** den Garten.
i) Kinder und Jugendliche können den Großeltern bei dem Umgang **(mit/in/an/für)** Technik helfen.
j) Ich schaue mir gern Filme **(in/an/auf/mit)** meinem iPad an.

Prüfungstipp

Don't forget to spend extra time revising the aspects of German which you find difficult. Remember: Übung macht den Meister! Practice makes perfect!

4. What words make up the following compound words, and what do they mean in English?

a) Vordergrund = _____+_____= _____________

b) Wochenende = _____+_____= _____________

c) Freizeit = _____+_____= _____________

d) Großeltern = _____+_____= _____________

e) kompromissbereit = _____+_____= _____________

f) Hintergrund = _____+_____= _____________

g) Freizeitkleidung = _____+_____= _____________

h) Privatsphäre = _____+_____= _____________

i) selbstständig = _____+_____= _____________

j) berufstätig = _____+_____= _____________

5. Note down for the underlined regular verbs: singular or plural, the tense and the infinitive.

a) Mein Großvater erzählt komische Geschichten.

b) Die Großeltern schenkten den Kindern Zeit.

c) Ich koche manchmal das Abendessen.

d) Wir feierten bis in die Nacht.

e) Meine Mutter sagte, dass ich launisch bin.

f) Er arbeitete an einer Tankstelle.

6. Note down the following information for the underlined irregular verbs: singular or plural, the tense and the infinitive.

a) Meine Großmutter sieht sehr modisch aus.

b) Meine Geschwister sind ganz lieb und lustig.

c) Mein Vater trägt eine Brille.

d) Wir spielen gern zusammen.

e) Mein Bruder hilft mir bei den Hausaufgaben.

f) Leider gibt es oft Streit zu Hause.

7. Lückentext: Fill in the blanks with the correct missing words from the box.

wir	**kommt**	**Ausgehen**	**über**	**gibt**
aus	**vor**	**hilfsbereit**	**kommen**	**ist**

Wir **1** _____________ meistens sehr gut miteinander **2** _____________ , denn meine Eltern sind tolerant und **3** _____________ . Es **4** _____ selten Streit zu Hause, denn meine Mutter ist sehr geduldig und mein Vater **5** _____ locker. Manchmal streiten wir **6** _____________ Hausarbeit, Noten, das **7** _____________ und Klamotten. Aber das **8** _____________ ja in jeder Familie **9** _____________ . Eigentlich verstehen **10** _____________ uns ganz gut.

Prüfungstipp

Grammar is an important part of your exam, so make sure you are familiar with the grammar terms in English and German.

Selbstbewertung: Ordinary Level

Vocabulary

1. If I can translate these nouns into German, I understand the nouns needed to describe my family. (1 mark each)

a) brother	**c)** brothers	**e)** mother	**g)** siblings	**i)** family
b) sister	**d)** sisters	**f)** father	**h)** parents	**j)** housework

Your score: ___ / 10

2. If I can translate these sentences into English, I am able to discuss myself and my family in German. (1 mark each)

a) Ich habe einen Bruder und eine Schwester.	**f)** John ist faul und lustig.
b) Sie heißen ...	**g)** Meine Eltern sind verständnisvoll.
c) Ich bin der/die Älteste/Jüngste/das Mittelkind.	**h)** Wir streiten über Taschengeld.
d) Wir kommen gut miteinander aus.	**i)** Wir streiten über Hausaufgaben.
e) Mary ist freundlich und nett.	**j)** Ich bin normalerweise lustig.

Your score: ___ / 10

Grammar

3. If I can conjugate the following verbs, I can express myself in the present tense. (5 marks for each verb)

   a) heißen (to be named): ich heiße, du ___ , er/sie/es ___ , wir ___ , ihr ___ , Sie/sie ___

   b) sein (to be): ich bin, du ___ , er/sie/es ___ , wir ___ , ihr ___ , Sie/sie ___

Your score: ___ / 10

4. If I can choose the correct verb, I understand irregular verbs in the present tense. (1 mark each)

a) Mein Vater **(fahrt/fährt)** mich zur Schule.	**f)** Wir **(tragen/trägen)** eine Uniform.
b) Der Junge **(lest/liest)** ein Buch.	**g)** Mein Vater **(gebt/gibt)** mir Taschengeld.
c) Ich **(sehe/siehe)** das schöne Bild.	**h)** Mein Bruder **(sprecht/spricht)** sehr laut.
d) Meine Schwester **(helft/hilft)** mir.	**i)** Die Katze **(schlaft/schläft)** immer.
e) Warum **(nehmst/nimmst)** du den Apfel?	**j)** Das Kind **(seht/sieht)** gern fern.

Your score: ___ / 10

5. If I can conjugate these verbs, I understand separable verbs. (2 marks each)

   a) Wir (auskommen) meistens gut miteinander.

   b) Ich (zuhören) gern Popmusik.

   c) Wir (aufräumen) das Klassenzimmer.

   d) Ich (aufmachen) das Fenster.

   e) Der Schüler (mitmachen) im Unterricht.

Your score: ___ / 10

What have I learned?	
What must I improve?	
What do I want to revise?	

Your total score: ___ / 50

Selbstbewertung: Higher Level

HL

1. If I can translate the following into German, I can express myself in the present tense. (1 mark each)

a) I have a brother and a sister.	**f)** John is always lazy and very funny.
b) There are five of us in the family.	**g)** My parents are understanding and tolerant.
c) I like being the eldest.	**h)** We argue about pocket money and going out.
d) Normally we get on well together.	**i)** We argue about housework and homework.
e) Mary is friendly and nice.	**j)** I can be a bit lazy at times.

Your score: ___ / 10

2. If I can translate the adjectives below, I can describe my family. (1 mark each)

a) Mein Bruder ist immer ____________ und sehr ____________ . (nice/friendly)

b) Meine Schwester ist ____________ und ____________ . (impatient/cheeky)

c) Meine Geschwister sind ____________ und ____________ . (good-humoured/funny)

d) Ich bin immer ____________ und meistens ____________ . (helpful/patient)

e) Meine Eltern sind beide sehr ____________ und ____________ . (tolerant/fair)

Your score: ___ / 10

3. If I can put the following verbs into the present tense, I can express myself in the present tense. (1 mark each)

a) Ich (heißen) Daire.	**f)** Wir (auskommen) gut miteinander.
b) Mein Vater (kochen) das Abendessen.	**g)** Ich (mithelfen) bei der Hausarbeit.
c) Meine Mutter (fahren) mich zur Schule.	**h)** Wir (sprechen) auf Deutsch.
d) Mein Bruder (sein) manchmal faul.	**i)** Der Hund (schlafen) in der Garage.
e) Meine Schwester (lesen) gern Romane.	**j)** Meine Mutter (geben) mir Taschengeld.

Your score: ___ / 10

4. If I can put these regular verbs into the imperfect tense, I understand the present and imperfect tenses. (1 mark each)

a) Ich kaufe ein neues Kleid.	**f)** Wir feiern Ostern zusammen.
b) Was brauchst du?	**g)** Worauf wartet ihr?
c) Er sucht einen Brieffreund.	**h)** Frau Schmidt, drücken Sie mir die Hand!
d) Die Frau bestellt einen Kaffee.	**i)** Die Kinder verstecken sich.
e) Das Kind spielt im Garten.	**j)** Ich übe Deutsch jeden Tag.

Your score: ___ / 10

5. If I can fill in the blanks, I understand the difference between verbs, nouns and articles. (2 marks each)

Fernbedienung   streiten   verstehen   einen   bin

Ich heiße Michael und ich **1** ____________ achtzehn Jahre alt. Ich habe **2** ____________ Bruder und eine Schwester. Eigentlich **3** ____________ wir uns alle sehr gut, denn wir sind gutmütig. Manchmal **4** ____________ wir uns über die **5** ____________ , aber ich glaube, das kommt in jeder Familie vor.

Your score: ___ / 10

What have I learned?	
What must I improve?	
What do I want to revise?	

Your total score: ___ / 50

02 Mein Wohnort

Learning Outcomes

- **Oral:** describing one's home place
- **Reading:** reading and discussing three texts about one's home place
- **Writing:** writing an opinion (**Äußerung**) about homelessness, a picture description and a letter about living in Ireland
- **Aural:** listening to and answering questions on four extracts about one's home place

Grammar

- Regular verbs in the perfect tense
- Irregular verbs in the imperfect and perfect tenses

Vocabulary

- Buildings, facilities and transport
- Geographical terms
- Likes and dislikes about city/country living

German Culture

- **Duzen and Siezen**: informal and formal terms of address
- **Wohngemeinschaften**: flat-sharing
- The population of Germany

Exam Tips

- Higher Level students should practise rephrasing German sentences.
- Make sure that you know the most common **sein** verbs in German.
- Make sure that you have a good command of vocabulary for a range of topics.

Mündliche Arbeit: Ihr Wohnort

Stellen Sie sich gegenseitig Fragen darüber, wo Sie leben.

1. Wo wohnen Sie?
2. Wohnen Sie gern hier?
3. Was gibt es hier zu tun?
4. Erzählen Sie mir ein bisschen über Ihr Dorf/Ihre Stadt.
5. Wo wollen Sie später wohnen?

Ich wohne ... **Ich möchte (nicht) ...**
Das ist/liegt ... **Ich fahre/komme ...**
Der Ort/Die Stadt/Das Dorf heißt ...
Ich mag ... **Es gibt (kein(e)) ...**
Hier gibt es ...

1. Wo wohnen Sie? *Where do you live?*	
Ich wohne einen Katzensprung von hier, also gehe ich immer zu Fuß zur Schule, auch wenn es regnet.	*I live a stone's throw away, so I always go to school on foot, even when it's raining.*
Ich wohne, wo sich Fuchs und Hase gute Nacht sagen.	*I live in the middle of nowhere.*
Der Ort/**die** Stadt/**das** Dorf heißt ...	*The town/city/village is called ...*
Ich wohne **auf dem** Land/**im** Dorf/**in der** Stadtmitte/**am** Stadtrand.	*I live in the country/in the village/in the city centre/ on the edge of town.*
Ich wohne in **einer** Wohnung/**einem** Einfamilienhaus/**einem** Reihenhaus/**einem** Bauernhaus.	*I live in an apartment/a detached house/a terraced house/a farmhouse.*
Ich wohne ... Minuten/Kilometer von hier entfernt.	*I live ... minutes/kilometres from here.*
Das liegt im Süden/im Westen/im Osten/im Norden.	*That is in the south/west/east/north.*
Das liegt in Südostirland/in Nordwestirland.	*That is in south-east Ireland/in north-west Ireland.*

2. Wie kommen Sie jeden Tag zur Schule? *How do you get to school every day?*	
Mein Vater/**Meine** Mutter fährt mich zur Schule.	*My father/my mother drives me to school.*
Ich habe mein eigenes Auto, also fahre ich zur Schule.	*I have my own car, so I drive to school.*
Ich komme mit dem Bus zur Schule. Die Fahrt dauert ... Minuten.	*I go to school by bus. The trip takes ... minutes.*
Ich wohne gleich um die Ecke, also gehe ich zu Fuß zur Schule.	*I live just around the corner, so I walk to school.*
Ich fahre mit dem Rad zur Schule, aber wenn es regnet, fährt meine Mutter mich im Auto.	*I cycle to school, but when it rains, my mother drives me in the car to school.*

3. Wohnen Sie gern hier? *Do you like living here?*	
Ich wohne (nicht) gern hier, denn es ist immer/nie was los.	*I (don't) like living here as there is always something/ never anything going on.*
Meine Freunde wohnen ganz in der Nähe.	*My friends live nearby.*
Die Umgebung ist wunderschön und ich mache gern lange Spaziergänge.	*The area is beautiful and I like taking long walks.*
Ich wohne nicht gern hier, denn es gibt nichts zu tun.	*I don't like living here because there is nothing to do.*
Ich mag meinen Wohnort, aber ich freue mich auf das Leben in der Stadt.	*I like where I live, but I'm looking forward to city life.*
Die Nachbarn sind freundlich. Jeder kennt jeden.	*The neighbours are friendly. Everyone knows everyone.*
Das Nachtleben ist lebendig.	*The nightlife is lively.*

4. Erzählen Sie mir ein bisschen über die Umgegung/die Stadt/das Dorf! *Tell me a bit about the area/the town/the village!*	
Hier gibt es viel/nichts zu tun.	*There is a lot/nothing to do here.*
Es gibt viele Vereine für Jugendliche, einen Golfplatz, ein Schwimmbad und viele Geschäfte, also langweilt man sich nie.	*There are a lot of clubs for young people, a golf course, a swimming pool and a lot of shops, so one is never bored.*
Es gibt ungefähr 30.000 Einwohner hier.	*There are about 30,000 inhabitants here.*
Die Einkaufsmöglichkeiten sind sehr gut.	*The shopping opportunities are very good.*
Man muss in die Stadt fahren, wenn man etwas unternehmen will.	*You have to go into town if you want to do something.*
Zum Glück sind die Busverbindungen sehr gut./ Leider sind die Busverbindungen sehr schlecht.	*Luckily, the bus connections are very good./ Unfortunately, the bus connections are very bad.*
Hier gibt es **einen** Sportplatz/**eine** Eisdiele/**ein** Kino/viele Geschäfte.	*There is a sports ground/an ice-cream parlour/a cinema here./There are many shops here.*
Es gibt keine Einrichtungen für Jugendliche.	*There are no facilities for young people.*
Es gibt gute Sportmöglichkeiten, aber wenn man sich nicht für Sport interessiert, dann gibt es wenig für Jugendliche.	*There are good sports opportunities, but if you are not interested in sport, then there is not much for young people.*
Es fehlt uns an Sporthallen, denn in Irland kann man sich nie auf das Wetter verlassen.	*We have a lack of indoor sports facilities because in Ireland one can never rely on the weather.*

Was für Einrichtungen gibt es in Ihrem Wohnort?

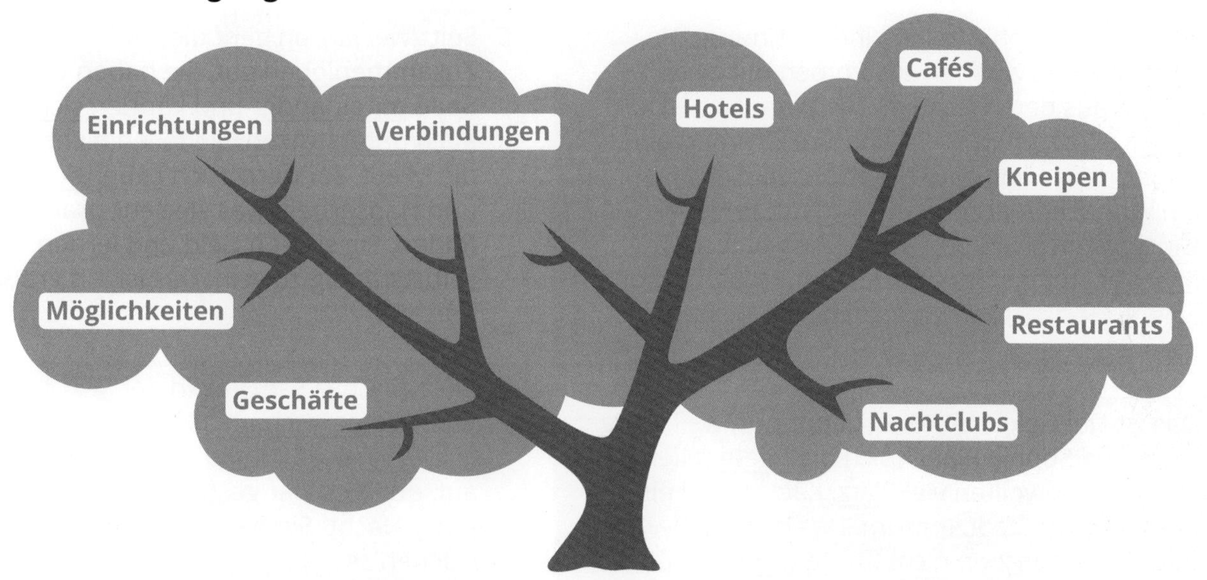

Übersetzen Sie die folgenden Sätze. Translate the following sentences.

1. Ich möchte so schnell wie möglich von hier wegkommen, denn das Dorf/die Stadt/der Ort ist todlangweilig.
2. Ich will später in einer Stadt wohnen. Ich finde die städtische Lebensweise spannend.
3. Ich will unbedingt hier wohnen, da ich mich hier heimisch fühle. Jeder kennt jeden.
4. Ich bin noch nicht sicher, wo ich mich niederlassen will.
5. Hier ist die Landschaft atemberaubend schön. Ich mag die reine Natur.
6. Ich könnte mich überall wohlfühlen. Hauptsache ist, man hat Freunde in der Nähe.
7. Ich will die Welt bereisen. Ich habe keine Lust, mich irgendwo niederzulassen.
8. Wo Familie und Freunde sind, da ist mein Zuhause.

 Remember that you can use these expressions in your written work as well as your oral work.

Text 1: Glücklich in der Wohngemeinschaft

Beantworten Sie die folgenden Fragen:

1. Was machen die Frauen? Wo sind sie?
2. Was für Kleidung tragen sie?
3. Was essen und trinken sie?
4. Was sieht man im Hintergrund?
5. Was sieht man im Vordergrund?

Vorarbeit *Preparation*

1. **Finden Sie diese Ausdrücke im Text!** Find these expressions in the text!
   - **A** ... plus ... electricity, heating ...
   - **B** ... that only works ...
   - **C** They ... learn to be independent.
   - **D** Whoever has time does the shopping.
2. **Finden Sie das Deutsche für die Wörter unten!** Find the German for the words below.
   - **A** inner city/share/kitchenette/animal shelter/square metres
   - **B** financially feasible/close friends/rent/space/the two
   - **C** housework/living together/support each other/living expenses/with each other
   - **D** finally/flat share/relaxed/separate/cash boxes

A Marga und Sophie teilen eine Wohnung. Die zwei Freunde wohnen zusammen mit zwei Katzen aus dem Tierheim. Die Wohnung ist 110 Quadradmeter groß. Es gibt fünf Zimmer, ein Badezimmer und eine Toilette, zwei Schlafzimmer, ein Wohnzimmer mit Kochnische. Sie haben Glück, denn sie haben auch einen Balkon. Die Miete kostet im Monat 1.500 Euro plus Telefon, Strom, Heizkosten, mitten in der Münchner Innenstadt.

B Das ist viel Geld – und das klappt nur, weil Marga Jäger und Sophie Planck sich die Miete teilen. Marga: „Wir wollten viel Platz, Katzen und eine Wohnung im Stadtzentrum. Das ist für eine Person in München nicht finanzierbar." Sophie: „Weil wir eng befreundet sind, ist es praktisch, zusammen zu wohnen. Und es macht Spaß, wenn man zusammen wohnt." Die beiden gehen gerne auf Partys oder geben selbst eine Party in ihrer Wohnung.

C Seit zwei Jahren geht dieses Zusammenleben gut. Sie haben viel Spaß miteinander und können sich auch unterstützen. Sie teilen nicht nur die Miete, sondern auch Lebenskosten und Hausarbeit, was sie sehr praktisch finden. Sie sparen Geld und lernen, selbstständig zu sein. Das ist ein großer Vorteil.

D Ein typischer Samstag in der Wohngemeinschaft: es ist 15 Uhr. Endlich stehen Marga und Sophie auf, denn es war gestern eine lange Party-Nacht. Sie hatten viel Spaß und wachen sehr langsam auf. Marga kauft Brötchen und Croissants und Sophie kocht Kaffee. Die Freundinnen teilen die Hausarbeit ganz locker. Sie haben keine getrennten Kassen. Wer Zeit hat, kauft ein.

OL Ordinary Level Questions

1. Choose a suitable heading for each paragraph from the box below and give reasons for your choice in English.

Gestern gab es eine Party	Marga und Sophie sind gute Freunde	Die Freundinnen wohnen im Stadtzentrum	Sie wohnen seit zwei Jahren zusammen

OL Ordinary Level Questions

2. Answer the following questions in English.
   a) Where do Marga and Sophie live? Give **three** details. A
   b) What kind of accommodation did Marga and Sophie want? B
   c) What do Marga and Sophie share? Give **three** details. C
   d) At what time do Marga and Sophie typically get up on Saturdays? D

3. Complete the following sentences based on Text 1.
   a) Marga und Sophie **(kaufen/suchen/verkaufen/mieten)** eine Wohnung.
   b) Marga und Sophie gehen gern **(zu/auf/in/an)** Partys.
   c) Sie leben **(seit/für/vor/nach)** zwei Jahren zusammen.
   d) Marga und Sophie stehen nach einer Party spät **(an/um/auf/nach)**.

HL Higher Level Questions

1. Beantworten Sie folgende Fragen auf Deutsch!
   a) Mit wem wohnt Marga? Beschreiben Sie mit **mehreren** Details die Wohnung! A
   b) i) Warum teilen Marga und Sophie die Wohnung (**3** Gründe)? B
      ii) Woher weiß man, dass Marga und Sophie Partys gern haben (**2** Gründe)? B
   c) i) Wie lange wohnen Marga und Sophie zusammen? C
      ii) Was teilen Marga und Sophie? C
   d) i) Was machen Marga und Sophie typischerweise samstags? D
      ii) Wer kauft bei ihnen ein? D
2. Answer the following questions in English.
   a) i) Describe the apartment which Marga and Sophie share. Give **five** details. A
      ii) How much does the apartment cost each month, and what costs are extra? A
      iii) Where did Marga and Sophie get their cats? A
   b) i) How can Marga and Sophie afford their apartment? B
      ii) Why is it practical for Marga and Sophie to live together? Give **two** reasons. B
   c) What do Marga and Sophie share? C
   d) i) Why do they usually get up late on Saturdays? D
      ii) Give **three** examples which indicate that Marga and Sophie are comfortable living together. D
3. Woraus bestehen folgende Wörter, und was bedeuten sie im Text?
   a) Heizkosten = _______+_______= _______
   b) Stadtzentrum = _______+_______= _______
   c) Haushaltsplan = _______+_______= _______
   d) Lebenskosten = _______+_______= _______
4. Put the following underlined regular verbs into the imperfect tense.
   a) Marga und Sophie teilen eine Wohnung.
   b) Und es macht Spaß, zusammen zu wohnen.
   c) Marga kauft Brötchen und Croissants und Sophie kocht Kaffee.

Kulturecke

3.7 million people live in Berlin, Germany's capital city. With some 83 million people, Germany has the largest population in the European Union, but it's in decline. Germany has one of the world's lowest birth rates, and the government predicts that the population could drop to 67 million by 2060. On average, German women have their first child at 30 and statistically have 1.4 children.

Grammatik: Zeitformen/Tenses

p. 41 (Übung macht den Meister)

Imperfect Tense: Irregular Verbs

In the imperfect tense there is often a vowel change to the infinitive stem: for example, **lesen** becomes **las-** and **fahren** becomes **fuhr-**. These vowel changes are varied and have to be learned by heart.

You add the endings: **-**, **-st**, **-**, **-en**, **-t**, **-en**.

lesen	fahren	fliegen	laufen
ich las-	ich fuhr-	ich flog-	ich lief-
du l**ast**	du f**uhrst**	du fl**ogst**	du l**iefst**
er/sie/es/man las-	er/sie/es/man fuhr-	er/sie/es/man flog-	er/sie/es/man lief-
wir l**asen**	wir f**uhren**	wir fl**ogen**	wir l**iefen**
ihr l**ast**	ihr f**uhrt**	ihr fl**ogt**	ihr l**ieft**
Sie/sie l**asen**	Sie/sie f**uhren**	Sie/sie fl**ogen**	Sie/sie l**iefen**

Put the following bracketed verbs into the imperfect tense.

1. Meine Mutter (fahren) mich zur Schule.	*My mother drove me to school.*
2. Peter und ich (treffen) uns in der Bibliothek.	*Peter and I met at the library.*
3. Wie (finden) du den Film?	*How did you find the film?*
4. Ich (sprechen) viel Deutsch in Österreich.	*I spoke a lot of German in Austria.*
5. Es (geben) ein Kino hier.	*There was a cinema here.*
6. Wir (trinken) oft Kaffee ohne Milch.	*We often drank coffee without milk.*
7. Die Kinder (rufen) Schimpfwörter.	*The children shouted swear words.*
8. Der Mann (gehen) den Weg entlang.	*The man went along the path.*

Imperfect Tense: Irregular Separable Verbs

Put the bracketed verbs into the imperfect tense. Remember to put the separable prefix at the end of the sentence.

1. Ich (annehmen) die Einladung.	*I accepted the invitation.*
2. Er (aufstehen) spät.	*He got up late.*
3. Die Frau (abgeben) die Aufgabe.	*The woman returned the work.*
4. Wir (weiterfahren) langsam.	*We slowly drove on.*
5. Das Konzert (stattfinden) in Dublin.	*The concert took place in Dublin.*

Imperfect Tense: Irregular Inseparable Verbs

Put the bracketed verbs into the imperfect tense.

1. Ich (beschreiben) das Foto.	*I described the photo.*
2. Was (erfahren) du?	*What did you discover?*
3. Das Mädchen (bestehen) die Prüfung.	*The girl passed the exam.*
4. Der Junge (benehmen) sich gut.	*The boy behaved well.*
5. Das Essen (gefallen) mir sehr.	*I liked the food a lot.*

02.01 Hörverständnis Teil 1

Vorarbeit *Preparation*

passend	*suitable*	**zufällig**	*by chance*	**einziehen**	*to move in*
sich leisten	*to afford*	**Rücken**	*back*	**kennenlernen**	*to get to know*
sich bewerben	*to apply*	**bügeln**	*to iron*	**Altersheim**	*retirement home*

CL Ordinary + Higher Level Questions

Note: O = Ordinary; H = Higher

1. Why can Thomas not find a suitable room? Give **one (O)/two (H)** details.
2. **a)** When did Susi find her room?
   b) Where did she find out about the room? Give **one (O)/two (H)** details.
3. Under this scheme, with whom do students live? What must they do in exchange for not paying rent?
4. **a)** Give **two (O)/three (H)** details about Frau Knecht.
   b) What does she need help with? Give **two (O)/three (H)** details.
5. When did Susi move in? Name one advantage each for Frau Knecht and Susi.

02.02 Hörverständnis Teil 2

Vorarbeit *Preparation*

Grillfete	*barbecue party*	**rollstuhlgerecht**	*wheelchair-accessible*	**lecker**	*delicious*
behilflich	*helpful*	**Zugang**	*access*	**Gerichte**	*dishes*
begeistert	*excited*	**Anlagen**	*facilities*	**bestätigen**	*to confirm*
Verwandte	*relative*	**Vegetarier**	*vegetarian*	**Unwetter**	*storm*

OL Ordinary Level Questions

1. How many people will be going to the restaurant?
2. What **two** issues does the caller mention?
3. When will the woman call back?
4. What is the **name** and **number** of the caller?

HL Higher Level Questions

1. Using ***key phrases***, write down **in German** the key information from the conversation.
   - The name of the person **making** the call
   - The reason for the call
   - Details regarding further contact
   - The caller's phone number

Gesprächsnotiz

Anruf von: ________________ Gesprächsanlass: ________________

Der Anrufer
- erwartet morgen einen Rückruf ☐
- wird so schnell wie möglich angerufen ☐
- bekommt nächste Woche einen Rückruf ☐
- bekommt übermorgen einen Rückruf ☐

Kontaktnummer: *Vorwahl* ________ *Rufnummer* ______________

2. Write down **three** examples of the language which show that the caller is **pleased**.

Text 2: Der Kältebus bringt Wärme

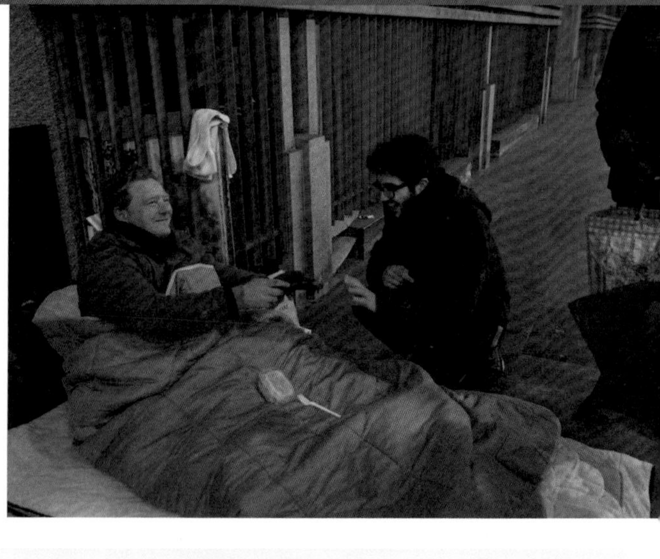

Bitte beantworten Sie die folgenden Fragen:

1. Wie ist das Wetter?
2. Wie sieht der Obdachlose aus?
3. Was verteilen die freiwilligen Helfer?
4. Was sieht man im Hintergrund?
5. Was sieht man im Vordergrund?

Vorarbeit *Preparation*

1. **Finden Sie diese Ausdrücke im Text!** Find these expressions in the text.
   - **A** Whoever needs medical help is cared for by doctors.
   - **B** ... otherwise I won't wake up tomorrow.
   - **C** He has packed his possessions in three bags.
   - **D** This winter many refugees will need help.
   - **E** Every guest is greeted with a handshake.
2. **Finden Sie das Deutsche für die Wörter unten!** Find the German for the words below.
   - **A** protected/cared for/outside/the homeless/emergency overnight accommodation
   - **B** to provide/shivers/home/necessities/wrapped up
   - **C** steals/belongings/misfortune/stores/died
   - **D** poor people/survive/following/frozen to death
   - **E** advice/cheap/dessert/offers

A In Berlin leben etwa 11.000 Menschen ohne Wohnung. Sobald es draußen gefährlich kalt wird, schicken wir den Kältebus durch die Straßen. Wir bringen die Obdachlosen zu einer Notübernachtung. Wer medizinische Hilfe braucht, wird von Ärzten betreut. In den letzten Jahren haben wir zehntausenden obdachlosen Menschen geholfen und sie vor dem Tod durch Erfrieren geschützt.

B Mit Decken, Schlafsäcken und warmer Kleidung an Bord fährt der Kleinbus jeden Abend um 18 Uhr los, um Menschen, die sich selbst nicht schützen können, mit dem Notwendigsten zu versorgen. „Heute komme ich mit euch mit. Ich darf hier nicht einschlafen, sonst wache ich morgen nicht mehr auf." Das sagt Ingo, 58 Jahre alt. Er zittert, obwohl er in Decken eingewickelt ist. Sein Zuhause ist eine alte Parkbank in Berlin.

C Menschen wie Ingo suchen Wärme, wenn es draußen kalt ist. Ingos Unglück begann, als seine Frau starb. Er verlor Freunde, die Arbeit und dann auch seine Wohnung. 14 Jahre lebt Ingo schon auf der Straße. Tagsüber sammelt er Flaschen. Sein Hab und Gut hat er in drei Tüten verpackt und lagert es um die Parkbank herum. Wenn er den Park tagsüber verlässt, hat er Angst, dass jemand seine Tüten stiehlt.

D Viele Menschen wie Ingo überleben im Winter, weil es den Kältebus gibt. 1994 war ein Obdachloser in Berlin erfroren. Im folgenden Jahr begann dieser Service für Obdachlose. Letztes Jahr hat der Service mehr als 2.300 Menschen betreut und 30.800 Übernachtungen gezählt. Die Zahl der betreuten Obdachlosen, der Armen und osteuropäischen Reisenden liegt bei mehr als 5.000. In diesem Winter werden viele Flüchtlinge Hilfe brauchen.

E Der Service bietet nicht nur Notübernachtung und warme Kleidung, sondern auch billiges Essen und Beratung. 50 Cent kostet die Suppe, ein kleiner Salat 30 Cent, das warme Menü zwei Euro. Frisch gebackenen Kuchen und Nachtisch gibt's für 60 Cent. Jeder Gast wird mit Handschlag begrüßt.

OL Ordinary Level Questions

1. Answer the following questions in English.
   a) How many people in Berlin are homeless according to the article? A
   b) What does the bus have on board to give to the homeless people? Give **three** details. B
   c) How long has Ingo been living on the streets? C
   d) In what year did the service for the homeless begin? D
   e) What food does the service offer and how much does it cost? E
2. True or false?
   a) In recent years the *Kältebus* has provided help for ten thousand homeless people.
   b) The bus departs every evening at 8 o'clock.
   c) Ingo's misfortune began when his parents died.
   d) In 1994 a homeless person froze to death in Berlin.
   e) The service offers cheap food.
3. Choose the correct prepositions.
   a) Der Kältebus wird **(auf/durch/in/an)** die Straßen geschickt.
   b) Ingo ist **(in/mit/für/an)** Decken eingewickelt.
   c) Er lagert seine Sachen **(hinter/in/um/an)** die Parkbank herum.
   d) Das Leben ist schwierig **(am/um/für/im)** Winter.
   e) Jeder wird **(mit/gegen/zum/am)** Händedruck begrüßt.

HL Higher Level Questions

1. Beantworten Sie folgende Fragen auf Deutsch und in Ihren eigenen Worten.
   a) i) Wann wird der Kältebus durch die Straßen geschickt? A
      ii) Wohin werden die Obdachlosen gebracht? A
   b) i) Warum fährt der Bus mit Decken, Schlafsäcken und warmer Kleidung an Bord? B
      ii) Warum soll Ingo nicht einschlafen? B
   c) i) Wann begann Ingos Unglück und was verlor er? (**Mehrere** Details!) C
      ii) Wo lagert er sein Hab und Gut? C
   d) i) Wie viele Menschen betreut der Service? D
      ii) Wer noch wird diesen Winter Hilfe brauchen? D
   e) Was bietet der Service? (**3** Details) E
2. Answer the following questions in English.
   a) i) What does this service provide to homeless people? Give **two** details. A
      ii) When does it provide this service? A
   b) Give **three** details about Ingo. B
   c) i) What does Ingo do during the day? C ii) What is Ingo afraid of? C
   d) How many people did the service care for last year, and how many places in overnight accommodation were provided? D
   e) Apart from emergency accommodation and warm clothing, what else does the service provide? Give **three** details. E
3. Was passt zusammen?

1. Obdachlose brauchen Hilfe,	**A** um Obdachlose zu versorgen.
2. Der Bus fährt los,	**B** nachdem ein Obdachloser erfroren war.
3. Weil Ingo kein Zuhause hat,	**C** wenn es draußen kalt ist.
4. Der Service begann,	**D** und jeder wird herzlich begrüßt.
5. Das Essen ist billig	**E** schläft er auf einer Parkbank.

Prüfungstipp

It is important for Higher Level students to practise rephrasing German sentences.

Use the question to rephrase: **Wann wird der Bus durch die Straßen geschickt? → Der Bus wird durch die Straßen geschickt, sobald es draußen kalt wird.**

Change nouns and pronouns: **Die Helfer bringen die Obdachlosen zu einer Notübernachtung. → Sie bringen sie zu einer Notübernachtung.**

Change word order: **Ich darf hier nicht einschlafen, sonst wache ich morgen nicht mehr auf. → Ingo wacht morgen nicht auf, wenn er hier einschläft.**

OL Äußerung zum Thema: Ordinary Level

You are interviewing Ingo. Complete his dialogue based on the information given in Text 2.

Sie: Wie alt sind Sie?
Ingo: ______________________________
Sie: Wo wohnen Sie?
Ingo: ______________________________
Sie: Wie lange leben Sie jetzt auf der Straße?
Ingo: ______________________________
Sie: Wann begann Ihr Unglück?
Ingo: ______________________________
Sie: Was machen Sie während des Tages?
Ingo: ______________________________

HL Äußerung zum Thema: Higher Level

Write 13 to 15 sentences, answering the questions below.

- Beschreiben Sie das Foto oben in **drei bis vier** Sätzen.
- Warum gibt es so viele obdachlose Menschen, Ihrer Meinung nach? Nennen Sie **zwei** Gründe.
- Wie kann man den Obdachlosen helfen? Geben Sie **zwei** Beispiele.
- Würden Sie gern eine eigene Wohnung haben? Nennen Sie **zwei** Vorteile und **zwei** Nachteile, eine eigene Wohnung zu haben oder eine Wohnung zu teilen.

Nützliche Sätze/Useful Sentences

Tip: Use sentences from the oral section and the texts for your written work.

Obdachlosigkeit ist ein wachsendes Problem, denn viele Leute können sich die Hypothek nicht leisten und dann wird ihr Haus wieder in Besitz genommen.	*Homelessness is a growing problem because many people can't afford the mortgage and then their house is repossessed.*
Leider gibt es nicht genug Notschlafstellen, also müssen viele unter Brücken oder in Türeingängen schlafen.	*Unfortunately, there are not enough emergency shelters, so many people have to sleep under bridges or in doorways.*
Kinder, die in Notschlafstellen wohnen, finden es sehr schwierig, ihre schulischen Leistungen beizubehalten.	*Children who live in emergency shelters find it very difficult to maintain their academic performance.*
Wir müssen die wohltätigen Organisationen, die den Obdachlosen helfen, unterstützen.	*We must support the charitable organisations which help the homeless.*
Zur Zeit gibt es einen Wohnungsmangel und deshalb geraten Menschen in Obdachlosigkeit.	*At the moment there is a housing shortage and therefore people are becoming homeless.*
Zuhause habe ich nicht genug Privatsphäre.	*I don't have enough privacy at home.*
Man lernt haushalten, wenn man auszieht.	*You learn to budget when you move out.*
Ich träume von meinen eigenen vier Wänden.	*I dream about having my own place.*
Ich möchte auf eigenen Beinen stehen. Die Selbstständigkeit ist für mich sehr wichtig.	*I want to stand on my own two feet. Independence is very important to me.*
Bei Hotel Mama wohnt man sehr bequem.	*Living at home is very comfortable.*

Translate the following sentences into English:

1. Ich würde bestimmt meine Familie vermissen.
2. Man bezahlt keine Miete oder Rechnungen.
3. Von Zuhause ausziehen ist ein großer Schritt.
4. Ausziehen kostet einfach zu viel.

Grammatik: Zeitformen/Tenses

p. 41 (Übung macht den Meister)

Perfect Tense: Regular Verbs

The perfect tense of regular verbs is formed with **haben** plus the past participle. To form the past participle, put **ge-** in front of the infinitive of the verb and replace the *-(e)n* with **-t**: sag*en* becomes **gesagt**; mach***en*** becomes **gemacht**. The past participle goes to the end of its own clause.

Simple: **Ich habe Reis gekocht**

Inseparable: **Sie hat die Geschichte erzählt**

Separable: **Er hat das Fenster aufgemacht**

machen (to do)		**mitmachen** (to participate)	
ich **habe** ... **gemacht**	wir **haben** ... **gemacht**	ich **habe** ... **mitgemacht**	wir **haben** ... **mitgemacht**
du **hast** ... **gemacht**	ihr **habt** ... **gemacht**	du **hast** ... **mitgemacht**	ihr **habt** ... **mitgemacht**
er/sie/es/man **hat** ... **gemacht**	Sie/sie **haben** ... **gemacht**	er/sie/es/man **hat** ... **mitgemacht**	Sie/sie **haben** ... **mitgemacht**

Put the following bracketed verbs into the perfect tense.

1. Die Zeiten (ändern) sich.	*The times have changed.*
2. Ich (arbeiten) dieses Jahr fleißig.	*I worked hard this year.*
3. Die Lehrerin (klagen) über die schlechten Noten.	*The teacher complained about the bad grades.*
4. Wir (feiern) Weihnachten groß.	*We really celebrated Christmas.*
5. Was (fragen) du?	*What did you ask?*

Perfect Tense: Regular Separable Verbs

Put the bracketed verbs into the correct form in the perfect tense.

1. Ich (abholen) das Kind um 2 Uhr.	*I picked the child up at 2 o'clock.*
2. Wir (ausräumen) das Zimmer.	*We cleared out the room.*
3. Mein Vater (einkaufen) am Wochenende.	*My father went shopping at the weekend.*
4. Die Kinder (nachmachen) uns.	*The children imitated us.*
5. Wann (ausruhen) du dich?	*When did you rest?*

Perfect Tense: Regular Inseparable Verbs

Put the bracketed verbs into the correct form in the perfect tense. Inseparable verbs do not take **ge-** in the past participle.

1. Meine Eltern (behandeln) mich wie ein Kleinkind.	*My parents treated me like a small child.*
2. Was (entdecken) ihr?	*What did you discover?*
3. Der Lehrer (unterrichten) Englisch jahrelang.	*The teacher taught English for years.*
4. Das Kind (verstecken) sich im Garten.	*The child hid in the garden.*
5. Ich (entschuldigen) mich beim Rektor.	*I apologised to the principal.*

Some verbs are known as 'mixed verbs' because they behave as if they are both regular and irregular at the same time. Here are six common mixed verbs:

bringen > brachte > gebracht
denken > dachte > gedacht
kennen > kannte > gekannt
nennen > nannte > genannt
rennen > rannte > gerannt
wissen > wusste > gewusst

Text 3: Neue Nachbarn

Beantworten Sie die folgenden Fragen:

1. Was machen die Frau und das Mädchen?
2. Wie sind sie bekleidet?
3. Wie fühlen sie sich, Ihrer Meinung nach?

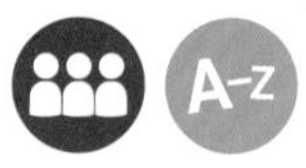

Vorarbeit *Preparation*

Finden Sie das Deutsche für die Wörter unten. Find the German for these words below.

A single/storey/curious/removal van

B drawer/busies herself/address with **du**/conversation

C misses/delighted/printed/down

D died/considers/worries/meets

E hugs/getting on/peace/is happy

Karin Ernst (amended)

A Franziska schaut neugierig aus dem Küchenfenster. Ein großer Möbelwagen steht unten vorm Haus. Oben ziehen die neuen Nachbarn ein. „Ich werde ihnen eine Tasse Kaffee anbieten." Franziska nimmt den Hausschlüssel und geht eine Etage höher. Sie klingelt. „Guten Tag. Ich bin Ihre Nachbarin aus der zweiten Etage. Ich heiße Franziska Erdmann." „Ich heiße Saskia Fischer. Das ist meine Tochter Merle", sagt die junge Frau. „Ich wollte Sie zu einer Tasse Kaffee einladen. Ihren Mann natürlich auch." „Ich wohne mit Merle hier allein. Als alleinerziehende Mutter. Aber wir kommen ganz gut zurecht, nicht wahr, Merle?" fragt sie ihre Tochter. „Gerne nehme ich Ihre Einladung an."

B Franziska geht zurück in ihre Wohnung und bald klingelt es. Die Nachbarin und Merle kommen herein. Sie haben ein angenehmes Gespräch. „Ich muss jetzt wieder an die Arbeit", sagt Frau Fischer. „Merle, wir müssen nach Hause." „Kann ich hierbleiben?" fragt Merle. „Klar kannst du hierbleiben und ich glaube, wir sollten uns alle duzen", lacht Franziska. „Wir werden uns öfter sehen." „Was machst du am liebsten?" fragt Franziska. „Am liebsten male ich." In einer Schublade finden sie Papier und Stifte. Merle beschäftigt sich mit den Buntstiften. „Wie zauberhaft", ruft Franziska. Nach einer Weile hat Merle genug vom Malen. „Hast du Bücher?" fragt sie. „Natürlich haben wir Bücher", sagt Björn. „Bei uns schreibt Franziska selber Geschichten für Kinder. Willst du eine hören?" „Gerne", freut sich Merle.

C Später kommt Merles Mutter herunter. „Mama", ruft Merle, „weißt du, dass Franziska selber Geschichten schreibt?" Björn hat für Merle eine Geschichte am Computer ausgedruckt. „Vielleicht könnte Merle Bilder dafür malen. Björn und ich sind ganz begeistert von ihren Zeichnungen", antwortet Franziska. „Da haben wir aber Glück gehabt, daß wir jetzt solche netten Nachbarinnen haben." Sie freut sich, dass jetzt ein Kind im Haus wohnt. Die eigenen Kinder und Enkel vermisst sie sehr.

D Einige Wochen später trifft Franziska Saskia und Merle vor dem Haus. „Ist etwas los?" fragt Franziska, denn sie sieht, dass Saskia besorgt ist. „Ach, ich kann dich doch nicht mit meinen Sorgen stören", antwortet Saskia. „Wozu sind wir Nachbarinnen?" bittet Franziska. Saskia erklärt, dass sie für ein paar Tage ins Krankenhaus muss. „Nichts Großes, aber ich weiß nur nicht, wohin mit Merle." Franziska überlegt. „Können deine Eltern nicht kommen?" „Ich habe keine Eltern mehr. Die sind bei einem Autounfall ums Leben gekommen", antwortet Saskia. „Mama", sagt Merle. „Ich gehe zu Franziska und Björn."

E Sonntagmorgen gehen Franziska und Björn nach oben und klingeln. Björn nimmt Merles Tasche. Franziska umarmt Saskia. „Tschüss, Mama. Wir besuchen dich im Krankenhaus." Am nächsten Tag machen sich Merle und Franziska nachmittags auf den Weg zum Krankenhaus. Saskia freut sich, als sie Merle wiedersieht! „Und wie kommt ihr zurecht?" fragt sie Franziska. „Es geht wunderbar." „Mama, es ist ganz prima bei Franziska und Björn. Du kannst in aller Ruhe wieder gesund werden."

OL Ordinary Level Questions

1. a) Give **two** details about Franziska's new neighbours. A
   b) What is Merle's favourite pastime? B
   c) Why is Franziska happy that a child is living in the house? C
   d) What is Saskia worried about, and what solution does Merle come up with? D
   e) When do Franziska and Merle go to the hospital? E

2. Choose a suitable heading for each paragraph from the box below and explain your choice in English.

   Merle malt sehr gern | **Saskia muss ins Krankenhaus gehen** | **Franziska vermisst ihre Enkelkinder** | **Die neuen Nachbarn ziehen ein** | **Franziska und Merle besuchen Saskia**

3. Select the correct prepositions for the following sentences.
   a) Franziska will die neuen Nachbarn **(bei/für/zum/mit)** Kaffee einladen.
   b) Merle malt **(an/für/mit/auf)** den Buntstiften.
   c) Björn hat für Merle eine Geschichte **(am/im/vom/beim)** Computer ausgedruckt.
   d) Saskia will Franziska nicht **(bei/an/zu/mit)** ihrem Kram stören.
   e) Franziska und Merle machen sich **(an/auf/vor/durch)** den Weg zum Krankenhaus.

CL Ordinary + Higher Level

Lückentext: Fill in the blanks with the correct words.

alt **mich** **uns** **werden** **Klasse**

Neulich sind neue Nachbarn neben **1** ______________ eingezogen. Die Familie ist sehr nett und der Sohn ist genauso **2** ______________ wie ich. Er wird in meine **3** ______________ in die Schule gehen. Es freut **4** ______________, dass ich jetzt einen neuen Freund habe. Im Sommer **5** ______________ wir viel zusammen unternehmen.

HL Higher Level Questions

1. Beantworten Sie folgende Fragen auf Deutsch und in Ihren eigenen Worten.
   a) Wer gehört zur Familie Fischer? A
   b) Was für eine Geschichte liest Franziska vor? B
   c) Warum haben Franziska und Björn Glück? C
   d) Warum ist Saskia besorgt? Welche Lösung schlägt Merle vor? D
   e) Wie fühlt sich Saskia, wenn sie Merle sieht? E

2. Answer the following questions in English.
   a) Where exactly do the new neighbours live? A
   b) What does Merle do after her mother goes home? Give details. B
   c) i) What does Franziska think of Merle's drawings? C
      ii) What is Franziska pleased about, and why?
   d) What problem does Saskia have, and how is the problem resolved? D
   e) Find **three** examples in the text which show that the new neighbours are becoming close friends.

3. Put the following underlined regular verbs into the perfect tense.
   a) Franziska schaut aus dem Küchenfenster.
   b) Am liebsten male ich.
   c) Merle beschäftigt sich mit den Buntstiften.
   d) Die eigenen Kinder und Enkel vermisst sie sehr.
   e) Franziska überlegt.
   f) Saskia freut sich.

Kulturecke

The verb **siezen** means addressing somebody with the formal **Sie**. The verb **duzen** means addressing somebody with the informal **du**. To be on the safe side, always address people with **Sie** unless they invite you to use **du**. In Germany teachers address students over the age of 16 with **Sie**.

Grammatik: Zeitformen/Tenses

p. 41 (Übung macht den Meister)

Perfect Tense: Irregular Verbs

The perfect tense of irregular verbs is formed with **haben** plus the past participle of the verb. Their past participles do not follow the same pattern as regular verbs, so you will need to learn them.

Most irregular past participles end with **-en**.

Sein is used instead of **haben** where the verb involves motion, for example, **fahren** (to go/drive).

lesen (to read)		**fahren** (to travel)	
ich habe ... geles**en**	wir haben ... geles**en**	ich **bin** ... gefahr**en**	wir **sind** ... gefahr**en**
du hast ... geles**en**	ihr habt ... geles**en**	du **bist** ... gefahr**en**	ihr **seid** ... gefahr**en**
er/sie/es/man hat ... geles**en**	Sie/sie haben ... geles**en**	er/sie/es/man **ist** ... gefahr**en**	Sie/sie **sind** ... gefahr**en**

1. Put the following irregular verbs into the perfect tense. Do you need **haben** or **sein**?

a) Wir (gehen) in die Stadt.	*We went into town.*
b) Ich (lesen) viele Bücher.	*I've read a lot of books.*
c) Was (essen) du?	*What did you eat?*
d) Das Kind (trinken) viel Milch.	*The child drank a lot of milk.*
e) Wann (beginnen) der Unterricht?	*When did the lesson begin?*

2. Irregular separable verbs: Ich habe das Buch vorgelesen.

Put the following irregular separable verbs into the perfect tense. Do you need **haben** or **sein**?

a) Wir (einsteigen) in den Bus.	*We got on the bus.*
b) Ich (hochladen) viele Fotos auf Instagram.	*I uploaded many photos to Instagram.*
c) Die Kinder (teilnehmen) am Unterricht.	*The children participated in the lesson.*
d) Wann (raustragen) du den Müll?	*When did you take out the rubbish?*
e) Die Familie (losfahren) spät am Abend.	*The family set off late in the evening.*

3. Irregular inseparable verbs: Er hat davon erfahren.

Put the following irregular inseparable verbs into the perfect tense. Do you need **haben** or **sein**?

a) Das Mädchen (beschreiben) das Bild.	*The girl described the picture.*
b) Wir (besprechen) das Thema im Unterricht.	*We discussed the topic in class.*
c) Ich (bestehen) darauf.	*I insisted on it.*
d) (Genießen) du den Austausch?	*Did you enoy the exchange?*
e) Ich (entscheiden) mich für einen anderen Kurs.	*I've decided on a different course.*

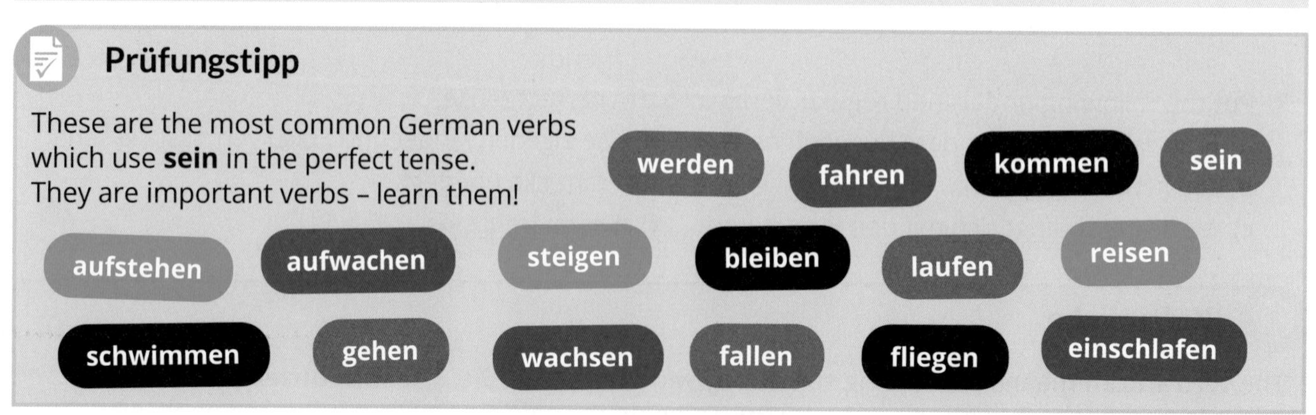

02.03 Hörverständnis Teil 3

Vorarbeit *Preparation*

Gesicht	*face*	**sauer sein**	*to be angry*	**sich leisten**	*to afford*
verlassen	*to leave*	**recht haben**	*to be right*	**Kurbad**	*spa*
Lehre	*apprenticeship*	**Einwohner**	*inhabitants*	**heimisch**	*at home*
Festland	*mainland*	**ziehen**	*to move*	**Insel**	*island*

Ordinary + Higher Level Questions

1. **a)** The conversation is between:
   i) a parent and teenage child ☐ **iii)** a boyfriend and girlfriend ☐
   ii) a teacher and student ☐ **iv)** two classmates ☐
   b) Find **one (O)/two (H)** detail(s) from the conversation to support your choice.
2. **a)** Which word best describes the female speaker's attitude during the conversation?
   i) pleased ☐ **iii)** apologetic ☐
   ii) angry ☐ **iv)** shocked ☐
   b) Write down **one (O)/two (H)** detail(s) from the conversation to support your choice.
3. What do we learn about the island of Wangerooge? Give **one (O)/two (H)** detail(s).
4. What does the male speaker decide to do over the next few years? Give **one (O)/two (H)** detail(s).

02.04 Hörverständnis Teil 4

Vorarbeit *Preparation*

entdecken	*to discover*	**Probefahrt**	*test drive*	**Gewitter**	*thunderstorm*
ausrauben	*to rob*	**Rentnerin**	*pensioner*	**fehlen**	*to lack*
Schmuck	*jewellery*	**Führerschein**	*driving licence*	**Trickdieb**	*swindler*
verschwinden	*to disappear*	**Schmuggel**	*smuggling*	**schätzen**	*to estimate*

Ordinary + Higher Level Questions

1. Who was robbed on Thursday, and what was taken?
2. **a)** With how many cars did the confidence man disappear? What was the financial value of the cars?
   b) What had the confidence man presented to the dealers?
3. **a)** Why are the police finding it difficult to combat human trafficking? Give **one (O)/two (H)** detail(s).
   b) What is the cost of human trafficking, according to the text?
4. **a)** What is the weather forecast for today? Give **two (O)/three (H)** details.
   b) What is the forecast for tomorrow? Give **two (O)/three (H)** details.

Prüfungstipp

Temperatures nearly always come up in the aural section:
1° **ein Grad** *one degree*
-12° **minus zwölf Grad** *minus twelve degrees*
+15° **plus fünfzehn Grad** *plus fifteen degrees*

Schriftliche Produktion: Ordinary Level

Write a letter to your pen pal, Karl(i). Complete the first paragraph by correctly inserting the sentence halves below. Then follow the instructions.

Ich freue mich immer **Ich muss jetzt** **aber ich vermisse meine Freunde**
in ein neues Haus umgezogen **der gestern angekommen ist**

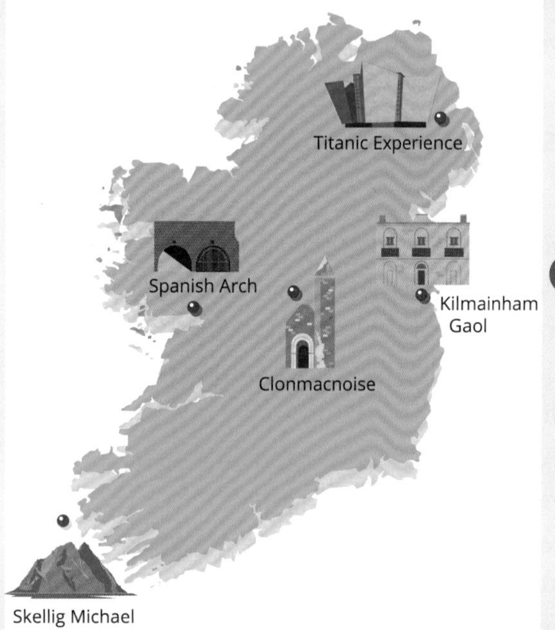

Liebe(r) Karl(i),

vielen Dank für deinen Brief, _______________ . _______________ , von dir zu hören. Wie du weißt, sind wir neulich _______________ . Das neue Haus ist schön und groß, _______________ . _______________ in eine neue Schule gehen.

Now continue the letter.

- Describe the exact location of your new house.
- Describe what you like and don't like about your new house.
- Say what there is for young people to do in the area.
- Mention one thing you like and one thing you dislike about the area.
- Describe how you will go to your new school (on foot, by car, bike or bus).
- Write a suitable closing sentence.

HL Schriftliche Produktion: Higher Level

Reply in German to your pen pal's letter. Give detailed answers to the questions.

Liebe(r) _______________ ,

endlich habe ich wieder Zeit dir zu schreiben! Aber ehrlich gesagt schreibe ich gerade heute, weil ich eine Bitte habe. Ich muss nämlich einen Aufsatz über Irland für die Schule schreiben. Hilfst du mir dabei? Erstens, erzähl' mir ein bisschen über deinen Wohnort. Wo liegt es genau? Wie viele Einwohner gibt es?

Was für Einrichtungen gibt es dort für Jugendliche? Und was fehlt euch? Wie du weißt, wohne ich auf dem Land, aber ich würde viel lieber in der Stadt wohnen, weil es da jede Menge zu tun gibt. Und du, wo würdest du lieber wohnen? Auf dem Land oder in der Stadt? Und warum?

In der Schule lernen wir viel über England, aber nicht viel über Irland. Kannst du mir ein bisschen über die geografische Lage erzählen? Wie viele Einwohner gibt es eigentlich in Irland? Und wie heißt die Hauptstadt?

Meine Englischlehrerin hat uns erzählt, dass Irland „die grüne Insel" genannt wird. Stimmt es, dass die irische Landschaft so schön ist? Was sollte man als Tourist in Irland unbedingt sehen? Ich hoffe nämlich, dass ich im Sommer zu dir kommen kann. Ich will nicht nur meine Sprachkenntnisse verbessern, sondern auch ein bisschen vom Land erfahren. Erzähl' mir, was ich unbedingt sehen muss! Jetzt muss ich leider wieder an die Arbeit. Schreib' mir bald!

Dein(e) Karl(i)

Prüfungstipp

Big German cities: **Berlin**, **Hamburg**, **München**, **Köln**, **Frankfurt am Main**, **Essen**, **Stuttgart**

Germany's important rivers: **Die Donau**, **der Rhein**, **die Elbe**, **die Oder**, **die Mosel**

Germany's important forests: **Der Schwarzwald**, **der Harz**, **der Bayerische Wald**

Übung Macht den Meister!

Write the sentences in your copy, inserting the correct form of the verb. Then translate them.

A Imperfect Tense: Irregular Verbs

1. Ich (bleiben) für eine Woche in Köln.
2. Warum (kommen) der Mann nach Hause?
3. Wir (nehmen) Hustensaft gegen Husten.
4. Der Mann (fahren) gern Motorrad.
5. Die Kinder (sitzen) im Kreis.
6. Der Schüler (schreiben) oft Aufsätze.
7. Ich (wissen) nichts davon.

B Imperfect Tense: Irregular Separable Verbs

1. Ich (abgeben) die Hausaufgaben.
2. Die Leute (einsteigen) in den Bus.
3. Der Unterricht (anfangen) um 8 Uhr.
4. Wir (ausgehen) immer am Wochenende.
5. Du (raustragen) den Müll.
6. Ihr (teilnehmen) am Unterricht.
7. Das Kind (vorlesen) eine Geschichte.

C Imperfect Tense: Irregular Inseparable Verbs

1. Der Lehrer (verlieren) die Geduld.
2. Ich (erfahren) viel über Deutschland.
3. Mein Nachbar (gewinnen) im Lotto.
4. Das Schloss (befinden) sich an der Küste.
5. Der Mann (bewerben) sich um die Stelle.
6. Wir (unterhalten) uns in der Pause.
7. Das Kind (versprechen), brav zu sein.

D Perfect Tense: Regular Verbs

1. Ich (antworten) die Frage.
2. Wir (feiern) Erntedankfest im November.
3. Meine Mutter (färben) sich ihre Haare.
4. Das Kind (fühlen) sich krank.
5. Wir (üben) jeden Tag die deutsche Grammatik.
6. Mein Bruder (lachen) immer.
7. Ich (lernen) das neue Gericht.

E Perfect Tense: Regular Separable Verbs

1. Ich (ablehnen) die Einladung zur Party.
2. Wir (ausräumen) den Dachboden.
3. Mein Freund (herüberschauen) zu mir.
4. Du (ausruhen) dich gut in den Sommerferien.
5. Der Schüler (aufwachen) spät für die Prüfung.
6. Ihr (abmachen) einen Termin beim Zahnarzt.
7. Meine Mutter (einkaufen) am Wochenende.

F Perfect Tense: Regular Inseparable Verbs

1. Was (bedeuten) der Satz auf Englisch?
2. Meine Eltern (beruhigen) mich immer.
3. Was (entdecken) du in Österreich?
4. Ich (erwarten) bessere Noten.
5. Der Laptop (gehören) meinem Bruder.
6. Die Frau (beschweren) sich über den Lärm.
7. Ich (gewöhnen) mich an den Schuldruck.

G Perfect Tense: Irregular Verbs

1. Meine Mutter (geben) mir kein Taschengeld.
2. Wir (sehen) den neuen Film im Kino.
3. Letzten Sommer (fahren) sie nach Spanien.
4. Sie (pl.) (bleiben) dort für drei Wochen.
5. Der Mann (essen) viel Wurst und Sauerkraut.
6. Die Kinder (trinken) viel Sprudelwasser.
7. Wann (fliegen) du nach Frankreich?

H Perfect Tense: Irregular Separable Verbs

1. Ich (aufstehen) spät am Wochenende.
2. Das Kind (anziehen) sich schnell.
3. Was (herausfinden) du?
4. Das Mädchen (aufschreiben) die Nummer.
5. Das Konzert (stattfinden) im August.
6. Ich (vorschlagen) viele Themen für das Projekt.
7. Wir (niederlassen) uns auf dem Land.

I Perfect Tense: Irregular Inseparable Verbs

1. Glücklicherweise (bestehen) ich die Prüfung.
2. Was (geschehen) letzte Woche in der Schule?
3. Meine kleine Schwester (übertreiben) immer.
4. Der Mann (unterschreiben) den Vertrag.
5. Der Junge (verstehen) die Hausaufgaben.
6. Der Hund (verschwinden) um die Ecke.
7. Das Mädchen (besitzen) viele Schmuckstücke.
8. Der Unterricht (beginnen) um 9 Uhr.

Für die Prüfung/Exam Focus

1. Was passt zusammen?

1. Weil immer viel los ist,	**A** die die Touristen anlocken.
2. In Irland gibt es viele Sehenswürdigkeiten,	**B** weil das Dorf todlangweilig ist.
3. In Zukunft möchte ich in der Stadt wohnen,	**C** wohne ich gern hier.
4. Ich will so schnell wie möglich von hier weg,	**D** möchte ich eine eigene Wohnung haben.
5. Wenn ich einundzwanzig Jahre alt bin,	**E** aber die Miete in der Stadt ist sehr teuer.

2. Was passt zusammen?

1. Wenn das Wetter gut ist,	**A** gehen wir ins Kino oder ins Café.
2. Hier gibt es viele Einrichtungen für Teenager,	**B** und man kann lange Spaziergänge machen.
3. Wenn das Wetter schlecht ist,	**C** denn ich wohne gleich um die Ecke.
4. Die Landschaft ist sehr malerisch	**D** spielen wir Fußball im Park.
5. Ich gehe zu Fuß zur Schule,	**E** also will ich mich hier niederlassen.

3. Select the correct prepositions for the following sentences.

a) Wir wohnen in einer Wohnsiedlung **(um/am/im/über)** Stadtrand.

b) Ich würde lieber **(in/an/auf/hinter)** dem Land wohnen.

c) Zum Glück habe ich ein eigenes Zimmer **(im/am/zum/um)** Dachboden.

d) Leider gibt es **(zur/in/nach/an)** Zeit viele obdachlose Menschen.

e) Jeder **(an/in/auf/bei)** der Nachbarschaft ist ganz freundlich und hilfsbereit.

4. What words make up the following compound words, and what do they mean in English?

a) Privatleben = ______+______= ______________

b) Großstadt = ______+______= ______________

c) haushalten = ______+______= ______________

d) Privatsphäre = ______+______= ______________

e) Westküste = ______+______= ______________

f) teilnehmen = ______+______= ______________

5. Note for the underlined regular verbs: singular or plural, the tense and the infinitive.

a) Wir haben ein Museum besucht.

b) Ich lerne fleißig in der Schule.

c) Was kriegtest du zum Geburtstag?

d) Meine Großeltern wohnen auf dem Land.

e) Die Kinder spielten im Garten.

f) Was habt ihr in der Schule gelernt?

6. Note down the following information for the underlined irregular verbs: singular or plural, the tense and the infinitive.

a) Ich bin in die Stadt gegangen.

b) Wir tranken eine Tasse Kaffee.

c) Du fährst gern Rad.

d) Das Mädchen las gern in der Bibliothek.

e) Wir sind in einem Hotel geblieben.

f) Wann triffst du dich mit Karl?

7. Lückentext: Fill in the blanks with the correct missing words from the box.

vermisse	**für**	**müssen**	**Nachbarn**	**gehe**	**meine**	**denn**	**auf**	**jeden**	**die**

Ich wohne gern hier, **1** ________ die Landschaft ist wunderschön. Die **2** ________ sind freundlich und jeder kennt **3** ________. Es gibt gute Einrichtungen **4** ________ Jugendliche und man kann leicht in **5** ________ Stadt fahren. Aber ich werde von hier wegziehen **6** ________, wenn ich **7** ________ die Uni **8** ________. Natürlich **9** ________ ich dann **10** ________ Familie!

Selbstbewertung: Ordinary Level

OL

Vocabulary

1. If I can translate these sentences into English, I can describe where I live. (1 mark each)

a) Ich wohne auf dem Land.	**f)** Es gibt ... Einwohner hier.
b) Es gibt viel für Jugendliche hier.	**g)** Die Busverbindungen sind sehr gut.
c) Ich gehe zu Fuß zur Schule.	**h)** Ich fahre im Auto/Bus zur Schule.
d) Es gibt gute Einkaufsmöglichkeiten hier.	**i)** Leider gibt es kein Kino hier.
e) Ich würde lieber auf dem Land wohnen.	**j)** Ich mag mein Schlafzimmer.

Your score: ___ / 10

2. If I can translate these nouns into German, I can describe where I live. (1 mark each)

a) football pitch	**c)** neighbourhood	**e)** apartment	**g)** shops	**i)** swimming pool
b) cinema	**d)** flat-sharing	**f)** house key	**h)** facilities	**j)** city centre

Your score: ___ / 10

Grammar

3. If I can put these regular verbs into the perfect tense, I can express myself in the perfect tense. (1 mark each)

a) Ich wohne seit Jahren auf dem Land.	**f)** Ich surfe jeden Tag im Internet.
b) Ich mache Spaziergänge im Park.	**g)** Ich koche das Mittagessen.
c) Meine Freunde und ich spielen Fußball.	**h)** Ich spare mein Taschengeld.
d) Ich lerne fleißig jeden Abend.	**i)** Ich kaufe ein neues Handy.
e) Wir hören gern Popmusik.	**j)** Ich dusche mich jeden Tag.

Your score: ___ / 10

4. If I can choose the correct form of **sein** or **haben**, I can use irregular verbs in the perfect tense. (1 mark each)

a) Wir **(haben/sind)** nach Hause gefahren.	**f)** Wir **(haben/sind)** nach Bonn geflogen.
b) Wir **(haben/sind)** viel Wurst gegessen.	**g)** Ich **(habe/bin)** ein gutes Buch gelesen.
c) Er **(hat/ist)** eine Woche geblieben.	**h)** Ich **(habe/bin)** einen Film gesehen.
d) Ich **(habe/bin)** viel Cola getrunken.	**i)** Wir **(haben/sind)** in die Stadt gegangen.
e) Ich **(habe/bin)** im Meer schwimmen gegangen.	**j)** Ich **(habe/bin)** viel Deutsch gesprochen.

Your score: ___ / 10

5. If I can choose the correct preposition, I can correctly describe where I live. (1 mark each)

a) Ich wohne **(in/auf/an)** der Stadt.	**f)** Ich wohne **(in/auf/an)** dem Land.
b) Ich gehe **(auf/in/zu)** Fuß zur Schule.	**g)** Wir gehen **(an/in/auf)** die Disco.
c) Wir spielen Fußball **(am/ab/im)** Park.	**h)** Wir gehen oft **(ans/ins/aufs)** Kino.
d) Ich wohne **(im/an/um)** die Ecke.	**i)** Ich stehe **(um/im/am)** 7 Uhr auf.
e) Ich wohne **(im/bei/zu)** meinen Eltern.	**j)** Karl liegt **(am/im/um)** Krankenhaus.

Your score: ___ / 10

What have I learned?	
What must I improve?	
What do I want to revise?	

Your total score: ___ / 50

Selbstbewertung: Higher Level

HL

1. If I can translate these sentences into German, I can express myself in the present tense. (1 mark each)

a) There are many facilities here.	**f)** There is nothing to do here.
b) I go into town as often as possible.	**g)** I live right around the corner.
c) The landscape is beautiful.	**h)** Everybody knows everyone, which I like.
d) I normally go to school on foot.	**i)** There is a cinema, a golf course and cafes.
e) The nightlife in the city is exciting.	**j)** On Saturday we go to the cinema or disco.

Your score: ___ / 10

2. If I can put these sentences into the imperfect tense, I can express myself in the imperfect tense. (1 mark each)

a) Ich gehe oft in die Stadt.	**f)** Ich esse gern Pommes.
b) Wir treffen uns im Café.	**g)** Wir fliegen nach Frankreich.
c) Meine Schwester spricht fließend Deutsch.	**h)** Du schreibst einen Aufsatz.
d) Es gibt viel zu tun.	**i)** Der Unterricht beginnt um 9 Uhr.
e) Mein Vater trinkt viel Kaffee.	**j)** Ich lese gern Zeitschriften.

Your score: ___ / 10

3. If I can put these sentences into the perfect tense, I can express myself in the perfect tense. (1 mark each)

a) Ich lerne fleißig für das Abitur.	**f)** Ich schreibe einen deutschen Aufsatz.
b) Ich übe die deutschen Zeitformen.	**g)** Wir sprechen im Unterricht auf Deutsch.
c) Wir fahren nach Deutschland.	**h)** Wir fliegen im Flugzeug.
d) Wir erleben die deutsche Kultur.	**i)** Wir essen Bratwurst mit Sauerkraut.
e) Wir bleiben in einer Jugendherberge.	**j)** Der Austausch lohnt sich.

Your score: ___ / 10

4. If I can give the number, tense and infinitive of these verbs, I understand the present, imperfect and perfect tenses. (2 marks for each verb)

a) Wir sind nach Spanien geflogen.	**d)** Die Kinder haben Milch getrunken.
b) Ich lerne viel Deutsch.	**e)** Mein Vater fuhr das neue Auto.
c) Meine Schwester ging in die Stadt.	

Your score: ___ / 10

5. If I can correctly fill the gaps, I understand word functions. (1 mark each)

Großstadt nach meine wenn gehe mich wohne in im gibt

Ich heiße Anna und ich **1** _____ in einer kleinen Stadt **2** _____ Südwestirland. Wenn das Wetter gut ist, **3** _____ ich zu Fuß zur Schule, aber **4** _____ das Wetter schlecht ist, fährt **5** _____ mein Vater **6** _____ Auto. Ich wohne gern hier, denn **7** _____ Freunde wohnen in der Umgebung, aber wenn ich älter bin, möchte ich **8** _____ Dublin umziehen. Ohne Zweifel **9** _____ es mehr Freizeitaktivitäten in einer **10** _____ .

Your score: ___ / 10

What have I learned?	
What must I improve?	
What do I want to revise?	

Your total score: ___ / 50

03 In meiner Freizeit

Learning Outcomes

- **Oral:** discussing leisure activities
- **Reading:** reading and answering questions on three texts about leisure activities
- **Writing:** writing an opinion (**Äußerung**), describing a picture and writing a letter about leisure time
- **Aural:** listening to and answering questions on four extracts about leisure activities

Grammar

- Regular verbs in the pluperfect tense
- Irregular verbs in the pluperfect tense
- The future tense

Vocabulary

- Naming leisure activities
- Describing leisure activities

German Culture

- **Muttizettel:** how young people are allowed to spend their freetime in Germany
- German specialist schools

Exam Tips

- Push up your expression mark by using adjectives.
- When you start a sentence with **weil**, **wenn**, **als**, remember to use verb, verb: **Wenn das Wetter gut ist, spiele ich gern Fußball**.
- Underline five phrases which you can adapt for your oral and written work.

Mündliche Arbeit: In meiner Freizeit

Beantworten Sie die folgenden Fragen:

Was machen Sie gern?

Interessieren Sie sich für Sport und Musik?

Wie ruhen Sie sich aus?

Was machen Sie gern in Ihrer Freizeit?

Sehen Sie gern fern?

1. Was machen Sie gern? *What do you like doing?*	
Ich bin (nicht) sehr sportlich und hier in Irland haben wir ein/kein reiches Angebot an Sportmöglichkeiten.	*I am (not) very sporty and here in Ireland we (do not) have a rich selection of sports facilities.*
Am Wochenende spiele ich Camogie oder Fußball, egal ob das Wetter gut oder schlecht ist, denn ich finde es wichtig, körperlich fit zu sein.	*At the weekends I play camogie or football, no matter whether the weather is good or bad, because I find it important to be physically fit.*
Meine Lieblingssportart ist ______________ .	*My favourite type of sport is ______________ .*
Hier gibt es leider einen Mangel an Freizeitmöglichkeiten. Man muss in die Stadt fahren, wenn man etwas unternehmen will.	*Unfortunately, there is a lack of free time activities here. You have to go into town if you want to do something.*
Einkaufen ist mein Lieblingshobby. Das würde ich gern jeden Tag machen. Leider schwimme ich aber nicht in Geld.	*Shopping is my favourite hobby. I would like to do that every day. But unfortunately, I'm not swimming in money.*
Ich habe einen großen Freundeskreis und wir unternehmen viel zusammen.	*I have a large circle of friends and we do a lot together.*
Ich gehe jeden Tag mehrere Stunden auf Facebook/Snapchat/Instagram. Ich glaube, ich bin fast handysüchtig.	*I go on Facebook/Snapchat/Instagram for several hours every day. I think I'm almost addicted to my phone.*
Ich surfe wahnsinnig gern im Internet. Das macht immer viel Spaß.	*I'm crazy about surfing the internet. That's always a lot of fun.*
Ich faulenze gern, also verbringe ich viel Zeit beim Fernsehen oder am Computer/Handy.	*I like to laze around, so I spend a lot of time with the television or on the computer/my phone.*
Ich telefoniere/Skype/Facetime zwischen einer und anderthalb Stunden pro Tag. Wenn ich nicht in der Schule bin, ist das Handy mein ständiger Begleiter.	*I telephone/Skype/Facetime for between an hour and an hour and a half every day. When I'm not at school, the phone is my constant companion.*

2. Wie ruhen Sie sich gern aus? *How do you like to relax?*	
Ich erlebe gern die Natur, also gehe ich regelmäßig mit dem Hund spazieren.	*I like experiencing nature, so I regularly go walking with the dog.*
Der Mensch braucht Entspannung. Ich höre gern Musik auf meinem Handy, wenn ich mich ausruhen will.	*Everybody needs relaxation. I like listening to music on my phone when I want to relax.*
Ich finde es wichtig, meine Freizeit zu genießen.	*I think it's important to enjoy my free time.*
Es ist wichtig abzuschalten.	*It's important to switch off.*
Am allerliebsten gehe ich in die Disco und mache mich locker. Ich schwinge gern das Tanzbein.	*I like going to the disco most of all and letting my hair down. I like to dance the night away.*

2. Wie ruhen Sie sich gern aus? *How do you like to relax?*	
Ich habe dieses Jahr keine Zeit für Hobbys, denn ich stehe unter viel Druck, gute Noten zu bekommen.	*I have no time for hobbies this year because I'm under a lot of pressure to get good grades.*
Im Sommer, wenn ich mehr Freizeit habe, kann ich mich gut ausruhen.	*In the summer, when I have more free time, I can well and truly relax.*
Ein Leben ohne mein Haustier kann ich mir gar nicht vorstellen. Ich habe meinen Hund/meine Katze so lieb.	*I really can't imagine a life without my pet. I so love my dog/my cat.*
Ich bin eine Leseratte. Im Moment lese ich _______________, was wirklich spannend ist.	*I'm a bookworm. At the moment I'm reading _______________, which is really exciting.*
Ich spiele unheimlich gern Computerspiele.	*I love playing computer games.*
Es ist sehr wichtig, sich zu entspannen, denn sonst kann man den alltäglichen Stress nicht abbauen.	*It is very important to relax because otherwise one can't relieve everyday stress.*

3. Sehen Sie gern fern? *Do you like to watch television?*	
Ich sehe leidenschaftlich gern fern. Meine Lieblingssendung ist _______________, denn ich finde die Sendung lustig und unterhaltsam.	*I love watching TV. My favourite programme is _______________ because I find the programme funny and entertaining.*
Das Fernsehen verdummt oft den Menschen, denn die meisten Sendungen sind einfach blöd.	*Television often dulls the mind because most programmes are simply stupid.*
Ich sehe gern Filme auf Netflix.	*I like watching films on Netflix.*
Ich sehe normalerweise pro Tag eine halbe Stunde fern, an den Wochenenden mehr.	*I normally watch half an hour of television a day, more at the weekends.*
Ich schwärme für „Game of Thrones".	*I'm crazy about* Game of Thrones.

4. Was bedeuten diese Sätze auf Englisch? *What do these sentences mean in English?*

a) Ich bin musikalisch/künstlerisch begabt. Musik/Kunst mache ich leidenschaftlich gern.

b) Ich spiele Klavier, aber nur aus Spaß und Vergnügen.

c) Ich bin sehr kreativ. Wenn ich male, kann ich meine Gedanken und Gefühle ausdrücken.

d) Ich bin ein begeisterter Rockmusikfan.

e) Ich höre gern Musik, aber ich spiele kein Instrument.

Übersetzen Sie zu zweit die folgenden Ausdrücke. In pairs translate the following expressions.

1. Weil ich gar nicht sportlich bin, ist es mir egal, ob das Wetter gut oder schlecht ist.
2. Wenn es regnet, wird das Spiel entweder abgesagt oder verschoben.
3. Ich glaube, dass das Nichtstun sehr entspannend ist. Meine Freunde und ich hängen gern in der Stadt rum.
4. Ich entspanne mich am besten beim Schwimmen oder Joggen.
5. Der Mensch muss sich ausruhen.

Prüfungstipp

Use the sentences on pages 46 and 47 to write about your free time. Keep these paragraphs for your oral work.

Push up your expression mark by using adjectives: **spannend**, **lustig**, **unterhaltsam**.

When you start a sentence with **weil**, **wenn**, **als**, remember to use verb, verb: **Wenn das Wetter gut ist, spiele ich gern Fußball.**

Text 1: Sina besucht eine Eliteschule

Bitte beantworten Sie die folgenden Fragen:

1. Was sieht man auf dem Bild?
2. Was machen die jungen Frauen?
3. Wie sehen sie aus?
4. Wie fühlen sie sich, Ihrer Meinung nach?

Vorarbeit *Preparation*

1. **Finden Sie diese Ausdrücke im Text!** Find these expressions in the text.
   A For 18-year-old Sina, school must be on the sidelines.
   B When you have experienced that once, you don't want anything else.
   C But the absenteeism slowly became too much.
   D Handball and school are equally important to me.
   E It is very important to her ... to also have an additional career option.
2. **Finden Sie das Deutsche für die Wörter unten!** Find the German for the words below.
   A pivot player/club/national division/level
   B Czech Republic/strength training/offers
   C so-called/before/Leaving Certificate exams/oral
   D grinds/away matches/fit/rules
   E professionals/pass (exam)/dreams/hardly

A Für die 18-Jährige Sina muss die Schule nebenbei laufen, denn sie spielt Handball in der ersten Bundesliga. Von 8 bis 16 Uhr geht sie zur Schule und ab 18.30 Uhr steht sie als Kreisläuferin des Buxtehuder Sport Vereins in der Halle. Handball auf diesem Niveau, das bedeutet für die Spielerin viel Zeit: 16 Stunden pro Woche Training, fünfmal abends, dreimal vormittags. Dazu kommen ein bis zwei Spiele pro Woche. Seit 2009 ist die 18-jährige Junioren-Nationalspielerin. „Die Sporthalle ist schon mein zweites Zuhause", sagt Sina.

B Ein normales Schülerleben mit Partys und viel Freizeit vermisst sie manchmal: „Der Handball ermöglicht mir ja auch besondere Momente", sagt sie und erzählt von der Junioren-Europameisterschaft in Tschechien. „Wenn du das einmal erlebt hast, willst du nichts anderes." Ab und zu wünscht sie sich ein normales Leben. „Ich bin gerade am Knie verletzt und habe neben der Rehabilitation aus Krafttraining und Schwimmen etwas mehr Zeit für meine Freunde."

C Sie hat schon ihre Abiturprüfungen in Sporttheorie, Politik und Englisch gemacht. Sie macht bald die mündliche Prüfung in Mathe. Im April kommen noch zwei Sportprüfungen in Schwimmen und Handball. Ihre Schule in Hamburg ist eine sogenannte Eliteschule des Sports. Im ganzen Land gibt es rund 40 Eliteschulen. Für Sina ist ihr Alltag jetzt viel besser: „Vorher war ich auf einer normalen Schule, aber die Fehlzeiten wurden langsam zu viel."

D An den Eliteschulen des Sports sind die Regeln weniger stark. Unterrichtsmaterial wird online gestellt, und es gibt Nachhilfestunden. „Bei Auswärtsspielen habe ich immer meinen Laptop dabei und versuche, zu lernen oder meine Hausaufgaben zu machen. Handball und Schule sind für mich gleichwertig, beides muss passen", erzählt Sina.

E In der Frauenhandball-Bundesliga gibt es kaum Profis, und die Bezahlung ist nicht genug. Deshalb sagt Sina, „Ich möchte jetzt erst mal mein Abitur bestehen, wieder fit werden und dann entweder Architektur oder Sport studieren." Es ist ihr sehr wichtig nicht nur ihre Träume zu erfüllen, sondern auch eine zusätzliche Berufsoption zu haben.

OL Ordinary Level Questions

1. **a)** Why does Sina's schooling come second to sport? A **b)** Of which league is she a member? A
2. Fill in the required information in the box below.

Sina starts school at:	Time spent training	How often?	Name of sports club

3. Are these statements true or false?
   a) Sina pursues her academic schoolwork more than sport.
   b) Sina trains for 18 hours a week.
   c) She plays centre back on her team.
   d) Since 2008, she has been playing for the Junior National Team.
   e) Sina has injured her leg.
4. Select the correct prepositions for the following sentences.
   a) Sina geht **(von/zum/zur/mit)** Eliteschule.
   b) Sie spielt **(am/im/für/beim)** ihr Team.
   c) Sie macht Prüfungen **(mit/in/an/im)** Mathe und Sport.
   d) Sie macht ihre Hausaufgaben und lernt **(in/an/bei/für)** Auswärtsspielen.

HL Higher Level Questions

1. Beantworten Sie folgende Fragen auf Deutsch!
   a) Wie sieht Sinas Alltag aus? Geben Sie **vier** Details! A
   b) Was vermisst sie? B
   c) Welche Prüfungen hat Sina schon gemacht? Welche Prüfungen wird sie bald machen? C
   d) Warum ist ihr Alltag besser an dieser Eliteschule? D
   e) Warum will Sina entweder Architektur oder Sport studieren? E
2. Answer the following questions in English.
   a) Why is the sports hall Sina's second home? Support your answer with evidence. A
   b) What are the consequences of her injuring her knee? B
   c) Why was Sina's old school no longer suitable for her? C
   d) What are the benefits of the new school for Sina? D
   e) Why does Sina feel that it is important for her to have career options? E
3. Aus welchen Wörtern bestehen die zusammengesetzten Wörter und was bedeuten sie auf Englisch?
   a) vormittags = _____ + _____ = _____
   b) Schülerleben = _____ + _____ = _____
   c) Sportprüfungen = _____ + _____ = _____
   d) Unterrichtsmaterial = _____ + _____ = _____
   e) Berufsoption = _____ + _____ = _____
4. Put the underlined irregular verbs from Text 1 into the perfect tense.
   a) Von 8 bis 16 Uhr geht sie zur Schule.
   b) Diese kleine Pause genieße ich schon.
   c) Im ganzen Land gibt es rund 40 Eliteschulen.
   d) An den Eliteschulen des Sports sind die Regeln weniger stark.

Prüfungstipp

Avoid **'Ja/Nein'** answers in the oral. Always try to expand on your answer. Answer every question with three to five sentences. You can do this by giving examples and opinions. If you have fully answered the question, move the conversation on to a related topic. For example, if you have talked about your sporting activities, tell the examiner about the things you do when the weather is bad.

Grammatik: Zeitformen/Tenses

p. 61 (Übung macht den Meister)

Pluperfect Tense: Regular Verbs

The pluperfect tense can be translated as 'I had lived/I had watched'. In the pluperfect, the imperfect tense of **haben** is used, and the main verb will go to the end of the sentence as a past participle: **machen → gemacht**; **lachen → gelacht**.

ich **hatte** ... **getanzt**	wir **hatten** ... **gewohnt**
du **hattest** ... **gekauft**	ihr **hattet** ... **gespielt**
er/sie/es/man **hatte** ... **geweint**	Sie/sie **hatten** ... **gelacht**

Pluperfect Tense: Regular Verbs

Put the following bracketed regular verbs into the pluperfect tense.

1. Mein Vater (kaufen) schon das Auto.	*My father had already bought the car.*
2. Der Junge (lachen) laut.	*The boy had laughed out loud.*
3. Die Frau (machen) so viel Arbeit.	*The woman had done so much work.*
4. Die Kinder (lernen) fleißig für die Prüfung.	*The children had studied hard for the exam.*
5. Warum (weinen) das Mädchen?	*Why had the girl been crying?*
6. Ich (brauchen) ein neues Sporttrikot.	*I had needed a new sports jersey.*
7. Wir (grillen) Würste am Strand.	*We had barbecued sausages on the beach.*
8. Die Mädchen (reden) bis spät in die Nacht.	*The girls had talked until late in the night.*

Pluperfect Tense: Regular Separable Verbs

Put the following bracketed regular separable verbs into the pluperfect tense. Remember to put the 'ge' between the separable prefix and the main verb: **Ich hatte ... ausgemacht**.

1. Mein Vater (aufwärmen) schon das Essen.	*My father had already heated up the meal.*
2. Julia (zuhören) eigentlich im Unterricht.	*Julia had actually listened in class.*
3. Das Kind (umdrehen) sich schon.	*The child had already turned around.*
4. Wir (weiterspielen) auf dem Sportplatz.	*We had continued playing in the sports ground.*
5. Warum (anlächeln) mich das Mädchen?	*Why had the girl smiled at me?*
6. Wir (abmachen) einen Termin für Freitag.	*We had agreed an appointment for Friday.*
7. Klaus (mitmachen) beim Spiel.	*Klaus had participated in the game.*
8. Die Kinder (ausruhen) sich im Park.	*The children had relaxed in the park.*

Pluperfect Tense: Regular Inseparable Verbs

Put the following bracketed regular inseparable verbs into the pluperfect tense. Remember that the **be-**, **emp-**, **ent-**, **er-**, **ge-**, **miss-**, **ver-**, **zer-** verbs will not take a '**ge**', e.g. **ich hatte verkauft**.

1. Der Mann (besuchen) seine Mutter.	*The man had visited his mother.*
2. Die Frauen (verkaufen) schon die Kuchen.	*The women had already sold the cakes.*
3. Ich (erleben) schon eine neue Kultur.	*I had already experienced a new culture.*
4. Die Frau (beobachten) die Vögel.	*The woman had watched the birds.*
5. Der Film (begeistern) mich.	*The film had delighted me.*
6. Ute (entwickeln) einen neuen Trendsport.	*Ute had developed a new trend sport.*
7. Der Trainer (erwarten) zu viel von mir.	*The trainer had expected too much of me.*
8. Das Kind (beruhigen) sich endlich.	*The child had finally calmed down.*

03.01 Hörverständnis Teil 1

A-Z Vorarbeit *Preparation*

Herausforderung	*challenge*	**schützen**	*to protect*	**Mitgliedsregeln**	*membership rules*
Ausrüstung	*equipment*	**Wettbewerb**	*competition*	**Ellenbogenschützer**	*elbow pad*
verschieden	*different*	**teilnehmen**	*to take part*	**schicken**	*to send*
Helm	*helmet*	**Mitglied**	*member*	**Gern geschehen!**	*You're welcome!*

CL Ordinary + Higher Level Questions

1. Give **three (O)/five (H)** details about the skateboarder's equipment.
2. **a)** How much does the equipment cost? **b)** How often does he train?
3. **a)** What does the young skateboarder say about his club? Give **two (O)/three (H)** details.
   b) Which competitions does he take part in?
4. What advantages does the man see in being part of a skateboarding club? (**1 (O)/2 (H)** details)
5. **a)** How can one become a member of the club?
   b) What does one have to pay for? Give **one (O)/two (H)** details.

03.02 Hörverständnis Teil 2

A-Z Vorarbeit *Preparation*

Fundbüro	*lost property*	**Reißverschluss**	*zip*	**wiederkriegen**	*to get back*
Verlust	*loss*	**Portemonnaie**	*wallet*	**heulen**	*to howl*
melden	*to report*	**Schlüssel**	*keys*	**sich beruhigen**	*to calm down*
liegen lassen	*to leave behind*	**aufschreiben**	*to write down*	**aufschreiben**	*to write down*

OL Ordinary Level Questions

1. What does the caller want to report?
2. Where did the event happen?
3. Describe the item.
4. What is the **name** and **number** of the caller?

HL Higher Level Questions

1. Using ***key phrases***, write down **in German** the key information the caller provides:
   - the name of the person **making** the call
   - the reason for the call
   - details regarding further contact
   - the recipient's phone number

Gesprächsnotiz

Anruf von: ____________ Gesprächsanlass: ____________

- erwartet am Abend einen Rückruf ☐
- wird in zwei Tagen noch einmal anrufen ☐
- bekommt irgendwann einen Rückruf ☐
- wird auf der Webseite einen Kommentar hinterlassen ☐

Kontaktnummer: *Vorwahl* ____________ *Rufnummer* ____________

2. Write down **three** examples of the language which show that the caller is **agitated**.

Text 2: Ausgehen unter 18 – so feiern Jugendliche

  Bitte beantworten Sie die folgenden Fragen:

1. Wo sind die Jugendlichen?
2. Was machen sie?
3. Wie ist die Stimmung?
4. Wie sind sie bekleidet?
5. Gehen Sie gern in die Disco? Warum/warum nicht?

Vorarbeit *Preparation*

1. **Finden Sie diese Ausdrücke im Text!** Find these expressions in the text.
   - **A** The German Youth Protection Act
   - **B** Or they have a 'note from Mum' and a companion who is over 18.
   - **C** You only get into certain clubs at 18.
   - **D** My parents give me a lot of freedom when it comes to going out.
   - **E** It works like this.

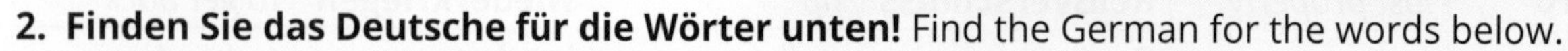

2. **Finden Sie das Deutsche für die Wörter unten!** Find the German for the words below.
   - **A** permission/regulates/to go out/to be allowed
   - **B** to name/unless/signature/the end
   - **C** monitored/to try out/certain/about it
   - **D** stupid/responsible/sang along
   - **E** to agree/sign/to leave/to accompany

© www.pasch-net.de (amended)

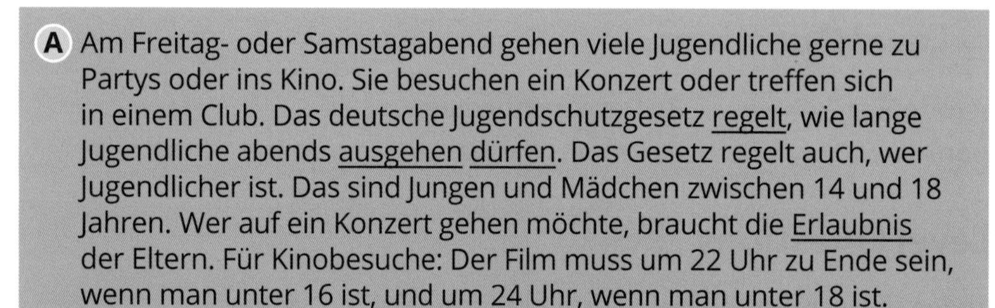

A Am Freitag- oder Samstagabend gehen viele Jugendliche gerne zu Partys oder ins Kino. Sie besuchen ein Konzert oder treffen sich in einem Club. Das deutsche Jugendschutzgesetz regelt, wie lange Jugendliche abends ausgehen dürfen. Das Gesetz regelt auch, wer Jugendlicher ist. Das sind Jungen und Mädchen zwischen 14 und 18 Jahren. Wer auf ein Konzert gehen möchte, braucht die Erlaubnis der Eltern. Für Kinobesuche: Der Film muss um 22 Uhr zu Ende sein, wenn man unter 16 ist, und um 24 Uhr, wenn man unter 18 ist.

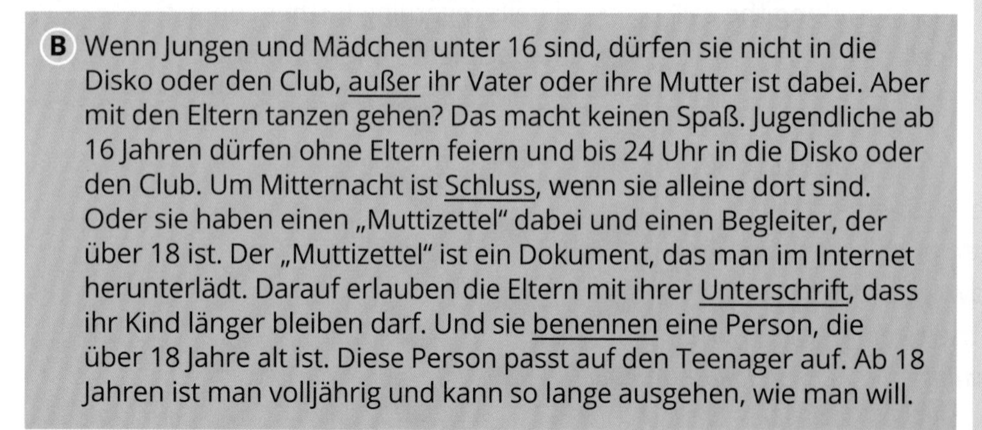

B Wenn Jungen und Mädchen unter 16 sind, dürfen sie nicht in die Disko oder den Club, außer ihr Vater oder ihre Mutter ist dabei. Aber mit den Eltern tanzen gehen? Das macht keinen Spaß. Jugendliche ab 16 Jahren dürfen ohne Eltern feiern und bis 24 Uhr in die Disko oder den Club. Um Mitternacht ist Schluss, wenn sie alleine dort sind. Oder sie haben einen „Muttizettel" dabei und einen Begleiter, der über 18 ist. Der „Muttizettel" ist ein Dokument, das man im Internet herunterlädt. Darauf erlauben die Eltern mit ihrer Unterschrift, dass ihr Kind länger bleiben darf. Und sie benennen eine Person, die über 18 Jahre alt ist. Diese Person passt auf den Teenager auf. Ab 18 Jahren ist man volljährig und kann so lange ausgehen, wie man will.

C **Karl mag Grillen, Konzerte und Technomusik:** Ich gehe sehr gerne mit meinen Freunden aus. Wir treffen uns im Park zum Grillen oder Picknicken. Manchmal gehen wir in Clubs und zu Konzerten. In bestimmte Clubs kommt man erst ab 18 rein. Das wird streng kontrolliert. Wenn ich 18 bin, möchte ich mal hin. Wenn alle immer darüber reden, möchte man das schon ausprobieren.

D Frederike mag Konzerte und darf lange ausgehen: Ich war mit drei Freundinnen bei einem Konzert von „Kraftklub". Das ist eine Band aus Chemnitz. Die Mutter von einer Freundin war auch dabei. Deshalb war es kein Problem reinzukommen. Es war toll! Alle haben laut mitgesungen und mitgetanzt. Wir waren erst um zwei Uhr nachts zu Hause. Meine Eltern lassen mir viel Freiraum beim Ausgehen. Ich muss nicht um Punkt zehn Uhr zu Hause sein. Sie wissen, dass ich verantwortungsbewusst bin und nichts Dummes tue.

E Paula tanzt gerne zu Musik aus den Charts: Wenn man noch nicht 18 ist, muss man Partys um Mitternacht verlassen. Außer man hat einen „Muttizettel". Er funktioniert so: Wenn einer in der Gruppe schon 18 ist, dann darf er drei andere Personen begleiten, die noch nicht 18 sind. Die Eltern der Minderjährigen müssen einverstanden sein und das auf dem „Muttizettel" unterschreiben. Den Zettel muss man den ganzen Abend dabeihaben. Wenn Freunde 18 werden, dann freuen sie sich immer und sagen: „Oh ja, ich kann jetzt deine Mutti sein!" Ich mag am liebsten Chartmusik oder Musik aus Lateinamerika. Da kann man tanzen und mitsingen.

OL Ordinary Level Questions

1. **a)** If you are under 16 in Germany, until what time are you allowed to go to the cinema? A
   b) Under what circumstances are under-16s allowed to go to a disco? B
   c) What does Karl like? C
   d) At what time did Frederike come home from the concert? D
   e) What does Paula like best of all? E
2. Are the following statements true or false?
   a) Jugendliche sind Jungen und Mädchen zwischen 12 und 18 Jahren.
   b) Ab 18 Jahren ist man volljährig und kann ohne Erlaubnis ausgehen.
   c) Karl geht gern mit seinen Freunden aus.
   d) Frederikes Eltern sind sehr streng.
3. Select the correct prepositions for the following sentences.
   a) Der Film muss **(am/im/vom/um)** 24 Uhr zu Ende sein, wenn man unter 18 ist.
   b) Jugendliche **(ab/von/mit/um)** 16 Jahren dürfen ohne Eltern feiern.
   c) Frederike war **(bei/mit/ohne/zu)** drei Freundinnen bei einem Konzert von „Kraftklub".
   d) Karl trifft sich mit seinen Freunden **(am/um/im/zum)** Park.

HL Higher Level Questions

1. Beantworten Sie folgende Fragen auf Deutsch!
   a) Was regelt das deutsche Jugendschutzgesetz? (**2** Beispiele!) A
   b) Was ist ein Muttizettel, und wo bekommt man einen Muttizettel? B
   c) Was macht Karl gern? C
   d) Warum hat Frederike viel Freiraum beim Ausgehen? Nennen Sie **mehrere** Gründe! D
   e) Warum freuen sich die Freunde, wenn sie 18 werden? E
2. Answer the following questions in English.
   a) What do young people need to go to a concert? How late may they stay at the cinema? A
   b) What are the laws regarding attending a disco for under-16s, over-16s and over-18s? B
   c) Why does Karl want to get into certain clubs? C
   d) Why did Frederike have no problem getting into the concert? D
   e) Explain how the Muttizettel works. E
3. Put the underlined regular verbs from Text 2 into the pluperfect tense.
   a) Sie besuchen ein Konzert.
   b) Das macht keinen Spaß.
   c) Alle haben ... mitgetanzt.
   d) Diese Person passt auf den Teenager auf.

OL Äußerung zum Thema: Ordinary Level

You are interviewing Paula. Complete Paula's dialogue using the information given in Text 2.

Sie: Was machst du gern?
Paula: ______________________________
Sie: Um wie viel Uhr muss man eine Party verlassen, wenn man nicht 18 Jahre alt ist?
Paula: ______________________________
Sie: Wie funktioniert ein „Muttizettel"?
Paula: ______________________________
Sie: Wie alt muss eine Begleitperson sein?
Paula: ______________________________
Sie: Was müssen die Eltern auf dem Zettel unterschreiben?
Paula: ______________________________

HL Äußerung zum Thema: Higher Level

Write 13 to 15 sentences, answering the questions below.

- Beschreiben Sie das Foto in **drei bis vier** Sätzen.
- Was machen deutsche Jugendliche gern am Wochenende, laut Text? Was machen Sie persönlich gern am Wochenende?
- Bis zu welchem Alter gilt man als Jugendlicher in Irland? Was darf man in Irland ab 16 machen/nicht machen?

Use sentences from the oral section and from the reading texts for your written work.

Nützliche Sätze/Useful Sentences

Im Vordergrund sieht man viele Jugendliche. Im Hintergrund sieht man einen DJ.	*In the foreground you see many young people. In the background one sees a DJ.*
Die jungen Leute tanzen ganz begeistert.	*The young people are dancing very enthusiastically.*
Man kann eine Disco-Kugel sehen.	*One can see a disco ball.*
Manche tragen Freizeitkleidung und andere sind schön bekleidet.	*Some are wearing casual clothes and others are dressed up.*
Es herrscht eine knisternde Atmosphäre.	*There is an electric atmosphere.*
Die Jugendlichen feiern gern und wir wissen, wie man Spaß haben kann.	*Young people like to celebrate and we know how to have fun.*
Jedem Tierchen sein Pläsierchen.	*Each to their own.*
Meine Freunde und ich gehen so oft wie möglich in die Disco.	*My friends and I go to the disco as often as possible.*
Ich bin ein richtiger Partylöwe und gehe gern mit Freunden aus.	*I'm a real party animal and like going out with friends.*
In der Regel gilt man in Irland bis zum Alter von 18 Jahren als Kind.	*As a rule, one is considered a child in Ireland until the age of 18.*
Natürlich ist der Verkauf von Alkohol und Zigaretten an Minderjährige verboten.	*Of course, the sale of alcohol and cigarettes to minors is forbidden.*
Man darf erst ab 18 zur Wahl gehen.	*You're only allowed to vote at 18.*

 Grammatik: Zeitformen/Tenses

p. 61 (Übung macht den Meister)

Pluperfect Tense: Irregular Verbs

Reminder: To form the pluperfect, use the imperfect tense of **haben** and the past participle. For more on irregular past participles, turn to page 38.

The pluperfect tense can be translated as 'I had sung/I had eaten'. Here are some examples of irregular verbs in the pluperfect tense:

ich **hatte** ... **getrunken**	wir **hatten** ... **gesungen**
du **hattest** ... **gegessen**	ihr **hattet** ... **geschrieben**
er/sie/es/man **hatte** ... **gelesen**	Sie/sie **hatten** ... **getroffen**

Verbs of motion use the imperfect tense of **sein** and the past participle (see page 58).

Put the bracketed irregular verbs into the pluperfect tense.

1. Ich (trinken) schon eine Cola.	*I had already drunk a Coke.*
2. Er (stehlen) am vorigen Tag ein Auto.	*He had stolen a car the previous day.*
3. Wir (schreiben) einen Beschwerdebrief.	*We had written a letter of complaint.*
4. Die Frau (lesen) schon den Roman.	*The woman had already read the novel.*
5. Meine Mutter (sehen) bestimmt den Film.	*My mother had definitely seen the film.*
6. Warum (verstehen) du die Regeln nicht?	*Why had you* (singular) *not understood the rules?*
7. Ina (entscheiden) sich für einen neuen Kurs.	*Ina had decided on a new course.*
8. Wir (sprechen) viel über das Thema.	*We had spoken a lot about the topic.*

Pluperfect Tense: Irregular Separable Verbs

Put the bracketed irregular separable verbs into the pluperfect tense. Remember to put the **ge-** between the separable prefix and the main verb: Ich hatte angefangen.

1. Ich (abschließen) schon die Tür.	*I had already locked the door.*
2. Es (anfangen) am vorigen Tag.	*It had begun the previous day.*
3. Wir (anziehen) uns schon um 7 Uhr.	*We had already got dressed by 7 a.m.*
4. Anna (vorlesen) schon den Roman.	*Anna had already read the novel aloud.*
5. Mein Vater (fernsehen) eine Stunde lang.	*My father had watched TV for an hour.*
6. Die Polizei (festnehmen) schon den Mann.	*The police had already arrested the man.*

Pluperfect: Irregular Inseparable Verbs

Put the bracketed irregular inseparable verbs into the pluperfect tense. Remember that inseparable verbs do not add a **-ge** to the beginning of the main verb: **ich hatte ... erfahren**.

1. Ich (erfahren) davon vor ein paar Tagen.	*I had learned about it a few days ago.*
2. Er (vergeben) mir erst gestern.	*He had only forgiven me yesterday.*
3. Wir (verfahren) uns in der Wüste.	*We had got lost in the desert.*
4. Susi (entscheiden) sich die Schule zu verlassen.	*Susi had decided to leave the school.*
5. Lea (erhalten) vor einer Woche den Brief.	*Lea had received the letter a week ago.*
6. Die Schüler (besprechen) das Thema.	*The students had discussed the topic.*

Prüfungstipp

It is important to practise the basic verbs. Many of these are irregular in English and German. However, you will come across them often, which will help you to master them.

Text 3: Julchen auf Eis

Beschreiben Sie, was Sie auf dem Bild sehen!

1. Wo sind die Kinder?
2. Was machen die Kinder?
3. Wie sind sie bekleidet?
4. Würden Sie gerne mal Schlittschuh fahren? Warum/warum nicht?

Vorarbeit *Preparation*

1. **Finden Sie diese Ausdrücke im Text!** Find these expressions in the text.
   - **A** Every year exactly the same thing happens.
   - **B** He feels sorry for her.
   - **C** It doesn't always have to be the majority that wins.
   - **D** She has got used to being disappointed again and again.
2. **Finden Sie das Deutsche für die Wörter unten!** Find the German for the words below.
   - **A** classmates/ice skating/hurts/choose/stupid
   - **B** interest/you're right/sad/looks at
   - **C** year before last/to suggest
   - **D** to be honest/hope/delicious

www.fuer-kinderrechte.de, 2010 (amended)

A Julchen hasst Schlittschuhlaufen. Wintersport ist nicht ihr Ding. Jedoch wählen die meisten ihrer Mitschüler einen Klassenausflug zur Eisbahn. Jedes Jahr passiert genau das Gleiche. Während die Mitschüler alle auf dem kalten, glatten Eis Schlittschuh laufen und lachen, ist Julchen nicht froh. Julchen möchte viel lieber ins Museum oder ins Kino gehen. Sie mag auch ins Theater gehen. „Blödes Eislaufen", denkt sie sich! „Ich langweile mich hier und alles tut mir weh! Das Eis ist ja doch hart. Ich will nach Hause!"

B Einer der Mitschüler, der Klausi, kommt auf Julchen zu und sagt, „Wie geht es dir, Julchen? Macht das Eislaufen dir keinen Spaß?" Julchen sagt nur, dass ihr Arm und Bein weh tun. Klausi guckt sie einen Moment an. Er versteht, dass Julchen Eislaufen nicht gernhat. Er hat Mitleid mit ihr. „Eislaufen ist toll, aber warum muss unser Klassenausflug immer der Ausflug zur Eisbahn sein?" fragt er sich. Er mag selber auch backen und wollte immer einen Tagesausflug zu einer Bäckerei machen um zu sehen, wie das funktioniert. Er geht zu den anderen und sagt, „Ich denke, Julchen sieht traurig aus und hat keinen Spaß beim Eislaufen." Die anderen sagen „Oh, da hast du recht. Das ist ja schlecht. Aber ich habe keine Lust ins Museum zu gehen. Das ist doch langweilig, oder?"

C Dann sagt Klausi, „Ich mag Eislaufen gehen, aber wenn Julchen es nicht mag, finde ich es unfair, dass wir das jedes Jahr machen. Ich denke, wir haben alle auch das recht nein zu sagen und andere Aktivitäten vorzuschlagen. Es muss ja nicht immer die Mehrheit sein, die gewinnt. Wir haben letztes Jahr und vorletztes Jahr doch schon unseren Klassenausflug zur Eisbahn gemacht."

D Julchen hört Klausi zu aber sie sagt nichts. Sie hat sich daran gewöhnt immer wieder enttäuscht zu sein. Ehrlich gesagt hatte sie keine Hoffnung auf einen anderen Schulausflug. Am nächsten Schultag bringt Klausi Kuchen für alle mit. Die Klasse sitzt zusammen und isst den leckeren Kuchen, während sie alle planen, das nächste Mal den Ausflug ins Nationalmuseum zu machen. Das ist immerhin ein Anfang, denkt Julchen und muss grinsen.

In English, we say 'You **are** right'. In German, we say 'You **have** right' – **du hast recht**. Here are some other expressions with **haben**. What do they mean?

Hunger haben Durst haben Lust haben Heimweh haben Glück haben Schmerzen haben

OL Ordinary Level Questions

1. Answer the following questions in English.
   a) Julchen does not like skating. Where would she prefer to go on a class trip? A
   b) Where would Klausi like to go on a class trip? B
   c) How many times has the class gone to the ice rink? C
   d) What does Klausi bring to school the next day? D
2. Choose a suitable heading for each paragraph and explain your choice in English.

Die anderen wollen nicht ins Museum gehen | Es ist unfair, immer das Gleiche zu machen | Julchen mag Eislaufen nicht | Nächstes Mal wird es anders sein

3. What belongs together?

1. Julchen ist nicht froh,	**A** weil sie traurig aussieht.
2. Klausi hat Mitleid mit Julchen,	**B** immer das Gleiche zu tun.
3. Die anderen glauben,	**C** denn Wintersport ist nicht ihr Ding.
4. Klausi findet es unfair,	**D** ins Museum gehen.
5. Nächstes Mal wird die Klasse	**E** dass ein Museum langweilig ist.

4. Complete the following sentences based on Text 3.
   a) Julchen möchte eher **(ins Kino/zur Schule/mit mir spazieren/zum Park)** gehen.
   b) Sie findet Eislaufen **(anspruchsvoll/interessant/blöd/lustig)**.
   c) Klausi hat Mitleid mit **(ihm/ihr/ihnen/Ihnen)**.
   d) Klausi hat **(eine Torte/ein Brot/Brötchen/einen Kuchen)** gebacken.

HL Higher Level Questions

1. Beantworten Sie folgende Fragen auf Deutsch und in Ihren eigenen Worten.
   a) Warum mag Julchen Eislaufen gehen nicht (**3** Gründe)? Was tut ihr weh? A
   b) Welche Frage hat Klausi Julchen gestellt? Wie hat Julchen auf diese Frage reagiert? B
   c) Was findet Klausi unfair, und warum? C
   d) Was macht Klausi danach? Warum hat er das gemacht? D
2. Answer the following questions in English.
   a) Why does Julchen hate skating (**3** reasons)? A
   b) What does Julchen say to Klausi about how she is feeling? What does Klausi say to the others? B
   c) Why does Klausi think the class should do a different class outing the next time? C
   d) What steps does he take to achieve this? D
   e) Julchen experiences a variety of emotions in the course of the story. Give **three** examples of both positive and negative emotions which she experiences.
3. Aus welchen Wörtern bestehen die zusammengesetzten Wörter? Was bedeuten sie auf Englisch?
   a) Wintersport = _____ + _____ = ________
   b) Klassenausflug = _____ + _____ = ________
   c) Mitleid = _____ + _____ = ________
   d) Schultag = _____ + _____ = ________
4. Put the regular and irregular bracketed verbs from Text 3 into the pluperfect tense.
   a) Julchen (langweilen) sich beim Eislaufen.
   b) Klausi (verstehen), dass Julchen unglücklich war.
   c) Wir (machen) jedes Jahr den gleichen Ausflug.
   d) Klausi (bringen) Kuchen in die Schule.

Grammatik: Zeitformen/Tenses

p. 61 (Übung macht den Meister)

The Pluperfect: Irregular Verbs

Remember that the pluperfect will use a form of **sein** instead of **haben** to express motion. The following forms of **sein** are used: **ich war**, **du warst**, **er/sie/es/man war**, **wir waren**, **ihr wart**, **Sie/sie waren**.

Verbs of motion: **bleiben**, **fahren**, **fallen**, **fliegen**, **gehen**, **kommen**, **laufen**, **reisen**, **schwimmen**

Put the bracketed verbs of motion into the pluperfect tense. Some of them are separable.

1. Der Vogel (wegfliegen) schnell.	*The bird had flown away quickly.*
2. Der Mann (entkommen) der Polizei.	*The man had escaped from the police.*
3. Wir (schwimmen) schon im Meer.	*We had already swum in the sea.*
4. Die Kinder (springen) aus dem Baum.	*The children had jumped out of the tree.*
5. Die Austauschgruppe (fliegen) nach Berlin.	*The exchange group had flown to Berlin.*

Future Tense

The future tense can be translated as 'I will sing/I will be singing'. In the future tense, the present tense of **werden** is used and the main verb goes to the end of the sentence in the **infinitive**:

ich **werde** ... **trinken**	ich **werde** ... **mitmachen**	ich **werde** ... **bestellen**
du **wirst** ... **sehen**	du **wirst** ... **ankommen**	du **wirst** ... **verkaufen**
er/sie/es/man **wird** ... **stehlen**	er/sie/es/man **wird** ... **abschreiben**	er/sie/es/man **wird** ... **empfehlen**
wir **werden** ... **tanzen**	wir **werden** ... **aufmachen**	wir **werden** ... **genießen**
ihr **werdet** ... **schreiben**	ihr **werdet** ... **zurückfliegen**	ihr **werdet** ... **vermissen**
Sie/sie **werden** ... **üben**	Sie/sie **werden** ... **einkaufen**	Sie/sie **werden** ... **überraschen**

Put the bracketed verbs into the future tense.

1. Ich (fahren) im Sommer ins Ausland.	*In the summer I will travel abroad.*
2. Wir (wohnen) in einem 4-Sterne-Hotel.	*We will stay in a four-star hotel.*
3. Mein Bruder und ich (schwimmen) im Meer.	*My brother and I will swim in the sea.*
4. Ich (essen) die einheimische Küche.	*I will eat the regional cuisine.*

Future Tense: Separable Verbs

Put the bracketed separable verbs into the future tense.

1. Ich (ausruhen) mich im Sommer gut.	*I will rest well in the summer.*
2. (Ausschlafen) du am Wochenende?	*Will you sleep in at the weekend?*
3. Er (ausprobieren) neue Gerichte.	*He will try out new dishes.*
4. Wann (vorbereiten) du dich auf die Prüfung?	*When will you prepare for the exam?*

Future Tense: Inseparable Verbs

Put the bracketed inseparable verbs into the future tense.

1. Ich (erleben) eine neue Kultur.	*I will experience a new culture.*
2. Wir (besichtigen) die Sehenswürdigkeiten.	*We will visit the sights.*
3. Der Junge (beeilen) sich.	*The boy will hurry.*
4. Die Schüler (übernachten) in einem Hotel.	*The students will overnight in a hotel.*

03.03 Hörverständnis Teil 3

Vorarbeit *Preparation*

die Nase voll haben	*to be fed up*	**wegen**	*because of*	**schaffen**	*to manage*
Jahreszeit	*time of year*	**Flug**	*flight*	**vorhaben**	*to plan*
sich freuen auf	*to look forward to*	**buchen**	*to book*	**genervt**	*annoyed*
anfangen	*to begin*	**reichen**	*to be enough*	**treffen**	*to meet*

Ordinary + Higher Level Questions

1. **a)** The conversation is between:
   i) two classmates ☐ **ii)** two students ☐ **iii)** a teacher and a parent ☐ **iv)** two parents ☐
   b) Find **one (O)/two (H)** details in the conversation that support your choice.
2. **a)** Which word best describes Dirk's attitude during the conversation?
   i) worried ☐ **ii)** frustrated ☐ **iii)** encouraging ☐ **iv)** tired ☐
   b) Write down **one (O)/two (H)** details from the conversation to support your choice.
3. Why is Dirk in a bad mood? Give **one (O)/two (H)** details.
4. What do the two students decide to do in the end? Give **one (O)/two (H)** details.

03.04 Hörverständnis Teil 4

Vorarbeit *Preparation*

Naturwissenschaften	*sciences*	**entgleisen**	*to derail*	**Gegenstand**	*object*
stattfinden	*to take place*	**passieren**	*to happen*	**Angriff**	*attack*
Zugunglück	*train accident*	**überwacht**	*monitored*	**regnerisch**	*rainy*
verletzt	*injured*	**werfen**	*to throw*	**wechselhaft**	*changeable*

Ordinary + Higher Level Questions

1. **a)** A competition for young scientists is taking place in Germany. Give **one (O)/two (H)** details.
   b) What does the first prize consist of?
2. **a)** Give **one (O)/two (H)** details about the train accident.
   b) What happened to the passengers?
3. **a)** Why are the police monitoring bridges? Give **one (O)/two (H)** details.
   b) According to the police, what motivates the culprits? Give **one (O)/two (H)** details.
4. **a)** What is the weather forecast for Saturday? Give details.
   b) What is the forecast for Sunday? Give details.

Prüfungstipp

There will always be a question on the weather, so these weather expressions are important.

Die Luftfeuchtigkeit bleibt hoch.	*Humidity remains high.*
Auch morgen ändert sich das Wetter wenig.	*The weather won't change much tomorrow.*
Die Temperaturen erreichen wieder 26 Grad.	*Temperatures will again reach 26 degrees.*

OL  Schriftliche Produktion: Ordinary Level

Write a letter to your pen pal, Karl(a). Complete the first paragraph by correctly inserting the sentence halves below. Then follow the instructions.

Ich bin so beschäftigt
wahnsinnig viel Spaß machen
auf ein Konzert zu gehen
wenn das Abitur vorbei ist
dir zu schreiben

Liebe(r) Karl(a),
endlich habe ich Zeit, ______________ . ______________ , denn wir haben jede Woche Klassenarbeiten. Ich werde mich freuen, ______________ . Aber jetzt will ich dir von meinen Plänen erzählen. Ich habe vor, mit zwei Freunden ______________ . Das wird ______________ !

Now continue the letter.

- Say when and where the concert will take place and describe how you will get there.
- Give **two** details about the two friends who are going with you.
- Describe which groups will be playing and which is your favourite group.
- Explain where you will stay the night and how much the entrance tickets cost.
- Write a suitable closing sentence.

HL Schriftliche Produktion: Higher Level

1. You have received the following letter from your pen pal. Reply in German.

Liebe(r) ______________ ,
endlich habe ich ein bisschen Zeit, mich zu entspannen und ich werde mir ein Buch aus der Bibliothek ausleihen. Könntest du mir ein Buch empfehlen? Welches und warum? Und du, was liest du gern? Alle meine Freunde haben einen Laptop und surfen ständig im Internet. Ich weiß nicht, ob das gut ist. Was meinst du? Ich finde das Internet auch super, aber abends lese ich lieber. Ich habe allerdings das Gefühl, dass heutzutage immer weniger Leute Bücher lesen. Wie ist es in Irland?

Ich muss dir was Spannendes erzählen. Meine Mutter hat neulich 700 Euro im Lotto gewonnen. Mit dem Gewinn wollen wir eine Woche in den Bergen verbringen! Spielt deine Familie EuroMillionen oder Lotto? Gibt es ein irisches Lotto? Was würdest du machen, wenn du im Lotto gewinnen würdest?

Danke für die Einladung nach Irland. Das will ich bestimmt machen, aber nicht diesen Sommer, denn ich sehe mir die Fußballeuropameisterschaft an. Ich hoffe, dass Deutschland Meister wird. Bist du auch so ein Fußballfanatiker wie ich? Welche Mannschaft unterstützt du? Ich verstehe Leute nicht, die Fußball nicht mögen. Du auch nicht? Wie hältst du dich fit?

Du hast auch geschrieben, dass du über Weihnachten auf ein Konzert gehen wirst. Wer wird auf der Bühne sein? Mit wem wirst du dahin fahren und wie viel werden die Eintrittskarten kosten? Erzähl mir davon. Jetzt mache ich Schluss, denn ich bin hundemüde.

Dein(e) Karl(a)

2. Translate these sentences into English.

1. Das Konzert wird im September stattfinden.	**6.** Natürlich gibt es ein irisches Lotto.
2. Viele berühmte Gruppen werden dort sein.	**7.** Ich würde die ganze Welt bereisen.
3. Wir werden auf dem Campinggelände zelten.	**8.** Ich würde einen Teil davon sparen.
4. Ich würde dir ______________ empfehlen.	**9.** Nein, ich bin kein großer Fußballfan.
5. Man entspannt sich gut beim Lesen.	**10.** Ich werde mit Freunden dahin fahren.

  Übung Macht den Meister!

Write the sentences in your copy, inserting the correct form of the verb. Then translate them.

A Pluperfect Tense: Regular Verbs

1. Ich (brauchen) gute Noten im Abitur.
2. Wann (feiern) man seinen Geburtstag?
3. Wer (fehlen) an diesem Tag?
4. Der Fernseher (funktionieren) leider nicht.
5. Wir (lieben) es eigentlich gern.

B Pluperfect Tense: Regular Separable Verbs

1. Ich (ausschalten) das Licht, um Strom zu sparen.
2. Das Kind (einpacken) schon seine Schulsachen.
3. Meine Eltern (ausruhen) sich an diesem Tag.
4. Wir (wegräumen) den Müll.
5. Er (zumachen) das Buch.

C Pluperfect Tense: Regular Inseparable Verbs

1. Der Schüler (verbessern) seine Deutschnoten.
2. Wir (übersetzen) das auf Deutsch.
3. Ich (gewöhnen) mich schon an die Arbeit.
4. Das Kind (entschuldigen) sich schon.
5. Wir (beeilen) uns.

D Pluperfect Tense: Irregular Verbs

1. Der Junge (fahren) Auto.
2. Was (lesen) das Kind?
3. Wir (essen) zu Mittag in der Kantine.
4. Die Katze (schlafen) dauernd vor dem Kamin.
5. Was (nehmen) du?

E Pluperfect Tense: Irregular Separable Verbs

1. Mein Bruder (mithelfen) nie zu Hause.
2. Wer (teilnehmen) am Wettbewerb?
3. Am Wochenende (ausschlafen) meine Mutter.
4. Ich (fernsehen) die ganze Nacht lang.
5. Mein Lehrer (aufgeben) zu viele Hausaufgaben.

F Pluperfect Tense: Irregular Inseparable Verbs

1. Wir (besprechen) wichtige Themen im Unterricht.
2. Das Mädchen (bewerben) sich um ein Praktikum.
3. Die Kinder (erhalten) viele Trophäen.
4. Mein Bruder (unterbrechen) mich.
5. Warum (empfehlen) du es mir?

G Pluperfect Tense: Irregular Verbs of Motion

1. Wir (fliegen) für eine Woche nach Spanien.
2. Wann (gehen) ihr in die Stadt?
3. Ich (bleiben) für einen Monat in Deutschland.
4. Der Junge (fahren) mit der Eisenbahn.
5. Wann (kommen) er nach Hause?

H Pluperfect Tense: Irregular Separable Verbs of Motion

1. Warum (weglaufen) der Mann?
2. Wir (ankommen) rechtzeitig um 8 Uhr.
3. Der Mann (losfahren) ohne seinen Pass.
4. Du (aussteigen) sehr schnell aus dem Bus.
5. Die Kinder (herumrennen) ganz wild im Garten.

I Pluperfect Tense: Irregular Inseparable Verbs of Motion

1. Die Frau (verschwinden) ganz plötzlich.
2. Der Dieb (entkommen) der Polizei.
3. Die Flüchtlinge (entfliehen) dem Krieg.
4. Ich wusste nicht, was (geschehen).
5. Alles (verlaufen) gut.

J Future Tense

1. Wir (dekorieren) den Weihnachtsbaum.
2. Der Kurs (dauern) vier Tage.
3. Ich (fühlen) mich erschöpft.
4. Meine Mutter (kaufen) viele Geschenke.
5. Mein Vater (kochen) Eintopf.

Für die Prüfung/Exam Focus

1. Was passt zusammen?

1. Am Wochenende gehe ich	**A** gehe ich gern einkaufen.
2. Wenn ich Geld habe,	**B** also spiele ich viel Rugby und Tennis.
3. Ich bin eigentlich ganz sportlich,	**C** mit meinen Freunden ins Kino.
4. Er ist an Sport nicht interessiert	**D** gehe ich gern auf Snapchat.
5. In meinem Zimmer	**E** aber er geht doch schon spazieren.

2. Was passt zusammen?

1. Ich bin relativ fit,	**A** mache ich viel Sport.
2. Um fit zu bleiben,	**B** denn ich gehe oft zum Fitnessstudio.
3. Am Samstagmorgen	**C** verbringe ich viel Zeit auf Snapchat.
4. Wenn ich Zeit habe,	**D** schlafe ich gern aus.
5. Seitdem ich ein neues Handy habe,	**E** mache ich einen langen Spaziergang.

3. Select the correct prepositions for the following sentences.

a) Ich gehe gern **(ins/in die/in den/zur)** Kino.

b) Meine Eltern haben viel Geduld **(zu/mit/in/auf)** mir.

c) Ich fahre gern **(mit/in/auf/an)** dem Rad aufs Land.

d) Wir sprechen **(über/durch/mit/in)** Gott und die Welt.

e) Ich interessiere mich **(für/in/um/an)** Kunst.

4. What words make up the following compound words, and what do they mean in English?

a) Klassenarbeit = _____+_____= ________

b) mitmachen = _____+_____= ________

c) Herbstferien = _____+_____= ________

d) fernsehen = _____+_____= ________

e) Höchsttemperaturen = _____+_____= ________

f) losfahren = _____+_____= ________

5. Indicate for the underlined regular verbs the number, tense and infinitive.

a) Mein Bruder hatte komische Geschichten erzählt.

b) Die Eltern haben den Kindern Zeit geschenkt.

c) Ich werde das Abendessen kochen.

d) Wir tanzten bis in die Nacht.

e) Meine Mutter sagt, dass ich launisch bin.

f) Meine Schwester arbeitet bei einer Tankstelle.

6. Indicate for the underlined irregular verbs the number, tense and infinitive.

a) Meine Tante hatte sehr modisch ausgesehen.

b) Die Eltern haben den Kindern Bücher gegeben.

c) Mein Vater hat eine Brille getragen.

d) Wir hatten gern Zeit zusammen verbracht.

e) Leider wird es Streit zu Hause geben.

7. Lückentext: Fill in the blanks with the correct missing words from the box.

Filme gehen Spaß in Bühnenauftritte Interessen für Proben macht aus

Wir **1** ________ jedes Wochenende **2** ________ , denn wir sehen uns leidenschaftlich gern **3** ________ an. Wir haben die gleichen **4** ________ , und haben viel **5** ________ zusammen. Wir interessieren uns alle **6** ________ Musik, und spielen **7** ________ einer Band! Wir machen täglich **8** ________ , denn wir machen oft **9** ________ . Das **10** ________ unheimlich viel Spaß.

Selbstbewertung: Ordinary Level

OL

Vocabulary

1. If I can translate theses sentences into English, I can express myself in the present tense. (1 mark each)

a) Ich spiele Fußball.	**f)** Es ist sehr lustig.
b) Wir gehen ins Kino.	**g)** Ich spiele gern Computerspiele.
c) Wir trinken einen Kaffee im Café.	**h)** Ich sehe gern fern.
d) Ich lese gern Bücher.	**i)** Meine Lieblingssendung ist ...
e) Mein Lieblingsfilm heißt ...	**j)** Die Sendung ist spannend.

Your score: ___ / 10

2. If I can translate these nouns into German, I understand the main nouns to describe hobbies. (1 mark each)

a) leisure activities	**c)** programme	**e)** barbecues	**g)** concert	**i)** abroad
b) computer games	**d)** activity	**f)** friends	**h)** cinema	**j)** TV

Your score: ___ / 10

Grammar

3. If I can choose the correct form of **sein** or **haben**, I can use irregular verbs in the pluperfect tense. (1 mark each)

a) Ich **(hatte/war)** nach Bonn gefahren.	**f)** Wir **(hatten/waren)** mit dem Zug gefahren.
b) Wir **(hatten/waren)** viel Wurst gegessen.	**g)** Ich **(hatte/war)** einen guten Film gesehen.
c) Wir **(hatten/waren)** ins Kino gegangen.	**h)** Ich **(hatte/war)** einen Brief geschrieben.
d) Mark **(hatte/war)** Deutsch gesprochen.	**i)** Ich **(hatte/war)** eine Woche geblieben.
e) Anna **(hatte/war)** Tee getrunken.	**j)** Er **(hatte/war)** mir ein Buch gegeben.

Your score: ___ / 10

4. If I can put these verbs into the future tense, I can describe my future. (2 marks each)

a) gehen: ich _____ ____________

b) fahren: ich _____ ____________

c) machen: wir _____ ____________

d) wohnen: wir _____ ____________

e) bleiben: ich _____ ____________

Your score: ___ / 10

5. If I can choose the correct preposition, I can correctly describe my free time activities. (1 mark each)

a) Ich gehe oft **(im/in/zur)** die Stadt.	**f)** Ich bin **(am/im/um)** 10 Uhr zu Hause.
b) Ich gehe oft **(am/an/auf)** Facebook.	**g)** Ich gehe gern **(ins/im/zum)** Kino.
c) Ich surfe **(im/am/um)** Internet.	**h)** Ich gehe **(auf/an/in)** ein Konzert.
d) Ich treffe mich mit Freunden **(im/um/an)** Park.	**i)** Ich brauche gute Noten **(am/im/zum)** Abitur.
e) **(Im/Um/Am)** Samstag gehe ich aus.	**j)** Ich interessiere mich **(an/für/in)** Musik.

Your score: ___ / 10

What have I learned?	
What must I improve?	
What do I want to revise?	

Your total score: ___ / 50

Selbstbewertung: Higher Level

HL

1. If I can put these sentences into the pluperfect, I understand the pluperfect tense. (1 mark each)

a) Ich bin in die Stadt gegangen.	**f)** Wir haben uns ausgeruht.
b) Ich habe viele Freunde getroffen.	**g)** Ihr habt uns besucht.
c) Wir haben einen Kaffee getrunken.	**h)** Meine Eltern haben mir Geld gegeben.
d) Wir sind aufs Land gefahren.	**i)** Ich bin im Meer schwimmen gegangen.
e) Was hast du gemacht?	**j)** Wir sind spät angekommen.

Your score: ___ / 10

2. If I can translate these sentences into German, I can use the pluperfect tense. (2 marks each)

a) He had already departed. (abfahren)	**d)** I had already been in Germany. (sein)
b) I had forgotten my passport. (vergessen)	**e)** She had heard the news. (hören)
c) She had lost her purse. (verlieren)	

Your score: ___ / 10

3. If I can translate these sentences, I can express myself in the future tense. (1 mark each)

a) I will relax in the summer. (ausruhen)	**f)** I will buy a new phone. (kaufen)
b) We will travel to Spain. (fahren)	**g)** We will celebrate together. (feiern)
c) I will arrive tomorrow. (ankommen)	**h)** We will see my grandparents. (sehen)
d) I will spend time abroad. (verbringen)	**i)** He will set off tomorrow. (losfahren)
e) I will invite all my friends. (einladen)	**j)** I will try out rugby. (ausprobieren)

Your score: ___ / 10

4. If I can give the number, tense and infinitive of these verbs, I understand the tenses. (2 marks each)

a) Wir <u>sind</u> nach Hause <u>gefahren</u>.	**d)** Das Mädchen <u>spielt</u> gern Fußball.
b) Wo <u>warst</u> du?	**e)** Die Kinder <u>hatten</u> ein Eis <u>gegessen</u>.
c) Ich <u>werde</u> mein Deutsch <u>verbessern</u>.	

Your score: ___ / 10

5. If I can correctly fill in the gaps below, I understand word functions. (1 mark each)

fahre spannend Handballclubs Freunden interessant ins Lesen gehe Mitglied sehr

Ich bin **1** _____ unternehmungslustig. Ich **2** _____ jeden Tag joggen und bin **3** _____ eines **4** _____. Wenn ich Zeit habe, gehe ich gerne mit meinen **5** _____ ins Kino. Eigentlich mag ich auch **6** _____. Ich finde Romane aller Art sehr **7** _____ und **8** _____. Manchmal **9** _____ ich mit meinen Freunden **10** _____ Ausland.

Your score:

What have I learned?	
What must I improve?	
What do I want to revise?	

Your total score: ___ / 50

04

Schule

Learning Outcomes

- **Oral work:** discussing and comparing school life in Germany and Ireland
- **Reading:** reading and answering questions on three texts about school life in Germany and Ireland
- **Writing:** writing an opinion (**Äußerung**), describing a picture and writing a letter about school life
- **Aural:** listening to and answering questions on four extracts about school life

Grammar

- Modal verbs in the present tense
- Modal verbs in the imperfect tense
- Infinitive phrases
- The conditional

Vocabulary

- Talking about school subjects
- Describing and comparing the school day, homework, stress and holidays in Germany and Ireland
- Discussing school activities
- Explaining the impact of school life on pupils

German Culture

- School holidays in Germany
- **Hauptschulen**, **Realschulen**, **Gymnasien**
- **Numerus Clausus**

Exam Tips

- Increase your expression mark by using adverbs and adjectives.
- Try to include the conditional in your oral and written work. It is a good way to push up your expression mark.

Mündliche Arbeit: Mein Schulleben

Bitte beantworten Sie die folgenden Fragen:

Welche Fächer lernen Sie gern/nicht gern und warum?

Wie finden Sie die Vorschriften an dieser Schule?

Was machen Sie in den Pausen?

Wie sieht ein typischer Schultag aus?

1. Welche Fächer lernen Sie? *Which subjects are you studying?*	
Natürlich mache ich die Pflichtfächer, Englisch, Irisch und Mathe. Meine Wahlfächer sind BWL, Chemie, Holzarbeit und offensichtlich Deutsch.	*Of course, I do the compulsory subjects, English, Irish and Maths. My optional subjects are Business, Chemistry, Woodwork and, obviously, German.*
Ich mache Grundkurs Mathe. Ich mache Leistungskurs in allen anderen Fächern.	*I do Ordinary Level Maths. I do Higher Level in all the other subjects.*
Geschichte ist mein Lieblingsfach. Ich finde dieses Fach interessant und nützlich.	*History is my favourite subject. I find this subject interesting and useful.*
Biologie und Deutsch sind meine Lieblingsfächer, weil ich gute Noten in diesen Fächern bekomme.	*Biology and German are my favourite subjects because I get good grades in these subjects.*
Ich mag Englisch nicht, weil ich es kompliziert finde.	*I don't like English because I find it complicated.*
Ich hasse Chemie, denn ich kann es einfach nicht begreifen.	*I hate Chemistry because I just can't understand it.*
Ich habe Physik gewählt. Ich habe nicht gewusst, wie schwer es in der Oberstufe ist. Jedoch finde ich das Fach faszinierend/spannend/anspruchsvoll.	*I chose Physics. I didn't know how difficult it is at Senior Cycle. However, I find the subject fascinating/exciting/challenging.*
Eigentlich finde ich das Fach schwierig/trocken/langweilig/verwirrend.	*Actually, I find the subject difficult/dry/boring/confusing.*
Ich mache Musik, denn da bin ich gut drin.	*I do Music because I am good at it.*

2. Welche Fächer werden angeboten? *Which subjects are offered?*	
Hier gibt es ein großes Angebot an Fächern.	*Here there is a wide choice of subjects.*
Natürlich werden die Pflichtfächer, Englisch, Irisch und Mathe, angeboten.	*Of course, the mandatory subjects, English, Irish and Maths, are offered.*
Glücklicherweise kann man hier zwei Fremdsprachen wählen.	*Luckily, you can choose two modern languages here.*
Auch werden die Naturwissenschaften, Biologie, Chemie und Physik, angeboten.	*The sciences, Biology, Chemistry and Physics, are also offered.*
Man kann Kunst, BWL, Musik, Holzarbeit, Metallarbeit, Agrarwissenschaft und Buchhaltung lernen.	*One can study Art, Business, Music, Woodwork, Metalwork, Agricultural Economics and Accounting.*
Ich glaube, es ist wichtig eine gute Fächerauswahl zu haben, denn das wird den Schülern helfen ihre Leidenschaft zu finden.	*I think it is important to have a good choice of subjects because that will help the pupils to find their passion.*

3. Was sind die Regeln an dieser Schule? *What are the rules in this school?*	
Erstens muss man die Schuluniform tragen. Ich finde die Uniform praktisch, denn man weiß immer, was man tragen wird. Jeder sieht gleich aus und das mag ich.	*Firstly, one must wear the school uniform. I find the uniform practical because you always know what you're going to wear. Everyone looks the same and I like that.*
Persönlich mag ich die Uniform nicht. Sie ist unbequem und hässlich. Im Winter ist die Uniform nicht warm genug und im Sommer ist sie zu warm.	*Personally, I don't like the uniform. It is uncomfortable and ugly. In winter the uniform isn't warm enough and in summer it is too warm.*
Ich gehe gern in diese Schule, aber ich würde lieber in eine getrennte Schule gehen. Ich finde die Mädchen/Jungen eine große Ablenkung von der Schularbeit.	*I like going to this school, but I would prefer to go to a single-sex school. I find the girls/boys a big distraction from schoolwork.*
Ich gehe nicht gern in diese Schule, weil sie eine reine Mädchenschule ist. Ich würde lieber eine gemischte Schule besuchen.	*I don't like going to this school because it is an all-girls school. I would rather attend a mixed school.*
Es gibt hier viele Schulregeln. Kaugummi, Zigaretten, Alkohol und Drogen sind natürlich verboten. Man muss auch pünktlich und höflich sein.	*There are a lot of rules here. Chewing gum, cigarettes, alcohol and drugs are of course forbidden. One must also be punctual and polite.*
Handys und Mobbing sind nicht erlaubt.	*Mobile phones and bullying are forbidden.*
Wenn man die Regeln missachtet, kriegt man eine Warnung. Wenn man das nochmal macht, muss man nachsitzen. In ernsteren Fällen lässt der Schulleiter/die Schulleiterin die Eltern in die Schule kommen. Es kommt aber selten zu einem Verweis.	*If one breaks the rules, one gets a warning. If one does it again, one gets detention. In more serious cases, the principal will call the parents into school. It rarely ever comes to an official warning letter though.*
Die Schule ist nicht zu streng. Hier gibt es eine gute Atmosphäre. Ich mag diese Schule, denn ich habe viele Freunde hier und die Lehrer sind hilfsbereit und verständnisvoll.	*The school isn't too strict. Here there is a good atmosphere. I like this school because I have many friends here and the teachers are helpful and understanding.*

4. Übersetzen Sie die folgenden Sätze.

a) Jeden Morgen stehe ich um 7 Uhr auf. Ich wasche mich und ziehe mich an. Danach esse ich mein Frühstück und meine Mutter fährt mich mit dem Auto zur Schule.

b) Die Schule beginnt pünktlich um 9 Uhr und jede Stunde dauert vierzig Minuten.

c) Mittwochs haben wir Halbtagsschule, was ich toll finde.

d) In der kleinen Pause esse ich ein Butterbrot und ich rede mit meinen Freunden. Wir spielen auf dem Schulhof Fußball. In der großen Pause gehen wir ins Dorf/in die Stadt und kaufen Pommes. Die lange Pause dauert eine Stunde.

e) Nach der Schule ruhe ich mich ein bisschen aus. Dann mache ich meine Hausaufgaben. Das dauert zwei bis drei Stunden jeden Tag. Natürlich lerne ich auch am Wochenende.

f) Wir haben viele moderne Einrichtungen hier, wie zum Beispiel einen Sportplatz, eine Turnhalle, eine Bibliothek, eine Kantine, ein Sprachlabor und einen Computerraum. Jedes Klassenzimmer hat ein interaktives Whiteboard.

g) Nach der Schule lerne ich für zwei Stunden unter Aufsicht in der Schule. Da kann ich mich gut auf die Arbeit konzentrieren, denn es gibt keine Ablenkungen.

h) Die Lehrer geben immer zu viel auf. Ich habe nie genug Zeit, um zu lernen.

i) Zwar gibt es viel Arbeit, aber man gewöhnt sich schnell daran.

j) Hoffentlich wird sich die Arbeit lohnen.

Text 1: Mein Sohn schwänzt die Schule

Bitte beantworten Sie die folgenden Fragen:

1. Was sieht man auf dem Bild?
2. Was macht der Junge gerade?
3. Wohin fährt er, Ihrer Meinung nach?
4. Wie fühlt er sich, Ihrer Meinung nach?

Vorarbeit

1. Finden Sie diese Ausdrücke im Text!
   - **A** But I can't get through to him.
   - **B** ... the gang pulls one down ...
   - **C** The young people must come to a decision themselves.
   - **D** It is very important ...
   - **E** It helps if a boy has a mentor ...
2. Finden Sie das Deutsche für die Wörter unten!
   - **A** manages/overload/school-leaving qualification/skips (school)/to mature/bullying
   - **B** feels/undisturbed/professional/conversely/reasons
   - **C** school experiences/dilemma/from a certain age/force/relationship/extent
   - **D** cry for help/to solve together/refusal to go to school/solutions
   - **E** role model/supports/reasonable/turned around (changed)

A Langeweile, Überforderung oder Mobbing: Es gibt viele Gründe fürs Schulschwänzen. Die Elternfrage: Vor kurzem habe ich erfahren, dass mein Sohn (15) regelmäßig die Schule schwänzt. Jetzt fürchte ich natürlich, dass er seinen Schulabschluss nicht schafft. Ich komme aber nicht an ihn heran. Was kann ich tun? Mein Kind, ein Schulschwänzer! Wenn Eltern das realisieren, ist es zuerst ein kleiner Schock. Der Schulbesuch ist nicht nur Pflicht, sondern auch wichtig, um persönlich und intellektuell zu reifen. Wenn der Schulabschluss darunter leidet, wird es schwer sein, einen guten Beruf zu erlernen.

B Tausende von Eltern sind Jahr für Jahr mit dem Schulschwänzen konfrontiert. Mögliche Gründe fürs Schulschwänzen: Man wird oder fühlt sich gemobbt, die Clique zieht einen runter, in der Familie gibt es Konflikte. Manche Jugendlichen sehen keine berufliche Perspektive, ein anderer ist vielleicht überfordert oder umgekehrt gelangweilt – andere möchten ganz einfach ungestört am PC surfen und spielen.

C Diese sind wichtige Fragen: Seit wann existiert das Problem, in welcher Form, in welchem Ausmaß? Wie waren die bisherigen Schulerfahrungen? Was sind seine Wünsche für die Zukunft? Wie ist die Beziehung zwischen Sohn und Eltern? Die Zwickmühle bei diesem Problem: Man kann Jugendliche ab einem gewissen Alter kaum mehr zu etwas zwingen. Die Jugendlichen müssen selbst zu einer Entscheidung kommen. Der erste Schritt ist das Schwänzen als Symptom zu sehen.

D Schulverweigerung ist eine Revolte, ein Hilferuf. Ganz wichtig ist es, wieder miteinander ins Gespräch zu kommen und gemeinsam Lösungen auszusuchen. Eltern können den Sohn auch selbst zur Schule bringen. Und mit dem Klassenlehrer erörtern, wie man das Problem zusammen lösen kann.

E Gibt es einen Onkel, Opa oder Freund der Familie, der mit dem Schüler reden könnte? Es nützt, wenn ein Junge einen Mentor als positives Rollenvorbild hat. Ich kenne viele Jugendliche, die innerhalb kurzer Zeit wie umgedreht waren, wenn sie gespürt haben, sie kommen mit einem Mann gut aus, der vernünftig ist, und der sie unterstützt.

© Michael Felten, *Zeit Online*, 18 Jan. 2018 (amended)

OL Ordinary Level Questions

1. a) Name **two** reasons why pupils skip school, according to the article.
   b) What question do parents ask with regard to this matter?
2. Fill in the required information in the box below.

How often the son skips school A	**Two** important questions to ask C	**One** thing parents can do D	Name **three** possible role models E

3. Which of these statements are true or false?
   a) The mother is worried that her son will not finish his schooling.
   b) Hundreds of parents are confronted with this problem.
   c) Some young people don't see bright career opportunities ahead of them.
   d) It is recommended that parents discuss the problem with their child.
   e) A good male role model can have a very positive effect on a boy.
4. Select the correct prepositions for the following sentences.
   a) Der Schulabschluss leidet viel **(von/unter/mit/aus)** Schuleschwänzen.
   b) Es gibt eine Zwickmühle **(mit/an/bei/für)** diesem Problem.
   c) Die Eltern sollten **(mit/im/für/bei)** dem Klassenlehrer sprechen.
   d) Man muss miteinander **(ans/ins/fürs/um)** Gespräch kommen.

HL Higher Level Questions

1. Beantworten Sie folgende Fragen auf Deutsch!
   a) i) Wovor hat die Mutter Angst? A
      ii) Wie reagieren die Eltern meist auf die Tatsache, dass ihre Kinder die Schule schwänzen? Geben Sie **zwei** Details! A
   b) Welche Gründe für das Schuleschwänzen werden im Text genannt? Geben Sie **vier** Details! B
   c) Wie sollte man auf dieses Problem reagieren? Geben Sie **drei** Details! C
   d) Nennen Sie **zwei** Dinge, die die Eltern machen könnten, um das Problem zu lösen. D
   e) Was für einen Einfluss kann ein positives Rollenvorbild auf einen Teenager haben? E
2. Answer the following questions in English.
   a) Name the **two** reasons why regular school attendance is necessary. A
   b) Name the **four** main reasons why pupils may skip school. B
   c) Which questions need to be asked when a pupil skips school regularly? C
   d) Which **three** actions can be taken by parents to resolve this problem? D
   e) According to the text, what effect can a positive role model have on a teenager? E
3. Aus welchen Wörtern bestehen die zusammengesetzten Wörter und was bedeuten sie auf Englisch?
   a) Schulabschluss = _____ + _____ = ________
   b) Schuleschwänzen = _____ + _____ = ________
   c) Hilferuf = _____ + _____ = ________
   d) Rollenvorbild = _____ + _____ = ________
4. Put the regular and irregular underlined verbs from Text 1 into the pluperfect tense.
   a) Ihr Sohn geht nicht oft in die Schule.
   b) Man fühlt sich gemobbt.
   c) Die Sache ist so wichtig.
   d) Der Mann hat den Jungen unterstützt.

Prüfungstipp

Increase your expression mark by using adverbs and adjectives.

Grammatik: Modalverben/ Modal Verbs

p. 81 (Übung macht den Meister)

Present Tense: Modal Verbs

There are six modal verbs. These verbs are 'helper' verbs. They require an infinitive verb, which goes to the end of the phrase. Watch their endings: **-**, **-st**, **-**, **-en**, **-t**, **-en**.

müssen (to have to/must)	**wollen** (to want to)	**können** (to be able to)	**dürfen** (to be allowed to)	**mögen** (to like)	**sollen** (to ought to)
ich muss-	ich will-	ich kann-	ich darf-	ich mag-	ich soll-
du mu**sst**	du wi**llst**	du ka**nnst**	du da**rfst**	du ma**gst**	du soll**st**
er/sie/es/man muss-	er/sie/es/ man will-	er/sie/es/man kann-	er/sie/es/man darf-	er/sie/es/man mag-	er/sie/es/man soll-
wir müss**en**	wir woll**en**	wir könn**en**	wir dürf**en**	wir mög**en**	wir soll**en**
ihr müss**t**	ihr woll**t**	ihr könn**t**	ihr dürf**t**	ihr mög**t**	ihr soll**t**
Sie/sie müss**en**	Sie/sie woll**en**	Sie/sie könn**en**	Sie/sie dürf**en**	Sie/sie mög**en**	Sie/sie soll**en**

Put these modal verbs into the present tense.

1. Ich (wollen) gute Noten in Deutsch bekommen.	*I want to get good grades in German.*
2. Dieses Jahr (müssen) wir ständig lernen.	*This year we have to study all the time.*
3. In der Pause (dürfen) man in die Stadt gehen.	*In the break one is allowed to go into town.*
4. Natürlich (sollen) man im Unterricht mitmachen.	*Of course one should participate in class.*
5. Ich (können) die Aussprache gar nicht verstehen.	*I can't understand the pronunciation.*
6. Zum Glück (mögen) ich meine Lehrer.	*Luckily, I like my teachers.*
7. Wir (wollen) eine Abi-Fahrt machen.	*We want to do a Leaving Cert trip.*
8. Ihr (können) viele Redewendungen lernen.	*You* (plural) *can learn many idioms.*

Imperfect Tense: Modal Verbs

It is more common to form German modal verbs in the imperfect tense when talking about the past.

müssen	**wollen**	**können**	**dürfen**	**mögen**	**sollen**
ich musste	ich wollte	ich konnte	ich durfte	ich mochte	ich sollte
du musstest	du wolltest	du konntest	du durftest	du mochtest	du solltest
er/sie/es/man musste	er/sie/es/man wollte	er/sie/es/man konnte	er/sie/es/man durfte	er/sie/es/man mochte	er/sie/es/man sollte
wir mussten	wir wollten	wir konnten	wir durften	wir mochten	wir sollten
ihr musstet	ihr wolltet	ihr konntet	ihr durftet	ihr mochtet	ihr solltet
Sie/sie mussten	Sie/sie wollten	Sie/sie konnten	Sie/sie durften	Sie/sie mochten	Sie/sie sollten

Put these modal verbs into the imperfect tense.

1. Ich (müssen) eine Uniform in der Schule tragen.	*I had to wear a uniform at school.*
2. Ich (wollen) einen Austausch machen.	*I wanted to do an exchange.*
3. Man (dürfen) seine eigene Kleidung tragen.	*One was allowed to wear one's own clothes.*
4. Ich (mögen) das deutsche Essen sehr.	*I really liked the German food.*
5. Leider (können) wir keinen Schulausflug machen.	*Unfortunately, we couldn't do a school trip.*
6. Du (sollen) auf die Prüfung vorbereiten.	*You should prepare for the exam.*
7. Er (wollen) eine gemischte Schule besuchen.	*He wanted to attend a mixed school.*
8. Wir (müssen) viele Klassenarbeiten schreiben.	*We had to do many class tests.*

04.01 Hörverständnis Teil 1

Vorarbeit

Rektorin	*principal*	**Zeugnis**	*report card*	**Proben**	*rehearsals*
insgesamt	*altogether*	**Komponisten**	*composers*	**ehrgeizig**	*ambitious*
sogenannten	*so-called*	**Geige**	*violin*	**erfolgreich**	*successful*
Internat	*boarding school*	**üben**	*to practise*	**Staat**	*state*

CL Ordinary + Higher Level Questions

1. Give **three (O)/five (H)** details about the school.
2. **a)** What do the music students do in the mornings?
   b) Apart from composers, what other types of musicians are mentioned?
3. What do we learn about the students? **Give two (O)/three (H) details.**
4. What supports are available to help with the cost of attending this school? Give **one (O)/two (H)** details.

04.02 Hörverständnis Teil 2

Vorarbeit

verbinden	*to connect*	**eine Vier**	*a H4*	**besprechen**	*to discuss*
sich beruhigen	*to calm down*	**Englischarbeit**	*English test*	**gegen**	*against*
weitererzählen	*to pass a message*	**Note**	*grade*	**Mühe**	*effort*
notieren	*to make a note*	**empört**	*to be outraged*	**erhalten**	*to receive*

OL Ordinary Level Questions

1. Whom does the caller wish to speak to?
2. Which school subject is the caller referring to?
3. Describe the issue the caller has.
4. What is the **name** and **number** of the caller?

HL Higher Level Questions

1. Using ***key phrases***, write down in **German** the key information the caller provides:
   - the name of the person **making** the call
   - the reason for the call
   - details regarding further contact
   - the caller's phone number

Gesprächsnotiz
Anruf von: ______________ Gesprächsanlass: ______________
Der Anrufer:
- erwartet heute Morgen einen Rückruf ☐
- wird in zwei Tagen noch einmal anrufen ☐
- bekommt irgendwann einen Rückruf ☐
- bekommt morgen eine E-Mail ☐

Kontaktnummer: *Vorwahl* ______________ *Rufnummer* ______________

2. Write down **three** examples of the language which show that the caller is **stressed**.

Text 2: Wie bekomme ich Lust auf Lernen

Beantworten Sie die folgenden Fragen:

1. Was sieht man auf dem Bild?
2. Wo sind die Jugendlichen?
3. Was machen sie?
4. Wie ist die Stimmung?

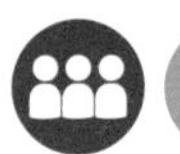 

Vorarbeit

1. Finden Sie diese Ausdrücke im Text!
   - **A** One nearly always has to force oneself to study.
   - **B** A good start is half the battle.
   - **C** The teachers will prepare one for it.
   - **D** Nobody would be capable of ...
   - **E** One gets all the important material summarised.
2. Finden Sie das Deutsche für die Wörter unten!
   - **A** reward/distraction/cheat sheet/to harm
   - **B** to choose/specific/leads (to)/summary
   - **C** along with that/material/curricula/to shine
   - **D** capable/in one go/revision/to recommend
   - **E** to offer/extra tuition/advantage/to consolidate

ABItipps.de (amended)

A Zum Lernen muss man sich fast immer zwingen. Gut ist, wenn man sich klar macht, wofür man lernt. In erster Linie natürlich für sich selbst. Man will schließlich Erfolg haben! Man kann sich eine Belohnung für bestimmte Lernerfolge einplanen. Zum Beispiel Freunde treffen, Entspannung in Form von Sport, einkaufen gehen, spazierengehen. Es hilft auch vielen Jugendlichen, das Lernen nicht im eigenen Zimmer zu machen und stattdessen am Esstisch zu lernen. So hat man keine Ablenkung von den spannenderen Dingen im Schlafzimmer. Und wenn man den Computer und das Handy ausschaltet, hat man Ruhe von Facebook, WhatsApp, Snapchat usw. Um eine Pause vom Lernen zu machen, würde es eine gute Idee sein, Sport zu treiben. Es würde auch nicht schaden beim Spazieren mit Spickzettel alles zu wiederholen. Man kann auch seine eigene Stimme beim Lernen aufnehmen und dann Podcasts hören.

C Die Vorbereitung zum Abitur beginnt eigentlich mit dem Start in der ersten Klasse. Wer von Anfang an den Stoff lernt kann damit am Ende der Schulzeit glänzen. Je mehr Stoff man in frühen Jahren schon gelernt hat, desto weniger muss man am Ende lernen. Die Vorbereitungsphase auf das Abitur beginnt in den letzten zwei Schuljahren. Die Lehrpläne zeigen, was in den Prüfungen aufkommen kann. Die Lehrer werden einen darauf vorbereiten. Nebenbei gibt es auch noch Lernhilfen, die eine Ergänzung sein können.

B Einfach ohne Plan mit dem Lernen zu beginnen führt oft nicht zum großen Erfolg. Man lernt lieber das, was man gerne macht, als das, was man nötig hat. Das Lernen ordentlich durchzuplanen und bestimmte Fächer und Themen pro Tag zu wählen ist eine gute Idee. Eine gute Vorbereitung ist die halbe Miete. Man kann sehr gut mit Lernkarten lernen. So soll man Kärtchen mit den Themen erstellen. Dann hat man eine klasse Zusammenfassung, um alles zu wiederholen.

D Einige Wochen vor dem Abitur gibt es eine Zeit des intensiven Lernens und Wiederholens des Schulstoffs. Aber keiner würde fähig sein, wochenlang am Stück an den Büchern zu sitzen. Es würde sich empfehlen Zeit zum Entspannen einzuplanen. Viele lernen am effizientesten, wenn sie von Beginn an einen strikten Lernplan haben.

E Immer mehr Abiturienten wollen bei der Vorbereitung auf das Abitur Nachhilfestunden. Viele wollen dadurch ihren Stoff festigen oder die Themen behandeln, die sie nicht richtig verstehen. Nachhilfe kann nicht schaden! Bei der wöchentlichen Nachhilfe paukt man den Stoff. Eine beliebte Nachhilfeform sind Seminare in den Ferien. Meist finden einige Wochen vor dem Abi statt. Der Vorteil ist, dass man alles Wichtige zusammengefasst bekommt. Das frischt das Wissen auf. Es gibt Anbieter wie StudyHelp, die Mathe-Abi-Crashkurse anbieten.

OL Ordinary Level Questions

1. **a)** Name **three** rewards one could give oneself for achieving a learning goal. **A**
   b) What is suggested in the text as being the most important factor in one's learning? **B**
   c) According to the text, when does studying for the Leaving Certificate begin? **C**
   d) What does the text say about trying to study everything in one go for weeks on end? **D**
2. Are the following statements true or false?
   a) Der Computer ist eine Ablenkung vom Lernen.
   b) Das chaotische Lernen kann zum großen Erfolg führen.
   c) Je mehr man frühzeitig lernt, desto besser.
   d) Viele möchten Nachhilfe bekommen.
3. Select the correct prepositions for the following sentences.
   a) Man sollte **(am/im/vom/um)** Tisch im Esszimmer sitzen, wenn man lernen will.
   b) Wenn man das Lernen plant, führt das oft **(vom/im/am/zum)** Erfolg.
   c) **(Bei/Mit/Ohne/Am)** Ende der Schulzeit muss man viel lernen.
   d) **(Am/Um/Zur/Zum)** Entspannen sollte man spazierengehen.
   e) Die Vorbereitung **(in/bei/für/auf)** das Abitur ist anstrengend.

HL Higher Level Questions

1. Beantworten Sie folgende Fragen auf Deutsch!
   a) Nennen Sie **drei** Schritte, die man machen kann, um besser lernen zu können! **A**
   b) Wie macht man am besten einen Lernplan? Warum ist das so? **B**
   c) Was kann man sonst machen, um sein Wissen zu vertiefen? **C**
   d) Beschreiben Sie die beste Methode, laut Text, den Lernstoff zu wiederholen. **D**
   e) Warum wollen so viele Abiturienten Nachhilfe in ihren Fächern bekommen? **E**
2. Answer the following questions in English.
   a) What should students do with their computer and smartphone, and why? **A**
   b) Why is it important to have a study plan? **B**
   c) Name **three** sources that will help students to prepare for their examinations. **C**
   d) Apart from studying, what are students recommended to do and why? **D**
   e) Give **two** reasons why grind courses and seminars may be of benefit to students. **E**
3. Aus welchen Wörtern bestehen die zusammengesetzten Wörter, und was bedeuten sie auf Englisch?
   a) Lernerfolge = ______ + ______ = ______
   b) Zusammenfassung = ______ + ______ = ______
   c) Vorbereitungsphase = ______ + ______ = ______
   d) Nachhilfestunden = ______ + ______ = ______
4. Put the underlined modal verbs from Text 2 into the imperfect tense.
   a) Zum Lernen muss man sich fast immer zwingen.
   b) Man will schließlich Erfolg haben!
   c) Man kann sich eine Belohnung für bestimmte Lernerfolge einplanen.
   d) So soll man Kärtchen mit den Themen erstellen.

 OL Äußerung zum Thema: Ordinary Level

You are interviewing a pupil. Complete the dialogue, using the information given in Text 2.

Sie: Du bist im Abiturjahr. Wie belohnst du dich für Lernerfolge?

Schüler: ______________________________

Sie: Hast du einen Lernplan?

Schüler: ______________________________

Sie: Wie viele Themen lernst du am Stück?

Schüler: ______________________________

Sie: Konzentrierst du dich auf nur ein Thema oder auf ein Fach?

Schüler: ______________________________

Sie: Was machst du sonst, um alles zu lernen?

Schüler: ______________________________

 HL Äußerung zum Thema: Higher Level

Write 13 to 15 sentences, answering the questions below.

- Beschreiben Sie das Foto oben in **drei bis vier** Sätzen.
- Stehen junge Leute heutzutage unter viel Stress in der Oberstufe? Was kann man gegen den Schulstress machen?
- Gibt es große Unterschiede zwischen den deutschen und irischen Schulsystemen? Wo würden Sie lieber in die Schule gehen, in Deutschland oder in Irland, und warum?

 Nützliche Sätze

Bestimmt! Wir stehen unter viel Druck im Abijahr. Ich bin immer erschöpft. Leider geben die Lehrer zu viel auf. Ich habe nie genug Zeit für die Hausaufgaben.	*Definitely! We're under a lot of pressure during the Leaving Cert. I'm always exhausted. Unfortunately, the teachers give too much homework. I never have enough time for the homework.*
Zwar gibt es viel Arbeit, aber man gewöhnt sich daran.	*While there is a lot of work, you get used to it.*
Hoffentlich wird sich die Arbeit lohnen.	*Hopefully the hard work will pay off.*
Und wie! Erstens haben wir einen langen Schultag im Vergleich zu Deutschland. Die deutsche Schule fängt um 8 Uhr an, aber endet normalerweise um eins oder zwei.	*Loads! Firstly, we have a long school day in comparison to Germany. German school begins at 8 o'clock but is normally finished by 1 or 2 o'clock.*
Die deutschen Schüler haben mehr Freizeit als wir.	*German students have more free time than we do.*
In Deutschland dauern die Sommerferien nur sechs Wochen, aber wir haben drei Monate schulfrei.	*In Germany the summer holidays only last six weeks, but we have three months off school.*
Es gibt mehr Vorschriften an irischen Schulen. Ich würde also lieber in Deutschland in die Schule gehen, denn die Stimmung ist lockerer und man kann nachmittags viel mehr unternehmen.	*There are more rules in Irish schools. I would therefore rather go to school in Germany, because the atmosphere is more relaxed and in the afternoons you can do a lot more.*
Ich glaube, Schüler haben es in Irland besser. Man kann sich in den langen Sommerferien gut entspannen. Aber die Schulen sind alle gemischt in Deutschland. Auch muss man keine Uniform tragen.	*I think pupils have it better in Ireland. One can really relax in the long summer holidays. However, schools are all mixed in Germany. Also, one doesn't have to wear a uniform.*

Grammatik: Infinitivsätze/Infinitive Phrases

p. 81 (Übung macht den Meister)

Infinitive phrases are phrases where the verb stays in the infinitive form. If you are not using a modal verb, you must put **zu** in front of the infinitive. **Zu + infinitive** will always be the last element in a sentence. If a separable prefix is used in the infinitive, the **zu** is inserted between the prefix and the stem.

Ich kann Deutsch sprechen. (Modal verb) **Ich hoffe, Deutsch zu sprechen** (Infinitive phrase)

Es macht Spaβ, eine Fremdsprache **zu lernen**.	*It is fun to learn a foreign language.*
Es macht keinen Spaβ, eine Klassenarbeit **zu machen**.	*It is no fun to do a class test.*
Es ist schwierig, Grammatik **zu üben**.	*It is difficult to practise grammar.*
Ich habe keine Lust, Physik **zu lernen**.	*I have no interest in studying Physics.*
Es ist nicht einfach, gute Noten **zu bekommen**.	*It is not easy to get good grades.*
Ich habe vor, Jura und Deutsch **zu studieren**.	*I intend to study Law and German.*
Ich hoffe, im Abitur gut **abzuschneiden**.	*I hope to do well in the Leaving Cert.*
Peter hat vor, im Ausland **zu studieren**.	*Peter intends to study abroad.*

1. Add the correct form of the infinitive phrase to these sentences.

a) Ich habe begonnen, für die Schule (lernen).	*I have begun to study for school.*
b) Die Kinder fangen an, Korbball (spielen).	*The children begin to play basketball.*
c) Die Schüler hören auf, den Aufsatz (schreiben).	*The students stop writing the essay.*
d) Der Lehrer hat beschlossen, den Jungen (bestrafen).	*The teacher decided to punish the boy.*
e) Ich habe vergessen, das Formular (ausfüllen).	*I forgot to fill out the form.*
f) Mein Lehrer schlägt vor, einen Austausch (machen).	*My teacher suggests doing an exchange.*
g) Das Mädchen verspricht ihrer Mutter, brav (sein).	*The child promises her mother to be good.*
h) Ich versuche, meine Deutschkenntnisse (verbessern).	*I try to improve my knowledge of German.*

2. Complete the following sentences using **zu** plus infinitive.

a) Es macht Spaβ, ...	*It is fun ...*	**e)** Es ist Zeit, ...	*It is time ...*
b) Es ist schön, ...	*It is lovely ...*	**f)** Ich versuche, ...	*I try ...*
c) Ich habe Lust, ...	*I'm interested in ...*	**g)** Man hofft, ...	*One hopes ...*
d) Ich finde es schwer, ...	*I find it difficult ...*	**h)** Meine Schwester hat vor, ...	*My sister intends to ...*

Prüfungstipp

Revise grammar points from previous chapters by searching for examples of them in reading texts. For example, look through an earlier text and find modal verbs or infinitive phrases. Finding correct examples confirms your understanding.

Kulturecke

There are three types of German secondary schools. The **Hauptschule** teaches the same subjects as the **Realschule** and **Gymnasium**, but at a slower pace and with more vocational-style courses which lead to an apprenticeship. **Realschule** students can either go on to vocational training or a **Gymnasium**. The **Gymnasium**, which focuses on academic learning, leads to the **Abitur** and prepares students for university. **Numerus Clausus** (closed number) means that places are restricted for popular courses such as medicine or law, so students with the best **Abitur** results are accepted onto the course.

Text 3: Der Verweis

Beantworten Sie die folgenden Fragen:

1. Beschreiben Sie, was Sie auf dem Bild sehen!
2. Warum bekommt diese Person einen Verweis, Ihrer Meinung nach?
3. Gibt es so was oft an irischen Schulen?
4. Wie wird man in Irland bestraft, wenn man die Regeln missachtet?

Vorarbeit

1. Finden Sie diese Ausdrücke im Text!
   - **A** Her heart was racing ...
   - **B** Roswita got a fright ...
   - **C** The principal signed the sheet.
   - **D** ... had not been successful enough.
   - **E** She felt content once again.
2. Finden Sie das Deutsche für die Wörter unten!
   - **A** official warning/school record/signature
   - **B** school report/tears/nodded
   - **C** handed over/signed/to solve/closed
   - **D** had failed/disbelievingly/dead/dreams
   - **E** forced/to enter/breakup/memory

A Roswita aus der 7b war auf dem Weg zum Büro der Schulleitung. Ihr Herz raste und ihre Wangen glühten. Sie wusste, warum die Schulleiterin mit ihr sprechen wollte. „Ja", dachte sie, „ja, ich habe die Unterschrift meines Vaters auf dem Zeugnis gefälscht, und, ja, ich weiß auch, dass man dafür einen Verweis bekommt. Und dieser Verweis steht in der Schulakte, das weiß ich."

B Roswita dachte an ihre Eltern. Jetzt musste sie nicht nur die Fünf in Latein erklären, sondern auch den Verweis. Ihre Augen füllten sich mit Tränen. Das Mädchen stand vor der Tür. Sie klopfte. Roswita erschrak, als sie die Stimme der Schulleiterin hörte. „Du weißt, warum ich dich rufen ließ?" fragte die Rektorin, Mater Maria. Das Mädchen nickte. „Und du weißt auch, was es bedeutet, eine Unterschrift zu fälschen." Sie nickte wieder. „Nun Roswita, erkläre mir bitte, warum du das gemacht hast", sagte die Nonne. Das Mädchen sagte ihr, „Ich hatte Angst, meinen Eltern das Zeugnis mit der Fünf zu zeigen, Mater Maria."

C Die Schulleiterin schloss für einen Moment die Augen, und als sie die Augen öffnete, konnte sie nur die Marienstatue auf ihrem Schreibtisch sehen. „... ich hatte so große Angst, Mater Maria..." wiederholte eine Stimme in ihrem Kopf. Plötzlich wusste sie, wie sie das Problem lösen konnte. Sie stand auf, holte ein weißes Blatt Papier und den Schulstempel und setzte sich an ihren Schreibtisch. Das Mädchen sah, wie die Direktorin das Blatt unterschrieb. „Nun geh, Kind, und bring es mir morgen unterschrieben zurück", sagte sie, indem sie Roswita ein neues Zeugnis übergab.

D Roswita starrte ungläubig auf das neue Zeugnis. Da war die schreckliche Fünf im Fach Latein zu lesen, aber der Platz für die Unterschrift des Vaters war frei. Die Rektorin stand am Fenster ihres Büros und schaute auf den Schulgarten. Sie dachte an den Tag, an dem sie die Schule verlassen musste. Ihre Träume von einem Studium waren für immer tot. Ihre Lehrerin hatte die gefälschte Unterschrift unter der Note Sechs auf der Mathematikarbeit gesehen. Sie hatte auch solche große Angst vor der Reaktion ihres Vaters, dem erfolgreichen Professoren, weil sein einziges Kind in der Schule durchgefallen war. Sie hatte so viel Angst, dass er wieder denken würde, dass seine Tochter nicht erfolgreich genug gewesen war.

E Lange stand die Rektorin noch am Fenster und dachte darüber nach. Den Verweis von der Schule, den Bruch mit ihren Eltern und die Erinnerung an den Tag, an dem ihre Eltern sie gezwungen hatten, Nonne zu werden. Sie wurde gezwungen, in dieses Kloster einzutreten. Doch dann sah sie die Madonna auf ihrem Schreibtisch und sie fühlte sich wieder zufrieden.

Anita Voncina, 5 July 2015 (amended)

OL Ordinary Level Questions

1. **a)** Where was Roswita going that made her feel so nervous? A
   b) Why was Roswita in trouble? What explanation did she give for her actions? B
   c) What had the principal done when she was a pupil, and why had she done it? D
   d) When the principal looked at the Madonna again in the end, how did she feel? E
2. Choose a suitable heading for each paragraph and explain your choice in English.

Die Schulleiterin ist jetzt froh | **Roswita hat Angst vor ihren Eltern** | **Die Direktorin trifft eine Entscheidung** | **Roswita geht zur Schulleitung** | **Roswita bekommt ein neues Zeugnis**

3. What words make up the following compound words, and what do they mean in English?
   a) Unterschrift = ______ + ______ = ______
   b) Schulakte = ______ + ______ = ______
   c) Marienstatue = ______ + ______ = ______
   d) Mathematikarbeit = ______ + ______ = ______
4. Select the correct prepositions for the following sentences.
   a) Roswita ist nervös, denn sie muss **(zum/zur/ins/um)** Direktoriat.
   b) Sie weiß, dass der Verweis **(am/in der/im/an der)** Schulakte steht.
   c) Sie schloss **(in/nach/für/vor)** einen Augenblick die Augen.
   d) Sie hatte Angst **(von/für/vor/vom)** ihm.

HL Higher Level Questions

1. Beantworten Sie die folgenden Fragen auf Deutsch und in Ihren eigenen Worten.
   a) Wohin musste Rowita gehen? Wie fühlte sie sich zu dieser Zeit? Geben Sie **zwei** Details! A
   b) Was hat die Rektorin Roswita gefragt? Wie hat Roswita auf diese Frage reagiert? B
   c) Wie hat die Schulleiterin auf die Antwort von Roswita reagiert? C
   d) Woran dachte die Rektorin? E
2. Answer the following questions in English.
   a) Describe exactly how Roswita felt as she was heading to her destination. A
   b) What did Mother Maria ask her? B
   c) What did Mother Maria decide to do after looking at the statue of the Virgin Mary on her desk? C
   d) Describe Mother Maria's personal memory of not doing well in school one year. D
3. What belongs together?

1. Man darf nicht	**A** sobald sie ihre Stimme gehört hatte.
2. Sie kriegte einen Schreck,	**B** die Unterschrift der Eltern fälschen.
3. Als die Nonne ihre Augen öffnete,	**C** vor ihrem Vater.
4. Roswita hatte Angst	**D** als sie ins Kloster eintreten musste.
5. Die Rektorin dachte an den Tag,	**E** sah sie die Madonna.

4. Note down for the underlined verbs: singular or plural, the tense and the infinitive.
   a) Sie wusste, warum die Rektorin mit ihr sprechen wollte.
   b) Roswita dachte an ihre Eltern.
   c) Sie stand auf.
   d) Ihre Träume waren für immer tot.

 Grammatik: Der Konditional/The Conditional

p. 81 (Übung macht den Meister)

The conditional mood can be translated as 'I would live/I would watch'. To form the conditional, the conditional form of **werden** is used. The main verb goes to the end of the sentence in the infinitive form: **machen**, **lachen**, **sagen**. Regular and irregular verbs are formed in the same way.

ich **würde ... tanzen**	wir **würden ... sprechen**
du **würdest ... fahren**	ihr **würdet ... spielen**
er/sie/es/man **würde ... weinen**	Sie/sie **würden ... gehen**

Try to include the conditional in your oral and written work. It is a good way to push up your expression mark.

Put the following bracketed regular verbs into the conditional.

1. Mein Vater (kaufen) das Auto.	*My father would buy the car.*
2. Der Junge (lachen) laut.	*The boy would laugh out loud.*
3. Die Frau (machen) so viel Arbeit.	*The woman would do so much work.*
4. Die Kinder (lernen) fleißig für die Prüfung.	*The children would study hard for the exam.*
5. Warum (weinen) die Kinder?	*Why would the children cry?*
6. Er (brauchen) ein neues Sporttrikot.	*He would need a new sports jersey.*

Conditional Tense: Separable Verbs

Put the following bracketed regular separable verbs into the conditional. Remember to put the whole separable verb to the end in the infinitive form: **ausgehen**, **zusammenfahren**, **abfahren**.

1. Mein Vater (aufwärmen) das Essen.	*My father would heat up the meal.*
2. Julia (zuhören) eigentlich im Unterricht.	*Julia would actually listen in class.*
3. Das Kind (umdrehen) sich immer.	*The child would always turn around.*
4. Wir (weiterspielen) im Park.	*We would continue to play in the park.*
5. Warum (anlächeln) mich das Mädchen?	*Why would the girl smile at me?*
6. Wir (abmachen) einen Termin für Freitag.	*We would agree an appointment for Friday.*
7. Klaus (ausprobieren) Radfahren.	*Klaus would try out cycling.*
8. Die Kinder (ausruhen) sich im Park.	*The children would relax in the park.*
9. Ich (vorstellen) mir das anders.	*I would imagine it differently.*
10. Meine Eltern (umbauen) den Dachboden.	*My parents would convert the attic.*

Conditional Tense: Inseparable Verbs

Put the following bracketed regular inseparable verbs into the conditional.

1. Der Mann (besuchen) seine Mutter.	*The man would visit his mother.*
2. Die Frauen (verkaufen) die Kuchen.	*The women would sell the cakes.*
3. Ich (erleben) eine neue Kultur.	*I would experience a new culture.*
4. Die Frau (beobachten) die Vögel.	*The woman would watch the birds.*
5. Der Film (begeistern) mich.	*The film would delight me.*
6. Ute (entwickeln) einen neuen Trendsport.	*Ute would develop a new trend sport.*
7. Der Trainer (erwarten) zu viel von mir.	*The trainer would expect too much of me.*
8. Das Kind (beruhigen) sich.	*The child would calm down.*

04.03 Hörverständnis Teil 3

Vorarbeit

Spinnst du?	*Are you crazy?*	**vermeiden**	*to avoid*
ahnen	*to guess*	**regeln**	*to take care of*
ehrlich	*honestly*	**Eindruck**	*impression*
angucken	*to look at*	**schüchtern**	*shy*
peinlich	*embarrassing*	**überzeugt**	*convinced*
ständig	*constantly*	**bitten**	*to ask*

CL Ordinary + Higher Level Questions

1. **a)** The conversation is between two speakers called Birgit and Julia. They are:
   i) classmates ☐ **ii)** sisters ☐ **iii)** a teacher and a parent ☐ **iv)** two parents ☐
   b) Find **one (O)/two (H)** details in the conversation to support your choice.
2. What does the first speaker (Birgit) suggest doing that day? Whom does she want to invite and why? Give **one (O)/two (H)** details.
3. According to the conversation, how could Julia and Jan help each other? Give **one (O)/two (H)** details.
4. **a)** Which word best describes Birgit's attitude during the conversation?
   i) angry ☐ **ii)** frustrated ☐ **iii)** encouraging ☐ **iv)** tired ☐
   b) Write down **one (O)/two (H)** details from the conversation to support your choice.

04.04 Hörverständnis Teil 4

Vorarbeit

Fremdsprachenwahl	*choice of foreign language*	**zunehmen**	*to increase*	**Stau**	*traffic jam*
Kindertagesstätten	*nurseries*	**feststellen**	*to determine*	**schaffen**	*to accomplish*
Raucherecke	*smoking corner*	**Gesetz**	*law*	**weniger**	*less*
Aufnahme	*uptake*	**gefolgt von**	*followed by*	**regnerisch**	*rainy*

CL Ordinary + Higher Level Questions

1. **a)** What are the results of the study on pupils' choices of foreign languages? Give **one (O)/two (H)** details.
   b) What is said about the uptake of Latin and Greek?
2. **a)** What will be taking effect in German schools?
   b) Where else will this be taking effect?
3. What is happening on German motorways at the moment and why? Give **two (O)/three (H)** details.
4. According to the study, why is it important to keep the school starting age at six years in Germany?
5. **a)** What is the weather forecast for today? Give **two (O)/three (H)** details.
   b) What is the forecast for tomorrow? Give **two (O)/three (H)** details.

OL Schriftliche Produktion: Ordinary Level

Write a letter to your pen pal. Complete the first paragraph by correctly inserting the sentence halves.

die nette Einladung **sein** **viel Spaß machen** **Endlich habe ich Zeit** **Ich war so müde**

Hallo aus Irland! ______________ dir zu schreiben! ______________ nach den langen Sommerprüfungen. Es würde mir ______________ , dich in Deutschland zu besuchen. Vielen Dank für ______________ . Das wird toll______________ !

Now continue the letter.

- Say how long the summer holidays will last.
- Give **two** details about the hobbies you will pursue after finishing all your exams.
- Say how many classes you have every day and how long they last.
- Say how long you spend on your homework.
- Say when you would like to go to Germany and how long you would like to stay.
- Mention what you would like to do when you're there.
- Write a suitable closing sentence.

HL Schriftliche Produktion: Higher Level

Reply in German to your pen pal's letter.

Liebe(r) ______________ ,

endlich sind die Klassenarbeiten vorbei! Ich bin total erschöpft! Sag mal, wie findest du unser Prüfungssystem im Vergleich zum irischen? Welches System würdest du lieber haben und warum?

Im Großen und Ganzen herrscht eine gute Stimmung an deutschen Schulen. Ich glaube, das liegt am kurzen Schultag und an der kontinuierlichen Beurteilung. Wie ist deine Meinung dazu? Wie kommst du mit dem ganzen Schulstress zurecht? (Schulalltag, kontinuierliche Beurteilung, Hausaufgaben, Noten, usw.)

Danke für die Einladung nach Irland. Das werde ich bestimmt machen! Wie wäre es mit Juni? Ich würde gerne vom 10. bis zum 20. Juni bleiben. Ich hoffe, das wird euch gut passen! Ich würde sehr gerne im Meer schwimmen gehen, radfahren und natürlich mit deinen Freunden in der Stadt herumhängen. Du, würdest du diesen Sommer auch ein paar Wochen bei mir in Deutschland verbringen? Das würde so viel Spaß machen. Was hältst du davon? Was würdest du gerne in Deutschland alles unternehmen und wann würdest du hierherkommen?

Du hast auch geschrieben, dass du zu Ostern sogenannte Wiederholungsseminare besucht hast. Erzähl mir alles davon! Wie war es? Wo war es? Was sind die Vorteile, einen Wiederholungskurs zu machen?

Ich freue mich riesig auf deine Antwort! Lass bald von dir hören!

Dein(e) Uli

Übung Macht den Meister!

Write the sentences in your copy, inserting the correct form of the verb. Then translate them.

A Present Tense: Modal Verbs

1. Ich (wollen) nach Deutschland fahren.
2. Du (müssen) dieses Jahr fleiβig lernen.
3. Man (können) im Unterricht gut aufpassen.
4. Der Schüler (sollen) pünktlich sein.
5. Die Lehrerin (mögen) das neue Buch.
6. Er (dürfen) seine eigene Kleidung tragen.
7. Wir (müssen) jetzt zum Unterricht kommen.
8. Ihr (können) den Lernstoff wiederholen.

B Imperfect Tense: Modal Verbs

1. Wir (dürfen) keinen Kaugummi kauen.
2. Ich (sollen) fleiβiger lernen.
3. Die Schüler (müssen) Hausaufgaben machen.
4. Warum (wollen) du Geschichte lernen?
5. Der Lehrer (können) den Brief übersetzen.
6. Die Schülerin (mögen) das Fach nicht.
7. Ich (dürfen) in der Bibliothek lernen.
8. Wann (können) du den Aufsatz schreiben?

C Present Tense: Infinitive Phrases

1. Ich hoffe, gute Noten im Abitur (bekommen).
2. Er beabsichtigt, in Limerick (studieren).
3. Hannah hat vor, ins Ausland (fahren).
4. Du hast vergessen, deine Mutter (anrufen).
5. Deutsche Wortstellung ist schwer (verstehen).
6. Ich habe keine Zeit, mich (ausruhen).
7. Wir haben Interesse, einen Austausch (machen).
8. Die Schüler versuchen, Deutsch (beherrschen).

D Conditional Tense: Regular Verbs

1. Ich (brauchen) gute Noten im Abitur.
2. Wann (feiern) man seinen Geburtstag?
3. Wer (danken) ihm?
4. Warum (funktionieren) es nicht?
5. Wir (lieben) es eigentlich gern.
6. Ich (spielen) gern Karten.
7. Die Schüler (reisen) gern nach Deutschland.
8. Wann (machen) du die Hausaufgaben?

E Conditional Tense: Regular Separable Verbs

1. Ich (ausschalten) das Licht.
2. Das Kind (einpacken) seine Schulsachen.
3. Meine Eltern (ausruhen) sich am Abend.
4. Wir (wegräumen) gern den Müll.
5. Er (vorbereiten) sich gern auf die Prüfung.
6. Man (weitermachen) gern mit der Arbeit.
7. Er (anrufen) sie gern.
8. Sie (mitmachen) gern im Deutschunterricht.

F Conditional Tense: Regular Inseparable Verbs

1. Der Schüler (verbessern) gern seine Noten.
2. Wir (übersetzen) das ins Deutsche.
3. Ich (gewöhnen) mich schon an die Arbeit.
4. Das Kind (entschuldigen) sich.
5. Wir (beeilen) uns.
6. Wie viel Geld (verdienen) du?
7. Die Lehrerin (betonen) die Grammatik.
8. Ich (begrüßen) meinen Austauschpartner.

G Conditional Tense: Irregular Verbs

1. Der Junge (fahren) gern Auto.
2. Was (lesen) das Kind gern?
3. Was (essen) wir zu Mittag in der Kantine?
4. Mein Bruder (helfen) mir bei der Arbeit.
5. (Nehmen) du das letzte Stück Kuchen?
6. Ich (trinken) gern eine Limonade.
7. Er (stehlen) ein Auto.
8. Wir (schreiben) einen Beschwerdebrief.

H Conditional Tense: Irregular Separable Verbs

1. Warum (weglaufen) der Mann?
2. Wir (ankommen) rechtzeitig um 8 Uhr.
3. Der Mann (losfahren) jetzt.
4. Du (aussteigen) in der Stadt aus dem Bus.
5. Die Kinder (herumrennen) im Garten.

I Conditional Tense: Irregular Separable Verbs

1. Die Frau (verlieren) nicht ihr Portemonnaie.
2. Der Dieb (entkommen) leicht der Polizei.
3. Die Flüchtlinge (entfliehen) dem Krieg.
4. Ich wusste nicht, was danach (geschehen).
5. Der Mann (verjagen) nie die Kinder.

Für die Prüfung

1. Was passt zusammen?

1. Wenn ich mehr Zeit hätte,	**A** würde ich Nachhilfe in Mathe bekommen.
2. Wenn ich Geld hätte,	**B** würde ich mehr Sport treiben.
3. Ich würde es viel lieber haben,	**C** die Altstadt zu besuchen.
4. Er würde es sehr interessant finden,	**D** müssen die Eltern sofort in die Schule kommen.
5. Wenn man beim Mobbing erwischt wird,	**E** in Deutschland in die Schule zu gehen.

2. Select the correct prepositions for the following sentences.

a) Ich lerne gern Irisch, denn ich bin gut **(ins/in die/im/zum)** Fach.

b) Meine Eltern verstehen, dass ich **(zu/unter/in/auf)** viel Stress stehe.

c) Ich fahre **(mit/in/auf/an)** dem Bus zur Schule.

d) Am Wochenende ruhe ich mich **(mit/bei/in/durch)** mir zu Hause aus.

e) Wir lernen zusammen **(an der/im/in der/neben dem)** Bibliothek.

3. What words make up the following compound words, and what do they mean in English?

a) Prüfungssystem = _____ + _____ = _____

b) Schulabschluss = _____ + _____ = _____

c) Wahlfach = _____ + _____ = _____

d) Pflichtfächer = _____ + _____ = _____

4. Put in the correct form of the present tense of the modal verb to complete the sentence.

a) Ich ____________ (wollen) gute Noten bekommen.

b) Ich ____________ (müssen) mein Deutsch verbessern.

c) ____________ (Können) du mir helfen?

d) Meine Eltern sagen, ich ____________ (sollen) mehr lernen.

5. Complete the sentences, using an infinitive phrase.

a) Ich war überrascht, ____________ . (hören/von dir)

b) Du hast versprochen, ____________ . (anrufen/uns)

c) Ich hoffe, ____________ . (gut abschneiden/im Abitur)

d) Was beabsichtigst du, ____________ ? (studieren/nächstes Jahr)

e) Ich habe vor, ____________ . (fahren/nach Griechenland)

6. Rewrite the underlined verbs in the conditional.

a) Wir verbringen gern Zeit zusammen.

b) Leider gibt es Streit zu Hause.

c) Mein Bruder hilft mir.

d) Wir sprechen auf Deutsch.

7. Lückentext: Fill in the blanks with the correct missing words from the box.

regelmäßig verbringe Interesse studieren Fremdsprachen seit verbessern ist Beruf Noten

Normalerweise **1** ______ ich vier Stunden bei den Hausaufgaben. Ich lerne **2** ______ , denn ich will gute **3** ______ bekommen, so dass ich an der Uni **4** ______ kann. Ich habe viel **5** ______ an Kunst, also male ich jeden Tag, um meine Fähigkeiten zu **6** ______ . Ich lerne auch leidenschaftlich gern Musik, und spiele **7** ______ vier Jahren Klavier! Außer Kunst und Musik lerne ich auch gern **8** ______ , denn sie sind nützlich im **9** ______ . Das **10** ______ sehr wichtig.

Selbstbewertung: Ordinary Level

Vocabulary

1. If I can translate these sentences, I can discuss school in German. (1 mark each)

a) Chemie ist mein Lieblingsfach.	**f)** Ich gehe gern in die Schule.
b) In Irland gibt es einen langen Schultag.	**g)** Ich besuche eine gemischte Schule.
c) Ich mache Grundkurs Irisch.	**h)** Ich lerne nicht gern Mathe.
d) Wir bekommen viele Hausaufgaben.	**i)** Ich finde Englisch schwierig.
e) In Irland trägt man eine Uniform.	**j)** Ich finde BWL interessant und praktisch.

Your score: ___ /10

2. If I can translate these nouns into German, I understand the nouns needed to describe school life. (1 mark each)

a) lesson	**c)** study plan	**e)** class test	**g)** subject	**i)** canteen
b) homework	**d)** report card	**f)** school rules	**h)** Leaving Certificate	**j)** holidays

Your score: ___ /10

Grammar

3. If I can use the correct form of these verbs, I understand modal verbs. (1 mark each)

a) Ich _____ Deutsch sprechen. (wollen)	**f)** Wir _____ Limonade trinken. (mögen)
b) Du _____ mir helfen. (können)	**g)** Ihr _____ uns besuchen. (können)
c) Mein Bruder ___ arbeiten. (müssen)	**h)** Du _____ Englisch lernen. (wollen)
d) Meine Schwester _____ ein Eis essen. (dürfen)	**i)** Die Kinder _____ in die Schule gehen. (müssen)
e) Das Kind _____ viel lernen. (sollen)	**j)** Ich _____ in die Stadt gehen. (dürfen)

Your score: ___ /10

4. If I can put **zu** in the correct position, I understand how to form infinitive phrases. (1 mark each)

a) Ich hoffe, gute Noten bekommen.	**f)** Ich habe vor, nach Deutschland fahren.
b) Ich beabsichtige, fleißig lernen.	**g)** Hast du Lust, in die Stadt fahren?
c) Es ist schwierig, Deutsch lernen.	**h)** Es macht Spaß, Deutsch lernen.
d) Ich versuche, eine Eins kriegen.	**i)** Hast du Lust, mit mir lernen?
e) Es ist leicht, die Sprache beherrschen.	**j)** Ich habe keine Lust, Deutsch sprechen.

Your score: ___ /10

5. If I can put these verbs into the conditional, I can describe what I would like to do. (2 marks each)

a) I would go. (gehen)	**d)** We would live. (wohnen)
b) We would travel. (fahren)	**e)** I would stay. (bleiben)
c) I would do. (machen)	

Your score: ___ /10

What have I learned?	
What must I improve?	
What do I want to revise?	

Your total score: ___ /50

Selbstbewertung: Higher Level

HL

1. If I can put these verbs into the imperfect (p. 30), I understand mixed verbs. (1 mark each)

a) Wir denken über die Zukunft.	**f)** Wie nennt ihr den Hund?
b) Kennst du meine Lehrerin?	**g)** Ich verbringe den Sommer im Ausland.
c) Ich bringe meine Schultasche mit.	**h)** Ich weiß nichts davon.
d) Der Hund rennt im Garten.	**i)** Wie lange brennt das Feuer?
e) Leider weiß ich nichts darüber.	**j)** Wie viel Geld bringt die Tombola ein?

Your score: ___ / 10

2. If I can put these verbs into the perfect (p. 35), I understand mixed verbs. (1 mark each)

a) Ich denke oft darüber.	**f)** Die Lehrerin bringt uns viel bei.
b) Wir verbringen viel Zeit auf dem Land.	**g)** Er denkt über das Projekt nach.
c) Er weiß viel über die Kultur.	**h)** Ich bringe mein Regenzeug mit.
d) Die Kinder kennen den Mann.	**i)** Das Feuer brennt weiter.
e) Die Schüler rennen im Park.	**j)** Mein Opa nennt mich „Liebling".

Your score: ___ / 10

3. If I know which sentences need **zu**, I understand modal verbs and infinitive phrases. (1 mark each)

a) Ich hoffe, gute Noten _______ bekommen.	**f)** Ich habe vor, nach Berlin _______ fahren.
b) Ich kann die Grammatik _______ verstehen.	**g)** Ich beabsichtige, fleißig _______ lernen.
c) Kannst du mir _______ helfen?	**h** Hast du Lust, in die Stadt _______ fahren?
d) Es ist schwierig, Deutsch _______ lernen.	**i)** Ich muss jeden Tag viel _______ lernen.
e) Es macht Spaß, Deutsch _______ lernen.	**j)** Ich möchte auf die Uni _______ gehen.

Your score: ___ / 10

4. If I can translate these sentences into German, I can use the conditional. (2 marks each)

a) He would like to go to university.	**d)** I would like to go to Germany. (fahren)
b) I would like to improve my grades.	**e)** That would be fun.
c) She would help me with the homework.	

Your score: ___ / 10

5. If I can correctly fill in the gaps, I understand the difference between verbs and adjectives. (1 mark each)

lerne wahr um gut gehört
mache lernen fassen wiederholen bitte

Ich bin **1** ______ in Physik. Also **2** ______ ich es jeden Tag gern. Ich habe **3** ______ , man lernt immer zuerst, was man gern hat. Das ist eigentlich **4** ______! Wenn ich eine Klassenarbeit **5** ______ , mag ich mit Freunden das Thema **6** ______. Wir **7** ______ alles zusammen und **8** ______ es zu Hause. Manchmal **9** ______ ich meinen Lehrer **10** ___ Hilfe.

Your score: ___ / 10

What have I learned?	
What must I improve?	
What do I want to revise?	

Your total score: ___ / 50

05 Sprachenlernen

Learning Outcomes

- **Oral:** discussing language learning
- **Reading:** reading and discussing three texts on language learning
- **Writing:** writing an opinion (**Äußerung**), a picture description and letter on language learning
- **Aural:** listening to and answering questions on four extracts on languages

Grammar

- Word order
- Conjunctions

Vocabulary

- Language learning in the classroom, on exchanges and courses
- Advantages and difficulties of learning a foreign language

German Culture

- Experiences of exchanges

Exam Tips

- Practise speaking German with your classmates as often as possible.
- Work on your pronunciation. Good online dictionaries will show you how to pronounce difficult words.
- Practise German word order. To get a good expression mark in your written work, you need a good command of word order.

Mündliche Arbeit: Sprachenlernen

Stellen Sie sich gegenseitig alle Fragen unten. Schreiben Sie sie auf.

Wie finden Sie Deutsch?

Was ist schwierig an der deutschen Sprache?

Finden Sie Deutsch einfach oder schwer?

Warum lernen Sie Deutsch?

Was machen Sie im Deutschunterricht?

Wie lernt man am besten eine Sprache?

1. Wie finden Sie Deutsch? *How do you find German?*	
Ich lerne Deutsch seit fünf/sechs Jahren. Ich mag Deutsch, denn es ist eine logische Sprache. Obwohl man viel lernen muss, gibt es nicht zu viele Ausnahmen.	*I've been learning German for five/six years. I like German because it is a logical language. Although there is a lot to learn, there aren't too many exceptions.*
Deutsch ist eine nützliche Sprache und man bekommt leichter eine Stelle, wenn man Deutsch beherrscht. In Irland gibt es viele deutsche Firmen.	*German is a useful language and you can get a job more easily if you have mastered German. In Ireland there are many German firms.*
Ich mag Deutsch nicht, denn ich bin nicht sprachlich begabt. Ich habe Deutsch gewählt, weil ich Französisch hasse.	*I don't like German, because I'm not good at languages. I chose German because I hate French.*
Ich finde Deutsch eine wunderschöne Sprache. Ich lerne auch Französisch, denn ich habe ein feines Gehör für Sprachen. Ich möchte Sprachen auf der Uni studieren.	*I think German is a beautiful language. I'm also learning French because I have a good ear for languages. I would like to study languages at university.*
Ich finde Deutsch schwierig. Die Grammatik ist sehr kompliziert, besonders die Fälle. Die Wortstellung ist unmöglich.	*I find German difficult. The grammar is very complicated, especially the cases. The word order is impossible.*
Leider finde ich Deutschunterricht langweilig. Es gibt immer zu viel zu lernen.	*Unfortunately, I find German class boring. There is always too much to learn.*
Unsere Lehrerin ist fantastisch. Sie erklärt alles ganz deutlich.	*Our teacher is fantastic. She explains everything very clearly.*

2. Was ist schwierig an der Sprache? *What is difficult about the language?*	
Ich kann mir die vielen Vokabeln nie merken.	*I can never remember all the vocabulary.*
Die deutsche Aussprache ist ziemlich leicht, aber die Hörverständnisse sind manchmal knifflig. Die Menschen sprechen sehr schnell und es ist schwierig, alles mitzubekommen.	*The German pronunciation is quite easy, but the listening comprehensions are sometimes tricky. The people speak very quickly and it is difficult to understand everything.*
Die Grammatik geht über meinen Verstand.	*The grammar goes over my head.*
Ich finde die Fälle und die Zeiformen richtig verwirrend.	*I find the cases and the tenses really confusing.*

3. Warum lernen Sie Deutsch? *Why are you learning German?*	
Ich habe Deutsch gewählt, denn ich finde die deutsche Aussprache leichter als die französische Aussprache.	*I chose German because I find the German pronunciation easier than the French pronunciation.*
Ich hatte keine Wahl, denn Deutsch ist Pflichtfach an dieser Schule.	*I had no choice because German is a compulsory subject at this school.*
Ich glaube, Fremdsprachen sind sehr wichtig in der heutigen Gesellschaft. Man hat bessere Berufschancen, wenn man eine Fremdsprache spricht.	*I think foreign languages are very important in today's society. One has better job opportunities if you speak a foreign language.*
Manche Kurse an der Uni verlangen einen Abschluss in einer Fremdsprache.	*Some university courses require a foreign language at Leaving Cert.*
Eigentlich lerne ich drei Fremdsprachen, Deutsch, Englisch und Irisch. Ich stamme ursprünglich aus Litauen und habe erst mit zehn Jahren Englisch und Irisch gelernt.	*Actually, I learn three foreign languages, German, English and Irish. I come from Lithuania originally and I only learned English and Irish at the age of ten.*

Übersetzen Sie die folgenden Sätze.

4. Was machen Sie im Deutschunterricht? *What do you do in German class?*
a) Im Deutschunterricht lernen wir Grammatik und üben die mündliche Arbeit.
b) Wir lesen Texte und schreiben Briefe und Aufsätze. Natürlich machen wir auch Hörverständnisse.
c) Wir lernen über die deutsche Kultur.
d) Wir üben regelmäßig für die mündliche Prüfung.
e) Im Übergangsjahr haben wir einen Film gesehen. Der Film hieß „Good Bye Lenin!"
f) Wir haben viel über die deutsche Geschichte und Kultur gelernt.

5. Wie lernt man am besten eine Sprache? ***How can one best learn a language?***	
Ich glaube, man lernt eine Sprache am besten, wenn man das Land besucht. Ein Austausch ist eine gute Methode, eine Sprache zu lernen.	*I believe you best learn a language when you travel to the country. An exchange is a good method of learning a language.*
Im Übergangsjahr habe ich einen Austausch in München gemacht. Meine Gastfamilie war echt lieb und ich habe meine Deutschkenntnisse verbessert. Seit dem Austausch finde ich Deutsch viel leichter.	*In Transition Year I did an exchange in Munich. My host family was really lovely and I improved my knowledge of German. Since the exchange, I find German much easier.*
Leider habe ich keinen Austausch gemacht, aber ich habe einen deutschen Sommerkurs gemacht. Ich habe viel gelernt und der Kurs hat Spaß gemacht.	*Unfortunately, I haven't done an exchange, but I did do a German summer course. I learned a lot and the course was fun.*
Ich bekomme Nachhilfestunden in Deutsch, denn ich finde Deutsch sehr schwierig.	*I get grinds in German because I find German very difficult.*
Ein Sprachkurs im Ausland ist sinnvoll, denn dann erlebt man auch die Kultur.	*A language course abroad is worthwhile because then one also experiences the culture.*

Prüfungstipp

A German Film

You may be asked to talk about a German film. While you don't need to answer this question, it is useful to prepare a few sentences. Here are some sample questions and answers:

Examiner: Haben Sie einen deutschen Film gesehen?

Candidate: Ja, im Übergangsjahr haben wir „Good Bye Lenin!" gesehen. Der Film war sehr lustig, aber ich habe auch viel über die deutsche Geschichte und Kultur gelernt.

Examiner: Haben Sie den Film auf Englisch oder auf Deutsch gesehen?

Candidate: Der Film war auf Deutsch aber es gab Untertitel auf Englisch. Das hat mir viel geholfen.

Text 1: Welche Sprachen lernen Europäer?

  Bitte beantworten Sie die folgenden Fragen:

1. Was sieht man auf dem Foto?
2. Wo wurde dieses Foto aufgenommen?
3. Was macht die Frau?
4. Beschreiben Sie die europäische Fahne!

Vorarbeit

1. Finden Sie diese Ausdrücke im Text!
   - **A** The holiday season thereby throws a light on the question.
   - **B** The government in Paris wants to get rid of bilingual classes.
   - **C** Languages which are similar to one's own are also often taught.
   - **D** And therefore the language is firmly established in the country's schools.
2. Finden Sie das Deutsche für die Wörter unten!
   - **A** linguistic/crisscross/travels/confusion
   - **B** decide/Education Minister/conversely
   - **C** useful/effort/differences/countries in a crisis
   - **D** longing/foreign worker/war/history/popular

A Es ist Sommer, Urlaubszeit: Man reist von Deutschland nach Italien, von Italien nach Frankreich, von Frankreich nach Großbritannien, von Großbritannien nach Schweden, und kreuz und quer über den Kontinent. Die Reisezeit ist gleichzeitig eine der sprachlichen Verwirrung. Parlez-vous Deutsch? Sprechen Sie italiano? Where is the next Bushaltestelle? Sorry, aber my Englischunterricht ist lange her. Die Urlaubssaison wirft damit ein Licht auf die Frage: Welche Sprachen lernen junge Europäer in der Schule?

B Die Regierung in Paris will die Zweisprachen-Klassen abschaffen. Die Deutschlehrer in Frankreich protestierten und in Berlin sagt Bundesbildungsministerin Johanna Wanka: „Wir brauchen einen starken Deutschunterricht in Frankreich und einen guten Französischunterricht in Deutschland." In Frankreich lernen inzwischen 37 Prozent der Schüler Spanisch, nur rund 14 Prozent entscheiden sich für Deutsch. Umgekehrt haben mehr als ein Viertel der Schüler in Deutschland Französischunterricht.

C Englisch dominiert in Europas Klassenzimmern. Doch in der zweiten und dritten Reihe zeigen sich interessante Unterschiede zwischen den Ländern. Welche Sprache neben Englisch auf dem Stundenplan der Schulen steht, ist oft eine praktische Entscheidung. Wie groß ist der Aufwand, die Sprache zu erlernen? Wie nützlich ist sie? Wo will ich vielleicht eines Tages arbeiten oder studieren? Sprachen aus wirtschaftlich prosperierenden Ländern sind attraktiver als die von Staaten in einer Krise. Sprachen des Nachbarlandes werden eher gelernt als exotische Sprachen. Sprachen, die der eigenen ähnlich sind, werden auch oft unterrichtet.

D Die Geschichte spielt auch eine Rolle: Deutsch zum Beispiel ist vor allem populär in vielen Ländern Osteuropas. Zur Zeit des Kalten Krieges wurde in vielen Staaten neben Russisch auch Deutsch gelernt. Viele griechische Schüler lernen Deutsch. Nach dem Zweiten Weltkrieg kamen viele Griechen als Gastarbeiter nach Deutschland. Auch deswegen ist die Sprache in den Schulen des Landes stark verankert. Spanisch ist als Fremdsprache zwar in vielen Ländern populär, aber in Schweden und Norwegen ist Spanisch unter den Schülern besonders beliebt. Vielleicht spielt im hohen Norden die Sehnsucht nach dem Süden und der Sonne eine besondere Rolle.

Bernd Kramer, *Spiegel Online*, 27 Aug. 2015 (amended)

OL Ordinary Level Questions

1. Answer the following questions in English.
   a) What time of year does this article focus on? What question does this article address? A
   b) According to the text, what percentage of French students learn Spanish and German? B
   c) Which language dominates European classrooms? Name **one** reason, according to the text, for choosing a particular foreign language. C
   d) Why, according to the text, is Spanish particularly popular in Sweden and Norway? D
2. Are the following statements true or false?
   a) Im Sommer reist man quer durch Europa.
   b) Alle deutschen Schüler lernen Französisch.
   c) Viele Schüler lernen Englisch als Fremdsprache.
   d) Viele griechische Schüler lernen Spanisch.
3. What words make up the following compounds, and what do the compound words mean in English?
   a) Urlaubszeit = ______ + ______ = ______
   b) Deutschunterricht = ______ + ______ = ______
   c) Nachbarland = ______ + ______ = ______
   d) Muttersprache = ______ + ______ = ______
4. Select the correct prepositions for the following sentences.
   a) Welche Sprachen lernen junge Europäer **(an/um/für/in)** der Schule?
   b) Viele Schüler entscheiden sich **(mit/für/gegen/um)** Englisch.
   c) **(Auf/An/In/Für)** dem Lehrplan stehen verschiedene Sprachen.
   d) Spanisch ist **(an/in/auf/mit)** vielen Ländern beliebt.

HL Higher Level Questions

1. Beanworten Sie folgende Fragen auf Deutsch!
   a) Was macht man im Sommer? Welche Frage wird zu dieser Jahreszeit gestellt? A
   b) Warum protestierten die Deutschlehrer in Frankreich? Wie viele deutsche Schüler lernen Französisch? B
   c) Aus welchen Gründen lernen Schüler eine bestimmte Sprache, laut Text? (**3** Details) C
   d) Wie spielt die Geschichte eine Rolle bei der Wahl der Fremdsprachen? D
2. Answer the following questions in English.
   a) What question does the holiday season raise? A
   b) Why did German teachers in France protest recently? B
   c) According to the text, what are the practical reasons for choosing a foreign language? C
   d) How can a country's history affect the choice of foreign languages? Give **two** concrete examples. D
3. Was passt zusammen?

1. Wenn man durch Europa reist,	**A** aber nur 14% lernen Deutsch.
2. 37% der französischen Schüler lernen Spanisch,	**B** andere Fremdsprachen sind auch beliebt.
3. Englisch ist die Hauptfremdsprache aber	**C** denn viele Griechen kamen früher nach Deutschland.
4. Die Fremdsprachenwahl	**D** wird man sprachlich verwirrt.
5. Deutsch ist populär in Griechenland,	**E** ist eine praktische Entscheidung.

4. Note down for the underlined regular verbs the number, the tense and the infinitive.
   a) Die Urlaubssaison wirft ein Licht auf die Frage.
   b) Die Deutschlehrer in Frankreich protestierten.
   c) Sprachen, die der eigenen ähnlich sind, werden oft unterrichtet.
   d) Viele Griechen kamen nach Deutschland.

Grammatik: Wortstellung/Word Order

p. 101 (Übung macht den Meister)

Word Order 1

The verb is **the second unit** of language in a sentence. *The first unit* of language in a sentence can be the person(s) or thing(s) doing the verb (called the subject) or an expression of time, place or manner:

Meine Freunde und ich **gehen** jedes Wochenende in die Stadt. *Zu Hause* **gibt** es manchmal Krach.

In den Sommerferien **arbeite** ich an einer Tankstelle.

Put the bracketed verb into the present tense and the correct position. Translate the sentences.

1. Meistens ich gern Deutsch (lernen).	**4.** Leider ich nicht sprachlich begabt (sein).
2. In der Schule wir die Aussprache (üben).	**5.** Im Unterricht wir über die Kultur (lernen).
3. Ich die Grammatik kompliziert (finden).	**6.** Ich das Wesentliche (verstehen).

Word Order 2

When there are two verbs in a clause or sentence, the **first verb** is the second unit of language and the *second verb* goes to the end.

Jeden Tag **muss** ich drei bis vier Stunden lang *lernen*. Nächstes Jahr **werde** ich auf die Uni *gehen*.

Ich **bin** letztes Jahr in die Schweiz *gefahren*.

Complete these sentences using the perfect tense, a modal verb or the future tense.

1. Im Übergangsjahr wir nach Berlin (gehen).	**4.** Wir in die Schule (dürfen/gehen).
2. Du die Vokabeln fleißig (müssen/lernen).	**5.** Ich viele Bratwürste (essen).
3. Ich die Grammatik (beherrschen).	**6.** Ich in den Ferien nach Köln (fahren).

Word Order 3

In a subordinate clause, the verb always goes to the end. A subordinate clause begins with a word like **weil** (because), **wenn** (if), **obwohl** (although), **als** (when). If you begin the sentence with a main clause, the verb is the second unit in the main clause, but the verb in the subordinate clause goes to the end:

Ich lerne dieses Jahr fleißig (main clause), **weil ich gute Noten im Abi möchte** (subordinate clause).

Ich wohne gern hier (main clause), **weil es hier viele Freizeitmöglichkeiten gibt** (subordinate clause).

Put the verbs into the correct position in the sentence. Then translate the sentences into English.

1. Ich jeden Tag Vokabeln, weil ich gute Noten bekommen. (lerne/will)
2. Ich Deutsch, obwohl ich die Grammatik schwierig. (mag/finde)
3. Wir Hörverständnisse, damit wir unsere Sprachkenntnisse verbessern. (machen/können)
4. Ein Sprachkurs eine gute Idee, weil man intensiver. (ist/lernt)
5. Ich im Abitur gut abschneiden, damit ich auf die Uni gehen. (will/kann)

If you begin a sentence with a subordinate clause, the subordinate clause sends its verb to the end of its clause. This clause is followed by a comma and the verb and the rest of the main clause.

Obwohl wir viel lernen müssen (subordinate clause), **mag ich das Fach** (main clause).

Als ich in Bonn war (subordinate clause), **habe ich viel Deutsch gelernt** (main clause).

Put the verbs into the correct position in the sentence. Then translate the sentences into English.

1. Weil die Leute so schnell, ich die Hörverständnisse schwierig. (sprechen/finde)
2. Nachdem ich nach Deutschland gefahren, sich meine Deutschkenntnisse verbessert. (bin/haben)
3. Wenn ich regelmäßig, ich alles. (lerne/begreife)
4. Als ich klein, wir nach Österreich gefahren. (war/sind)
5. Obwohl die Zeitformen schwierig, die deutsche Aussprache ziemlich leicht. (sind/ist)

05.01 Hörverständnis Teil 1

Vorarbeit

Heimweh haben	*to be homesick*	**Geschlechter**	*genders*	**Magister**	*Masters*
Sozialwissenschaften	*social sciences*	**klingen**	*to sound*	**Stipendium**	*grant*
gesetzestreu	*law-abiding*	**schimpfen**	*to give out*	**höflich**	*polite*
Wie super!	*How wonderful!*	**ausdrücken**	*to express*	**heimisch**	*at home*

CL Ordinary + Higher Level Questions

1. a) What do we learn about Liya? Give **two (O)/four (H)** details.
   b) Why does she want to study in Germany? Give **one (O)/three (H)** details.
2. How long has she been learning German? What does she say about the German language?
3. What helps Liya cope with homesickness?
4. Mention **two (O)/four (H)** things Liya says about the German people.
5. What has helped Liya to integrate into German life? Give **one (O)/three (H)** details.

05.02 Hörverständnis Teil 2

Vorarbeit

zur Weißglut bringen	*to enrage*	**versprechen**	*to promise*	**wütend**	*angry*
rausgeschmissen	*thrown away*	**einstellen**	*to employ*	**schicken**	*to send*
Geldverschwendung	*waste of money*	**ausgebildet**	*trained*	**Chef**	*boss*

OL Ordinary Level Questions

1. The caller is ringing about his daughter. What is the daughter's involvement with Alpha?
2. Why is the caller so annoyed? Give **three** details.
3. What is the name and phone number of the caller?
4. The phone call is to:
   a) a secondary school ☐ **b)** a hotel ☐ **c)** a language school ☐ **d)** a university ☐

HL Higher Level Questions

1. Using ***key phrases***, write down **in German** the key information from the conversation.
   - The name of the **caller**
   - The reason for the call
   - Details regarding further contact
   - The caller's phone number

Gesprächsnotiz
Anruf von: ____________________ Gesprächsanlass: ____________________
Der Anrufer:
- wird nächste Woche kontaktiert ☐
- erhält einen Rückruf ☐
- wird eine SMS erhalten ☐
- ruft heute Nachmittag wieder an ☐

Telefonnummer des Anrufers: ____________________

2. Write down **three** examples of the language used to express the caller's **dissatisfaction**.

Text 2: Wie lernt man am besten Vokabeln?

Bitte beantworten Sie die folgenden Fragen:

1. Was sehen Sie auf dem Bild?
2. Was machen die Jugendlichen?
3. Ist es schwer, eine Fremdsprache zu lernen?
4. Wie lernen Sie am besten Vokabeln?

Vorarbeit

1. Finden Sie diese Ausdrücke im folgenden Text!
   - **A** They have one thing in common.
   - **B** The effort for this method is big.
   - **C** The sentence doesn't have to make sense.
   - **D** ... who get stressed from studying.
   - **F** ... and all over again.
   - **G** Memory becomes much stronger ...
2. Finden Sie das Deutsche für die Wörter unten!
   - **A** Danish/to line up/to swot/subsequent
   - **B** concepts/memory/picture cards/visually
   - **C** mnemonic/to save (information)
   - **D** headphones/strengthens/fans/tries out
   - **E** rewards/free/chosen/sounds/beneficial
   - **F** frequently/to recite/to absorb
   - **G** to remember/uses/in front/scored

A Acht Schüler der zwölften Klasse treten zum Praxistest an. Sie haben eines gemeinsam: Sie können kein Dänisch. Heute aber sollen sie hundert dänische Wörter lernen. Eine Stunde lang büffeln die Schüler nach verschiedenen Prinzipien. Ein anschließender Vokabeltest zeigt, was die beste Methode ist, um viele Vokabeln schnell zu lernen.

B **Lernen mit Bildern** Frank, 18, und Lukas, 18, lernen mit 100 *Bilderkärtchen*. Der Aufwand für diese Methode ist groß, denn für jedes Wort braucht man ein Bild. Der Vorteil: Das Gedächtnis funktioniert visuell besser. Es ist aber schwer, abstrakte Begriffe bildlich zu präsentieren.

C **Assoziationssätze** Ima, 17, und Patrick, 18, arbeiten mit Assoziationen. Das Wort wird mit seiner Übersetzung durch eine Eselsbrücke verbunden. Der Satz muss nicht Sinn machen, hilft aber die Information zu speichern.

D **Superlearning** Ute, 17, entspannt sich mit Dänisch, denn sie probiert das Superlearning aus. Anhänger dieser Lernmethode glauben, dass die Entspannung das Gedächtnis verstärkt. Ihre Dänisch-Vokabeln hört sie sich über Kopfhörer an. Diese Methode ist gut für Menschen, die vom Lernen gestresst sind.

E **Die Vokabeltrainer-App** Marilla, 17, lernt mit einem Vokabeltrainer auf dem Handy. Die kostenlose App hat ausgewählte Vokabeln. Der Lernprozess ist wie ein Spiel. Der Spaß am Handy ist förderlich. Kleine Belohnungen wie Sterne und Geräusche motivieren Lernende.

F **Die Vokabel-Liste** Wolfgang, 17, und Laura, 18, bekommen nur eine Liste mit den hundert Vokabeln. Sie lernen, wie sie es zu Hause immer tun: durchlesen, zuhalten, aufsagen – und wieder von vorn. Das Kurzzeitgedächtnis kann die Vokabeln auf diese Weise aufnehmen. Aber Vokabeln kommen nur in das Langzeitgedächtnis, wenn sie häufig gebraucht werden.

G **Auswertung:** „Das Gedächtnis wird viel stärker, wenn man Assoziationen verwendet. Die Technik wirkt auch langfristig. Die Vokabeltrainer-App ist die zweitbeste Strategie. Doch nach ein paar Tagen vergisst man viel." Die Assoziations-Methode liegt klar vorn, die Schüler wussten nach einer Stunde mehr als 90 Prozent der Vokabeln. Mit der Bilder-Methode konnten sich die Schüler etwa 80 Prozent der Wörter merken, etwas schlechter schnitten die Vokabel-Liste und das Superlearning ab. Die Assoziations-Methode ist also der Gewinner.

Carola Padtberg, *Spiegel Online*, 3 Nov. 2014 (amended)

OL Ordinary Level Questions

1. a) What class do these students belong to? What language are they learning? A
   b) What is being tested in this exercise? A
   c) How are the various methods evaluated? A
2. Fill in the following grid.

	Who is using this method?	How does it work?	How effective is it?
a) Lernen mit Bildern			
b) Assoziationssätze			
c) Superlearning			
d) Die Vokabeltrainer-App			
e) Die Vokabel-Liste			

3. Select the correct answer.
   a) Es ist schwer, für jedes Wort ein **(Tier/Bild/Konzept/Foto)** zu finden.
   b) Eine Eselsbrücke hilft die **(Konzentration/Hausaufgabe/Vokabel/Lehrerin)** zu speichern.
   c) Die Entspannung verstärkt das **(Gehirn/Lernen/Risiko/Gedächtnis)**.
   d) Mit einer Vokabel-Liste kommen nur häufig **(gebrauchte/gemeldete/geschriebene/gelesene)** Vokabeln ins Langzeitgedächtnis.
4. Separate these compound words into their components and translate them into English.
   a) Vokabeltest = _____ + _____ = _____
   b) durchlesen = _____ + _____ = _____
   c) Kurzzeitgedächtnis = _____ + _____ = _____
   d) zweitbeste = _____ + _____ = _____

HL Higher Level Questions

1. Beanworten Sie folgende Fragen auf Deutsch!
   a) Was haben die acht Schüler gemeinsam? Was machen sie heute, laut Text? A
   b) Was ist der Vorteil beim Lernen mit Bildern? Was ist der Nachteil dabei? B
   c) Wie funktionieren Assoziationssätze? C
   d) Für wen ist das Superlearning eine gute Methode? D
   e) Laut Text, was ist die beste Methode, Vokabeln zu lernen? G
2. Answer the following questions in English.
   a) What are the students doing, and for how long? A
   b) What is difficult about *Lernen mit Bildern*? B
   c) How does the word association method work, according to the text? C
   d) What motivates people using the vocabulary training app? E
   e) Which method was found to be most successful? Give details. G
3. Was passt zusammen?

1. Die Schüler lernen dänische Wörter,	**A** weil das Gedächtnis visuell funktioniert.
2. Lernen mit Bildern ist eine gute Methode,	**B** hilft er, Informationen zu speichern.
3. Obwohl der Merksatz Unsinn sein kann,	**C** wenn man Assoziationen benutzt.
4. Die Vokabeltrainer-App macht Spaß,	**D** bevor sie einen Vokabeltest machen.
5. Man kann das Gedächtnis verbessern,	**E** denn man bekommt kleine Belohnungen.

4. Complete the following sentences by placing the bracketed verbs into the appropriate clause.
   a) Obwohl die Schüler kein Dänisch, sie dänische Vokabeln. (sprechen/lernen)
   b) Weil man für jedes Wort ein Bild finden, der Aufwand sehr groß. (muss/ist)
   c) Lernende motiviert, wenn sie kleine Belohnungen. (sind/bekommen)

OL Äußerung zum Thema: Ordinary Level

You are interviewing Ima from Text 2. Complete Ima's dialogue based on the information given in Text 2.

Sie: Wie alt sind Sie?
Ima: ______________________________
Sie: Was sollen Sie heute machen?
Ima: ______________________________
Sie: Womit arbeiten Sie?
Ima: ______________________________
Sie: Muss der Merksatz Sinn machen?
Ima: ______________________________
Sie: Ist die Assoziationsmethode eine gute Methode, eine Fremdsprache zu lernen?
Ima: ______________________________
Sie: Vielen Dank für das Gespräch.

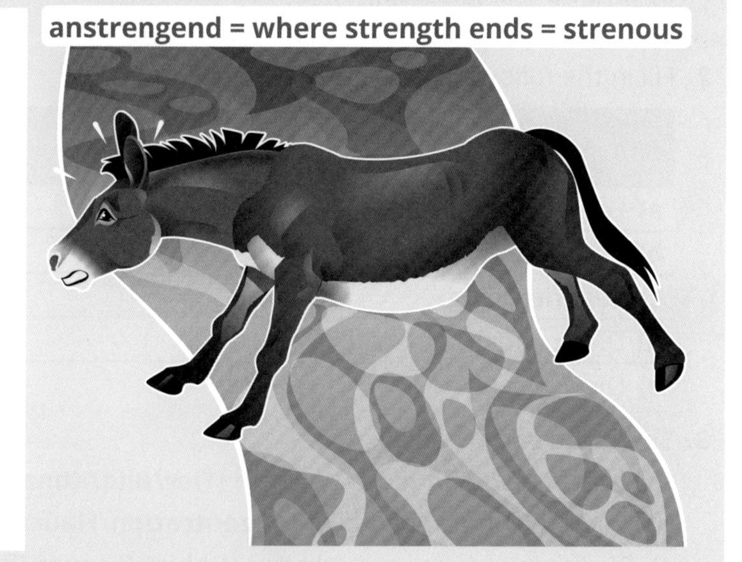

HL Äußerung zum Thema: Higher Level

Write 13 to 15 sentences, answering the questions below.

- Beschreiben Sie das Bild oben in **drei bis vier** Sätzen.
- Glauben Sie, dass Deutsch eine schwierige Sprache ist? Begründen Sie Ihre Meinung und geben Sie **zwei** Beispiele.
- Warum ist es wichtig, Ihrer Meinung nach, eine Fremdsprache zu lernen? Nennen Sie **zwei** Gründe, warum/warum nicht. Was sind, Ihrer Meinung nach, die besten Methoden, eine Fremdsprache zu lernen? Geben Sie **zwei** Beispiele.

Nützliche Sätze

Auf dem Bild sieht man einen Esel. Seine Beine überbrücken einen kleinen Bach. Das Bild ist lustig aber auch einprägsam.	*On the picture one sees a donkey. Its legs are straddling a small stream. The picture is funny but also memorable.*
Ich finde Deutsch eine anspruchsvolle Sprache.	*I find German a challenging language.*
Es gibt so viele Regeln und Ausnahmen, die ich mir nie merken kann.	*There are so many rules and exceptions which I can never remember.*
Die Geschlechter sind mir ein reines Rätsel.	*The genders are a pure puzzle to me.*
Es ist schwierig, die Umlaute richtig auszusprechen.	*It is difficult to pronounce the umlauts correctly.*
Alle Sprachen sind schwer zu lernen, aber es lohnt sich bestimmt, eine Sprache zu beherrschen.	*All languages are difficult to learn, but it is certainly worthwhile mastering a language.*
Man kann sich leichter mit Einheimischen unterhalten, wenn man die Sprache spricht.	*One can talk more easily with local people if one speaks the language.*
Fremdsprachen sind oft förderlich für die Karriere.	*Foreign languages are often beneficial for one's career.*
Sprachenlernen hält dein Gehirn auf Trab.	*Learning languages keeps your mind alert.*
Mit jeder Sprache, die man lernt, erweitert man den Horizont und lernt eine neue Kultur kennen.	*With every language that you learn, you broaden your horizons and get to know a new culture.*

Grammatik: Wortstellung/Word Order

p. 101 (Übung macht den Meister)

Word Order 4

In German, time expressions come first in a sentence. The manner in which an action is done comes next and after the verb. 'Manner' means how or with whom an action is done (by car; with my friends; by bus, etc.) The place where an action occurs comes after 'manner'.

Thus, the rule is: (first) **Time** (second) **Manner** (third) **Place**.

Ich gehe jeden Tag (time) **zu Fuß** (manner) **zur Schule** (place).

If you have more than one expression of time, you use the more general one first:

Ich komme **1** jeden Tag **2** früh **3** um 8.45 in der Schule an.

Put the bracketed Time Manner Place expressions in the correct position. Then translate.

1. Wir fahren (ins Ausland/im Sommer/oft).	**5.** Ich gehe (gern/immer) in die Schule.
2. Ich stehe (leider/um 7 Uhr/jeden Tag) auf.	**6.** Ich war (in Deutschland/im Übergangsjahr).
3. Ich gehe (in die Stadt/am Wochenende/immer).	**7.** Die Kinder spielen (im Park/im Sommer).
4. Ich lerne (für eine Stunde/jeden Tag) Vokabeln.	**8.** Ich sehe (zwei Stunden/jeden Abend) fern.

Konjunktionen/Conjunctions

Co-ordinating Conjunctions

The verb remains the second idea in both clauses, just as in English.

und and **aber** but **sondern** but rather **denn** because **oder** or

Dieses Jahr lerne ich fleißig, **denn** ich möchte gute Noten bekommen.

Rewrite the sentence pairs into one sentence using co-ordinating conjunctions. Then translate.

1. Ich mag Deutsch. Es ist eine schöne Sprache.	**5.** Ich lerne allein. Ich lerne mit meinen Freunden.
2. Ich spreche oft Deutsch. Ich mache viele Fehler.	**6.** Ich mag Sprachen. Ich bin sprachlich begabt.
3. Ich lerne Vokabeln. Ich übe die Grammatik.	**7.** Ich mag Deutsch. Die Grammatik ist kompliziert.
4. Ich mache keine Hausaufgaben. Ich sehe fern.	**8.** Wir schreiben Briefe. Wir sprechen auf Deutsch.

Subordinating Conjunctions

A subordinating conjunction joins a subordinate clause to a main clause: My mother will love me **if I get good grades**. In German, the subordinating conjunction always sends the verb to the end of its own clause:

Ich will Lehrerin werden, **weil** ich gern mit anderen arbeiten möchte.

Wenn man sich für Fremdsprachen interessiert, muss man einfach ins Ausland fahren.

als when	**da** since	**nachdem** after	**ohne dass** without	**weil** because
als ob as if	**damit** in order that	**ob** whether	**sobald** as soon as	**seit(dem)** since
bevor before	**dass** that	**obgleich** although	**sodass** so that	**wenn** if
bis until	**falls** in case that	**obwohl** although	**während** while	**wie** how

Rewrite the sentence pairs into one sentence using subordinating conjunctions. Then translate.

1. Mir gefällt die Schule. Meine Freunde sind hier.	**5.** Ich habe Hausaufgaben gemacht. Ich ruhe mich aus.
2. Ich mag Deutsch. Ich finde es schwierig.	**6.** Ich pauke ständig. Ich bekomme gute Noten.
3. Der Kurs ist lang. Der Lehrer gibt viel auf.	**7.** Ich schlafe ein. Ich lerne Vokabeln.
4. Ich lerne fleißig. Ich bekomme schlechte Noten.	**8.** Ich bekomme gute Noten. Ich freue mich.

Text 3: Der Alltag wie ihn mancher kennt

Bitte beantworten Sie die folgenden Fragen:

1. Was sehen Sie auf dem Foto?
2. Was macht das Mädchen?
3. Wie fühlt sie sich?
4. Wie finden Sie das Lernen?

Vorarbeit

1. Finden Sie diese Ausdrücke im Text!
   - **A** She was lost in thought.
   - **B** ... it was double Dutch to her.
   - **C** As always, she was right.
   - **D** There would be trouble!
   - **E** ... the homework wasn't checked today.
   - **F** Was she simply jinxed?
2. Finden Sie das Deutsche für die Wörter unten!
   - **A** pushed/dreams/continue/confused
   - **B** make an effort/get grounded/solve
   - **C** explain/different/understood
   - **D** feverishly/missed/nearly/alarm clock
   - **E** staring/survived/desperately/spent
   - **F** completed/prayed/decided/exhausted

A Sie war gerade mit ihren Gedanken woanders. Sie fragte sich, „Wie wird es in meiner Lieblingsserie wohl weitergehen?" Plötzlich wurde sie von ihrer Klassenkameradin aus den Träumen geschubst. Verwirrt schaute sie die Nachbarin an, die auf eine Textstelle im Mathebuch zeigte. Sie begann vorzulesen.

B Als einige Jungen zu lachen begannen, wurde ihr klar, dass sie die Aufgabe lösen sollte. Die Lehrerin machte sich eine Notiz in ihrem Heft. „Wieder eine schlechte Note", dachte sie. Am Ende der Stunde sagte ihr die Lehrerin, „Wenn du dich nicht mehr anstrengst, muss ich deine Eltern anrufen." So etwas erlebte sie ja fast jeden Tag. Die Französischstunde war auch nicht besser, denn sie verstand wieder nur Bahnhof. Als sie zu Hause ankam, hielt sie ihre Arbeit mit einer Vier in der Hand. Sie dachte, sie würde Hausarrest und Fernsehverbot bekommen.

C Wie immer hatte sie recht. Wie sollte es denn anders sein? Zu Hause setzte sie sich an den Schreibtisch um Vokabeln zu lernen. Vielleicht verstand sie dann, was der Lehrer von ihr wollte. Sie fragte sich, „Warum kann es mein Lehrer nicht genauso erklären, wie es hier so gut erklärt steht?" Sie blickte aus dem Fenster und sah die Nachbarskinder beim Spielen.

D Am nächsten Morgen klingelte der Wecker. Sie aß eine Scheibe Toast, steckte sich einen Apfel in die Tasche und rannte zum Bus, den sie fast verpasst hätte. Vielleicht lag es daran, dass der Busfahrer sie erkannte und geduldig auf sie wartete. Sie lächelte ihm zu und setzte sich auf einen freien Sitzplatz. Da hatte sie das Gefühl etwas vergessen zu haben. Tatsächlich fehlten ihr die Mathe-Hausaufgaben. Das gäbe Ärger! Sie holte ihr Heft und einen Kugelschreiber heraus und suchte fieberhaft nach den Lösungen. Beinahe hätte sie die Haltestelle verpasst. Sie sprang aus dem Bus.

E Zum Glück kam sie nicht zu spät. Die Mathe-Stunde überstand sie, denn die Hausaufgaben wurden heute nicht kontrolliert. Schlimmer war der Englisch-Vokabeltest. Sie saß nun verzweifelt vor einem Stück Papier. Den Rest des Schultages verbrachte sie damit ganz konzentriert in ihre Bücher zu starren.

F Als sie abends erschöpft im Bett lag, dachte sie noch lange über den Tag nach. War sie einfach ein Pechvogel? Sie beschloss der Sonne morgen richtig „Hallo" zu sagen, sich mehr Zeit zu lassen um zu frühstücken. Ihre Zeitschriften würde sie nach der Schule kaufen, und abends kontrollieren ob alle Hausaufgaben erledigt sind. Sie betete für einen besseren Tag.

Sarah Sangmeister, 2002 (amended)

Ordinary Level Questions

1. a) What was the girl thinking about during the Maths class? A
   b) What does the teacher say to her, and what mark did she get in the French class? B
   c) What did the girl want to learn, and what distracted her from learning? C
   d) i) Why did she not miss the bus? ii) What had she forgotten? D
   e) i) Why did the girl survive the Maths class? ii) How did she feel about the English class? E
   f) How did she decide to change things that evening? Give details. F
2. Choose a suitable heading for each paragraph and explain your choice in English.

Sie steht zu spät auf

Sie versteht den Englischtest nicht

Wird die Lehrerin die Eltern anrufen?

Das Mädchen kriegt Hausarrest

Morgen wird sie positiv sein

Soll sie im Mathebuch vorlesen?

3. True or false?
   a) Das Mädchen begann, die Aufgabe zu lösen.
   b) Das Mädchen bekam eine schlechte Note.
   c) Sie setzte sich vor den Fernseher.
   d) Sie verstand den Englischtest nicht.
4. Select the correct prepositions for the following sentences.
   a) Ihre Nachbarin zeigte **(an/auf/in/mit)** eine Textstelle im Mathebuch.
   b) Die Lehrerin schrieb eine Notiz **(an/auf/in/um)** ihrem Heft.
   c) Das Mädchen blickte **(aus/am/im/um)** dem Fenster.
   d) Der Wecker klingelte **(um/im/am/vom)** nächsten Tag.

HL Higher Level Questions

1. Beantworten Sie folgende Fragen auf Deutsch.
   a) Worüber dachte das Mädchen im ersten Absatz? A
   b) Woher weiß man, dass das Mädchen keine gute Schülerin war? B
   c) Was sah das Mädchen, als sie aus dem Fenster blickte? C
   d) Was versuchte das Mädchen im Bus zu machen? D
   e) Wie fand das Mädchen den Englisch-Vokabeltest? E
   f) Was würde das Mädchen morgens anders machen, und warum? F
2. Answer the following questions in English.
   a) What did the girl do when her neighbour roused her from her daydream? A
   b) What kind of a day had the girl had? Give **three** examples. B
   c) What did she ask herself when she sat down to learn vocabulary? C
   d) Why, according to the text, did the bus driver wait for her? D
   e) Why did the Maths class go better than expected? E
   f) What conclusion did the girl come to when considering the course of her day? F
   g) The girl experiences a lot of confusion and a lack of understanding. Find **three** examples in the text which reveal this.
3. Was passt zusammen?

1. Sie dachte,	**A** was der Lehrer von ihr will.
2. Die Lehrerin wird ihre Eltern anrufen,	**B** denn sie machte die Mathe-Hausaufgaben.
3. Sie versteht nicht,	**C** dass sie vorlesen sollte.
4. Sie hätte fast die Haltestelle verpasst,	**D** betet sie für einen besseren Tag.
5. Bevor sie einschläft,	**E** wenn sie sich nicht mehr anstrengt.

Grammatik: Konjunktionen/Conjunctions

p. 101 (Übung macht den Meister)

Adverbial Conjunctions

Adverbial conjunctions are immediately followed by the verb.

also therefore	**da*** then, so	**dennoch** yet	**so** and so
auch also	**daher** therefore	**deshalb** therefore	**sonst** otherwise
auch nicht not either	**dann** then	**(je)doch** however	**trotzdem** in spite of that
außerdem besides	**darum** therefore	**kaum** hardly	**zwar** while it is true

Es gibt viele Freizeitsaktivitäten, **deshalb** wohne ich gern hier.

* **da** has three meanings: 'because' (subordinating conjunction); 'then, so' (adverbial conjunction); 'there' (adverb).

Rewrite the sentence pairs into one sentence using subordinating conjunctions. Then translate into English.

1. Ich tue mein Bestes. Ich finde Deutsch schwierig.	**5.** Der Lehrer ist hilfsbereit. Der Kurs ist lang.
2. Ich lerne jeden Tag. Ich behalte nichts im Kopf.	**6.** Ich will Jura studieren. Ich muss viel lernen.
3. Ich stehe um 8 Uhr auf. Ich ziehe mich an.	**7.** Ich lerne viel. Ich hoffe, mein Ziel zu erreichen.
4. Mathe ist wichtig. Es ist ein Pflichtfach.	**8.** Mein Lehrer ist gut. Er ist auch streng.

Correlative Conjunctions

These conjunctions come in pairs, one for each clause: '**Either** you tidy your room, **or** you're grounded!'

entweder ... oder either ... or	**nicht nur ... sondern auch** not only ..., but also
je ... desto the ..., the	**sowohl ... als auch** both ... and
mal ... mal sometimes ..., sometimes	**weder ... noch** neither ... nor

Je mehr Deutsch ich lerne, **desto** besser ist es für mich.

Rewrite the sentence pairs into one sentence using correlative conjunctions. Then translate into English.

1. Ich lerne viel. Ich bekomme schlechte Noten.	**5.** Ich mag Irisch nicht. Ich mag Deutsch nicht.
2. Ich lerne Deutsch. Ich bekomme gute Noten.	**6.** Ich lerne viel. Ich werde müde.
3. Ich esse in der Kantine. Ich gehe ins Dorf.	**7.** Ich mag Deutsch. Deutsch nervt mich.
4. Ich lerne in der Schule. Ich lerne zu Hause.	**8.** Ich schneide gut ab. Ich wiederhole das Abitur.

Um ... zu

um ... zu means '(in order) to'. In German, the expression 'in order' cannot be left out. The verb 'to buy' in the example is in the infinitive because of **zu** and goes to the end of the sentence:

Ich gehe in die Stadt um eine Jeans zu kaufen. I am going into town in order to buy a new pair of jeans.

Ich gehe ins Sportgeschäft, um das neue Trikot anzuprobieren. I go into the sports shop in order to try on the new jersey.

Rewrite the sentence pairs into one sentence using **um ... zu**. Then translate them into English.

1. Ich sehe fern. Ich ruhe mich aus.	**5.** Ich gehe ins Café. Ich trinke einen Kaffee.
2. Ich gehe ins Dorf. Ich treffe mich mit Hannah.	**6.** Ich lerne jeden Abend. Ich mache Fortschritte.
3. Ich trainiere jeden Tag. Ich will fit sein.	**7.** Frank lernt fleißig. Er will eine Eins bekommen.
4. Ich gehe ins Kino. Ich will einen Film sehen.	**8.** Wir hören CDs an. Wir bessern unser Deutsch auf.

05.03 Hörverständnis Teil 3

Vorarbeit

die Qual der Wahl	*the agony of choice*	**Berufsberater**	*guidance counsellor*	**Notendurchschnitt**	*grade average*
ersticken	*to suffocate*	**Beratung**	*advice*	**BAföG**	*grant*
zugeben	*to admit*	**beschweren**	*to complain*	**unterstützen**	*to support*
recherchieren	*to research*	**einstellen**	*to employ*	**schenken**	*to give*

CL Ordinary + Higher Level Questions

1. **a)** The conversation is between:
   - **i)** a brother and a sister ☐
   - **ii)** a teacher and student ☐
   - **iii)** two Leaving Certificate students ☐
   - **iv)** two classmates ☐

   b) Find **one (O)/two (H)** details in the conversation that support your choice.
2. **a)** Which word best describes the male speaker's attitude during the conversation?
   i) depressed ☐ **ii)** angry ☐ **iii)** apologetic ☐ **iv)** frightened ☐

   b) Write down **one (O)/two (H)** details from the conversation to support your choice.
3. What information is the male speaker looking for? Write down **one (O)/three (H)** details.
4. What solution does the female speaker propose? Give **one (O)/two (H)** details.

05.04 Hörverständnis Teil 4

Vorarbeit

Ausbildung	*education*	**sperren**	*to close*	**Forscher**	*researcher*
tätig	*active*	**Überholen**	*overtaking*	**eindeutig**	*clearly*
weiblich	*female*	**zusammenstoßen**	*to collide*	**Schweigen**	*silence*
Mangelwaren	*to be scarce*	**als üblich**	*than usual*	**mäßig**	*moderate*

CL Ordinary + Higher Level Questions

1. **a)** How many women and men are employed as teachers?
   b) What percentage of Leaving Certificate students are girls?
2. **a)** For how long was the road closed? **b)** How many people were injured?
3. **a)** How many seconds are needed for love at first sight to occur, according to the text?
   b) How do girls react if they like a boy, according to the text?
4. **a)** What is the weather forecast for today? Give **two (O)/three (H)** details.
   b) What is the forecast for tomorrow? Give **two (O)/three (H)** details.

Prüfungstipp

German fractions often come up in the aural section.

0,9	**null Komma neun**	*point nine*	⅓	**ein Drittel**	*a third*
¼	**ein Viertel**	*a fourth*	¾	**drei Viertel**	*three quarters*
⅖	**zwei Fünftel**	*two fifths*	1 ½	**eineinhalb/anderthalb**	*one and a half*

OL Schriftliche Produktion: Ordinary Level

Write a letter to your pen pal, Anton(ia). Complete the first paragraph by correctly inserting the sentence halves below. Then follow the instructions.

nicht so viel kontinuierliche Beurteilung zu haben wie wir **so viel Spaß machen**
weil ich mit meinen Klassenarbeiten fertig bin **einen Sprachkurs in Berlin**

Hallo aus Dundalk!

Wie geht es dir? Mir geht es echt gut, ______________ . Du hast Glück, ______________ ! Aber jetzt will ich dir alles erzählen. Ich habe vor, mit zwei Freunden ______________ zu machen. Das wird ______________ !

Now continue the letter.

- Say when and where the course will take place.
- Give **two** details about the two friends who are going with you.
- Describe what you will be doing on the course.
- Describe where you will be staying.
- Invite your German friend to visit you in Berlin.
- Write a suitable closing sentence.

HL Schriftliche Produktion: Higher Level

Reply in German to your pen pal's letter. Give detailed answers to the questions.

Liebe(r) ______________ ,

endlich habe ich Zeit dir zu schreiben! Wie geht es dir nach deinen Sommerprüfungen? Mir geht es echt gut, denn meine mündlichen Prüfungen sind endlich vorbei!

Du hattest auch eine mündliche Prüfung in Deutsch und Irisch, oder? Wie bereitest du dich darauf vor? Und klappt das gut?

Alle meine Freunde haben einen Sprachkurs gemacht, um ihre Sprachkenntnisse zu verbessern. Ich nicht, denn es kostet zu viel Geld. Ich lerne alles, was wir im Unterricht machen und das reicht mir. Und du, was ist für dich der beste Weg eine Fremdsprache zu lernen?

Ich habe einen Schüleraustausch gemacht und habe das super gefunden. Würdest du gerne so was machen, oder nicht? Und warum?

Wie ist es eigentlich in Irland, was Fremdsprachen überhaupt angeht? Welche Sprachen werden angeboten und wie viele kann man für das Abitur lernen? Wie ist deine Meinung dazu?

Jetzt mache ich Schluss. Schreib bald zurück!

Dein(e) Anton(ia)

Nützliche Sätze

Übersetzen Sie die folgenden Sätze.

1. Ich übe regelmäßig die mündliche Sprache, entweder allein oder zu zweit.
2. Man soll Kontakt zu einem Muttersprachler aufnehmen.
3. In der Schule lernen wir die Grundsteine, um die Sprache verstehen zu können.
4. Ich würde sehr gern einen Austausch machen, denn da erlebt man auch die Kultur.
5. Ich finde es gut, dass jetzt eine Vielfalt an Fremdsprachen angeboten wird.

Übung Macht den Meister!

A Word Order 1

Put the bracketed verb in the correct position and conjugation. Then translate the sentences.

1. Jeden Tag ich fleißig in der Schule (lernen).	**5.** Mein Bruder nicht so oft für die Schule (pauken).
2. Im Unterricht wir die Grammatik (üben).	**6.** Wir uns regelmäßig deutsche CDs (anhören).
3. Am Wochenende wir Briefe (schreiben).	**7.** In der Schule die Regeln ganz streng (sein).
4. Ich so oft wie möglich auf Deutsch (sprechen).	**8.** Wie du die deutsche Aussprache (finden)?

B Word Order 2

Complete these sentences using the perfect tense, a modal verb or the future tense. Then translate the sentences.

1. Ich gute Noten im Abitur (müssen/bekommen).	**5.** Wir letzten Sommer nach Berlin (sein/fahren).
2. Ich dieses Jahr fleißig (haben/lernen).	**6.** Ich die Grammatik nicht (können/begreifen).
3. Ich Deutsch an der Uni (werden/studieren).	**7.** Ich jeden Tag neue Vokabeln (werden/lernen).
4. Mein Bruder das Abitur (werden/wiederholen).	**8.** Ich viele Redewendungen (haben/hören).

C Word Order 3

Complete the following sentences. Then translate them.

1. Ich brauche gute Noten im Abitur, da ...	**5.** Ich lerne besser, wenn ...
2. Die Schüler reisen nach Deutschland, weil ...	**6.** Wenn ich Freizeit habe, ...
3. Es regnete stark, als ...	**7.** Da die Zeitformen kompliziert sind, ...
4. Wir lernen eigentlich gern Deutsch, weil ...	**8.** Als ich jünger war, ...

D Um ... zu

Join the following sentence halves and translate the sentences.

1. Ich schaltete das Licht aus,	**A** um die Kultur zu erleben.
2. Das Kind packt schon seine Schulsachen ein,	**B** um sie ins Kino einzuladen.
3. Meine Eltern ruhen sich an diesem Tag aus,	**C** um Strom zu sparen.
4. Wir räumen den Müll weg,	**D** um den Garten aufzuräumen.
5. Er bereitet sich auf die Prüfung vor,	**E** um damit bald fertig zu sein.
6. Man macht schon mit der Arbeit weiter,	**F** um Energie zu tanken.
7. Er ruft sie an,	**G** um eine gute Note zu bekommen.
8. Wir haben einen Austausch gemacht,	**H** um für die Schule organisiert zu sein.

E Word Order 4

Translate the following sentences into German.

1. Firstly, we write down useful vocabulary.	**6.** Sometimes we listen to CDs.
2. Then we write useful sentences.	**7.** Occasionally we go to the computer room.
3. After that we interview each other in pairs.	**8.** Mostly we speak in German.
4. Usually we practise for fifteen minutes.	**9.** Every day I learn vocabulary.
5. Often we practise via Skype.	**10.** At the weekend I write a letter.

Für die Prüfung

1. Was passt zusammen?

1. Hier werden zwei Fremdsprachen angeboten,	**A** lerne ich am vorigen Abend für mehrere Stunden.
2. Wenn ich eine Prüfung schreibe,	**B** also habe ich einen Schüleraustausch gemacht.
3. Ich bin Feuer und Flamme für Deutsch,	**C** doch man muss nur eine Sprache wählen.
4. Wenn man Interesse an Sprachen hat,	**D** da wir jetzt in der EU leben.
5. Jeder sollte Fremdsprachen lernen,	**E** sollte man einen Schüleraustausch machen.

2. Was passt zusammen?

1. Ich tue mein Bestes im Fach Deutsch,	**A** lerne ich jeden Tag.
2. Um fit in Deutsch zu sein,	**B** um die Sprache zu beherrschen.
3. Ich spreche viel Deutsch,	**C** denn ich finde die Umlaute schwierig.
4. Wenn ich nervös bin,	**D** um eine gute Note zu bekommen.
5. Ich konzentriere mich auf die Aussprache,	**E** interviewe ich mich selbst.

3. Select the correct prepositions for the following sentences.

a) Ich spreche gern Deutsch **(ins/in die/in den/im)** Unterricht.

b) Meine Lehrerin hat einen Schüleraustausch **(an/vor/für/auf)** uns organisiert.

c) Ich fahre gern **(mit/in/ins/an)** Ausland.

d) Im Übergangsjahr sind wir **(mit/bei/in/durch)** dem Flugzeug nach Berlin geflogen.

e) Wir gingen jeden Tag **(in die/im/zum/neben dem)** Schule.

f) Auch gingen wir **(im/zum/mit dem/auf dem)** Museum.

4. What words make up the following compound words, and what do they mean in English?

a) Muttersprache = _____ + _____ = ________

b) aussprechen = _____ + _____ = ________

c) Fremdsprache = _____ + _____ = ________

d) weiterstudieren = _____ + _____ = ________

e) Schüleraustausch = _____ + _____ = ________

f) wegreisen = _____ + _____ = ________

5. Match the sentence halves and translate the sentences into English.

1. Wenn ich im Unterricht bin,	**A** muss ich alle Fragen beantworten.
2. Obwohl ich viel Grammatik lerne,	**B** lerne ich viele Redewendungen.
3. Nachdem ich alle Rollenspiele geübt habe,	**C** passe ich immer gut auf.
4. Weil ich deutsche Filme gern sehe,	**D** mache ich immer noch Fehler.
5. Wenn ich den Brief schreibe,	**E** übe ich sie mit einem Klassenkameraden.

6. Replace the underlined conjunction with the bracketed word, adjust the word order and translate.

a) Der Junge joggt gern aber er schwimmt viel lieber. (jedoch)
b) Das Kind isst gern Pommes Frites, weil sie gut schmecken. (denn)
c) Der Junge wirft den Ball und er rennt danach. (dann)
d) Ich finde die Schule langweilig, obwohl ich viele Freunde hier habe. (jedoch)
e) Ich mache zwei Stunden Hausaufgaben und ich lerne für eine Stunde. (dann)

Selbstbewertung: Ordinary Level

Vocabulary

1. If I can translate theses sentences into English, I can talk about learning languages. (1 mark each)

a) Ich spreche Deutsch und Irisch.	**f)** Es ist sehr interessant.
b) Ich übe jeden Tag.	**g)** Wir machen Hörverständnisse.
c) Wir haben einen Austausch gemacht.	**h)** Ich finde die Grammatik schwierig.
d) Ich übe Rollenspiele am Wochenende.	**i)** Ich finde die Aussprache leicht.
e) Ich spreche gern Deutsch.	**j)** Französisch und Deutsch sind sehr populär.

Your score: ___ / 10

2. If I can translate these nouns into German, I understand the main nouns to describe language learning. (1 mark each)

a) school exchange	**d)** language course	**g)** pronunciation	**i)** grammar
b) oral exam	**e)** foreign languages	**h)** vocabulary	**j)** accent
c) German class	**f)** native language		

Your score: ___ / 10

Grammar

3. If I can conjugate these verbs in the **ich** form in the present and perfect tenses, I can talk about my experiences of learning a language. (1 mark for each tense)

a) schreiben (I write; I have written)	**d)** lesen (I read; I have read)
b) sprechen (I speak; I have spoken)	**e)** lernen (I learn; I have learned)
c) hören (I listen; I have listened)	

Your score: ___ / 10

4. If I can choose the correct conjunction, I can use complex sentences. (2 marks each)

a) Ich finde Deutsch schwierig, **(denn/weil)** die Grammatik ist kompliziert.

b) Ich lerne gern Deutsch, **(denn/weil)** die Sprache interessant ist.

c) Wir stehen unter viel Druck, **(denn/weil)** es gibt viel zu lernen.

d) Ich übe die mündliche Sprache, **(denn/weil)** die mündliche Prüfung wichtig ist.

e) Die Hörverständnisse sind schwierig, **(denn/weil)** die Leute sehr schnell sprechen.

Your score: ___ / 10

5. If I can choose the correct preposition, I understand the prepositions needed to describe learning languages. (1 mark each)

a) Ich interessiere mich **(in/auf/für/an)** Deutsch.	**f)** Ich möchte **(im/am/ans/ins)** Ausland fahren.
b) Ich mache immer **(in/im/am/für)** Unterricht mit.	**g)** Sprachen sind wichtig **(für/an/in/vor)** die Zukunft.
c) Ich lerne Deutsch **(für/an/seit/um)** sechs Jahren.	**h)** Ich sehe gern Filme **(an/in/von/auf)** Netflix.
d) Wir lernen viel **(über/von/auf/mit)** die Kultur.	**i)** Wir sind **(nach/zu/in/auf)** Deutschland gefahren.
e) Wir sehen einen Film **(in/auf/bei/an)** Deutsch.	**j)** Ich lerne jeden Tag **(um/für/mit/an)** zwei Stunden.

Your score: ___ / 10

What have I learned?	
What must I improve?	
What do I want to revise?	

Your total score: ___ / 50

Selbstbewertung: Higher Level

HL

1. If I can translate these sentences into German, I understand the use of verbs with co-ordinating conjunctions. (2 marks each)

   a) He learned the vocabulary and she listened to CDs.

   b) I like German because it is interesting.

   c) I practised a lot but I found the exam hard.

   d) She likes to play the piano or she likes to go for walks.

   e) He didn't do his homework but rather he watched TV.

Your score: ___ / 10

2. If I can translate these sentences into German, I understand the use of verbs with subordinating conjunctions. (2 marks each)

   a) He went on the exchange because he wanted to improve his German.

   b) I like the grammar although it is difficult.

   c) She will go to Germany when she has the money.

   d) Since she was a child, she has loved speaking Irish.

   e) We went on the school exchange when we were in Transition Year.

Your score: ___ / 10

3. If I can translate these sentences into German, I understand the use of verbs after adverbial conjunctions. (2 marks each)

   a) He learned the vocabulary, then he wrote it out.

   b) The Leaving Certificate is important, therefore I study every day.

   c) There is a lot of pressure but in spite of that I like going to school.

   d) My German teacher is strict, however she is also fair.

   e) I'm looking forward to college, yet I will miss school.

Your score: ___ / 10

4. If I can correctly combine and translate these sentences, I understand the **um … zu** construction. (2 marks each)

   a) Wir lesen Texte. Wir lernen über die Kultur.

   b) Wir üben Grammatik. Wir wollen korrekt sprechen.

   c) Ich gehe in die Schule. Ich will meine Freunde sehen.

   d) Ich mache einen Austausch. Ich spreche Deutsch.

   e) Ich esse viel Gemüse. Ich will gesund sein.

Your score: ___ / 10

5. If I can correctly fill in the gaps below, I understand word functions. (1 mark each)

manchmal in auf die jeden Lesen ich Film sehe Grammatik

Ich bin gut **1** ______ Deutsch. Ich übe die Sprache **2** ______ Tag und schreibe immer neue Vokabeln **3** ______ . Ich finde das **4** ______ interessant, aber ich finde die **5** ______ schwierig. **6** ______ sind die CDs ein bisschen schwierig. Ich finde **7** ______ Kultur super und **8** ______ mag das Essen. Manchmal **9** ______ ich einen guten **10** ______ mit deutschen Untertiteln.

Your score:

What have I learned?	
What must I improve?	
What do I want to revise?	

Your total score: ___ / 50

06

Im Ausland

Learning Outcomes

- **Oral:** discussing school exchanges, holidays and studying abroad
- **Reading:** reading and answering questions on three texts about time abroad
- **Writing:** writing an opinion (**Äußerung**), describing a picture and writing a letter about being abroad
- **Aural:** listening to and answering questions on four extracts about life abroad

Grammar

- Gender of nouns, singular and plural
- Case system: the nominative, accusative, dative and genitive
- Indefinite articles, negative articles and possessive adjectives

Vocabulary

- Discussing time abroad
- Describing the importance of gaining international experience

German Culture

- Tourism in Germany
- Food and drink
- Studying and voluntary work

Exam Tips

- Use German idioms in your oral and written work.
- Revise a chosen grammar point by searching for examples of it in the reading comprehensions. Add these examples to your grammar revision copybook.
- Improve your expression by adapting sentences from the oral and reading sections.

Mündliche Arbeit: Im Ausland

Stellen Sie sich gegenseitig alle Fragen unten. Schreiben Sie sie auf.

Würden Sie gern ins Ausland fahren?

Wohin in Deutschland würden Sie gern einmal reisen? Warum?

Kennen Sie ein deutsches Fest?

Was ist/war im alltäglichen Leben dort anders?

Waren Sie schon mal in Deutschland/Österreich/in der Schweiz? Wo?

Wie feiert man Weihnachten/Silvester/Karneval/Ostern in Deutschland?

Wie ist das Essen?

1. Würden Sie gern ins Ausland fahren? *Would you like to go abroad?*	
Ich würde gern nach Berlin fahren. Ich interessiere mich sehr für deutsche Kultur.	*I would like to go to Berlin. I'm very interested in German culture.*
Ich möchte gern das Brandenburger Tor und Checkpoint Charlie besuchen.	*I would like to visit the Brandenburg Gate and Checkpoint Charlie.*
Ich war noch nie in Deutschland, aber ich möchte später ein paar Jahre in Deutschland verbringen, um Arbeitserfahrung zu sammeln.	*I've never been to Germany, but I would like to spend a few years in Germany later in order to get work experience.*
Sicher freue ich mich riesig auf einen Aufenthalt im Ausland!	*Of course I'm really looking forward to a stay abroad!*
Wenn ich ganz viel Geld hätte, würde ich ohne Zweifel nach Griechenland reisen.	*If I had a lot of money, without a doubt I would travel to Greece.*
Wenn ich im Lotto gewinnen würde, würde ich zu den Galapagos Inseln reisen, weil mich dort die Tiere interessieren.	*If I won the lotto, I would go to the Galapagos Islands because I find the animals there interesting.*
Ich möchte sehr gern im Ausland studieren.	*I would really like to study abroad.*

2. Waren Sie schon mal im Ausland? *Have you ever been abroad?*	
Ich bin eine Reisetante/ein Reiseonkel.	*I'm a globetrotter.*
Wir waren oft in Spanien. Ich sehne mich immer nach der Sonne und dem Meer.	*We were often in Spain. I always long for the sun and the sea.*
Wir fahren so oft wie möglich ins Ausland.	*We go abroad as often as possible.*
Leider war ich noch nie im Ausland aber ich hoffe, in Zukunft ins Ausland zu fahren.	*Unfortunately, I have never been abroad, but I hope to go abroad in future.*
Im Übergangsjahr sind wir auf einer Klassenfahrt nach München gefahren. Ich habe bei einer sehr netten Gastfamilie gewohnt. Das war ein tolles Erlebnis und ich habe viel über Land und Leute gelernt. Ich bin immer noch in Kontakt mit **meinem** Austauschpartner/**meiner** Austauschpartnerin.	*In Transition Year we went on a school trip to Munich. I stayed with a very nice host family. That was a great experience and I learned a lot about the country and the people. I'm still in contact with my exchange partner.*
Leider habe ich keinen Austausch gemacht, aber ich habe einen deutschen Sommerkurs gemacht. Ich habe viel gelernt und der Kurs hat auch Spaß gemacht.	*Unfortunately, I haven't done an exchange, but I did do a German summer course. I learned a lot and the course was also fun.*

 Übersetzen Sie die folgenden Sätze.

3. Was haben Sie dort gemacht? *What did you do there?*	
a) Wir haben in einem schönen Hotel gewohnt.	**e)** Ich habe am Strand gelegen, um mich zu bräunen.
b) Wir sind jeden Tag im Meer schwimmen gegangen.	**f)** Ich habe das herrliche Wetter richtig genossen.
c) Abends sind wir ins Restaurant gegangen und haben leckeres Essen gegessen.	**g)** Das Essen hat mir gut gefallen.
d) Wir haben die Sehenswürdigkeiten gesehen.	**h)** Ich habe neue Leute kennengelernt.

4. Was halten Sie von einem Schüleraustausch? *What do you think of school exchanges?*	
Meine Gastfamilie war echt lieb und ich habe meine Deutschkenntnisse verbessert. Seit dem Austausch finde ich Deutsch viel leichter.	*My host family was really lovely and I improved my knowledge of German. Since the exchange, I find German much easier.*
Man lernt neue Sitten und Bräuche kennen und auch ein bisschen Umgangssprache.	*One learns about new customs and traditions and also a little bit of slang.*
Das Essen hat mir (nicht) geschmeckt. Ich finde Würste lecker/ekelhaft.	*I liked/didn't like the food. I find sausages tasty/ disgusting.*
Wir haben die Sehenswürdigkeiten besichtigt. Ich bin einkaufen gegangen. Ich bin in die deutsche Schule gegangen.	*We visited the sights. I went shopping. I went to a German school.*
Ich habe jeden Tag Deutsch gesprochen. Das hat mir viel in der Schule geholfen.	*I spoke German every day. That has helped me a lot in school.*
Leider habe ich nicht allzu viel Deutsch gelernt. Jedoch hat der Austausch viel Spaß gemacht.	*Unfortunately, I didn't learn too much German. Yet the exchange was a lot of fun.*
Ich habe den Austausch nicht gemacht, denn ein Austausch kostet viel Geld.	*I didn't do the exchange because an exchange costs a lot of money.*
Die Vorteile eines Austausches sind zahlreich.	*The advantages of an exchange are many.*
Erstens kann man den Horizont erweitern.	*Firstly, one can broaden one's horizons.*
Zweitens lernt man eine neue Kultur kennen, was einen reifer und toleranter macht.	*Secondly, one gets to know a new culture, which makes one more mature and tolerant.*
Drittens schließt man neue Freundschaften, hoffentlich lebenslange Freundschaften.	*Thirdly, one makes new friendships, hopefully friendships for life.*

5. Haben Sie vor, im Ausland zu leben? *Are you planning on living abroad?*	
Ich möchte für ein paar Jahre im Ausland wohnen, um Arbeitserfahrung zu sammeln.	*I would like to live abroad for a few years in order to get work experience.*
Ich werde bestimmt auswandern, denn es gibt bessere Berufschancen im Ausland.	*I will definitely emigrate because there are better career opportunities abroad.*
Wenn ich qualifiziert bin, kann ich nach England/ Australien/Deutschland auswandern, um Arbeit zu suchen.	*When I am qualified, I can emigrate to England/ Australia/Germany in order to look for work.*
Ich würde gern für ein paar Jahre im Ausland arbeiten, aber ich will mich bestimmt später in Irland niederlassen.	*I would like to work abroad for a couple of years, but later I definitely want to settle in Ireland.*

 Match these German idioms to their English translations. Use them in your oral and written work.

1. Ich verstehe nur Bahnhof.	**A** They're crazy.
2. Das ist mir Wurst.	**B** That's all double Dutch to me.
3. Sie haben einen Vogel.	**C** It doesn't matter to me.

 Text 1: Ab ins Ausland

Bitte beantworten Sie die folgenden Fragen:

1. Was sieht man auf dem Foto?
2. Was macht die Frau auf dem Foto?
3. Wie ist sie bekleidet?
4. Wo ist sie, Ihrer Meinung nach?

  Vorarbeit

1. Finden Sie diese Ausdrücke im Text!
   - **A** If you have the opportunity ...
   - **B** How about a job ... ?
   - **C** The participants must be prepared ...
   - **D** In Chile ... it is also easier to get a visa.
   - **E** ... young people from all over the world.
2. Finden Sie das Deutsche für die Wörter unten!
   - **A** stay/school fees/necessary/deal with
   - **B** suitable/take care of/food and board
   - **C** voluntary service/disabled/environmental protection
   - **D** frequently overrun/recommend/farm
   - **E** organisers/voluntary work/to be suitable

Eine Weile in einer anderen Kultur zu leben ist immer eine tolle Erfahrung

A 12 Monate Auslandsschuljahr: Wenn du die Möglichkeit hast, während der Schulzeit ein ganzes Jahr im Ausland zu verbringen, solltest du dich für einen Austausch bewerben. Beliebte Länder sind Australien, Kanada und Neuseeland. Dort kosten aber die Schulgebühren viel. Es ist etwas günstiger in Großbritannien, in den USA oder in Irland. Agenturen helfen beim Organisieren des Aufenthalts. Sie kümmern sich um das Visum, das außerhalb der Europäischen Union nötig ist. In vielen Ländern des englischsprachigen Raums ist es auch möglich, nur drei oder sechs Monate lang zu bleiben. Aber je länger, desto besser, denn erst ab einem Vierteljahr beginnt man langsam mit der Sprache warm zu werden.

B 10 Monate Au-pair: Du bist mit der Schule fertig und 18 Jahre alt? Wie wäre es mit einem Job als Kinderbetreuer? Als Au-pair betreust du die Kinder deiner Gastfamilie und hilfst bei der täglichen Hausarbeit mit. Dafür bekommst du Unterkunft, Verpflegung und Taschengeld. Die Agentur informiert über wichtige Themen wie Arbeitszeit, Versicherung und Taschengeld, und findet auch die passende Familie für dich.

C 6 Monate Freiwilligendienst: Ein Freiwilligendienst ist perfekt, um die Kultur kennenzulernen, denn du arbeitest in einem sozialen, kulturellen oder sportlichen Projekt oder im Natur- und Umweltschutz mit. Du arbeitest im Kindergarten oder an einer Schule mit, du betreust behinderte Menschen oder du kümmerst dich um Tiere. Du erhältst eine Unterkunft, Verpflegung und Reisekosten von der EU. Die Teilnehmer müssen für den Einsatz vorbereitet sein. Wenn man im Ausland dann Probleme hat, wird keine Agentur dich betreuen.

D 3 Monate Work and Travel: Als Work-and-Traveller reist du für einige Wochen in ein anderes Land und finanzierst deinen Aufenthalt durch Jobs – zum Beispiel als Mitarbeiter auf einem Bauernhof, in Restaurants oder Jugendherbergen. Länder wie Australien oder Neuseeland werden von Work-and-Travellern häufig überrannt, also ist es schwierig, dort Arbeit zu finden. Wir empfehlen, sich über andere Länder zu informieren. In Chile oder Japan ist es auch einfacher, ein Visum zu erhalten.

E 2 Wochen Workcamp: Eine Alternative für Jüngere sind die kurzen Workcamps. Du arbeitest mit anderen Jugendlichen aus der ganzen Welt in einem sozialen oder kulturellen Projekt, zum Beispiel im Natur- und Umweltschutz, und kannst nebenbei noch an einem Freizeitprogramm teilnehmen. Workcamps eignen sich prima, um erste Erfahrungen in der Freiwilligenarbeit zu sammeln. Die Veranstalter nehmen häufig schon Jugendliche ab 14 oder 15 Jahren auf.

© YAEZ (amended)

OL Ordinary Level Questions

1. **a)** Name the countries in which one could apply to do an exchange. (A)
   b) What is the usual length of stay allowed in some European countries? (A)
2. Write down the letter (A–E) from the comprehension on page 108 for the type of stay abroad where:
   a) The agency will inform you about insurance. ___
   b) You will not have direct help from any agency if you have a problem while abroad. ___
   c) You should find out more about less popular destination countries. ___
   d) The stay is suitable for getting experience of voluntary work. ___
   e) The longer you stay, the more it will improve your knowledge of the language. ___
3. What words make up the following compound words, and what do they mean in English?
   a) Umweltschutz = _____ + _____ = _____
   b) Ausland = _____ + _____ = _____
   c) Freiwilligenarbeit = _____ + _____ = _____
   d) Jugendherbergen = _____ + _____ = _____
   e) Gastfamilie = _____ + _____ = _____
4. Select the correct prepositions for the following sentences.
   a) Du wirst **(von/bei/in/mit)** der Arbeit mithelfen.
   b) Du arbeitest **(auf/in/mit/bei)** einem Projekt.
   c) Informiere dich **(über/mit/auf/an)** andere Länder!
   d) Du kannst **(in/an/bei/für)** zwei Wochen dort bleiben.

HL Higher Level Questions

1. Beantworten Sie folgende Fragen auf Deutsch!
   a) Beschreiben Sie genau den Auslandsaufenthalt im ersten Absatz! Geben Sie **drei** Details! (A)
   b) Was machen die Agenturen? (A)
   c) Laut Text, warum ist es vorteilhaft so lang wie möglich im Ausland zu bleiben? (A)
   d) Worüber informiert die Agentur im zweiten Absatz? (B)
   e) Warum müssen die Teilnehmer am Freiwilligendienst vorbereitet sein? (C)
   f) Warum ist es schwierig ein Visum in Australien zu erhalten? (D)
2. Answer the following questions in English.
   a) What is involved in a one-year stay abroad? Give **three** details. (A)
   b) Which tasks will be required of you as an au pair? (B)
   c) Name **five** tasks which you might do as a volunteer. (C)
   d) How will you finance yourself while travelling? Give details. (D)
   e) What are the advantages of work camps? (E)
3. Was passt zusammen?

1. Wenn man die Möglichkeit hat,	**A** beginnt man, die Sprache zu beherrschen.
2. Nach einem Vierteljahr	**B** um Erfahrung zu sammeln.
3. Die Agentur informiert über wichtige Themen	**C** Arbeit zu finden.
4. In manchen Ländern ist es schwierig,	**D** sollte man einen Austausch machen.
5. Workcamps sind ideal,	**E** und sucht eine passende Familie aus.

4. Identifizieren Sie die Zeitform der unterstrichenen Verben unten, ob Singular oder Plural und Infinitivform!
   a) Es <u>ist</u> etwas günstiger in Großbritannien, in den USA oder in Irland.
   b) Du <u>hilfst</u> bei der täglichen Hausarbeit <u>mit</u>.
   c) Du <u>erhältst</u> eine Unterkunft, Verpflegung und Reisekosten von der EU.
   d) Wenn man im Ausland dann Probleme hat, <u>wird</u> keine Agentur dich <u>betreuen</u>.

Grammatik: Genus/Gender – Masculine, Feminine, Neuter

p. 121 (Übung macht den Meister)

There are three genders of nouns in the German language: masculine, feminine and neuter. The gender of a noun can often be identified by its suffix, although there are some exceptions.

Maskulin **Masculine**	Feminin **Feminine**	Neutrum **Neuter**
-ant	-age	-ach
-ast	-e	-al
-en	-ei	-chen
-er	-enz	-ett
-ich	-heit	-ium
-ig	-ik	-lein
-ing	-in	Many nouns beginning with **Ge-**
-ismus	-ion	The young of animals
-ist	-keit	Names of cities and countries
	-schaft	Infinitives turned into nouns
	-tät	
	-ung	

Note: There are a few exceptions to nouns ending with **-en**. When the infinitive is capitalised and turned into a noun, it will be neuter:

das Wissen, das Sprechen, das Hören, das Lesen, das Essen, das Trinken.

-er exceptions: die Mutter, die Schwester, die Großmutter, das Fenster, das Wetter, das Zimmer.

1. Identify the gender of the following nouns according to their endings.

Fabrik	Kaninchen	Mannschaft	Übung	Geschenk
Schule	Tendenz	Freiheit	Fahrer	Studium
Qualität	Geschäft	Metzgerei	Feigling	Fähigkeit

2. Identify the gender of the following compound nouns by the ending of the second noun.

Fußballmannschaft	Ratgeber	Buchhandlung	Matheübung	Geburtstagsgeschenk
Austauschpartner	Federmäppchen	Klassenlehrer	Mitarbeiter	Lastwagen
Sonntagmorgen	Geschäftsführer	Landwirtschaft	Hausaufgabe	Aussprache

There are five main ways to form the plural of German nouns:

1. Add an **-e** ending to most masculine, very few feminine and some neuter nouns.
   Many will also take an umlaut on the first vowel: der Koch › die Köche; die Stadt › die Städte. Exceptions include: das Pferd › die Pferde; der Hund › die Hunde.
2. Add an **-er** ending with an umlaut over the first vowel for many neuter and some masculine nouns: das Haus › die Häuser; der Vater › die Väter; das Buch › die Bücher; das Schloss › die Schlösser.
3. Add an **-n/en** ending for nouns ending in **-e**, **-ung**, **-ik**, **-heit**, **-keit**: das Auge › die Augen; der Gedanke › die Gedanken; die Vorstellung › die Vorstellungen; die Fabrik › die Fabriken.
4. Add an **-s** for nouns of French or Italian origin: das Kino, das Hotel, das Café, das Restaurant, das Radio, die Disco, der Club, die CD, die DVD.
5. No change: das Mädchen › die Mädchen; der Onkel › die Onkel; der Lehrer › die Lehrer; der Schüler > die Schüler.

 06.01 Hörverständnis Teil 1

Vorarbeit

Schiedsrichter	*referee*	**anbieten**	*to offer*	**beeinflussen**	*to influence*
Tor	*goal*	**ehemalig**	*former*	**freiwillig**	*voluntary*

Ordinary + Higher Level Questions

1. **a)** Since when had Julian been in Ireland? **b)** When did he return to Germany?
2. What was he doing in Ireland?
3. Describe what the agencies do. Give **two (O)/three (H)** details.
4. Why did Julian choose Ireland? Give **two (O)/three (H)** details.
5. **a)** Which project did he choose?
   b) Describe his duties. Give **two (O)/three (H)** details.
6. **a)** What are the advantages of this work, according to Julian?
   b) What is he going to do now and why?

06.02 Hörverständnis Teil 2

Vorarbeit

Reisebüro	*travel agency*	**behilflich sein**	*to be of help*	**Flüge**	*flights*
erwarten	*to expect*	**im Alter von**	*aged ...*	**Tagesausflüge**	*day trips*
Abflüge	*departures*	**passend**	*suitable*	**Vormittag**	*morning*

Ordinary Level Questions

1. What does the caller want to do?
2. What is the caller's name?
3. **a)** How many students are in the group? **b)** Where are they going to and for how long?
4. What is the number and e-mail address of the caller?

Higher Level Questions

1. Using ***key phrases***, write down **in German** the key information from the conversation.
   - The name of the person **making** the call
   - The reason for the call
   - **Five** details of their conversation
   - Details regarding further contact
   - The recipient's phone number and e-mail address

Gesprächsnotiz

Anruf von: ____________________ Gesprächsanlass: ____________________

Der Anrufer bekommt:

- am Abend eine E-Mail ☐
- einen Anruf ☐
- morgen Vormittag eine E-Mail ☐
- morgen Nachmittag eine E-Mail ☐

Kontaktnummer: ____________________ E-Mailadresse: ____________________

2. In listening to the phone call for the ***third*** time, write down **three** examples of the language used (***expressions and phrases***) which show that the travel agent is **positive**.

Text 2: Studenten, stresst euch nicht im Auslandsstudienjahr

Bitte beantworten Sie die folgenden Fragen:

1. Was sieht man auf dem Bild?
2. Was machen sie?
3. Wie ist die Stimmung?
4. Wie sind sie bekleidet?
5. Haben Sie vor, im Ausland zu studieren?

Vorarbeit

1. Finden Sie diese Ausdrücke im Text!
   - **A** ... more popular than ever.
   - **B** Erasmus is above all one thing.
   - **C** ... not to take things so seriously.
   - **D** ... take their responsibilities seriously ...
   - **E** Europe used to be like that.
2. Finden Sie das Deutsche für die Wörter unten!
   - **A** Iceland/the third most popular/Arts
   - **B** independence/promotes/questionnaire
   - **C** presentation/lecture hall/pub
   - **D** university life/relaxed/hard work
   - **E** euro crisis/proof/to appear/becomes one

A Unter Studenten ist das Erasmus-Programm so beliebt wie noch nie. Erasmus ist das Austauschprogramm der Europäischen Union. Derzeit nehmen auch Universitäten außerhalb der EU, wie z. B. Island, Liechtenstein, Norwegen, die Schweiz und die Türkei, an dem Austauschprogramm teil. Allein 30.000 junge Menschen aus Deutschland gingen letztes Jahr für eine Studienzeit oder ein Praktikum ins Ausland. Die Erasmus-Teilnehmer wollen Wirtschafts-, Natur-, Sozial- oder Geisteswissenschaften studieren. Deutschland ist das drittbeliebteste Land für Erasmus-Studenten.

B Laut dem Leiter unterstützt und fördert das Erasmus-Programm Bildung und internationale Erfahrung. Er findet Jobperspektiven wichtig. Die Studenten denken aber auch an Spaß, an Urlaub und an Selbstständigkeit. Die Studenten möchten lieber einfach neue Leute kennenlernen. In einer Erasmus-Online-Erfahrungsumfrage heißt es: „Erasmus ist vor allem eins: Party, Party, Party!"

C Man schickt den Eltern Postkarten mit dem Kolosseum drauf und Grüßen: „Es geht mir gut, und ich lerne viel." Man lernt ja sowohl in der Kneipe als auch im Hörsaal, sowohl die Dinge nicht so ernst zu nehmen als auch fleißig zu sein. Man kann auch seine Sprachkenntnisse aufbessern. Die Erasmus-Studenten sind auf sowohl Spaß und Lernen motiviert. Dann und wann muss man ein Referat halten laut Professoren.

D Erasmus-Studenten sorgen für eine gelassene, europäische Stimmung sowie Zusammenarbeit und Fleiß. Das ist eine sehr gute Kombination. Erasmus-Studenten sollten aber auch den Uni-Alltag und ihre Verantwortungen ernst nehmen. Sie wollen natürlich am Strand liegen oder den Eiffelturm besichtigen, Menschen kennenlernen, tanzen gehen.

E Erasmus-Studenten zeigen, junge Menschen mögen in Europa leben. Und das ist in einer Zeit, in der Europa schon zum Synonym geworden ist für ein langweiliges Bürokratenmonster und die Euro-Krise. In Zeiten, in denen die Stabilität der EU unsicher geworden ist, wirken Erasmus-Studenten positiv, sogar romantisch. Europa war das auch mal. Sind diese Studenten der Beweis der Idee, dass man näher zusammenkommt und irgendwann eins wird?

Nora Gantenbrink, *Die Zeit* # 10/2012 (amended)

OL Ordinary Level Questions

1. a) Describe the Erasmus programme. Give **two** details. A
   b) What do students think about when they think of the Erasmus programme? B
   c) Which two places are mentioned as places of equal learning? C
   d) Name **one** academic activity and **one** leisure activity undertaken by students. D
2. Are the following statements true or false?
   a) Non-EU countries also take part in this programme.
   b) According to the Erasmus online survey, students are only interested in having fun.
   c) Erasmus students are not motivated to learn.
   d) One can visit the Eiffel Tower or lie on a beach.
3. Select the correct prepositions for the following sentences.
   a) Island nimmt **(am/im/vom/um)** Erasmus-Programm teil.
   b) Erasmus Studenten denken **(an/um/im/zum)** Spaß und Urlaub.
   c) Sie schicken Postkarten **(bei/mit/ohne/zu)** Fotos von Sehenswürdigkeiten.
   d) Die Studenten sorgen **(ab/von/mit/für)** eine gelassene Stimmung.
   e) Das ist ja **(an/um/im/in)** einer Zeit, wo viele Leute die EU nicht mögen.

HL Higher Level Questions

1. Beantworten Sie folgende Fragen auf Deutsch!
   a) Beschreiben Sie mit **mehreren** Details das Erasmus-Programm! A
   b) Was ist das Wichtigste am Erasmus-Progamm? Geben Sie **zwei** Details! B
   c) Wie stehen viele Studenten zum Erasmus-Programm? C
   d) Was ist, laut Text, die beste Kombination für Erasmus Studenten? D
   e) Warum ist, laut Text, die EU unsicherer geworden? E
2. Answer the following questions in English.
   a) Who exactly takes part in the Erasmus programme and what do they do? Give **five** details. A
   b) Compare the philosophy of the director and the participants of the Erasmus programme. B
   c) According to the text, what are the two places where students learn? C
   d) What qualities do the participants bring to the programme? What are their responsibilities? D
   e) Explain the meaning of the closing question in paragraph E. E
3. Was passt zusammen?

1. Das Erasmus-Programm wird	**A** aber sie sollten auch studieren.
2. Der Leiter findet Bildung wichtig,	**B** als auch studieren.
3. Die Studenten sind viel unterwegs,	**C** von der EU unterstützt.
4. Die Studenten sollten sowohl Spaß haben	**D** denn sie ist zu bürokratisch geworden.
5. Die EU ist nicht so beliebt,	**E** während Studenten mehr Wert auf Partys legen.

4. Replace the modal verbs below with the main verb + **gern**. Example: Die Teilnehmer **wollen** Sozialwissenschaften studieren: Die Teilnehmer studieren **gern** Sozialwissenschaften.
   a) Sie möchten neue Leute kennenlernen.
   b) Sie wollen natürlich am Strand liegen.
   c) Man muss ein Referat halten.
   d) Junge Menschen mögen in Europa leben.

Prüfungstipp

A good way to revise a passage is to see how you can adapt phrases. Unter Studenten ist das Erasmus-Programm so beliebt wie noch nie: Unter **Schülern** ist **Deutsch** so beliebt wie noch nie.

OL Äußerung zum Thema: Ordinary Level

You are interviewing an Erasmus student. Complete the dialogue using the information in Text 2.

Sie: Was studieren Sie?
Student: ______________________________
Sie: Gehen Sie auf viele Partys?
Student: ______________________________
Sie: Was ist Ihnen wichtiger, Partys oder das Studium?
Student: ______________________________
Sie: Halten Sie Referate an der Uni?
Student: ______________________________
Sie: Wohnen Sie gern hier?
Student: ______________________________

HL Äußerung zum Thema: Higher Level

Write 13 to 15 sentences, answering the questions below.

- Beschreiben Sie das Foto oben in **drei bis vier** Sätzen.
- Glauben Sie, dass das Erasmus-Programm eine gute Idee ist? Warum/warum nicht?
- Was lernt man, wenn man eine Zeitlang im Ausland verbringt?
- Was haben Sie über die deutsche Kultur gelernt? Wo haben Sie das gelernt?

Nützliche Sätze

Ich finde das Erasumus-Programm eine tolle Idee, denn man lernt Land und Leute kennen.	*I think the Erasmus programme is a brilliant idea because you get to know the country and the people.*
Ich glaube, dass das Erasmus-Programm eine gute Idee ist, aber ich persönlich würde so was nie machen. Ich bin nämlich ein Stubenhocker.	*I believe that the Erasmus programme is a good idea, but personally I would never do something like that. I'm a homebody.*
Ich will unbedingt das Erasmus-Jahr machen. Ich will eine neue Kultur erfahren und ich suche immer den Nervenkitzel.	*I definitely want to do the Erasmus year. I want to experience a new culture and I'm always looking for exciting experiences.*
Ich glaube, man lernt Toleranz und Offenheit, wenn man eine Zeit im Ausland verbringt.	*I believe one learns tolerance and openness when one spends time abroad.*
Ich habe gehört, dass man im Erasmus-Jahr viel Spaß hat. Ich bin Partylöwe und will bestimmt mitmachen!	*I've heard that one has a lot of fun during the Erasmus year. I'm a party animal and I definitely want to take part!*
Es ist immer vorteilhaft, neue Kontakte zu knüpfen.	*It's always advantageous to make new contacts.*
Man lernt flexibel und selbstständig zu sein und neue Situationen zu meistern.	*One learns to be flexible and independent and to master new situations.*
Ganz bestimmt wächst man als Mensch.	*One very definitely grows as a person.*
Wir haben in der Schule viel über das deutsche Schulsystem gelernt. Wir haben auch über die Feste, wie Karneval, Weihnachten und das Oktoberfest, gelernt.	*At school we learned a lot about the German school system. We also learned about the festivals, like Carnival, Christmas and Oktoberfest.*

Grammatik: Die Fälle/The Cases

p. 121 (Übung macht den Meister)

A noun denotes a person, place, thing, idea or concept:
man, Mary, school, book, imagination, philosophy. All nouns in German are capitalised.

There are four cases, or functions, for nouns in German:

1. Nominative case: The noun is doing the action (subject).
   Examples: Der Mann sang ein Lied. The man sang a song.

2. Accusative case: The action is being done to the noun (direct object).
   Examples: Sie kaufte ein Handy. She bought a phone.

3. Dative case: The noun is indirectly involved (indirect object). The dative conveys the meaning 'to', 'with', 'from'. Examples: Es gehört einer Frau. It belongs to a lady.

4. Genitive case: Possession. The noun either has 'of' directly in front of it, or an 's after it.
   Examples: Die Farbe eines Buchs. A book's colour/The colour of a book.

Decide the cases of the underlined nouns below.

1. Ein Mann trinkt einen Kaffee.	*A man is drinking a coffee.*
2. Ein Kind schreibt einen Brief.	*A child is writing a letter.*
3. Das Spielzeug gehört einem Kleinkind.	*The toy belongs to a small child.*
4. Ein Lehrer gibt einem Schüler eine Eins.	*A teacher gives an A to a pupil.*
5. Ein Junge kann den Standort eines Hauses finden.	*A boy can find the location of a house.*

Indefinite Articles

The case system affects the indefinite article 'a' or 'an'.

Case	Masculine	Feminine	Neuter	Plural
Nominative	ein Mann	ein**e** Frau	ein Kind	zwei Männer
Accusative	ein**en** Mann	ein**e** Frau	ein Kind	drei Frauen
Dative	ein**em** Mann	ein**er** Frau	ein**em** Kind	vier Kinder**n**
Genitive	ein**es** Mann**es**	ein**er** Frau	ein**es** Kind**es**	fünf Männer

Decide the case of each noun and fill in the correct form of the indefinite article 'a'.

1. ___ Mann (m) isst ___ Orange (f).	*A man eats an orange.*
2. ___ Kind (n) kauft ___ Handy (n).	*A child buys a mobile phone.*
3. Die Farbe ___ Buches (n) ist nicht wichtig.	*The colour of a book isn't important.*
4. Das ist das Handy ___ Kindes (n).	*That is a child's mobile phone.*
5. Thomas gibt ___ Mann (m) den ersten Preis.	*Thomas gives first prize to a man.*

Negative Articles

The negative of **ein**, **eine**, **ein** (**kein**, **keine**, **kein**, **keine**) follows the same case pattern.

Case	Masculine	Feminine	Neuter	Plural
Nominative	kein Mann	kein**e** Frau	kein Kind	kein**e** Männer
Accusative	kein**en** Mann	kein**e** Frau	kein Kind	kein**e** Frauen
Dative	kein**em** Mann	kein**er** Frau	kein**em** Kind	kein**en** Kinder**n**
Genitive	kein**es** Mann**es**	kein**er** Frau	kein**es** Kind**es**	kein**er** Männ**er**

Text 3: Andorra – Spanien; an der Grenze

Bitte beantworten Sie die folgenden Fragen:

1. Beschreiben Sie was Sie auf dem Bild sehen!
2. Was macht die Frau?
3. Wo ist sie?
4. Wie sieht die Frau aus?
5. Wie fühlt sie sich, Ihrer Meinung nach?

Vorarbeit

1. Finden Sie diese Ausdrücke im Text!
   - **A** It was the beginning of the 80s.
   - **B** Finally I was ready ...
   - **C** ... drove in the direction of ...
   - **D** He walked along the queue.
2. Finden Sie das Deutsche für die Wörter unten!
   - **A** located/the Pyrenees/it struck me/converted (money)
   - **B** continued/put/finished/recommended/looked around
   - **C** traffic jam/steeply downhill/customs officials/border/boot (of car)
   - **D** for the fright/border crossing/licence plate/expensive/barrier

Autorin: Doris E. M. Bulenda, 13 October 2017 (amended)

A Es war Anfang der 1980er Jahre. Ich fuhr mit dem Auto durch Frankreich, dann in die Pyrenäen nach Andorra. Andorra war wunderschön gelegen, eine wunderschöne Stadt in den Bergen. Also parkte ich und machte einen langen Spaziergang. Dabei fiel es mir auf, dass es eine Menge von Parfümerien gab. Ich schaute in die Schaufenster und rechnete die Preise um. Toll – das war alles so günstig.

B Schon ging ich in eine riesige Parfümerie und schaute mich um. Natürlich sah ich alles nicht nur an, sondern ich stellte das eine oder andere Parfüm auf die Theke, dann noch eins und noch eins. Die Verkäuferin kam an und empfahl mir noch dies und jenes. Schließlich war ich fertig, ich schrieb einen Scheck aus. Meine „Beute" wurde in vier oder fünf Plastiktüten verpackt. Ich brachte die Parfüms ins Auto, dann setzte ich den Stadtbummel fort. Zigaretten und alkoholische Getränke kaufte ich nicht, die waren in Spanien günstiger.

C Als ich wieder auf die Uhr schaute, war es schon Nachmittag. Ich setzte mich ins Auto und fuhr Richtung der spanischen Grenze. Da ging es steil bergab. Vor mir sah ich einen Stau vor der spanischen Grenze. Das war noch vor EU- und Schengen-Zeiten ... Langsam fuhr ich in Richtung Grenze. Ich sah, dass die Zollbeamten alle Autos genau kontrollierten, den Kofferraum öffneten. So langsam wurde ich immer nervöser – wie viel Parfüm durfte man eigentlich mitnehmen? Natürlich waren mir die genauen Zahlen nicht bekannt – aber trotzdem hatte ich Angst, viel zu viel gekauft zu haben.

D Dann, so circa 500 Meter vor der Grenzstation, kam ein Uniformierter die Straße hinauf und schaute sich die einzelnen Autos an. Er ging die Schlange entlang. Dann kam er zu mir, schaute auf mein deutsches Autokennzeichen und sagte, ich solle ihm folgen. Au, verdammt, das wird jetzt wohl teuer werden, dachte ich. Und dann brachte er mich zu einem Übergang, öffnete die Schranke und ließ mich ohne Kontrolle durchfahren. Ich lächelte den Uniformierten an, rief „muchas gracias" aus dem Fenster und hoffte, dass man nicht sehen könnte, wie erleichtert ich war. Ich war so froh ... Aber auf den Schrecken brauchte ich eine Pause im Restaurant, das ich im nächsten Dorf fand, und zwar ein großes Glas Wein!

OL Ordinary Level Questions

1. a) Where was the narrator going? Describe the route taken. A
   b) What did the narrator buy exactly? What did the narrator not buy and why? B
   c) What happened at the border? Give **two** details. C
   d) What did the uniformed customs official do? D
2. Choose a suitable heading for each paragraph and explain your choice in English.

Ich steckte im Stau | Unterwegs nach Andorra | Ich hatte Angst | Lust auf Parfüm

3. What words make up these compound words and what do they mean in English?
   a) Schaufenster = _____ + _____ = _____
   b) bergab = _____ + _____ = _____
   c) Grenzstation = _____ + _____ = _____
   d) mitnehmen = _____ + _____ = _____
4. Indicate if the following sentences are true or false.
   a) Die Erzählerin fuhr über Andorra nach Spanien.
   b) Sie wollte nicht nur Parfüm sondern auch Alkohol und Zigaretten kaufen.
   c) Der Zollbeamte kontrollierte das Auto der Erzählerin.
   d) Die Erzählerin trank später ein Glas Wein.
5. Indicate the correct answer.
   a) Die Erzählerin wollte **(in/zu/nach/an)** Spanien fahren.
   b) Sie fand eine Parfümerie **(in/im/nach/am)** Andorra.
   c) Sie schaute **(an/in/auf/für)** die Uhr.
   d) Sie steckte **(in/an/auf/zu)** einem langen Stau.

HL Higher Level Questions

1. Beantworten Sie folgende Fragen auf Englisch!
   a) Wohin fuhr die Erzählerin genau? Geben Sie mehrere Details! A
   b) Was kaufte sie in der Parfümerie und warum? Was kaufte sie nicht und warum? B
   c) Was entdeckte die Erzählerin nach dem Einkaufen? Wovor hatte sie Angst? C
   d) Was machte der Offizielle genau? Wie reagierte die Erzählerin darauf? D
2. Answer the following questions in English.
   a) What exactly does the narrator do on the journey? Give **four** details. A
   b) What does the saleswoman suggest to the narrator? B
   c) What does the narrator see when she comes to the border? C
   d) Why was the narrator nervous? What exactly did the official do? D
   e) The narrator becomes nervous as she comes to the border with Spain. The customs official is calm. Compare and contrast their reactions. Give **two** examples for each person.
3. Was passt zusammen?

1. Ich fuhr Richtung	**A** sah ich eine Parfümerie.
2. Auf dem Weg dahin	**B** über die Grenze fahren.
3. Hier kaufte ich eine Menge Parfüm,	**C** steckte ich in einem langen Stau.
4. An der Grenze zu Spanien	**D** Spaniens mit dem Auto los.
5. Der Offizielle ließ mich ohne Kontrolle	**E** denn alles war so günstig.

4. Indicate the gender of the underlined nouns.
   a) Ich machte einen langen Spaziergang.
   b) Vor mir sah ich einen Stau.
   c) Ich brauchte eine Pause im Restaurant.
   d) Ich trank ein Glas Wein.

Grammatik: Die Fälle/The Cases

p. 121 (Übung macht den Meister)

Reminder: there are four cases, or functions, for nouns in German:

1. Nominative case: The noun **is doing** the action.
   Examples: Der Student **schrieb** den Brief. The student **wrote** the letter.
2. Accusative case: The action **is being done to** the noun.
   Examples: Das Mädchen **hat** den Apfel **gegessen**. The girl **ate** the apple.
3. Dative case: The noun is indirectly involved and conveys the meaning 'to', 'with', 'from'.
   Examples: Der Lehrer **hat** es dem Kind **weggenommen**. The teacher **took** it from the child.
4. Genitive case: The noun either has '**of**' directly before it, or an 's after in English.
   Examples: Die Farbe **des** Kleid**es**. The colour **of** the dress.

Possessive Adjectives

The possessive adjectives: **mein** (my), **dein** (your – singular), **sein** (his), **ihr** (her), **sein** (its), **unser** (our), **euer** (your – plural), **Ihr** (your – polite) and **ihr** (their) follow the same case pattern as the indefinite article 'a'.

Case	Masculine	Feminine	Neuter	Plural
Nominative	mein Mann	mein**e** Frau	mein Kind	mein**e** Männer
Accusative	mein**en** Mann	mein**e** Frau	mein Kind	mein**e** Frauen
Dative	mein**em** Mann	mein**er** Frau	mein**em** Kind	mein**en** Kinder**n**
Genitive	mein**es** Mann**es**	mein**er** Frau	mein**es** Kind**es**	mein**er** Männer

Using the table above, fill in the following tables for **dein**, **sein** and **ihr**.

Case	Masculine	Feminine	Neuter	Plural
Nominative	dein Mann	deine Frau	dein Kind	deine Männer
Accusative				
Dative				
Genitive				

Case	Masculine	Feminine	Neuter	Plural
Nominative	sein Mann	seine Frau	sein Kind	seine Frauen
Accusative				
Dative				
Genitive				

Case	Masculine	Feminine	Neuter	Plural
Nominative	ihr Mann	ihre Frau	ihr Kind	ihre Kinder
Accusative				
Dative				
Genitive				

Hausaufgaben

Practise the case endings for the remaining possessive adjectives. Draw up similar tables for **unser** (our), **euer/eur-** (your – plural), **Ihr** (your – polite) and **ihr** (their) for masculine, feminine, neuter and plural nouns.

06.03 Hörverständnis Teil 3

Vorarbeit

kaum schaffen	*hardly manage*	**vorankommen**	*to make progress*	**Zeitverschwendung**	*waste of time*
verlangen	*to demand*	**ganz zu schweigen von**	*not to mention*	**Übersetzungen**	*translations*
ermöglichen	*to facilitate*	**nützlich**	*useful*	**Fremdsprachenaufenthalt**	*language programme*

CL Ordinary + Higher Level Questions

1. **a)** The conversation is between:
   i) two classmates **ii)** two students **iii)** a teacher and a parent **iv)** two parents
   b) Find **one (O)/two (H)** indications in the conversation to support your choice.
2. **a)** Which word best describes the female speaker's attitude during the conversation?
   i) worried **ii)** frustrated **iii)** encouraging **iv)** tired
   b) Write down **one (O)/two (H)** details from the conversation to support your choice.
3. What does the male speaker say to encourage the female speaker? Give **one (O)/two (H)** details.
4. What do the two of them decide to do in the end? Give one **(O)/two (H)** details.

06.04 Hörverständnis Teil 4

Vorarbeit

ist ... untergegangen	*sank*	**Mittelmeer**	*Mediterranean*	**Gewässer**	*waters*
Rettungen	*rescues*	**bundesweit**	*state-wide*	**Teilnahme**	*participation*
Verteidigungskräfte	*defence forces*	**Bildung**	*education*	**bewölkt**	*cloudy*
Menschen	*people*	**sind ertrunken**	*drowned*	**bedeckt**	*overcast*

CL Ordinary + Higher Level Questions

1. **a)** What will be taking place state-wide? Give **one (O)/two (H)** details.
   b) What is this initiative in aid of?
2. **a)** Give **one (O)/two (H)** details about the boat accident.
   b) What happened to the passengers?
3. **a)** What do thousands of Germans do every year? Give **one (O)/two (H)** details.
   b) Where do they pursue these activities?
4. **a)** What happened in Thailand and what caused it?
   b) Give **one (O)/two (H)** details of what happened to the people there.
5. **a)** What is the weather forecast for this morning? Give details.
   b) What is the forecast for the next few days?

Prüfungstipp

Look up the English meanings of these natural disasters.

Lawine	**Erdbeben**	**Hochwasser**	**Dürre**	**Waldbrand**	**Orkan**

Schriftliche Produktion: Ordinary Level

Write a letter to your pen pal, Martin(a). Complete the first paragraph by correctly inserting the sentence halves below. Then follow the instructions.

den ich letzte Woche erhalten habe **bei der Weinlese in Deutschland zu arbeiten** **so viel Spaß machen** **schöne Grüße aus Irland** **dich im Sommer zu sehen**

Liebe(r) Martin(a),

______________ ! Vielen Dank für deinen Brief, ______________ . Ich freue mich schon, ______________ . Aber jetzt will ich dir von meinen Plänen erzählen. Ich habe vor, mit zwei Freunden ______________ . Das wird ______________ !

Now complete the letter.

- Say when and where you intend to work in Germany.
- Give **two** details about the friends who are going with you.
- Describe what you hope to do in your free time in Germany.
- Say that you would like to meet him/her and say when.
- Say that you will get good work experience and hope to improve your German.
- Write a suitable closing sentence.

HL Schriftliche Produktion: Higher Level

Reply in German to your pen pal's letter. Give detailed answers to their questions.

Liebe(r) ______________ ,

schöne Grüße aus Deutschland! Wie geht es dir? Mir geht's sehr gut, besonders jetzt, denn die Prüfungen sind vorbei. Ich bin gerade bei der Planung meines Arbeitsaufenthalts in England. Ich kann es kaum erwarten! Und du, du hast auch vor, in den Sommerferien eine Zeitlang im Ausland zu verbringen! Erzähl mir alles!

Danke für die Einladung nach Irland. Das werde ich am Ende des Sommers bestimmt machen. Was soll ich mitbringen? Was könnten wir alles tun, wenn ich rüberkomme?

Ich freue mich darauf im Ausland zu arbeiten. Denkst du, es ist wichtig, Auslandserfahrung zu sammeln?

Du hast auch geschrieben, dass du zu Ostern in Frankreich warst. Mit wem bist du dorthin gefahren? Wie war es? Wo war es? Wie war das Wetter? Würdest du es jedem empfehlen dahin zu fahren? Warum (nicht)? Jetzt mache ich Schluss. Schreib bald zurück!

Dein(e) Martin(a)

Prüfungstipp

Go to the marking schemes on the State Examinations Commission website to get a better understanding of how the letter is marked.

At Honours Level, the examiners are usually looking for 25 relevant sentences. Each relevant sentence or expansion will get a content mark. If you have answered every question and expanded on your answers, you will generally have full or near full content marks. Your expression mark is also out of 25. If your German is very average, you will probably get 10–12 marks.

It is a good idea to be aware of your personal weaknesses and then to edit your written work with these weaknesses in mind. The most serious mistakes are word order and verb ending mistakes.

Make a checklist of your top three recurring mistakes and work on them.

Übung Macht den Meister!

1. Translate the sentences below into English and identify the case of each underlined noun.
2. Identify the gender and/or number of the nouns by their endings or the ending of the indefinite articles, negative articles or possessive adjectives.

A Indefinite Articles

1. Ich brauche eine gute Note in Deutsch.	**6.** Ein Teenager küsst ein Mädchen.
2. Ein Schüler hat einen Zehn-Euro-Schein.	**7.** So ein Hut gehört normalerweise einem Kind.
3. Ein Mädchen liest ein Buch.	**8.** Ein Autor eines Buches schreibt eine Zusammenfassung.
4. Ein Fernseher kostet vierhundert Euro.	**9.** Er wünscht einem Nachbarn gute Nacht.
5. Ein Kind isst eine Birne.	**10.** Eine Zusammenfassung eines Texts kann einem Leser helfen.

B Negative Articles

1. Ich brauche keine gute Note.	**6.** Der Junge sagte kein einziges Wort.
2. Der Junge hat kein Geld.	**7.** Wir haben keine Garage.
3. Die Schule hat keine Kantine.	**8.** Sag es keinem Menschen!
4. Kein Kind wagte es ein Wort zu sagen.	**9.** Die Kinder sahen keinen Fehler im Text.
5. Es gibt heute keine Schule.	**10.** Ich habe leider kein Fahrrad.

C Possessive Adjectives

1. Meine Mutter hilft meiner Schwester.	**6.** Euer neues Haus sieht super aus im Vergleich zu eurem alten Haus.
2. Dein Bruder hat sein Geld gefunden.	**7.** Eure Schule ist kleiner als meine Schule.
3. Seine Schule hat seinen Erfolg gefeiert.	**8.** Ihr Vater (sing.) mag seinen neuen Wagen sehr.
4. Ihre Kinder (pl.) sagten ihrer Mutter (sing.), was los war.	**9.** Ihre Schüler (pl.) fanden das Thema seines neuen Films sehr interessant.
5. Unsere Stadt ist schön.	**10.** Meine Schwester mag die Farbe meines Kleides nicht.

D Mixed Articles

Insert the correct indefinite article, negative article or possessive adjective.

1. Ich suche _____ neues Buch (n).	*I'm looking for a new book.*
2. _____ Vater (m) spielt sehr gern Golf.	*My father really likes playing golf.*
3. Ich gebe _____________ Schwester (f) das Geld.	*I'm giving your* (sing.) *sister the money.*
4. Ich mag die Farbe _____________ Rocks (m).	*I like the colour of your skirt.*
5. _____ neues Mädchen (n) kommt in die Schule.	*A new girl is coming to school.*
6. Der Junge hat _____ Aufsatz (m) geschrieben.	*The boy wrote no essay.*
7. _____ Mensch (m) war zu sehen.	*No person was to be seen.*
8. _____ Eltern (pl.) sind in die Stadt gegangen.	*Our parents went into town.*
9. Ich habe _____ Onkel (m) _____ Karte (f) geschickt.	*I sent my uncle a card.*
10. Wann hast du _____ Pass (m) verloren?	*When did you lose your passport?*

Für die Prüfung

1. Was passt zusammen?

1. Der Schultag ist länger in Irland	**A** werde ich ins Ausland fahren.
2. Wenn ich Geld habe,	**B** um meine Sprachkenntnisse zu verbessern.
3. Ich will im Ausland arbeiten,	**C** habe ich einen Laptop.
4. Er will neue Leute kennenlernen	**D** als in Deutschland.
5. In meinem Zimmer	**E** aber er geht nie aus.

2. Was passt zusammen?

1. Wir fahren oft ins Ausland,	**A** aber ich möchte gern hinfahren.
2. Wenn ich viel Geld hätte,	**B** um mein Deutsch zu verbessern.
3. Ich möchte im Ausland studieren,	**C** als ich in Deutschland war.
4. Ich habe viel Deutsch gelernt,	**D** denn es macht Spaß.
5. Ich war noch nie in Deutschland,	**E** würde ich ins Ausland fahren.

3. Select the correct preposition for the following sentences.

a) Ich möchte gern **(ins/in die/in den/zur)** Ausland fahren.

b) Sie würde gerne **(zu/im/in/auf)** Ausland arbeiten.

c) Er ist **(mit/in/auf/an)** seinem Austauschpartner sehr gut ausgekommen.

d) Nach dem Abitur will ich **(mit/bei/in/durch)** meinen Freunden eine Abifahrt machen.

4. What words make up the following compound words, and what do they mean in English?

a) Auslandserfahrung = ______ + ______ = ______

b) zusammenarbeiten = ______ + ______ = ______

c) Abifahrt = ______ + ______ = ______

d) Schüleraustausch = ______ + ______ = ______

5. Choose the correct possessive adjective.

a) Thomas spielt in einer Rockgruppe. **(Seine/Sein/Ihr)** Instrument (n) ist das Schlagzeug.

b) Madonna ist Sängerin. **(Seine/Ihr/Ihre)** Stil (m) ist provokativ.

c) Klaus spielt Gitarre. Er mag **(sein/seine/seinen)** Gitarre (f).

d) Klaus und Maria sind Geschwister. **(Ihr/Ihre/Seine)** Eltern (pl.) sind verständnisvoll.

6. Indicate the following for the underlined nouns: 1) singular/plural, 2. the case, 3. the gender.

a) Mein Bruder hatte seine Brieftasche verloren.

b) Ihre Lehrer (sing.) zeigen den Kindern viel Respekt.

c) Ein Mann gab seinem Freund Geld.

d) Eine Frau überquerte die Straße.

e) Unsere Mutter sagte den Kindern nichts.

f) Meine Nachbarn halfen der alten Frau.

7. Lückentext: Fill in the blanks with the correct missing words from the box.

Abifahrt	**Spaß**	**Oktoberfest**	**werden**	**dem**
meinen	**besichtigen**	**Alpen**	**in**	**auch**

Nach **1** ________ Abitur will ich mit **2** ________ Freunden eine **3** ________ machen. Wir **4** ________ nach Deutschland zum **5** ________ fahren. Wir werden viel **6** ________ haben, besonders **7** ________ den großen Bierzelten! Wir werden **8** ________ die Sehenswürdigkeiten **9** ________ und in den **10** ________ wandern gehen.

Selbstbewertung: Ordinary Level

OL

Vocabulary

1. If I can translate these sentences into English, I can discuss going abroad. (1 mark each)

a) Ich will ins Ausland fahren.	**f)** Ich mag das Essen.
b) Wir sind nach Spanien gefahren.	**g)** Ich gehe gern schwimmen.
c) Wir haben in einem Hotel gewohnt.	**h)** Ich möchte Berlin besuchen.
d) Das Wetter war sonnig.	**i)** Ich möchte im Ausland studieren.
e) Wir gehen auf viele Partys.	**j)** Wir haben viel über Deutschland gelernt.

Your score: ___ / 10

2. If I can translate these nouns, I can describe being abroad. (1 mark each)

a) abroad	**c)** gallery	**e)** weather	**g)** beach	**i)** invitation
b) language	**d)** culture	**f)** exchange	**h)** sights	**j)** airport

Your score: ___ / 10

Grammar

3. If I can conjugate these verbs in the perfect tense, I can express myself in the past. (1 mark each)

a) fahren (to travel): ich bin gefahren; du ______ ______; er/sie/es ______ ______; wir ______ ______; ihr ______ ______; Sie/sie ______ ______

b) essen (to eat): ich habe gegessen; du ______ ______; er/sie/es ______ ______; wir ______ ______; ihr ______ ______; Sie/sie ______ ______

Your score: ___ / 10

4. If I can choose the correct possessive adjective, I understand the nominative case and the accusative case. (1 mark each)

a) (Mein/Meine) Vater heißt Mike.	**f)** Ich mag **(mein/meinen)** Vater.
b) (Mein/Meine) Mutter heißt Anne.	**g)** Ich mag **(meine/meinen)** Mutter.
c) (Mein/Meine) Bruder heißt Sean.	**h)** Ich mag **(mein/meinen)** Bruder.
d) (Mein/Meine) Schwester heißt Rose.	**i)** Ich mag **(meine/meinen)** Schwester.
e) (Mein/Meine) Geschwister heißen Tom und Sharon.	**j)** Ich mag **(meine/meinen)** Geschwister.

Your score: ___ / 10

5. If I can choose the correct preposition, I can describe being abroad. (1 mark each)

a) Ich möchte **(in/um/zu/nach)** Deutschland fahren.
b) Ich interessiere mich sehr **(in/für/an/mit)** die deutsche Kultur.
c) Ich freue mich **(an/um/auf/in)** einen Aufenthalt in Berlin.
d) Ich möchte **(um/im/am/zum)** Ausland studieren.
e) Ich kann **(für/um/am/in)** zwei Wochen bleiben.
f) **(Um/Im/Am/Vom)** Sommer fliegen wir nach Spanien.
g) Jeden Abend gehen wir **(im/ins/an/ans)** Restaurant.
h) Später gehen wir **(an/in/auf/von)** die Disco.
i) Wir lernen in der Schule viel **(über/an/von/für)** Deutschland.
j) Ich will **(zu/mit/für/an)** zwei Freunden nach Portugal fahren.

Your score: ___ / 10

What have I learned?	
What must I improve?	
What do I want to revise?	

Your total score: ___ / 50

Selbstbewertung: Higher Level

HL

1. If I can identify the gender of these nouns and translate them, I can express myself accurately when talking about being abroad. (1 mark each)

a) Erfahrung	**c)** Ausland	**e)** Kultur	**g)** Sommerkurs	**i)** Ausflug
b) Abifahrt	**d)** Austausch	**f)** Übersetzung	**h)** Umgangssprache	**j)** Urlaub

Your score: ___ / 10

2. If I can turn these nouns into the plural form, I can express myself accurately when talking about things I do/did abroad. (1 mark each)

a) Ausflug	**c)** Austausch	**e)** Aufenthalt	**g)** Kultur	**i)** Sprache
b) Brauch	**d)** Sehenswürdigkeit	**f)** Mensch	**h)** Tradition	**j)** Unterkunft

Your score: ___ / 10

3. If I can identify the gender and case, I understand indefinite articles and possessive adjectives. (1 mark each)

a) Der Wagen <u>seines Vaters</u> ist sehr groß.	**f)** Das Haus <u>unserer Nachbarn</u> ist sehr schön.
b) <u>Mein Vater</u> ist sehr großzügig.	**g)** Die Frau macht mit <u>ihrem Kind</u> einen Spaziergang.
c) Ich möchte <u>einen Austausch</u> machen.	**h)** <u>Deine Eltern</u> wohnen in Spanien.
d) Meine Schwester wäscht <u>ihr Auto</u>.	**i)** Ich liebe <u>meine Katze</u>.
e) Meine Oma wohnt bei <u>meinem Onkel</u>.	**j)** <u>Meine Mutter</u> ist verständnisvoll.

Your score: ___ / 10

4. If I can correctly fill in the gaps below, I understand the difference between indefinite articles and possessive adjectives. (1 mark each)

meines ein unser meiner einen
einer meine einen mein meine

Ich habe letztes Jahr mit **1** _____ Klasse **2** _____ Schülerautausch gemacht. **3** _____ Lehrer hat den Austausch organisiert. **4** _____ besten Freunde haben alle den Austausch gemacht. Wir haben auch **5** _____ Tagesausflug in die Alpen gemacht. Ich habe **6** _____ Deutsch verbessert und **7** _____ Aussprache ist jetzt viel besser. Ich habe bei **8** _____ sehr netten Familie gewohnt. Das war die beste Erfahrung **9** _____ Lebens! **10** _____ Austausch lohnt sich ganz bestimmt.

Your score: ___ / 10

5. If I can translate these sentences into German, I understand the various cases of the indefinite article, the negative article and possessive adjectives. (2 marks each)

a) A man was eating an apple.	**d)** His sister did not drink a Coke.
b) A woman bought my car.	**e)** A boy sold his books to another pupil.
c) Her brother ate her sandwiches.	

Your score: ___ / 10

What have I learned?	
What must I improve?	
What do I want to revise?	

Your total score: ___ / 50

07

Zukunftspläne

Learning Outcomes

- **Oral:** describing future plans
- **Reading:** reading and discussing three texts about future plans
- **Writing:** writing one's opinion (**Äußerung**), describing a picture and writing a letter about future plans
- **Aural:** listening to and answering questions on four extracts about the future

Grammar

- Definite articles and demonstratives
- Accusative and dative prepositions
- Two-way and genitive prepositions

Vocabulary

- Study courses and career goals
- Making decisions
- Celebrating after the Leaving Certificate

German Culture

- **Numerus Clausus** and **BAföG**
- Impact of the German school system on career choices

Exam Tips

- Often a question will have more than one part. Highlight each part of the question and answer each part fully.
- When answering Higher Level Reading Comprehension 1 Question 4, you will need **three to four** examples to support your answer. Answer as precisely as possible in English. If you quote a German example, translate it into English.

Mündliche Arbeit: Ihre Zukunftspläne

Stellen Sie sich gegenseitig alle Fragen. Schreiben Sie sie auf.

Beschreiben Sie das Foto!

Wo sind die Schüler?

Was machen sie hier?

Waren Sie schon mal bei einem Tag der offenen Tür?

War es ein erfolgreicher Tag?

1. Was wollen Sie nächstes Jahr machen? *What do you want to do next year?*	
Ich möchte an der Universität in Limerick studieren. Ich will Wissenschaften studieren.	*I would like to study at the university in Limerick. I want to study Sciences.*
Ich hoffe, Jura zu studieren. Dafür brauche ich viele Punkte. Ich bin nicht sicher, ob ich das erreichen kann.	*I hope to study Law. I need a lot of points for that. I'm not sure if I can make it.*
Ich möchte Friseurin werden. Ich mache einen Kurs in Cork. Der Kurs dauert zwei Jahre.	*I would like to be a hairdresser. I'm doing a course in Cork. The course lasts two years.*
Wenn ich meine erste Wahl nicht schaffe, werde ich meine zweite Wahl machen.	*If I don't get my first choice, I will do my second choice.*
Ich will unbedingt Krankengymnastik studieren. Also, wenn ich nicht genug Punkte bekomme, werde ich das Abitur wiederholen.	*I definitely want to study physiotherapy. So, if I don't get enough points, I will repeat the Leaving Cert.*
Ich habe keine Ahnung, was ich nächstes Jahr machen werde.	*I have no idea what I will do next year.*
Ich will Geschäftsmann(frau)/Zahnarzt(ärztin)/Anwalt (Anwältin)/Kindergärtner(in) werden.	*I want to be a businessman/businesswoman/dentist/lawyer/nursery school teacher.*
Ich werde eine Lehre machen.	*I'll do an apprenticeship.*
Ich weiß nicht, was die Zukunft bringt.	*I don't know what the future holds.*
Das Abitur ist kein Zuckerschlecken, aber hoffentlich wird sich die Arbeit lohnen.	*The Leaving Cert is no joke, but hopefully the work will be worth it.*

2. Warum haben Sie diesen Kurs gewählt? *Why did you choose this course?*	
Ich möchte Lehrer(in) werden, denn ich komme gut mit Kindern aus. Dieser Kurs dauert vier Jahre und ich werde von Zuhause wegziehen müssen.	*I would like to be a teacher because I get on well with children. This course lasts for four years and I will have to move away from home.*
Ich habe vor, Medizin zu studieren, denn ich will Menschen helfen.	*I intend to study Medicine because I want to help people.*
Ich habe mich für diesen Kurs entschieden, denn ich interessiere mich wahnsinnig für Sprachen/Wissenschaft/Kunst.	*I decided on this course because I'm really interested in languages/science/art.*
Ich werde Informatik studieren. Die Technik erweitert sich von Tag zu Tag und gute Informatiker sind immer zu gebrauchen.	*I'm going to study IT. Technology is expanding from one day to the next and good computer people will always be needed.*
Es war schwierig, eine Entscheidung zu treffen.	*It was difficult to make a decision.*

Ich werde nach Dublin umziehen. Ich werde hoffentlich ein Haus mit Freunden teilen.	*I will move to Dublin. I will hopefully share a house with friends.*
Ich bin für so einen Beruf geeignet, denn ich bin geschickt im Umgang mit Menschen.	*I'm suitable for such a job because I'm good at dealing with people.*
Ich habe diesen Kurs gewählt, denn mit einem Abschluss als Diplom-Kauffrau bekomme ich sicher eine gute Stelle.	*I chose this course because I'll certainly get a good job with a business degree.*
Jeder möchte Arzt oder Anwalt sein, und niemand will noch als Klempner arbeiten.	*Everyone wants to be a doctor or a lawyer, and no one wants to work as a plumber any more.*

3. Was suchen Sie bei der Arbeit? *What are you looking for in your work?*	
Ich suche Sicherheit bei der Arbeit.	*I'm looking for security in work.*
Ich suche Abwechslung und Aufstiegsmöglichkeiten.	*I'm looking for variety and opportunities for promotion.*
Geld ist nicht das Wichtigste im Leben.	*Money is not the most important thing in life.*
Ich freue mich auf die Zukunft.	*I'm looking forward to the future.*
Jeder braucht einen erfüllenden Beruf.	*Everyone needs a fulfilling career.*
Ich suche eine Arbeit, die mir Spaß macht.	*I'm looking for a job which is fun.*
Wähle einen Beruf, den du liebst, und du brauchst keinen Tag in deinem Leben mehr zu arbeiten, wie der Spruch lautet.	*Choose a job that you love and you will never need to work a day in your life, as the saying goes.*
Ich möchte einen Beruf in Richtung Elektronik ergreifen, denn ich interessiere mich wahnsinnig dafür.	*I would like to go for a career in electronics because I'm really interested in it.*
Ich suche Arbeit, die Eigeninitiative erfordert.	*I'm looking for work which requires individual initiative.*

4. Wollen Sie eine Abifahrt machen? *Do you want to go on a trip after the Leaving Certificate?*	
Ich habe vor, mit Freunden nach Spanien zu fahren. Wir werden für eine Woche in einem Hotel wohnen.	*I intend to go to Spain with friends. We will stay in a hotel for a week.*
Nach dem Prüfungsstress muss man sich entspannen.	*After the stress of exams, you have to relax.*
Meine Freunde und ich sind feierwütig. Wir werden ganz einfach die Nacht zum Tag machen.	*My friends and I are party people. We will simply turn night into day.*
Bevor der Ernst des Lebens richtig beginnt, muss erstmal richtig gefeiert werden.	*Before the serious side of life really goes ahead, you first have to celebrate properly.*
Tagsüber werde ich mich am Strand sonnen. Abends gehen wir dann in die Disco und tanzen bis spät in die Nacht.	*During the day I'll sunbathe on the beach. Then in the evenings we will go to a disco and dance late into the night.*
Ich mache keine Abifahrt, denn ich muss mein Geld für die Uni sparen.	*I'm not going on a trip after the Leaving Cert because I need to save my money for university.*
Abends machen wir uns richtig locker.	*In the evenings we'll really let loose.*

Prüfungstipp

The oral exam is worth 100 marks and is broken down into three parts. It lasts 15 to 20 minutes. Part 1 is the general conversation, or **das Allgemeine Gespräch**. Part 1 is worth **40** marks out of 100 and will last between 4–7 minutes. You will be asked to talk about:

- You and your family
- Hobbies
- Learning German
- Future plans
- Where you live
- School
- Going abroad

Revise chapters 1–7 covering these topics to effectively prepare for your oral exam.

Text 1: Zukunftspläne von Jugendlichen

Bitte beantworten Sie die folgenden Fragen:

1. Was machen die Schüler?
2. Wo sind sie?
3. Was für Kleidung tragen sie?
4. Wie sehen die Schüler aus?

Vorarbeit

1. Finden Sie diese Ausdrücke im Text!
   - **A** I've thought about my future.
   - **B** I would have no interest in that.
   - **C** Furthermore, I like the people there.
   - **D** That was different for my mother.
   - **E** It worked for me.
2. Finden Sie das Deutsche für die Wörter unten!
   - **A** to look/to research/in any case
   - **B** grew into/agriculture/qualified
   - **C** grant/restricted places/finished/more open
   - **D** uncertain/busy/guidance counsellor
   - **E** attracts/mechatronics/design

Ruth Asan, *die taz*, 22 June 2014 (amended)

A Frieda Jäger, 17 Jahre, besucht die 11. Klasse eines Gymnasiums in Halle an der Saale: Natürlich habe ich mir schon Gedanken über meine Zukunft gemacht. Ich mache bald Abitur. Danach möchte ich auf jeden Fall studieren. Am liebsten würde ich später forschen, ich sehe mich im Labor stehen und durch Mikroskope gucken. Deswegen will ich etwas in Richtung Biologie studieren.

B Ich kann mir aber auch vorstellen, in die Landwirtschaft zu gehen, wie mein Vater. Das hat ja auch mit Biologie zu tun. Meine Eltern haben beide nicht studiert. Mein Vater ist in seiner Familie in die Landwirtschaft hereingewachsen, meine Mutter ist gelernte Friseurin. Das war damals ein guter Beruf. Heute arbeitet sie in der Chemiebranche. Da macht sie aber jeden Tag dasselbe, darauf hätte ich keine Lust.

C Meine Eltern unterstützen mich in meiner Entscheidung zu studieren. Ich soll aber auf jeden Fall etwas machen, womit man einen Job bekommt. Aber ich weiß ja auch nicht, wie der Arbeitsmarkt sein wird, wenn ich fertig mit dem Studium bin. Das weiß man ja nie. Es gibt viele Studienfächer, für die man heute extrem gute Noten braucht. Ärztin könnte ich wohl nicht werden. Aber ich will sowieso in Holland studieren, da gibt es keinen Numerus Clausus. Dort würde ich auch BAföG bekommen, in Deutschland nicht, weil meine Eltern zu viel verdienen. Außerdem gefallen mir die Menschen dort, die sind viel offener.

D Anna Cirtautas hat gerade ihr Abitur an einem Gymnasium gemacht: Wenn man ambitiös ist, kann man heute immer etwas finden. Da bin ich optimistisch. Bei meiner Mutter war das anders. Sie hatte eine unsichere Zukunft vor sich und konnte nicht das studieren, was sie wollte. Mein Vater konnte gar nicht studieren, weil sie so früh ein Kind bekommen haben. Seit der Oberstufe beschäftige ich mich intensiv mit meiner Zukunft. Meine Mutter ist Berufsberaterin für Abiturienten, sie informiert mich darüber.

E Ich habe in den letzten Jahren an vielen Workshops zur Berufsorientierung teilgenommen. Bei mir hat es funktioniert: Ich will Mechatronik studieren. Danach will ich Entwicklungsingenieurin werden. An dem Beruf reizt mich, dass man kreativ sein und viel reisen kann.

OL Ordinary Level Questions

1. **a)** What can Frieda see herself doing in future? A
   b) In what fields do her parents work? B
   c) Where does Frieda want to study and why? Give **two** reasons. C
   d) Why is Anna optimistic about the future? D
   e) Why is Anna excited about a career as a design engineer? Give **two** details. E
2. True or false?
   a) Frieda hat schon das Abitur gemacht.
   b) Frieda interessiert sich für Biologie.
   c) Frieda könnte Ärztin werden.
   d) Anna glaubt nicht, dass sie etwas finden wird.
   e) Anna weiß genau, was sie studieren will.
3. What words make up the following compounds, and what do they mean in English?
   a) Landwirtschaft = ______ + ______ = ______
   b) Chemiebranche = ______ + ______ = ______
   c) Arbeitsmarkt = ______ + ______ = ______
   d) Studienfächer = ______ + ______ = ______
4. Select the correct prepositions for the following sentences.
   a) Ich mache mir Gedanken **(von/für/über/an)** die Zukunft.
   b) Ich habe keine Lust **(an/auf/mir/für)** einen langweiligen Beruf.
   c) Man braucht gute Noten **(für/um/bei/zu)** viele Kurse.
   d) Ich werde mein Abitur **(in/an/am/zu)** einem Gymnasium machen.

HL Higher Level Questions

1. Beantworten Sie folgende Fragen auf Deutsch!
   a) Was für Zukunftspläne hat Frieda? Geben Sie mehrere Details! A
   b) Was machen ihre Eltern beruflich, und was hat ihre Mutter beruflich gemacht? B
   c) Was für ein Studium will Frieda machen? Wo will sie studieren, und warum? (**3** Details!) C
   d) i) Warum konnte Annas Vater nicht studieren? D
   ii) Wie bekommt Anna Informationen über Berufsmöglichkeiten? D
   e) Warum will Anna Mechatronik studieren? E
2. Answer the following questions in English.
   a) What does Frieda want to study and why? A
   b) Why doesn't Frieda want to follow her mother into the chemical industry? B
   c) i) What unknown does Frieda face when deciding on a course of studies? C
   ii) Why would she not get a grant in Germany? C
   d) How were things different for Anna's parents? D
   e) What has Anna done over the last few years? E
3. Was passt zusammen?

1. Frieda macht sich Gedanken über die Zukunft,	**A** weil sie die holländischen Menschen mag.
2. Frieda hat keine Lust,	**B** wo man kreativ sein und viel reisen kann.
3. Frieda will in Holland studieren,	**C** dass sie etwas finden wird.
4. Anna ist optimistisch,	**D** denn sie macht bald das Abitur.
5. Anna sucht einen Beruf,	**E** in der Chemiebranche zu arbeiten.

4. Geben Sie für die folgenden Nomen, ob Singular oder Plural, das Geschlecht und den Fall.
   a) Ich mache mir Gedanken über meine Zukunft.
   b) Danach möchte ich auf jeden Fall studieren.
   c) Darauf hätte ich keine Lust.
   d) Meine Eltern unterstützen mich.
   e) In Holland gibt es keinen Numerus Clausus.
   f) Anna hat ihr Abitur gemacht.

Grammatik: Die Fälle/The Cases

p. 141 (Übung macht den Meister)

1. Nominative case: The noun is doing the action.
2. Accusative case: The action is being done to the noun.
3. Dative case: The noun is indirectly involved and conveys the meaning 'to', 'with', 'from'.
4. Genitive case: The noun either has 'of ' directly before it or an 's after it in English.

Decide the cases of the underlined nouns below. Then translate the sentences into English.

1. Die Frau trinkt den Tee.	**5.** Der Teddy gehört dem Mädchen.
2. Das Kind isst das Brötchen.	**6.** Die Lehrerin gibt der Schülerin eine Eins.
3. Der Schüler schreibt den Aufsatz.	**7.** Die Mutter nimmt dem Kind das Buch weg.
4. Der Lastwagen überfährt den Hund.	**8.** Der Junge findet den Standort des Buches.

Definite Articles

The following table shows the effect of the cases on the definite article 'the' in front of a masculine, feminine, neuter or plural noun.

Case	Masculine: Mann	Feminine: Frau	Neuter: Kind	Plural: Männer, Frauen, Kinder
Nominative	der	die	das	die
Accusative	den	die	das	die
Dative	dem	der	dem	den
Genitive	des	der	des	der

Decide the case of each noun and fill in the correct form of the definite article 'the', using the table above as your guideline. Then translate the sentences into English.

1. ___ Junge (m) isst ___ Banane (f).	**5.** ___ Frau (f) braucht ___ Geld (n).
2. ___ Kind (n) kauft ___ Buch (n).	**6.** Die Farbe ___ Pullovers (m) ist schön.
3. ___ Tante (f) sieht ___ DVD (f) an.	**7.** Das ist das Fahrrad ___ Mannes (m).
4. ___ Mann (m) liest ___ Zeitschrift (f).	**8.** Thomas gibt ___ Frau (f) das Geschenk.

Demonstratives

Demonstratives – **dieser** (this or these), **jener** (that or those), **jeder** (each, every) and **welcher** (which) – follow the same pattern as the definite article ('the'):

Name	Masculine: Mann	Feminine: Frau	Neuter: Kind	Plural: Männer, Frauen, Kinder
Nominative	dieser	diese	dieses	diese
Accusative	diesen	diese	dieses	diese
Dative	diesem	dieser	diesem	diesen
Genitive	dieses	dieser	dieses	dieser

Hausaufgaben

In your copy fill in the chart for **jeder, jener** and **welcher**. Practise the case endings for demonstratives by taking sentences 1–8 from the exercise above and replacing the definite articles (the) with the demonstratives (this/that/every). They take the same endings for each case.

07.01 Hörverständnis Teil 1

Vorarbeit

sich engagieren für	*to be involved in*	**Entwicklungsländer**	*developing countries*	**Holz**	*wood*
reichlich	*copious*	**Spiegel**	*mirror*	**Zugang**	*access*
Sonnenstrahl	*sunray*	**Solarkocher**	*solar cooker*	**bauen**	*to build*
Kohlendioxid	*carbon dioxide*	**Einheimische**	*local people*	**zeigen**	*to show*

CL Ordinary + Higher Level Questions

1. How long has the vocational school been involved in helping the developing countries?
2. Why is solar energy an effective alternative? Give **two (O)/four (H)** details.
3. **a)** Describe the solar cooker. Give **one (O)/two (H)** details.
   b) Give **two (O)/four (H)** advantages of the solar cooker.
4. How do the workshops function? Give **two (O)/four (H)** details.

07.02 Hörverständnis Teil 2

Vorarbeit

schulden	*to owe*	**bedanken**	*to thank*	**versprechen**	*to promise*
Muskelkrampf	*muscle cramp*	**passieren**	*to happen*	**ertrinken**	*to drown*
retten	*to save*	**reagieren**	*to react*	**verdanken**	*to owe*
Rettungsschwimmer	*lifeguard*	**verbunden**	*appreciative*	**erreichen**	*to reach*

OL Ordinary Level Questions

1. Describe the young man whom the caller is looking for. Give **two** details.
2. What word best describes the caller's emotions?
   a) annoyed ☐ **b)** grateful ☐ **c)** happy ☐ **d)** confused ☐
3. What is the name and phone number of the caller?
4. The phone call is to: **a)** a school ☐ **b)** a police station ☐ **c)** a hospital ☐ **d)** a bank ☐

HL Higher Level Questions

1. Write down **in German** the key information:
   - the name of the **caller**
   - the reason for the call
   - details regarding the outcome
   - the caller's phone number

Gesprächsnotiz
Anruf von: ____________________ Gesprächsanlass: ____________________
Der Anrufer:
- wird morgen wieder telefonieren ☐
- wird morgen zurückgerufen ☐
- wird sobald wie möglich kontaktiert ☐
- wird von der Polizei gesucht ☐

Kontaktnummer: *Vorwahl* ____________ *Rufnummer* ____________________

2. Write down **three** examples of the language used which show that the caller is **grateful**.

Text 2: Wer bin ich, was kann ich?

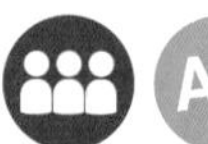 Bitte beantworten Sie die folgenden Fragen:

- Wo sind die Studenten?
- Was machen sie hier?
- Würden Sie gern auf die Uni gehen? Warum/warum nicht?

Vorarbeit

1. Finden Sie diese Ausdrücke im Text!
   - **A** ... many young people break into a rash.
   - **B** ... most lack knowledge about themselves.
   - **C** Nothing occurs to me.
   - **D** ... who is growing up without a father ...
   - **E** ... but at the moment that doesn't look good.
   - **F** ... one must use one's capabilities.
2. Finden Sie das Deutsche für die Wörter unten!
   - **A** employment agency/career advice
   - **B** to deny/encourage/decide
   - **C** over-stretched/average/independent
   - **D** to broaden/task/someone
   - **E** forklifts/minimum requirement/cleaner
   - **F** skills/to choose/feeling for language

A Na, was willst du später machen? Die Frage sorgt bei vielen Jugendlichen für Ausschlag – sie wissen es nicht. Die Kunden dieser Arbeitsagentur, das sind meist Menschen im Alter von 16 bis 25, mit Abitur. Das sind junge Menschen, die nicht wissen, was sie als Beruf ausüben möchten. Die Karriereberatung kostet 1.500 Euro, inklusive Nachfragen in den ersten zwölf Monaten danach.

B Ob Hauptschüler oder Abiturient, wenn sich Jugendliche für einen Beruf entscheiden, fehlt den meisten Wissen über sich selbst. Es fällt jedem Zweiten die Berufswahl schwer. Was kann ich überhaupt? Professionelle Beratungen versuchen, diese Frage zu klären. Niemand kann aber leugnen, dass das Elternhaus und die Schulform für die Zukunft von Schülern zählen – mehr als Noten, Interessen oder Talente. Eltern informieren Kinder über mögliche Berufe und fördern Talente.

C Mara, 17, hübsch, groß, ein Lächeln wie ein Model, enge Jeans zu weißer Strickjacke, weiß nicht, was sie mal machen oder wie sie leben will. „Mir fällt gar nichts ein", sagt sie. In der Schule ist Mara entweder gelangweilt oder überfordert, sie mag Geschichte, Deutsch, Theater und Sport. Ihre Hausaufgaben macht Mara, wenn sie Zeit hat, ihre Noten sind durchschnittlich, ihre Freizeit verbringt sie mit Sport, Lesen und Entspannen. Ihre Eltern erhoffen, dass sie einen Job findet, der ihr ein unabhängiges Leben ermöglicht.

D Djawad, 14, ein Junge, der ohne Vater aufwächst, wird nächsten Sommer die Schule beenden. Er möchte gern Arzt oder Pilot werden. Noch nie hat ihm jemand gesagt, dass das mit einem Hauptschulabschluss nicht möglich ist. Mit seiner Mutter, die in einer Parfümerie arbeitet, hat er noch nie über Berufsthemen gesprochen. Laut der Agentur, „Viele Kinder kennen die Berufswelt nur aus dem Fernsehen. Unsere Aufgabe ist den Horizont zu erweitern."

E Diren, 13, ist ein selbstbewusster Junge mit türkischem Hintergrund. Doch seine Schulnoten sind schlecht. Direns Eltern arbeiten viel, die Mutter als Reinigungskraft, der Vater fährt Gabelstapler. Er träumt davon, als Profifußballer Geld zu verdienen, alternativ könnte er sich Autoverkäufer vorstellen. Ein Realschulabschluss wäre dafür die Mindestvoraussetzung, doch momentan sieht es dafür nicht gut aus.

F Um die richtige Karriere zu wählen, muss man seine Potenziale ausnutzen. Wo diese liegen, soll man durch Persönlichkeitstests herausfinden. Diese Tests informieren über Temperament und Fähigkeiten in Mathe, logischem Denken und seinem Sprachgefühl. Man sollte auch mit einem Berufsberater ein Interview machen. Auch sind die Schulnoten wichtig.

Lena Greiner & Carola Padtberg, *Spiegel Online*, 14 Jan. 2015 (amended)

OL Ordinary Level Questions

1. a) Give **two** details about the customers of the employment agency. A
   b) According to the text, how many young people find it difficult to make a career choice? B
   c) What kind of a student is Mara? Give **three** details. C
   d) Djawad wants to be a doctor or pilot. Why will this not be possible? D
   e) Why is Diren not likely to fulfil his dreams? E
   f) According to the text, what should one do in order to choose the right career? F
2. Fill in the information required.

	Family background	What kind of student?	Career dreams
Mara			
Djawad			
Diren			

3. Select the correct prepositions for the following sentences.
   a) Viele junge Leute wissen nicht, was sie **(an/für/in/zu)** Zukunft beruflich machen wollen.
   b) Viele Jugendliche haben nicht genug Wissen **(an/über/durch/für)** sich selbst.
   c) Mara verbringt ihre Freizeit **(mit/an/in/bei)** Entspannen, Lesen und Sport.
   d) Manche Jugendliche kennen die Berufswelt nur **(im/am/auf/aus)** dem Fernsehen.
   e) Man kann seine Potenziale **(durch/mit/aus/an)** Persönlichkeitstests herausfinden.

HL Higher Level Questions

1. Beantworten Sie folgende Fragen auf Deutsch!
   a) Welche Frage ist für viele Jugendliche schwierig zu beantworten? A
   b) Was zählen am meisten für die Zukunft von Schülern? B
   c) Wie ist Mara in der Schule? Geben Sie **drei** Details! C
   d) Warum kann Djawad nicht Arzt oder Pilot werden? D
   e) Was machen Direns Eltern beruflich? Was will Diren selber beruflich machen? E
   f) Wie hilft ein Persönlichkeitstest, um die Berufswahl zu machen? F
2. Answer the following questions in English.
   a) How much does the career advice cost, and what is included in this price? A
   b) What are the strongest influences on a child's future? How do parents influence their children, according to the text? B
   c) What do Mara's parents hope for her? C
   d) What does the agency see as its task? D
   e) Why are Diren's professional dreams unrealistic? E
   f) Name **three** ways of refining a career choice, according to the text. F
3. Aus welchen Wörtern bestehen die folgenden Wörter? Was bedeuten sie auf Englisch?
   a) Elternhaus = _____ + _____ = _____
   b) Nachfragen = _____ + _____ = _____
   c) Berufswahl = _____ + _____ = _____
   d) aufwachsen = _____ + _____ = _____
   e) Autoverkäufer = _____ + _____ = _____
   f) Persönlichkeitstests = _____ + _____ = _____
4. Geben Sie für die Nomen an: ob Singular oder Plural, das Geschlecht und den Fall.
   a) Die Karriereberatung kostet 1.500 Euro.
   b) Jugendliche entscheiden sich für einen Beruf.
   c) Ihre Freizeit verbringt sie mit Sport.
   d) Kinder kennen die Welt aus dem Fernsehen.
   e) Seine Schulnoten sind schlecht.
   f) Man sollte ein Interview machen.

OL Äußerung zum Thema: Ordinary Level

You are interviewing Mara. Complete Mara's dialogue based on the information in Text 2.

Sie: Wie alt sind Sie?
Mara: ______________________
Sie: Wissen Sie schon, was Sie nach der Schulzeit machen wollen?
Mara: ______________________
Sie: Wie finden Sie die Schule?
Mara: ______________________
Sie: Wie sind Ihre Schulnoten?
Mara: ______________________
Sie: Was machen Sie gern in Ihrer Freizeit?
Mara: ______________________

HL Äußerung zum Thema: Higher Level

Write 13 to 15 sentences, answering the questions below.

- Beschreiben Sie das Foto rechts in **drei bis vier** Sätzen.
- Warum ist es schwierig, Ihrer Meinung nach, einen Studiengang oder einen Beruf zu wählen?
- Wie informiert man sich am besten über die Berufswahl?
- Was wollen Sie nach dem Abitur machen? Warum haben Sie sich dafür entschieden?

Nützliche Sätze

Heutzutage hat man wirklich die Qual der Wahl!	*Nowadays one is really spoiled for choice.*
Oft hat man Missverständnisse über bestimmte Berufe.	*Often one has misconceptions about particular careers.*
Nur eine Minderheit von Jugendlichen weiß genau, was sie machen will.	*Only a minority of young people know exactly what they want to do.*
Das Internet ist eine gute Informationsquelle.	*The internet is a good source of information.*
Man soll sich auf jeden Fall mit einem Berufsberater treffen, um nützliche Ratschläge zu kriegen.	*One should definitely meet with a guidance counsellor in order to get useful advice.*
Ich glaube, dass der Tag der offenen Tür eine tolle Idee ist. Da bekommst du einen besseren Überblick über die verschiedenen Kurse.	*I believe that Open Days are a brilliant idea. There you get a better overview of the different courses.*
Natürlich muss man seine Interessen und Stärken kennen.	*Of course, you have to know your interests and strengths.*
Je mehr du dich über den Wunschberuf informierst, desto besser.	*The more you inform yourself about your desired profession, the better.*

Kulturecke

Germany is seen as an attractive country for people who want to study abroad. Around 150 universities offer courses and degrees completely in English. There are also no tuition fees. While some universities are considering introducing tuition fees for international students, these fees will be low in comparison to other countries. At the moment graduate unemployment in Germany is the lowest in Europe.

Grammatik: Präpositionen/Prepositions

p. 141 (Übung macht den Meister)

Prepositions are words showing the relationship between nouns or pronouns: Is the dog **on** the table, **under** the table or **behind** the table? In German, prepositions affect the case of the noun or pronoun.

Accusative Prepositions

When you use the following prepositions, the noun or pronoun will always be in the accusative case.

bis until	**entlang** along	**gegen** against	**um** at, around, for
durch through	**für** for	**ohne** without	**wider** anti, against

Ich interessiere mich sehr für *die* **Umwelt.** (accusative, feminine)

1. Insert the correct indefinite article for the following sentences. Then translate the sentences.

a) Der Junge lief durch _____ Wald (m).	**e)** Er geht _____ Weg (m) entlang.
b) Ich bleibe für _____ Monat (m) hier.	**f)** Er wirft den Ball gegen _____ Wand (f).
c) Ich bitte um _____ Entschuldigung (f).	**g)** Die Kinder laufen durch _____ Spielplatz (m).
d) Ohne _____ Erlaubnis (f) sind Handys verboten.	**h)** Er bleibt bis _____ Wochenende (n).

2. Insert the correct definite article for the following sentences. Then translate the sentences.

a) Am Wochenende gehe ich _____ Fluss (m) entlang.	**e)** Die Eltern kümmern sich um _____ kranke Kind (n).
b) Ohne _____ Geld (n) kann ich nicht mitmachen.	**f)** Wir sind gegen _____ Krieg (m).
c) Vielen Dank für _____ Geschenk (n)!	**g)** Ich ging ohne _____ Buch (n) in die Schule.
d) Wir fahren immer durch _____ Stadt (f).	**h)** Wir machen die Prüfung wider _____ Willen (m) der Direktorin.

Dative Prepositions

When you use the following prepositions, the noun or pronoun will always be in the dative case.

aus out of, from	**bei** at, with	**mit** with	**seit** since	**zu** to
außer except, apart from	**gegenüber** opposite	**nach** to, after	**von** from, of	

Ich muss zu *dem* **Zahnarzt** (dative, masculine) **gehen.**

Note that **bei dem** may contract to **beim** and **zu dem/zu der** may contract to **zum/zur**.

1. Insert the correct indefinite article for the following sentences. Then translate the sentences.

a) Ich wohne bei _____ Freund (m).	**e)** Ich sehne mich nach _____ Urlaub (m).
b) Ich bin seit _____ Woche (f) krank.	**f)** Wir gehen zu _____ Party (f).
c) Mark kommt aus _____ fremden Land (n).	**g)** Sie erzählt uns von _____ Abenteuer (n).
d) Er geht mit _____ Rucksack (m) in Urlaub.	**h)** Der Junge strebt nach _____ guten Abitur (n).

2. Insert the correct definite article. Then translate the sentences.

a) Ich rede gern mit _____ Kind (n).	**e)** Die Schule liegt _____ Kirche (f) gegenüber.
b) Mein Vater arbeitet bei _____ Bank (f).	**f)** Der Direktor telefoniert mit _____ Mutter (f).
c) Ich sehne mich nach _____ Sommer (m).	**g)** Das Mädchen kommt aus _____ Türkei (f).
d) Hast du dich von _____ Grippe (f) erholt?	**h)** Ich gehe jeden Tag zu _____ Spielplatz (m).

Prüfungstipp

Revise all aspects of the course. Use past papers and the marking schemes.

Text 3: Der Weg vorwärts

Bitte beantworten Sie die folgenden Fragen:

1. Wen sieht man auf dem Bild?
2. Was machen die Schüler hier?
3. Ist eine Karrieremesse eine gute Idee?

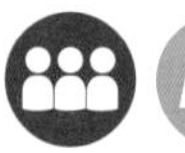 

Vorarbeit

1. Finden Sie diese Ausdrücke im Text!
   - **A** The whole class was talking about ...
   - **B** He was also our guidance counsellor.
   - **C** ... I was doing my homework diligently.
   - **D** ... firms, colleges and universities ...
   - **E** Everything was going very well.
2. Finden Sie das Deutsche für die Wörter unten!
   - **A** holidays/girlfriend/classmates/tanned
   - **B** Leaving Certificate students/career fair/involved
   - **C** gave up/H1s/prospects/made an effort/class tests
   - **D** representatives/rainy/distributed
   - **E** proceeded/sounded/relieved/talks

A Die ganze Klasse berichtete von ihren schönen Ferien. Manche waren in Spanien oder an der Nordseeküste gewesen. Andere waren sogar nach Griechenland gefahren. Sie waren alle froh und braungebrannt. Ich war nicht braun, wie die anderen Mädchen, denn ich war leider nur für ein paar Tage weggefahren. Einer meiner Klassenkameraden, Markus, hatte eine neue Freundin. Wir hatten dieselben Lehrer in allen Fächern.

B In Englisch und Erdkunde hatten wir wieder Herrn Becker und ich freute mich, denn er war einer der nettesten Lehrer an der Schule, und sicher einer der besten. Er war auch unser Berufsberater und hatte sich mit dem Schulblog beschäftigt. Dieses Jahr wollte er alle Abiturienten zur größten Karrieremesse im Bundesland bringen. Unser Blog handelte von diesem künftigen Besuch.

C Ich fühlte mich wohl, denn es ging mir prima. Ich schrieb meine ersten paar Klassenarbeiten und machte fleißig meine Hausaufgaben. Ich bekam schon einige Einser, was mich sehr motiviert hat. Um mich auf das Lernen in der Schule zu konzentrieren, gab ich meinen Job im örtlichen Supermarkt auf. Ich dachte, ich würde bessere Aussichten haben, wenn ich mich in der Schule bemühte.

D An einem regnerischen Tag im November brachte Herr Becker uns zur großen Karrieremesse in der Stadt. Überall gab es Stände, wo Firmen, Hochschulen und Universitäten Broschüren und weitere Informationen über mögliche Berufe verteilten. Die Vertreter sprachen mit den Messebesuchern und zeigten interessante Videos.

E Alles lief sehr gut. Die Vorträge waren super interessant und es gab eine Vielfalt an Berufsmöglichkeiten zu sehen. Plötzlich hörte ich im Vorbeigehen einen interessanten Podcast zum Thema Journalismus. Ich stoppte und hörte zu, wie der Alltag eines Journalisten ablief. Das klang so spannend, dass ich mit der Vertreterin dieses Kurses an der Universität sprechen musste. Sie hat mich gründlich darüber informiert und ich nahm einige Broschüren zum Lesen mit. Ich fühlte mich erleichtert, denn der Weg vor mir wurde plötzlich klar; ich würde Journalistin werden.

Prüfungstipp

Frequently occurring suffixes on adjectives will help you to identify them:

-ant (relevant, interessant) -ig (lustig, langweilig) -voll (anspruchsvoll, humorvoll)
-haft (ekelhaft, schmackhaft) -lich (nützlich, hässlich)

OL Ordinary Level Questions

1. a) Where had various class members gone on holiday? A
   b) Why was the narrator looking forward to English and Geography? Give **two** details. B
   c) What did the narrator do in order to concentrate on her school work? C
   d) What happened on a rainy day in November? Give **three** details. D
   e) What did the narrator decide after hearing an interesting podcast? E
2. Choose a suitable heading for each paragraph and give reasons for your choice in English.

Wir besuchen die Karrieremesse	Dieses Jahr machen wir das Abitur	Ich will Journalismus studieren	Die Ferien sind vorbei	Ich lernte fleißig in der Schule

3. Select the correct prepositions for the following sentences.
   a) Alle Schüler redeten **(an/von/an/für)** den Ferien.
   b) Herr Becker war bereit, sich **(für/an/mit/auf)** dem Schulblog zu beschäftigen.
   c) Ich gab meinen Job **(um/im/an/auf)** Supermarkt auf.
   d) Es war ein regnerischer Tag **(im/um/an/am)** November.
   e) Ich lernte über eine Vielfalt **(an/in/auf/von)** Berufsmöglichkeiten.
4. What words make up the following compounds, and what do they mean in English?
   a) Klassenkameraden = ______ + ______ = ______
   b) Berufsberater = ______ + ______ = ______
   c) Karrieremesse = ______ + ______ = ______
   d) Berufsmöglichkeiten = ______ + ______ = ______

HL Higher Level Questions

1. Beantworten Sie folgende Fragen auf Deutsch.
   a) Wovon berichtete die Klasse? Geben Sie **zwei** Details! A
   b) Wohin wollte Herr Becker die Abiturklasse bringen? B
   c) Woher weiß man, dass es der Erzählerin gut ging? C
   d) Beschreiben Sie die Karrieremesse! (**3** Details) D
   e) Was wollte die Erzählerin am Ende der Geschichte machen? E
2. Answer the following questions in English.
   a) What kind of holidays had the other students had? Why was the narrator not tanned? A
   b) What kind of teacher was Herr Becker? Give **four** details. B
   c) The narrator's school year gets off to a good start. Give **three** details. C
   d) What did the representatives at the different stands do? D
   e) How did the narrator find the talks? E
   f) The text explores expectations. Give **three** examples of language or content which raise the issue of expectations.
3. Was passt zusammen?

1. Ich fühlte mich wohl,	**A** um mehr Zeit für das Lernen zu haben.
2. Ich habe meinen Job aufgegeben,	**B** und die Vorträge waren interessant.
3. Wir sind zur Karrieremesse gegangen,	**C** denn ich bekam gute Noten.
4. Die Vertreter hatten Broschüren	**D** über das alltägliche Leben eines Journalisten.
5. Es gab einen interessanten Podcast	**E** um uns über Berufsmöglichkeiten zu informieren.

4. Geben Sie für die Nomen an: ob Singular oder Plural, das Geschlecht und den Fall.
   a) Er brachte die Abiturienten zur <u>Karrieremesse</u>.
   b) Ich konzentrierte mich auf das <u>Lernen</u>.
   c) Die <u>Vertreter</u> zeigten interessante Videos.
   d) Ich hörte einen interessanten <u>Podcast</u>.

Grammatik: Präpositionen/Prepositions

p. 141 (Übung macht den Meister)

Two-Way Prepositions

While some German prepositions always take the accusative or the dative case, certain prepositions can take either the accusative or the dative case. When they convey motion towards something, they take the accusative case. When they describe a fixed position, they take the dative case.

an at, on, on to, to	**in** in, into	**unter** under
auf on, on to, at, to	**neben** beside	**vor** in front of, before
hinter behind	**über** over	**zwischen** between

Note: **an dem** may be contracted to **am**, and **in dem** may be contracted to **im**. **In das** may be contracted to **ins**.

1. Decide whether these examples are accusative (direction) or dative (position).

a) Mein Geld ist auf der Bank.	**d)** Ich muss auf die Bank gehen.
b) Ich gehe oft ins Ausland.	**e)** Ich möchte im Ausland wohnen.
c) Ich gehe hinter das Haus.	**f)** Es gibt einen Garten hinter dem Haus.

2. Insert the correct definite article. Then translate the sentences.

a) Ich gehe gern in ___ Schule (f).	**e)** Er hängt das Bild an ___ Wand (f).
b) In ___ Schule (f) gibt es eine schöne Stimmung.	**f)** Viele Poster hängen an ___ Wand (f).
c) Mein Handy liegt auf ___ Tisch (m).	**g)** Die Kirche ist hinter ___ Rathaus (n).
d) Ich lege mein Buch auf ___ Tisch (m).	**h)** Ich setze mich neben ___ Mann (m).

Genitive Prepositions

The following prepositions always take the genitive case.

(an)statt instead of	**diesseits** this side of	**jenseits** that side of	**während** during the time of
außerhalb outside of	**innerhalb** inside of	**trotz** in spite of	**wegen** because of

Während ***der*** **Woche** (f) **lerne ich fleißig.** During the week I study hard.

Wegen ***des*** **schlechten Wetters** (n) **sehe ich fern.** Because of the bad weather I watch TV.

Trotz ***des*** **Drucks** (m) **gehe ich gern in die Schule.** In spite of the pressure I like going to school.

Insert the correct definite article. Then translate the sentences.

1. Ich wohne außerhalb ___ Stadt (f).	**5.** Ich war krank wegen ___ Grippe (f).
2. Trotz ___ des Wetters (n) wohne ich gern hier.	**6.** Wegen ___ Hitze (f) bräune ich mich.
3. Während ___ Wochenendes (n) ruhe ich mich aus.	**7.** Ich bin froh wegen ___ Schnees (m).
4. Das Spiel wird wegen ___ Regens (m) abgesagt.	**8.** Trotz ___ leckeren Essens (n) habe ich keinen Hunger.

A summary of German prepositions and the cases they govern:

Accusative	Dative	Two-Way	Genitive
bis	aus	an	(an)statt
durch	außer	auf	außerhalb
entlang	bei	hinter	diesseits
für	gegenüber	in	innerhalb
gegen	mit	neben	jenseits
ohne	nach	über	trotz
um	seit	unter	während
wider	von	vor	wegen
	zu	zwischen	

07.03 Hörverständnis Teil 3

Vorarbeit

Erfolg	*success*	**vorhaben**	*to intend*	**kriegen**	*to get*
sich verlassen auf	*to rely on*	**Lebenslauf**	*CV*	**klug**	*clever*

Ordinary + Higher Level Questions

1. **a)** The conversation is between:
   i) a brother and sister ☐ **iii)** two friends ☐
   ii) a teacher and a student ☐ **iv)** father and daughter ☐
   b) Find **one (O)/two (H)** details in the conversation that support your choice.
2. **a)** Which word best describes the male speaker's attitude early on in the conversation?
   i) frustrated ☐ **ii)** nervous ☐ **iii)** worried ☐ **iv)** excited ☐
   b) Write down **one (O)/two (H)** details from the conversation to support your choice.
3. What advice does the female speaker give the male speaker? Give **one (O)/three (H)** details.
4. What are they planning to do in August? Give **one (O)/two (H)** details.

07.04 Hörverständnis Teil 4

Vorarbeit

Wettbewerb	*competition*	**Erfindungen**	*discoveries*	**Teilnehmer**	*participants*
verschwinden	*to disappear*	**Tierarten**	*species of animals*	**Düngemittel**	*fertilisers*
Verlust	*loss*	**Ökosystem**	*ecosystem*	**unverzichtbar**	*indispensible*
Fluggesellschaften	*airlines*	**Schatten**	*shade*	**örtlich**	*locally*

Ordinary + Higher Level Questions

1. **a)** Where will the next young scientist competition be taking place?
   b) Who is this competition intended for? Give **two (O)/four (H)** details.
2. **a)** Why are animals, birds and insects disappearing? Give **one (O)/two (H)** details.
   b) By what percentage are they disappearing each year?
3. **a)** How much money did tourists spend in Germany last year?
   b) Why did more than half of them fly to Germany?
4. **a)** What weather is expected next week? Give **two (O)/four (H)** details.
   b) What recommendation is given for the weather alert?

There is always a weather section in the news. Make sure that you are familiar with weather-related vocabulary and include as many details as you can in your answers.

Blitz, m	*lightning*	**Nebel, m**	*fog*
Donner, m	*thunder*	**Orkan, m**	*hurricane*
Gefrierpunkt, m	*freezing point*	**Schneeregen, m**	*sleet*
Gewitter, n	*thunderstorm*	**Wolke, f**	*cloud*
Hitzewelle, f	*heatwave*	**bedeckt**	*overcast*

OL Schriftliche Produktion: Ordinary Level

Write a letter to your pen pal, Johann(a). Complete the first paragraph by correctly inserting the sentence halves below. Then follow the instructions.

der gestern angekommen ist
auf die Ferien **für die Uni**
schöne Grüße aus Irland
Sommerarbeit zu finden

Liebe(r) Johann(a),

______________! Vielen Dank für deinen Brief, ______________. Ich freue mich riesig ______________! Aber jetzt will ich dir von meinen Plänen erzählen. Ich habe vor, mit zwei Freunden in Deutschland ______________, um Geld ______________ zu verdienen.

Now continue the letter.

- Say when and where you are looking for summer jobs.
- Give **two** details about the friends who are going with you to Germany to visit Johann(a).
- Describe what you will do with the money that you will earn.
- Say when and how you will be travelling to Germany.
- Say that you all learned German in school and want to speak it when you go to Germany.
- Write a suitable closing sentence.

HL Schriftliche Produktion: Higher Level

Reply in German to your pen pal's letter. Give detailed answers to their questions.

Liebe(r) ______________,

hallo aus Deutschland! Wie geht es dir? Vielen Dank für deinen Brief, den ich vorgestern bekommen habe! Ich kann es kaum erwarten dich im August zu sehen! Und du, dein Abi ist schon vorbei, oder?! Was wirst du dann im Juli machen, während ich meine letzten Abiprüfungen mache?!

Danke für die Einladung nach Irland, die ich gerne annehme! Ich habe einige Ideen, was wir machen könnten, wenn ich in Irland bin, aber sag mal, was du für uns geplant hast!

Ich freue mich darauf selbstständiger zu werden und auf die Uni zu gehen. Wie ist es bei dir im Moment? Weißt du schon alles was du nach dem Abitur machen möchtest? Erzähl mal!

Du hast auch geschrieben, dass der Berufsberater an deiner Schule einen Besuch auf eine Karrieremesse organisiert hat. Mit wem bist du dorthin gefahren? Wie war es? Wo war es? Würdest du es jedermann empfehlen eine Karrieremesse zu besuchen? Warum (nicht)?

Lass bald von dir hören!

Dein(e) Johann/a

Kulturecke

In Deutschland gibt es ca. 400 Hochschulen, davon sind über 100 Universitäten, ca. 200 Fachhochschulen und ca. 50 Kunsthochschulen. Das Studienangebot in Deutschland ist riesig.

Übung Macht den Meister!

A Definite Articles

Identify whether the underlined nouns are singular or plural, their case and their gender.

1. Das Mädchen hat den Kuchen gekauft.
2. Der Mann arbeitet für die Firma.
3. Die Lehrerin gibt dem Kind eine gute Note.
4. Die Jacke des Kindes ist blau.
5. Der Hund der Familie ist weggelaufen.
6. Ich schenke dem Jungen das Geld.

B Definite Articles

Insert the correct definite article for each sentence.

1. ___ Sendung (f) ist spannend.
2. Um 7 Uhr klingelt ___ Wecker (m).
3. Ich nutze ___ Internet (n) jeden Tag.
4. Ich gebe ___ Kind (n) ein Geschenk.
5. Ich leihe ___ Frau (f) das Geld.
6. Wo ist das Auto ___ Mannes (m)?

C Demonstratives

Identify whether the underlined nouns are singular or plural, their case and their gender.

1. Dieser Mann braucht jenen Mantel.
2. Jene Frau steckte dieses Geld in die Tasche.
3. Diese Größe passt dieser Frau nicht.
4. Diese Kosten erstaunen jenen Lehrer.
5. Jenes Kind wird diese Banane essen.
6. Jede Person sollte zu jenen Kindern nett sein.

D Demonstratives

Insert the correct endings for the demonstratives.

1. Welch___ Mann (m) kommt herein?
2. Ich kenne dies___ Frau (f) nicht.
3. Welch___ (pl.) Schüler erhalten einen Preis?
4. Ich mag dies___ Jungen (m) sehr.
5. Jed___ Kind (n) will im Park spielen.
6. Wir geben jed___ Kind (n) ein Eis.

E Accusative Prepositions

Insert the correct article for these prepositions.

1. Vielen Dank **für** _____ Geschenk (n).
2. Das Kind rannte **um** _____ Ecke (f).
3. Die Kinder laufen **durch** _____ Park (m).
4. Ich gehe **ohne** mein___ Freund (m) spazieren.
5. Ich bleibe **für** ein___ Monat (m) in Berlin.
6. Das Buch handelt sich **um** ein___ Jungen (m).

F Dative Prepositions

Insert the correct article or ending for these prepositions.

1. Das Mädchen kommt **aus** ___ Türkei (f).
2. Anna wohnt **bei** ihr___ Mutter (f).
3. Ich fahre **mit** _____ Bus (m) zur Schule.
4. **Nach** _____ Schule (f) ruhe ich mich aus.
5. Hast du dich **von** _____ Grippe (f) erholt?
6. Hans wohnt **seit** ein___ Monat (m) bei uns.

G Two-Way Prepositions

Insert the correct article for these prepositions.

1. Ich will nächstes Jahr **auf** ___ Uni (f) gehen.
2. Mein Bruder studiert **an** ___ Uni (f) in Cork.
3. Ich stecke meine Schuhe **unter** ___ Bett (n).
4. Die Lehrerin steht **in** ___ Klassenzimmer (n).
5. Die Katze klettert **auf** ___ Baum (m).
6. Die Regeln **in** ___ Schule (f) sind streng.

H Genitive Prepositions

Insert the correct article for these prepositions.

1. **Wegen** ___ Wetters (n) bleibe ich zu Hause.
2. **Während** ___ Abends (m) lerne ich viel.
3. **Trotz** ___ Arbeit (f) bin ich glücklich.
4. **Während** ___ Ferien (pl.) reise ich gern.
5. **Trotz** ___ Preises (m) fahre ich nach Florida.
6. Ich bin **wegen** ___ Hitze (f) sehr müde.

You will often see German prepositions and their articles contracted:

an + dem = am	für + das = fürs	von + dem = vom
an + das = ans	in + dem = im	zu + dem = zum
bei + dem = beim	in + das = ins	zu + der = zur

Für die Prüfung

1. Was passt zusammen?

1. Wenn ich im Abitur gut abschneide,	**A** um Lehrer zu werden.
2. Ich werde nach Limerick umziehen müssen,	**B** möchte ich einen Musikkurs machen.
3. Als ich jung war,	**C** um meine Sprachkenntnisse zu verbessern.
4. Weil ich musikalisch begabt bin,	**D** werde ich Jura und Deutsch studieren.
5. Ich möchte in Deutschland studieren,	**E** wollte ich Polizist werden.

2. Was passt zusammen?

1. Ich werde das Abitur wiederholen,	**A** ist es nicht das A und O des Lebens.
2. Nach dem Studium	**B** dass ich jeden Tag lerne.
3. Obwohl Geld wichtig ist,	**C** wo nicht zu viel von mir verlangt wird.
4. Meine Eltern bestehen darauf,	**D** wenn ich nicht genug Punkte kriege.
5. Ich suche eine Stelle,	**E** möchte ich die Welt bereisen.

3. Select the correct prepositions for the following sentences.

a) Ich interessiere mich sehr **(in/auf/mit/für)** Informatik.
b) Ich freue mich sehr **(in/auf/für/an)** die Zukunft.
c) **(Mit/An/Zu/Auf)** einem guten Abschluss kann man bestimmt eine gute Stelle finden.
d) Ich muss **(zu/nach/in/auf)** Cork umziehen.
e) Man muss sich **(um/über/von/auf)** die verschiedenen Kurse informieren.
f) Ich mache mir oft Gedanken **(wegen/auf/für/über)** die Zukunft.

4. What words make up the following compound words, and what do they mean in English?

a) Zukunftspläne = ____ + ____ = ______
b) Berufsberater = ____ + ____ = ______
c) Abschlussprüfung = ____ + ____ = ______
d) ausüben = ____ + ____ = ______
e) Ferienabenteuer = ____ + ____ = ______
f) Lehrerzimmer = ____ + ____ = ______

5. Identify whether the underlined nouns are singular or plural, their gender and their case.

a) Ich suche <u>einen interessanten Beruf</u>.
b) <u>Eine gut bezahlte Stelle</u> ist wichtig.
c) Ich lerne sehr gern <u>Fremdsprachen</u>.
d) Ich übe die Sprache mit <u>meinem Freund</u>.
e) Wir gehen oft ins <u>Sprachlabor</u>.
f) Ich will <u>meinen Horizont</u> erweitern.

6. Insert the correct definite articles for the following sentences.

a) ___ Kurs (m) verlangt viele Punkte.
b) Ich möchte ___ Sprachkurs (m) machen.
c) Wir reden oft mit ___ Nachbarn (pl.).
d) Ich lerne fleißig für ___ Prüfung (f).
e) Ich finde ___ Rollenspiele (pl.) schwierig.
f) Ich verstehe den Akzent ___ Mannes (m) nicht.
g) Während ___ Woche (f) ist das Wetter heiß.
h) Wir spielen Fußball in ___ Park (m).
i) Klaus schenkt ___ Kind (n) ein Eis.
j) Morgen gehen wir zu ___ Tierarzt (m).

7. Lückentext: Fill in the blanks with the correct missing words from the box.

man	**jeder**	**kommt**	**entscheidet**	**sich**
erste	**muss**	**sondern**	**zum**	**zu**

Vor dem Abistress **1** ___ der Entscheidungsstress. Die Studienwahl ist eigentlich die **2** ___ Entscheidung, die man selbst treffen muss. Das Studium soll nicht nur Spaß machen, **3** ___ auch die Zukunft sichern. Bevor man **4** ___ für einen Studiengang **5** ___ , **6** ___ man sich gut darüber informieren. Natürlich sollte **7** ___ auch **8** ___ Berufsberater gehen, um nutzvolle Ratschläge **9** ___ kriegen. **10** ___ ist seines Glückes Schmied!

Selbstbewertung: Ordinary Level

OL

Vocabulary

1. If I can translate these nouns into German, I can describe future plans. (1 mark each)

a) Leaving Certificate	**c)** apprenticeship	**e)** businessman	**g)** course	**i)** decision
b) information	**d)** profession	**f)** careers advisor	**h)** security	**j)** career choice

Your score: ___ 10

2. If I can translate these sentences into English, I can discuss my future plans. (1 mark each)

a) Ich will auf die Uni gehen.	**f)** Ich ziehe nächstes Jahr nach Dublin um.
b) Ich möchte Informatik studieren.	**g)** Der Kurs dauert drei Jahre.
c) Ich brauche hohe Punkte für den Kurs.	**h)** Ich will selbstständig sein.
d) Ich will Menschen helfen.	**i)** Ich habe viel im Internet recherchiert.
e) Ich freue mich auf die Zukunft.	**j)** Ich hoffe, dass ich im Abi gut abschneide.

Your score: ___ 10

Grammar

3. If I can put these sentences into the future tense, I can discuss future plans. (1 mark each)

a) Ich mache einen Kurs in Dublin.	**f)** Ich verdiene viel Geld.
b) Ich recherchiere im Internet.	**g)** Ich gehe zum Berufsberater.
c) Ich lerne viel.	**h)** Ich mache einen Persönlichkeitstest.
d) Ich ziehe nach Limerick um.	**i)** Die Berufswahl ist schwierig.
e) Ich fahre ins Ausland.	**j)** Ich bekomme gute Noten.

Your score: ___ 10

4. If I can choose the correct preposition, I can describe my future plans. (1 mark each)

- **a)** Ich interessiere mich **(in/auf/für/an)** Kunst.
- **b)** Ich freue mich **(in/an/am/auf)** die Zukunft.
- **c)** Der Lehrer will **(mit/zu/an/für)** mir reden.
- **d)** Ich will **(ins/im/zu/nach)** Ausland fahren.
- **e)** Ich will **(nach/zu/zum/zur)** dem Abi studieren.
- **f)** Geld ist nicht das Wichtigste **(in/im/an/am)** Leben.
- **g)** Ich möchte **(auf/an/zu/bei)** jeden Fall studieren.
- **h)** Ich hätte keine Lust **(an/in/auf/zu)** Medizin.
- **i)** Man braucht gute Noten **(für/in/an/auf)** den Kurs.
- **j)** Ich nehme **(auf/an/in/am)** vielen Workshops teil.

Your score: ___ 10

5. If I can match the following sentences, I can use complex sentences. (2 marks each)

1. Ich will Krankenschwester werden,	**A** also will ich Wissenschaftler werden.
2. Ich will Grundschullehrer werden,	**B** werde ich einen Computerkurs machen.
3. Ich interessiere mich für Biologie,	**C** werde ich eine Lehre machen.
4. Weil ich Informatik gern habe,	**D** weil ich Menschen helfen will.
5. Wenn ich nicht genug Punkte bekomme,	**E** denn ich möchte mit Kindern arbeiten.

Your score: ___ 10

What have I learned?	
What must I improve?	
What do I want to revise?	

Your total score: ___ 50

Selbstbewertung: Higher Level

HL

1. If I can translate these words into German with the correct definite article, I can accurately describe my future plans. (1 mark each)

a) career choice	**c)** future	**e)** exam	**g)** profession	**i)** requirement
b) course	**d)** decision	**f)** apprenticeship	**h)** skills	**j)** CV

Your score: ___ 10

2. If I can translate these sentences into German, I can discuss my future plans. (1 mark each)

a) I'm going to study Arts.	**f)** I will move to Dublin to study.
b) There are lots of jobs in the area of science.	**g)** The course lasts three years.
c) I need three hundred points for the course.	**h)** I want to be independent.
d) I want to help people.	**i)** I researched courses on the internet.
e) I'm looking forward to the future.	**j)** I hope I'll do well in the Leaving Cert.

Your score: ___ 10

3. If I can choose the correct article, I understand accusative and dative prepositions. (1 mark each)

a) Ich entschuldige mich bei **(der/dem)** Lehrerin.
b) Ich lerne mit **(meinem/meiner)** Freund.
c) Er kommt aus **(eine/einer)** Großstadt.
d) Ich interessiere mich für **(den/der)** Beruf.
e) Nach **(das/dem)** Abitur entspanne ich mich.
f) Ich fahre mit **(der/dem)** Bus zur Schule.
g) Ich laufe durch **(den/dem)** Park.
h) Ich fahre seit **(einen/einem)** Monat Auto.
i) Ich muss zu **(den/dem)** Arzt gehen.
j) Das Auto prallte gegen **(den/dem)** Baum.

Your score: ___ 10

4. If I can choose the correct article, I understand two-way prepositions. (1 mark each)

a) Ich wohne in **(das/dem)** Dorf.
b) Sie geht in **(diesen/diesem)** Laden.
c) Ich werde auf **(die/der)** Uni gehen.
d) Ich gehe oft in **(die/der)** Stadt.
e) Das Buch liegt auf **(den/dem)** Tisch.
f) Er wirft die Tasche auf **(den/dem)** Tisch.
g) Die Kirche ist neben **(die/der)** Bibliothek.
h) Ein schönes Bild hängt an **(die/der)** Wand.
i) Das Kind klettert über **(die/der)** Mauer.
j) Es gibt viele Regeln in **(die/der)** Schule.

Your score: ___ 10

5. If I can identify the gender, number and case of the nouns, I understand articles. (1 mark each)

a) Ich mache das Abitur.	**f)** Ich interessiere mich für den Beruf.
b) Der Kurs dauert vier Jahre.	**g)** Ich rede mit dem Berufsberater.
c) Die Berufsberaterin hat mir geholfen.	**h)** Die Prüfungen werden bald beginnen.
d) Ich finde den Kurs anspruchsvoll.	**i)** Ich habe die Entscheidung getroffen.
e) Trotz der Punkte will ich Medizin studieren.	**j)** Ich muss in dem Fach gut abschneiden.

Your score: ___ 10

What have I learned?	
What must I improve?	
What do I want to revise?	

Your total score: ___ 50

08 Feiern und Feste

Learning Outcomes

- **Oral:** discussing celebrations and festivals; preparing for the project option
- **Reading:** reading and discussing three texts on celebrations and festivals
- **Writing:** writing an opinion (**Äußerung**) and describing pictures about celebrations
- **Aural:** listening to and answering questions on four extracts about celebrations

Grammar

- Personal pronouns
- Reflexive pronouns
- Relative pronouns

Vocabulary

- Describing festivals and celebrations
- Comparing festivals and celebrations in Ireland and Germany
- Discussing the origins of festival traditions

German Culture

- German festivals and celebrations
- Festivals and celebrations in German-speaking countries
- Assimilation of Irish celebrations into life in German-speaking countries

Exam Tips

- Pick two sentences from the comprehensions which show a difference between German and Irish festivals. Extend those sentences to draw comparisons between Germany and Ireland.
- Practise using reflexive pronouns and relative pronouns in your oral work.

Mündliche Arbeit: Feste und Feiern

Stellen Sie sich gegenseitig alle Fragen unten. Schreiben Sie die Antworten auf.

- Was feiern die Iren?
- Gibt es Unterschiede zwischen den deutschen und irischen Festen?
- Wie feiern Sie Weihnachten/Ostern/Ihren Geburtstag?
- Was für Feste feiern Sie in Irland?
- Wie und was feiern Sie am liebsten?
- Was ist Ihr Lieblingsfest?

1. Was feiern die Iren? *What do the Irish celebrate?*	
Ohne Zweifel sind die Hauptfeste in Irland Weihnachten, Ostern und unser Nationalfeiertag.	*Without a doubt, the main festivals in Ireland are Christmas, Easter and our national holiday.*
Sie werden alle mit einem Festessen, Geschenken und Familientreffen verbunden.	*They are all associated with a celebratory meal, presents and meeting family.*
Natürlich werden die Straßen und Häuser schön geschmückt und man feiert mit Musik, Weihnachtsmärkten, Ostereiern und Umzügen, je nach dem Festival.	*Of course, streets and houses are decorated beautifully and people celebrate with music, Christmas markets, Easter eggs and parades, depending on the festival.*
Man bekleidet sich schick und trägt Symbole der Feste, wie zum Beispiel Kleeblatt oder Koboldhüte.	*People dress nicely and wear symbols of the festival, for example, shamrock or leprechaun hats.*
In Irland liegt man viel Wert auf Tradition.	*In Ireland a lot of value is placed on tradition.*
Im Sommer kann man fast ohne Pause feiern, denn überall gibt es Festivals und Feste.	*In the summer one can almost celebrate without a break because there are festivals everywhere.*

2. Gibt es Unterschiede zwischen den deutschen und irischen Festen? *Are there differences between German and Irish festivals?*	
Wir feiern alle dieselben Hauptfeste, wie zum Beispiel Weihnachten, Silvester und Ostern.	*We all celebrate the same main festivals such as Christmas, New Year and Easter.*
Die Deutschen feiern ihren Tag der deutschen Einheit am dritten Oktober.	*Germans celebrate their national day of unity on the third of October.*
Meiner Meinung nach ist Deutschland der Ursprung der Weihnachtsmärkte und Wein- und Bierfeste, aber mittlerweile sind sie auch in Irland sehr beliebt geworden.	*In my opinion, Germany is the origin of Christmas markets and wine and beer festivals, but in the meantime, they have also become very popular in Ireland.*
In beiden Ländern gibt es riesige Musikfeste, wie zum Beispiel Rock am Ring in Deutschland und Electric Picnic in Irland.	*In both countries there are huge music festivals, for example, Rock am Ring in Germany and Electric Picnic in Ireland.*
Ich habe den Eindruck, dass die Deutschen gern feiern.	*I have the impression that the Germans like to celebrate.*

3. Wie und was feiern Sie am liebsten? *What do you like to celebrate the most, and how?*	
Mein absolutes Lieblingsfest ist ..., was ich mit meiner Familie und meinen Freunden gerne feiere.	*My absolute favourite festival is ... , which I like celebrating with my family and my friends.*
Natürlich gehen wir aus und feiern in einem Pub und danach in einem Nachtclub.	*Of course we go out and celebrate in a pub and afterwards in a night club.*

Write out your answer to Question 3 in the past tense and the future tense: **Wie und was haben Sie gefeiert?** (past tense) **Wie und was werden Sie feiern?** (future tense)

Prüfungstipp

The Project Option

Part 2 of your oral examination is either a project or picture sequence. If you choose the project option, you will focus on one project only, rather than on five possible picture sequences.

Form of the Project

- The project may be presented in a variety of forms: poster, wall chart, picture, scrapbook, video, etc.
- You will bring it to the examination and hand it to the examiner when asked.
- You may point to or refer to parts of your project during the examination.
- The project should be written/labelled/spoken in German on a Leaving Certificate German topic of interest to you.
- On average, it takes two minutes to present your project orally in sixteen sentences. Time yourself.
- Possible topic areas include: an aspect of German history, authors, artists, performers, composers, cities, geography, food, school, hobbies, sports, teams, sports stars, refugee camps, historical events.

Process and Marking

- There are **three** parts to the presentation of the project or picture sequence, each worth 10 marks.
- The total time of this section should be no longer than four to five minutes.

Part 1: Oral presentation of project for a maximum of two minutes = 10 marks

Part 2: Explanation of how you did the project and explaining details about it = 10 marks

a) Answering a question to further clarify something you mentioned in your project, for example:

Sie haben Ihr Projekt über Berlin geschrieben – haben Sie Berlin schon besucht? *You have written your project about Berlin – have you ever been to Berlin?*

Sie haben über das Fusion Festival geschrieben. Waren Sie selber je auf einem Musikfest? *You wrote about the Fusion Festival. Have you ever been to a music festival yourself?*

b) Answering a question about how you did the project, for example:

Woher haben Sie Ihre Informationen bekommen? *Where did you get the information from?*

Was haben Sie dabei gelernt? *What did you learn from it?*

Wie lange hat es gedauert das Projekt zu machen? *How long did it take to carry out the project?*

Warum haben Sie ein Projekt gemacht und nicht die Bildergeschichten? *Why did you choose a project and not the picture sequences?*

Part 3: Opinion on a related issue = 10 marks

Mir fällt bei Ihrem Projekt das Thema ... ein. Was meinen Sie dazu? *Your project makes me think of the topic of ... . What is your opinion on that?*

Sie haben geschrieben, wie ... in Deutschland ist. Wie ist es in Irland? *You wrote about what ... is like in Germany. What is it like in Ireland?*

✓ Find a topic relating to Germany which is of interest to you. Narrow the breadth of the topic down to two minutes' talking time. Keep a record of the work you do and make a note of any wider issues which you think could arise from your project. This will help you to prepare for the opinion question in Part 3. Even if you are taking the picture sequence option, you can still do a project and talk about it in the general questions section of your oral.

Text 1: Was ist der St. Patricks Day?

Bitte beantworten Sie die folgenden Fragen:

1. Was sehen Sie auf dem Foto?
2. Wo sind sie?
3. Was feiern sie?
4. Was sieht man im Hintergrund?
5. Wie ist die Stimmung?

Vorarbeit

1. Finden Sie diese Ausdrücke im Text unten!
   - **A** ... symbols like leprechauns and shamrock.
   - **B** To honour the patron saint ...
   - **C** It is the same everywhere.
   - **D** ... Irish treats are available.
   - **E** They celebrate their national saint.
2. Finden Sie die deutschen Wörter im Text unten!
   - **A** emigrated/holy (saint)/Christianity/named
   - **B** drummers/flag bearers/bagpipers
   - **C** parade/Ferris wheel/oysters/pinched/keg
   - **D** food colouring/pour/treats
   - **E** go on stage/brass orchestra/Mass

© dpa (amended) & © Christine Bazalka, www.meinbezirk.at (amended)

A Jedes Jahr feiern die Iren am 17. März ihren heiligen Patrick, der vor 1.600 Jahren am 17. März gestorben ist. Saint Patrick hatte das Christentum auf die „Grüne Insel" Irland gebracht und deshalb wurde der 17. März zum Nationalfeiertag ernannt. Seitdem feiern die Iren St. Patrick – immer in grün, der traditionellen irischen Farbe, und mit Symbolen wie Kobolden und Kleeblättern. Der irische Nationalfeiertag wird nicht nur in Irland gefeiert, er wird auch von Millionen ausgewanderten Iren in aller Welt gefeiert.

B Am Montag ziehen tausende Mitglieder irischer Vereine durch München. Seit 1996 findet die Parade dort statt. Grün, weiß, orange: Am Sonntag haben die irischen Nationalfarben Münchens Straßen bunt geschmückt. Zu Ehren des Schutzpatrons der Insel, Saint Patrick, zogen Dudelsackspieler, Trommler, Fahnenschwinger, Rugbyspieler und viele andere Mitglieder irischer Vereine durch die Stadt. 1.200 Menschen nahmen an der Parade teil, 20.000 Zuschauer verfolgten das Spektakel vom Straßenrand aus.

C Auch in Wien gibt es grünes Bier, grüne Brücken und einen traditionellen Umzug. Es gilt überall: Wer nicht grün trägt, darf gezwickt werden! Die Donaukanalbrücken, das Riesenrad und das Burgtheater werden grün beleuchtet. Es wird bei grünem Bier irischer Folk-Rock gespielt. Dazu kann man aus 40 verschiedenen Whiskey-Sorten wählen. Stouts vom Fass, irische Austern und eine irische Band kann man in jeder Kneipe genießen.

D Das Wiener Folk-Rock-Duo Those Angry Men spielt im Irish-Pub Wien. Der Abend beginnt um 18 Uhr mit einer Happy Hour; Guinness und irische Leckerbissen sind vorhanden. Im The Twins Pub wird der große Tag mit Livemusik und grünem Bier gefeiert. Wer zu Hause feiern möchte, kann grünes Bier ganz einfach selber machen: Bier ins Glas gießen und grüne Lebensmittelfarbe dazu.

E Das traditionelle Fest der Iren in Wien: Sie feiern ihren Nationalheiligen am Samstag, 19. März, mit einer Messe. Danach, ab 11.45 Uhr, beginnt ein Umzug. Für Musik und Unterhaltung sorgen die Irish Dance Schools in Vienna, das Wiener Blasorchester, die Vienna Pipes and Drums. Die irische Tanzgruppe Cumann Ceili Vin und die Band Pholc treten am Samstag, 19. März, ab 20 Uhr auf.

Ordinary Level Questions

1. **a)** When did St Patrick die and what did he bring to Ireland? A
   b) What colours are used to decorate the streets of Munich? Who takes part in the parade? B
   c) What becomes green in Vienna, and who provides the music? C
2. Are the following statements true or false?
   a) Der St. Patrick hat Christentum nach Irland gebracht.
   b) Der irische Nationalfeiertag wird in allen deutschen Städten gefeiert.
   c) Man färbt alle Getränke grün.
   d) Viele Brücken werden in Wien grün.
3. What words make up the following compound words, and what do they mean in English?
   a) Burgtheater = _____ + _____ = _____
   b) Schutzpatron = _____ + _____ = _____
   c) Blasorchester = _____ + _____ = _____
   d) Tanzgruppe = _____ + _____ = _____
4. Select the correct prepositions for the following sentences.
   a) Viele feiern den St. Patricks Day **(an/im/auf/in)** München.
   b) Die Wiener feiern den irischen Feiertag **(mit/für/gegen/um)** grünem Bier.
   c) **(Am/An/Im/In)** ersten Tag gibt es eine Messe.
   d) Der Abend beginnt **(im/um/am/zum)** 18 Uhr mit einer Happy Hour.

HL

Higher Level Questions

1. Beantworten Sie folgende Fragen auf Deutsch!
   a) Was hat St. Patrick nach Irland gebracht? Und wann war das genau? A
   b) Beschreiben Sie genau, was am Montag, laut Text, passiert. Geben Sie mehrere Details! B
   c) Wie wird St. Patricks Day in Wien gefeiert? Was passiert, wenn man Grün nicht trägt? C
   d) Was wird in den Wiener Kneipen organisiert? D
   e) Beschreiben Sie alles, was am 19. März in Wien passiert. E
2. Answer the following questions in English.
   a) What exactly do the Irish do to celebrate their national holiday? A
   b) Name the types of participants that take part in the parade in Munich. B
   c) How can one celebrate St. Patrick's Day at home? D
   d) Describe exactly what happens after Mass on 19 March. E
3. Was passt zusammen?

1. Der Schutzpatron Irlands	**A** nehmen am Umzug teil.
2. Viele Menschen aus irischen Clubs	**B** mit Umzügen, Biertrinken und Musik spielen.
3. In Wien mag man	**C** das Bier mit grüner Lebensmittelfarbe.
4. Man feiert den Tag	**D** hat das Christentum nach Irland gebracht.
5. Man färbt auch	**E** die Brücken grün machen.

4. Geben Sie für die Nomen an: ob Singular oder Plural, das Geschlecht und den Fall.
   a) Saint Patrick brachte das Christentum nach Irland.
   b) Seitdem feiern die Iren St. Patrick.
   c) Die Stadt wird in die Nationalfarbe getaucht.
   d) Tausende Mitglieder irischer Vereine ziehen durch München.
   e) Der Abend beginnt mit einer Happy Hour.
   f) Sie feiern ihren Nationalheiligen mit einer Messe.

Grammatik: Pronomen/Pronouns

p. 161 (Übung macht den Meister)

A pronoun replaces a noun, for example:

- 'The man' can be replaced with 'he', 'him', 'to him'.
- 'Mary' can be replaced with 'she', 'her', 'to her'.
- 'The teachers' can be replaced with 'they', 'them', 'to them'.

If a noun is masculine, it must remain masculine:

Der Wagen: Er (nominative) **fährt schnell** *He drives fast* **Ich mag** ihn (accusative) *I like him*

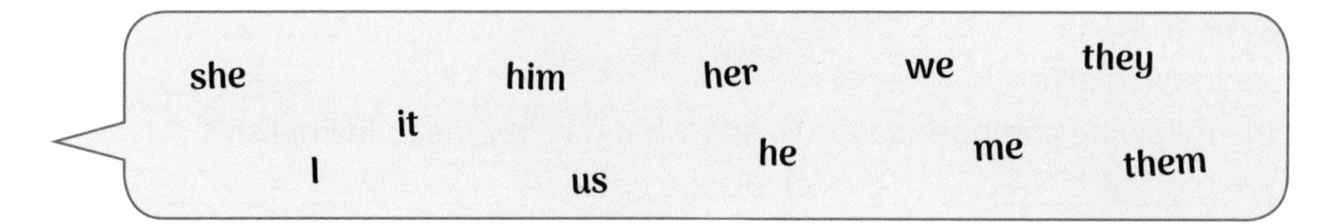

Like nouns, pronouns follow the German case system of the nominative, accusative and dative. However, the genitive case does not occur with pronouns. A quick reminder of the case system:

- The nominative case applies when the person or thing is doing the action in the sentence: I bought a car; He ate an apple; We went to school
- The accusative case applies when the action is done directly to the person or thing in the sentence: The girl bought it; The boy liked them; The artists drew us
- The dative case implies indirect action ('to', 'from', 'with'): My teacher gave the book to me; The man took the money from him; The children went with us

Personal Pronouns	Nominative	Accusative	Dative
I, me, to me	ich	mich	mir
you, you, to you (singular)	du	dich	dir
he, him, to him	er	ihn	ihm
she, her, to her	sie	sie	ihr
it, it, to it	es	es	ihm
we, us, to us	wir	uns	uns
you, you, to you (plural)	ihr	euch	euch
you, you, to you (polite)	Sie	Sie	Ihnen
they, them, to them	sie	sie	ihnen

1. Identify the case of the underlined pronouns in the sentences below. Are they singular or plural? Then translate the sentences.

a) Ich gebe ihm das Buch.	**e)** Er liest ihm eine Geschichte vor.
b) Du gibst mir das Geld.	**f)** Er sieht mich nicht.
c) Sie hilft mir.	**g)** Ihr liebt es.
d) Wir sehen ihn jetzt.	**h)** Sie trinken es gern.

2. Replace the bracketed nouns below with the correct personal pronouns. Make sure that they are correct in terms of number (singular or plural), gender and case. Then translate the sentences.

a) Ich gebe (dem Jungen) ein Eis.	**e)** Wir wollen (den Film) im Kino sehen.
b) (Der Mann) hat einen neuen Wagen gekauft.	**f)** (Das Buch) kostet zwanzig Euro.
c) Ich mag (die Lehrerin) sehr.	**g)** Wir helfen (den Kindern) oft.
d) Ich finde (den Schauspieler) langweilig.	**h)** Ich gehe mit (meinem Bruder) in die Stadt.

08.01 Hörverständnis Teil 1

Vorarbeit

begeisterte	*thrilled*	**Produzent**	*producer*	**Plattenvertrag**	*record deal*
aufgenommen	*recorded*	**Nachfolger**	*successor*	**übertragen**	*to broadcast*
beschloss	*decided*	**Vorstellung**	*performance*	**Jubiläum**	*anniversary*

CL Ordinary + Higher Level Questions

1. What do we learn about Laura? Give **two (O)/four (H)** details.
2. **a)** How did she come to be a musician? Give **one (O)/three (H)** details.
   b) How did she get her first record deal?
3. Describe her experience of participating in the competition. Give **two (O)/four (H)** details.
4. **a)** Mention **two (O)/four (H)** things which happened after the competition.
   b) Why did she stop taking part in competitions?
5. **a)** What are her feelings about solo and group recitals? Give **one (O)/two (H)** details for each.
   b) Who are her favourite composers and why? Give **one (O)/two (H)** details for each composer.

08.02 Hörverständnis Teil 2

Vorarbeit

erledigen	*to complete*	**bestätigen**	*to confirm*	**bestellen**	*to order*
abholen	*to collect*	**absagen**	*to cancel*	**Blumenhandlung**	*florist's shop*

OL Ordinary Level Questions

1. Why is the man calling, and when does the woman think she will be home?
2. The next phone call will be to:
   a) a restaurant ☐ **b)** a florist's shop ☐ **c)** a book shop ☐ **d)** a school ☐
3. What is the name and phone number of the business?

HL Higher Level Questions

1. Write down **in German** the key information from the conversation. Write ***key phrases***, not full sentences. The note should contain:
   - The name of the **caller**
   - The reason for the call
   - Details about the solution
   - The phone number mentioned

Gesprächsnotiz

Anruf von: ____________________ Problem: ____________________

Der Anrufer:

- ruft nächste Woche an
- erhält einen Rückruf von der Handlung
- wird eine SMS erhalten
- ruft heute bei der Blumenhandlung an

Telefonnummer: ____________________

2. In listening to the phone call for the ***third*** time, write down **three** examples of the language used (***expressions and phrases***) which show the caller's **tolerance** and **understanding**.

Text 2: Feste und Bräuche in Deutschland

Bitte beantworten Sie die folgenden Fragen:

1. Was machen diese Leute?
2. Wie sehen sie aus?
3. Wie ist die Stimmung?

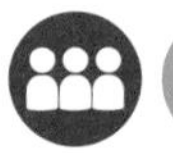 

Vorarbeit

Finden Sie das Deutsche für die Wörter unten!

A devil/curses/prayer/driven out/gather
B Lent/high point/Shrove Monday/dressed up
C Maypole/craftspeople/previous evening
D stream/roast chicken/every year
E emigrants/pre-Christian/spread
F boots/rod/recites/bad things
G church service/pitched/Nativity play/carols
H toasts/church bells/sparkling wine/ring out

www.derweg.org (amended)

A In der Nacht vom 30. April auf den 1. Mai ist die Walpurgisnacht. Im 1. Jahrhundert betete Sankt Walpurga für den Schutz der Menschen gegen Flüche. Durch ihr Gebet glaubte man, dass Dämonen vertrieben wurden. Seit dem 16. Jahrhundert feiern Hexen am selben Abend diese Nacht. Sie versammeln sich mit dem Teufel. Heute ist die Hexennacht als Tanz um ein Hexenfeuer in den Mai bekannt.

B Der Karneval ist die letzte wilde Zeit vor der Fastenzeit. In diesen Tagen wird mit Wein und Gesang gefeiert. Fast eine Woche lang sieht man verkleidete Menschen auf der Straße oder bei Festen. Höhepunkt ist ein langer Umzug mit vielen bunten Wagen und verkleideten Menschen am Rosenmontag. Die Schulen und die meisten Geschäfte sind an diesem Tag geschlossen.

C Am Vorabend des 1. Mai wird der Maibaum geschmückt. Größere Maibäume tragen oft auch Symbole von wichtigen Handwerkern. Man stellt den Maibaum auf und tanzt bis in die Nacht um den Baum um das Maifest zu feiern.

D Das Münchner Oktoberfest ist das größte Volksfest der Welt. Alljährlich strömen über 6 Millionen Besucher auf das Fest. Jährlich werden etwa 6 Millionen Maß Bier getrunken, ca. 500.000 Brathendl und ca. 200.000 Paar Schweinswürste gegessen.

E In vorchristlicher Zeit verabschiedeten sich die Kelten in der Nacht vom 31. Oktober zum 1. November vom Sommer und hießen den Winter willkommen. Irische Auswanderer brachten die Halloween-Bräuche mit in die USA. Dort verbreitete sich die Tradition. Besonderer Beliebtheit bei den Kindern ist das sogenannte trick or treat (Saures oder Süßes).

F Am 6. Dezember feiert man Nikolaus. Am Vorabend stellen die Kinder ihre Stiefel vor die Haustür. Sie möchten, dass der Nikolaus sie mit Leckerbissen füllt. Abends kommt der Nikolaus. Er hat eine Rute für die bösen Kinder bei sich und einen Sack voller kleiner Geschenke für die lieben Kinder. Aus einem großen Buch liest er ihnen vor, was sie für gute und böse Dinge getan haben.

G Ab Anfang Dezember werden Weihnachtsmärkte aufgeschlagen, Christbäume aufgestellt und geschmückt. Am Heiligen Abend versammeln sich Familien unter dem Christbaum und feiern. Viele Menschen gehen zum Gottesdienst in die Kirche. Dort singt man Lieder. Manchmal spielen die Kinder ein „Krippenspiel". Nach dem Gottesdienst ist es Zeit für die Geschenke. Am ersten Weihnachtstag geht das Feiern weiter. Man isst häufig Karpfen, Gans oder einen leckeren Braten.

H Am 31.12. ist der Silvestertag. Man feiert in fröhlicher Runde, und um 24 Uhr wünscht man sich ein frohes neues Jahr oder stößt bei einem Glas Sekt mit einem „Prost Neujahr" an. Überall fangen alle Kirchenglocken an zu läuten. Man sieht oft auch ein buntes Feuerwerk.

OL Ordinary Level Questions

1. a) What happens on 31 October? E
   b) When is St Nicholas' Day celebrated? F
   c) When will one start to see Christmas markets in Germany? G
   d) What do children sometimes do in church on Christmas Eve? G
2. Fill in the following grid.

Festival	Time of year	Three details about the event
Walpurgis Night		
Oktoberfest		
Halloween		
Christmas		
New Year's Eve		

3. Select the correct prepositions for the following sentences.
   a) Die Symbole **(vom/mit/von/im)** Handwerkern hängen am Maibaum.
   b) Der Nikolaus hat eine Rute **(bei/auf/hinter/neben)** sich.
   c) **(In/Auf/Ab/Mit)** dem Beginn Dezembers sieht man schon die Weihnachtsmärkte.
   d) **(Auf/An/Ab/Im)** Silvester trinkt man ein Glas Sekt.
4. Separate these compound words into their components and translate them into English.
   a) Gottesdienst = _____ + _____ = _____
   b) Christbaum = _____ + _____ = _____
   c) Hexenfeuer = _____ + _____ = _____
   d) Haustür = _____ + _____ = _____

HL Higher Level Questions

1. Beantworten Sie folgende Fragen auf Deutsch!
   a) Beschreiben Sie in Ihren eigenen Worten, wer Sankt Walpurga war. A
   b) Wie lange dauert das Fest vom Karneval? Wie wird es gefeiert? B
   c) Wann genau feiert man das Maifest? Wie feiert man das genau? C
   d) Warum wird Halloween gefeiert? Woher stammt diese Tradition? E
   e) Warum bringt Nikolaus am 6. Dezember eine Rute mit? F
   f) Was machen die Deutschen am Heiligen Abend? G
2. Answer the following questions in English.
   a) Explain the origin of Walpurgis Night. A
   b) What happens during Carnival? Give **four** details. B
   c) Which food and drink are consumed at the Oktoberfest? Give **three** details. D
   d) Describe in detail what happens on St Nicholas' Day. F
   e) What do Germans do on Christmas Eve? Describe a typical Christmas dinner in Germany. G
   f) Describe in detail what happens on New Year's Eve. H
3. Was passt zusammen?

1. Sankt Walpurga betete	**A** und gehen zum Umzug.
2. Die Menschen verkleiden sich	**B** die aus Irland stammten, gebracht.
3. Mehr als 6 Millionen Besucher kommen hierher	**C** für den Schutz der Menschen gegen Dämonen.
4. Halloween-Bräuche wurden von Menschen,	**D** während er Geschenke für die braven Kinder brachte.
5. Nikolaus brachte eine Rute für die bösen Kinder,	**E** um das Oktoberfest zu feiern.

OL Äußerung zum Thema: Ordinary Level

You are interviewing a German teenager. Complete his dialogue, based on the information given in Text 2.

Sie: Was ist Ihr Lieblingsfest?
Junge: ______________________________
Sie: Wie feiern Sie das?
Junge: ______________________________
Sie: Mit wem feiern Sie das?
Junge: ______________________________
Sie: Bekommen Sie Geschenke?
Junge: ______________________________
Sie: Was essen Sie gerne zu diesem Fest?
Junge: ______________________________
Sie: Vielen Dank für das Gespräch.

HL Äußerung zum Thema: Higher Level

Write 13 to 15 sentences, answering the questions below.

- Beschreiben Sie die Fotos oben in **drei bis vier** Sätzen.
- Welche Unterschiede gibt es zwischen Weihnachten in Irland und in Deutschland?
- Wie feiern Sie Weihnachten?

Nützliche Sätze

In Deutschland werden Geschenke am Heiligen Abend verschenkt.	*In Germany gifts are exchanged on Christmas Eve.*
Am ersten Weihnachtstag gibt es ein großes Festessen.	*On Christmas Day there is a big meal.*
Wir verbringen viel Zeit mit Freunden und Familien.	*We spend a lot of time with friends and family.*
Viele gehen zum Gottesdienst und singen Weihnachtslieder.	*Many go to church and sing carols.*
Wir essen Putenfleisch oder Lammfleisch mit Gemüse und Kartoffeln. Das ist lecker.	*We eat turkey or lamb with vegetables and potatoes. That is delicious.*
Ich kaufe Geschenke für meine Familie. Ich bekomme Geld, Kleidung und ein neues Handy zu Weihnachten.	*I buy presents for my family. I get money, clothes and a new mobile phone for Christmas.*

Kulturecke

Just as the different regions of Germany have their own customs and celebrations, so do Austria and Switzerland. Using the internet, do some research into traditional celebrations in different German-speaking countries.

Grammatik: Reflexivpronomen/ Reflexive Pronouns

p. 161 (Übung macht den Meister)

A reflexive pronoun involves the concept of 'self' and can replace a noun.

- 'The man' can be replaced with 'himself', 'to himself', 'with himself'.
- 'Mary' can be replaced with 'herself', 'to herself', 'with herself'.
- 'The teachers' can be replaced with 'themselves', 'to themselves', 'with themselves'.

Like nouns and personal pronouns, reflexive pronouns follow the German case system of the accusative and dative. However, the nominative and genitive cases do not occur with reflexive pronouns.

- Here is an example of the accusative case:
  Ich wasche mich = I wash myself
- The dative case is used when a body part is mentioned:
  Ich wasche mir die Haare = I wash my hair

Reflexive Pronouns	Accusative	Dative
myself, to myself	mich	mir
yourself, to yourself (singular)	dich	dir
himself, to himself	sich	sich
herself, to herself	sich	sich
itself, to itself	sich	sich
ourselves, to ourselves	uns	uns
yourselves, to yourselves (plural)	euch	euch
yourself, to yourself (polite)	sich	sich
themselves, to themselves	sich	sich

1. Here are some common examples of reflexive verbs. Identify the case of each reflexive pronoun. Then translate the sentences.

a) Ich stelle mich vor.	**e)** Sie waschen sich.
b) Er duscht sich.	**f)** Du wäschst dir die Haare.
c) Wir ziehen uns an.	**g)** Sie freut sich darüber.
d) Sie ziehen sich aus.	**h)** Er schaut sich einen Film an.

2. Insert the correct accusative or dative reflexive pronoun. Then translate the sentences.

a) Du hast _____ verletzt.	**e)** Er erinnert _____ daran.
b) Ich habe_____ das Bein verletzt.	**f)** Meine Mutter ärgert _____.
c) Wir amüsieren _____.	**g)** Wann wäschst du _____ die Haare?
d) Ich habe _____ erkältet.	**h)** Sie bewerben _____ um die Stelle.

In German, there are a lot more verbs with reflexive pronouns than in English. Here are the most common ones:

sich anhören to listen to	**sich eignen** to be suitable
sich anschauen to watch	**sich entspannen** to relax
sich ausruhen to rest	**sich freuen auf** to look forward to
sich bemühen to make an effort	**sich freuen über** to be glad about
sich duschen to shower	**sich interessieren für** to be interested in

Text 3: Am Nikolausabend

Bitte beantworten Sie die folgenden Fragen:

1. Beschreiben Sie, was Sie auf diesem Foto sehen!
2. Zu welcher Jahreszeit spielt sich die Geschichte ab?
3. Wie ist die Stimmung?

Vorarbeit

1. Finden Sie diese reflexiven Ausdrücke im Text!
   - **A** I pressed my nose against the cold glass.
   - **B** I started to feel better.
   - **C** I was delighted.
   - **D** ... without saying goodbye to us.
2. Finden Sie das Deutsche für die Wörter unten!
   - **A** clever/well behaved/began/rose
   - **B** figure/rose/punishes/kind
   - **C** turned the page/complaint/curl/listen
   - **D** behaviour/more heavily/flash/snow

Christine Herrmann, 3 December 2007 (amended)

A Vor vielen Jahren stand ich am Fenster in unserem Kinderzimmer und schaute hinaus. Zusammen mit meiner älteren Schwester drückte ich mir die Nase an dem kalten Glas. „Ist bald Weihnachten?" fragte ich meine Schwester, denn sie war ja alt und klug. „Heute ist ja erst Nikolausabend", verkündete sie. „Hmmm", meinte ich, „der Nikolaus kommt doch nicht hierhin, oder?" und langsam stieg die Angst in mir auf. Wenn er wirklich kommen würde, würde er wissen, dass ich ab und zu, aber nur ab und zu, nicht brav gewesen war. Ehrlich gesagt, schon öfter. „Ich weiß nicht", sagte sie. Draußen fing es an, zu schneien. „Ich schlafe ein", meinte ich, denn wenn ich schlief, würde mich der Nikolaus doch nicht wecken.

B Es klingelte an der Haustür und mein Herz klopfte stark. Jemand öffnete die Haustür. Ich hörte eine laute, tiefe Stimme und nun stieg pure Angst in mir hoch. Zu spät, Mama rief nach uns, wir sollten kommen. Wie gut, dass meine Schwester bei mir war, als wir vor dem riesigen dicken Nikolaus ankamen. Er hatte einen weißen Bart und ein rotes Gesicht. Er lächelte und seine Augen waren gütig. Ich fing an, mich besser zu fühlen. Aber halt! Wer war die schwarze Gestalt neben ihm? „Das ist Knecht Ruprecht, der bestraft die bösen Kinder mit der Rute!" sagte der Nikolaus und ich wurde immer nervöser. Hinter meiner Schwester war es etwas sicherer.

C Dann sah ich die Schuhe von Knecht Ruprecht, es waren rote Stiefel. Knecht Ruprecht war klein und ich sah eine goldene Locke unter seiner schwarzen Mütze. Was?! Knecht Ruprecht war eine Frau! „Aber der Knecht Ruprecht ist doch eine ..." – „Sei still!" sagte meine Schwester und gab mir einen Knuff. Der Nikolaus machte sein großes Buch auf und blätterte um. „Was?" fragte ich. Der Nikolaus hatte etwas gesagt und ich hatte nicht gehört. „Ich sehe hier, dass du nicht immer ohne Murren zu Bett gehst und mit dem Zähneputzen ist es auch stressig. Oft hörst du nicht zu", murmelte er. „Ansonsten warst du recht brav und deshalb bekommst du ein Geschenk von mir." Ich freute mich sehr! Ich war so erleichtert! Knecht Ruprechts blaue Augen blitzten freundlich. Er/sie wischte sich übers schwarze Gesicht. Dort, wo er/sie gewischt hatte, war nicht mehr so schwarz, aber ich wusste jetzt, warum.

D Die Auflistung des Verhaltens meiner Schwester war nicht so schnell zu Ende, wie die meine, aber endlich bekam auch sie ihr Geschenk. So, sie war auch ein braves Kind! Der Nikolaus und Knecht Ruprecht gingen einfach hinaus in den Winterabend, ohne sich von uns zu verabschieden. Der Schnee fiel stärker. Nur ab und zu sah man die roten Stiefel vom Knecht Ruprecht im Laternenlicht aufblitzen, als sie beide durch die Nacht weggingen.

OL Ordinary Level Questions

1. a) i) What question does the narrator ask? ii) What answer does his sister give? A
   b) Describe Nikolaus and Ruprecht, giving **two** details about each person. B C
   c) What did the narrator believe he had discovered about Ruprecht? C
   d) Describe the outdoor scene as Nikolaus and Ruprecht leave the narrator's home. D
2. Choose a suitable heading for each paragraph from the box below and explain your choice in English.

Nikolaus und Ruprecht kommen an	Nikolaus und Ruprecht gehen weg	Ich war erleichtert	Der 5. Dezember

3. Are the following statements true or false?
   a) Der Erzähler steht vor einem Fenster.
   b) Er hat keine Angst vor Nikolaus und Knecht Ruprecht.
   c) Er bekommt kein Geschenk.
   d) Nikolaus und Ruprecht winken dem Erzähler beim Weggehen zu.
4. Select the correct prepositions for the following sentences.
   a) Der Erzähler steht **(in/im/am/vor)** Kinderzimmer.
   b) Jemand klopft **(mit/von/an/durch)** der Tür.
   c) Er sah blonde Haare **(in/an/unter/über)** der Mütze.
   d) Sie gingen **(an/um/im/in)** den Abend hinaus.

HL Higher Level Questions

1. Beantworten Sie folgende Fragen auf Deutsch!
   a) Welche Frage stellt der Erzähler? Wie antwortet seine Schwester auf die Frage? A
   b) Beschreiben Sie genau, wie Nikolaus und Knecht Ruprecht aussehen! B C
   c) Warum fühlt sich der Erzähler so erleichtert? C
   d) Hat die Schwester sofort ihr Geschenk bekommen? Woher wissen Sie das? D
2. Answer the following questions in English.
   a) Where is the narrator and what does he do? Give a detailed description with **two** details each. A
   b) How does the narrator react when there is a knock at the door? Give **three** details. B
   c) What exactly does Nikolaus say to the narrator? C
   d) Describe in detail how Nikolaus and Ruprecht depart. D
   e) The narrator experiences a number of intense emotions. Give **three** examples of these intense emotions and explain the context of these emotions (can be *language use* and/or *content*).
3. Was passt zusammen?

1. Er kümmerte sich darum,	**A** sobald Nikolaus ihn anlächelte.
2. Er fühlte sich besser,	**B** und gingen in den Winterabend hinaus.
3. Er freute sich,	**C** dass Nikolaus auf ihn böse sein würde.
4. Sie verabschiedeten sich	**D** als er vom Nikolaus ein Geschenk bekam.

4. Indicate whether the following underlined pronouns are singular or plural, their case and the person to whom the pronoun refers.
   Example: **Ich stand am Fenster**: singular, nominative, refers to the narrator.
   a) Langsam stieg die Angst in mir auf.
   b) Er würde wissen, dass ich nicht immer brav war.
   c) Der Nikolaus würde mich nicht wecken.
   d) Mama rief nach uns.
   e) Wer war die Gestalt neben ihm?
   f) Sie gingen beide weg.

Grammatik: Relativpronomen/Relative Pronouns

p. 161 (Übung macht den Meister)

A relative pronoun can mean: who/which, whom, to whom/to which, whose/of which, that.

These pronouns always refer to the noun which comes directly before it in a sentence, for example:

- The man who bought the car is very happy.
- The man whom we saw leaving the building was found later that day.
- The man to whom the prize was given is an inventor.
- The man whose house is for sale hopes he will make a profit.

Note that relative pronouns match the gender and number of the noun they refer to.

Similar to nouns, pronouns and reflexive pronouns, relative pronouns follow the German case system. Relative pronouns can be used in the nominative, accusative, dative or genitive case.

Relative Pronouns	Male	Female	Neuter	Plural
who, which, that	der	die	das	die
whom, which, that	den	die	das	die
to/with/from whom/which	dem	der	dem	denen
whose, of which	dessen	deren	dessen	deren

Note that after a relative pronoun, the verb is placed at the end of the clause.

1. Identify the case, gender and number of the relative pronouns below. Then translate the sentences.

a) Das Kind, das ein Eis kauft, sieht froh aus.	**e)** Die Bücher, die Sie lesen, sind interessant.
b) Die Frau, die das Kleid anprobiert, ist schick.	**f)** Der Mann, dem du das Buch gegeben hast, ist froh.
c) Die Frau, die ich sah, hatte blonde Haare.	**g)** Die Schüler, denen der Lehrer die Noten gab, waren erleichtert.
d) Das Buch, das ich verloren hatte, wurde gefunden.	**h)** Die Frau, der ich erste Hilfe leistete, hat sich erholt.

2. Insert the correct relative pronouns for the sentences below. Then translate the sentences.

a) Danke für den Brief, ______ (m) heute angekommen ist.	**e)** Was ist das Fach, ______ (n) du am liebsten hast?
b) Wo ist die Schule, ______ (f) du besuchst?	**f)** Die Jungen, von ______ (pl.) er spricht, sind begabt.
c) Der Lehrer, ______ (m) die Kinder danken, ist nett.	**g)** Ich mag das Kind, ______ (n) immer höflich ist.
d) Meine Tante, ______ (f) Haus in Kerry liegt, ist krank.	**h)** Der Mann, ______ (m) Auto ich fahre, ist freundlich.

Hausaufgaben

Practise using simple relative pronouns in your oral and written work:

Meine Schwester, die vierzehn ist, heißt Ellen. My sister, who is 14, is called Ellen.

Das Fach, das ich am schwierigsten finde, ist Mathe. The subject that I find the hardest is Maths.

08.03 Hörverständnis Teil 3

Vorarbeit

herumlaufen	*to run around*	**Feuerwerk**	*fireworks*	**führen**	*to lead*
deprimierend	*depressing*	**verletzt**	*injured*	**einläuten**	*to ring in*
neugierig	*curious*	**erleben**	*to experience*	**vernünftiger**	*more sensibly*
übertreiben	*to exaggerate*	**unangenehm**	*unpleasant*	**betrunken**	*drunk*

CL Ordinary + Higher Level Questions

1. **a)** The conversation is between:
   i) friends ☐ **ii)** schoolmates ☐ **iii)** Leaving Certificate students ☐ **iv)** teammates ☐
   b) Find **one (O)/two (H)** details in the conversation that support your choice.
2. **a)** Which word best describes the female speaker's attitude during the conversation?
   i) depressed ☐ **ii)** angry ☐ **iii)** apologetic ☐ **iv)** frightened ☐
   b) Write down **one (O)/two (H)** details from the conversation to support your choice.
3. How does the male speaker try to change the female speaker's mind? Write down **one (O)/three (H)** details.
4. What solution does the male speaker propose? Give **one (O)/two (H)** details.

08.04 Hörverständnis Teil 4

Vorarbeit

verehren	*to honour*	**betreuen**	*to care for*	**beten**	*to pray*
vertreiben	*to drive out*	**genießen**	*to enjoy*	**Schweinehaxe**	*pork knuckle*
Feinkost	*gourmet foods*	**gönnen**	*to indulge in*	**zauberhaft**	*magical*
Reibekuchen	*potato fritters*	**Holzbuden**	*wooden huts*	**verhungern**	*to starve*

CL Ordinary + Higher Level Questions

1. **a)** Name the two groups of people who celebrate Walpurgis Night.
   b) What does each group celebrate on Walpurgis Night?
2. **a)** How many people visit the Oktoberfest each year?
   b) How many come from abroad to the festival?
   c) What food and drink is available at the festival?
3. **a)** What is being celebrated in Bamberg? Give details. **b)** How long will it last?
4. **a)** Describe the Christmas market scene in Trier. Give **three (O)/five (H)** details.
   b) Name **i)** the food and drink and **ii)** the Christmas items mentioned.
5. **a)** What is the weather forecast for today? Give **two (O)/three (H)** details.
   b) What warning is given? Give **two (O)/three (H)** details.

Schriftliche Produktion: Ordinary + Higher Level

Das Projekt, Teil 1: Presentation

If you have decided to do the project instead of picture sequences in your oral examination, use the sentences below as a resource to write **16 (OL)/25 (HL) sentences** on your topic.

Ich habe ein Projekt gemacht. Ich habe es dabei.	*I did a project. I have it here with me.*
Mein Projekt handelt von Weihnachten/Ostern/ einem Musikfest namens ... /der Stadt Berlin.	*My project is about Christmas/Easter/a music festival called ... /about the city of Berlin.*
... ist/war ein wohlbekannter Musiker/ Komponist/Künstler/Dichter/Sportler, der in ... geboren wurde.	*... is/was a well-known musician/composer/artist/ poet/sportsman who was born in ...*

Das Projekt, Teil 2: Clarification

In part 2 you will clarify aspects of the project and explain the process involved in carrying it out.

Ich wollte das Projekt machen, weil ich mich für Geschichte/Musik/Sport interessiere.	*I wanted to do the project because I'm interested in history/music/sport.*
Ich habe drei Monate daran gearbeitet.	*I worked on it for three months.*
Ich habe zu Hause/in der Bibliothek/im Deutschunterricht daran gearbeitet.	*I worked on it at home/in the library/in German class.*
Ich habe viel im Internet recherchiert.	*I did a lot of research on the internet.*

Das Projekt, Teil 3: Elaboration

In part 3 you will answer questions on topics arising from the project.

Ich habe viel über ... gelernt.	*I learned a lot about ...*
Bei uns ist es ebenso/Bei uns ist es ganz anders.	*It's the same for us/It's very different for us.*
Es gibt ähnliche Musikfeste hier in Irland.	*There are similar music festivals here in Ireland.*

HL Schriftliche Produktion: Higher Level

Bitte beantworten Sie die folgenden Fragen:

1. Beschreiben Sie, was Sie auf dem Foto sehen!
2. Welche traditionellen Feste feiert man in Irland?
3. Wie feiern Sie Weihnachten und Silvester?
4. Ist Weihnachten zu kommerziell geworden?
5. Gibt es gute Musikfeste in Irland? Waren Sie je auf einem Konzert?

Nützliche Sätze

Man sieht nur die Hetze auf den Straßen und die ganze Weihnachtskauferei.	*One only sees rushing in the streets and all this Christmas shopping.*
Man kauft oft zu viele Geschenke. Meiner Meinung nach ist das nicht der Sinn von Weihnachten.	*One often buys too many presents. In my opinion, that is not the point of Christmas.*
Man sollte mehr Wert auf Familie und Freunde legen als auf Geschenke. Man sollte auf die Armen und Einsamen in unserer Gesellschaft achten.	*One should place more importance on family and friends than on presents. One should pay attention to the poor and the lonely in our society.*

Übung Macht den Meister!

A Personal Pronouns

1. Identify the gender, number and case (nominative, accusative, dative) of the personal pronouns below.
2. Write the sentences in your copy and translate them.

a) Ich brauche dich.
b) Wir feiern es.
c) Sie treffen ihn.
d) Er gab mir das Geld.
e) Sie versprach es ihm.
f) Du hast es ihr gegeben.
g) Ihr habt es ihnen geschenkt.

3. Replace the nouns below with the correct personal pronoun, according to gender, number and case.

a) Jonas schaltet das Licht aus.
b) Das Kind packt seine Schulsachen ein.
c) Meine Eltern rufen Michael an.
d) Meine Freunde und ich räumen den Müll weg.
e) Brigitte macht die Prüfung.
f) Suzanne und Jan sehen den Film.
g) Mein Vater kauft ein Auto.

B Reflexive Pronouns

1. Insert the correct reflexive pronoun, according to gender, number and case.

a) Michael duscht ___ .
b) Wir freuen ___ auf die Zukunft.
c) Ich gewöhne ___ schon an die Arbeit.
d) Das Kind entschuldigt ___ .
e) Wir beeilen ___ .
f) Man Vater rasiert ___ jeden Morgen.
g) Sie waschen ___ am Morgen.

2. Insert the correct dative reflexive pronoun.

a) Der Junge wäscht ___ die Haare.
b) Wir haben ___ alle das Gesicht gewaschen.
c) Das Mädchen hat ___ den Finger verletzt.
d) Die Katze leckt ___ die Pfoten.
e) Sie bürsten ___ die Haare.
f) Ich rieb ___ die Augen.
g) Wann wäschst du ___ die Hände?

C Relative Pronouns

1. Insert the correct relative pronoun, according to gender, number and case.

a) Ich sehe den Jungen, ___ mir geholfen hat.
b) Das Haus, ___ ich mag, ist in der Bachstraße.
c) Die Frau, ___ mir half, steht da drüben.
d) Die Stadt, ___ ich am liebsten habe, heißt Trier.
e) Die Schüler, ___ die Prüfung machen, sind klug.
f) Die Lehrer, ___ das Fach unterrichten, sind nett.
g) Das Kind, ___ ich das Eis gab, ist lieb.

2. Insert the correct relative pronoun, according to gender, number and case.

a) Der Mann, ___ ich das Buch gab, stand da.
b) Die Frau, ___ Tasche verloren ist, ist wütend.
c) Die Studenten, ___ der Dozent die Noten gab, sind froh.
d) Die Jungen, ___ Fahrräder gestohlen wurden, gingen zur Polizeiwache.
e) Der Polizist, ___ Erfolg anerkannt wird, ist stolz.
f) Der Film, ___ ich am liebsten habe, heißt ...
g) Die Frau, mit ___ ich rede, ist launisch.

3. Identify the number, gender and case of the following relative pronouns.

a) Die Person, mit der ich das Haus teile, kommt aus Deutschland.
b) Das Auto, das ich besitze, ist sehr alt.
c) Die Gegend, in der ich wohne, heißt Ballincollig.
d) Der Schüler, der zu spät kommt, wird beschimpft.
e) Wer hat meine Filzstifte, die auf der Theke lagen?
f) Die Freunde, mit denen ich gern ausgehe, sind ein bisschen verrückt.
g) Meine Eltern wollen mit dem Mädchen sprechen, das mich schikaniert hat.
h) Die Firma, die diese Software entwickelt, heißt IBM.
i) Ich kenne seit Jahren den Freund, bei dem ich für eine Woche wohne.
j) Was wisst ihr über den Mann, der jetzt bei der Zeitung arbeitet?

Für die Prüfung

1. Was passt zusammen?

1.	In Irland werden	**A**	feiern die Deutschen eher den Tag der deutschen Einheit.
2.	Während die Iren den Nationalfeiertag groß feiern,	**B**	sind sie auch in Irland beliebt.
3.	Obwohl Deutschland das Heimatland des Weihnachtsmarkts ist,	**C**	Weihnachten, Ostern, Halloween und der Nationalfeiertag groß gefeiert.
4.	In Deutschland findet die Bescherung am Heiligen Abend statt,	**D**	sondern auch in Deutschland und Österreich.
5.	St. Patricks Day wird nicht nur in Irland gefeiert,	**E**	während sie am ersten Weihnachtstag in Irland stattfindet.

2. Match the sentence halves. Translate the sentences into English and identify the gender, case and number of the underlined personal pronouns in each sentence.

1.	Ich möchte	**A**	einen Abi-Ball zu organisieren.
2.	Um meinen Geburtstag zu feiern,	**B**	und was werdet ihr alles machen?
3.	Wir haben vor,	**C**	gehen wir ins Restaurant.
4.	Wenn ich mit dem Abitur fertig bin,	**D**	dich nach Irland zum Besuch einladen.
5.	Wann werdet ihr das Fest feiern,	**E**	werde ich eine Abi-Fahrt machen.

3. Select the correct reflexive pronouns for the following sentences.

a) Ich verhalte **(mich/mir/dich/sich)** gut im Unterricht.

b) Meine Klassenkameraden benehmen **(mich/euch/sich/uns)** sehr gut in der Schule.

c) Wir freuen **(euch/uns/sich/mich)** riesig auf euren Besuch!

d) Er hat **(sich/dich/mir/mich)** beim Lehrer entschuldigt.

e) Sie können **(euch/dich/sich/mich)** duschen, wenn Sie wollen.

f) Die Kinder interessieren **(sich/dich/mir/mich)** für Geschichte.

g) Wir verstehen **(uns/sich/euch/mich)** relativ gut.

h) Freut ihr **(mich/dich/euch/sich)** auf den Abi-Ball?

4. What words make up the following compound words, and what do they mean in English?

a) anfangen = _____ + _____ = ________

b) Hauptfeste = _____ + _____ = ________

c) Heimatland = _____ + _____ = ________

d) Nationalfeiertag = _____ + _____ = ________

e) Weihnachtsmarkt = _____ + _____ = ________

f) Gottesdienst = _____ + _____ = ________

g) Abi-Ball = _____ + _____ = ________

h) stattfinden = _____ + _____ = ________

5. Select the correct prepositions for the following sentences.

a) Ich interessiere mich **(mit/bei/für/auf)** deutsche Sitten und Bräuche.

b) Meine Klassenkameraden entschuldigen sich **(über/für/von/bei)** dem Mathelehrer.

c) Wir freuen uns riesig **(an/auf/zu/nach)** euren Besuch!

d) Er hat sich **(über/für/von/bei)** dem Fußballspielen verletzt.

e) Sie können **(mit/bei/für/auf)** mir wohnen, wenn Sie wollen.

f) Die Kinder haben sich gut **(von/neben/auf/unter)** der Grippe erholt.

g) Wir verstehen uns gut **(über/für/mit/bei)** den Lehrern.

Selbstbewertung: Ordinary Level

Vocabulary

1. If I can translate theses sentences into English, I can express myself in the present tense. (1 mark each).

a) Wir feiern Weihnachten, Ostern, Halloween und St. Patrick's Day.	**f)** Sie feiern auch Walpurgnisnacht und den Nikolaustag.
b) Mein Lieblingsfestival ist Electric Picnic.	**g)** Die Deutschen feiern die gleichen Feste.
c) Ich kaufe Geschenke für meine Familie.	**h)** Wir gehen zum Gottesdienst.
d) Wir schmücken den Weihnachtsbaum.	**i)** Wir geben einander Geschenke.
e) Wir essen ein Festessen.	**j)** Wir machen viel Spaß.

Your score: ___ / 10

2. If I can translate these nouns into English, I understand the main nouns needed to describe festivals. (1 mark each)

a) Nationalfeiertag	**c)** Fest	**e)** Weihnachten	**g)** Geschenke	**i)** Festessen
b) Umzug	**d)** Gottesdienst	**f)** Ostern	**h)** Stimmung	**j)** Silvester

Your score: ___ / 10

Grammar

3. If I can conjugate these verbs in the **ich** and **wir** forms in the present tense, I can talk about my experiences of Irish and German festivals and celebrations. (1 mark each)

a) feiern: ich ____________ wir ____________
b) schenken: ich ____________ wir ____________
c) essen: ich ____________ wir ____________
d) kaufen: ich ____________ wir ____________
e) schmücken: ich ____________ wir ____________

Your score: ___ / 10

4. If I can choose the correct reflexive pronoun, I understand reflexive pronouns. (1 mark each)

a) Ich freue **(mich/mir)** auf Weihnachten.	**f)** Ich höre **(mich/mir)** gern Popmusik an.
b) Im Sommer ruhe ich **(mich/mir)** aus.	**g)** Ich dusche **(mich/mir)**.
c) Wir amüsieren **(sich/uns)** gern.	**h)** Ich wasche **(mich/mir)** die Haare.
d) Wir interessieren **(sich/uns)** für Festivals.	**i)** Meine Eltern und ich verstehen **(sich/uns)**.
e) Ich sehe **(mich/mir)** gern Filme an.	**j)** Wir unterhalten **(sich/uns)** in der Pause.

Your score: ___ / 10

5. If I can put these verbs into the future tense, I can describe a future celebration. (1 mark each)

a) feiern: ich _____ ____________ **f)** singen: ich _____ ____________
b) essen: ich _____ ____________ **g)** freuen: ich _____ ____________
c) trinken: ich _____ ____________ **h)** schmücken: ich _____ ____________
d) tanzen: ich _____ ____________ **i)** lachen: ich _____ ____________
e) gehen: ich _____ ____________ **j)** spielen: ich _____ ____________

Your score: ___ / 10

What have I learned?	
What must I improve?	
What do I want to revise?	

Your total score: ___ / **50**

Selbstbewertung: Higher Level

HL

1. If I can translate these sentences into German, I recognise the importance of personal pronouns in the nominative, accusative and dative cases. (2 marks each)

a) He bought her a book.	**d)** I would like to invite you to the party.
b) We will give them flowers.	**e)** I will go with them on holiday.
c) Will you (singular) come with us to the concert?	

Your score: ___ / 10

2. If I can translate these sentences into German, I recognise the importance of reflexive pronouns in the accusative and dative cases. (2 marks each)

a) I am looking forward to the holiday.	**d)** I have washed my hair.
b) He apologised to the teacher.	**e)** Then I dressed myself.
c) They dress up as witches.	

Your score: ___ / 10

3. If I can translate these sentences into German, I recognise the importance of relative pronouns in the nominative and accusative cases. (2 marks each)

a) My favourite festival is St Patrick's Day, which takes place on the 17th of March.

b) I have a brother who is called Frank.

c) My favourite celebrations are birthdays, which I celebrate with my friends and family.

d) I have two brothers who are called Frank and Paul.

e) The subject which I like the most is German.

Your score: ___ / 10

4. If I can translate the verbs below into English, I understand the simple, separable and inseparable verbs used to describe festivals and celebrations. (1 mark each)

a) aufstellen	**d)** sich verkleiden	**g)** sich freuen auf	**i)** sich ankleiden
b) einkaufen gehen	**e)** einladen	**h)** feiern	**j)** besuchen
c) schenken	**f)** schmücken		

Your score: ___ / 10

5. If I can correctly fill in the gaps below, I understand the difference between verbs, nouns, pronouns, articles, adjectives and prepositions. (1 mark each)

feiern mit ins befreundet uns eine gleichen dass macht Geschenke

Ich feiere am liebsten **1** ______ meinen Freunden. Normalerweise **2** ______ wir unsere Geburtstage zusammen, was natürlich viel Spaß **3** ______. Meistens gehen wir **4** ______ Kino und ins Restaurant. Wir schenken einander **5** ______ und **6** ______ Geburtagskarte. Ich finde es toll, **7** ______ wir zusammen feiern, denn wir sind so gut **8** ______ und haben die **9** ______ Interessen. Wir verstehen **10** ______ echt gut und haben immer viel Spaß zusammen.

Your score: ___ / 10

What have I learned?	
What must I improve?	
What do I want to revise?	

Your total score: ___ / 50

09 Die große Arbeitswelt

Learning Outcomes

- **Oral:** discussing the world of work and the picture sequence
- **Reading:** reading and discussing three texts on the working world
- **Writing:** writing an opinion (**Äußerung**), picture descriptions and a letter on working life
- **Aural:** listening to and answering questions on four extracts on work

Grammar

- The dative case
- Prepositional verbs in the accusative and dative

Vocabulary

- Work and career
- Part-time work and work experience
- Job possibilities abroad

German Culture

- The German economy
- **Das Freiwillige Soziale Jahr** (voluntary social year)
- Gender and work

Exam Tips

- When you first read the letter, look out for questions which require the past tense. Use the perfect tense to answer them. Remember that verbs of motion use **sein**.
- If you see any form of **würden** in the letter, use the conditional in your answer:

  Wie würden deine Eltern reagieren?
  Meine Eltern würden schlecht reagieren.

Prüfungstipp

The Picture Sequence

Part 2 of your oral examination is **either** a project **or** a picture sequence. Both are 30 marks each.

Form of the Picture Sequence

- There will be five picture cards, each with five to six pictures, which you will receive well before the oral exam.
- On the day of the exam, these cards will be face down on the table. You will choose one at random.
- The examiner will ask you to narrate the story depicted on the card before asking you a series of follow-up questions.
- It is important to remember to narrate the picture sequence with the emphasis on the story actions.

Process and Marking

- There are three parts to the presentation of the picture sequence, each worth 10 marks.
- The total time of this section should be no longer than four to five minutes.
- Try to answer every question with two to four sentences.

Part 1: Narration of picture sequence and explanation = 10 marks

Narrate the picture story in 10–15 sentences for Ordinary Level and 15–20 sentences for Higher Level. The examiner will ask you to explain some aspect of the story not dealt with in the narration. You might be asked to describe how someone is dressed, what is on the table, how the teacher will react.

Part 2: Future projection = 10 marks

The examiner may ask you questions such as:

- **Wie geht die Geschichte weiter?** *How does the story continue?*
- **Was passiert in Zukunft?** *What happens in future?*

Use the future tense for the future projection: **In Zukunft wird Maria alles mit ihren Eltern besprechen. Zusammen werden sie eine Lösung finden.**

Part 3: Opinion on a related issue = 10 marks

Picture sequences explore several themes. These could be bullying, school rules, family relationships, the use of mobile phones. It is a good idea to prepare a few sentences on possible opinion questions.

The issues are topical and also appear in the written exam. If you don't understand a question, ask:

Könnten Sie die Frage bitte wiederholen? *Please could you repeat the question?*

Ich verstehe die Frage nicht. *I don't understand the question.*

Wie bitte? *Pardon me?*

Prüfungstipp

This picture is typical of the first of five or six pictures on a picture sequence card. Become familiar with your picture sequences as soon as possible. Make sure that you regularly practise all of them, including the ones which you do not like. Below are guidelines for answering at Ordinary and Higher Level.

Part 1: Narration

Aim to have three to four sentences for each picture on the card.

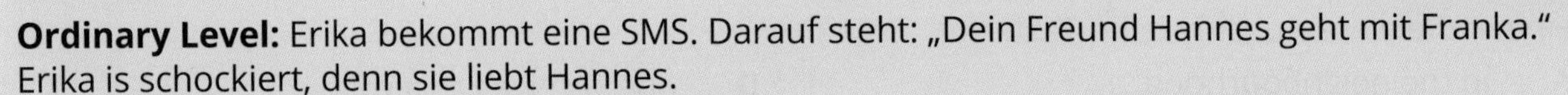

Ordinary Level: Erika bekommt eine SMS. Darauf steht: „Dein Freund Hannes geht mit Franka." Erika is schockiert, denn sie liebt Hannes.

Higher Level: Es ist 7 Uhr 30 und Erika wacht auf. Sie hat eben eine SMS bekommen. Sie liest die Nachricht: „Dein Freund Hannes geht mit Franka." Erika ist ganz schockiert, denn sie ist tief in Hannes verliebt und Franka ist ihre beste Freundin.

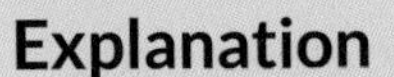

Explanation

Prepare for possible questions on each picture.

„Wie sieht das Schlafzimmer aus?" *What does the bedroom look like?*

Ordinary Level: Das Schlafzimmer ist schön. Es gibt viele Poster und Bücher.

Higher Level: Das Schlafzimmer sieht sehr gemütlich aus. Es gibt viele Poster an der Wand und ein großes Foto von Erika und Hannes. Es gibt ein Bücherregal mit vielen Büchern. Es gibt Schminke und einen kleinen Spiegel auf der Kommode.

Part 2: Future Projection

Prepare three to four sentences on what happens next.

„Wie geht die Geschichte weiter?" *How does the story continue?*

Ordinary Level: Erika und Thomas sprechen mit ihren Eltern und ihren Lehrern. Sie werden eine Lösung finden.

Higher Level: Erika und Thomas werden ihren Eltern über die zwei SMS erzählen. Sie werden auch am nächsten Tag mit den Lehrern darüber reden. Zusammen werden sie eine Lösung finden. Mobbing soll man nie tolerieren.

Part 3: Opinion

„Kommt Mobbing oft in Schulen vor?" *Does bullying happen often in schools?*

Ordinary Level: Es gibt nicht viel Mobbing hier. Jeder ist sehr freundlich hier.

Higher Level: Leider kommt Mobbing oft vor. Schüler werden gehänselt oder sogar ausgegrenzt, vielleicht weil sie anders sind. Zum Glück gibt es nicht viel Mobbing in dieser Schule, denn wir achten auf einander.

„Wofür benutzen Sie ein Handy?" *What do you use your mobile for?*

Ordinary Level: Ich schicke SMS. Ich bleibe in Kontakt mit meinen Eltern und meinen Freunden.

Higher Level: Ich benutze mein Handy jeden Tag. Ich surfe im Internet damit und ich gucke mir Filme darauf an. Natürlich schicke ich auch SMS. Ein Leben ohne Handy kann ich mir gar nicht vorstellen.

„Mit wem sprechen Sie, wenn Sie ein Problem haben?" *Who do you speak to when you have a problem?*

Ordinary Level: Ich spreche mit meinen Eltern, wenn ich ein Problem habe. Meine Eltern sind sehr verständnisvoll.

Higher Level: Zum Glück kann ich immer mit meinen Eltern sprechen, denn sie haben ein offenes Ohr für mich. Ich habe auch gute Freunde, mit denen ich über alles sprechen kann. Es ist wichtig, ein Problem zu besprechen, denn geteiltes Leid ist halbes Leid.

Text 1: Geld verdienen nebenbei

 Bitte beantworten Sie die folgenden Fragen:

1. Was sehen Sie auf dem Foto?
2. Was trägt er?
3. Was macht der Junge, Ihrer Meinung nach?

Vorarbeit

1. Finden Sie diese Ausdrücke im Text!
   A ... in the neighbourhood ...
   B Grocery shops ... are available.
   C ... with a bit of luck and above all hard work ...
   D ... one receives as a rule ...
   E There are apps today for nearly every purpose.
2. Finden Sie das Deutsche für die Wörter unten!
   A delivery/stories/occasional/to distribute
   B as long as/hourly wage/luxury/tips/at least
   C cleaning/further/mowing the lawn
   D warehouse worker/discount/retail/goods
   E questionnaires/connection/participation/work equipment

In Deutschland haben mehr als drei Millionen Personen eine zweite berufliche Tätigkeit.

www.heimarbeit.de (amended)

A In der Nachbarschaft

Jobs in der Nachbarschaft sind ebenfalls sehr beliebt. Hier gibt es nicht nur die Gartenarbeit oder das Babysitting, sondern auch Jobs für zwischendurch wie das Austragen von Zeitungen. Babysitten ist ein Klassiker unter den Nebenjobs. Die Aufgaben sind klar definiert: Man kümmert sich um die Kinder einer Familie. Oft sieht man einfach fern, bereitet Essen zu, und liest Geschichten vor oder spielt mit den Kindern. Wer lieber morgens arbeitet, für den ist das Austragen von Zeitungen eine gute Wahl. Dort soll man dann Zeitungen, Zeitschriften oder Werbeprospekte in die Briefkästen verteilen.

B Nebenjobs im Restaurant, im Café oder im Supermarkt

Restaurant und Cafés sind eine erstklassige Möglichkeit für einen Nebenjob. Neben einem guten Stundenlohn kann man auch noch Trinkgeld bekommen. Zumindest solange man im direkten Kontakt mit den Gästen arbeitet. Wer in der Küche arbeitet, hat diesen Luxus aber leider nicht immer. Lebensmittelgeschäfte wie Lidl und Aldi stehen zur Auswahl.

C Garten- und Haushaltsarbeiten und Nachhilfe geben

Eine weitere Möglichkeit ist die Hilfe im Garten oder im Haushalt in der Nachbarschaft, zum Beispiel Einkaufen, Rasenmähen, Putzen, und so weiter... Auch kann man mit etwas Glück und vor allem tüchtiger Arbeit bis zu 10 Euro pro Stunde verdienen. Nachhilfe geben ist auch eine gute Methode, nebenbei Geld zu verdienen. Ein Stundenlohn kann zwischen 7 und 10 Euro liegen – besonders schön ist aber, dass es sehr flexibel ist.

D Nebenbei Geld verdienen im Mode-Einzelhandel

Wenn man Mode liebt, gibt es verschiedene Aufgaben wie zum Beispiel Lagerarbeiter, die Annahme der Ware, die Beratung der Kunden oder den Verkauf an der Kasse. Kleiner Bonus: Als Mitarbeiter erhält man in der Regel exklusive Rabatte für eigene Einkäufe.

E Nebenbei von Zuhause aus Geld verdienen

Auch von Zuhause aus kann man Geld verdienen. Die wichtigsten Arbeitsmittel sind der Computer und ein Anschluss zum Internet. Vor allem für Mütter ist ein Nebenjob von Zuhause aus sehr interessant. Aber auch für andere. Auf Platz eins steht die Teilnahme an Online-Umfragen. Auf Platz zwei steht das Testen verschiedener Produkte von Zuhause. Apps gibt es heute für fast jeden Zweck. Unter anderem gibt es auch Apps, mit denen man sich Geld verdienen kann.

OL Ordinary Level Questions

1. a) Give **three** examples of neighbourhood jobs mentioned in the text. A
   b) According to the text, when does one receive tips? B
   c) How much can one earn giving grinds? C
   d) What bonus do people working in retail normally receive? D
   e) For whom is a home-based part-time job most interesting? E
2. Choose the correct preposition.
   a) Als Babysitter kümmert man sich **(für/an/um/mit)** die Kinder.
   b) Im Café bekommt man oft Trinkgeld, wenn man Kontakt **(mit/auf/für/an)** den Kunden hat.
   c) Man braucht **(für/vor/durch/im)** allem fleißige Arbeit, wenn man gut verdienen will.
   d) Wenn man im Mode-Einzelhandel arbeitet, könnte man **(an/in/bei/zu)** der Kasse arbeiten.
   e) Man braucht einen Anschluss **(im/am/zum/um)** Internet, wenn man zu Hause arbeitet.
3. What words make up the following compound words, and what do they mean in English?
   a) Gartenarbeit = _____ + _____ = _____
   b) Arbeitsstelle = _____ + _____ = _____
   c) Stundenlohn = _____ + _____ = _____
   d) Mitarbeiter = _____ + _____ = _____
   e) Zuhause = _____ + _____ = _____

HL Higher Level Questions

1. Beantworten Sie folgende Fragen auf Deutsch.
   a) Was für Jobs kann man in der Nachbarschaft kriegen? Geben Sie mehrere Beispiele! A
   b) Wie bekommt man am besten Trinkgeld? B
   c) Warum ist Nachhilfe geben vorteilhaft? Nennen Sie **zwei** Gründe! C
   d) Was für Arbeit kann man im Mode-Einzelhandel machen? D
   e) Für wen ist ein Nebenjob von Zuhause aus sehr interessant? E
2. Answer the following questions in English.
   a) According to the text, what **three** tasks might a babysitter do? A
   b) Why do restaurants and cafes offer attractive part-time work? B
   c) What types of neighbourhood jobs are available? Name **three**. C
   d) Name **four** tasks one might do when working in retail, according to the text. D
   e) What are the top **two** jobs which one can do from home? E
3. Was passt zusammen?

1. Viele Menschen haben einen Nebenjob,	**A** wenn man gern früh aufsteht.
2. Man kann Zeitungen austragen,	**B** kann man auch Trinkgeld bekommen.
3. Wenn man mit den Gästen arbeitet,	**C** wenn man im Mode-Einzelhandel arbeitet.
4. Man bekommt Rabatte,	**D** braucht man einen Anschluss zum Internet.
5. Wenn man von Zuhause aus arbeitet,	**E** um mehr Geld zu verdienen.

4. Geben Sie für die Nomen an: ob Singular oder Plural, bei Singular das Geschlecht, den Fall.
   a) Jobs in der Nachbarschaft sind beliebt.
   b) Man kümmert sich um die Kinder.
   c) Man kann an der Kasse arbeiten.
   d) Es gibt Apps für fast jeden Zweck.

Kulturecke

Make use of rich German idioms in your spoken and written work.

Die Kirche im Dorf lassen literally: to leave the church in the village, meaning: don't get carried away

Der Film war nur OK. Lass die Kirche im Dorf. The film was only ok. Don't get carried away.

Grammatik: Der Dativfall/The Dative Case

p. 181 (Übung macht den Meister)

- The dative case is used for the indirect object and usually conveys the meaning: 'to', 'from', 'by' (to the child, from the boy, by car): **Ich gebe dem Kind** (dat.) **das Buch** (acc.).
- The dative case is used after dative prepositions (see page 135): **Du gehst** *mit* **mir einkaufen**.
- The dative case is used with two-way prepositions when describing fixed positions (see page 138): **Ein schöner Garten liegt hinter dem Haus**.
- The dative case is also used after certain verbs and expressions, which are listed below.

Verbs Followed by the Dative Case

antworten to answer	**geschehen** to happen	**raten** to advise
danken to thank	**glauben** to believe	**schaden** to harm, to damage
gefallen to like, to be pleasing to	**gratulieren** to congratulate	**schmecken** to taste
gehören to belong to	**helfen** to help	**verzeihen** to pardon, to forgive
gelingen to succeed	**passen** to fit, to suit	**wehtun** to hurt

Ich helfe meiner Mutter (f., dat.) **mit der Hausarbeit** *I help my mother with the housework*

Insert the correct dative forms for the following sentences.

1. Ich rate _____ tüchtig zu arbeiten.	*I advise the boy to work hard.*
2. Gefällt _____ das deutsche Essen?	*Do you* (plural) *like German food?*
3. Gehört _____ das schöne neue Auto?	*Does the lovely new car belong to you* (polite)?
4. Das Kleid passt _____ sehr gut.	*The dress really suits the girl.*
5. Luftverschmutzung schadet _____ Umwelt.	*Air pollution damages the environment.*
6. Die Spritze hat _____ wehgetan.	*The injection hurt the lady.*
7. Ich glaube _____ einfach nicht.	*I simply don't believe the girl.*
8. Wir gratulieren _____ Kind zum Geburtstag.	*We congratulate the child on its birthday.*

Expressions with the Dative Case

Mir ist kalt/heiß. I feel cold/hot.	**Das macht mir Spaß.** That's fun for me.
Es fällt mir ein. It occurs to me.	**Das ist mir egal.** That's all the same to me.
Es tut mir leid. I'm sorry.	**Das ist uns behilflich.** That's helpful to us.
Es kommt mir vor, dass ... It seems to me that ...	**Das ist ihm bekannt.** That is known to him.
Wie geht's dir? How are you?	**Ich bin dir dankbar.** I'm grateful to you.
Sie ist ihrem Vater ähnlich. She resembles her father.	**Das reicht mir.** That's enough for me.

Insert the correct pronoun for the following dative expressions.

1. Das ist _____ behilflich.	*That is helpful to me.*
2. Es tut _____ leid.	*He is sorry.*
3. Wie geht es _____?	*How are you* (polite)?
4. Das macht _____ Spaß.	*That's fun for us.*
5. Das ist ___ bekannt.	*That is known to her.*
6. Das ist ___ egal.	*That's all the same to you* (singular).
7. Ich bin _____ sehr dankbar.	*I am very grateful to you* (plural).
8. Es fällt _____ ein, dass er lernen muss.	*It occurs to him that he must study.*

09.01 Hörverständnis Teil 1

Vorarbeit

begreifen	*to understand*	**Abfliegen**	*takeoff*	**Schritte**	*steps*
Umstände	*conditions*	**Voraussetzung**	*requirement*	**beweisen**	*to prove*

CL Ordinary + Higher Level Questions

1. **a)** What does Josef do as a profession?
   b) How long has he been doing this, and how long had he dreamed of pursuing this career?
2. Name the tests he had to go through before starting this career. What other requirements are mentioned? Give **one (O)/two (H)** details.
3. How long did his course last, and how much did the course cost?
4. What does he enjoy about his work? Give **one (O)/two (H)** details.
5. Describe his working week in detail. Give **two (O)/three (H)** details.

09.02 Hörverständnis Teil 2

Vorarbeit

Ingenieurwesen	*engineering*	**GmbH**	*Ltd*	**Stellenangebot**	*vacancy*
sich erkundigen	*to enquire*	**Termin**	*appointment*	**mitteilen**	*to inform*
Entwicklung	*development*	**beteiligt**	*involved*	**sich bewerben**	*to apply*

OL Ordinary Level Questions

1. What information is the caller looking for? What is the caller's name?
2. Where does the woman suggest the caller look?
   a) a library ☐ **b)** a telephone book ☐ **c)** a website ☐ **d)** an information office ☐
3. What is the caller's number?

HL Higher Level Questions

1. Using ***key phrases***, write down **in German** the key information from the conversation:
   - the name of the **caller**
   - the reason for the call
   - **four** details of their conversation
   - details regarding further contact
   - the caller's phone number

Gesprächsnotiz

Anruf von: ______________ Gesprächsanlass: ______________

Der Anrufer:

- ruft später zurück ☐
- erwartet einen Rückruf ☐
- wird eine E-Mail erhalten ☐
- wird eine SMS erhalten ☐

Kontaktnummer: ______________

2. Write down **three** examples of the language used (***expressions and phrases***) which show that the caller is **eager** to stress the importance of his request.

Text 2: Möglichkeiten für ein Gap Year

Bitte beantworten Sie die folgenden Fragen:

1. Was macht die Frau auf diesem Foto?
2. Wo ist sie?
3. Was sieht man im Hintergrund/Vordergrund?

Vorarbeit

1. Finden Sie diese Ausdrücke im Text!
   - **A** Not only does one gather work experience ...
   - **B** ... which particularly interests you ...
   - **C** So the gap very quickly becomes a career booster.
   - **D** ... to realise a long-cherished dream.
2. Finden Sie das Deutsche für die Wörter unten!
   - **A** now or never/perpetual/to attain/manages/enables
   - **B** worker/be worthwhile/knows the ropes/business/pay attention
   - **C** to use/satisfied/to advance/time out/resigned/mentally
   - **D** local people/poor/prefer/accepts/work out

A Reisen

Am beliebtesten für ein Gap Year ist ein Work and Travel Programm, denn es ermöglicht einem mit einem Visum ein oder zwei Jahre in einem Land wie Australien, Neuseeland, Kanada usw. zu arbeiten und das Land zu bereisen. Man sammelt nicht nur Arbeitserfahrung und verbessert seine Sprachkenntnisse, sondern kann auch das Reisen durch Gelegenheitsjobs finanzieren. Man kann auch eine Sprache lernen. Heutzutage kommt man nicht mehr ohne Englisch aus. Ein Sprachkurs kann Ihnen helfen die Grammatik zu verstehen. Ein Sprachlehrer kann Ihnen dabei helfen die richtige Aussprache zu erlangen. Jetzt oder nie: Wer schon immer mal eine Weltreise machen wollte, der sollte dafür ein Gap Year machen. Wer Vollzeit arbeitet, der weiß, dass man nicht ewig Urlaub nehmen kann.

B Praktikum, Workshops oder Seminare

Gerade nach dem Abitur oder dem Bachelor kann sich ein Praktikum im Ausland oder in der Heimat lohnen. Wer mehr als drei Monate für ein Praktikum investieren möchte, der sollte darauf achten, dass das Praktikum bezahlt wird. Nach drei Monaten ist jeder Praktikant bestens eingearbeitet und dient dem Unternehmen als Arbeitskraft. Ein Workshop oder Seminar zu einem Thema, welches Sie brennend interessiert, kann Sie erfüllen. Einige Beispiele hierfür können ein Kochkurs in Asien, eine Barkeeper Ausbildung in Irland oder ein Kunstkurs irgendwo auf der Welt sein.

C Beruflich weiterbilden

Wer in seinem jetzigen Beruf eigentlich zufrieden ist und nur eine kurze Auszeit haben möchte, der kann die Zeit auch nutzen, um die Karriere voranzubringen. So wird die Lücke ganz schnell zum Karrierebooster. Wer innerlich seinen jetzigen Job schon gekündigt hat, aber noch nicht weiß, wie es beruflich weitergehen soll, der kann ein Gap Year für die Berufsfindung nutzen.

D Persönliche Projekte

Ein Gap Year ist dazu da, dass man sich Zeit für sich nimmt, um seine Beziehung zu retten, für jemanden da zu sein, oder einen lang gehegten Traum zu verwirklichen. Ein Jahr ist eine gute Zeit, um zu sehen, ob es mit einer selbstständigen Tätigkeit klappen kann. Als Freelancer ist man sein eigener Chef und entscheidet welchen Auftrag man annimmt und welchen nicht. Eine selbstlose Möglichkeit, um sein Gap Year zu nutzen, ist Freiwilligenarbeit. Beachten sollte man, dass einige Organisationen freiwillige Helfer in einigen armen Ländern bevorzugen, anstatt die Einheimischen auszubilden und anständig zu bezahlen.

Auslandskarriere.de (amended)

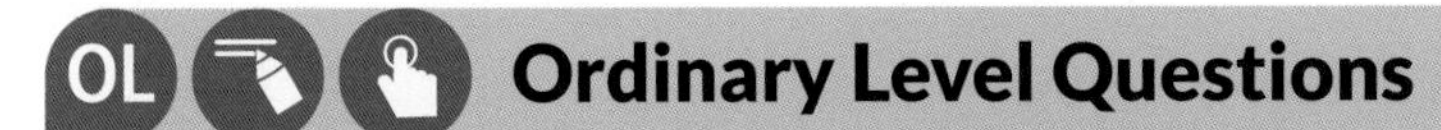

Ordinary Level Questions

1. a) What is the most popular choice for a gap year, according to the text? A
   b) The text mentions three possible courses one could do during a gap year. What are they? B
   c) If one is not happy with one's job, how can a gap year be helpful, according to the text? C
   d) As a freelancer, what can one decide? D
2. True or false?
   a) Mit einem Visum darf man in Kanada arbeiten.
   b) Nach dem Abitur muss man ein Praktikum machen.
   c) Man kann sich beruflich weiterbilden.
   d) Als Freelancer hat man einen Chef.
3. Complete the following sentences based on Text 2.
   a) Ein Sprachlehrer hilft bei der **(Arbeit/Aussprache/Reise/Berufswahl)**.
   b) Ein Praktikum ist eine gute Möglichkeit nach dem **(Schultag/Neujahr/Abitur/Sommer)**.
   c) Ein Gap Year kann den **(Chef/Teilzeitjob/Mensch/Beruf)** voranbringen.
   d) Man kann seine **(Träume/Ausbildung/Hoffnung/Organisationen)** verwirklichen.
4. Choose the correct preposition.
   a) Man kann das Reisen **(mit/durch/für/an)** Teilzeitjobs finanzieren.
   b) Ein Praktikant ist **(nach/in/für/an)** drei Monaten eingearbeitet.
   c) Das Gap Year wird **(zu/zum/für/in)** Karrierebooster.
   d) Man nimmt Zeit **(mit/an/in/für)** sich selbst.

HL Higher Level Questions

1. Beantworten Sie folgende Fragen auf Deutsch.
   a) Nennen Sie **zwei** Vorteile bei einem Work and Travel Programm. A
   b) Worauf sollte man achten, wenn man ein Praktikum macht? B
   c) Wie kann man ein Gap Year nutzen, wenn man beruflich unzufrieden ist? C
   d) Nennen Sie **zwei** Vorteile, wenn man als Freelancer arbeitet. D
2. Answer the following questions in English.
   a) Why are work and travel programmes so popular? Give **three** reasons. A
   b) According to the text, when is a good time to do work experience at home or abroad? B
   c) According to the text, how can one use this time out for one's career? Give **two** options. C
   d) What must one be mindful of when considering voluntary work abroad? D
3. Aus welchen Wörtern bestehen die folgenden Wörter? Was bedeuten sie auf Englisch?
   a) Sprachkenntnisse = ______ + ______ = ______
   b) Weltreise = ______ + ______ = ______
   c) Kochkurs = ______ + ______ = ______
   d) Freiwilligenarbeit = ______ + ______ = ______
4. Geben Sie für die Nomen an, ob Singular oder Plural, bei Singular das Geschlecht, den Fall.
   a) Man kann eine Sprache lernen.
   b) Ein Praktikum in der Heimat lohnt sich.
   c) Das Praktikum soll bezahlt werden.
   d) Viele wollen einen Traum verwirklichen.

Kulturecke

The German **Freiwillige Soziale Jahr** (voluntary social year – **FSJ** for short) is a social educational year for people aged 17–27. Young people can work in a range of areas, including hospitals, youth welfare organisations and nursing homes. It is an excellent opportunity to gain practical experience while contributing to the community and gaining insight into different professions.

OL Äußerung zum Thema: Ordinary Level

You are interviewing a young person who is doing a work and travel programme. Complete the dialogue using the information given in Text 2.

Sie: In welche Länder kann man mit diesem Programm fahren?
Jugendlicher: ______________________________
Sie: Für wie lange kann man dort arbeiten?
Jugendlicher: ______________________________
Sie: Wie kann man das Reisen finanzieren?
Jugendlicher: ______________________________
Sie: Kann man auch seine Sprachkenntnisse verbessern?
Jugendlicher: ______________________________
Sie: In welches Land wollen Sie persönlich fahren?
Jugendlicher: ______________________________

HL Äußerung zum Thema: Higher Level

- Beschreiben Sie die Bilder unten in **drei bis vier** Sätzen.
- Finden Sie, dass ein „Gap Year" vorteilhaft ist? Geben Sie **zwei** Gründe warum/warum nicht.
- Was wollen Sie persönlich nach dem Studium machen?
- Was für Arbeit wollen Sie in Zukunft ergreifen? Was ist für Sie wichtig bei der Arbeit?

Nützliche Sätze

Ich glaube, man wird reifer, wenn man neue Erfahrungen hat.	*I believe you become more mature when you have new experiences.*
Ich finde es gut, wenn man etwas Positives zur Gesellschaft beiträgt.	*I find it good when one makes a positive contribution to society.*
Ich finde das Gap Year eine reine Zeitverschwendung. Ich will gleich mit dem Studium anfangen.	*I find the gap year a pure waste of time. I want to start my studies right away.*
Wenn man eine Pause von dem Lernen macht, kann es schwierig sein, sich wieder daran zu gewöhnen.	*When you take a break from studying, it can be hard to get used to it again.*
Leider habe ich keine Ahnung, was für Arbeit ich machen will. Aber das hat noch Zeit.	*Unfortunately, I have no idea what kind of work I want to do. But there's still time.*
Am wichtigsten ist, dass die Tätigkeit Freude macht.	*The most important thing is that you enjoy your job.*
Nette Kollegen und Kolleginnen sind mir wichtig.	*Nice colleagues are important to me.*
Ich suche ein gutes Arbeitsklima und Wertschätzung.	*I'm looking for a good working atmosphere and appreciation.*

Grammatik: Verben + Präpositionen/ Verbs + Prepositions

p. 181 (Übung macht den Meister)

Verbs + Prepositions + Accusative

Some verbs have set meanings if accompanied by a particular preposition: to pay attention to, to be delighted about, etc. These German verbs are followed by prepositions which take the accusative case:

Verb + An + Accusative

denken an to think of	**glauben an** to believe in
sich erinnern an to remember	**schreiben an** to write to
sich gewöhnen an to get used to	

Verb + Auf + Accusative

achten auf to pay attention to	**hoffen auf** to hope for
antworten auf to answer	**sich konzentrieren auf** to concentrate on
aufpassen auf to mind	**reagieren auf** to react to
sich freuen auf to look forward to	**warten auf** to wait for

Verb + Für + Accusative

sich begeistern für to get enthusiastic about	**sich entscheiden für** to decide on
sich eignen für to be suitable for	**sich interessieren für** to be interested in
sich engagieren für to be involved with	**sorgen für** to take care of

Verb + Über + Accusative

sich ärgern über to get annoyed about	**klagen über** to complain about
sich beschweren über to complain about	**lachen über** to laugh about
diskutieren über to discuss	**sich streiten über** to fight about
sich freuen über to be pleased about	**sich wundern über** to wonder at
sich informieren über to inform oneself about	

Verb + Um + Accusative

sich bemühen um to make an effort for	**kämpfen um** to struggle for
bitten um to ask for	**kümmern um** to care for
sich handeln um to be about	

1. Insert the correct prepositions and then translate the following sentences.

a) Ich interessiere mich _____ die Umwelt.	**e)** Ich habe mich _____ den Kurs entschieden.
b) Ich passe _____ meine kleine Schwester auf.	**f)** Ich freue mich ___ die Ferien.
c) Meine Mutter ärgert sich _____ meine Noten.	**g)** Wir hoffen _____ gutes Wetter.
d) Ich konzentriere mich _____ die Aussprache.	**h)** Im Deutschunterricht diskutieren wir _____ vieles.

2. Insert the correct definite or indefinite articles and then translate the following sentences.

a) Ich hoffe auf ___ gutes Ergebnis (n).	**e)** Man gewöhnt sich an ___ Arbeit (f).
b) Das Buch handelt sich um _____ Held (m).	**f)** Er eignet sich für _____ Kurs (m).
c) Wir freuen uns auf _____ Sommer (m).	**g)** Ich konzentriere mich auf _____ Grammatik (f).
d) Wir ärgern uns über _____ Schuldruck (m).	**h)** Man hat sich über _____ Austausch (m) informiert.

Text 3: Arbeitswelt im Wandel

Bitte beantworten Sie die folgenden Fragen:

1. Was machen die Leute auf diesem Foto?
2. Wo sind sie?
3. Was macht die Person hinter dem Schalter?
4. Wie fühlen sich die Menschen, die Schlange stehen?

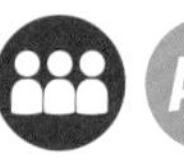 

Vorarbeit

1. Finden Sie diese Ausdrücke im Text!
   A ... all joy was lost.
   B That does it.
   C ... working ... for decades.
   D ... I was told.
2. Finden Sie das Deutsche für die Wörter unten!
   A daylight/growls/tolerate/employees/economy
   B introduced/to master/briskly/queues/compatible/demands
   C educated/features/dreadful/further training/technician
   D to retire/changes/to facilitate/value/radio practitioner

A Die Wirtschaft brummt bedrohlich. Täglich gute Zahlen zum deutschen Arbeitsmarkt und zur Wirtschaft. Gut für wen eigentlich? Viele Arbeitnehmer stellen fest, dass ihr Job immer stressiger wird ... Beim Brötchenholen wunderte ich mich. „Guten Tag, meine Liebe", begrüßt mich normalerweise die Verkäuferin unten im Kaufhaus mit einem Lächeln. An diesem Tag aber packte sie ohne ein Wort zu sagen die Brötchen ein. „Sieben Wochen ohne richtiges Wochenende", sagte sie, „immer nur der Sonntag frei. Das halte ich nicht mehr aus." Sechs Tage die Woche ohne Tageslicht zu arbeiten, da ging auch ihr die Freude aus.

B Ein paar Tage später kaufte ich am Bahnhof meine Fahrkarten für die Weihnachtsreisen. Die Dame am Schalter war freundlich, nur fragte ich mich warum es ihr so lange gedauert hat, meine Fragen nach Preisen und Abfahrtszeiten zu beantworten. „Jetzt reicht's", sagte sie ihrer Kollegin. Dann ging es plötzlich zackig. Ich blickte hinter mir. „Die Schlangen werden noch länger?", fragte ich sie und sie nickte. Sie versuchte das neue Computersystem zu beherrschen. „Warum denn dann die Neuerung?", wunderte ich mich. Sie seufzte. Man wolle neue Kolleg/innen schnell einarbeiten können, erklärte sie mir. Das alte System habe eine längere Einarbeitungszeit gebraucht und das sei mit den Anforderungen des zukünftigen Arbeitsmarkts nicht mehr vereinbar. „Aber wenn die da oben wüssten, wie es hier am Schalter zugeht, hätten sie diese Änderung nie eingeführt", versicherte sie mir.

C Ich musste an das Gespräch mit einer Technikerin vom Radio vor ein paar Monaten denken. Eine gut ausgebildete Frau, seit Jahrzehnten in Radioproduktionen tätig. Seit Kurzem aber sollten die Journalisten ihre Beiträge auch technisch „selbst fahren". Der Stress und die Frustration für die Journalisten und die Techniker waren schrecklich. Die Techniker sollten nun mit Digitalisierungen und Podcasts arbeiten, hatten aber keine berufliche Weiterbildung dafür.

D Diese Veränderungen kamen gar nicht vom Radiofach, wurde mir erzählt. Kein Hörfunkpraktiker würde so was machen, nur der Manager würde das machen. Und was wissen die Manager von der praktischen Arbeit? Fast wöchentlich gibt es neue Arbeitsanforderungen, die die Arbeit erleichtern sollen, die aber nur Schwierigkeiten machen. Zuerst haben die Techniker erzählt, sie und ihre Kollegen seien wütend und frustriert. Sie fühlten sich unsicher und ängstlich. Wo war der Wert für ihren Beruf geblieben? „Und irgendwann denkt man dann: ich kann es kaum erwarten, in die Rente zu gehen. Die Zeiten, in denen man die Arbeit geliebt hat, sind vorbei."

© Bernadette Conrad, *Zeit Online*, 27 Dec. 2017 (amended)

OL Ordinary Level Questions

1. a) How long has the shop assistant been working without a proper weekend? A
   b) What was the narrator buying a few days later and where was she? B
   c) What were the technicians now supposed to work with? C
   d) According to the text, why are managers not the best people to initiate changes? D
2. Choose a suitable heading for each paragraph and explain your choice in English.

Ich will in die Rente gehen	Die Journalisten und Techniker werden frustriert	Auch am Wochenende arbeiten	Die Systeme sind nicht vereinbar

3. What words make up these compound words, and what do they mean in English?
   a) Arbeitsmarkt = _____ + _____ = _____
   b) Weihnachtsreisen = _____ + _____ = _____
   c) Jahrzehnte = _____ + _____ = _____
   d) Arbeitsanforderungen = _____ + _____ = _____
4. Select the correct prepositions for the following sentences.
   a) Die Verkäuferin arbeitet seit Wochen **(mit/auf/ohne/um)** richtiges Wochenende.
   b) Die Erzählerin kaufte Fahrkarten **(im/am/um/an)** Bahnhof.
   c) Der Stress **(an/auf/in/für)** die Journalisten und Techniker war schlimm.
   d) Die Erzählerin will **(an/um/in/auf)** die Rente gehen.

HL Higher Level Questions

1. Beantworten Sie folgende Fragen auf Deutsch.
   a) Wie geht es zur Zeit der Wirtschaft? A
   b) Warum dauert es so lange, bis die Dame die Fragen beantworten kann? B
   c) Warum war die Technikerin frustriert? C
   d) Woran denkt man, wenn man sich bei der Arbeit unsicher fühlt? D
2. Answer the following questions in English.
   a) According to the text, what is causing many employees to find their work more stressful? A
   b) Why were the queues getting longer at the station? Give **three** details. B
   c) How have the demands of work changed for journalists, according to the text? C
   d) Some people can hardly wait to retire. What explanation does the text give? D
   e) The text suggests that work is not always a positive experience. Identify **three** examples (***in language or content***) which put work in a negative light.
3. Was passt zusammen?

1. Der Job wird stressiger,	**A** konnte sie die Fragen nicht beantworten.
2. Die Verkäuferin hält es nicht mehr länger aus,	**B** die die Arbeit schwierig machen.
3. Obwohl die Dame am Schalter freundlich war,	**C** dass sie sechs Tage ohne Tageslicht arbeitet.
4. Jetzt sollen die Journalisten technisch arbeiten,	**D** weil die Wirtschaft brummt.
5. Es gibt ständig neue Anforderungen,	**E** obwohl sie keine Weiterbildung dafür haben.

4. Indicate for the underlined words whether they are singular or plural, their gender and the case.
   a) Die Verkäuferin begrüßte mich.
   b) Ich kaufte meine Fahrkarten.
   c) „Jetzt reicht's", sagte sie ihrer Kollegin.
   d) Ich musste an das Gespräch denken.
   e) Die Techniker fühlten sich unsicher.
   f) Wo war der Wert für ihren Beruf geblieben?

Remember to use the reading texts to revise grammar from previous chapters. Find two examples of relative pronouns in Paragraph D.

Grammatik: Verben + Präpositionen/ Verbs + Prepositions

p. 181 (Übung macht den Meister)

Verbs + Preposition + Dative

Some verbs have set meanings if accompanied by a particular preposition: to suffer from, to take part in, to begin with. These German verbs are followed by prepositions which take the dative case:

Verb + An + Dative

leiden an to suffer from	**sterben an** to die from	**teilnehmen an** to take part in

Verb + Aus + Dative

bestehen aus to consist of

Verb + Mit + Dative

anfangen mit to begin with	**sprechen mit** to talk with
aufhören mit to stop doing	**übereinstimmen mit** to agree with
rechnen mit to bank on	**sich unterhalten mit** to talk with

Verb + Nach + Dative

sich erkundigen nach to enquire about	**riechen nach** to smell of	**streben nach** to strive for
fragen nach to ask about	**schmecken nach** to taste of	
greifen nach to reach for	**sich sehnen nach** to long for	

Verb + Von + Dative

abhängen von to depend on	**erzählen von** to tell of	**überzeugen von** to convince of
abraten von to discourage from	**sprechen von** to speak about	**wissen von** to know about
sich erholen von to recover from	**träumen von** to dream of	

Verb + Vor + Dative

Angst haben vor to be afraid of	**retten vor** to rescue from
sich fürchten vor to be afraid of	**warnen vor** to warn of

Verb + Zu + Dative

beitragen zu to contribute to	**führen zu** to lead to	**passen zu** to suit
sich eignen zu to be suitable for	**gehören zu** to belong to	**zwingen zu** to force

1. Insert the correct prepositions and translate the following sentences.

a) Ich unterhalte mich _____ meinen Freunden.	**e)** Ich sehne mich _____ Weihnachten.
b) Du eignest dich _____ dieser Arbeit.	**f)** Ich habe dir _____ dem Urlaub erzählt.
c) Ich habe Angst _____ der Prüfung.	**g)** Sie nimmt _____ dem Projekt teil.
d) Meine Mutter leidet _____ Kopfschmerzen.	**h)** Ich weiß nichts _____ diesem Film.

2. Insert the correct endings to the articles or pronouns. Then translate the following sentences.

a) Das trägt zu d___ Problemen (pl.) bei.	**e)** Das hängt von d___ Ergebnissen (pl.) ab.
b) Wir nehmen an d___ Projekt (n) teil.	**f)** Ich fürchte mich vor d___ Dunkelheit (f).
c) Ich stimme mit dein___ Meinung (f) überein.	**g)** Ich eigne mich zu dies___ Beruf (m).
d) Du fragst nach d___ Austausch (m).	**h)** Ich spreche gern mit mein___ Freunden (pl.).

09.03 Hörverständnis Teil 3

Vorarbeit

Arbeitspraktikum	*work experience*	Lebenslauf	*CV*	Dozent	*lecturer*
Maschinenbau	*mechanical engineering*	**Empfehlungsbrief**	*letter of recommendation*	**glatt ablaufen**	*to go smoothly*
unterbrechen	*to interrupt*	**begabt**	*talented*	**aufgeschlossen**	*open to*

CL Ordinary + Higher Level Questions

1. **a)** The conversation is between:
   i) teacher and student **ii)** schoolmates **iii)** mother and son **iv)** university students
   b) Find **one (O)/two (H)** details in the conversation that support your choice.
2. **a)** Which word best describes the female speaker's attitude during the conversation?
   i) depressed **ii)** angry **iii)** nervous **iv)** excited
   b) Write down **one (O)/two (H)** details from the conversation that support your choice.
3. How does the male speaker react to the female speaker's news? Give **one (O)/three (H)** details.
4. What did the female speaker have to do? Give **one (O)/two (H)** details.

09.04 Hörverständnis Teil 4

Vorarbeit

Überqueren	*crossing*	überfahren werden	*to be run over*	Sanitäter	*paramedic*
blendend	*blinding*	**Massenkarambolage**	*pile-up*	**Verletzung**	*injury*
prallen	*to crash*	**abschleppen**	*to tow away*	**kamen ums Leben**	*lost their lives*
Lastwagen	*truck*	**Geschwindigkeit**	*speed*	**Schiene**	*rail*

CL Ordinary + Higher Level Questions

1. **a)** Describe what happened to the tour guide. **b)** How many tourists were in her group?
2. **a)** What caused the pile-up on the motorway? **b)** What did the emergency services have to do?
3. Describe the accident on the A8. Give **three (O)/five (H)** details.
4. **a)** How did the train driver lose control of the train? **b)** What happened to the passengers?
5. What is today's weather forecast? Give **two (O)/three (H)** details.

It is important to know traffic terms, as they are often mentioned in the news.

Wie heißt das auf Englisch?

1. Der Fahrer kam ums Leben.	**A** I don't recognise the number plate.
2. Er hat Fahrerflucht begangen.	**B** The car skidded.
3. Ich erkenne das Kennzeichen nicht.	**C** The driver lost his life.
4. Der Wagen kam ins Schleudern.	**D** We had a breakdown.
5. Wir hatten eine Autopanne.	**E** He committed a hit-and-run.

Schriftliche Produktion: Ordinary Level

Write a letter to your pen pal. Complete the first paragraph by correctly inserting the sentence halves below. Then follow the instructions.

dass ich großes Glück gehabt habe | **bei Familie Müller in Bern**
in der Zeitung gesehen | **ich dir aus der Schweiz schreibe**
aber ich hätte nie gedacht, dass es in der Schweiz sein würde

Liebe(r) Martin(a),

du bist sicher überrascht, dass ______________ . Ich bin hier als Au-pair ______________ . Ich wollte ja diesen Sommer arbeiten, ______________ . Mein Vater hatte die Anzeige der Familie ______________ . Ich muss wirklich sagen, ______________ .

Now continue the letter.

- Describe the work you do in the family and give details about the children in your care.
- Mention **two** things you like about the family.
- Mention **two** things that you have done with the children so far.
- Say that you are doing a German course in your free time.
- Ask if Martin(a) can visit you in Bern in July.
- Write a suitable closing sentence.

HL Schriftliche Produktion: Higher Level

Reply in German to your pen pal's letter. Give detailed answers to the questions.

Liebe(r) ...,

endlich kriegst du wieder Post von mir. Stell dir vor! Gestern hatte ich ein Vorstellungsgespräch für einen Nebenjob als Sprachassistent. Eine Sprachschule in der Stadt bietet Wochenendkurse für Ausländer, die ihr Deutsch verbessern möchten. Hast du einen Nebenjob? Arbeitest du an Wochenenden oder hast du sie frei? Was machst du, um Geld zu verdienen? Arbeiten viele Schüler während der Sommerferien?

Nach dem Abitur will ich freiwillig in einem Entwicklungsland arbeiten. Würdest du auch so was machen? Warum/warum nicht? Was lernt man deiner Meinung nach bei so einer Erfahrung?

Ich habe vor, eine Ausbildungsmesse in Hannover zu besichtigen. Sie läuft vom 3. bis zum 4. März. Ich weiß noch nicht genau, was ich nach der Schule machen möchte. Was hast du nach den Prüfungen vor? Ausbildung oder Studium? Oder erst mal ab ins Ausland? Wie hast du dich über Berufsmöglichkeiten informiert? Erzähl mir davon!

Gibt es immer noch stereotypische Männer- und Frauenberufe in deinem Land? Wie findest du das? Würdest du einen Beruf wählen, der typisch männlich/weiblich ist? Welchen, und warum?

Jetzt muss ich Schluss machen.

Dein(e) Martin(a)

Nützliche Sätze

Ich habe vor, auf die Uni zu gehen.	*I intend to go to university.*
Jetzt hat jeder die Möglichkeit, seine Träume zu verfolgen.	*Now everyone has the opportunity to pursue their dreams.*
Stereotypische Männer- und Frauenberufe gehören zu der Vergangenheit.	*Stereotypical men's and women's jobs belong in the past.*
Es gibt immer noch diverse Berufe, die von einem Geschlecht dominiert werden.	*There are still various professions which are dominated by a particular gender.*

  Übung Macht den Meister!

A Dative Verbs

1. Insert the correct definite article.

a) Ich helfe _____ Frau (f).
b) Das Kind dankt _____ Mann (m).
c) Das Kleid gefällt _____ Mädchen (n).
d) Das Buch gehört _____ Jungen (m).
e) Zigaretten schaden _____ Gesundheit (f).
f) Wir gratulieren ___ Schülern (pl.).
g) Ich glaube _____ Kind (n) nicht.
h) Der Kuchen schmeckt _____ Lehrerin (f) nicht.

2. Insert the correct endings for the possessive adjectives.

a) Ich antworte mein___ Vater (m).
b) Der Junge dankt sein___ Eltern (pl.).
c) Sie gratuliert ihr___ Freundin (f).
d) Ich glaube dein___ Bruder (m).
e) Der Zahnarzt hilft mein___ Schwester (f).
f) Das Gepäck gehört unser___ Großeltern (pl.).
g) Die Landschaft gefällt Ihr___ Freunden (pl.).
h) Das Essen schmeckt ihr___ Freunden (pl.).

B Dative Expressions

Insert the correct personal pronouns.

a) Das reicht _____ . *That's enough for her.*
b) Es geht _____ gut. *I'm well.*
c) Es tut _____ leid. *He is sorry.*
d) Das macht _____ Spaß. *That's fun for them.*
e) Ich bin _____ dankbar. *I'm grateful to you* (polite).
f) Das ist _____ bekannt. *That is known to us.*
g) _____ ist heiß. *You're* (sing.) *feeling hot.*
h) Es geht _____ schlecht. *He is sick.*

Accusative prepositions
für, um

Two-way prepositions
an, auf, über, vor

Dative prepositions
aus, mit,
nach, von, zu

C Prepositional Verbs in the Accusative

1. Insert the correct preposition.

a) Der Film handelt sich _____ einen Mann.
b) Ich begeistere mich _____ Musik.
c) Ich bemühe mich _____ meine Aussprache.
d) Wir informieren uns _____ die Umwelt.
e) Der Lehrer klagt _____ schlechte Noten.
f) Wir streiten uns _____ Hausarbeit.
g) Er denkt _____ den Austausch.
h) Wir engagieren uns _____ die Nachbarschaft.

2. Insert the correct endings for the possessive adjectives.

a) Ich denke oft an mein___ Brieffreund (m).
b) Wir warten auf unser___ Lehrerin (f).
c) Er begeistert sich für sein___ Projekt (n).
d) Wir lachen über ihr___ komischen Hund (m).
e) Die Kinder streiten sich über ihr___ Zimmer (n).
f) Ich erinnere mich an dein___ Geburtstag (m).
g) Wir achten auf unser___ Lehrer (m).
h) Der Lehrer klagt über ihr___ Benehmen (n).

D Prepositional Verbs in the Dative

1. Insert the correct prepositions.

a) Ich unterhalte mich _____ meinen Freunden.
b) Sie hat Angst _____ Spinnen.
c) Er fängt _____ dem Lernen an.
d) Ich träume _____ der Zukunft.
e) Das Zimmer riecht _____ Zigaretten.
f) Manche greifen _____ Drogen.
g) Armut führt oft _____ Hoffnungslosigkeit.
h) Er erzählt uns _____ der deutschen Kultur.

2. Insert the correct definite articles.

a) Ich leide an _____ Grippe (f).
b) Ich spreche mit _____ Nachbarn (pl.).
c) Wir erkundigen uns nach _____ Austausch (m).
d) Das hängt von _____ Noten (pl.) ab.
e) Ich weiß nichts von _____ Projekt (n).
f) Ich habe Angst vor _____ Prüfung (f).
g) Er griff nach _____ Koffer (m).
h) Sie sehnt sich nach _____ Urlaub (m).

Für die Prüfung

1. Was passt zusammen?

1. Nebenjobs sind attraktiv,	**A** aber oft führt sie nur zu Schwierigkeiten.
2. Digitalisierung soll die Arbeit erleichtern,	**B** denn die Wirtschaft boomt zur Zeit.
3. Jetzt gibt es längere Arbeitsstunden,	**C** weil man mehr Geld verdienen kann.
4. Es gibt jetzt weniger Arbeitslose,	**D** die richtige Stelle zu finden.
5. Es kann sehr schwierig sein,	**E** und die Pendelzeiten sind auch länger.

2. Was passt zusammen?

1. Ich will ein Praktikum machen,	**A** was uns Spaß macht.
2. Ich arbeite samstags an einer Tankstelle,	**B** werde ich einen Ferienjob suchen.
3. Wir sollen das machen,	**C** die gut bezahlt wird.
4. Weil ich für den Führerschein sparen will,	**D** weil ich das Geld brauche.
5. Ich suche Arbeit,	**E** um Arbeitserfahrung zu sammeln.

3. Insert the correct prepositions for the following sentences.

a) Ich freue mich **(auf/am/für/in)** die Zukunft.

b) Er interessiert sich **(an/am/für/in)** den Kurs.

c) Wir streiten uns **(an/in/über/für)** Klamotten.

d) Ich spreche **(mit/für/in/an)** dir.

e) Erinnerst du dich **(für/in/an/bei)** den Mann?

f) Wir ärgern uns **(an/über/in/am)** die Arbeit.

4. What words make up the following compound words, and what do they mean in English?

a) Arbeitserfahrung = _____ + _____ = ________

b) Nebenjob = _____ + _____ = ________

c) erstklassig = _____ + _____ = ________

d) Stundenlohn = _____ + _____ = ________

e) Mitarbeiter = _____ + _____ = ________

f) Arbeitsklima = _____ + _____ = ________

5. Indicate for the underlined verbs the tense, the infinitive and whether they are singular or plural.

a) Sie fühlten sich unsicher.

b) Man hat die Arbeit geliebt.

c) Was wissen die Manager von der Arbeit?

d) Da ging ihr die Freude aus.

e) Sie wird in Rente gehen.

f) Ich hatte eine Fahrkarte gekauft.

6. Indicate for the underlined nouns the gender, the case and whether they are singular or plural.

a) Ich lerne fleißig für die Prüfung.

b) Mein Vater hat ein gutes Gehalt.

c) Die Arbeit wird sich lohnen.

d) Meine Mutter macht viele Überstunden.

e) Ich brauche einen neuen Laptop.

f) Nach dem Abitur will ich auf die Uni gehen.

7. Lückentext: Fill in the blanks with the correct missing words from the box.

wichtig habe eigene sein können
Zukunft mich gute aber und

Ich **1** _____ klare Vorstellungen von meiner **2** _____ . Ich sehne **3** _____ nach Sicherheit. Ich will eine **4** _____ Arbeit und eine **5** _____ Familie haben. Ich empfinde einen starken Leistungsdruck **6** _____ ich habe mich daran gewöhnt. Ich will sparsam **7** _____ und mir gleichzeitig etwas leisten **8** _____ . Werte wie Toleranz **9** _____ Freiheit sind mir **10** _____ .

Selbstbewertung: Ordinary Level

OL

Vocabulary

1. If I can translate these sentences into English, I can talk about work. (2 marks each)

a) Meine Eltern haben lange Arbeitsstunden.

b) Ich suche einen Nebenjob, um Geld zu verdienen.

c) Ich weiß noch nicht, was für Arbeit ich machen will.

d) Ich arbeite samstags im Supermarkt um die Ecke.

e) Ich bediene die Kunden und ich räume die Regale ein.

Your score: ___ / 10

2. If I can translate these nouns into German, I understand the language of work. (1 mark each)

a) voluntary work	**c)** economy	**e)** CV	**g)** training	**i)** salary
b) work experience	**d)** money	**f)** saleswoman	**h)** tips	**j)** dream

Your score: ___ / 10

Grammar

3. If I can choose the correct preposition, I can accurately talk about work. (1 mark each)

a) Ich will **(im/am)** Ausland arbeiten.	**f)** Ich habe Angst **(über/vor)** der Zukunft.
b) Ich bin **(an/für)** die Arbeit geeignet.	**g)** Ich spreche **(um/mit)** meinen Eltern.
c) Ich weiß nichts **(an/von)** dem Beruf.	**h)** Ich freue mich **(an/auf)** die Arbeit.
d) Ich denke oft **(an/zu)** die Zukunft.	**i)** Ich hoffe **(auf/für)** eine gute Stelle.
e) Ich begeistere mich **(für/an)** Kunst.	**j)** Ich bemühe mich **(an/um)** gute Noten.

Your score: ___ / 10

4. If I can conjugate these verbs in the **ich** and **wir** forms in the present tense, I can talk about the world of work. (1 mark each)

a) arbeiten	ich _____	wir _____
b) verdienen	ich _____	wir _____
c) bedienen	ich _____	wir _____
d) finanzieren	ich _____	wir _____
e) sich interessieren	ich _____ mich	wir _____ uns

Your score: ___ / 10

5. If I can put these past tense sentences into the present tense, I understand the perfect and present tenses. (1 mark each)

a) Ich habe lange daran gearbeitet.	**f)** Wir haben einen Lebenslauf geschrieben.
b) Ich habe viel Geld verdient.	**g)** Wir haben Überstunden gemacht.
c) Ich habe die Reise selbst finanziert.	**h)** Wir haben die Kunden bedient.
d) Ich habe viel Deutsch gelernt.	**i)** Wir haben mit dem Chef gesprochen.
e) Ich habe ein Praktikum gemacht.	**j)** Wir haben über die Zukunft diskutiert.

Your score: ___ / 10

What have I learned?	
What must I improve?	
What do I want to revise?	

Your total score: ___ / 50

Selbstbewertung: Higher Level

HL

1. If I can translate these sentences into German, I understand dative verbs. (1 mark each)

a) I don't believe you (sing.).	**f)** The book belongs to me.
b) He thanks the woman.	**g)** What happened to him?
c) I help my brother.	**h)** Ice cream tastes good to me.
d) I congratulate the child.	**i)** My mother advises me to rest.
e) The colour suits her.	**j)** He forgives her.

Your score: ___ / 10

2. If I can translate these sentences, I understand dative expressions. (1 mark each)

a) That's all the same to me.	**f)** He is thankful to her.
b) He feels cold.	**g)** That's fun for you.
c) She feels hot.	**h)** That's enough for him.
d) How are they?	**i)** That's helpful to me.
e) He is sorry.	**j)** That's known to her.

Your score: ___ / 10

3. If I can put in the correct prepositions, I understand prepositional verbs in the accusative. (1 mark each)

a) Wir freuen uns _____ den Sommer.	**f)** Sie hofft _____ gute Noten.
b) Ich denke oft _____ dich.	**g)** Er bittet mich _____ Hilfe.
c) Ich interessiere mich _____ Medizin.	**h)** Wir streiten uns _____ Klamotten.
d) Ich eigne mich _____ Informatik.	**i)** Er ist _____ den Beruf geeignet.
e) Er beschwert sich _____ das Essen.	**j)** Ich bitte dich _____ Hilfe.

Your score: ___ / 10

4. If I can put in the correct prepositions, I understand prepositional verbs in the dative. (1 mark each)

a) Ich spreche _____ meinen Freunden.	**f)** Meine Eltern warnen mich _____ Drogen.
b) Das schmeckt _____ Zitronen.	**g)** Ich habe mich _____ der Grippe erholt.
c) Er leidet _____ einer Erkältung.	**h)** Er fängt _____ dem Aufsatz an.
d) Sie hat Angst _____ Ratten.	**i)** Das Lernen führt _____ guten Noten.
e) Ich erkundige mich _____ dem Job.	**j)** Ich leide _____ Leistungsdruck.

Your score: ___ / 10

5. If I can correctly fill in the gaps below, I understand word functions. (1 mark each)

süß lieber gutbezahlte Entspannung denn möchte ich und ist das

Natürlich hoffe **1** _____ , eine **2** _____ Stelle zu bekommen. Aber Geld **3** _____ nicht das A und O des Lebens. Ich suche auch Sicherheit **4** _____ Zufriedenheit bei der Arbeit. Ich **5** _____ nette Arbeitskollegen haben. Ich würde **6** _____ keine Überstunden machen, **7** _____ der Mensch braucht **8** _____ , aber wie **9** _____ Spruchwort lautet, Arbeit macht das Leben **10** _____ .

Your score: ___ / 10

What have I learned?	
What must I improve?	
What do I want to revise?	

Your total score: ___ / 50

10

Jugendthemen

Learning Outcomes

- **Oral:** discussing young people's issues
- **Reading:** reading and discussing three texts about young people
- **Writing**: writing an opinion (**Äußerung**), a picture description and letter about young people's issues
- **Listening:** listening to and answering questions on four extracts about issues that young people face

Grammar

- Adjectives and adjective endings
- Comparative and superlative adjectives
- No article + adjective + noun
- Simple, comparative and superlative adverbs

Vocabulary

- Discussing topics of interest for young people (friendship, coming of age, body art)
- Cyber bullying, alcohol, drugs, the media
- Describing one's personal experience of issues that affect young people

German Culture

- Age limit for drinking alcohol
- Legal rights when one comes of age

Exam Tips

- Set up a personal revision schedule built around the general conversation topics, picture sequences and role plays.
- Use plenty of adjectives and adverbs to improve your expression mark.
- Practise the techniques described on page 187 on a role play of your choice.

Mündliche Arbeit: Jugendthemen

Übersetzen Sie die Meinungen unten, die mit den Bildergeschichten, bzw. Ihrem Projekt, zu tun haben, ins Englische. Diskutieren Sie diese Meinungen.

Alkohol und Drogen

Frage: Warum greifen Jugendliche zu Alkohol oder Drogen?

Meinung: Meiner Meinung nach greifen manche Jugendliche zu Alkohol oder Drogen, um dem Schulstress zu entfliehen. Andere probieren sie aus Neugier oder wegen Druck. Sie wollen machen was alle machen. Andere meinen, dass es cool ist und denken über die Gefahren nicht nach.

Stress

Frage: Stehen manche Jugendliche unter Stress, und warum?

Meinung: Ohne Zweifel stehen manche Jugendliche unter Stress. Schuld sind oft Schulstress, Klassenarbeiten oder Streit zu Hause. Viele Jugendliche wollen selbstständiger werden und das kann zu Problemen mit Erwachsenen führen. Andere machen sich Sorgen um die Zukunft, denn sie wissen nicht, was sie nach dem Abitur machen werden.

Freundschaft

Frage: Wie wichtig ist eine gute Freundschaft?

Meinung: Eine gute Freundschaft ist unheimlich wichtig, besonders wenn man ein Problem hat. Oft kann man seine Probleme mit den Eltern nicht besprechen. Ein guter Freund/eine gute Freundin sollte zuverlässig sein. Gute Freundschaften helfen einem den Alltagsstress abzubauen.

Die Medien

Frage: Spielen die Medien eine Rolle in Ihrem Leben?

Meinung: Ganz bestimmt spielen die Medien eine wichtige Rolle. Manchmal haben die Medien einen positiven Einfluss, denn sie können über die Gesundheit aufklären. Aber oft schaffen die Medien ein Zerrbild. Berühmte Menschen werden als Vorbilder betrachtet und Jugendliche versuchen dann, sie nachzuahmen. Heutzutage gibt es ein großes Problem mit Bulimie und Magersucht, denn junge Mädchen und Jungen wollen wie ihre Vorbilder aussehen.

Volljährigkeit

Frage: Was darf man mit 18 in Irland machen?

Meinung: Mit 18 ist man schon volljährig. Man darf in Irland mitstimmen, was eine gewisse Verantwortung mit sich bringt. Natürlich darf man Alkohol trinken, was zu Problemen führen kann, wenn man auch den Führerschein gemacht hat. Man hat auch das Recht zu heiraten. Mit diesen neuen Rechten kommt aber auch viel Verantwortung.

Tattoos und Piercings

Frage: Was halten Sie von Tattoos oder Piercings?

Meinung: Das ist eine Geschmacksfrage. Ich finde Körperkunst abscheulich. Ohne die richtige Hygiene kann man leicht infiziert werden. Meine Eltern würden darauf sehr schlecht reagieren. Da gäbe es Krach zu Hause! Meine Mutter würde richtig sauer auf mich sein. Es ist ja auch schwierig, eine Tätowierung zu entfernen. Und man muss damit ewig leben. Das ist bestimmt nichts für mich.

Use the paragraphs above as a guide to form your opinions for your written work. You will be awarded high marks if you can give three opinions and three reasons for each opinion.

Prüfungstipp

Role Plays for the Oral Examination

You will be given **five role-play cards** well in advance of your oral examination. The **top half** of the role-play card consists of:

1. a summary in German of the role play, and
2. **five** sets of instructions to follow, each comprising **four** short tasks.

The **bottom half** is the English translation of the German above. You will choose one role play from five, face down, and you will have one minute to prepare. You retain the card throughout the role play.

Here is an example of the German summary in the **top half** of the role-play card:

Sie arbeiten im Sommer als Fremdenführer/in für eine irische Reisegesellschaft. Sie begleiten eine Gruppe von deutschsprachigen Bustouristen auf einer Rundreise durch Irland. Sie selbst hatten eine kleine Verspätung und merken bereits bei der Abfahrt vom Flughafen: Es gibt einen schwierigen Touristen/eine schwierige Touristin in der Gruppe! Sie versuchen, mit diesem Problem fertigzuwerden.

In the **bottom half** is the English translation:

You are working for the summer as a tourist guide for an Irish travel company. You are guiding a group of German-speaking tourists on a bus tour through Ireland. You were a little delayed and when leaving the airport, you notice: there is a difficult tourist in the group! You try to deal with the problem.

Here is an example of a set of **instructions**, listed a) to d) here for clarification purposes:

a) Begrüßen Sie die Reisegruppe und stellen Sie sich vor: **b)** Name, **c)** Ihre Aufgabe ... .
d) Kommentieren Sie das Wetter.

In the bottom half of the role-play card is the **English**:

1. a) Greet the group, introduce yourself: b) name, c) your task ... . d) Comment on the weather.

Techniques for using the German/English instructions on your role-play card

Technique 1

You are often instructed to greet someone, give your name and say why you are there: **Guten Tag! Ich heiße ... und ich bin ihr Fremdenführer auf dieser Rundreise durch Irland.** *Note: your reason for being there is taken directly from the summary.*

Technique 2

Use the instructions in your answer by changing **Sie** to **ich** + verb ending **-en** to **-e** (but keep an eye out for irregular verbs such as **wissen** and modal verbs): **Nennen Sie die Gründe. Entschuldigen Sie sich.** *Give your reasons and apologise.* ➔ **Ich entschuldige mich! Ich war verspätet, da ich ...**

Practise these techniques on a role play of your choice.

Technique 3

If you are asked to explain, describe, or ask or answer questions, you will often answer using the same noun/pronoun and verb ending on the card, e.g.:

Fragen Sie, wie die Reise bisher war. *Ask how the trip has been so far.* ➔ **Wie war die Reise bisher?** *How has the trip been so far?*

Sagen Sie, warum alle Touristen bisher zufrieden waren. *Say why all tourists have been happy so far* ➔ **Alle Touristen waren bisher zufrieden, denn ...**

Technique 4

If you form a sentence from a set of incomplete phrases, you will often need the verbal expressions: **Es ist/es gibt/wir sollten** (it is/there is (are)/we should). For example:

(**erstklassiges Hotel** ... **erstmal entspannen** ... **tolles Essen** ...) (*first class hotel ... firstly relax ... great food*) ➔ **Es ist ein erstklassiges Hotel, Frau Braun. Wir sollten uns erstmal entspannen. Es gibt hier auch tolles Essen.**

Text 1: Die größten Sorgen der Teenager

Bitte beantworten Sie die folgenden Fragen:

1. Was sieht man auf dem Foto?
2. Was machen die Jugendlichen?
3. Wo sind sie, Ihrer Meinung nach?
4. Was sieht man im Vordergrund/Hintergrund?

Vorarbeit

1. Finden Sie im Text die Synonyme für die Ausdrücke unten.
   - **A** ... , die ihnen sehr viel bedeuten ...
   - **B** Die Jugendlichen sorgen sich darum, ...
   - **C** Junge Leute verstehen, dass ...
   - **D** Je früher desto besser ...
   - **E** ... alle haben sich ihre Zukunft bereits perfekt ausgedacht ...
   - **F** Manche benehmen sich gern indifferent.
2. Finden Sie das Deutsche für die Wörter unten.
   - **A** more and more aware/take seriously
   - **B** peers/sensitive/recognition
   - **C** to support/experiences of success
   - **D** get into trouble/to plan poorly/sensibly
   - **E** transform/encourage/circle of acquaintances
   - **F** feel/vulnerable/most important thing

www.neuropool.com (amended)

A Als Teenager werden sich die Jugendlichen ihrer Umgebung und ihrer eigenen Person immer bewusster. Das führt oft zu Sorgen, die für die Teenager extrem wichtig sind, und die Eltern und Lehrer sollten die Sorgen der jungen Menschen ernst nehmen.

B Die Jugend macht sich Sorgen, was die anderen über sie denken. Sie sind auch sehr empfindlich, was ihre eigene Identität angeht. Auf keinen Fall möchte sie von ihren Altersgenossen in negativem Licht gesehen werden. Die Suche nach Anerkennung kann dazu führen, dass sie mit Drogen anfangen.

C Jugendliche sind darüber im Klaren, dass gute Noten ihnen Türen zu einer besseren Zukunft öffnen können. Die meisten Jugendlichen sorgen sich um ihre Schulnoten. Gute Noten bringen ihnen Anerkennung bei den Lehrern und geben ihnen Erfolgserlebnisse. Es ist wichtig, die Jugendlichen dort zu fördern, wo sie Spaß und Talent haben, anstatt Zeit in die nicht so geliebten Fächer zu investieren.

D Jugendliche verplanen ihre Zeit oft doppelt und dreifach und geraten dann in Not, denn sie entdecken, sie können alles nicht gleichzeitig machen. Lieber früher als später sollten Kinder lernen, ihre Zeit sinnvoll einzuteilen und Prioritäten zu setzen. Sie müssen lernen, dass das Leben viele Möglichkeiten bietet, aber dass sie nur einige wählen sollten.

E Scheinbar hat jeder Freund seine Zukunft schon genau geplant, nur man selbst weiß nicht, was zu tun. Die Eltern sollten sie stets an ihre guten Qualitäten erinnern, so dass sie sich auf diese konzentrieren und sie in eine berufliche Wahl verwandeln können. Eltern sollten Teenager ermutigen mit anderen über ihre Zukunft zu sprechen und einen großen Bekanntenkreis aufzubauen. Bei der Berufswahl helfen gute soziale Beziehungen. Es fällt einem oft auf, was die richtige Möglichkeit ist, wenn man die Augen offenhält.

F Teenager geben sich gerne gleichgültig den Eltern gegenüber, doch im Innern sind sie sehr verletzlich. Sie spüren finanzielle und emotionelle Krisen sehr intensiv. Das Allerwichtigste ist sie zu lieben, öfters Zeit zu nehmen um ihnen zuzuhören und über die Möglichkeiten zu einer Lösung zu reden.

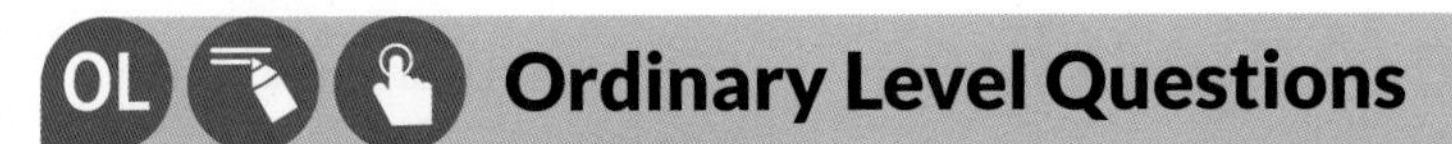

Ordinary Level Questions

1. **a)** Give **two** details about this article. **b)** Who should take young people's worries seriously? A
2. In paragraphs C to F, name **a)** each issue experienced by young people; **b)** the reason it exists; **c)** the possible solution given.
3. Are the following statements true or false?
   a) Young people become more and more aware of the world around them.
   b) Young people don't care what others think about them.
   c) They understand that good grades can make their future brighter.
   d) They have no problem doing many things at the same time.
   e) They feel that everyone has planned out their future in detail except for themselves.
4. Select the correct prepositions for the following sentences.
   a) Die Jugendlichen sorgen sich **(um/über/unter/an)** ihre Zukunft.
   b) Es ist ihnen wichtig, was andere **(über/unter/im/beim)** sie denken.
   c) Sie verstehen, dass gute Noten wichtig **(mit/von/an/für)** ihre Zukunft sein können.
   d) Eltern sollten mit ihrem Teenager **(auf/um/über/zum)** seine Probleme sprechen.

HL Higher Level Questions

1. Beantworten Sie folgende Fragen auf Deutsch!
   a) Was sollten die Eltern ernst nehmen? A
   b) Laut Text, warum greift die Jugend zu Drogen? B
   c) Warum sind gute Noten wichtig? C
   d) Was müssen Kinder lernen? (**2** Details) D
   e) Was wird über Zukunftspläne der Jugend gesagt? E
   f) Welche Gefühle haben junge Leute, laut Text? F
2. Answer the following questions in English.
   a) What is one worry for young people, according to the text? Give details. B
   b) According to the text, what **two** things cause worries for young people? B C
   c) Give **three** reasons why young people worry about grades, according to the text. C
   d) **i)** How do teenagers sometimes run into timing difficulties? **ii)** What solution is suggested? D
   e) Give **three** examples of how a teenager might be steered towards making a good career choice. E
   f) Name **three** pieces of advice given to parents with regard to their teenage children. F
3. Finden Sie im Text das passende Synonym für die angegebenen Wörter.
   A Mensch **C** Ergebnisse **E** Beziehungen
   B Gleichaltrige **D** Gelegenheiten **F** oft
4. Was passt zusammen?

1. Junge Leute machen sich Sorgen	**A** was einem bei der Berufswahl helfen kann.
2. Sie wissen,	**B** spüren Teenager sehr intensiv.
3. Man sollte einen Bekanntenkreis aufbauen,	**C** wo ihr Teenager offenbar Talente hat.
4. Die Eltern sollten immer wieder sagen,	**D** dass man immer gute Noten lobt.
5. Ob eine Krise emotionell oder finanziell ist,	**E** über viele Sachen.

5. Geben Sie für die unterstrichenen Nomen jeweils an: ob Singular oder Plural; bei Singular das Geschlecht; den Fall (Nominativ, Akkusativ, Dativ, Genitiv).
   a) Die Jugendlichen werden sich ihrer Umgebung immer bewusster.
   b) Sie wollen nicht von ihren Altersgenossen im negativen Licht gesehen werden.
   c) Gute Noten können Türen öffnen.
   d) Jugendliche müssen ihre Zeit sinnvoll einplanen.
   e) Man sollte einen großen Bekanntenkreis aufbauen.

Grammatik: Adjektive/Adjectives

p. 201 (Übung macht den Meister)

An adjective describes a noun: tall, large, red, funny, scary, faithful, boring.

If the German adjective comes after the *noun* it describes, it will look as follows:

Die Gebäude **sind hässlich** *The buildings* are ugly   *Der Junge* **ist freundlich** *The boy* is friendly

Examples of adjectives:

Colours	Taste	Size	Weather	Appearance	Qualities	Moods
red	delicious	tall	foggy	beautiful	cheeky	delighted
dark	tasty	slim	windy	ugly	arrogant	sad
light	disgusting	deep	freezing	strong	sweet	depressed
coloured	fresh	huge	cool	attractive	calm	thrilled

Match the following adjectives with the English adjectives above.

Farbe	Geschmack	Größe	Wetter	Aussehen	Werte	Launen
dunkel	lecker	tief	frierend	hässlich	frech	traurig
hell	ekelhaft	schlank	kühl	schön	ruhig	froh
gefärbt	frisch	riesig	nebelig	stark	eingebildet	erfreut
rot	schmackhaft	groß	windig	anziehend	niedlich	deprimiert

Comparative and Superlative Adjectives

The comparative of the adjective appears as: bigger, smaller, more exciting. In German, this is formed by adding **-er** to the adjective: **schlank → schlanker**; **interessant → interessanter**

The superlative of the adjective appears as: biggest, smallest, most exciting. In German, this is formed by adding **-st** or **-est** to the adjective: **schlank → schlankest-**; **interessant → interessantest-***

* The dash means you must add the appropriate ending, depending on gender, number and case.

Regular simple, comparative and superlative adjectives are formed as follows:

1. Simple Adjective	2. Comparative of Adjective	3. Superlative of Adjective
klein small	**kleiner** smaller	**kleinst-** smallest
schön beautiful	**schöner** more beautiful	**schönst-** most beautiful
dünn thin	**dünner** thinner	**dünnst-** thinnest

Irregular simple, comparative and superlative adjectives are formed as follows:

1. Simple Adjective	2. Comparative of Adjective	3. Superlative of Adjective
alt old	**älter** older	**ältest-** oldest/eldest
jung young	**jünger** younger	**jüngst-** youngest
groß big/tall	**größer** bigger/taller	**größt-** biggest/tallest
lang long	**länger** longer	**längst-** longest
kurz short	**kürzer** shorter	**kürzest-** shortest
gut good	**besser** better	**best-** best

Translate these sentences into English.

1. Mein Bruder ist drei Jahre älter als ich.	**5.** Das war die schönste Geschichte der Welt.
2. Ich finde Mathe interessanter als Grammatik.	**6.** Die Sommerferien sind länger in Irland.
3. Ich bin vier Jahre jünger als er.	**7.** Der deutsche Schultag ist kürzer.
4. Was ist anspruchsvoller, Irisch oder Englisch?	**8.** Ich bin das älteste Kind in meiner Familie.

10.01 Hörverständnis Teil 1

Vorarbeit

Zwerg	*dwarf*	**Verdacht**	*suspicion*	**Drohung**	*threat*
hochnäsig	*stuck up*	**einschüchtern**	*to intimidate*	**verbergen**	*to hide*
Selbstzweifel	*self-doubt*	**Scham**	*shame*	**feige**	*cowardly*

CL Ordinary + Higher Level Questions

1. **a)** What details does Anke give about herself? **b)** When did she become a victim of cyber bullying?
2. What was the typical content of the negative posts which she received?
3. Why did her friend have a suspicion about who the bully might be? Give **one (O)/two (H)** details.
4. Why, according to Anke, is cyber bullying on the increase? Give **one (O)/two (H)** details.
5. The interviewer says that comments and threats do not stop when one goes home. What was Anke's reaction? Give **two (O)/three (H)** details.
6. How did she overcome this problem? What advice does she give?

10.02 Hörverständnis Teil 2

Vorarbeit

Polizeiwache	*police station*	**Zeugin**	*witness*	**Angriff**	*attack*
Dämmerung	*dusk*	**versprechen**	*to promise*	**einkreisen**	*to surround*
schlagen	*to hit*	**Verbrechen**	*crime*	**verschwinden**	*to disappear*

OL Ordinary Level Questions

1. What does the caller ask?
2. What is the caller's name?
3. What does the caller want to report?
4. What is the caller's phone number?
5. The caller:
   a) will ring back later ☐
   b) is expecting a callback ☐
   c) will receive an e-mail ☐

HL Higher Level Questions

1. Using ***key phrases***, write down **in German** the key information the caller provides:
   - the name of the person **making** the call
   - the reason for the call
   - **four** details of their conversation
   - details regarding further contact
   - the caller's phone number

Gesprächsnotiz

Anruf von: ____________________ Gesprächsanlass: ____________________

Der Anrufer:

- ruft später zurück ☐
- erwartet einen Rückruf ☐
- wird eine E-Mail erhalten ☐
- wird morgen angerufen ☐

Kontaktnummer: ____________

2. Write down **three** examples of the language used which show that the caller is **anxious**.

Text 2: Noch kein Abi, trotzdem Boss

Bitte beantworten Sie die folgenden Fragen:

1. Was sehen Sie auf dem Foto?
2. Wie sieht der Junge aus und wie alt ist er?
3. Was macht er gerade, und warum?

Vorarbeit

1. Finden Sie diese Ausdrücke im folgenden Text!
   - **A** ... to place advertising messages.
   - **B** ... to the round of talks ...
   - **C** Most of his employees are the same age ...
   - **D** ... they are the customers of the future.
   - **E** With the change of user behaviour ...
   - **F** His business idea is timely.
2. Finden Sie das Deutsche für die Wörter unten!
   - **A** target group/above all/stage
   - **B** founded/business manager/trade fair
   - **C** trainees/belongs to/businesses
   - **D** prefer/complain/successful/to upload
   - **E** advertising industry/generational change
   - **F** main office/customers/lack

Nina Piatscheck, *Zeit Campus* # 1/2018 (amended)

A Alle sind gekommen, um Charles auf der Bühne zu sehen: einen Jungen in hellgrauen Basketball-Sneakern und Pullover von Ralph Lauren. „Ich bin Charles Bahr, und ich bin 15 ...", sagt er. Der Moderator fragt, ob Facebook noch relevant sei. „Meine Mutter ist den ganzen Tag auf Facebook", sagt Charles. „Wenn Sie eine ältere Zielgruppe erreichen wollen: sicherlich." Für Charles sind Podcasts, Snapchat und Instagram vor allem eins: Chancen, Werbebotschaften zu platzieren.

B Deshalb hat Deutschlands größte Messe für digitales Marketing ihn zur Gesprächsrunde *The Brand Disrupters: For Millennials, from Millennials* eingeladen. Der CEO von Twitter spricht hier, die Geschäftsführerin von Facebook und die Marketingchefin von Ikea. Und auch Charles Bahr, Schüler und Deutschlands jüngster Agenturchef: Mit 14 gründete er seine Social-Media-Agentur Tubeconnect Media. „Mein Team und ich wissen, wie man Marketing auf Social Media macht."

C Charles gehört zur Generation Z. Die meisten seiner Angestellten sind Gleichaltrige und jobben auf Projektbasis, ohne feste Arbeitszeiten. Volljährig sind nur zwei in seinem Geschäft. Zehn- bis zwölfjährige Praktikanten arbeiten auch mit dem Team. Die Bewerbungsgespräche führt Charles auf dem Schulhof. Charles will Unternehmen erzählen, auf welchen Plattformen er und seine Freunde unterwegs sind, wie sie diese nutzen, was sie gut finden.

D Seine jungen Praktikanten verbringen viel Zeit damit, auf musical.ly eigene Playback-Videos zu ihren Lieblingssongs hochzuladen. Er und seine gleichaltrigen Freunde bevorzugen Instagram und Snapchat. Oft klagen Erwachsene, sie könnten Snapchat und musical.ly gar nicht verstehen. Für viele Unternehmen sind Teenager aber eine relevante Zielgruppe, weil sie die Kunden der Zukunft sind. Deshalb ist Charles erfolgreicher Berater.

E Charles arbeitet auch an Projekten mit Kunden. Für die Berliner Shoppingplattform Yeay haben er und sein Team Influencer auf YouTube und musical.ly ausgesucht. Heute gibt es Tausende Kanäle allein auf YouTube. Mit dem Wechsel des Nutzerverhaltens findet in der Werbebranche ein Generationswechsel statt. Junge Menschen gründen neue Agenturen und werden gebucht, da sie die Entwicklungen im digitalen Marketing mitgestalten.

F Viele ältere Kölner-Messebesucher wollen Charles kennenlernen. Auch Niels Alzen, Kreativchef der Werbeagentur Scholz & Friends mit Sitz in Hamburg, die Montblanc, Opel und die Berliner Philharmoniker zu ihren Kunden zählt. „Seine Geschäftsidee ist zeitgemäß. Er baut Brücken, wo sie uns fehlen", sagt Alzen. Besonders im digitalen Marketing sei ein Diskurs mit der Zielgruppe wichtig.

OL Ordinary Level Questions

1. a) Give **five** details about Charles Bahr. A
   b) Name the people who are at the round of talks. B
   c) Give details about the people he works with. C
   d) What do his trainees generally do? D
   e) Which projects has he worked on? E
   f) Who wants to get to know Charles? F
2. Choose the correct answer.
   a) Charles ist **(Chef/Arbeiter/Schüler/Student)** einer Werbeagentur.
   b) Die Marketingchefin von IKEA ist gekommen **(an/um/zu/mit)** von Charles Bahr zu lernen.
   c) Charles macht **(Jobinterviews/Projekte/Prüfungen/Hausaufgaben)** in der Schule.
3. What words make up these compounds and what do they mean in English?
   a) hellgrau = _____ + _____ = _____
   b) Marketingchefin = _____ + _____ = _____
   c) Arbeitszeiten = _____ + _____ = _____
   d) Geschäftsidee = _____ + _____ = _____

HL Higher Level Questions

1. Beantworten Sie folgende Fragen auf Deutsch und in Ihren eigenen Worten!
   a) i) Geben Sie mehrere Details über Charles. A
   ii) Warum sind Podcasts, Instagram und Snapchat ihm wichtig? (**2** Gründe) A
   b) Was für eine Messe wird hier beschrieben? Geben Sie **drei** Details. B
   c) i) Was wissen Sie über die Menschen, die bei Charles arbeiten? (**4** Details) C
   ii) Was macht Charles genau? C
   d) Was machen **i)** die jüngeren Arbeiter und **ii)** die älteren Arbeiter in dieser Firma? D
2. Answer the following questions in English.
   a) According to Charles, what should marketers focus on with **i)** older people and **ii)** younger people? A
   b) Why exactly did Charles found this company? B
   c) Why is his company so successful? C
   d) Which project has Charles worked on? Why is it so successful? E
   e) What exactly does Alzen say about Charles and his company? F
3. Was passt zusammen?

1. Charles findet Snapchat und Instagram	**A** sind zwischen zehn und zwölf Jahren alt.
2. Er hat sein Unternehmen gegründet,	**B** gehen die Jüngeren auf Videowebseiten.
3. Viele der Arbeiter, die bei ihm arbeiten,	**C** denn die Jugend ist die Hauptzielgruppe der Werbungsbranche.
4. Während Charles auf Snapchat geht,	**D** super zum Platzieren von Werbungen.
5. Er wird oft gebucht,	**E** da er soziale Medien versteht.
6. Viele Geschäftsführer besuchen die Messe,	**F** um über digitales Marketing zu lernen.

4. Give the simple form of the adjective in the expressions below. Example: **ein toller Junge** = **toll**
   A **eine ältere Zielgruppe** an older target group = _____
   B **größte Messe für digitales Marketing** biggest trade fair for digital marketing = _____ + _____
   C **Die meisten Angestellten** Most employees = _____
   D **Seine jungen Praktikanten** His young trainees = _____
   E **Junge Menschen gründen neue Agenturen** Young people are founding new companies = _____ + _____
   F **Besonders im digitalen Marketing** Especially in digital marketing = _____

OL Äußerung zum Thema: Ordinary Level

You are interviewing Charles Bahr. Complete the dialogue based on the information given in Text 2.

Sie: Wie alt sind Sie?

Charles: ______________________________

Sie: Wie alt sind die Leute, die für Sie arbeiten?

Charles: ______________________________

Sie: Wo führen Sie ihre Bewerbungsgespräche?

Charles: ______________________________

Sie: Was suchen Sie im Internet, wenn Sie arbeiten?

Charles: ______________________________

Sie: Warum wollen die großen Chefs mit Ihnen sprechen?

Charles: ______________________________

HL Äußerung zum Thema: Higher Level

Use sentences from the oral section on page 186 to help you write this **Äußerung**.

- Beschreiben Sie das Foto rechts in **drei bis vier** Sätzen.
- Was halten Sie vom Cybermobbing? Begründen Sie Ihre Meinung.
- Was sonst für Probleme haben junge Leute heutzutage? Geben Sie Beispiele. Wie könnte man diese Probleme lösen?

Wir kriegen dich noch!

Nützliche Sätze

Cybermobbing ist heutzutage ein wachsendes Problem.	*Nowadays, cyberbullying is a growing problem.*
Schüler werden gehänselt oder sogar ausgegrenzt, vielleicht weil sie anders sind.	*Students are teased or even excluded, perhaps because they are different.*
Wir müssen das Problem offen besprechen, denn Vorbeugen ist besser als Heilen.	*We must discuss the problem openly because prevention is better than cure.*
Die Folgen können richtig ernst sein.	*The consequences can be really serious.*
Das Opfer des Mobbings wird oft zum Außenseiter und das führt zu Depressionen und Hoffnungslosigkeit.	*The victim of bullying often becomes an outsider and that leads to depression and hopelessness.*
Leider begehen die Opfer manchmal sogar Selbstmord, denn sie sehen keinen Ausweg.	*Unfortunately, the victims sometimes even commit suicide because they can't see an escape.*
Man soll den Kopf nicht in den Sand stecken.	*One shouldn't hide one's head in the sand.*
Sie sind in einem Teufelskreis gefangen.	*They are caught in a vicious cycle.*

Kulturecke

Wenn man in Deutschland volljährig wird:

- Darf man hochprozentigen Alkohol kaufen und öffentlich trinken.
- Darf man ab 18 mehr als 40 Stunden pro Woche arbeiten.
- Darf man heiraten falls beide Partner volljährig sind.
- Darf man ohne Begleitung fahren, wenn man den Führerschein schon gemacht hat.
- Darf man ausgehen solange man will und sich jeden Film ansehen.
- Wird die Schulpost nun direkt zu den Schülern gehen.
- Hat man das volle Wahlrecht.

Grammatik: Adjektive/Adjectives

p. 201 (Übung macht den Meister)

Adjective before the Noun

When an adjective comes before the described noun, it takes on the **gender** (masculine/feminine/neuter), **number** (singular or plural) and **case** of the noun. Turn to page 115 for a reminder of the German case system. Example: **Das kleine Kind isst den leckeren Apfel** →

a) **kleine** = neuter, singular, nominative **b)** **leckeren** = masculine, singular, accusative

1 Definite Article + Adjective + Noun

This applies to definite articles (**der**, **die**, **das**, **die**) and demonstratives (**dieser/jener/jeder** – **diese/jene/jede**).

	Masculine	Feminine	Neuter	Plural
Nominative	der kluge Mann	die kluge Frau	das kluge Kind	die klugen Männer
Accusative	den klugen Mann	die kluge Frau	das kluge Kind	die klugen Frauen
Dative	dem klugen Mann	der klugen Frau	dem klugen Kind	den klugen Kindern
Genitive	des klugen Mannes	der klugen Frau	des klugen Kindes	der klugen Männer

Decide the gender, number and case of the adjectives in bold print below.

1. Der **coole** Mann trinkt den **heißen** Kaffee.	**4.** Die **interessierten** Schüler lasen die **alten** Bücher.
2. Das **neue** Auto überfährt den **alten** Mann.	**5.** Dieser **coole** Lehrer hat den **netten** Schüler gelobt.
3. Das **rote** Rad gehört dem **netten** Mädchen.	**6.** Die **alte** Frau sah die Farbe des **neuen** Autos.

2 Indefinite Article + Adjective + Noun

This applies to indefinite articles, negative articles (**kein**) and possessive articles (**mein**, **dein**, **sein**, etc).

	Masculine	Feminine	Neuter	Plural
Nominative	ein kluger Mann	eine kluge Frau	ein kluges Kind	keine klugen Frauen
Accusative	einen klugen Mann	eine kluge Frau	ein kluges Kind	keine klugen Kinder
Dative	einem klugen Mann	einer klugen Frau	einem klugen Kind	keinen klugen Männern
Genitive	eines klugen Mannes	einer klugen Frau	eines klugen Kindes	keiner klugen Frauen

Decide the gender, number and case of the adjectives in bold print below.

1. Ein **junges** Kind sucht sein **altes** Buch.	**4.** Dein **kleiner** Sohn hat einen **schönen** Preis.
2. Ein **alter** Mann dankt einer **netten** Frau.	**5.** Ein **netter** Lehrer gibt dem Schüler eine **gute** Note.
3. Die **nette** Frau hilft einem **lieben** Kind.	**6.** In unserer **großen** Stadt gibt es ein **altes** Museum.

3 No Article + Adjective + Noun

	Masculine	Feminine	Neuter	Plural
Nominative	kluger Mann	kluge Frau	kluges Kind	kluge Kinder
Accusative	klugen Mann	kluge Frau	kluges Kind	kluge Männer
Dative	klugem Mann	kluger Frau	klugem Kind	klugen Frauen
Genitive	klugen Mannes	kluger Frau	klugen Kindes	kluger Kinder

Decide the gender, number and case of the adjectives in bold print below.

1. **Warme** Milch schmeckt mir nicht.	**4.** **Schwüles** Wetter bringt Gewitter.
2. **Fettes** Essen schadet der Gesundheit.	**5.** Von **veganem** Essen werde ich nicht satt.
3. Ich mag **gesellige** Tiere.	**6.** Für **guten** Apfelsaft braucht man gute Äpfel.

Text 3: Freundschaft

  Bitte beantworten Sie die folgenden Fragen:

1. Was machen die zwei Mädchen?
2. Wo sind sie, glauben Sie?
3. Wie fühlen sich die Mädchen, Ihrer Meinung nach?

Vorarbeit

1. Finden Sie diese Ausdrücke im Text!
   - **A** But now everything was going wrong.
   - **B** ... is this all my fault?
   - **C** ... what's wrong with Mai?
   - **D** She turned pale.
   - **E** To stick together, even if it was very hard.
2. Finden Sie das Deutsche für die Wörter unten.
   - **A** honesty/sandpit/fought/trust/strangers
   - **B** disappeared/annoy/insulted/sad/tears
   - **C** move house/horrified/It depends
   - **D** behaved/heatedly/say goodbye/doorbell
   - **E** understood/grow apart/true/manage

Maria Peters, 18 Oct. 2006 (amended)

A „Freundschaft..." Für Mieke war es nicht nur ein Wort. Freundschaft war für sie alles. Es bedeutete Vertrauen, Ehrlichkeit und Spaß. Doch jetzt lief alles schief. Ihre beste Freundin Mai war sauer auf sie, aber Mieke konnte nicht verstehen warum. Mai und Mieke waren die typischen besten Freunde, die sich schon seit dem Sandkasten kannten. Nie hatten sie sich gestritten. Vor einigen Tagen war noch alles in Ordnung und nun waren sie wie wildfremde Menschen.

B „Was habe ich dir eigentlich getan?", fragte sie. „Ich weiß nicht wovon du redest", antwortete Mai und rannte weg. Schnell lief Mieke ihr nach. „Mai, ich will dich nicht ärgern, aber bin ich an all dem hier schuld?" Mai schüttelte den Kopf. Plötzlich brach sie in Tränen aus. Leise sagte sie „Ich kann es nicht" und verschwand. „Und das nach all den Jahren", sagte Mieke beleidigt und traurig. Deprimiert ging sie in den Unterricht. Ein langer Tag lag vor ihr.

C „Hallo", begrüßte sie ihre Mutter. „Weißt du schon, was mit Mai ist?", fragte ihre Mutter. „Was?" „Mais Mutter hat einen neuen Job bekommen." „Das ist toll", sagte Mieke. „Es kommt drauf an. Für euch beiden nicht. Sie müssen umziehen. Und ziemlich weit weg", sagte ihre Mutter. „Was?", fragte Mieke. Das war es, was Mai ihr nicht sagen konnte. „Und wann genau?", fragte sie. „Spätestens in zwei Tagen", antwortete ihre Mutter. Mieke war entsetzt.

D Plötzlich rannte Mieke aus der Tür und zu dem weißen Haus, das neben ihrem stand. Hitzig drückte sie auf die Klingel. Mai öffnete die Tür. Sie wurde blass, als sie Mieke sah. „Was tust du hier?", fragte sie. „Meine beste Freundin verabschieden. Oder wolltest du gehen, ohne mir was zu sagen?", antwortete sie. „Ich wollte es dir erzählen", sagte sie. „Ganz ehrlich." „Wolltest du wirklich gehen, ohne dich zu verabschieden?", sagte sie. „Nein, aber ich wusste nicht, wie ich es sagen sollte. Wir waren bis jetzt noch nie lange getrennt...", machte sie weiter. „Der Gedanke daran macht mich genauso verrückt." Jetzt bemerkte Mieke, wie kindisch sie sich verhalten hatte.

E „Mensch Mai ... Eines kann ich dir versprechen. Nämlich, dass wir Freunde bleiben", sagte Mieke. „Wir schreiben uns und wir mailen uns, okay?" „Ich habe noch zwei Tage, dann fahren wir schon", bemerkte Mai. „Denkst du nicht, dass wir uns auseinanderleben? Ich meine, du wirst wieder eine beste Freundin finden und ich sicher auch." „Mai ... du wirst immer meine beste Freundin bleiben, verstanden? Das schaffen wir. So, wie wir sonst auch immer alles schaffen." Dann fingen die beiden an, Mais Sachen zusammenzupacken. Nun ging alles viel schneller, da sie zu zweit waren. „Freundschaft", murmelte Mieke. Das war die wahre Bedeutung von Freundschaft. Zusammenzuhalten, auch wenn es sehr schwerfiel.

OL Ordinary Level Questions

1. a) Describe the friendship between Mieke and Mai. Give **two** details. A
   b) Mieke notices that Mai was acting differently. What did she ask Mai? Give **two** details. B
   c) i) How did Mieke find out what was wrong with Mai? C
      ii) What was the problem? C
   d) What exactly did Mieke do after she discovered the reason for Mai's behaviour? D
   e) Mai is worried that she and Mieke will grow apart. What does Mieke say in response? E
2. Choose a suitable heading for each paragraph and explain your choice in English.

Mais Mutter hat eine neue Stelle	Mieke besucht Mai	Sie packen Mais Sachen zusammen ein	Mai und Mieke sind beste Freundinnen	Mieke versteht nicht, warum Mai so schlecht gelaunt ist

3. What belongs together?

1. Seit ihrer Kindheit	**A** jedoch hat Mieke keine Idee warum.
2. Eines Tages ist Mai schlecht gelaunt,	**B** dass sie ihre beste Freundin verlieren wird.
3. Mieke sagt ihrer Mutter,	**C** sind Mai und Mieke gut befreundet.
4. Mai hat Angst,	**D** immer Freundinnen zu bleiben.
5. Mai und Mieke versprechen einander	**E** dass sie nicht weiß, was mit Mai los ist.

4. Select the correct prepositions for the following sentences.
   a) Mai und Mieke sind **(seit/bei/für/am)** ihrer Kindheit beste Freundinnen.
   b) Mieke weiß nicht, was **(mit/vor/an/für)** Mai los ist.
   c) Miekes Mutter sagt, dass Mai **(von/aus/auf/in)** hier wegziehen wird.
   d) Mai und Mieke werden **(in/an/ohne/für)** immer Freundinnen bleiben.

HL Higher Level Questions

1. Beantworten Sie folgende Fragen auf Deutsch!
   a) Wie würde Mieke ihre Freundschaft mit Mai beschreiben? Schreiben Sie **drei** Sätze (Präsens) in *Ich*-Form. A
   b) Eines Tages ist Mai schlecht gelaunt. Wie reagiert Mieke darauf? B
   c) Was entdeckt Mieke während des Gesprächs mit ihrer Mutter? (**2** Details) C
   d) Was macht sie dann genau? Geben Sie **drei** Details. D
   e) Was versprechen sich die Mädchen im letzten Absatz? E
2. Answer the following questions in English.
   a) How well do Mai and Mieke know each other? Give several details. A
   b) What does Mieke ask Mai, and how does she react when Mai runs away? B
   c) Give **five** details about the conversation between Mieke and her mother. C
   d) Mai explains to Mieke how she feels about the situation. Give several details about her feelings. D
   e) The text explores the theme of friendship. Give **four** examples in the last paragraph that are a good sign that Mai and Mieke will remain friends. E
3. Translate the following adjectives from the text into English. How effective are they in supporting the topic of friendship in the text?
   a) sauer b) traurig c) entsetzt d) blass e) wahr
4. Decide the gender, number and case of the underlined adjectives below.
   a) Ein <u>langer</u> Tag lag vor ihr.
   b) Mais Mutter hat einen <u>neuen</u> Job bekommen.
   c) Mieke rannte zu dem <u>weißen</u> Haus.
   d) Du bist meine <u>beste</u> Freundin.

Grammatik: Adjektive + Adverbien/ Adjectives + Adverbs

p. 201 (Übung macht den Meister)

Quantities + Adjective + Noun

The **expressions of quantity** listed below may have an article or possessive adjective in front of them. Depending on which article or possessive adjective is used, one of the three tables on page 195 will apply.

all- all	beid- both	manch- some	solch- such	viel- much/many*	wenig- few*

*viel and wenig do not always take endings in the singular.

Die vielen jungen Leute lernen Deutsch. (Page 195, Table 1, nominative, plural)

Ich suche **einen solchen Rock**. (Page 195, Table 2, accusative, masculine singular)

Viele junge Leute lernen Deutsch. (Page 195, Table 3, nominative, plural)

Adverbs

An adverb describes a verb or an adjective. In English, adverbs often end with -ly: luckily, recently. Other adverbs which do not end with -ly are: often, seldom, as well, also, very.

A few German adverbs may look like adjectives, but when used with a verb or an adjective, they have a meaning of -ly. For example, **nervös** can mean the adjective 'nervous' or the adverb 'nervously'.

1. Translate into English the following German adverbs. They have been grouped by category.

a) Speed: plötzlich, zögernd, schnell, langsam	**e) Comparing and contrasting:** auch, dennoch, jedoch, sehr
b) Negatives: nimmer, nicht, nie, gar nicht, ungern, nicht gern	**f) Mood:** nervös, erschreckt, enttäuscht, entzückt, leider
c) Causal: also, deshalb, daher, deswegen, dadurch	**g) Time:** bald, oft, öfters, manchmal, neulich, immer, normalerweise, genau, gerade
d) Locational: da drüben, dort, dorthin, dort oben, oben, unten, hinten, hier	**h) Qualities:** leise, laut, intelligent

2. Using the list above, complete the sentences by inserting an appropriate adverb.

a) Er rannte _____ aus der Tür.	**e)** Wir wohnen _____ seit vier Jahren.
b) Sie schrie _____ vor Schreck.	**f)** Ich stehe _____ um 9 Uhr auf.
c) Sie las die Geschichte _____ vor.	**g)** Ich träume _____ .
d) Er fuhr sehr _____ die Straße entlang.	**h)** Sie ging sehr _____ aus dem Zimmer.

Comparative and Superlative Adverbs

The comparative of the adverb appears as: quicker, slower. In German, this is formed by adding **-er** to the adverb: **schnell → schneller; langsam → langsamer**

The superlative of the adverb appears as: quickest, slowest, most exciting. This is formed by adding **am -sten** to the adverb: **schnell → am schnellsten; langsam → am langsamsten**

Here are some common irregular comparatives and superlatives:

gern → lieber → am liebsten
gut → besser → am besten
oft → öfter → am öftesten
viel → mehr → am meisten

Prüfungstipp

A revision schedule can help you to plan your time. This is particularly important when preparing for your oral exam. Ten minutes a day on oral work will be much more effective than three hours once a week. Make sure that your revision schedule covers every topic.

10.03 Hörverständnis Teil 3

Vorarbeit

keine Sorge	*no worries*	**erleichtert**	*relieved*	**Treff**	*get together*
umgezogen	*moved house*	**gern haben**	*to like*	**aufnehmen**	*to accept*
klappen	*to work out*	**sich einleben**	*to settle in*	**schaffen**	*to manage*

CL Ordinary + Higher Level Questions

1. **a)** The conversation is between:
   i) two classmates ☐ **iii)** a teacher and a student ☐
   ii) two college students ☐ **iv)** a parent and a child ☐
   b) Find **one (O)/two (H)** details in the conversation that support your choice.
2. **a)** Which word best describes the first speaker's attitude during the conversation?
   i) delighted ☐ **ii)** worried ☐ **iii)** sad ☐ **iv)** happy ☐
   b) Write down **one (O)/two (H)** details from the conversation to support your choice.
3. What does the second speaker say to encourage the first speaker? Give **two (O)/three (H)** details.
4. How does the second speaker feel at the end? Give **one (O)/two (H)** details.

10.04 Hörverständnis Teil 4

Vorarbeit

Kultusministerium	*Department of Education*	**Niveau**	*level*	**drinnen**	*inside*
bestehen	*to exist*	**Notnummer**	*emergency number*	**süchtig**	*addicted*
draußen	*outside*	**Entzug**	*withdrawal*	**einteilen**	*to allocate*

CL Ordinary + Higher Level Questions

1. **a)** Describe the study commissioned by the Department of Education. Give **one (O)/two (H)** details.
   b) What solutions are suggested by the study? Give **one (O)/two (H)** details.
2. Describe the campaign in Güdingen. Give **two (O)/three (H)** details.
3. **a)** Describe the summer camp in Ingolstadt. Give **two (O)/three (H)** details.
   b) Give details about whom it is for and how long it will last.
4. **a)** What is the purpose of the recovery centre?
   b) Give details of what the participants will do at the centre. Give **three (O)/four (H)** details.
5. What is the weather forecast? Give **four (O)/five (H)** details.

Expressions of time

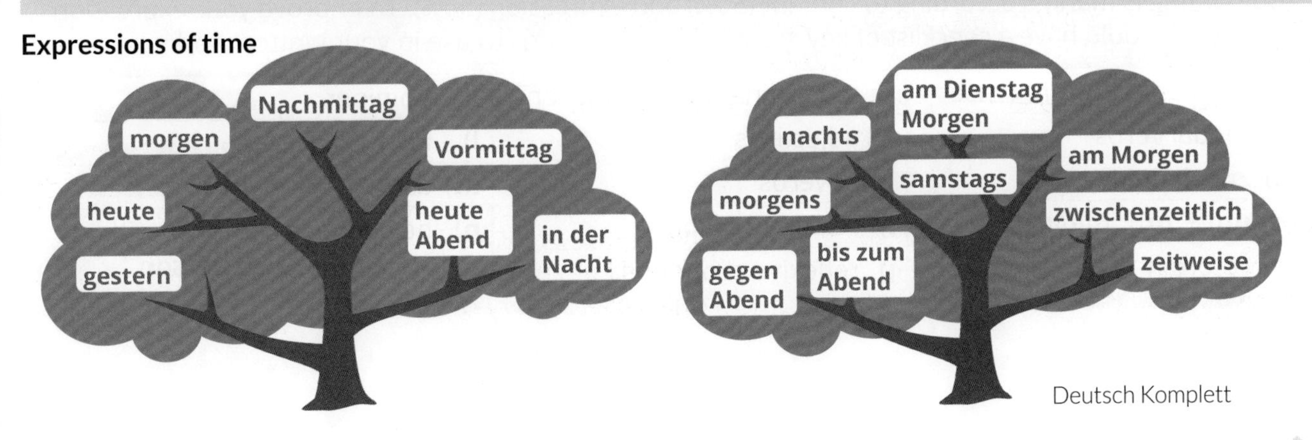

OL Schriftliche Produktion: Ordinary Level

Use the oral work section on page 186 to help you write a letter to your pen pal, Denis/Denise. Complete the first paragraph by inserting the correct phrases from the box. Then follow the instructions.

letzten Juli 18 geworden **ein Auto** **eine Antwort auf deinen Brief zu schreiben** **meinen Führerschein gemacht** **mich gefreut von dir zu hören**

Liebe(r) Denis/Denise,

endlich habe ich die Zeit gefunden, ______________ . Wie geht's? Mir geht's bestens. Ich habe ______________ . Wie du weißt, bin ich ______________ . Letzte Woche habe ich ______________ ! Meine Eltern haben mir ______________ geschenkt!

Now continue the letter.

- Describe your car (brand, colour, electronic features).
- Say that the driving test was hard but that you are very happy.
- Say the present from your parents was fantastic.
- Say that you have a part-time job and can pay for the costs.
- Invite your friend on a visit to Ireland.
- Write a suitable closing sentence.

HL Schriftliche Produktion: Higher Level

Benutzen Sie die Ausdrücke auf Seite 186 um die folgenden Fragen zu beantworten.

1. Beschreiben Sie in **vier bis fünf** Sätzen, was Sie auf dem Foto sehen.
2. Warum greifen Jugendliche zu Alkohol oder Drogen? Nennen Sie **zwei** mögliche Gründe. Wie sieht die Situation in Irland aus? Schreiben Sie **zwei** Sätze.
3. Stehen Jugendliche heutzutage unter zu viel Stress, Ihrer Meinung nach? Warum, glauben Sie, ist das so? Nennen Sie **zwei** mögliche Gründe. Wie könnte man den Stress abbauen? Geben Sie **zwei** mögliche Lösungen.
4. Wie wichtig ist eine gute Freundschaft? Wie verbringen Sie Zeit mit Ihren Freunden? Wie feiern Sie mit Ihren Freunden?
5. Was bedeutet Volljährigkeit für Sie? Erklären Sie Ihre Meinung in **zwei** Sätzen. Wie wird die Volljährigkeit normalerweise in Irland gefeiert?

Prüfungstipp

Your writing is marked according to content (50%) and expression (50%). To improve your expression mark, you should have a checklist of key grammatical structures to use in your written work:

a) use of past/future tense	**f)** subordinating conjunctions	**k)** opinions
b) modal verbs	**g)** adjectives	**l)** idioms
c) **zu** + infinitive	**h)** adverbs	**m)** the conditional
d) **um** + **zu** + infinitive	**i)** relative pronouns	**n)** beginning a sentence with an adverb + verb + person
e) co-ordinating conjunctions	**j)** reflexive pronouns	

Übung Macht den Meister!

A Adjectives after the Noun

Übersetzen Sie die folgenden Sätze ins Englische.

1. Ich finde Deutsch nützlich.
2. Ich denke, der Film war toll.
3. Manche finden das schwierig.
4. Mein bester Freund ist lustig.
5. Der Unterricht ist interessant.
6. Das Thema ist sehr kompliziert.

B Comparative Adjectives

Translate the sentences into German.

1. English is more challenging than History.
2. Chemistry is harder than Biology.
3. Irish is easier than French.
4. The school day here is longer.
5. Their holidays are much shorter than ours.
6. My brother is one year older than me.

C The/This/That + Adjective + Noun

Insert the correct adjective ending.

1. Der neu_ Schüler ist hier.
2. Was ist das deutsch___ Wort für „adjective"?
3. Ich finde diese körperlich___ Arbeit schwer.
4. Sie sieht dieses arm___ Kind auf dem Boden.
5. Wir essen dieses altgebacken___ Brot nicht.
6. Er gibt jenem klug___ Jungen den Preis.

D The/This/That + Adjective + Noun

Replace *the* + adjective + noun with:

a) *this* + adjective + noun, and then with

b) *that* + adjective + noun

1. Der kluge Junge kriegt eine Eins.
2. Die nette Lehrerin kommt gleich.
3. Der ältere Bruder grinst.
4. Das ist ein altes Schloss aus der alten Zeit.
5. Er fängt die wilde Katze.
6. Sie nimmt den roten Hut der alten Frau mit.

E Negative Article/Possessive Adjective + Adjective + Noun

Replace *a* + adjective + noun with:

a) negative article + adjective + noun, and then with

b) *my/your/his* ... + adjective + noun

1. Ein literarischer Wettbewerb ist toll.
2. Ich habe einen kleinen Bruder.
3. Mary mag ein kaltes Bier.
4. Jan trinkt einen heißen Kaffee.
5. Das ist ein cooler Podcast.
6. Ich lese gerade ein interessantes Buch.

F A/An + Adjective + Noun

Insert the correct adjective ending.

1. Ich kaufe einen kurz___ Rock.
2. Ein lang___ Rock gefällt mir nicht.
3. Hast du eine schön___ Reise gehabt?
4. Heike ist ein nett___ Mädchen.
5. Er wohnt in einem groß___ Haus.
6. Das ist eine sehr gut___ Idee.

G No Article + Adjective + Noun

Insert the correct adjective ending.

1. Ich mag heiß___ Kaffee (m).
2. Grün___ Tee (m) schmeckt auch gut.
3. Man soll alt___ Papier (n) recyceln.
4. Nach schwer___ Gewittern (pl.) scheint die Sonne.
5. Die Jacke ist aus echt___ Leder (n).
6. Dicht___ Nebel (m) liegt über der Stadt.

H Adverbs

Insert the most appropriate adverb for each sentence.

1. Die Zeiten ändern sich _____ .
2. Wir dekorieren _____ den Weihnachtsbaum.
3. Der Unterricht wird _____ enden.
4. Ich fühle mich _____ sehr krank.
5. Die Schülerin mag Fremdsprachen _____ .
6. Meine Mutter kauft _____ viele Geschenke.

Für die Prüfung

1. Was passt zusammen?

1. Die meisten Jugendlichen wollen	**A** auf die Zukunft.
2. Viele Jugendliche freuen sich riesig	**B** dass eine gute Freundschaft sehr wichtig ist.
3. Manche haben Angst	**C** weil sie dem Schulalltag entfliehen wollen.
4. Niemand kann leugnen,	**D** sich einfach mit Freunden ausruhen.
5. Einige trinken Alkohol,	**E** vor schlechten Noten im Abitur.

2. Was passt zusammen?

1. Ich gehe mit meinen Freunden aus,	**A** cool aus.
2. Meiner Meinung nach sehen Tattoos	**B** einfach um Spaß zu haben.
3. Nasenpiercings	**C** darf man Auto fahren.
4. Wenn ich ein Tattoo bekommen würde,	**D** finde ich eigentlich hässlich.
5. Wenn man volljährig wird,	**E** wären meine Eltern echt sauer auf mich.

3. Select the correct adjectives for the following sentences.

a) Ich gehe gern mit meiner **(netten/netter/nette)** Mutter dahin.

b) Sie hat Vertrauen zu ihrem **(älteren/älterem/älterer)** Sohn.

c) Ich passe auf meine **(kleinen/kleine/kleiner)** Schwester auf.

d) Die Großeltern helfen ihrer **(liebe/lieben/lieber)** Enkelin.

e) Wir lernen **(interessante/interessantes/interessanter)** Fakten.

f) Der Opa geht mit einem **(alter/altem/alten)** Stock.

4. What words make up the following compound words and what do they mean in English?

a) Sandkasten = _____ + _____ = __________

b) wegziehen = _____ + _____ = __________

c) Vorarbeit = _____ + _____ = __________

d) Prüfungstipp = _____ + _____ = __________

e) Hörverständnis = _____ + _____ = __________

f) Wettbewerb = _____ + _____ = __________

5. Identify the gender and case of the underlined adjectives.

a) Sie erzählt eine lustige Geschichte.

b) Wir feierten die ganze Nacht durch.

c) Die Eltern schenken ihr ein tolles Geschenk.

d) Ich rede oft mit meinem lieben Freund.

e) Ich mag die Farbe deiner coolen Jacke.

f) Ich schreibe nach den Tests einen langen Brief.

6. Translate these common adverbs into English.

a) also **b)** schnell **c)** auch **d)** jedoch **e)** jetzt **f)** deswegen **g)** nun **h)** leider **i)** bald **j)** oft

7. Lückentext: Fill in the blanks with the correct missing words from the box.

warm	**nach**	**lokalen**	**nette**	**manchmal**

1 _____ gehen wir zusammen ins Kino oder in die Kneipe. Im Sommer fahren wir in Urlaub **2** _____ West Cork. Wenn das Wetter **3** _____ ist, zelten wir auf einem schönen Campingplatz, wo wir viele **4** _____ Jugendliche treffen. Wenn es regnet oder sehr kalt ist, schauen wir uns Filme allerart an. Wir hängen auch herum und trinken einen Kaffee im **5** _____ Café.

Selbstbewertung: Ordinary Level

OL

Vocabulary

1. If I can translate theses sentences into English, I can talk about young people's issues. (1 mark each)

a) Viele Jugendliche trinken Alkohol.	**f)** Mein Schlafzimmer ist groß und hell.
b) Ich trinke nur ein Bier, wenn ich ausgehe.	**g)** Mobbing ist natürlich verboten.
c) Mein bester Freund heißt Alex.	**h)** Manche Jugendliche sind gestresst.
d) Meine beste Freundin ist sehr lustig.	**i)** Wir wollen selbstständiger werden.
e) Mein bester Freund hört mir immer zu.	**j)** Ich habe mein Profil auf privat gestellt.

Your score: ___/10

2. If I can translate these nouns into English, I understand the main nouns relating to young people's issues. (1 mark each)

a) Abiturprüfung	**d)** Freundeskreis	**g)** Computersucht	**i)** Drogenhändler
b) Netzwerk	**e)** Nasenpiercing	**h)** Ausgehen	**j)** Anruf
c) Handymobbing	**f)** Notnummer		

Your score: ___/10

Grammar

3. If I can conjugate these verbs in the **ich** form in the present and perfect tenses, I can talk about my personal experiences. (1 mark for each tense)

a) erfahren: I learn ____________ I have learned ____________

b) sehen: I see ____________ I have seen ____________

c) kennenlernen: I get to know ____________ I got to know ____________

d) gehen: I go ____________ I went ____________

e) haben: I have ____________ I had ____________

Your score: ___/10

4. If I can translate the following, I understand adjectives. (2 marks each)

a) Ich finde Deutsch cool, denn die Kultur ist interessant.

b) Ich lerne gern Deutsch, weil die Sprache schön ist.

c) Mein bester Freund ist lustig und freundlich.

d) Meine jüngere Schwester hat lange, blonde Haare und blaue Augen.

e) Ich mag ein leckeres Eis essen.

Your score: ___/10

5. If I can choose the correct adverb, I understand the adverbs used to describe young people's issues. (1 mark each)

a) Ich lerne **(also/sehr)** neue Leute kennen.	**f)** Ich will **(gern/fast)** ins Ausland fahren.
b) Ich gehe **(oft/langsam)** mit Freunden aus.	**g)** Freundschaft ist **(sehr/gern)** wichtig.
c) Wir sprechen **(fast/oft)** über die Ferien.	**h)** Ich danke dir **(sehr/oft)** für deine Hilfe.
d) Ich gehe **(jedoch/gern)** in die Schule.	**i)** Ich habe **(bald/neulich)** das Abi gemacht.
e) Wir sehen **(gerne/drüben)** Filme.	**j)** Die Tests sind **(immer/plötzlich)** stressig.

Your score: ___/10

What have I learned?	
What must I improve?	
What do I want to revise?	

Your total score: ___/50

Selbstbewertung: Higher Level

HL

1. If I can translate these sentences into German, I understand the use of nouns with adjectives. (2 marks each)

a) She finds the homework difficult.	**d)** School can be stressful.
b) I find the listening comprehensions easier.	**e)** Alcohol can be very dangerous.
c) I think that bullying is terrible.	

Your score: ___ / 10

2. If I can translate these sentences into German, I understand the use of adjectives before the noun. (2 marks each)

a) I went to a wild party.	**d)** My best friend is funny and entertaining.
b) Some were drinking hot chocolate.	**e)** We talk about interesting topics.
c) I like hanging out with my best friends.	

Your score: ___ / 10

3. If I can translate these sentences into German, I understand the use of adjectives in a variety of contexts. (2 marks each)

a) Her younger sister is a best friend of my older brother.
b) Many young people like to meet new people.
c) Other young people can be shy.
d) All young people find the Leaving Certificate challenging.
e) His older brother has got his second driving licence.

Your score: ___ / 10

4. If I can correctly fill in the gaps below, I understand the difference between adjectives and adverbs. (1 mark each)

zuverlässig hoffentlich gerne ungeduldig ernstes
immer gleichen cooles kommenden neue

Mein Freund Justus ist **1** _____ **2** _____ . Wenn ich ein **3** _____ Problem habe, kann ich es mit ihm besprechen. Er ist nie **4** _____ und hört mir **5** _____ zu. Wir machen viel zusammen, denn wir haben die **6** _____ Interessen. Wir werden im **7** _____ Sommer auf ein **8** _____ Musikfest in Galway gehen. Wir werden auf dem Konzertgelände zelten und **9** _____ viele **10** _____ Leute kennenlernen.

Your score: ___ / 10

5. If I can correctly translate these sentences into German, I understand the use of adverbs. (1 mark each)

a) I usually get on with everyone.	**f)** Because of that, I don't drink.
b) I often go out with my friends.	**g)** Of course, I don't drink and drive.
c) I would never take drugs.	**h)** Unfortunately, some do drink and drive.
d) Normally I drink two beers.	**i)** Some also take drugs.
e) However, I have my driving licence now.	**j)** Luckily, my friends are responsible.

Your score: ___ / 10

What have I learned?	
What must I improve?	
What do I want to revise?	

Your total score: ___ / **50**

11 Die großen Ansprüche unserer Zeit

Learning Outcomes

- **Oral:** discussing global issues; revise oral topics from Chapters 1 and 2
- **Reading:** reading and discussing three texts on global issues
- **Writing:** writing an opinion (**Äußerung**), picture descriptions and a letter on global issues
- **Aural:** listening to and answering questions on four extracts on world issues

Grammar

- Forming questions with a verb
- The interrogative **wer** (who) and **welcher**, **welche**, **welches** (which)
- Uses of **wo-** + preposition
- Uses of **da-** + preposition

Vocabulary

- War, racism and violence
- Mass migration
- Refugees and economic migrants

German Culture

- Refugees in Germany
- Smoking and drinking

Exam Tips

- Don't confuse **wo** (where) and **wer** (who). This is a common mistake!
- Create a list of the grammar points you learn and use it as a checklist to help improve your expression mark in the exam.

Text 1: Was tun?

  Bitte beantworten Sie die folgenden Fragen:

1. Was sehen Sie auf dem Foto?
2. Wogegen protestieren sie?
3. Was sieht man im Hintergrund ?

Vorarbeit

1. Finden Sie diese Ausdrücke im Text!
   - **A** ... a big increase in migrants from these areas ...
   - **B** The gap between poor and rich ...
   - **C** They feel disappointed by their governments.
   - **D** The missing values of the powerful
   - **E** The spread of fake news on the net
   - **F** ... the desired living standard of Westerners ...
2. Finden Sie das Deutsche für die Wörter unten!
   - **A** violence/tensions/are increasing/social
   - **B** immigrate/emigrate/governments
   - **C** economic policies/trust/to secure
   - **D** appointed/population/angry
   - **E** rumours/attacks/missing/bomb attack
   - **F** is changing/Near East/war/meanwhile

HuffPost Edition Deutschland, 15 Nov. 2013 (amended)

A Kulturelle Spannungen

Die Spannungen im Mittleren Osten und in Nordafrika steigen. Wegen der Instabilität gibt es eine große Zunahme an Migranten aus diesen Gebieten nach Europa und das führt langsam zu gesellschaftlichen Spannungen. Diese Spannungen können leicht zu Gewalt führen.

B Der Unterschied zwischen Arm und Reich wird immer größer

Viele Jugendliche sind arbeitslos. Was können Regierungen in Zukunft tun, um jungen Menschen wieder Hoffnung zu geben? Viele müssen auswandern um ihren Beruf auszuüben. Andere wandern ein, um Stellen zu nehmen, die Jugendliche nicht nehmen wollen.

C Kein Vertrauen in die Wirtschaftspolitik

Studien zeigen, dass Menschen unter 50 Jahren viel kritischer gegenüber der Wirtschaftspolitik ihres Landes stehen als die ältere Generation. Sie machen sich Gedanken darüber, wie der Staat ihre finanzielle Zukunft sichern kann. Besonders Jugendliche vertrauen den Politikern ihres Landes nicht. Sie fühlen sich von ihren Regierungen enttäuscht.

D Die fehlenden Werte bei Machthabern

Jugendliche sind böse auf ihre Regierung. Es scheint vielen Jugendlichen, dass die Menschen, die Chefs in der Politik und der Wirtschaft sind, eher für sich arbeiten als für die Bevölkerung, die sie angestellt hat.

E Die Verbreitung von Falschinformationen aus dem Netz

Wie schützt man sich gegen Angriffe aus dem Internet? Es gibt immer mehr Kriminalität und Mobbing im World Wide Web. Falschinformationen aus dem Netz gelten als großer Missbrauch, zum Beispiel, nach dem Bombenanschlag auf den Bostoner Marathon gab es Twitter-Gerüchte, dass ein vermisster Student dafür verantwortlich sei. Obwohl das Gerücht falsch war, hatte sich der Tweet schon längst viral verbreitet. Man muss das stoppen.

F Was zu tun?

Wir sind mittlerweile global vernetzt, also weiß jeder, was auf der Welt los ist, ob es um Probleme im Nahosten, den Krieg oder den erwünschten Lebensstandard der Westler angeht, unsere Welt verändert sich schnell. Diese Probleme sieht man als die wichtigsten Aufgaben der Politik an.

OL Ordinary Level Questions

1. a) Where are tensions rising, according to the text? A
   b) What is the biggest problem for young people? B
   c) How does the younger generation feel about the economic policies of their country? C
   d) Why are young people angry with their government? D
2. True or false?
   a) Es gibt keine Probleme im Mittelosten und in Afrika.
   b) Arbeitslosigkeit ist nur ein kleines Problem unter den Jugendlichen.
   c) Viele Jugendliche sind mit der Wirtschaftspolitik zufrieden.
   d) Die Chefs in der Politik arbeiten für die Menschen, die sie angestellt haben.
3. What words make up the following compound words, and what do they mean in English?
   a) Mittelosten = _____ + _____ = _____
   b) Nordafrika = _____ + _____ = _____
   c) Wirtschaftspolitik = _____ + _____ = _____
   d) Lebensstandard = _____ + _____ = _____
   e) Bombenanschlag = _____ + _____ = _____
   f) Nahosten = _____ + _____ = _____
4. Choose the correct preposition.
   a) Viele Migranten **(von/bei/in/aus)** armen Gebieten fliehen nach Europa.
   b) **(In/An/Um/Zum)** Zukunft müssen Regierungen jungen Menschen Hoffnung geben.
   c) Junge Menschen fühlen sich **(durch/wegen/von/auf)** ihren Regierungen enttäuscht.
   d) Viele Jugendliche sind böse **(mit/auf/in/aus)** die Regierung.

HL Higher Level Questions

1. Beantworten Sie folgende Fragen auf Deutsch.
   a) Nennen Sie die möglichen Folgen, laut Text, der großen Zunahme an Migration nach Europa. A
   b) Was machen Jugendliche heutzutage um Arbeit zu finden? B
   c) Warum fühlen sich die Jugendlichen von der Wirtschaftspolitik enttäuscht? C
   d) Was halten manche Jugendliche von den Machthabern in ihrem Land? D
   e) Erklären Sie die Gerüchte, die erwähnt werden, und die Folge davon. E
2. Answer the following questions in English.
   a) What may lead to serious tensions? A
   b) Which reasons are given for young Germans emigrating? B
   c) Give **three** details about how young people feel about their government. C
   d) Why are young people angry with their government? D
   e) What must be stopped, according to the text? E
   f) What problems are seen as the most important tasks of politics, according to the text? F
3. Was passt zusammen?

1. Der Krieg im Mittelosten	**A** ihre Regierung nichts macht um ihnen zu helfen.
2. Viele Jugendliche denken, dass	**B** weiß jeder, was für Probleme es in der Welt gibt.
3. Sie fühlen sich	**C** werden missbraucht.
4. Falschinformationen im Internet	**D** von der Wirtschaftspolitik ihres Landes enttäuscht.
5. Da wir heute global vernetzt sind,	**E** hat zu einer Zunahme an Migration geführt.

4. Insert the correct adjective endings.
   a) Die arbeitslos___ Jugendlichen wandern aus, um ihren Beruf auszuüben.
   b) Die Regierungen sollen den jung___ Menschen Hoffnung geben.
   c) Die jünger___ Generation ist viel kritischer gegenüber der Politik als die ältere Generation.
   d) Ein falsch___ Gerücht kann sich im Netz schnell verbreiten.

Grammatik: Fragen Stellen/Forming Questions

p. 219 (Übung macht den Meister)

As in English, you can form a question in German by starting with the *verb*, followed by the noun or pronoun:

Geht **das Kind jetzt?** *Is* the child going now? *Kommst* **du mit?** *Are* you coming with us?

Turn the following statements into questions, using the examples above as a guide.

1. Es gibt viel zu tun.	**5.** Du lernst viel.
2. Viele Menschen sind obdachlos.	**6.** Seine Schwester heißt Sharon.
3. Die Leute wohnen hier.	**7.** Der Briefträger kommt jeden Tag.
4. Wir werden in der Stadt feiern.	**8.** Der Hund hat die ganze Nacht gebellt.

Interrogative Pronouns

The interrogative **wer?** follows the case system in the masculine form, as shown in the table. With interrogative pronouns, gender and number are not significant. However, the case is essential.

Case	Interrogative	Translation
Nominative	wer?	*who?*
Accusative	wen?	*whom?*
Dative	wem?	*to/with/from whom?*
Genitive	wessen?	*whose?*

Turn the statements below into questions, using the underlined part of the sentence as a clue to the case.

Example: Das ist sein Buch. *That is his book.* → Wessen Buch ist das? *Whose book is that?*

1. Sie hat den Film gesehen.	**5.** Ich arbeite für die Frau.
2. Er hat den Mann gesehen.	**6.** Die Frau klopft an die Tür.
3. Der Mann geht in die Stadt.	**7.** Siehst du das Kind?
4. Er spricht mit der Frau.	**8.** Das ist Julias Heft.

Welcher, Welche, Welches (Which)

Welcher follows the **der**, **die**, **das** case system (see page 130).

Insert the correct form of **welch-** in the sentences below.

1. Für welch___ Auto interessieren Sie sich?	**5.** Welch___ Film gefällt dir am besten?
2. An welch___ Uni studierst du?	**6.** Mit welch___ Jungen hast du getanzt?
3. Welch___ Mann magst du?	**7.** Welch___ Geschenk hast du gekauft?
4. Welch___ Leute werden uns besuchen?	**8.** Über welch___ Lehrer ärgerst du dich?

Interrogatives

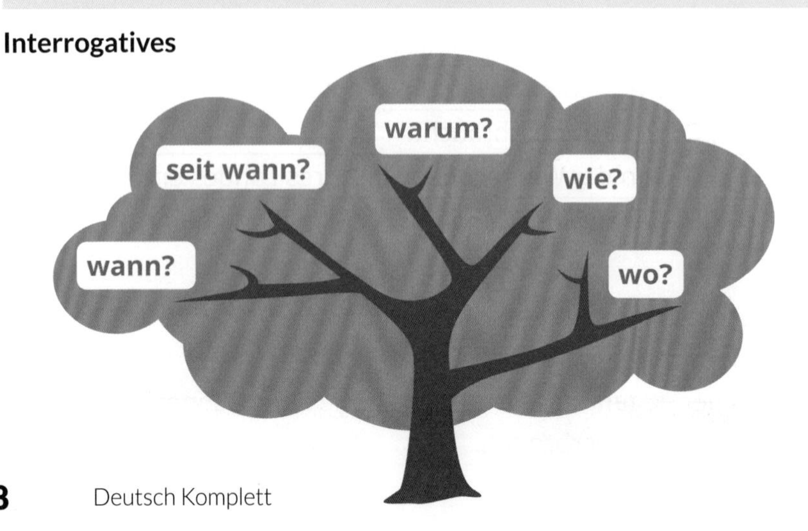

Common mistakes made by English speakers include mixing up **wo** (where) and **wer** (who) and making over-complicated questions. Avoid these errors in your work!

11.01 Hörverständnis Teil 1

Vorarbeit

störte	*disturbed*	**geerbt**	*inherited*	**Hilfsaktionen**	*aid projects*
hoffnungslos	*hopeless*	**Treffpunkt**	*meeting place*	**Fähigkeiten**	*skills*
selbstbewusst	*confident*	**keinen Bock**	*no desire*	**vermitteln**	*to liaise*
Energiequellen	*energy sources*	**beitragen**	*to contribute*	**leiten**	*to direct*

CL Ordinary + Higher Level Questions

1. **a)** What is this project about? **b)** How did it start and who had the idea?
2. What is the aim of the project? How many people use the service? Give **one (O)/two (H)** details.
3. Where does the project take place and how did the organiser get the venue?
4. **a)** Who funds the project? Give **one (O)/two (H)** details. **b)** How does the project operate?
5. Who is involved in the day-to-day running of the project? Give **two (O)/three (H)** details.

11.02 Hörverständnis Teil 2

Vorarbeit

Diebstahl	*theft*	**Bushaltestelle**	*bus stop*	**Führerschein**	*driver's licence*
griff	*grabbed*	**unangenehm**	*unpleasant*	**verschwunden**	*disappeared*
Anschlag	*attack*	**geguckt**	*looked*	**entsetzt**	*horrified*
Gedächtnis	*memory*	**Augenbrauenpiercing**	*eyebrow piercing*	**fummelte**	*fumbled*

OL Ordinary Level Questions

1. Why is the caller telephoning?
2. What is the caller's name and number?
3. The caller was:
   a) in a shop ☐ **b)** on a bus ☐ **c)** at a bus stop ☐ **d)** in a train station ☐

HL Higher Level Questions

1. Using ***key phrases***, write down **in German** the key information the caller provides:
   - the name of the person **making** the call
   - the reason for the call
   - **four** details of their conversation
   - details regarding further contact
   - the caller's phone number

Gesprächsnotiz

Anruf von: ____________________ Gesprächsanlass: ____________________

Der Anrufer:

- ruft später zurück ☐
- wird zurückgerufen ☐
- wird morgen zurückrufen ☐
- wird eine SMS erhalten ☐

Kontaktnummer: ____________________

2. Write down **three** examples of the language used which show the caller is **upset**.

Text 2: Ich sehne mich nach einem Ort, den ich Zuhause nennen kann

Bitte beantworten Sie die folgenden Fragen:

1. Was machen die Leute auf diesem Foto?
2. Wo sind sie?
3. Was tragen sie?

Vorarbeit

1. Finden Sie diese Ausdrücke im Text!
   - **A** We all need a home.
   - **B** ... they feel uprooted.
   - **C** ... I hardly slept.
   - **D** That must urgently be changed.
2. Finden Sie das Deutsche für die Wörter unten!
   - **A** war/refugees/under-age/to offer
   - **B** approval/training/accepted/vocational school
   - **C** share/flight/communal accommodation
   - **D** social worker/founded/suitable/goal

Sophie Martin, 9 Nov. 2017 (adapted)

A Um Alternativen für junge Flüchtlinge anzubieten, wurde Anfang 2016 das Projekt Zimmerfrei gegründet. Es vermittelt Zimmer an minderjährige Flüchtlinge. Wir alle brauchen ein Zuhause. „Für mich ist es der Ort, wo ich lebe", sagt Nadia. „Und das nicht nur, weil ich dort eine Wohnung habe, sondern meine Familie, Freunde und auch meine Arbeit." Doch was ist mit denjenigen, die kein Zuhause haben? So geht es den vielen Flüchtlingen, die nach Deutschland gekommen sind. Sie haben ihr Zuhause durch Krieg und Terror verloren.

B „Ich heiße Nadia und bin jetzt seit zwei Jahren in Deutschland. Für meine Eltern ist es schwieriger sich zu integrieren. Ich glaube, sie fühlen sich entwurzelt. Für mich ist es leichter hier in Hamburg, weil ich noch so jung bin. Ich lerne die deutsche Sprache, besuche die Berufsschule, will danach eine Ausbildung machen. Ich habe Pläne hier in Deutschland", sagt Nadia. Alleine Hamburg hat in den letzten zwei Jahren mehr als 32.000 Flüchtlinge aufgenommen. Nach der Anerkennung besuchen die Flüchtlinge einen Integrationskurs.

C „Als wir in Deutschland angekommen sind, waren wir in einer Sammelunterkunft. Es war laut und schmutzig. Ich hatte Ängste, Depressionen, und ich habe kaum geschlafen", sagt Nadia. Diese Probleme kennt auch Mara aus Ghana. Sie lebt in einem Frauenhaus, sucht eine Wohnung für sich und ihren Sohn. „Wir teilen uns die Küche und das Bad. Es wird viel gestohlen. Ich fühle mich oft gestresst. Ich habe eine gefährliche Flucht von Ghana bis nach Deutschland hinter mir. Ich glaube, wenn ich eine eigene Wohnung hätte, würde ich auch Deutsch schneller lernen, denn ich könnte mich besser konzentrieren."

D Von der schwierigen Wohnsituation in Hamburg weiß auch das Projekt Zimmerfrei. Zimmerfrei, das Anfang 2016 gegründet wurde, hat das Ziel, geeignete Zimmer und kleine Appartements für minderjährige Flüchtlinge zu finden. „Wir wollen den Jugendlichen die Möglichkeit geben, in Hamburg richtig zu leben", erklärt Anne Plehn. Die Sozialpädagogin arbeitet seit Juli 2016 für Zimmerfrei: „Das muss dringend geändert werden."

Prüfungstipp

In your **Äußerung** or the **Schriftliche Produktion**, you might be asked to describe a picture of mass migration, economic immigrants, protests or war. Use the resources in this chapter to express your opinion on these issues.

OL Ordinary Level Questions

1. **a)** Give **two** details about the Zimmerfrei project. (A)
   b) How have **i)** Nadia and **ii)** her parents settled in? (B)
   c) Give **two** details about where they first lived in Germany. (C)
   d) What does the organisation find for refugees under the age of 18? (D)
2. True or false?
   a) Für Nadia ist ihr Zuhause nur eine Wohnung.
   b) 32.000 Flüchtlinge wohnen in Hamburg.
   c) Die erste Unterkunft war ruhig und sauber.
   d) Man sucht Wohnungen für alle Flüchtlinge.
3. Complete the following sentences, based on Text 2.
   a) Viele Flüchtlinge haben ihre **(Geld/Auto/Heimat/Wohnwagen)** verlassen.
   b) Nadia geht zur Zeit auf die **(Uni/Schule/Gymnasium/Berufsschule)**.
   c) In der ersten Unterkunft hatte Nadia **(Spaß/Angst/Hunger/einen Job)**.
   d) Es ist **(schwierig/leicht/unmöglich/sehr einfach)** eine Wohnung in Hamburg zu finden.
4. Choose the correct preposition.
   a) **(Mit/Durch/Für/An)** Nadia ist ihr Zuhause, wo ihre Familie ist.
   b) Nadias Eltern fanden es nicht so einfach sich **(nach/in/für/an)** die Gesellschaft zu integrieren.
   c) Mara sucht ein Zuhause **(zu/zum/für/in)** ihren Sohn.
   d) Sie möchte **(mit/an/in/für)** einer eigenen Wohnung leben.

HL Higher Level Questions

1. Beantworten Sie folgende Fragen auf Deutsch.
   a) Sie waren neulich beim Projekt Zimmerfrei. Was erzählen Sie Ihrer Familie und Freunden über Zimmerfrei? (A)
   b) Beschreiben Sie, wie **i)** Nadia und **ii)** ihre Eltern sich integriert haben. (B)
   c) Unter welchen Lebensumständen wohnte Nadia in der Sammelunterkunft? (C)
   d) Nennen Sie **zwei** Ziele des Projekts. (D)
2. Answer the following questions in English.
   a) What have refugees lost in their homeland and what reasons are given for this? (A)
   b) Give details about Nadia's future plans. (B)
   c) Give details about the stress Mara says that she is under. (C)
   d) What does the social worker say? (D)
3. Was passt zusammen?

1. Viele Flüchtlinge sind	**A** weil ihre Unterkunft sehr laut und schmutzig war.
2. Nadias Eltern hatten Heimweh	**B** so dass sie richtig in Deutschland leben können.
3. Nadia hatte Depressionen,	**C** und konnten sich nicht integrieren.
4. Sie wollen eine Wohnung für sie finden,	**D** wegen Kriegs nach Deutschland gekommen.

4. Welches Fragewort würden Sie benutzen, um nach den unterstrichenen Wörtern zu fragen?
   a) Wir brauchen ein Zuhause.
   b) Ich bin seit zwei Jahren in Deutschland.
   c) Ich fühle mich oft gestresst.
   d) Es wurde 2016 gegründet.

German uses many more reflexive verbs than English. It is a good idea to highlight these verbs when you come across them and to use them in your oral and written work.

sich sehnen | sich integrieren | sich fühlen | sich teilen | sich konzentrieren

OL Äußerung zum Thema: Ordinary Level

You are interviewing Nadia. Complete the dialogue, using the information given in Text 2.

Sie: Seit wann bist du hier in Deutschland?
Nadia: ______________________________
Sie: Wohnst du hier mit deiner Familie?
Nadia: ______________________________
Sie: Wie war es in der Sammelunterkunft?
Nadia: ______________________________
Sie: Wie heißt die Organisation, die euch geholfen hat?
Nadia: ______________________________
Sie: Wie hilft diese Organisation den Flüchtlingen?
Nadia: ______________________________

HL Äußerung zum Thema: Higher Level

Sehen Sie sich die Fotos rechts an.

- Beschreiben Sie die Fotos rechts in jeweils **drei** Sätzen.
- Welche sozialen Probleme werden hier geschildert?
- Was gibt es sonst für Probleme in unserer Welt, mit denen wir uns befassen sollten?

Nützliche Sätze

Translate the sentences below into English.

1. Auf dem ersten Bild kann man viele Menschen sehen, die protestieren.
2. Sie halten Plakate mit Slogans, wie ... hoch.
3. Ohne Zweifel sehen sie alle wütend/besorgt aus.
4. Im Vordergrund/im Hintergrund tragen einige Menschen Plakate in der Hand.
5. Ich glaube, sie wollen Ausländer vertreiben.
6. Meiner Meinung nach muss man lernen Kompromisse zu schließen.
7. Gewalt kann nicht die Antwort sein.

Prüfungstipp

In the exam, your oral and written work is marked according to content (a mark awarded for each sentence which is relevant to the topic). There is always a maximum number of marks which the examiner will be allowed to award you for content, so there is no point writing more sentences than required.

You will also be marked according to expression (a mark awarded for the extent and variety of structures and expressions which you use). Create a list of grammar points which you have learned and use it as an expression and structures checklist to add to your work.

Grammatik: Fragen Stellen/Forming Questions

p. 219 (Übung macht den Meister)

1 Wo + Preposition: Direct Question

The German interrogative (question word) **wo** may have a preposition attached to it.
When combined with a preposition, **wo** can often mean 'what'. For example:

What is he afraid of? (of what?) **Wovor hat er Angst?**

If **wo** is combined with a preposition which begins with a vowel, then an extra *'r' will be added:* **wor-**.

wodurch?	*by which means?*	**womit?**	*with what?*	**worin?**	*in what?*
wofür?	*for what?*	**wonach?**	*what for? what of?*	**worüber**	*about what?*
wogegen?	*against what?*	**woran?**	*at what? / in what?*	**worum?**	*about what?*
woher?	*from where?*	**worauf?**	*on what? / for what?*	**wovon?**	*of what?*
wohin?	*where to?*	**woraus?**	*of what? / from where?*	**wozu?**	*why?*

Turn the statements below into questions.

Example: Ich will **über** das Problem sprechen. ➔ **Worüber** willst du sprechen?

1. Er hat was gegen den Film.	**6.** Ich bitte dich um Hilfe.
2. Ich habe Angst vor Hunden.	**7.** Ich warte auf den Bus.
3. Ich freue mich auf die Ferien.	**8.** Sie ist mit den Hausaufgaben fertig.
4. Der Kurs geht um Goethe.	**9.** Ich verstehe nichts von diesem Thema.
5. Es besteht aus Metall.	**10.** Meine Eltern bestehen auf gutes Benehmen.

2 Wo + Preposition: Implied Question

Wo + preposition can also be used to form an implied question. An implied question does not use a question mark.

I don't know what he is talking about (about what). **Ich weiß nicht, worüber er spricht**.

When **wo** + preposition is used to form an implied question, it sends the verb to the end of its clause. This also applies to simple interrogatives such as **wer**, **was**, **wann**, **wo**, **wie**, **warum** when they form an implied question:

Ich weiß, wo du wohnst. **Ich verstehe, was du meinst.**

Translate the following implied questions into English.

1. Sie versteht nicht, worüber er spricht.	**4.** Er weiß, worum es geht.
2. Sie weiß nicht, wovor er Angst hat.	**5.** Er wusste nicht, wohin er es nehmen sollte.
3. Der Fall, worauf sich das bezieht, ist ernst.	**6.** Wir hatten keine Idee, woher sie kam.

3 Was für ein? *What kind of?*

With the phrase **was für ein ... ?** the **für** does not necessarily cause the accusative case. The case used in the following noun will depend on the function of the noun in the sentence.

Was für ein Junge (nom.) ist er? *What kind of a boy is he?*

Was für einen Jungen (acc.) magst du? *What kind of boy do you like?*

Mit was für einem Jungen (dat.) tanzt sie? *With what kind of boy is she dancing?*

To answer a question, you can use **ja** (yes), **nein** (no), or **doch** (but yes, contradicting a negative).

Hast du den Film gesehen? **Ja**, ich habe den Film gesehen.

Hast du das Buch gelesen? **Nein**, ich habe das Buch nicht gelesen.

Kommt Laura **nicht** zur Party? **Doch**, Laura kommt zur Party.

Text 3: Der Alptraum

Vorarbeit

1. Finden Sie diese Ausdrücke im Text!
   - **A** I have dreamed about this recently.
   - **B** We're sorry, it's already assigned.
   - **C** ... suddenly the window pane shattered ...
   - **D** We have nothing against foreigners.
   - **E** Did you have a bad dream?
2. Finden Sie das Deutsche für die Wörter unten!
   - **A** asylum seekers/Westerners/traditional dress
   - **B** finally/sprayed on/entered/watched
   - **C** flames/crashed/flew in/at home
   - **D** belongs/dead/dreadful/understand
   - **E** refugee shelter/alarmed/sobbed/burnt

© Gudrun Pausewang, 2014 (amended)

A Ich habe schon oft geträumt, ganz allein zwischen Eskimos, Indianern oder Chinesen zu sein. So was habe ich kürzlich geträumt: Ich war im Ausland. Es muss ein afrikanisches Land gewesen sein, denn die Leute dort waren fast alle in traditioneller afrikanischer Tracht. Wir waren die einzigen Westler. Aber dieser Traum war ganz anders, denn meine Eltern, mein Bruder Michael und ich – waren dort nicht als Touristen, sondern als Asylbewerber! Ich weiß nicht, warum wir aus Deutschland geflüchtet waren. Krieg? Hunger?

B Als wir einen Laden betraten, beobachtete uns der Verkäufer. In einem Restaurant wollten wir einen Teller Suppe essen. Aber sobald der Kellner uns sah, stellte er ganz schnell auf alle Tische Schilder, worauf das Wort RESERVIERT stand. Und wer hätte gewusst, wie schwierig es sein konnte, eine Wohnung zu finden! Wir fanden keine. Überall, wo man eine Wohnung angeboten hat, hörten wir: »Es tut uns leid, sie ist schon vergeben.« Schließlich hatten wir doch noch Glück. Es waren nur zwei kleine Zimmer und eine Küche, aber besser als gar nichts. Das Bad mussten wir mit einer anderen Familie teilen. Im selben Haus wohnten noch Italiener, Franzosen, Engländer und Polen. Und auf der Hauswand, gleich unter unserem Fenster, stand groß hingesprüht: AUSLÄNDER RAUS!

C Zum Glück ging's mir ok in der Schule, denn die Kinder spielten mit mir in der Pause und erklärten mir alles, was ich nicht verstand. Da war ich sehr froh. Aber in der Nacht, daheim, als wir schon schliefen, splitterte plötzlich die Fensterscheibe, gerade über meinem Bett. Etwas flog herein und krachte fürchterlich, und bald stand der ganze Raum in Flammen. Mein Bett stand in Flammen. Auch ich selbst stand in Flammen. Und ich schrie und schrie und hatte Schmerzen. Ich hörte meine Eltern und Michael »Nina! Nina!« schreien, aber sie konnten mir nicht helfen.

D Und dann war ich tot. Ich konnte mich selber sehen, weil es ja ein Traum war. Meine Eltern weinten. Michael aber rief: »Ich will nicht in diesem schrecklichen Land bleiben!« Draußen standen viele Leute vor dem Haus. Ein paar von ihnen legten Blumen unter das Fenster. Andere hörte ich sagen: »Wir haben ja nichts gegen Ausländer« oder »Hoffentlich begreifen sie es bald, dass jeder eben in sein eigenes Land gehört.«

E Ich wachte auf. »Was ist denn?« fragte Mutti erschrocken. »Du hast ja so geschrien! Hast du was Schlimmes geträumt?« »Ich bin verbrannt!« schluchzte ich.« »Aber Ninakind«, sagte Mutti und nahm mich in den Arm, »Wie kommst du nur darauf?« Es wurde ganz hell in meinem Zimmer. Durchs Fenster sah ich Michael im Garten joggen. Aber an der Wand des Asylantenheimes stand AUSLÄNDER RAUS!

OL Ordinary Level Questions

1. Describe the beginning of the dream which Nina had. Give **three** details. (A)
2. Name **one** negative experience that Nina and her family had in the dream. (B)
3. Choose a suitable heading for each paragraph and explain your choice in English.

Die Wohnung steht in Flammen | **Der Alptraum beginnt** | **Die Wohnungssuche** | **Mutti rettet Nina** | **Die Eltern weinen**

4. Separate these compound words into their components and translate them into English.
   a) Asylbewerber = _____ + _____ = ________
   b) Hauswand = _____ + _____ = ________
   c) Fensterscheibe = _____ + _____ = ________
   d) Asylantenheim = _____ + _____ = ________
5. Indicate whether the following sentences are true or false according to the text.
   a) Nina und ihre Familie waren dort als Touristen.
   b) Wenn sie in einem Restaurant essen wollten, wurde ihnen gesagt, die Tische seien gebucht.
   c) Ninas Schlafzimmer stand in Flammen.
   d) Durch ihr Schlafzimmerfenster kann Nina ein Asylantenheim sehen.

CL Ordinary + Higher Level

Lückentext: Fill in the blanks with the correct missing words from the box below.

flog **schlimmen** **plötzlich** **gegen** **Schlafzimmer** **wer**

Ich hatte gestern Abend einen **1** _____ Traum. Ich schlief in meinem **2** _____ , als ich **3** _____ einen lauten Krach hörte. Ein Stein **4** _____ über meinen Kopf und schlug **5** _____ die Wand. Ich wusste nicht, **6** _____ den Stein geworfen hatte. Dann wachte ich auf.

HL Higher Level Questions

1. Beantworten Sie die folgenden Fragen auf Deutsch!
   a) Wo befand Nina sich in ihrem Traum? Geben Sie **zwei** Details! (A)
   b) Was hat der Kellner gemacht, sobald Nina mit ihrer Familie ins Restaurant gingen? (B)
   c) Beschreiben Sie genau, was Nina in dieser Nacht passiert ist. (C)
   d) Wie reagierten die Einheimischen auf das Feuer? Geben Sie **zwei** Details. (D)
   e) Wie reagierte die Mutter auf das Schreien von Nina? Geben Sie **drei** Details. (E)
2. Answer the following questions in English.
   a) Give **five** details about the beginning of Nina's dream. (A)
   b) Describe their new-found accommodation in detail. (B)
   c) What did Nina see when she woke up and how did she react? Give **four** details. (C)
   d) Give details about how each family member reacted to the fire. (D)
   e) What did Nina say to her mother about the dream? (E)
3. Was passt zusammen?

1. Nina war nicht als Touristin,	**A** was laut krachte.
2. Sie fanden eine Unterkunft,	**B** aber die Unterkunft war sehr klein.
3. Eines Nachts flog etwas durch das Fenster,	**C** sondern als Asylbewerberin dort.
4. Nina dachte,	**D** sah sie ein Asylantenheim durch das Fenster.
5. Nachdem sie aufgewacht war,	**E** dass sie tot war.

4. Use examples of content or language style from the text to show how the narrator creates tension and fear.

11.03 Hörverständnis Teil 3

Vorarbeit

Verdacht	*suspicion*	**erwischt**	*caught*	**zufällig**	*by chance*
Alkoholgeruch	*smell of alcohol*	**in seinem Atem**	*on his breath*	**fast**	*almost*
sich besaufen	*to booze*	**häufig**	*frequently*	**besprechen**	*to discuss*

CL Ordinary + Higher Level Questions

1. **a)** The conversation is between:
   i) a teacher and student ☐ **iii)** employer and employee ☐
   ii) friends ☐ **iv)** college students ☐
   b) Find **one (O)/two (H)** details in the conversation that support your choice.
2. **a)** Which word best describes the female speaker's attitude during the conversation?
   i) depressed ☐ **ii)** indifferent ☐ **iii)** happy ☐ **iv)** worried ☐
   b) Write down **one (O)/two (H)** details from the conversation to support your choice.
3. How does the male speaker react to the female speaker? Give **two (O)/three (H)** details.
4. What did the female speaker agree to do? Give **one (O)/two (H)** details.

11.04 Hörverständnis Teil 4

Vorarbeit

Rauchen	*smoking*	**gesundheitsschädlich**	*harmful to health*	**Verkauf**	*sale*
Gefahren	*dangers*	**sich mit ... befassen**	*to deal with*	**entdeckt**	*discovered*
ernst	*serious*	**Minderjährige**	*minors*	**leer**	*empty*
Lastwagen	*truck*	**wurde ... verhaftet**	*was arrested*	**Bergland**	*mountainous area*

CL Ordinary + Higher Level Questions

1. Name the issue mentioned in the first news item. Give **one (O)/two (H)** reason(s) why it is important.
2. What are experts discussing in Köln? Give **two (O)/three (H)** details.
3. Describe in detail what police officials discovered. Give **two (O)/four (H)** details.
4. What is the weather forecast? Give **three (O)/four (H)** details.

Prüfungstipp

Most ordinal numbers (first, second, third, etc.) are easy in German. You add **-te** or **-ste** if the number ends in **-g. 5: fünf → fünfte; 10: zehn → zehnte; 23: dreiundzwanzig → dreiundzwanzigste**

The three exceptions are: 1: eins → erste; 3: drei → dritte; 7: sieben → siebte

Grammatik: Präpositionen/Prepositions

p. 219 (Übung macht den Meister)

Da + Preposition

When attached to a preposition, the word **da** can mean 'it', 'this', 'that' or 'there'.

Note that if the preposition attached to **da** begins with a vowel, the letter -r is placed between the two words, as shown in the table below.

Frequently Occurring Da + Prepositions

dafür *for it*	**dahin** *to it, to there*	**daran** *on it, from it*	**darüber** *about it, above it*	**davon** *from it, of it*
dagegen *against it*	**dahinter** *behind it*	**darauf** *on top of this, on (to) it, about it*	**darum** *about it, around it*	**davor** *in front of it, from it*
daher *from there*	**daneben** *beside it, next to it*	**darin** *in it*	**darunter** *under it*	**dazwischen** *between them*

1. The '**da** + preposition' in the second sentence of each example replaces the underlined section in the first sentence. Translate the sentences into English.

a) Wir sprechen über eine interessante Fernsehsendung. → Wir sprechen darüber.

b) Mein Bruder leidet an Diabetes. → Mein Vater leidet auch daran.

c) Ich habe gegen die vorgeschlagene Regelung gewählt. → Ich habe dagegen gewählt.

d) Wir freuen uns auf die Reise nach Spanien. → Wir freuen uns darauf.

e) Ich freue mich über meine guten Noten in Deutsch. → Ich freue mich darüber.

2. Replace the underlined expressions below with the appropriate '**da** + preposition'.

a) Sie spricht über ihr Leben.	**d)** Er ist nach Paris gefahren.
b) Er schlug gegen den Baum.	**e)** Er setzte sich auf eine Bank.
c) Sie ging hinter das Haus.	**f)** Ich freue mich auf die Reise.

Common prepositional verbs

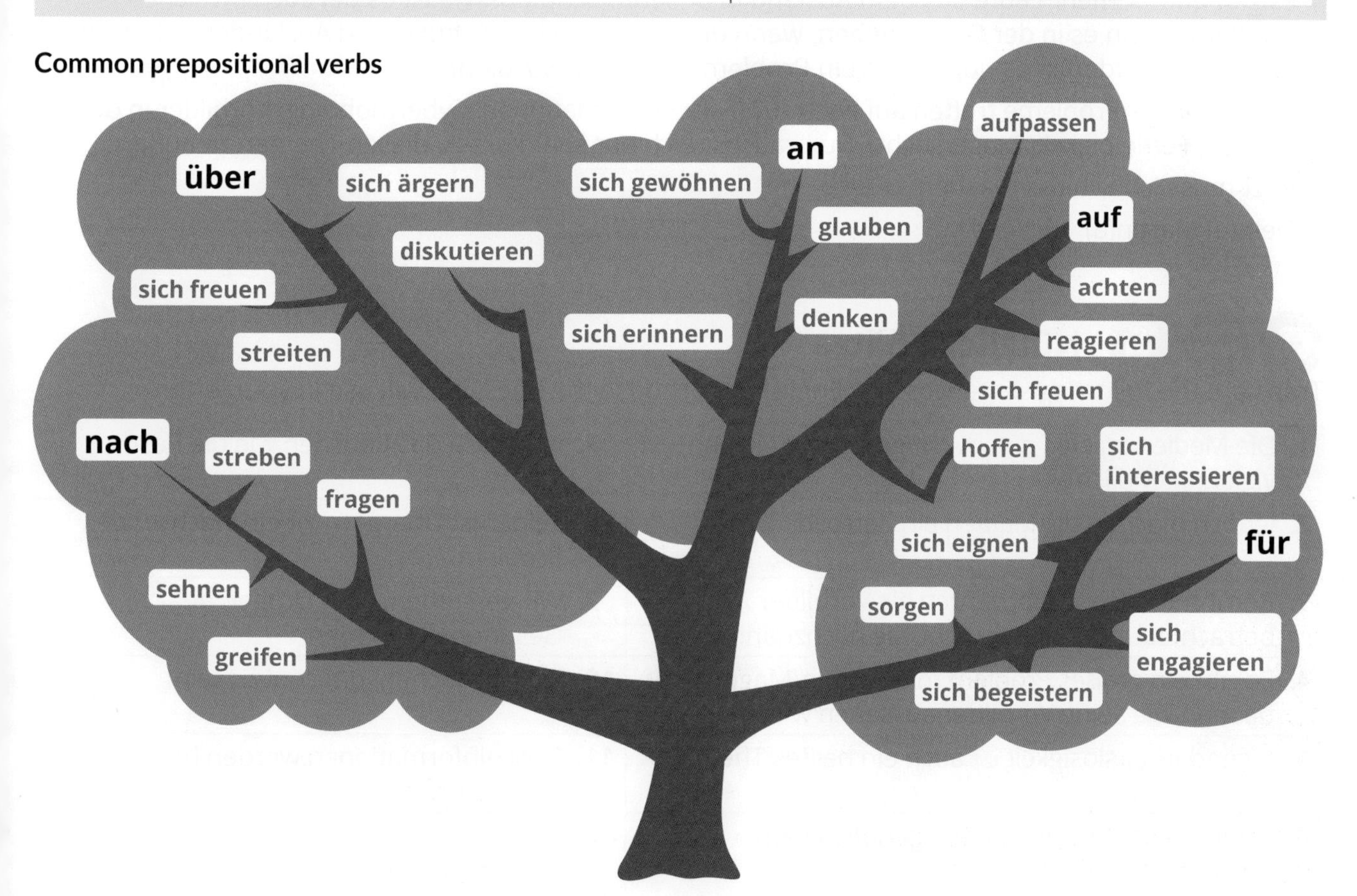

OL Schriftliche Produktion: Ordinary Level

Write a letter to your pen pal. Complete the first paragraph by correctly inserting the sentence halves below. Then follow the instructions.

dir einen Brief zu schreiben **mit meinen Freunden nach Österreich** **bin ich mit dem Abitur fertig** **riesig auf die Ferien** **ausruhen**

Liebe(r) Martin(a),

endlich habe ich Zeit, ______________ . Jetzt ______________ ! Ich freue mich ______________ . Ich will mich auch ______________ , bevor ich in Urlaub fahre. Ja, ich fahre im Juli ______________ .

Now continue the letter.

- Say that you studied a lot and you are tired now.
- Mention that you go out with your friends to relax and what you do when you go out.
- Briefly, give your opinion on smoking or drinking alcohol.
- Ask if you can visit your pen pal in Vienna in July.
- Write a suitable closing sentence.

HL Schriftliche Produktion: Higher Level

Reply in German to your pen pal's letter. Give detailed answers to the questions.

Liebe(r) ...,

endlich habe ich Zeit dir wieder zu schreiben.

Du, ich mache ein Projekt zum Thema „Die heißen Themen der europäischen Jugendlichen", und ich wollte dir ein paar Fragen dazu stellen. Ich hoffe, es macht dir nichts aus! Also, Frage eins: Trinken die irischen Jugendlichen viel? Wie ist es eigentlich bei euch? Frage zwei: Rauchen auch viele irische Jugendliche? Erzähl mir alles!

Es gibt immer mehr Leute aus dem Ausland in unseren Schulen. Wie ist es bei euch? Welche Probleme kann es in der Schule geben, wenn die einheimischen Schüler und Ausländer sich nicht gut kennen? Oder ist es überhaupt ein Problem in irischen Schulen?

Was sonst für Probleme treffen auf euch zu? (Falschinformationen, Cybermobbing, Vorbilder in den Medien, Fettleibigkeit, Magersucht). Du brauchst dich nur sehr kurz zu diesen Themen zu äußern.

Jetzt muss ich Schluss machen.

Dein(e) Martin(a)

Nützliche Sätze

Translate the following sentences into English and choose the ones you will use in your letter.

1. Die Medien spielen eine wichtige Rolle im Leben vieler Jugendlicher.	**7.** Ich hasse das Rauchen wie die Pest!
2. Jedoch machen die Medien ein Zerrbild.	**8.** Leider ist Übergewicht ein wachsendes Problem.
3. Berühmte Menschen werden als Vorbilder betrachtet und man versucht, sie nachzuahmen.	**9.** Wir verstehen, dass Drogen der Gesundheit schaden.
4. Es gibt ein großes Problem mit Bulimie/Magersucht, da man wie seine Vorbilder aussehen will.	**10.** Einige rauchen, um cool zu sein.
5. Jugendarbeitslosigkeit ist auch ein heißes Thema.	**11.** Falschinformationen werden heutzutage weit verbreitet.
6. Leider besaufen sich viele Jugendliche am Wochenende.	**12.** Wir müssen alle zusammenarbeiten, um Cybermobbing zu stoppen.

Übung Macht den Meister!

A Forming Questions

1. Translate the following questions into English.

a) Hast du Spaß gehabt?	**f)** Würdest du gerne im Ausland arbeiten?
b) Seid ihr mit dem Bus gefahren?	**g)** Bist du mit den Prüfungen fertig?
c) Wirst du mit Freunden dahin gehen?	**h)** Magst du Deutsch?
d) Werdet ihr zelten gehen?	**i)** Möchtest du ins Kino gehen?
e) Würdest du mir einen Gefallen tun?	**j)** Willst du einkaufen gehen?

2. Insert the appropriate interrogative.

a) _____ machen Sie in Ihrer Freizeit?	**f)** _____ Menschen sind das?
b) _____ sieht er aus?	**g)** _____ kommt auf die Party?
c) _____ fährst du in Urlaub?	**h)** _____ weinst du?
d) _____ beginnt der Schultag?	**i)** _____ lernst du Deutsch?
e) _____ wohnen Sie?	**j)** _____ ist Ihr Lieblingsfach?

3. Fill in the appropriate case of the interrogative 'who'.

a) _____ hast du gesehen?	**f)** _____ hilfst du gerade?
b) Mit _____ fahrt ihr nach Dublin?	**g)** Für _____ ist das gemeint?
c) _____ Buch ist das?	**h)** _____ hat den Hund geschlagen?
d) _____ ist das?	**i)** Mit _____ machen Sie den Austausch?
e) Von _____ spricht er?	**j)** Auf _____ warten Sie?

4. Insert the correct '**wo** + preposition'.

a) Ich spreche über mein Leben. _____ sprichst du?	**e)** Er will in die Stadt gehen. _____ will er gehen?
b) Ich warte auf den Bus. _____ wartest du?	**f)** Er kommt aus Island. _____ kommt er?
c) Er setzte sich auf das Sofa. _____ setzte er sich?	**g)** Es geht um Geld. _____ geht es?
d) Sie freut sich auf die Zukunft. _____ freut sie sich?	**h)** Es besteht aus Gold. _____ besteht es?

5. Insert the correct '**wo** + preposition' or interrogative in the implied questions below.

a) Ich weiß nicht, _____ er kommt.	*I don't know where he comes from.*
b) Ich verstehe, _____ ihr redet.	*I understand what you* (pl.) *are talking about.*
c) Er fragte mich, _____ ich tat.	*He asked me what I was doing.*
d) Ich wusste nicht, _____ er wartete.	*I didn't know what he was waiting for.*
e) Er erklärte, _____ er das machte.	*He explained why he was doing that.*

B Prepositions

Put in the correct '**da** + preposition' below.

a) Ich leide an der Grippe. Ich leide _____ .	**e)** Ich weiß nichts von dem Projekt. Ich weiß nichts _____ .
b) Ich spreche über das Problem. Ich spreche _____ .	**f)** Ich habe Angst vor der Prüfung. Ich habe Angst _____ .
c) Er hat Interesse an dem Austausch. Er hat Interesse _____ .	**g)** Er griff nach dem Koffer. Er griff _____ .
d) Das hängt von den Noten ab. Es hängt _____ ab.	**h)** Sie sehnt sich nach dem Urlaub. Sie sehnt sich _____ .

Für die Prüfung

1. Was passt zusammen?

1. Es kann zu Problemen führen,	**A** dass Krieg zu vielen Problemen führt.
2. Niemand kann leugnen,	**B** mit dem man sich befassen muss.
3. Arbeitslosigkeit ist ein Problem,	**C** weil sie oft denken, es sieht cool aus.
4. Junge Leute trinken Alkohol,	**D** wenn zu viele Flüchtlinge kommen.
5. Manche rauchen,	**E** einfach um abzuschalten.

2. Was passt zusammen?

1. Ich weiß nicht,	**A** worum sie sich handeln.
2. Es gibt so viele Regeln, dass ich nicht weiß,	**B** wofür du lernst?
3. Weißt du,	**C** wohin er geht.
4. Sie wissen nicht,	**D** was ich machen soll.
5. Er hat keine Ahnung,	**E** wohin sie fahren wollen.

3. Insert the correct prepositions for the following sentences.

a) Ich warte **(auf/am/für/in)** den Bus.

b) Er interessiert sich **(an/am/für/in)** Sport.

c) Sie streiten sich **(an/in/über/für)** Geld.

d) Ich spreche **(mit/über/in/im)** sein Leben.

e) Erinnerst du dich **(für/in/an/bei)** den Film?

f) Sie informiert sich **(an/über/in/am)** den Krieg.

g) Sie ärgern sich **(an/über/in/am)** ihre Noten.

h) Ihr konzentriert euch **(an/auf/für/mit)** die Arbeit.

4. What words make up the following compound words, and what do they mean in English?

a) worüber = _____ + _____ = _____

b) woher = _____ + _____ = _____

c) wohin = _____ + _____ = _____

d) woraus = _____ + _____ = _____

e) wovon = _____ + _____ = _____

f) wofür = _____ + _____ = _____

5. Indicate whether the underlined verbs are singular or plural, the tense and the infinitive.

a) Sie reagieren unsicher.

b) Er hat das Geld genommen.

c) Was weißt du von der Geschichte?

d) Wir fuhren in die Stadt.

e) Ich werde ins Ausland fahren.

f) Ich hatte mein Auto verkauft.

6. Indicate whether the underlined nouns are singular or plural, the gender and the case.

a) Ich mache viel in der Schule.

b) Ich habe einen guten Job bekommen.

c) Die Stunden dauern vierzig Minuten.

d) Ich esse wenig Süßigkeiten.

e) Ich brauche einen neuen Laptop.

f) Nach der Schulzeit will er hier bleiben.

g) In der Nacht hörte ich einen lauten Krach.

h) Es gibt viele Probleme in der Welt.

i) Ich verstehe das Problem nicht.

j) Ich möchte gegen die Regelung wählen.

7. Lückentext: Fill in the blanks with the correct missing words from the box below.

intolerant sind Bestes unsere Probleme mich wo finde sein wie

Ich **1** _____ es traurig, dass es so viele **2** _____ auf der Welt gibt. Ich sehne **3** _____ nach einer Welt, **4** _____ der Frieden herrscht. **5** _____ können wir **6** _____ Probleme lösen? Ich tue mein **7** _____ verständnisvoll zu **8** _____ , aber viele Menschen **9** _____ irgendwie **10** _____ . Das ist schade.

Selbstbewertung: Ordinary Level

OL

Vocabulary

1. If I can translate theses sentences into English, I can talk about social problems. (1 mark each)

a) Es gibt viel Arbeitslosigkeit.	**f)** Es gibt immer Kriege auf der Welt.
b) Jugendliche trinken viel.	**g)** Viele Flüchtlinge kommen nach Europa.
c) Sie rauchen auch.	**h)** Sie haben kein Zuhause mehr.
d) Es gibt viele Proteste.	**i)** Viele verdienen nicht genug Geld.
e) Man protestiert gegen die Banken.	**j)** Viele Ausländer wohnen hier.

Your score: ___ / 10

2. If I can translate these nouns into German, I understand the main nouns needed to describe social problems. (1 mark each)

a) foreigner	**d)** to protest	**g)** to work	**i)** smoking
b) war	**e)** unemployment	**h)** drugs	**j)** role model
c) refugee	**f)** alcohol		

Your score: ___ / 10

Grammar

3. If I can conjugate these verbs in the 'they' form in the present and perfect tenses, I can talk about social problems. (1 mark for each tense)

a) finden: they find ______________ they found ______________
b) trinken: they drink ______________ they drank ______________
c) rauchen: they smoke ______________ they smoked ______________
d) protestieren: they protest ______________ they protested ______________
e) suchen: they look for ______________ they looked for ______________

Your score: ___ / 10

4. If I can choose the correct conjunction, I can use complex sentences. (2 marks each)

a) Es ist nicht einfach, **(denn/weil)** es viel Arbeitslosigkeit gibt.
b) Viele Flüchtlinge kommen hierher, **(denn/weil)** es gibt Krieg in ihrem Land.
c) Wir stehen unter Druck, **(denn/weil)** wir müssen ihnen helfen.
d) Sie trinken viel, **(denn/weil)** es macht sie locker.
e) Man muss das Problem lösen, **(denn/weil)** es ist eine tragische Situation.

Your score: ___ / 10

5. If I can choose the correct preposition, I understand the prepositions needed to describe social problems. (1 mark each)

a) Er interessiert sich **(für/an)** Politik.	**f)** Er findet die Lösung **(für/an)** das Problem.
b) Ich mache **(bei/für)** Hilfsprojekten mit.	**g)** Er konzentriert sich **(in/auf)** die Zukunft.
c) Ich will **(mit/seit)** den Leuten arbeiten.	**h)** Ich hoffe **(von/auf)** Frieden auf der Welt.
d) Ich lerne viel **(über/am)** neue Menschen.	**i)** Wir sind **(in/auf)** das Konzert gegangen.
e) Wir sehen einen Film **(über/auf)** den Rassismus in Südafrika.	**j)** Ich lerne **(um/für)** zwei Stunden jeden Tag.

Your score: ___ / 10

What have I learned?	
What must I improve?	
What do I want to revise?	

Your total score: ___ / 50

Selbstbewertung: Higher Level

HL

1. If I can translate these sentences into German, I can discuss social issues. (2 marks each)

   a) Because of war, many refugees come to Europe.
   b) There are so many asylum seekers in this country.
   c) It is hard to find accommodation.
   d) They find it difficult to integrate.
   e) We must find a solution to this serious problem.

Your score: ___ / 10

2. If I can translate these sentences into German, I can describe social problems. (2 marks each)

   a) I think that the situation is very serious.
   b) The EU has to do something to resolve the problem before it is too late.
   c) There is unfortunately a lot of unemployment in Europe.
   d) More information is needed in schools about the dangers of drugs and alcohol.
   e) The influence of multimedia has both advantages and disadvantages.

Your score: ___ / 10

3. If I can translate these sentences into German, I understand interrogatives. (2 marks each)

a) Why are there so many wars in the world?	**d)** Who will try to fix this?
b) Are you interested in politics?	**e)** Have you tried to find a job?
c) What can we do to solve the issue?	

Your score: ___ / 10

4. If I can correctly fill in the gaps below, I understand word functions. (1 mark each)

um es wer nach aber zwar
ökonomische Flüchtlinge dass Krieges

Ich finde **1** _____ schockierend, **2** _____ so viele Leute wegen eines **3** _____ fliehen müssen. Niemand kann leugnen, dass jedermann zusammensitzen muss **4** _____ eine Lösung zu finden. Mittlerweile strömen tausende von Menschen **5** _____ Europa. Manche sind **6** _____Flüchtlinge, **7** _____ viele sind **8** _____ Migranten. Man muss feststellen, **9** _____ die ökonomischen Migranten sind, und wer die echten **10** _____ sind.

Your score: ___ / 10

5. If I can turn these sentences into questions and statements using **wo** and **da**, I can use prepositional questions and statements to write about social problems. (2 marks each)
   Example: Ich will mit dir über das Problem sprechen.
   a) Worüber willst du mit mir sprechen? **b)** Ich will darüber sprechen.

   a) Man muss nach Lösungen suchen.
   b) Man redet viel von der Migrantenproblematik.
   c) Wir müssen die Kinder vor Gewalt im Internet schützen.
   d) Eltern sollten sich mehr über die Gefahren des Internets informieren.
   e) Man sollte sich auf das wachsende Problem der Fettleibigkeit konzentrieren.

Your score: ___ / 10

What have I learned?	
What must I improve?	
What do I want to revise?	

Your total score: ___ / 50

12 Die Medien

Learning Outcomes

- **Oral:** discussing young people and new technology; revise topics from Chapters 1 to 4
- **Reading:** reading and discussing three texts on multimedia
- **Writing:** writing an opinion (**Äußerung**), a picture description and letter on technology
- **Aural:** listening to and answering questions on four extracts on technology

Grammar

- The imperative
- The subjunctive

Vocabulary

- The pros and cons of technology and the internet
- Popular online activities

German Culture

- German texting slang
- German-speaking countries and regions

Exam Tips

- When you first read your letter, look out for the questions which require the past tense. You will use the perfect tense.
- Remember that verbs of motion use **sein** in the perfect tense.
- The best way to prepare for your oral examination is to revise and rehearse for five minutes a day with a conversation partner.

Text 1: Therapie gegen Computersucht

 Bitte beantworten Sie die folgenden Fragen:

1. Was sehen Sie auf dem Foto?
2. Was tut der Junge?
3. Wie sieht er aus?

Vorarbeit

1. Finden Sie diese Ausdrücke im folgenden Text.
   - **A** He's falling further back at school ...
   - **B** ... to limit their media consumption.
   - **C** The youth welfare services got involved ...
   - **D** That wasn't enough.
   - **E** Reasons for addiction ...
2. Finden Sie das Deutsche für die Wörter unten!
   - **A** addiction/gambles/despair
   - **B** therapy centre/taken in/supervised
   - **C** fate/member/school qualification
   - **D** recognition/sense of reality/real/directed at
   - **E** communal/getting used to/overload

© dpa (amended)

A Thomas hängt nur noch am Computer, zockt die halbe Nacht lang Onlinespiele. Er rutscht in der Schule weiter ab und hat kein Interesse mehr an früheren Hobbys. Viele Eltern verzweifeln an diesem exzessiven Spielekonsum. Dann kann nur eine Therapie die Jugendlichen aus ihrer Sucht holen.

B In Dortmund gibt es eine Therapieeinrichtung für computersüchtige Jugendliche. Der Name „Auxilium Reloaded" bedeutet „Neustart". In der betreuten Wohngruppe werden insgesamt 14 junge Leute zwischen 15 bis 25 Jahren aufgenommen. Sie kommen aus ganz Deutschland und bleiben ein bis eineinhalb Jahre. Nur eine Stunde täglich dürfen sie auf dem Smartphone spielen. Sie müssen lernen, ihren Medienkonsum einzuschränken.

C Mit fünfzehn ist Lukas das jüngste Mitglied der Wohngruppe für computersüchtige Jugendliche. Der zwanzigjährige Justin und Lukas sprechen freiwillig über ihr Schicksal. „Ich bin selbst auf die Idee gekommen", sagt Justin. Bei Lukas griff das Jugendamt ein. Justin ist seit Juli in der Wohngruppe. Einen Schulabschluss hat er nicht.

D Justin hat mit einer PlayStation angefangen. Das reichte nicht. Er wollte online zocken, also hat er Egoshooter gespielt. Die Anerkennung der anonymen Mitspieler macht süchtig. Echte Freunde gibt es nicht. Dort landen junge Menschen, die bei Onlinespielen den Zugang zur Realität verloren haben. Mädchen gibt es noch nicht, weil die Onlinespiele mehr auf Jungs ausgerichtet sind.

E Gründe der Sucht sind: Überlastung in der Schule oder Mobbing. Nach der Diagnose folgt die Therapie. Man muss lernen den Tag-Nacht-Rhythmus wieder hinzubekommen. An Smartphone oder Computer kommen die Bewohner nur eine Stunde am Tag. Gemeinsames Kochen und Einkaufen gehört zur Gewöhnung an die reale Welt. Und bald geht es in die Realschule. Die Schule abschließen will auch Justin.

Prüfungstipp

The topic of multimedia may come up in the opinion question, the picture sequence or your project. In your **Äußerung** or the **Schriftliche Produktion** section, you may be asked to describe a picture of people using various multimedia items.

OL Ordinary Level Questions

1. **a)** How does Thomas spend his nights? A
   b) What is the purpose of the therapy centre? B
   c) How old are Lukas and Justin? C
   d) What do gamers tend to lose over time? D
2. Choose the correct preposition.
   a) **(Für/An/Um/Mit)** 20 ist Justin computersüchtig.
   b) Es gibt ein Therapiezentrum **(an/in/bei/zu)** Dortmund.
   c) Lukas und Justin sprechen **(über/vor/durch/im)** ihre bisherigen Lebenserfahrungen.
   d) Justin begann **(mit/auf/für/an)** einer PlayStation.
3. What words make up the following compound words, and what do they mean in English?
   a) Therapieeinrichtung = ___ + ___ = ___
   b) computersüchtig = ___ + ___ = ___
   c) Wohngruppe = ___ + ___ = ___
   d) Einkaufen = ___ + ___ = ___

CL Ordinary + Higher Level

Lückentext: Fill in the blanks with the correct missing words from the box below.

persönlichen vorsichtig ich Musik Stunden

Ich verbringe zwei bis drei **1** ___ pro Tag am Computer. Manchmal gehe ich in Chats aber ich bin immer **2** ___ . Ich mache keine **3** ___ Daten sichtbar. Wenn es merkwürdige Kontakte gibt, breche **4** ___ sie sofort ab. Ich kaufe gern online ein, ich lade **5** ___ herunter und ich sehe Filme auf Netflix.

HL Higher Level Questions

1. Beantworten Sie folgende Fragen auf Deutsch.
   a) i) **Justin** spricht über sich. Was erzählt er? Schreiben Sie **vier** Sätze (Präsens) in *Ich*-Form. D
   ii) **Thomas** spielt dauernd Onlinespiele. Beschreiben Sie genau die Konsequenzen davon. A
   b) Geben Sie mehrere Details über die Wohngruppe. B
   c) Wie wurden Justin und Lukas in die Wohngruppe aufgenommen? C
   d) Nennen Sie **zwei** Elemente des Onlinespielens, die einen süchtig machen können. D
   e) Laut Text, wie wird der Alltag in der Wohngruppe verbracht? Geben Sie **drei** Details. E
2. Answer the following questions in English.
   a) What are the consequences of Thomas playing online games? Give **two** details. A
   b) Give **three** details about the therapy centre. B
   c) How long has Justin been at the centre and what does he not have at the moment? C
   d) Explain how, according to the text, gamers can lose a sense of reality. D
   e) What is the purpose of doing things together in the group? What does Justin hope to achieve? E
3. Was passt zusammen?

1. Viele Eltern verzweifeln,	**A** kommen aus ganz Deutschland.
2. Die Mitglieder der Wohngruppe	**B** dass er selbst auf die Idee gekommen ist.
3. Justin sagt,	**C** jedoch reichte das nicht.
4. Er begann mit einer PlayStation,	**D** nur eine Stunde lang ihr Smartphone benutzen.
5. Die Bewohner dürfen pro Tag	**E** da ihr Kind zu viel Zeit beim Onlinespielen verbringt.

4. Geben Sie für die Nomen an: ob Singular oder Plural, bei Singular das Geschlecht, den Fall.
   a) Es gibt eine Therapieeinrichtung.
   b) Mobbing in der Schule

Grammatik: Der Imperativ/The Imperative

p. 237 (Übung macht den Meister)

The imperative is used to give a command: Go to the supermarket; Let's go to the cinema.
A command can be made to you (singular); you (plural); us; or you (polite).

To form the imperative of regular verbs, take the present tense verb and drop **du** and the **-st** verb ending; drop **ihr**; invert **wir gehen** to **gehen wir**; invert **Sie gehen** to **gehen Sie**.

du gehst ➔ Geh! wir gehen ➔ Gehen wir! ihr geht ➔ Geht! Sie gehen! ➔ Gehen Sie!

You (Singular)		We: Let's		You (Plural)		You (Polite)	
Bring!	*Bring!*	Bringen wir!	*Let's bring!*	Bringt!	*Bring!*	Bringen Sie!	*Bring!*
Schreib!	*Write!*	Schreiben wir!	*Let's write!*	Schreibt!	*Write!*	Schreiben Sie!	*Write!*

The imperative of most irregular verbs is also formed using the present tense of the verb in the **du**, **wir**, **ihr** and **Sie** forms:

Present tense: **du gibst** ➔ Imperative: **Gib!**

wir geben ➔ Geben wir! **ihr gebt ➔ Gebt!** **Sie geben ➔ Geben Sie!**

You (Singular)		We: Let's		You (Plural)		You (Polite)	
Gib!	*Give!*	Geben wir!	*Let's give!*	Gebt!	*Give!*	Geben Sie!	*Give!*
Sprich!	*Speak!*	Sprechen wir!	*Let's speak!*	Sprecht!	*Speak!*	Sprechen Sie!	*Speak!*
Lies!	*Read!*	Lesen wir!	*Let's read!*	Lest!	*Read!*	Lesen Sie!	*Read!*
Nimm!	*Take!*	Nehmen wir!	*Let's take!*	Nehmt!	*Take!*	Nehmen Sie!	*Take!*

Insert the correct imperative forms for the following sentences.

1. ___ lauter!	*Speak louder!* (you, singular)
2. ___ weg!	*Go away!* (you, plural)
3. ___ das laut vor!	*Read that aloud!* (you, polite)
4. ___ eine!	*Take one!* (you, singular)
5. ___ das auf!	*Let's write that down!*
6. ___ genau zu!	*Listen carefully!* (you, polite)
7. ___ leise!	*Speak quietly!* (you, plural)
8. ___ mir zehn Euro!	*Give me ten euros!* (you, singular)

Note that the verbs **sein** and **haben** are an exception and take the following form in the imperative:

You (Singular)		We: Let's		You (Plural)		You (Polite)	
Sei!	*Be!*	Seien wir!	*Let's be!*	Seid!	*Be!*	Seien Sie!	*Be!*
Hab!	*Have!*	Haben wir!	*Let's have!*	Habt!	*Have!*	Haben Sie!	*Have!*

Insert the correct imperative forms for the following sentences.

1. ___ ruhig!	*Be quiet!* (you, plural)
2. ___ ___ aufmerksam!	*Let's be attentive!*
3. ___ brav!	*Be well behaved!* (you, singular)
4. ___ ___ fleißig!	*Be hard-working!* (you, polite)
5. ___ höflich!	*Be polite!* (you, singular)
6. ___ nicht misstrauisch!	*Don't be suspicious!* (you, plural)
7. ___ lieb zu deiner Mutter!	*Be nice to your mother!* (you, singular)

12.01 Hörverständnis Teil 1

Vorarbeit

wirbelnd	*whirling*	**Technologiewelle**	*wave of technology*	**Kenntnisstand**	*level of knowledge*
aktualisieren	*to update*	**Veränderungen**	*changes*	**geringer**	*lower*

CL Ordinary + Higher Level Questions

1. a) How long has Frau Miele been working at the company?
   b) What technological changes have made her work stressful? Give **two (O)/three (H)** details.
2. According to Frau Miele, what personal quality is necessary for success?
3. How does Frau Miele intend to change her career direction?
4. What recommendation does she give the listeners? Give **one (O)/two (H)** details.
5. What factors sound attractive to her in her future work? Give **one (O)/two (H)** details.

12.02 Hörverständnis Teil 2

Vorarbeit

umbuchen	*to transfer*	**buchstabieren**	*to spell*	**Abflug**	*departure*
erlassen	*to waive*	**Zusatz**	*supplement*	**empfehlen**	*to recommend*
Bildschirm	*screen*	**überprüfen**	*to check*	**bestätigen**	*to confirm*

OL Ordinary Level Questions

1. What departure and return dates has the caller booked?
2. What does the caller wish to do?
3. What is the caller's name and telephone number?
4. The customer is complaining about:
   a) a strike ☐ **b)** a supplementary charge ☐ **c)** a delay ☐ **d)** no connecting flight ☐

HL Higher Level Questions

1. Using ***key phrases***, write down **in German** the key information the caller provides:
   - the name of the person **making** the call
   - the reason for the call
   - **four** details of their conversation
   - details regarding further contact
   - the caller's phone number

Gesprächsnotiz

Anruf von: ______________________ Gesprächsanlass: ______________________

Der Anrufer:
- ruft später zurück ☐
- erwartet einen Rückruf ☐
- wird eine E-Mail erhalten ☐
- wird eine SMS erhalten ☐

Kontaktnummer: ______________________

2. Write down **three** phrases which show the caller is **eager** to stress the importance of his request.

Text 2: Hilfe! Ich habe aus Versehen das Internet gelöscht!

Bitte beantworten Sie die folgenden Fragen:

1. Was machen die Leute auf diesem Foto?
2. Beschreiben Sie sie!
3. Wie fühlen sie sich, und warum?

Vorarbeit

1. Finden Sie diese Ausdrücke im folgenden Text.
   - **A** ... a young man makes fun of his mother.
   - **B** It won't work without help.
   - **C** Messages can be sent ... at lightning speed.
   - **D** ... all of the functions ... no longer work.
   - **E** They become the new 'illiterates'.
2. Finden Sie das Deutsche für die Wörter unten!
   - **A** overwhelmed/usage/to use/hopelessly
   - **B** adult education centres/overnight
   - **C** commands/input device/storing data
   - **D** emergency/to remove/fraudulent/protection
   - **E** recognise/society/excluded/exchanged

A Ein junger Mann macht sich über seine Mutter lustig. Für die Generation 60+ ist es aber schwierig, den Computer zu benutzen. Maria K. und ihr Mann Christian sind beide Mitte 70. Sie sind aktiv, betreiben Sport und gehen viel auf Reisen. Doch beim Umgang mit ihrem Computer fühlen sie sich hoffnungslos überfordert. „Ich habe mein ganzes Leben lang alles selber gemacht. Sogar unseren DVD-Player habe ich selbst installiert. Aber wenn ich mich vor den Computer setze, fühle ich mich wie ein Computer-Dummy", erklärt Christian.

B Ohne Hilfe geht es nicht! Wer im Alter den Computer verstehen will, braucht Unterstützung. Am besten sollte der hilfreiche Verwandte oder Nachbar dabei sein. Dann braucht man viel Geduld. Den Umgang eines Computers lernt man nicht von heute auf morgen. Computer-Gruppen gibt es in jeder Stadt. Da die Teilnehmer die gleichen Probleme haben, können sie einander helfen. Dann macht das Lernen mehr Spaß. Es gibt viele Computerkurse bei den Volkshochschulen.

C Die Mouse ist ein Eingabegerät. Mit einem Druck auf die linke Seite oder rechte Seite werden Befehle auf dem Computer ausgeführt. Ein USB-Stick verbindet den Computer mit einem anderen Gerät. Ein USB-Stick wird auch zum Speichern genützt. E-Mails sind elektronische Post. Mitteilungen können blitzschnell über das Internet versendet werden. Auch können Bilder und Videos versendet werden.

D Der Virus macht einen Computer krank. Das bedeutet, dass sämtliche Fähigkeiten eines Computers nicht mehr funktionieren. Im Notfall muss ein Computer-Spezialist den Virus entfernen. Einen Virus holt man sich über unsichere E-Mails oder Internetseiten. Zum Schutz dagegen gibt es Anti-Virus-Programme. Phishing ist der betrügerische Versuch über gefälschte Webseiten oder E-Mails an persönliche Daten zu kommen.

E Viele Informationen werden elektronisch ausgetauscht. Manche Senioren werden also von unserer virtuellen Gesellschaft ausgegrenzt. Sie werden zu den neuen „Analphabeten" der modernen Gesellschaft. Doch das muss nicht sein. Bitte liebe Senioren, habt keine Angst vor dem Computer und Internet. Mit Hilfe und Übung kann jeder die Welt der neuen Medien benutzen. Ihr werdet bald erkennen, wie hilfreich und spannend es ist einen Computer zu benutzen und die Welt des World Wide Webs zu besuchen. Habt Geduld, Rom ist auch nicht an einem Tag erbaut worden.

http://www.tipps-vom-experten.de/senioren-am-computer/ (amended)

OL Ordinary Level Questions

1. a) What age are Maria and Christian? A
   b) Who can help older people to master computers? B
   c) What can a USB stick be used for? C
   d) How do viruses occur, according to the text? D
   e) According to the text, how will seniors find using a computer after a bit of help and practice? E
2. True or false?
   a) Ältere Menschen benutzen gern den Computer.
   b) Es gibt Computerkurse in den Grundschulen.
   c) Ein USB-Stick verbindet den Computer mit dem Internet.
   d) Anti-Virus-Programme schützen gegen einen Virus.
   e) Senioren müssen nicht ausgegrenzt werden.
3. Complete the following sentences.
   a) Für ältere Menschen ist es schwierig den **(DVD-Player/Computer/Laptop/Bildschirm)** zu benutzen.
   b) Es gibt Computer-Gruppen in **(jedem Dorf/jedem Land/jeder Stadt)**.
   c) Ein USB-Stick hilft beim **(Speichern/Lernen/Betrug)**.
   d) Ein Virus ist **(gefährlich/behilflich/Hoffnung/hoffnungslos)**.
4. Choose the correct preposition.
   a) Der Zugang **(ans/am/an/zum)** Internet ist schwierig für Christian.
   b) Es gibt viele Computerkurse **(in/bei/an/mit)** den Volkshochschulen.
   c) Die Mouse ist **(mit/an/durch/von)** einem Kabel verbunden.
   d) E-Mails werden **(mit/über/von/durch)** das Internet versendet.

HL Higher Level Questions

1. Beantworten Sie folgende Fragen auf Deutsch.
   a) Maria K. und ihr Mann stellen sich vor. Schreiben Sie **drei** Sätze (Präsens) in *Wir*-Form. A
   b) Wie kann man den Umgang mit Computer lernen? Nennen Sie **drei** Möglichkeiten. B
   c) Was kann man per E-Mail machen? C
   d) Was bedeutet Phishing? D
   e) Warum sollen, laut Text, Senioren Geduld haben? E
2. Answer the following questions in English.
   a) Why does Christian feel like a computer dummy? Give **three** details. A
   b) According to the text, what do older people need when learning to use a computer? B
   c) According to the text, what does the mouse allow one to do? C
   d) How is phishing described in the text? Give **two** details. D
   e) Why, according to the text, is it important that seniors learn to use these new media? E
3. Match the German terms with the English words.

1. Bildschirm	**2.** Tastatur	**3.** Webseite	**4.** Anschluss	**5.** Gerät	**6.** Kabel
A connection	**B** cable	**C** device	**D** screen	**E** keyboard	**F** website

4. Welches Fragewort würden Sie benutzen, um nach den unterstrichenen Wörtern/Wortgruppen zu fragen? Schreiben Sie die jeweilige Frage auf!
   a) Christian hat <u>seinen DVD-Player</u> selbst installiert.
   b) Computer-Gruppen gibt es <u>in jeder Stadt</u>.
   c) Ein USB-Stick verbindet den Computer <u>mit einem anderen Gerät</u>.
   d) Im Notfall muss <u>ein Computer-Spezialist</u> den Virus entfernen.
   e) Manche Senioren werden also <u>von unserer virtuellen Gesellschaft</u> ausgegrenzt.

OL Äußerung zum Thema: Ordinary Level

You are interviewing Christian. Complete the dialogue, using the information in Text 2.

Sie: Wie heißen Sie?
Christian: ______________________
Sie: Wie alt sind Sie?
Christian: ______________________
Sie: Was machen Sie und Ihre Frau gern?
Christian: ______________________
Sie: Was haben Sie selbst installiert?
Christian: ______________________
Sie: Warum fühlen Sie sich wie ein Computer-Dummy?
Christian: ______________________

HL Äußerung zum Thema: Higher Level

- Beschreiben Sie das Foto rechts in **drei bis vier** Sätzen.
- Schreiben Sie **drei bis vier** Sätze über Ihren eigenen Internetgebrauch.
- Welche Risiken stellt das Internet für Kinder und Jugendliche dar? Nennen Sie **drei bis vier** Beispiele.

Nützliche Sätze

Übersetzen Sie die folgenden Meinungen ins Englische.

1. Ich benutze Kurznachrichtendienste wie SMS oder WhatsApp und ich surfe mobil im Netz.
2. Snapchat ist nützlich, um Partys und Geburtstage zu organisieren.
3. Das Internet kann positiv genutzt werden, indem man für die Schule recherchiert, Referate vorbereitet, sich Tipps für Bewerbungen anguckt oder auch Kontakt zu Freunden aufbaut.
4. Ich verbringe mehrere Stunden jeden Tag im Internet, denn ich sehe mir gern Filme auf Netflix an und ich lade Musik runter.
5. Ein Leben ohne das Internet kann ich mir nicht vorstellen!
6. Ich nutze mein Handy, um meinen Freunden Nachrichten zu schicken und mit ihnen über WhatsApp kostenlos zu telefonieren.
7. Man muss vorsichtig sein, dass Leute nicht zu Opfern der Gewalt oder des Cybermobbings werden.
8. Manche Jugendliche machen intime Fotos von sich selbst und versenden sie per Handy an Freunde und Bekannte.
9. Das Problem ist, dass diese Bilder auch oft dann im Internet landen, in sozialen Netzwerken oder Foto-Communitys, und dann für Peinlichkeit sorgen.

Kulturecke

Translate these German text-speak abbreviations.

1. akla – alles klar?
2. bb – bis bald
3. kA– keine Ahnung
4. wamaduheu? – was machst du heute?
5. DN – du nervst
6. G&K – Gruß und Kuss
7. (G)LG – (ganz) liebe Grüße
8. gn8 – gute Nacht
9. hdl – hab dich lieb
10. MAD – mag dich

Grammatik: Konjunktiv II/Subjunctive 2

p. 237 (Übung macht den Meister)

The subjunctive is not a tense, but a mood. Remember, tense refers to time (past, present or future). The subjunctive mood is outside time, because it is used for conditional or imaginary situations, wishes or suggestions. It does not imply fact.

Hypothetical situations: Wenn ich reich wäre, würde ich ein großes Haus kaufen. *If I were rich, I would buy a big house.*

Doubt: Ich weiß nicht, ob das eine gute Idee wäre. *I don't know if that would be a good idea.*

Wishes, using haben, sein, mögen, wollen or wünschen: Was hättest du gern? *What would you like?*

Politeness, using modal verbs: Könntest du? *Could you?* **Möchtest du?** *Would you like to?*

After the expression **'as if'/ 'if only': Wenn ich das nur gewusst hätte!** *If I had only known that!*

In English the subjunctive is now used primarily with the verb 'to be' and our modal verbs.

You **are** hard-working ➔ fact; If you **were** hard-working, ≠ fact.

I **can** speak Russian ➔ fact; If I **could** speak Russian, ≠ fact.

The subjunctive is used more frequently in German than in English. Subjunctive 2 is the most common form in German and it is formed from the imperfect form of the verb. An umlaut is used with the vowels **a**, **o** and **u**.

haben	sein	mögen	können	werden
ich hätte	ich wäre	ich möchte	ich könnte	ich würde
du hättest	du wär(e)st	du möchtest	du könntest	du würdest
er/sie/es hätte	er/sie/es wäre	er/sie/es möchte	er/sie/es könnte	er/sie/es würde
wir hätten	wir wären	wir möchten	wir könnten	wir würden
ihr hättet	ihr wär(e)t	ihr möchtet	ihr könntet	ihr würdet
Sie/sie hätten	Sie/sie wären	Sie/sie möchten	Sie/sie könnten	Sie/sie würden

1. Identify the subjunctive verbs in the following sentences. Then translate them.

a) Es wäre toll, wenn du mich besuchen würdest.
b) Wenn ich mehr Zeit hätte, würde ich fleißiger lernen.
c) Was würdest du machen, wenn du Bundeskanzler von Deutschland wärest?
d) Wenn ich an deiner Stelle wäre, würde ich einen Austausch machen.
e) Ich würde eine Weltreise machen, wenn ich viel Geld hätte.
f) Ich wünschte, ich hätte Ferien.
g) Wenn ich im Urlaub wäre, läge ich den ganzen Tag am Strand.
h) Könnten Sie das bitte wiederholen?
i) Wenn ich gut Deutsch sprechen könnte, bekäme ich immer gute Noten.
j) Hätten Sie gern ein Stück Kuchen?

2. Translate the following sentences into English.

a) Das wäre undenkbar.	**f)** Wenn ich das Wort nur wüsste!
b) Ich könnte ins Ausland fahren.	**g)** Ich hätte noch einen Wunsch.
c) Ich hätte gern ein neues Auto.	**h)** Das wäre fantastisch!
d) Möchtest du gern nach Spanien fliegen?	**i)** Ich möchte im Lotto gewinnen.
e) Ich würde dir gerne helfen.	**j)** Ich hätte lieber einen anderen Kurs.

When learning vocabulary, prioritise any words which you use a lot in German. If you learn five new words a day, six days a week, you will have learned 120 new words in a month!

Text 3: Wie Computerspiele erfunden wurden

Bitte beantworten Sie die folgenden Fragen:

1. Was sehen Sie auf dem Bild?
2. Wie sehen die Teufel aus?
3. Was für eine Stimmung gibt es hier?

Vorarbeit

1. Finden Sie diese Ausdrücke im folgenden Text.
   - **A** There was hustle and bustle in hell.
   - **B** ... must deliver results quickly!
   - **C** That sounds good!
   - **D** He neglects his real work ...
   - **E** Brilliant!
   - **F** ... where I can shoot down others.
2. Finden Sie das Deutsche für die Wörter unten!
   - **A** nightmare/commanded/invention
   - **B** input/accomplished/keeps from
   - **C** connects/clapped/idiot/distraction
   - **D** foregoes/masters/sacrifices/challenges
   - **E** interjected/cruel/pointless/user
   - **F** knight/sighed/fighters/slave

Alexander Vogt, 27 Nov. 2017 (amended)

A In der Hölle herrschte Betriebsamkeit. Satan hatte seinen Chefstrategen Luzifer, Azazel und Beelzebub befohlen, sich einer neuen Erfindung der Menschen anzunehmen, des „Personal Computers". Diese Erfindung sollte zu seinem schlimmsten Alptraum werden.

„COMPUTER SOLLEN SCHADEN!" schrie Satan.

„Jawohl", erwiderte Luzifer. „Computer werden schaden! Wir erfinden etwas!" „Sie stehen bald in jedem Haushalt", sagte Azazel, „sie erleichtern die Arbeit. Mit ihnen schaffen die Menschen mehr Arbeit in weniger Zeit!"

B „Dann schreiben wir ein Programm, das wie Arbeit aussieht, aber das den Menschen von der Arbeit abhält!", erklärte Luzifer. „Das Programm muss schnell Ergebnisse liefern! So hat der Mensch das Gefühl, etwas geleistet zu haben! Wir schreiben ein Programm, das ständig Ergebnisse ausspuckt. Für die kleinste Eingabe bekommt er Belohnungen!"

C „Das klingt gut!", lächelte Beelzebub. „Wenn es fertig ist, darf ich es auch haben?"

„Nein, du Trottel! Das Programm ist doch gefährlich und kein Spiel!"

„Das ist es!" rief Luzifer. „Wir programmieren ein Spiel! Etwas, das der Mensch nicht mit Arbeit verbindet! Das ist mein Plan: Der Mensch startet unser Computerspiel, weil er Entspannung oder Ablenkung sucht."

„Mit guter Musik! Und mit schönen bunten Bildchen!", klatschte Beelzebub.

D „Je besser der Mensch es beherrscht, desto schwieriger wird es. Er muss sich richtig damit beschäftigen, um die neuen Herausforderungen zu meistern. Er bekommt das Gefühl, immer besser in dieser „Arbeit" zu werden, besser als andere, die das gleiche Spiel spielen. Der Mensch opfert Zeit, um sich zu verbessern. Er vernachlässigt seine echte Arbeit, seine sozialen Kontakte, verzichtet auf Schlaf!"

E „Das ist grausam! Genial!", staunte Azazel. „Im Prinzip ist das „Spiel" ein Virus nicht für den PC, sondern für den PC Nutzer! Unser Spiel bringt den PC Nutzer dazu, die gleichen sinnlosen Arbeiten unendlich zu wiederholen!"

„Einen Fehler hat das Spiel", warf Azazel ein. „Nicht alle Menschen werden auf dieses „Spiel" reinfallen."

F Luzifer seufzte. „Man kann nicht alles haben. Immerhin die Hälfte der Menschen wird zum Sklaven des Spiels. Für alle soll etwas dabei sein! Für Mathematiker, für Fantasie Fans, für Sportler, für Kämpfer, für Musiker, für Idioten ..."

„Ich möchte ein Ritter sein, der Prinzessinnen rettet", sagte Beelzebub.

„Für mich ein Spiel, wo ich andere abknallen kann!", forderte Azazel.

„Ich mache mich sofort an die Arbeit", versprach Luzifer.

OL Ordinary Level Questions

1. a) According to Azazel, how will computers help people? A
   b) Name **two** features of the program Lucifer wants to write. B
   c) What **two** features does Beelzebub want added to the game? C
   d) What will this game force people to neglect? D
   e) According to Azazel, which people will be interested in this game? E
   f) Name **five** types of people for whom this game is intended. F
2. Choose a suitable heading for each paragraph and explain your choice in English.

Luzifer macht sich an die Arbeit
Man wird belohnt
Das Spiel ist gefährlich
Bald gibt es Computer überall
Das Spiel hat einen Fehler
Der Mensch will das Spiel meistern

3. Choose the correct preposition.
   a) Der Computer soll **(in/für/zu/um)** einem Alptraum werden.
   b) Der Spieler bekommt eine Belohnung **(mit/für/an/in)** die kleinste Eingabe.
   c) Luzifer programmiert ein Spiel **(an/um/für/mit)** Musik und Bildern.
   d) Das Spiel ist **(an/in/um/für)** Wirklichkeit Arbeit.

HL Higher Level Questions

1. Beantworten Sie folgende Fragen auf Deutsch.
   a) Was weiß Azazel über PCs? Geben Sie **drei** Details. A
   b) Warum muss das Programm Ergebnisse schnell liefern? B
   c) Warum will Luzifer ein Spiel programmieren? C
   d) Was passiert, laut Text, wenn der Mensch versucht sich beim Spiel zu verbessern? D
   e) Was für einen Fehler hat das Spiel? Glauben Sie, dass Azazel recht hat? Warum/warum nicht? E
   f) Beelzebub und Azazel wollen auch mitspielen. Was wollen sie bei so einem Spiel? F
2. Answer the following questions in English.
   a) What command did Satan give his chief strategists? Give **three** details. A
   b) The devils decide to write a program. Name **three** features of this program. B
   c) Why would a person start the computer game, according to Lucifer's plan? C
   d) Why, according to the text, will people spend more and more time on the game? D
   e) To what extent is the game a virus? E
   f) The devils are attempting to endanger the human race. Identify **four** examples (in language or content) which put their work in a negative light.
3. Was passt zusammen?

1. Luzifer wird etwas erfinden,	**A** denn er sucht Ablenkung und Entspannung.
2. Das Programm spuckt Ergebnisse aus,	**B** weil nicht alle Interesse daran haben.
3. Der Mensch wird das Spiel spielen,	**C** sodass der Mensch eine Belohnung kriegt.
4. Der Mensch vernachlässigt seine Arbeit,	**D** das den Menschen schaden wird.
5. Nicht alle Menschen werden reinfallen,	**E** um sich beim Spiel zu verbessern.

4. Geben Sie für die **Verben** an: den Infinitiv des Verbs; die Zeitform; ob Singular oder Plural.
   a) Satan hatte eine Erfindung befohlen.
   b) Das Programm hält einen von der Arbeit ab.
   c) Beelzebub unterbrach Luzifer.
   d) Luzifer versprach, die Arbeit zu machen.

Grammatik: Konjunktiv I/Subjunctive 1

p. 237 (Übung macht den Meister)

Subjunctive 1 is used for indirect speech, to report what someone has said. You are most likely to come across it in news articles.

Direct speech: Tom said, 'I am hungry.' Indirect speech: Tom said he was hungry.

Subjunctive 1 is not as common as subjunctive 2. While subjunctive 2 is formed from the imperfect, subjunctive 1 is formed from the infinitive of the verb. To form subjunctive 1, remove the **-en** from the infinitive and add these endings. Only **sein** does not follow this pattern.

haben	machen	geben	sollen	sein
ich hab**e**	ich mach**e**	ich geb**e**	ich soll**e**	ich sei
du hab**est**	du mach**est**	du geb**est**	du soll**est**	du sei(e)st
er/sie/es hab**e**	er/sie/es mach**e**	er/sie/es geb**e**	er/sie/es soll**e**	er/sie/es sei
wir hab**en**	wir mach**en**	wir geb**en**	wir soll**en**	wir seien
ihr hab**et**	ihr mach**et**	ihr geb**et**	ihr soll**et**	ihr seiet
Sie/sie hab**en**	Sie/sie mach**en**	Sie/sie geb**en**	Sie/sie soll**en**	Sie/sie seien

1. Identify the following statements as direct speech or indirect speech.

a) Die Frau sagte, „Ich bin müde."	**f)** Der Mann antwortete, er solle sofort gehen.
b) Das Kind behauptet, es habe Hunger.	**g)** Klaus antwortete, „Ich muss jetzt lernen."
c) Die Polizei berichtet, es gebe einen Unfall.	**h)** Der Mann sagt, er fühle sich sehr jung.
d) Der Mann klagte, er sei angegriffen worden.	**i)** Die Kinder behaupten, sie seien im Kino.
e) Marta sagte, „Ich komme spät nach Hause."	**j)** Der Lehrer sagt, „Ich habe den Brief gelesen."

2. Identify the subjunctive in the sentences below and decide whether subjunctive 1 or 2 is used.

a) Mary sagt, sie sei hübsch.	**f)** Mein Lehrer sagt, ich sei faul und frech.
b) Markus sagt, Detlev wäre intelligent.	**g)** Die Aufgabe wäre zu schwierig, glaube ich.
c) Hans sagte, er habe von Anna geträumt.	**h)** Frank sagt, er würde ins Kino gehen.
d) Könntest du das Fenster zumachen?	**i)** Da gäbe es Ärger zu Hause!
e) Wenn ich nur genug Geld hätte!	**j)** Hoch lebe das Geburtstagskind!

3. Turn the indirect speech into direct speech, as in the example:
Mary sagt, sie sei hübsch. ➔ Mary sagt, „Ich bin hübsch."

a) Er meinte, er habe fleißig gearbeitet.	**f)** Anna meint, sie sei musikalisch begabt.
b) Anna sagt, ihr Vater arbeite in einem Hotel.	**g)** Der Mann erklärte, er habe kein Geld.
c) Er sagte, der Fernseher funktioniere nicht.	**h)** Die Frau sagte, sie wolle uns helfen.
d) Sie fragte mich, ob ich Hunger hätte.	**i)** Hans sagte, er werde uns besuchen.
e) Uwe behauptet, er habe die Arbeit gemacht.	**j)** Maria meint, Klaus lüge.

12.03 Hörverständnis Teil 3

Vorarbeit

Wandel	*change*	**aufteilen**	*to split up*	**berichten**	*to report*
gefährden	*to endanger*	**Termintreue**	*stick to times*	**geringer**	*briefer*
Schiedsrichter	*referee*	**Abkürzung**	*abbreviation*	**Mitteilung**	*communication*

CL Ordinary + Higher Level Questions

1. **a)** The conversation is between:
   i) a teacher and students ☐ **ii)** schoolmates ☐ **iii)** neighbours ☐ **iv)** college students ☐
   b) Find **one (O)/two (H)** details in the conversation that support your choice.
2. **a)** Which word best describes the second speaker's attitude during the conversation?
   i) frustrated ☐ **ii)** relieved ☐ **iii)** nervous ☐ **iv)** interested ☐
   b) Write down **one (O)/two (H)** details from the conversation to support your choice.
3. What tasks are given to each group? Give **two (O)/four (H)** details.
4. Most speakers are very positive about the influence of media on written German. Give **two (O)/four (H)** details.

12.04 Hörverständnis Teil 4

Vorarbeit

begeistert	*inspired*	**beweisen**	*to prove*	**niedrig**	*low*
Erstattung	*refund*	**gefälscht**	*fake*	**Verschlüsselung**	*encryption*
Kennwörter	*passwords*	**Milliarde**	*billion*	**örtlich**	*local*

CL Ordinary + Higher Level Questions

1. **a)** What is the title of the project week? **b)** When and where will it take place?
2. How many Germans shop online, and why do they do this? Give **two (O)/three (H)** details.
3. **a)** What is the value of the online shops? **b)** Which online shops profit most?
4. **a)** What are experts warning about? Give **two (O)/three (H)** details.
   b) What prevention measure is suggested?
5. What is the weather forecast for today? Give **three (O)/four (H)** details.

Kulturecke

In welchen Ländern ist Deutsch die offizielle Sprache, und wo wird Deutsch häufig gesprochen?

Deutsch ist die offizielle Sprache in Belgien (zusammen mit Niederländisch und Französisch), Deutschland, Liechtenstein, Luxemburg (zusammen mit Luxemburgisch und Französisch), Österreich und der Schweiz (zusammen mit Französisch, Italienisch und Rätoromanisch).

Deutsch ist auch die offizielle Sprache in Gebieten in Brasilien, Italien, Polen und der Slowakei.

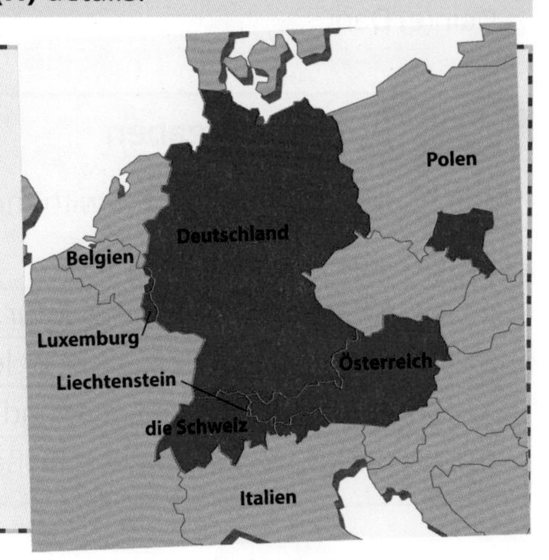

OL  Schriftliche Produktion: Ordinary Level

Write a letter to your pen pal. Complete the first paragraph by correctly inserting these sentence halves. Then follow the instructions.

etwas gewonnen **dass ich mich dazu gemeldet habe** **Heute Morgen habe ich** **vor Freude** **tolle Nachrichten**

Liebe(r) Dani,

ich habe ___________ ! ___________ einen Brief bekommen. Ich habe einen Wettbewerb gewonnen. Ich habe noch nie ___________ ! Außerdem hatte ich ganz vergessen, ___________ . Und jetzt habe ich den ersten Preis erhalten. Ich bin ganz verrückt ___________ !

Now continue the letter.

- Give details about the competition (type of competition, how you heard about it, your prize).
- Mention that you must collect your prize (when, where) and describe how you will get there (car, bus, train, bike...).
- Explain how you are going to celebrate (**feiern**) and with whom (family, friends).
- Describe what you will do with the prize money (holiday, new phone, new clothes...).
- Ask them if they have ever won a competition.
- Write a suitable closing sentence.

HL Schriftliche Produktion: Higher Level

Reply in German to your pen pal's letter. Give detailed answers to the questions.

Liebe(r) ...,

ich habe mich über deinen letzten Brief gefreut. Tut mir leid, dass ich mich so lange nicht gemeldet habe, aber nun endlich bekommst du ein Lebenszeichen von mir.

Endlich funktioniert meine Facebookseite wieder! Hast du dein eigenes Profil? Welche Infos sind wichtig auf einem Profil? Ich habe neulich gelesen, dass von den 15- bis 16-Jahre alten Jugendlichen ein Viertel täglich sechs oder mehr Stunden vor dem Computer sitzt. Verbringst du viel Zeit am Computer? Spielst du Computerspiele oder was machst du am Computer?

Ich schwärme für Technologie, jedoch hat die Sache natürlich einen Aber. Zurzeit ist Mobbing per Handy ein wachsendes Problem in Deutschland. Ist das auch der Fall in Irland? Was kann man tun, um dieses Problem zu lösen? Werden bei euch Computer im Unterricht eingesetzt? Haben alle Schüler Zugang zu Breitband? Benutzen alle Schüler den Computer zu Hause? Glaubst du, dass der Computer irgendwann den Lehrer ersetzt? Warum/warum nicht?

Was für positive und negative Erfahrungen hast du mit der Technologie gemacht? Was sind deiner Meinung nach die Chancen und die Gefahren der Technologie? Was könnte man tun, um die Gefahren zu reduzieren?

Schreib bald wieder – mein Briefkasten verhungert! Ich freue mich auf einen altmodischen Brief ☺

Dein(e) Dani

Hausaufgaben

Match these German idioms with their English translations.

1. Ich habe Schwein gehabt.	**A** While there's life, there's hope.
2. Ich bin Feuer und Flamme dafür.	**B** The early bird catches the worm.
3. Es hofft der Mensch solange er lebt.	**C** It's a drop in the ocean.
4. Morgenstund hat Gold im Mund.	**D** I was lucky.
5. Das ist ein Tropfen auf den heißen Stein.	**E** I'm passionate about it.

Übung Macht den Meister!

A The Imperative

1. Turn the following commands into the **du**, **ihr** and **wir** forms of address.

a) Öffnen Sie die Tür!	**f)** Hören Sie gut zu!
b) Schließen Sie das Fenster!	**g)** Beantworten Sie die Fragen dazu!
c) Stehen Sie auf!	**h)** Beschreiben Sie sich!
d) Setzen Sie sich!	**i)** Fangen Sie jetzt an!
e) Schalten Sie den Computer ein!	**j)** Schreiben Sie eine Äußerung!

2. Turn the following statements into the imperative 'Let's ...' form.

a) Wir trinken einen Kaffee.	**f)** Wir schreiben einen Aufsatz.
b) Wir gehen in die Disco.	**g)** Wir reden ständig auf Deutsch.
c) Wir feiern am Samstag.	**h)** Wir lernen fleißig.
d) Wir kaufen ein Geschenk für Hannah.	**i)** Wir spielen Computerspiele.
e) Wir essen eine Pizza.	**j)** Wir sehen einen Film auf Netflix.

B Subjunctive 2

1. Join the sentence halves.

1. Ich würde dir helfen,	**A** könnten wir in die Stadt fahren.
2. Wäre Paul hier,	**B** aber ich bin dazu zu müde.
3. Ich würde mein Zimmer aufräumen,	**C** würde ich einen Laptop kaufen.
4. Wenn ich viel Geld hätte,	**D** wenn ich die Tickets kaufen würde.
5. Er würde mitkommen,	**E** wenn ich gut in Deutsch wäre.

2. Use the subjunctive 2 of the bracketed verbs to complete the polite requests.

a) (Können) Sie mir bitte helfen?	**f)** (Können) du mir die Butter reichen?
b) (Werden) Sie mir einen Tee aufgießen?	**g)** Was (werden) ihr gern trinken?
c) (Mögen) du mit mir in die Stadt fahren?	**h)** Er (haben) gern eine Cola.
d) (Haben) ihr Zeit, mit mir zu reden?	**i)** (Können) ihr mir bei der Hausarbeit helfen?
e) Ich (haben) gern noch ein Bier.	**j)** (Mögen) Sie lieber Tee oder Kaffee?

3. Use the subjunctive 2 of the bracketed verb to complete these **als ob** (as if) sentences.

a) Sie benimmt sich, als ob sie die Chefin (sein).	**f)** Sie tut so, als ob sie mich nicht sehen (werden).
b) Er tut so, als ob er kein Geld (haben).	**g)** Er sieht aus, als ob er nicht geschlafen (haben).
c) Walter tut so, als ob er die Antwort (wissen).	**h)** Sie nickte, als ob sie verstanden (haben).
d) Sie redet, als ob sie meine Freundin (sein).	**i)** Er reagierte, als ob er stolz darauf (sein).
e) Es sieht aus, als ob er hier wohnen (werden).	**j)** Die Leute lachen, als ob es komisch (sein).

C Subjunctive 1

These statements are examples of indirect speech. Turn them into direct speech.

1. Sie sagt, der Mann lüge.	**6.** Der Mann behauptete, es gebe kein Glück.
2. Er meinte, es sei zu spät.	**7.** Das Mädchen sagte, sie sei eingeschlafen.
3. Frank behauptet, er habe das Buch gelesen.	**8.** Der Junge meint, er verstehe die Grammatik.
4. Monika sagte, sie kenne den Mann nicht.	**9.** Der Mann klagt, das Handy funktioniere nicht.
5. Die Frau meint, der Wagen koste zu viel.	**10.** Die Kinder sagen, sie seien müde.

Für die Prüfung

1. Was passt zusammen?

1. Mobbing kommt leider oft vor,	**A** denn bösartige SMS werden geschickt.
2. Schüler werden gehänselt,	**B** wenn man anonym ist.
3. Handymobbing ist ein ernstes Problem,	**C** nur weil sie anders sind.
4. Es ist leicht zu tun,	**D** dass niemand ausgegrenzt wird.
5. Wir müssen sicherstellen,	**E** und die Folgen können richtig ernst sein.

2. Was passt zusammen?

1. Fast jeder besitzt ein eigenes Handy	**A** der mit allem ausgestattet ist.
2. Ich kenne viele Eltern,	**B** wie man ein Handy vernünftig benutzt.
3. Ein Smartphone ist wie ein Taschencomputer,	**C** und die meisten davon sind Smartphones.
4. Junge Kinder wissen oft nicht,	**D** kann ich Apps leicht herunterladen.
5. Da ich ein Smartphone habe,	**E** die ihren Kleinkindern ein Handy geben.

3. Insert the correct prepositions for the following sentences.

a) Ich surfe gern **(am/im/um/zum)** Netz.

b) Ich sehe Filme **(am/im/um/auf)** YouTube.

c) Ich gewöhne mich **(an/in/auf/für)** die Arbeit.

d) **(Auf/An/Um/In)** dem Bild gibt es eine Frau.

e) Computer stehen **(in/im/um/am)** jedem Haus.

4. What words make up the following compound words, and what do they mean in English?

a) Technologiewelle = ___ + ___ = ___

b) Bildschirm = ___ + ___ = ___

c) Virenprogramm = ___ + ___ = ___

d) Kennwort = ___ + ___ = ___

e) Zugang = ___ + ___ = ___

f) herunterladen = ___ + ___ = ___

5. Put the underlined regular and irregular verbs into the imperfect tense.

a) Ich bekomme eine teure Handyrechnung.

b) Ich benutze Twitter nie.

c) Die ältere Generation mag Facebook nicht.

d) Viele Leute recherchieren im Internet.

e) Das Internet vergisst nie.

f) Wir laden gern Musik herunter.

6. Indicate whether the underlined nouns are singular or plural, their gender and their case.

a) Ich finde das Internet toll.

b) Das Handy ist aus dem Leben nicht wegzudenken.

c) Ich habe immer das Handy in der Tasche.

d) Man wird bestraft, wenn man beim Fahren mit einem Handy erwischt wird.

7. Lückentext: Fill in the blanks with the correct missing words from the box below.

Kontakt	**sondern**	**mit**	**mehrmals**	**zu**	**weil**
Jugendlichen	**Generation**	**oder**	**gleichen**		

80 Prozent der **1** ________ besuchen soziale Netzwerke täglich oder **2** ________ die Woche. Soziale Netzwerke gehören zu unserer **3** ________ . Wir sind nicht nur Konsumenten von Informationen, **4** ________ auch Gestalter von Web-Inhalten – seien es Texte, Fotos **5** ________ Videos. Besonders beliebt sind soziale Netzwerke, **6** ________ sie die Möglichkeit bieten, **7** ________ Menschen von überall auf der Welt in **8** ________ zu treten, solche mit **9** ________ Interessen zu finden und in Echtzeit mit ihnen **10** ________ kommunizieren.

Selbstbewertung: Ordinary Level

OL

Vocabulary

1. If I can translate these sentences into English, I can talk about social media. (2 marks each)

a) Ich benutze mein Handy jeden Tag.

b) Ich sehe gern Filme auf Netflix.

c) Ich poste Videos und Fotos auf Facebook.

d) Ich schaue mir gern Profile von Freunden an.

e) Ich habe mein Profil auf privat gestellt.

Your score: ___ / 10

2. If I can translate these nouns into German, I understand the language of technology. (1 mark each)

a) computer game	**c)** mobile phone	**e)** screen	**g)** protection	**i)** virus
b) text message	**d)** cyber bullying	**f)** website	**h)** network	**j)** keyboard

Your score: ___ / 10

Grammar

3. If I can choose the correct preposition, I can talk accurately about technology. (1 mark each)

a) Ich recherchiere **(im/am/um/zum)** Internet.	**f)** Ich schwärme **(mit/an/auf/für)** WhatsApp.
b) Ich sehe gern Filme **(in/auf/an/für)** YouTube.	**g)** Facebook ist ein Ding **(mit/an/auf/für)** Eltern.
c) Es gibt ein Handyverbot **(in/an/um/am)** der Schule.	**h)** Wir verstehen viel **(an/in/von/um)** Technologie.
d) Jeder ist **(bei/aus/auf/an)** Facebook.	**i)** Ich bin täglich **(mit/an/auf/für)** Instagram.
e) Wir benutzen Computer **(am/um/in/im)** Unterricht.	**j)** Man bleibt in Kontakt **(mit/an/auf/für)** Freunden.

Your score: ___ / 10

4. If I can conjugate these verbs in the **ich** and **wir** forms in the present tense, I can talk about the world of technology. (1 mark for each answer)

a) benutzen ich _____ wir _____

b) herunterladen ich _____ wir _____

c) recherchieren ich _____ wir _____

d) bekommen ich _____ wir _____

e) verstehen ich _____ wir _____

Your score: ___ / 10

5. If I can put these present tense sentences into the perfect tense, I understand the past and present tenses. (1 mark each)

a) Ich kaufe ein neues Handy.	**f)** Wir arbeiten an einem Projekt.
b) Ich sehe einen Film auf Netflix.	**g)** Wir kaufen Kleider online.
c) Ich surfe im Internet.	**h)** Wir haben interaktive Whiteboards.
d) Ich bleibe in Kontakt mit Freunden.	**i)** Wir recherchieren im Internet.
e) Ich benutze jeden Tag den Laptop.	**j)** Wir schauen uns gern Filme an.

Your score: ___ / 10

What have I learned?	
What must I improve?	
What do I want to revise?	

Your total score: ___ / 50

Selbstbewertung: Higher Level

HL

1. If I can translate these sentences into German, I understand the imperative. (1 mark each)

a) Open the door! (you, singular)	**f)** Sit down! (you, polite)
b) Write a letter! (you, plural)	**g)** Describe the photo! (you, polite)
c) Switch on the computer! (you, polite)	**h)** Give me the homework! (you, plural)
d) Give me the phone! (you, singular)	**i)** Switch off the computer! (you, singular)
e) Answer the questions! (you, plural)	**j)** Describe yourself! (you, singular)

Your score: ___ / 10

2. If I can translate these sentences, I understand the use of 'Let's ... '. (1 mark each)

a) Let's write to each other.	**f)** Let's go shopping online.
b) Let's watch a film.	**g)** Let's switch the computer off.
c) Let's put our profile on private.	**h)** Let's download music.
d) Let's change our passwords.	**i)** Let's upload photos.
e) Let's play a computer game.	**j)** Let's write a text message.

Your score: ___ / 10

3. If I can insert the correct form of the verb, I understand subjunctive 2. (1 mark each)

a) Ich (mögen) einen neuen Laptop.	**f)** Wir (können) über Skype sprechen.
b) (Können) ihr mir helfen?	**g)** Ich (werden) eine E-Mail schicken.
c) Ich (haben) lieber ein Smartphone.	**h)** Wir (sein) froh, euch kennenzulernen.
d) Ein iPad (sein) toll.	**i)** Es (können) sehr nützlich sein.
e) Er (mögen) ein neues Handy.	**j)** Welches Computermodell (haben) du lieber?

Your score: ___ / 10

4. If I can put the indirect speech into direct speech, I understand subjunctive 1. (1 mark each)

a) Sie sagt, sie spreche oft mit Ahmed.	**f)** Er sagt, ein Smartphone lohne sich.
b) Er meint, Computerspiele machen süchtig.	**g)** Sie meint, soziale Medien seien gefährlich.
c) Er sagt, sein Handy funktioniere nicht.	**h)** Er sagt, Mobbing führe zu Gewalt.
d) Sie sagte, sie habe Fotos hochgeladen.	**i)** Sie sagt, sie möge lieber einen iPad.
e) Er meint, es könne ein Irrtum sein.	**j)** Er meint, das Internet sei notwendig.

Your score: ___ / 10

5. If I can correctly fill in the gaps below, I understand word functions. (1 mark each)

aber **überwiegend** **das** **Kommunikation** **desto**
übertreffen **Medien** **aufbaut** **mehr** **Informationen**

Die modernen **1** ___ bieten nicht nur Unterhaltung, **2** ___ und Informationen – sie sind aus dem Leben nicht **3** ___ wegzudenken. **4** ___ Internet kann **5** ___ positiv sein, indem man **6** ___ für die Schule recherchiert, Referate vorbereitet, sich Tipps für Bewerbungen anguckt oder auch Kontakt zu Freunden **7** ___ . Bestimmt gibt es Gefahren, **8** ___ die Chancen digitaler Medien **9** ___ die Risiken. Je früher die Schüler mit dem Umgang der Technik vertraut werden, **10** ___ besser.

Your score: ___ / 10

What have I learned?	
What must I improve?	
What do I want to revise?	

Your total score: ___ / 50

13 Die Gesundheit

Learning Outcomes

- **Oral:** discussing health and fitness; revise oral topics from Chapters 5–8 and role plays
- **Reading:** reading and discussing three texts on health and fitness
- **Writing:** writing an opinion (**Äußerung**), a picture description and letter on health
- **Aural:** listening to and answering questions on four extracts on health

Grammar

- The present passive
- The imperfect passive
- Nationalities and countries

Vocabulary

- Health
- The fitness industry

German Culture

- Traditional food and modern food trends
- German cooking shows

Exam Tips

- A daily five-minute conversation in German will not only improve your spoken German, but will also boost your fluency and confidence.
- Use online audio scripts to revise key vocabulary.
- Using good grammatical structures, like the passive, will improve your expression mark.

Text 1: Wer Kochsendungen sieht, kocht nicht

Bitte beantworten Sie die folgenden Fragen:

1. Was sehen Sie auf dem Foto?
2. Was tun diese Menschen?
3. Wo sind sie?

Vorarbeit

1. Finden Sie diese Ausdrücke im Text!
   - **A** Things are getting greasy and hot again.
   - **B** The artificial flames ensure ...
   - **C** ... cooking fanatics rip ... recipes out ...
   - **D** The main thing – it is cheap.
   - **E** Variety is the open secret.
2. Finden Sie das Deutsche für die Wörter unten!
   - **A** studio audience/amazed/thundering/anecdotes/entertaining
   - **B** own/passionate/flame strengths/induction plates (hobs)/meat grinders
   - **C** additional/fridges/a new dish/self-breaded/end of one's life
   - **D** to bread/swings/damn/insist on/carbohydrates
   - **E** provide/daily/time pressure/delivery services/professionals

A Jetzt wird es wieder fettig und heiß. In deutschen Fernsehküchen ist das Gemüse König. Wenn die Köche dem staunenden Fernsehvolk ihre kulinarische Philosophie erklären, dann dankt das Studiopublikum mit donnerndem Applaus. Um unterhaltsam zu sein, erzählen die Köche Anekdoten, während sie eine gefüllte Hühnerbrust mit selbstgemachten Fettuccinen vorbereiten.

B Sie müssen leidenschaftliche und hochmotivierte Hobbyköche sein, denn sie besitzen Küchengeräte aller Art, Reiskocher und Fleischwölfe, einen Herd von Samsung mit blauen LEDs, die unter die Induktionsflächen gepackt werden und schon leuchten sie in unterschiedlich großen Flammenstärken auf. Die künstlichen Flammen sorgen für das romantische Gefühl. Und der Preis? 3.000 Euro.

C In den Regalen deutscher Küchen stehen so viele Kochbücher, dass sie bis ans Lebensende jeden Tag ein neues Gericht zubereiten können. Trotzdem reißen heimische Kochfanatiker zusätzliche Rezepte aus den Kochmagazinen aus, während in den meisten deutschen Kühlschränken eher gefrorenes Schnitzel und künstliche Fleisch- und Milchprodukte zu finden sind, als ein gutes Stück Parmesan oder selbstpaniertes Schnitzel.

D Das Verhältnis vieler Menschen zu ihrem Essen pendelt zwischen zwei Extremen. Die einen kümmern sich gar nicht darum, was und wie viel sie essen. Hauptsache – es ist billig. Sie trauen sich auch nicht selber ein Schnitzel zu panieren. Die anderen machen aus jedem Essen eine Wissenschaft, befolgen ständig neue Regeln, verdammen mal Eier, mal Butter, mal Milch, mal Zucker, mal Kohlenhydrate oder bestehen auf allerfeinsten Zutaten.

E Fast alle leiden unter dem permanenten Zeitdruck, was das alltägliche Kochen fast unmöglich macht. Und worauf das tägliche, gesunde Essen wirklich ankommt, weiß jeder Mensch. Öfter mal Obst und Gemüse essen, dafür weniger Zucker, weniger Fleisch und weniger Fett. Abwechslung heißt das offene Geheimnis. Und Kochen ist einfach wie nie. Webseiten, Blogs und Apps versorgen die Ess- und Gourmetwelt jederzeit mit Rezepten. Lieferservices bringen gestressten Berufstätigen Rezepte und die Zutaten inklusive an die Haustür. Mein Motto: Wenn im Fernsehen wieder eine Küchenshow läuft, dann drücken Sie den Schalter auf AUS! Wer Kochsendungen sieht, kocht nicht.

Olaf Lüken, 4 Feb. 2018 (amended)

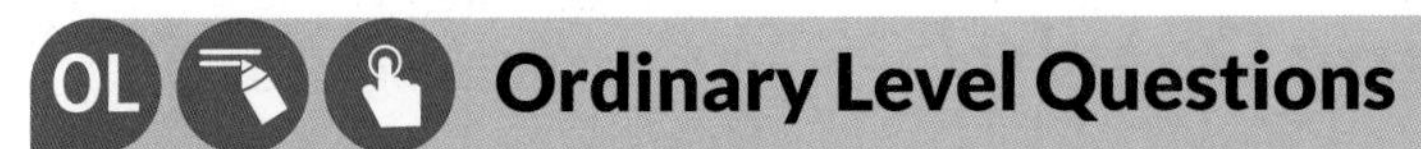

Ordinary Level Questions

1. a) Name **two** dishes which are in at the moment. A
   b) Name **two** kitchen gadgets which every cooking show seems to feature. B
   c) What items do many German kitchens have too many of? C
   d) What **two** extremes can be found in current German eating habits? D
   e) Give **two** tips which promote healthy eating, according to the text. E
2. True or false?
   a) Fernsehköche müssen unterhaltsam sein.
   b) Ein Induktionsherd kostet 2.000 Euro.
   c) In vielen deutschen Kühlschränken findet man künstliche Fleisch- und Milchprodukte.
   d) Alle befolgen die neusten Essregeln.
   e) Laut Text, wenn man sich Kochshows ansieht, kocht man nicht.
3. What words make up the following compound words, and what do they mean in English?
   a) Kochbücher = ___ + ___ = ___
   b) Fernsehköche = ___ + ___ = ___
   c) Kühlschränke = ___ + ___ = ___
   d) Lieferservice = ___ + ___ = ___

HL Higher Level Questions

1. Beantworten Sie folgende Fragen auf Deutsch.
   a) Was machen die Köche, um unterhaltsam zu sein? A
   b) Welche Küchengeräte werden im Text genannt? B
   c) i) Was machen viele Kochfanatiker? ii) Was steht doch meist in ihren Kühlschränken? C
   d) Wie macht man aus jedem Essen eine Wissenschaft? D
   e) Welche Kochtipps gibt der Autor dem Leser weiter? E
2. Answer the following questions in English.
   a) Besides cooking, describe in detail what the show host does during a programme. A
   b) Give **four** details about the oven described. B
   c) How do many Germans show an interest in cooking? What food ends up in most fridges? C
   d) Give **three** details each about the two types of extremes when it comes to food. D
   e) What is the author's motto about cooking? E
3. Was passt zusammen?

1. Die wichtigsten Zutaten	**A** weil sie unterhaltsam sein müssen.
2. Die Fernsehköche müssen hochmotiviert sein,	**B** einer der besten Wege gesund zu essen.
3. Auf den Regalen stehen viele Kochbücher,	**C** dass das Essen billig ist.
4. Manche finden es wichtig,	**D** sind Gemüsesorten.
5. Ohne Zweifel ist selber Kochen	**E** aber man isst künstliche Fleischprodukte.

4. Geben Sie für die unterstrichenen Nomen an: Singular oder Plural, das Geschlecht, den Fall.
   a) Die Köche bereiten eine gefüllte Hühnerbrust mit selbstgemachten Fettuccinen vor.
   b) Die künstlichen Flammen sorgen für das romantische Gefühl.
   c) In den Regalen deutscher Küchen stehen viele Kochbücher.
   d) Das Verhältnis vieler Menschen zu ihrem Essen pendelt zwischen zwei Extremen.

Prüfungstipp

A five-minute daily conversation in German with a classmate on the topics discussed in Chapters 5–8 will keep these topics fresh for the role plays/picture sequences or project.

Grammatik: Das Präsens Passiv/ The Present Passive

p. 255 (Übung macht den Meister)

The active voice involves subject-verb-object, or nominative-verb-accusative:

Der Mann (nom.) **kauft einen Wagen** (acc.). *The man buys a car.*

The passive voice is used when you want to emphasise the action, rather than the person doing that action:

Ein Wagen wird gekauft. *A car is bought.*

In German the present passive is formed with the present tense of **werden** + the past participle of the main simple, separable or inseparable verb, which is placed at the end of the sentence:

ich werde ... gelobt.	*I am being praised.*	wir werden ... befreit.	*we are being freed.*
du wirst ... verhaftet.	*you are being arrested.*	ihr werdet ... eingeladen.	*you are being invited.*
er/sie/es wird ... geschützt.	*he/she/it is protected.*	Sie/sie werden ... gemobbt.	*you/they are bullied.*

In order to introduce the agent (the person/thing doing the verb), use **von** + the dative case to express 'by' a person or something living; use **durch** + the accusative case to express 'by' a thing.

Du wirst von der Polizei geschützt. *You are protected by the police.*

Er wird durch Blei vergiftet. *He is being poisoned by lead.*

When an active sentence is turned into a passive one, the object of the sentence becomes the subject of the new sentence. This means that the object now moves into the nominative case.

Identify the passive in the following sentences (any form of **werden** and past participle).

1. Ich werde von vier Polizisten umringt.	*I am being surrounded by four police officers.*
2. Sie wird vom Zollbeamten angehalten.	*She is stopped by the customs official.*
3. Wir werden von jenen Kindern gemobbt.	*We are being bullied by those children.*
4. Er wird von Bienen angegriffen.	*He is being attacked by bees.*
5. Das Auto wird durch eine Firma gemietet.	*The car is being rented by a firm.*
6. Der Mann wird von den Reportern befragt.	*The man is being interviewed by the reporters.*
7. Die Kinder werden von dem Mann gerettet.	*The children are being rescued by the man.*
8. Die Migranten werden in Hotels untergebracht.	*The migrants are being accommodated in hotels.*

There are three steps to turning the active voice into the passive voice.

1. Turn the accusative into the nominative, because the passive voice turns the object of the sentence into the subject (be careful with masculine words).
2. Conjugate **werden**: do you need the singular **wird** or the plural **werden**?
3. Turn the active verb into its past participle form. Is the past participle regular or irregular?

Use these three steps to turn the following active voice sentences into passive voice sentences.

1. Das Studiopublikum applaudiert die Köche.
2. Hobbyköche besitzen Küchengeräte aller Art.
3. Kochfanatiker reißen Rezepte aus den Kochmagazinen aus.
4. Die anderen machen aus jedem Essen eine Wissenschaft.
5. Lieferservices bringen Rezepte und die Zutaten an die Haustür.
6. Die Zuschauer loben den Koch.
7. Man soll den Schalter ausschalten.
8. Die Frau brät das Schnitzel.

13.01 Hörverständnis Teil 1

Vorarbeit

Forschung	*research*	**Verallgemeinerung**	*generalisation*	**Bedürfnisse**	*needs*
Einstellung	*attitude*	**überzeugen**	*to convince*	**fördern**	*to support*
Verhalten	*behaviour*	**Ernährung**	*nutrition*	**eingehen auf**	*to respond to*

CL Ordinary + Higher Level Questions

1. What topic has Herr Mannhenke been invited to discuss?
2. What does Herr Mannhenke say with regard to young people and their attitude to health?
3. What suggestions does he make for useful ways to guide young people to a healthy lifestyle?
4. According to a questionnaire, what are many young people interested in?
5. What has been organised as a result? Give **two (O)/three (H)** details.

13.02 Hörverständnis Teil 2

Vorarbeit

Ängste	*fears*	**sich wandeln in**	*to turn into*	**Begeisterung**	*enthusiasm*
klug	*smart*	**wegblasen**	*to blow away*	**Zaubertrick**	*magic trick*
absteigen	*to be relegated*	**Alpträume**	*nightmares*	**Kraft**	*strength*

OL Ordinary Level Questions

1. Why is Claudia worried?
2. What does Jana say to calm Claudia down?
3. The callers are:
   a) classmates ☐ **b)** best friends ☐ **c)** teammates ☐ **d)** a trainer and a player ☐
4. What is Maria's number?

HL Higher Level Questions

1. Using ***key phrases***, write down **in German** the key information the caller provides:
   - the name of the person **making** the call
   - the reason for the call
   - **four** details of their conversation
   - details regarding further contact
   - Maria's phone number

Gesprächsnotiz
Anruf von: ________________ Gesprächsanlass: ________________
Der Anrufer:
- ruft Maria an ☐
- wird Maria eine SMS senden ☐
- wird Maria eine WhatsApp-Nachricht senden ☐
- wird mit Maria nicht kommunizieren ☐

Kontaktnummer: ________________

2. In listening to the phone call for the ***third*** time, write down **three** examples of the language used (***expressions and phrases***) which show how Jana **calms** Claudia down.

Text 2: Jugendliche im Fitnessstudio

Bitte beantworten Sie die folgenden Fragen:

1. Wo wurde das Foto aufgenommen, Ihrer Meinung nach?
2. Gehen Sie auch gern ins Fitnessstudio? Warum/warum nicht?

Vorarbeit

1. Finden Sie diese Ausdrücke im Text!
   - **A** ... to build up muscles and break down fat.
   - **B** ... belongs to an increasing number of ...
   - **C** I would like to get heavier (fatter).
   - **D** You can die from it.
   - **E** ... feel good in their skin.
2. Finden Sie das Deutsche für die Wörter unten!
   - **A** effort/sweat/almost/body
   - **B** fits into/protein/satisfaction
   - **C** to prevent/power training/stamina training
   - **D** supplements/target group/abuse
   - **E** to lose weight/turkey breast/path

A Simon und Tamim schwitzen fast täglich im Fitnessstudio. Sie wollen „den Körper ausdefinieren", sagen sie, und haben einen strengen Ernährungsplan. 900.000 Jugendliche gehen zum Krafttraining. „Es ist viel Aufwand", sagt Simon, 15. Der Gymnasiast geht seit einem halben Jahr ins Fitnessstudio, um Muskeln aufzubauen und Fett abzubauen. Sechsmal pro Woche trainiert er.

B Bis vor kurzem hat Simon morgens gar nichts gegessen. Heute steht er auf, um sich Eier zu kochen. Genau 150 Gramm Eiweiß soll er essen. Er bereitet sich Brote vor, denn das Essen in der Schule passt nicht in den Ernährungsplan. „Es ist ein Gefühl von Genugtuung, wenn man sieht, wie andere in unserem Alter die Form verlieren, während wir uns gerade ausdefinieren", sagt Simon. Er gehört zu einer steigenden Zahl von Jugendlichen, die versuchen, ihre Körper auszudefinieren.

C Michael Sauer, der Dopingexperte, möchte verhindern, dass Jugendliche dem Muskelaufbau mit Pulvern und Tabletten nachhelfen. In Schulen wird er oft mit kuriosen Fragen konfrontiert: „Ich möchte gern dicker werden, wie schaffe ich das? Ich kann essen, was ich will, ich bleibe dünn", fragt ein Junge. Sauer erklärt ihm, dass weniger Ausdauer- und mehr Kraftsport helfen könnte, die Muskeln aufzubauen.

D Michael Sauer macht Präventionsunterricht an Schulen. Er sagt: „Wenn wir mit den Jugendlichen über Medikamentenmissbrauch sprechen, können wir nicht sagen: Davon kannst du sterben. Dann hört mir keiner zu. Wir versuchen zu sagen: Wenn du deinen Körper nutzt, dann brauchst du keine Zusatzmittel zu nehmen." Für Discount-Fitnessketten wie McFit sind Jugendliche eine Zielgruppe. In einer Studie mit 400 Jugendlichen gab jeder Zweite an, dass er auf körperliche Fitness und Gesundheit achten würde.

E Simon und Tamim fühlen sich wohl in ihrem Körper. „Beim Sport können wir super abschalten. Wir bleiben fit und sehen gut aus", sagt Tamim. Simon hat ein konkreteres Ziel vor Augen: „Ich wollte abnehmen, deswegen esse ich gesund. Morgens meistens was mit Vollkorn, mittags was Leichtes und abends Putenbrust. Ich habe schon fünf Kilo runter." Es entwickelt sich schnell eine „Zweck-Mittel-Mentalität". Um weniger zu essen, greift man zu Diätdrinks oder Pillen. Ein Eiweißshake macht mehr Sinn als vier Liter Milch am Tag zu trinken. Fitness für gutes Aussehen ist für die Jugendlichen auch Identitätsarbeit. Sie verbringen viel Zeit im Studio. Je intensiver sich ein Athlet über seine Körperoptik definiert, desto schwieriger wird es, den Pfad wieder zu verlassen.

Maria Timtschenko, *Spiegel Online*, 9 Dec. 2013 (amended)

Ordinary Level Questions

1. **a)** Give **two** details about the strength training which Simon and Tamim do. A
   b) What food does Simon prepare? Give **two** details. B
   c) According to Michael Sauer, how can one best build up muscles? C
   d) What type of lessons does Michael Sauer give and what is his main message? D
2. True or false?
   a) 900.000 young people neglect their fitness levels.
   b) Simon has to eat 150 g of carbohydrates every day.
   c) Michael Sauer is often asked about the best way to put on weight.
   d) Michael Sauer tells young people about the abuse of medication.
3. Complete the following sentences, based on Text 2.
   a) Viele Jugendliche achten auf ihre **(Fitness/Hobbys/Noten/Freunde)**.
   b) Simon kocht **(Wasser/eine Suppe/Eier/Kartoffeln)**.
   c) Die Sportbegeisterung hat **(nur/viele/vier/nicht nur)** gute Seiten.
   d) Wenn man seinen Körper nutzt, braucht man **(keine/einige/viele/sehr viele)** Medikamente.
4. Choose the correct preposition.
   a) Simon geht **(mit/seit/an/auf)** sechs Monaten ins Fitnessstudio.
   b) Michael Sauer wird oft **(zu/mit/für/in)** interessanten Fragen konfrontiert.
   c) Jugendliche sind die Zielgruppe **(mit/an/in/für)** Fitnessketten.
   d) **(Mit/Beim/Bei/An)** Sport bleiben wir fit und sehen gut aus.

HL Higher Level Questions

1. Beantworten Sie folgende Fragen auf Deutsch.
   a) Simon stellt sich vor. Schreiben Sie **fünf** kurze informative Sätze (Präsens) in *Ich*-Form. A
   b) Geben Sie **drei** Details über die Morgenroutine von Simon. B
   c) Was will Michael Sauer verhindern? C
   d) Nennen Sie, was Michael Sauer den Jugendlichen sagt und auch nicht sagt. D
   e) Wie fühlen sich die zwei Jungen? E
2. Answer the following questions in English.
   a) Give **four** details about the effort which Simon says is involved in his weight training. A
   b) Describe in detail the food he prepares in the morning. B
   c) What does Michael Sauer try to prevent? C
   d) What exactly does Sauer say about the lessons he gives? D
   e) Give **four** details about what both boys think about this sport and what they do to achieve this. E
3. Was passt zusammen?

1. Viele Jugendliche begeistern sich	**A** bauen die zwei Jungs ihre Muskeln auf.
2. Während andere ihre Form verlieren,	**B** aber auch schlechte.
3. Dieser Hobby-Sport hat gute Seiten,	**C** für den Trendsport Krafttraining.
4. Niemand wird einem zuhören,	**D** dass sie gut aussehen.
5. Die beiden Jungen freuen sich,	**E** wenn man sagte, man sterbe davon.

4. Geben Sie für die Verben an: den Infinitiv des Verbs; die Zeitform; ob Singular oder Plural.
   a) Vor kurzem hat Simon morgens gar nichts gegessen.
   b) In Schulen wird Michael Sauer oft mit kuriosen Fragen konfrontiert.
   c) Wir bleiben fit und sehen gut aus.

OL Äußerung zum Thema: Ordinary Level

You are interviewing Simon. Complete the dialogue, using the information given in Text 2.

Sie: Seit wann gehst du ins Fitnessstudio?
Simon: ______________________________
Sie: Wie alt bist du?
Simon: ______________________________
Sie: Was isst du, wenn du trainierst?
Simon: ______________________________
Sie: Wer macht Krafttraining mit dir?
Simon: ______________________________
Sie: Wie oft trainiert ihr?
Simon: ______________________________

HL Äußerung zum Thema: Higher Level

Write 13 to 15 sentences, answering the questions below.

- Beschreiben Sie das Foto rechts in **drei bis vier** Sätzen.
- Wo ist der Mann, Ihrer Meinung nach?
- Achten viele Jugendliche heutzutage auf ihr Aussehen? Warum (nicht), Ihrer Meinung nach?
- Was für Probleme kann es beim Körperkrafttraining geben?

Nützliche Sätze

Übersetzen Sie folgende Sätze.

1. Auf dem Bild kann man einen Jungen sehen, der Krafttraining macht.
2. Er hebt Gewichte und macht Gerätetraining.
3. Er sieht fit und gesund aus.
4. Heutzutage begeistern sich viele Jugendliche für Krafttraining, da sie gut aussehen wollen.
5. Natürlich wollen sie auch fit bleiben, jedoch ist für sie ihr Aussehen das Wichtigste.
6. Für manche ist dieser sogenannte Hobby-Sport zu einem ganzen Lebensstil geworden.
7. Einige verlieren auch den Kontakt zu Freunden, die sich nicht so sehr für Krafttraining interessieren.

Hausaufgaben

Match these German idioms with their English meanings.

1. Ich bin gesund wie ein Fisch im Wasser.	**A** *Eat breakfast like a king, lunch like a prince and dinner like a beggar.*
2. Ohne Fleiß kein Preis.	**B** *Your health is your wealth.*
3. Man ist, was man isst.	**C** *You can have too much of a good thing.*
4. Frühstücken wie ein Kaiser, Mittagessen wie ein König und Abendessen wie ein Bettler.	**D** *No pain, no gain.*
5. Gesunder Mann, reicher Mann.	**E** *I'm fit as a fiddle.*
6. Allzuviel ist ungesund.	**F** *The first step is the hardest.*
7. Der erste Schritt ist der schwerste.	**G** *You are what you eat.*
8. Was man sät, so wird man ernten.	**H** *There's a limit to everything.*
9. Die Bäume wachsen nicht in den Himmel.	**I** *You reap what you sow.*

Grammatik: Das Präteritum Passiv/ Imperfect Passive

p. 255 (Übung macht den Meister)

Reminder: The passive voice is used when we want to emphasise the action or the object:

Der Mann wurde verhaftet. *The man was being arrested.*

In German the imperfect passive is formed with the imperfect tense of **werden** + the past participle of the simple, separable or inseparable verb, which is placed at the end of the sentence:

ich wurde ... verhaftet	*I was being arrested*	wir wurden ... befreit	*we were freed*
du wurdest ... geschützt	*you were protected*	ihr wurdet ... eingeladen	*you were being invited*
er/sie/es wurde ... gelobt	*he/she/it was praised*	Sie/sie wurden ... gemobbt	*you/they were bullied*

In order to introduce the agent (the person or thing doing the verb), use **von** + dative case to express 'by' a person or living thing; use **durch** + accusative case to express 'by' a thing.

Ich wurde von dem Rektor gelobt. *I was praised by the principal.*

Sie wurde durch den Strom getötet. *She was killed by the electricity.*

Remember that when you turn a sentence into the passive, the person or thing to whom the verb is being done in the active voice (object) is placed first in the sentence, becoming the subject in the passive. This means that the noun or pronoun is in the nominative case.

Identify **a)** the imperfect passive of the verb in each sentence below, **b)** the 'doer' of the verb and which case it is in, **c)** the person or thing to which the verb is being done and which case it is in.

1. Das Essen wurde von dem Koch serviert.	*The food was served by the cook.*
2. Das Zimmer wurde von den Kindern aufgeräumt.	*The room was tidied by the children.*
3. Aufsätze wurden von den Schülern geschrieben.	*Essays were written by the pupils.*
4. Der Wagen wurde von der Mutter gefahren.	*The car was being driven by the mother.*
5. Die Äpfel wurden von dem Jungen gestohlen.	*The apples were stolen by the boy.*
6. Die Stadt wurde im Jahr 1450 gegründet.	*The city was founded in 1450.*
7. Der Kuchen wurde von dem Mädchen gegessen.	*The cake was eaten by the girl.*
8. Die Waren wurden durch Schiffe transportiert.	*The goods were transported by ships.*

For a reminder of the three steps needed to form the passive voice, turn to page 244.

Use these three steps to turn the following imperfect active sentences into imperfect passive sentences.

1. Simon kochte Eier.	**5.** Schüler stellten Sauer kuriose Fragen.
2. Er bereitete sich Brote vor.	**6.** Du brauchtest keine Zusatzmittel.
3. Andere verloren die Form.	**7.** Abends aß Simon Putenbrust.
4. Simon definierte seinen Körper aus.	**8.** Die Jungen verbrachten viel Zeit im Studio.

Prüfungstipp

Using simple examples of the passive will push up your expression marks. When you come across a passive expression, try to adapt it for your own use.

Im Unterricht wird nur Deutsch gesprochen.	*Only German is spoken in class.*
Rom wurde nicht an einem Tag erbaut.	*Rome wasn't built in a day.*
Die Armen werden immer noch benachteiligt.	*The poor are still being disadvantaged.*
Nicht genug wird für die Umwelt getan.	*Not enough is being done for the environment.*
Strenge Gesetze sollten eingeführt werden.	*Strict laws should be brought in.*

Text 3: Unfair – Eine Fußballgeschichte

  Bitte beantworten Sie die folgenden Fragen:

1. Was sehen Sie auf dem Bild?
2. Wie sieht der Trainer aus?
3. Was macht er, und warum macht er das?
4. Was für Kleidung tragen die Schüler?

Vorarbeit

1. Finden Sie diese Ausdrücke im Text!
   - **A** ... to tear us to shreds.
   - **B** You're a disgrace ...
   - **C** The trainer was fuming.
   - **D** ... their trainer had already thrown in the towel.
   - **E** Nothing can go wrong.
2. Finden Sie das Deutsche für die Wörter unten!
   - **A** be relegated/most experienced/opponent
   - **B** goal/swerved/attack/rejoicing/cursed
   - **C** recognised/changed/two classes up
   - **D** phone calls/promotion/discovered
   - **E** down a league/gave up/victory/position

© Marco Wittler – www.366geschichten.de (amended)

A »Heute müssen wir gewinnen. Davon hängt die Zukunft der Mannschaft ab«, sagte der Trainer. »Gewinnen wir, bleiben wir in der Liga. Wenn ihr verliert, steigen wir ab.« Aber was sollten sie machen? Paul, der Mannschaftskapitän, sah die anderen Jungs an. Jeder wusste, dass es schon vorbei war. Sie wussten, dass der Gegner stärker war. »Die werden alles tun, um uns in der Luft zu zerreißen. Sie sind die beste und erfahrenste Mannschaft. Sie sind alle größer als wir. Wir haben keine Chance aber was haben wir zu verlieren?«

B Das Spiel begann und der erste Ansturm kam auf sie zu. Es dauerte keine Minute, bis das erste Tor fiel. Der Trainer fluchte laut. Schließlich schoss Paul den Ball ins Netz. Der Jubel unter den Jungen war groß. Die Stürmer des Gegners waren entschlossen, ein Tor zu schießen. Pauls Abwehrspieler waren so eingeschüchtert, dass sie vor Angst auswichen. Der Ball ging ins Netz. Es stand zwei zu eins. Die erste Halbzeit war vorbei. Der Trainer wartete wütend in der Kabine. »Ihr seid eine Schande für den ganzen Sport. So einen schlechten Fußball habe ich noch nie gesehen.«

C Die zweite Halbzeit wurde angepfiffen. Doch das Spiel änderte sich nicht. Die Gastmannschaft war viel zu stark. Am Ende stand es acht zu eins. Pauls Mannschaft hatte das Spiel verloren. Der Trainer kochte vor Wut. Ein paar Tage später kam ein neuer Schüler auf Pauls Schule. Paul erkannte ihn vom letzten Fußballspiel. Er war der beste Stürmer. Paul dachte, dass der Junge in seine Klasse kommen würde. Aber das passierte nicht. In der Pause entdeckte er den Stürmer. Der stand bei den Schülern, die zwei Klassen höher waren.

D »Was, der ist so alt? Das darf doch nicht sein.« Nach der Schule erzählte Paul seinen Eltern davon. »Er ist zwei Klassen über mir. Er ist viel zu alt, um gegen uns zu spielen.« Pauls Vater ging sofort ans Telefon und machte einige Telefonate. Am Wochenende trafen sich die Jungen am Sportplatz. Sie hatten bereits erfahren, dass ihr Trainer das Handtuch geworfen hatte. »Paul, ohne Trainer werden wir noch schlechter. Dann schaffen wir den Aufstieg nie.«

E In diesem Moment kamen die Eltern. »Wie ihr wisst, gab es bei eurem letzten Spiel ein Problem mit dem Alter der Spieler. Dadurch durften drei Stürmer nicht mehr mitspielen. Viele Spiele von ihnen wurden annulliert. Die Mannschaft wird eine Liga nach unten gestuft. Dadurch bleibt ihr, wo ihr seid.« Die Jungen jubelten. »Da euer letzter Gegner sehr unfair gespielt hat und deren Trainer nichts davon wusste, gab er dort sein Amt auf. Er will euch zum Sieg verhelfen.« Dann kam der neue Trainer und begrüßte seine neue Mannschaft mit einem Lächeln. »Dann kann nichts mehr schief gehen«, sagte Paul.

OL Ordinary Level Questions

1. **a)** Give **two** details about what the trainer said to his team. A
   b) What did the trainer say to the team at half-time? B
   c) What did Paul realise a couple of days later about the striker of the opposing team? C
   d) What did Paul's father do when he heard the news? D
   e) Why had their new trainer resigned from his last position? E
2. Choose a suitable heading for each paragraph and explain your choice in English.

Der Trainer ist wütend | Der gegnerische Stürmer ist zu alt | Der Trainer gibt sein Amt auf | Das Team bleibt in der Liga | Wir werden das Spiel verlieren

3. Separate these compound words into their components and translate them into English.
   a) Ansturm = ___ + ___ = ___
   b) Abwehrspieler = ___ + ___ = ___
   c) Fußballspiel = ___ + ___ = ___
   d) Trainingszeit = ___ + ___ = ___
4. Are the following sentences true or false?
   a) Der Trainer sagt dem Team, sie werden das Spiel gewinnen.
   b) In der Halbzeit sagt der Trainer, dass das Team sehr gut gespielt hat.
   c) Das gegnerische Team gewinnt, acht zu eins.
   d) Der letzte Trainer hat sein Amt aufgegeben.
   e) Der neue Trainer begrüßt das Team mit einem Lächeln.

HL Higher Level Questions

1. Beantworten Sie die folgenden Fragen auf Deutsch!
   a) Was hat der Trainer seinem Team gesagt? Geben Sie **vier** Details. A
   b) Wie hat der Trainer auf das erste Tor vom gegnerischen Team reagiert? B
   c) Was hat Paul über einen der Spieler des gegnerischen Teams entdeckt? C
   d) Beschreiben Sie genau, was Paul seinen Eltern erzählt hat. D
   e) Wie hat das Team auf die gute Nachricht reagiert? E
2. Answer the following questions in English.
   a) Give **three** details about how Paul and his team felt about the opposing team. A
   b) Describe in detail how the opposing team scored their second goal. B
   c) How did the match end? Give **three** details. C
   d) How did Paul's father react and what did the team discover at the next training session? D
   e) The text explores strong emotions. Give **four** examples of such emotions and what causes them.
3. Was passt zusammen?

1. Unser Trainer hat uns gesagt,	**A** und ohne zu warten schoss ihn ins Netz.
2. Wir hatten Angst vor dem anderen Team,	**B** sondern ins andere Klassenzimmer.
3. Ich hatte plötzlich den Ball	**C** dass wir heute gewinnen müssten.
4. Der Stürmer ging nicht in meine Klasse,	**D** aber jetzt war ein neuer da.
5. Der alte Trainer hatte schon aufgegeben,	**E** da sie alle viel größer als wir waren.

4. Schreiben Sie die folgenden unterstrichenen Verben **im Präsens**.
   a) Der erste Ansturm kam auf sie zu.
   b) Schließlich schoss Paul den Ball ins Netz.
   c) Es stand zwei zu eins.
   d) Paul erkannte den neuen Schüler.
   e) Er dachte, er würde in seine Klasse kommen.
   f) Paul rannte nach Hause.

13.03 Hörverständnis Teil 3

Vorarbeit

Krafttraining	*strength training*	**aufbauen**	*to build up*	**proteinreich**	*protein rich*
Brust	*chest*	**abbauen**	*to break down*	**Kost**	*diet*
sattmachen	*to satisfy*	**Ausdauer**	*endurance*	**Dauerläufe**	*endurance runs*

Ordinary + Higher Level Questions

1. **a)** The conversation is between:
   i) a teacher and student ☐ **ii)** friends ☐ **iii)** brothers ☐ **iv)** college students ☐
   b) Find **one (O)/two (H)** details in the conversation that support your choice.
2. **a)** Which word best describes Stefan's attitude to fitness training?
   i) depressed ☐ **ii)** indifferent ☐ **iii)** happy ☐ **iv)** curious ☐
   b) Write down **one (O)/two (H)** details from the conversation that support your choice.
3. How does Nikolaus react to Stefan's comments? Give **two (O)/three (H)** details.
4. What do they decide to do? Give **one (O)/two (H)** details.

13.04 Hörverständnis Teil 4

Vorarbeit

europäisch	*European*	**Schuldenkrise**	*debt crisis*	**jeder Vierte**	*one in four*
Armut	*poverty*	**sechseinhalb**	*six and a half*	**bedroht**	*threatened*
ausgegrenzt	*excluded*	**Steroide**	*steroids*	**Diätpillen**	*diet pills*
in Sicht	*in sight*	**Hitzewelle**	*heatwave*	**Fachleute**	*experts*

Ordinary + Higher Level Questions

1. What situation faces 26 million children and young people? Give **two (O)/three (H)** details.
2. Describe in detail the worrying situation that many young Germans aged 20–24 find themselves in.
3. Give **two (O)/three (H)** details about young people in Germany and fitness studios.
4. What is the attitude of many young Germans to health and healthy eating?
5. What is the weather forecast? Give **three (O)/four (H)** details.

Kulturecke

Match the following traditional German food and drink with their respective photos.

Lübecker Marzipan | Weißwurst und Brezeln | Christstollen
Pharisäer | Currywurst mit Pommes Frites | Wiener Schnitzel

Grammatik: Länder und Nationalitäten/ Countries and Nationalities

p. 255 (Übung macht den Meister)

Land	**Sprache**	**Person, m.**	**Person, f.**	**Personen, pl.**	**Adjektiv nach/ vor dem Nomen**
Country	*Language*	*Person, m.*	*Person, f.*	*People, pl.*	*Adjective, after/ before the noun*
Deutschland	Deutsch	der Deutsche/ ein Deutscher	die Deutsche eine Deutsche	die Deutschen viele Deutsche	deutsch *OR* deutsch- + *Adjective ending*
Irland	Irisch	der Ire/ Irländer ein Ire/ Irländer	die Irin/ Irländerin eine Irin/ Irländerin	die Iren/Irländer viele Iren/Irländer viele Irinnen/ Irländerinnen	irisch *OR* irisch-
Österreich	Deutsch	der/ein Österreicher	die/eine Österreicherin	die/viele Österreicher(innen)	österreichisch *OR* österreichisch-
die Schweiz	Deutsch Französisch Italienisch	der/ein Schweizer	die/eine Schweizerin	die/viele Schweizer(innen)	schweizerisch *OR* schweizerisch-
Frankreich	Französisch	der/ein Franzose	die/eine Französin	die/viele Franzosen die/viele Französinnen	französisch *OR* französisch-
Italien	Italienisch	der/ein Italiener	die/eine Italienerin	die/viele Italiener(innen)	italienisch *OR* italienisch-
Amerika	Englisch	der/ein Amerikaner	die/eine Amerikanerin	die/viele Amerikaner(innen)	amerikanisch *OR* amerikanisch-
Spanien	Spanisch	der/ein Spanier	die/eine Spanierin	die/viele Spanier(innen)	spanisch *OR* spanisch-
Schweden	Schwedisch	der/ein Schwede	die/eine Schwedin	die/viele Schweden/ Schwedinnen	schwedisch *OR* schwedisch-

Create your own table of countries, languages, people (m., f., pl.) and adjectives, using the table above.

1. **Similar to Irland:** England, Holland, Island, Grönland
2. **Similar to Spanien:** Belgien, Bosnien, Malaysien, Indonesien
3. **Similar to Österreich:** Japan, Luxemburg
4. **Similar to Amerika:** Mexiko
5. **Similar to Schweden:** Finnland, Polen, Russland, Dänemark, Schottland, Rumänien, Tschechien

Some places require a definite article in front of them. Here is a selection:

Masculine	**Feminine**	**Neuter**	**Plural**
der Irak	die Schweiz	das Baltikum	die Vereinigten Staaten
der Libanon	die Türkei		die Niederlande
der Sudan	die Europäische Union		die Philippinen

Continue this list in your copy.

OL Schriftliche Produktion: Ordinary Level

Write a letter to your pen pal. Complete the first paragraph by correctly inserting the sentence halves below. Then follow the instructions.

in den Ferien **kaum erwarten** **in einer Kochschule** **von dir zu hören** **Wir werden viel zusammen machen**

Liebe(r) Martin(a),

schön, ____________________ . Toll, dass du uns ____________________ besuchen wirst! ____________________ und du wirst meine Freunde kennenlernen. Ich freue mich selbst auf einen Kochkurs, den ich ____________________ machen werde. Ich kann es ____________________ !

Now continue the letter.

- Say that your favourite subjects are Home Economics and Biology.
- Mention that you eat healthily. Name **two** things you eat or drink.
- Say that you like to keep fit. Give **two** examples of how you achieve this.
- Say when and where the cookery course is.
- Write a suitable closing sentence.

HL Schriftliche Produktion: Higher Level

Reply in German to your pen pal's letter. Give detailed answers to the questions.

Liebe(r) ...,

ich hoffe, es geht dir und deiner Familie gut! Du wirst einen Kochkurs machen! Erzähl mir alles!

Es gibt immer mehr Leute hier in Deutschland, die gesund essen, und Kochsendungen sind total beliebt. Wie ist es bei euch in Irland? Persönlich esse ich nicht so gesund, aber ich versuche mich doch schon fit zu halten. Und du, bist du dafür auch begeistert? Haben irische Jugendliche Interesse an Fitness und Gesundheit?

Bei uns werden junge Leute immer mehr von Idolen beeinflusst, besonders was ihr Aussehen und ihren Lebensstil angeht. Ist das auch so bei euch? Was hältst du eigentlich davon?

In meiner Schule gibt es eine Kantine, aber die Gerichte in der Kantine haben einen sehr schlechten Ruf – sie sind fettig und geschmacklos! Gibt es Kantinen in irischen Schulen? Was für Essen wird angeboten? Gibt es eine Initiative zur gesunden Ernährung an der Schule?

An meiner Schule werden Sport und Sportleistungen großgeschrieben. Wie wichtig ist Sport bei dir an der Schule? Glaubst du, dass genug Sport im Stundenplan steht? Wie bleibst du fit? Oder hast du überhaupt Interesse daran? Jetzt muss ich Schluss machen.

Dein(e) Martin(a)

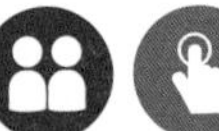

Nützliche Sätze

Übersetzen Sie folgende Sätze auf Englisch.

1. Um sich fit zu halten, gehen viele Jugendliche heutzutage ins Fitnessstudio.
2. Immer mehr Leute legen Wert auf viel frisches Bio- Gemüse und -Obst.
3. Man vermeidet auch künstliche Lebensmittelzusätze, Fett und Zucker.
4. Manche versuchen ihre Vorbilder nachzuahmen, was ihren Lebensstil und ihr Aussehen angeht.
5. Jeder weiß, dass das Aussehen der Stars durch Photoshop verändert wird.
6. Trotzdem wollen viele Jugendliche wie diese Vorbilder aussehen.
7. Manche Jugendliche achten aus Gesundheitsgründen auf ihr Aussehen.
8. Viele bleiben nur wegen ihres Aussehens fit.

Übung Macht den Meister!

A Present Passive

Turn the following present tense sentences into the present passive.

1. Man isst hier gesunde Gerichte.	**6.** Man befolgt strikte Regeln.
2. Jugendliche schätzen ihre Gesundheit.	**7.** Die Medien beeinflussen die Jugend.
3. Ich vermeide fettiges Essen.	**8.** Ich esse viel Obst und Gemüse.
4. Man trinkt viel Wasser.	**9.** Man verändert das Aussehen der Topstars.
5. Die Schule legt viel Wert auf Sport.	**10.** Junge Leute verbringen viel Zeit online.

B Imperfect Passive

Turn the following imperfect sentences into the imperfect passive.

1. Man aß dort vegetarische Gerichte.	**6.** Bewegung spielte eine entscheidende Rolle.
2. Jugendliche fanden gesunde Ernährung wichtig.	**7.** Viele Jugendliche kauften Sporttrikots.
3. Man aß viel Eiweiß.	**8.** Manche Jugendliche tranken zu viel Alkohol.
4. Man vermied zu viel Zucker.	**9.** Die Kinder aßen viel Fastfood.
5. Jugendliche entwickelten gesunde Essgewohnheiten.	**10.** Man bot Sportunterricht an.

C Present and Imperfect Passive

Turn the following present and imperfect passive sentences into the active voice.

1. Die Frau wurde von der Polizei verhaftet.	**6.** Diese Marke wird in Online-Shops verkauft.
2. Der Junge wird vom Präsidenten gelobt.	**7.** Fritz wird vom Chef angestellt.
3. Der Mann wurde durch einen Unfall getötet.	**8.** Die Menschen wurden vom Mann gefilmt.
4. Zwei Tonnen Kokain wurden von der Polizei beschlagnahmt.	**9.** Die Regeln werden von den Sportlern strikt befolgt.
5. Zehn Millionen DVDs wurden weltweit verkauft.	**10.** Das Auto wurde von Dieben gestohlen.

D The Passive

Translate the following passive sentences into English.

1. Er wurde beobachtet.	**6.** Ein Mädchen wurde verletzt.
2. Wir wurden verfolgt.	**7.** Drei Menschen werden von den Zollbeamten befragt.
3. Die Drogen wurden in einem Auto entdeckt.	**8.** Die Täter werden ins Gefängnis gebracht.
4. Täglich werden Menschen getötet.	**9.** Die zwei Frauen wurden bestraft.
5. Menschen werden ermordet.	**10.** Die Soldaten wurden erschossen.

E Nationalities

Insert the appropriate word (country, language, person, adjective).

1. ___ sind gastfreundlich.	*The Germans are friendly.*
2. Ich mag ___ Essen.	*I like German food.*
3. Ich finde ___ leicht.	*I find German easy.*
4. ___ ist ein schönes Land.	*Austria is a beautiful country.*
5. ___ Küche ist lecker.	*Austrian cuisine is delicious.*
6. ___ sind sehr politisch engagiert.	*The Irish are very involved in politics.*
7. ___ Jugendliche gehen gern in die Kneipe.	*Irish young people like going to the pub.*
8. Camogie ist eine ___ Sportart.	*Camogie is an Irish sport.*

Für die Prüfung

1. Was passt zusammen?

1. Viele Jugendliche gehen ins Fitnessstudio,	**A** nur weil sie gut aussehen wollen.
2. Einige bleiben fit,	**B** da sie gute Ernährung wichtig finden.
3. Andere essen gesund,	**C** von Steroiden und Diätpillen informieren.
4. Manche greifen zu Steroiden,	**D** um ihre Muskeln aufzubauen.
5. Man muss sich über die Gefahren	**E** um ihre Muskeln auszudefinieren.

2. Was passt zusammen?

1. Um mich fit zu halten,	**A** also esse ich viel Obst und Gemüse.
2. Ich lege viel Wert auf gesundes Essen,	**B** nur um gut auszusehen.
3. Ich esse lieber Bio-Lebensmittel,	**C** denn er will Profi-Sportler werden.
4. Viele Jugendliche befolgen strikte Essregeln,	**D** gehe ich regelmäßig ins Fitnessstudio.
5. Er geht jeden Tag zum Fitnesstraining,	**E** um Zusatzstoffe zu vermeiden.

3. Insert the correct prepositions for the following sentences.

a) Ich lege viel Wert **(auf/am/für/in)** mein Aussehen.

b) Er interessiert sich **(an/am/für/in)** Fitness.

c) Sie sehen schöne Fotos ihrer Vorbilder **(an/in/im/auf)** Internet.

d) Ich spreche viel **(mit/über/in/im)** die Gefahren von Steroiden.

e) Wir haben Interesse **(für/in/an/bei)** diesem Lebensstil.

f) Sie informiert sich **(an/über/in/am)** Diätpillen und Steroide.

4. What words make up the following compound words, and what do they mean in English?

a) Fitnessstudio = ___ + ___ = ___

b) proteinreich = ___ + ___ = ___

c) fettarm = ___ + ___ = ___

d) zuckerreich = ___ + ___ = ___

e) aufbauen = ___ + ___ = ___

f) abbauen = ___ + ___ = ___

5. Indicate whether the underlined verbs are in the present or imperfect passive.

a) Die Jugendlichen <u>wurden gesehen</u>.

b) Der Mann <u>wurde gekidnappt</u>.

c) Was <u>wird getan</u> um dieses Problem zu lösen?

d) Wir <u>werden verfolgt</u>.

e) Du <u>wirst bestraft</u>.

f) Das Handy <u>wird verkauft</u>.

6. Translate the following passive sentences into German.

a) The culprit was arrested by the police.

b) The drugs were found in a car.

c) The diet pills were sold online.

d) People are being killed every day.

e) Young people are harmed by the drug.

f) The stars are being followed by their fans.

7. Lückentext: Fill in the blanks with the correct missing words from the box.

Irland	**deutsche**	**Iren**	**Englisch**	**Deutscher**
deutsches	**Irisch**	**Deutsch**	**irisches**	**irische**

Ich bin **1** ________ aber wohne seit acht Jahren in **2** ________ . Ich kann fließend **3** ________ sprechen aber **4** ________ ist natürlich meine Muttersprache. Ich esse gern **5** ________ Essen aber ich vermisse die **6** ________ Küche schon, besonders **7** ________ Brot. In der Schule lerne ich auch **8** ________ , aber ich finde die **9** ________ Grammatik kompliziert. Ich finde die **10** ________ aber sehr lustig und freundlich.

Selbstbewertung: Ordinary Level

OL

Vocabulary

1. If I can translate theses sentences into English, I can talk about health and fitness. (1 mark each)

a) Ich bleibe gern fit und gesund.	**f)** Irische Jugendliche essen relativ gesund.
b) Ich trinke viel Wasser, wenn ich Sport treibe.	**g)** Sie mögen es auch, Fotos ihrer Vorbilder im Internet zu sehen.
c) Ich rauche nicht.	**h)** Viele Jugendliche finden ihr Aussehen wichtig.
d) Ich trinke nur wenig Alkohol.	**i)** Manche gehen zum Fitnessstudio.
e) Ich mache gern Sport.	**j)** Einige nehmen Steroide und Diätpillen.

Your score: ___ / 10

2. If I can translate these nouns into German, I understand the main nouns needed to describe health and fitness. (1 mark each)

a) health	**c)** gym	**e)** vegetables	**g)** sugar	**i)** meat
b) fitness	**d)** fruit	**f)** fat	**h)** carbohydrates	**j)** appearance

Your score: ___ / 10

Grammar

3. If I can conjugate these verbs in the 'they' form in the present and perfect tenses, I can talk about health and fitness. (1 mark for each tense)
   a) gehen: they go ___________ they went ___________
   b) nehmen: they take ___________ they took ___________
   c) essen: they eat ___________ they ate ___________
   d) denken: they think ___________ they thought ___________
   e) trainieren: they train ___________ they trained ___________

Your score: ___ / 10

4. If I can choose the correct conjunction, I can use complex sentences. (2 marks each)
   a) Ich finde mein Aussehen wichtig, **(also/um)** bleibe ich fit.
   b) Viele Jugendliche gehen zum Fitnessstudio, **(also/um)** fit zu werden.
   c) Jugendliche nehmen Diätpillen, **(also/um)** gut auszusehen.
   d) Wir essen viel Obst und Gemüse, **(also/um)** gesund zu bleiben.
   e) Ich esse viel Protein, **(also/um)** sind meine Muskeln ausdefiniert.

Your score: ___ / 10

5. If I can choose the correct preposition, I understand the prepositions needed to describe health and fitness. (1 mark each)

a) Ich interessiere mich nicht **(in/auf/für/an)** Fitness.	**f)** Man sollte sich **(für/an/in/über)** die Gefahren informieren.
b) Ich mache schon Sport **(in/bei/für/an)** der Schule.	**g)** Ich schwimme täglich **(an/in/für/auf)** 30 Minuten.
c) Jedoch konzentriere ich mich nicht **(mit/auf/an/seit)** mein Aussehen.	**h)** Ich bin ein großer Fan **(an/von/der/vom)** klassischen Musik.
d) Man sollte nicht so viel Interesse **(über/im/am/in)** Aussehen haben.	**i)** Sie gehen jeden Tag **(zu/in/auf/ins)** Fitnessstudio.
e) Ich sehe viele retuschierte Fotos **(über/von/bei/an)** den Stars.	**j)** Ich verfolge die Olympischen Spiele **(auf/zu/mit/in)** großem Interesse.

Your score: ___ / 10

What have I learned?	
What must I improve?	
What do I want to revise?	

Your total score: ___ / 50

Selbstbewertung: Higher Level

HL

1. If I can translate these sentences into German, I can use verbs and adjectives to describe health and fitness issues. (2 marks each)

   a) Personally I go to the gym three times a week to stay fit.
   b) Many young people are interested in their appearance.
   c) Some young people keep fit in order to look good.
   d) Others keep fit in order to stay healthy.
   e) Unfortunately, some young people take dangerous steroids to build up their muscles.

Your score: ___ / 10

2. If I can translate these sentences into German, I can use verbs, adverbs and conjunctions to describe health and fitness. (2 marks each)

   a) They should inform themselves about the dangers of steroids and diet pills.
   b) More information should be provided about the consequences of taking drugs.
   c) I firmly believe that there should be more sport on school timetables.
   d) Nobody can deny that young people are often influenced by the stars.
   e) They try to imitate the stars, even if their photos have been airbrushed.

Your score: ___ / 10

3. If I can translate these sentences into German, I understand how to use the passive. (2 marks each)

a) Young people are influenced by the media.	**d)** They were found by the police.
b) Diet pills are being bought online every day.	**e)** They are being harmed by the drugs.
c) People were filmed at the party.	

Your score: ___ / 10

4. If I can correctly fill in the gaps below, I understand word functions. (1 mark each)

versuche mich Woche essen negativen an über Fett kann gesund

Ich trainiere dreimal die **1** ___________ um **2** ___________ fit zu halten. Ich **3** ___________ auch wenig **4** ___________ und mehr Protein zu **5** ___________ . Ich habe viel Interesse **6** ___________ Fitness, denn man **7** ___________ viel mehr schaffen, wenn man **8** ___________ ist. Man muss die Jugendlichen von den **9** ___________ Konsequenzen von Steroiden bewusst machen, und sie auch **10** ___________ die Realität von retuschierten Fotos informieren.

Your score: ___ / 10

5. If I can translate these sentences into German, I can talk about nations, nationalities, languages and culture. (2 marks each)

   a) I come from Poland but I have been living in Ireland for the last four years.
   b) My mother tongue is Irish but I speak English most of the time.
   c) I have been learning German for four years and find German culture very interesting.
   d) The Germans are very friendly and hard-working, just like the Irish.
   e) German food is delicious, especially German sausages and bread.

Your score: ___ / 10

What have I learned?	
What must I improve?	
What do I want to revise?	

Your total score: ___ / 50

14 Umwelt

Learning Outcomes

- **Oral:** discussing environmental issues; revise picture sequences and role plays
- **Reading:** reading and discussing three texts on the environment
- **Writing:** writing an opinion (**Äußerung**), a picture description and letter about the environment
- **Aural:** listening to and answering questions on four extracts on the environment

Grammar

- Negation: **nicht** and **kein**
- Alternative forms of negation
- Difficult words and false friends

Vocabulary

- Naming environmental issues
- Solutions to environmental issues

German Culture

- German environmental awareness
- German idioms

Exam Tips

- Gather as many expressions as you can from the listening and reading comprehensions and use them in your oral and written work.
- Add each new grammar point to your grammar checklist. This will help you use a wide variety of grammatical structures in both your oral and written work.
- Add a selection of negative and positive expressions to your oral and written work in order to improve your expression mark.

Text 1: 10 Tipps, wie wir die Umwelt schützen können

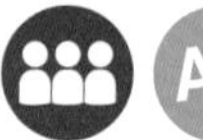 Bitte beantworten Sie die folgenden Fragen:

1. Was sieht man auf dem Bild?
2. Wie sieht die Landschaft aus?
3. Was machen die Menschen?

Vorarbeit

1. Finden Sie diese Ausdrücke im Text!
   - **A** Forego packaging ...
   - **B** ... everything is available at all times.
   - **C** ... because they are out of date.
   - **D** That saves ... a lot of exhaust fumes ...
   - **E** ... that mould forms on the walls of the room(s).
2. Finden Sie das Deutsche für die Wörter unten!
   - **A** to create/worn out/reusable/rags
   - **B** fuel consumption/more sustainably
   - **C** use/exception/be disposed of
   - **D** public transport/multiple sockets
   - **E** fling open/electricity consumption

Antenne Niedersachsen website (amended)

A **Weniger Müll verursachen:** Es ist wichtig, den Müll drastisch zu reduzieren. Ihr solltet beim Einkaufen möglichst wenige Produkte kaufen, die in Plastik eingepackt sind. Verpacke deine Einkäufe in einer wiederverwertbaren Stofftasche. Verzichtet auf Verpackungen wie To-Go-Becher für Kaffee.

Dinge wiederverwenden: Nutzt Behälter, die man wiederverwenden kann, und Materialien, die sich recyceln lassen. Ausgediente T-Shirts sind noch gut, um als Lappen benutzt zu werden.

B **Weniger konsumieren:** In unserer Gesellschaft steht uns jederzeit alles zur Verfügung. Deshalb kauft man oft mehr als man benötigt. Die jährlichen Trends sind für viele verlockend. Da diese Waren produziert und transportiert werden müssen, fallen entsprechend CO_2-Emissionen und Müll an. Tragt eure Kleidung länger anstatt sie jedes Jahr gegen neue auszutauschen.

Nachhaltiger essen: Ihr könnt die Umwelt schützen, wenn ihr weniger Fisch und Meeresfrüchte esst. Ein Großteil der Fischbestände ist durch Überfischung bedroht. Greift lieber zu regionalen Lebensmitteln, die nicht für einen enormen Spritverbrauch gesorgt haben.

C **Weniger Lebensmittel wegwerfen:** Im Supermarkt könnt ihr darauf achten, wie viel ihr einkauft. Viele Lebensmittel müssen im Müll entsorgt werden, weil sie abgelaufen sind. Man sollte nur das kaufen, was tatsächlich auch gebraucht wird.

Wasser sparen: Viele lassen das Wasser laufen, wenn sie sich beim Duschen einseifen oder die Zähne putzen. Baden verbraucht mehr Wasser als Duschen. Deswegen sollten Vollbäder die Ausnahme sein.

D **Weniger Auto fahren:** Wenn ihr zu Fuß gehen oder mit dem Rad fahren könnt, solltet ihr auf das Auto verzichten. Das erspart der Luft eine Menge Abgase und spart Sprit. Ihr könnt die öffentlichen Verkehrsmittel nutzen.

Strom sparen: Benutzt nur Lampen mit LED-Technik oder Energiesparlampen. Das senkt die Kosten auf der Stromrechnung und ist gut für die Umwelt. Elektronische Geräte verbrauchen im Standby-Modus immer noch Strom. Steckt solche Geräte in Mehrfachsteckdosen mit einem zentralen Schalter ein!

E **Energie sparen:** Wer richtig lüftet, kann viel Heizenergie sparen. Reißt mehrmals am Tag die Fenster für ein paar Minuten auf. Das verhindert, dass sich an den Zimmerwänden Schimmel bildet. Um die Heizkosten und die Umweltbelastung durch CO_2 zu senken, kann man die Raumtemperatur um nur 1 Grad Celsius herunterdrehen. Der Kühlschrank ist ein großer Stromfresser. Wer in Urlaub fährt, sollte den Kühlschrank ganz abschalten, um den Stromverbrauch zu reduzieren.

OL Ordinary Level Questions

1. a) According to the text, what are **two** ways one can reduce rubbish? A
   b) Name **two** methods for consuming less, according to the text. B
   c) Name **two** methods suggested by the text for saving water. C
   d) Name **two** suggested methods for saving electricity. D
   e) According to the text, what is **one** method for saving on heating costs? E
2. True or false?
   a) Du sollst deine Einkäufe in Plastiktüten einpacken.
   b) Man muss nicht jedes Jahr neue Kleidung kaufen.
   c) Wenn man Wasser spart, schützt man die Umwelt.
   d) Wenn man mit dem Auto fährt, schützt man die Umwelt.
   e) Man kann die Heizkosten reduzieren, wenn man die Raumtemperatur aufdreht.
3. What words make up the following compound words, and what do they mean in English?
   a) Überfischung = ___ + ___ = ___
   b) Lebensmittel = ___ + ___ = ___
   c) wegwerfen = ___ + ___ = ___
   d) Kühlschrank = ___ + ___ = ___
4. Select the correct prepositions for the following sentences.
   a) **(Am/Im/Um/Beim)** Einkaufen soll man auf möglichst wenig Verpackung achten.
   b) Die Fischbestände werden **(durch/von/für/gegen)** Überfischung bedroht.
   c) Man kann **(mit/an/beim/für)** Duschen Wasser sparen.
   d) Man soll so oft wie möglich **(an/auf/um/in)** das Auto verzichten.

HL Higher Level Questions

1. Beantworten Sie folgende Fragen auf Deutsch!
   a) Wie kann man, laut Text, weniger Müll verursachen? Geben Sie **drei** Beispiele! A
   b) Wie kann man, laut Text, weniger konsumieren? Geben Sie **drei** Beispiele! B
   c) Geben Sie **drei** Beispiele, wie man weniger Wasser verbrauchen könnte! C
   d) Wie kann man Strom sparen? Geben Sie mehrere Beispiele! D
   e) Warum ist es vorteilhaft, die Fenster regelmäßig aufzureißen? E
2. Answer the following questions in English.
   a) Give **two** examples given in the text of household items which can be recycled. A
   b) When goods are transported, what **two** consequences does this have on the environment? B
   c) According to the text, how could one throw away less food? C
   d) Name **two** techniques mentioned in the text for saving electricity. D
   e) Name **two** methods for reducing heating costs. E
3. Was passt zusammen?

1. Wir sollen Plastik vermeiden,	**A** was man wirklich braucht.
2. Wenn man nachhaltiger isst,	**B** wenn man zu Fuß geht oder mit dem Rad fährt.
3. Man soll nur das kaufen,	**C** wenn man richtig lüftet.
4. Man spart Abgase,	**D** um Müll zu reduzieren.
5. Man kann viel Heizenergie sparen,	**E** schützt man die Umwelt.

4. Geben Sie für die unterstrichenen Nomen an: ob Singular oder Plural, bei Singular das Geschlecht, den Fall.
   a) Es ist wichtig, den Müll zu reduzieren.
   b) Heuzutage steht alles zur Verfügung.
   c) Stellt das Wasser einfach ab.
   d) Das ist gut für die Umwelt.

Grammatik: Verneinung/Negation

p. 273 (Übung macht den Meister)

Kein means 'no', 'not a' and 'none'. **Kein** is used to negate a noun.

Es gibt keine Äpfel. There are no apples.

Gibt es Äpfel? Nein, es gibt keine. Are there apples? No, there are none.

The endings to **kein** change according to the number, the gender and the case of the noun. The endings follow the same pattern as the indefinite article (see page 115).

Add the correct ending to **kein** in the following sentences.

1. Ich habe kein___ Wagen.	**6.** Ich habe kein___ Frau getroffen.
2. Mein Vater ist kein___ Geschäftsmann.	**7.** Warum hast du kein___ Projekt gemacht?
3. Kein___ Mädchen kommen zu der Party.	**8.** Ich kenne leider kein___ deutschen Filme.
4. Ich habe kein___ Menschen davon erzählt.	**9.** Thorsten redet mit kein___ Schüler.
5. Er mag kein___ Bananen.	**10.** Heute ist kein___ schöner Tag.

You should use **nicht** with:

- **A verb: Ich tanze nicht.** I don't dance.
- **An adjective or adverb: Diese Avocado ist nicht reif.** This avocado isn't ripe.
- **A noun** with a definite article (**der, die, das**): **Ich kenne das Buch nicht.** I don't know the book.
- **A noun with a possessive adjective** (**mein**, **dein**, etc.): **Das ist nicht dein Handy.** That's not your phone.

Decide whether to use **nicht** or the appropriate form of **kein** in the following sentences.

1. Ich habe ___ Freizeit im Moment.	**6.** Deine Freunde sind ___ nett.
2. Es ist dunkel und ich kann ___ sehen.	**7.** Leider hat er ___ viel Zeit.
3. Das Kind will ___ schlafen.	**8.** Er spricht ___ Russisch.
4. Ich interessiere mich ___ für Golf.	**9.** Meine Schwester hat ___ Kinder.
5. Er kauft ___ Wagen.	**10.** Die Geschichte ist ___ wahr.

Nicht will usually precede the specific word that is being negated.

In a sentence with one verb, put **nicht** at the end of the phrase:

Ich sehe ihn nicht. I don't see him.

In a sentence with more than one verb, put **nicht** before the second verb:

Ich habe ihn heute nicht gesehen. I haven't seen him today.

Place **nicht** directly after the verb **sein**:

Ich bin nicht reich. I'm not rich.

Place **nicht** before the adverb:

Ich esse nicht viel. I don't eat much.

If **nicht** is used earlier in a sentence, it is used for extra emphasis.

In Irland isst man **nicht** gern Pizza.

Turn the following statements into the negative.

1. Ich mag Mathe.	**6.** Er ist letztes Jahr nach Italien gefahren.
2. Ich habe Maria gestern gesehen.	**7.** Otto ist launisch.
3. Ich bin verwirrt.	**8.** Sie hat die Hausaufgaben gemacht.
4. Ich lerne fleißig.	**9.** Hanna trinkt oft Kaffee.
5. In Irland isst man gern Pizza.	**10.** Wir gehen in die Stadt.

14.01 Hörverständnis Teil 1

Vorarbeit

Grafschaft	*county*	**anerkannt**	*recognised*	**mittelalterlich**	*medieval*
Felseninsel	*rocky island*	**Kalkstein**	*limestone*	**Halbinsel**	*peninsula*
unterirdisch	*underground*	**überschüttet**	*showered*	**Höhle**	*cave*
Kloster	*monastery*	**Weltnaturerbe**	*World Heritage site*		

CL Ordinary + Higher Level Questions

1. What do we find out about Sylvia and her job? Give **two (O)/four (H)** details.
2. What can visitors experience **a)** in Kerry and **b)** in Clare? Give **two (O)/four (H)** details.
3. How does Sylvia describe the Burren? Give **three (O)/five (H)** details.
4. **a)** What can visitors do in Galway? Give **one (O)/two (H)** details.
   b) What information is given about Cork? Give **two (O)/four (H)** details.
5. How can one get further information?

14.02 Hörverständnis Teil 2

Vorarbeit

öko	*eco*	**Terminkalender**	*schedule*	**verdrehen**	*to twist*
Ölleck	*oil spill (small)*	**bestätigen**	*to confirm*	**entsetzt**	*appalled*
Stellungnahme	*statement*	**strömen**	*to stream*	**Ölpest**	*oil spill (big)*

OL Ordinary Level Questions

1. With whom does the caller wish to speak, and what is the caller's profession?
2. What is the caller's surname and e-mail address?
3. The caller is complaining about:
   a) high oil prices ☐ **b)** an oil spill ☐ **c)** a strike ☐ **d)** oil restrictions ☐

HL Higher Level Questions

1. Using ***key phrases***, write down **in German** the key information the caller provides:
   - the name of the person **making** the call
   - the reason for the call
   - **four** details of their conversation
   - details regarding further contact
   - the recipient's e-mail address

Gesprächsnotiz

Anruf von: ______________ Gesprächsanlass: ______________

Die Anruferin:

- wird heute eine E-Mail schicken ☐
- erwartet morgen keine E-Mail ☐
- wird eine E-Mail erhalten ☐
- wird eine SMS erhalten ☐

E-Mailadresse: ______________________________

2. Write down **three** examples of the language which show the caller's **concern**.

Text 2: Umweltkatastrophe im Regenwald

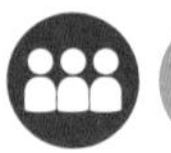  Bitte beantworten Sie die folgenden Fragen:

1. Was sehen Sie auf diesem Foto?
2. Was machen die Männer?
3. Was ist hier passiert, Ihrer Meinung nach?

Vorarbeit

1. Finden Sie diese Ausdrücke im Text!
   - **A** Highly poisonous substances ...
   - **B** ... about the earth's ecological wealth.
   - **C** ... the alleged perpetrator of the disaster ...
   - **D** The environmental activist demands ...
2. Finden Sie das Deutsche für die Wörter unten!
   - **A** dams/washed away/foreseeable/mine
   - **B** is reporting about/experienced/ever
   - **C** agriculture/earthquake/disaster
   - **D** damages/comparable/to redress

A Hochgiftige Substanzen strömen seit einer Woche in den Ozean an der brasilianischen Küste. Im November sind zwei Dämme eines Bergwerkes im Südosten Brasiliens gebrochen. Millionen von Kubikmetern Wasser voller Arsen und anderer Gifte haben ein Dorf weggespült. Dabei sind 17 Menschen getötet worden. Überall liegen tote Fische. Die Folgen dieser Umweltkatastrophe sind noch nicht absehbar.

B Ein brasilianischer Umweltaktivist macht gerade eine Dokumentation über den ökologischen Reichtum der Erde. Jetzt berichtet er über diese Situation in Brasilien. Er behauptet, es sei die größte ökologische Katastrophe, die das Land jemals erlebt habe. Es lebt nichts mehr in diesem Fluss.

C Die Minenfirma, die der angebliche Verursacher der Katastrophe sei, übernimmt keine Verantwortung für das Unglück.
Die Chefs der Minenfirma behaupten, ein Erdbeben habe den Dammbruch ausgelöst.
Der Umweltaktivist behauptet auch, dass aggressive, intensive Landwirtschaft dafür verantwortlich sei.

D Um die Schäden zu beseitigen, sind 1,25 Milliarden Dollar notwendig.
Der Umweltaktivist fordert, dass die multinationale Firma sofort handelt: Das Desaster in Brasilien ist vergleichbar mit der Explosion der Ölplattform „Deepwater Horizon" im Golf von Mexiko. British Petroleum musste eine Entschädigung von mehreren Milliarden Dollar zahlen. Großfirmen müssen in Zukunft verantwortlicher handeln.

Kulturecke

Wie können Sie persönlich die Umwelt schützen? Übersetzen Sie ins Englische!

- Man sollte auf erneuerbare Energie umsteigen.
- Gute Wärmedämmung heißt kleinere Energierechnungen.
- Man sollte abschalten, anstatt ein Gerät auf Standby zu stellen.
- Ich versuche Müll zu vermeiden, indem ich so viel wie möglich recycle.
- Man sollte regional und saisonal einkaufen, um Verschmutzung zu reduzieren.
- Wir müssen immer umweltfreundlich handeln.
- Ich bevorzuge natürliche Produkte, wie Holz statt Plastik.
- Wenn man Produkte mit Umwelt-Gütesiegeln kauft, trägt man positiv zur Umwelt bei.

OL Ordinary Level Questions

1. a) Where are the poisonous materials coming from, according to the text? A
   b) How does the environmental activist describe the scene? Give **two** details. B
   c) What was the cause of the dam breaking, according to the owners of the mining company? C
   d) How much money is needed to rectify the damages done? D
2. True or false?
   a) Die giftigen Substanzen fließen in den Fluss.
   b) Der Umweltaktivist macht gerade einen Dokumentarfilm.
   c) Die Besitzer der Firma sagen, dass ein Erdbeben den Unfall verursacht hat.
   d) Das Desaster in Brasilien war schlimmer als das Desaster im Golf von Mexico.
3. What words make up the following compounds? What do they mean in English?
   a) Kubikmeter = ___ + ___ = ___
   b) Minenfirma = ___ + ___ + ___ = ___
   c) Dammbruch = ___ + ___ = ___
   d) Ölplattform = ___ + ___ = ___
4. Select the correct prepositions for the following sentences.
   a) Millionen **(von/an/vom/am)** Kubikmetern dieser Giftsubstanzen haben das Dorf weggespült.
   b) Der Aktivist sieht **(an/aus/mit/an)** seinen eigenen Augen das Desaster.
   c) Die Minenfirma übernimmt keine Verantwortung **(an/für/in/mit)** das Unglück.
   d) Das Desaster **(in/im/an/am)** Brasilien war schlimm.

HL Higher Level Questions

1. Beantworten Sie folgende Fragen auf Deutsch.
   a) Beschreiben Sie genau das Desaster in Brasilien. A
   b) Wer berichtet über das Desaster? Geben Sie **zwei** Details! B
   c) Wer ist laut dem Umweltaktivisten für das Desaster verantwortlich? C
   d) Womit hat der Aktivist das Desaster in Brasilien verglichen? D
2. Answer the following questions in English.
   a) Give **four** details about the disaster and its consequences. A
   b) Give details about the activist's reaction to the disaster. B
   c) How did the mining company react to the disaster? C
   d) Give details about the costs needed to deal with the disaster. D
3. Was passt zusammen?

1. Seitdem zwei Dämme gebrochen sind,	**A** wegen der giftigen Substanzen.
2. Der Aktivist ärgert sich sehr	**B** dass ein Erdbeben das Desaster verursacht habe.
3. Die Bergbaufirma behauptet,	**C** strömen giftige Substanzen in den Ozean.
4. Nichts mehr lebt in dem Fluss	**D** um die Schäden zu überwinden.
5. Über eine Milliarde Dollar sind erforderlich,	**E** über das Desaster.

4. Geben Sie für die Verben an: Zeitform, ob Singular oder Plural, Infinitivform.
   a) Im November sind zwei Dämme einer Mine im Südosten Brasiliens gebrochen.
   b) Ein brasilianischer Umweltaktivist berichtete über das Desaster.
   c) Der Aktivist schickt der multinationalen Firma eine klare Herausforderung.
   d) 1,25 Milliarden Dollar sind notwendig, um die Schäden zu beseitigen.

OL  Äußerung zum Thema: Ordinary Level

You are interviewing the activist. Complete the dialogue, using the information from Text 2.

Sie:	Was machen Sie beruflich?
Aktivist:	______________________
Sie:	Beschreiben Sie das Desaster in Brasilien!
Aktivist:	______________________
Sie:	Wer ist für das Desaster verantwortlich, glauben Sie?
Aktivist:	______________________
Sie:	Was behauptet die Minenfirma?
Aktivist:	______________________
Sie:	Wie viel Geld würde man brauchen, um die Kosten des Desasters zu bezahlen?
Aktivist:	______________________

HL Äußerung zum Thema: Higher Level

Write 13 to 15 sentences, answering the questions below.

- Beschreiben Sie das Foto rechts in **drei bis vier** Sätzen.
- Was für Umweltprobleme gibt es heutzutage?
- Was kann man tun, um diese Probleme zu lösen?
- Was tun Sie persönlich, um die Umwelt zu schützen?

 Nützliche Sätze

Übersetzen Sie folgende Sätze ins Englische.

1. Auf dem Bild sieht man einen Fluss, der in den Tropen ist.
2. Der Fluss wird offensichtlich durch giftige Substanzen verseucht.
3. In unseren Flüssen und Seen kommt es zum Fischsterben.
4. Vielleicht liegt das Problem an Pestiziden und Giftstoffen, die aus Fabriken in den Fluss fließen.
5. Ohne Zweifel belasten Pestizide und Düngemittel unsere Gewässer und Lebensräume.
6. Heutzutage gibt es ernste Umweltprobleme, wie zum Beispiel die Verseuchung unserer Flüsse und Meere, ganz zu schweigen von der Luftverschmutzung.
7. Es sollte so viel wie möglich recycelt werden, um die riesigen Müllberge zu reduzieren.
8. Man sagt, dass Klimawandel Extremwetter verursacht, aber ich bin nicht völlig davon überzeugt.
9. Wenn Plastiktüten im Meer landen, bedrohen sie die Tiere, die dort leben.
10. Das kann katastrophale Auswirkungen auf unsere Welt haben.
11. Nachhaltig leben ist die neue Herausforderung mit großen Chancen für uns alle.
12. Es gibt ständig Umweltberichte mit klassischen Themen wie Abfall, Waldsterben oder nachhaltige Lebensweise in den Medien.
13. Niemand kann abstreiten, dass Tier- und Vogelarten ausgerottet werden.
14. Müll und Abwasser verseuchen unsere Flüsse und Meere.
15. Unsere Meere versinken im Plastikmüll.
16. Man kann nur schwer die Auswirkungen dieser Verschmutzung schätzen.
17. Zu Hause trennen wir den Müll und sparen so viel Wasser wie möglich.
18. Die Zahl der Anti-Dumping-Fälle nimmt zu.
19. Meiner Meinung nach sollten wir alle besser auf das Anti-Dumpinggesetz achten.
20. Ohne Zweifel ist die Kernkraftenergie zu riskant.
21. Ich bin davon überzeugt, dass saubere Energiequellen notwendig sind.
22. Beim Zähneputzen drehe ich immer den Wasserhahn ab.

Grammatik: Verneinung/Negation

p. 273 (Übung macht den Meister)

Alternative Methods of Negation

Negation	Example
nie never	**Er kommt** nie. He never comes.
niemals never	**Sie redet** niemals. She never talks.
niemand nobody	Niemand **kann es tun.** Nobody can do it.
nirgendwo nowhere	**Es liegt** nirgendwo. It's nowhere.
nicht ... sondern not ... but rather	**Ich habe** nicht **Samstag frei,** sondern **Sonntag.** I am not free on Saturday but rather on Sunday.
nicht nur ... sondern auch not only ... but also	**Ich habe** nicht nur **am Montag frei,** sondern auch **am Dienstag.** I am not only free on Monday but also on Tuesday.
nicht mehr no more/ no longer	**Wir haben** kein **Brot** mehr. We have no more bread. **Er arbeitet hier** nicht mehr. He doesn't work here any longer.
noch nicht not yet	**Ich bin** noch nicht **fertig.** I'm not finished yet.
weder ... noch neither ... nor	**Wir haben** weder **Brot** noch **Käse.** We have neither bread nor cheese.
nichts nothing	**Er hat** nichts **gesehen.** He didn't see anything.
doch yes, on the contrary	**Kommst du nicht mit?** Doch, **ich komme mit.** Are you not coming with us? Yes, I am.

Negatives and Positives

Negative	Positive
nie; **nimmer**; **niemals** never	**immer** always
niemand nobody	**jemand** someone **jedermann** everyone
nirgendwo nowhere	**irgendwo** somewhere **überall** everywhere

Prüfungstipp

Add a selection of negative and positive expressions to your oral and written work in order to improve your expression mark.

Turn the following sentences from the negative into the positive.

1. Ich bin nie faul.	**5.** Das Kind hat nichts gemacht.
2. Niemand hat ihn gesehen.	**6.** Ich werde niemals Ski fahren.
3. Das ist nirgendwo zu finden.	**7.** Die Polizei hat niemanden verhaftet.
4. Ich mag weder Tee noch Kaffee.	**8.** Man konnte sich nirgendwo verstecken.

Kulturecke

What do these German idioms mean in English?

1. Das ist nicht mein Bier.	**A** Nothing ventured, nothing gained.
2. Ich bin keine Kuh, die man melken kann.	**B** Time waits for no man.
3. Danach kräht kein Hahn mehr.	**C** There's no time like the present.
4. Wer nicht wagt, der nicht gewinnt.	**D** That's not my business.
5. Was du heute kannst besorgen, das verschiebe nicht auf morgen.	**E** The apple doesn't fall far from the tree.
6. Die Uhr bleibt stehen, aber die Zeit nicht.	**F** I'm not made of money.
7. Kümmere dich nicht um ungelegte Eier.	**G** Don't count your chickens before they hatch.
8. Der Apfel fällt nicht weit vom Stamm.	**H** No one gives a hoot about that any more.

Text 3: Die Abenteuer eines Seefahrers

Bitte beantworten Sie die folgenden Fragen:

1. Was sieht man auf dem Bild?
2. Wie ist das Wetter?
3. Ist das Schiff in Gefahr, Ihrer Meinung nach?

Vorarbeit

1. Finden Sie diese Ausdrücke im Text!
   - **A** One of my biggest adventures required ...
   - **B** At a distance of one kilometre we set anchor.
   - **C** ... and gave them to the locals.
   - **D** ... the boat could break into pieces.
   - **E** ... with my upper body ... over the railing ...
2. Finden Sie das Deutsche für die Wörter unten!
   - **A** rainforest/survived/air/nightmare
   - **B** asked/crew/groceries/bay/did
   - **C** already/invited/gratitude/boat driver/jetty
   - **D** storm/tropics/steamboat/reached
   - **E** sailor/accelerated/ghost ship/ship's goblin

A Eines meiner größten Abenteuer erforderte ganz viel Glück, denn ich habe es fast nicht überlebt. Wir fuhren dicht an der westafrikanischen Küste entlang, so dass wir das Grün des Regenwaldes sehen konnten, während Albatrosse dem Schiff folgten. Sie schienen in der Luft zu stehen. Die Sonne schien, und wer wüsste, dass der nächste Hafen zu einem Alptraum für mich werden sollte.

B Man konnte in der Bucht einige Hütten sehen. Mit einer Entfernung von einem Kilometer warfen wir die Anker. Die Mannschaft diskutierte, ob wir ins blaue Wasser springen sollten oder nicht. Der Chefsteward bat mich zum Kapitän zu kommen, denn der Koch, der der wichtigste Mann neben dem Kapitän an Bord ist, hatte eine Liste von Lebensmitteln, die ich holen musste. Ich tat, was ich konnte, denn meine Besatzung war ja auch noch da.

C Also fuhr ich mit dem Boot zum afrikanischen Dorf. Ich hatte nach einer Stunde mehrere 50 kg Säcke gefüllt und gab sie den lokalen Bewohnern. Als das Motorboot wieder da war, erklärte mir der Bootsführer, dass ich aus Dankbarkeit für die Säcke mit Essen an Land eingeladen war. Als wir am Steg anlegten, wurde ich bereits von einem der Besucher empfangen. Am Ende des Abends zeigte er mir die Sehenswürdigkeiten seines Dorfes. Dann lud er mich zur Übernachtung in sein Haus ein.

D Dann schlief ich bis in den frühen Morgen. Wer einmal ein heftiges Unwetter mit Gewittern und Regen in den Tropen erlebt hat, weiß, wie schlecht das sein kann. Ich stand an der Tür und beobachtete das Inferno der Natur. „Bei dem Wetter können Sie jetzt nicht zurück aufs Schiff", meinte der General. Aber dann rannte ich los und erreichte das Motorboot. Auf dem Weg zum Schiff konnten wir den Dampfer durch das Unwetter gar nicht sehen. Es war so wild, dass wir Angst hatten, dass das Boot in die Brüche gehen könnte.

E Er gab Gas und wir sprangen wie wild durch die Wellen. Das Schiff rollte schwer im Wasser. Es sah wie ein Geisterschiff ohne Mannschaft aus. Ich versuchte an die Leiter zu kommen um an Bord zu gehen. Ich sprang, als ich sicher war, dass ich sie fassen konnte. Aber ich war doch erschrocken, als ich gegen das Schiff prallte. Als ich oben ankam und mich mit dem Oberkörper einfach über die Reling zog, sah ich vor mir einen Matrosen. Er erschrak, weil er glaubte, der Klabautermann stehe ihm gegenüber. Er hätte mich vor Angst fast erschossen! „Stopp!", rief ich laut und sagte ihm meinen Namen. In der Nacht lichteten wir die Anker, neuen Abenteuern entgegen.

© Meinhard Pahlke, 21 Sept. 2012 (amended)

Ordinary Level Questions

1. a) Give **two** details about what the narrator can see from his ship. A
   b) Where did the narrator and the crew put down their anchors? B
   c) Why did the locals invite the narrator on land? C
   d) What did the general say to the narrator as he looked out at the raging storm? D
   e) Give **two** details about how he got back to his ship. E
2. Choose a suitable heading for each paragraph and explain your choice in English.

Endlich wieder an Bord	Die Einheimischen laden mich ein	Der Kapitän bittet mich zu kommen	Die schöne Küste Westafrikas	Der Sturm beginnt

3. Indicate whether the following sentences are true or false according to the text.
   a) Sie konnten den Regenwald sehen.
   b) Der Koch bat ihn zum Kapitän zu kommen.
   c) Er fuhr mit dem Schiff zum Hafen.
   d) Das Wetter war super schön.
   e) Er prallte gegen das Schiff.
4. Separate these compound words into their components and translate them into English.
   a) Lebensmittel = ___ + ___ = ___
   b) Geisterschiff = ___ + ___ = ___
   c) Motorboot = ___ + ___ = ___
   d) Oberkörper = ___ + ___ = ___

Higher Level Questions

1. Beantworten Sie die folgenden Fragen auf Deutsch!
   a) Beschreiben Sie genau die Aussicht, die man vom Schiff sehen konnte. A
   b) Warum wurde der Erzähler gebeten, zum Kapitän zu kommen? B
   c) Beschreiben Sie, wie der Erzähler ans Land kam. C
   d) Beschreiben Sie genau das Unwetter. D
   e) Wie hat der Erzähler sein Schiff wieder erreicht? E
2. Answer the following questions in English.
   a) Give **three** details which make the scene seem exotic. A
   b) What did the narrator have to do, and why? B
   c) How did the local people greet the narrator, and why? C
   d) Describe in detail the weather conditions the narrator experienced. D
   e) How exactly did he reach his ship and what happened when he got on board? E
   f) Give **four** examples of content and language which show that the narrator finds himself in a tense situation.
3. Was passt zusammen?

1. Vom Schiff konnten wir	**A** hätte ein Matrose mich fast erschossen.
2. Der Kapitän wollte mit mir sprechen,	**B** um Lebensmittel zu kaufen.
3. Weil ich den Bewohnern Lebensmittel gab,	**C** wurde ich zur Übernachtung eingeladen.
4. Ich fuhr mit dem Boot in die Bucht,	**D** den schönen Regenwald sehen.
5. Während ich an Bord kletterte,	**E** also ließ er mich zu sich kommen.

4. Schreiben Sie die unterstrichenen Verben **im Präsens**.
   a) Wir <u>fuhren</u> an der Küste entlang.
   b) Die Sonne <u>schien</u>.
   c) Der Steward <u>bat</u> mich zu kommen.
   d) Dann <u>schlief</u> ich bis in den frühen Morgen.
   e) Ich <u>stand</u> an der Tür.
   f) Es <u>sah</u> wie ein Geisterschiff <u>aus</u>.

Grammatik: Schwierige Wörter/Difficult Words

p. 273 (Übung macht den Meister)

about	**Es war** gegen **Mittag.** It was about midday.
	Ich bleibe ungefähr **eine Woche.** I'm staying about a week.
	Wovon **spricht er?** What is he talking about?
	Ich lese ein Buch über **Deutschland.** I'm reading a book about Germany.
	Ich wollte eben **gehen.** I was about to go.
home	**Ich gehe jetzt** nach Hause. I'm going home now.
	Ich lerne lieber zu Hause. I prefer studying at home.
to know	**Ich** kenne **den Mann nicht.** I don't know the man.
	Ich weiß, **wo die Schule liegt.** I know where the school is located.
	Ich verstehe **wenig davon.** I know little about it.
only	**Es ist** erst **August.** It's only August.
	Das Kleid kostet nur **30 Euro.** The dress only costs 30 euros.
	Sie allein **versteht das Problem.** Only she understands the problem.
to spend	**Ich** gebe **viel Geld dafür aus.** I spend a lot of money on it.
	Wir verbringen **Zeit bei den Großeltern.** We spend time with the grandparents.
that	**Ich glaube,** dass **wir vernünftig sein sollten.** I believe that we should be sensible.
	Ich kann das **nicht verstehen.** I can't understand that.
	Das Mädchen, das **Anna heißt, ist nett.** The girl that (who) is called Anna is nice.
when	Als **ich jung war, wohnten wir in Cork.** When I was young, we lived in Cork.
	Wenn **das Wetter gut ist, gehe ich in den Park.** When the weather is good, I go to the park.
	Ich weiß nicht, wann **sie kommt.** I don't know when she is coming.

False Friends

German word	English translation	English word	German translation
aktuell	current	**actually**	eigentlich
also	therefore	**also**	auch
Art	type	**art**	Kunst
bekommen	to receive	**to become**	werden
Billion	trillion	**billion**	Milliarde
Brand	fire	**brand**	Marke
brav	well behaved	**brave**	mutig
Chef	boss	**chef**	Koch
Gift	poison	**gift**	Geschenk
Gymnasium	secondary school	**gym**	Fitnessstudio
Kind	child	**kind (type)**	Art
Kollege	colleague	**college**	Hochschule
komisch	strange	**funny**	lustig
Noten	grades	**notes**	Notizen
Pension	B&B	**pension**	Rente
sensibel	sensitive	**sensible**	vernünftig
Rat	advice	**rat**	Ratte

14.03 Hörverständnis Teil 3

Vorarbeit

geschmolzen	*melted*	**Klimawandel**	*climate change*	**Sonnenflecken**	*sunspots*
Schneekanonen	*snow cannons*	**vermeiden**	*to avoid*	**Waldbrände**	*forest fires*
erkunden	*to investigate*	**Erderwärmung**	*global warming*	**überzeugt**	*convinced*

CL Ordinary + Higher Level Questions

1. **a)** The conversation is between:
   i) a teacher and student ☐ **iii)** a parent and child ☐
   ii) friends ☐ **iv)** employer and employee ☐
   b) Find **one (O)/two (H)** details in the conversation that support your choice.
2. **a)** Which word best describes Michael's views on the impact of global warming?
   i) doubtful ☐ **ii)** certain ☐ **iii)** angry ☐ **iv)** uninterested ☐
   b) Write down **one (O)/two (H)** details from the conversation to support your choice.
3. How does Mareike react to Michael's comments? Give **two (O)/three (H)** details.
4. What do they agree on in the end? Give **one (O)/two (H)** details.

14.04 Hörverständnis Teil 4

Vorarbeit

Bohrloch	*borehole*	**versiegeln**	*to seal*	**Leck**	*leak*
Verzweiflung	*despair*	**absehbar**	*foreseeable*	**Kabeljau**	*cod*
Wittling	*whiting*	**betroffen**	*affected*	**nachhaltig**	*sustainable*
Verseuchung	*contamination*	**umstritten**	*disputed*	**Vergiftung**	*poisoning*
vor Gericht	*in court*	**Entschädigungs-zahlungen**	*damages*	**Schuld**	*blame*
Aufräumaktionen	*clean-up campaigns*	**Bestände**	*stocks*	**örtlich**	*local*

CL Ordinary + Higher Level Questions

1. **a)** What problem is being caused by a borehole made by an oil company in America?
   b) What attempt is being made to fix the problem? What do experts think of its effectiveness?
2. Give **two (O)/three (H)** details about what is happening in the Baltic Sea.
3. What exactly has happened in a river in Guatemala and what are the consequences of this event?
4. According to the experts, how much has been spent on the clean-up operation for the nuclear accident and what criticism is made about the clean-up itself?
5. What is the weather forecast? Give **three (O)/four (H)** details.

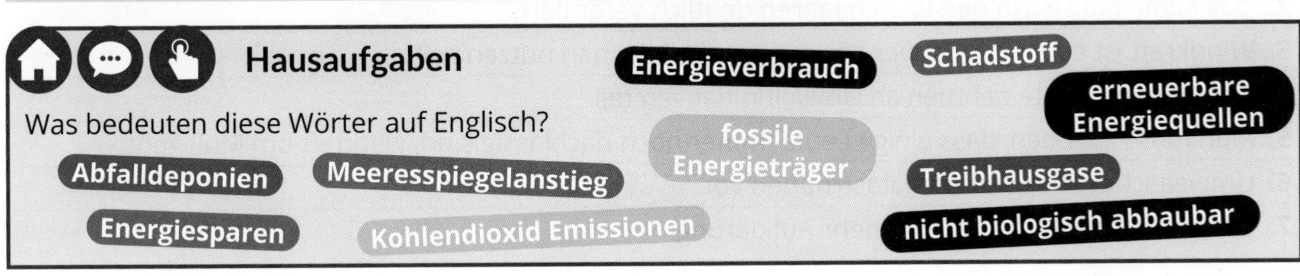

OL  Schriftliche Produktion: Ordinary Level

Write a letter to your pen pal. Complete the first paragraph by correctly inserting the sentence halves below. Then follow the instructions.

an einer Umweltinitiative **mir zu schreiben** **Erzähl mir**
sehr wichtig **einen Brief von dir zu bekommen**

Liebe(r) Martin(a),

schön, dass du wieder Zeit hattest, ________. Ich freue mich immer, ________. Du nimmst ________ teil. Das ist toll! ________ von deinen Aktivitäten. Ich finde es ________ die Umwelt zu schützen.

Now continue the letter.

- Say that you participate in an environment group in your school.
- Mention **two** things your group does to promote environmental protection.
- Say what you do at home to protect the environment.
- Say why you think it is important to protect the environment.
- Write a suitable closing sentence.

HL Schriftliche Produktion: Higher Level

Reply in German to your pen pal's letter. Give detailed answers to the questions.

Liebe(r) ...,

ich hoffe, es geht dir gut! Bald werde ich mit der Schule fertig sein. Ich kann es kaum erwarten!

In deinem letzten Brief hast du gesagt, dass du dich für die Umwelt engagierst. Was machst du eigentlich? Nimmst du an einer Umweltinitiative teil? Erzähl' mir darüber!

Ich denke, es ist wichtig sein Bestes zu tun um die Umwelt zu schützen, denn wir sollten natürlich den nächsten Generationen eine heile Welt hinterlassen. Und du, warum begeisterst du dich für den Umweltschutz? Glaubst du, dass wir alle mehr tun können um die Umwelt zu schonen? Ich versuche recyceltes Papier zu kaufen. Und du, was machst du in deinem alltäglichen Leben um die Umwelt zu schützen?

In Deutschland will man in den nächsten Jahren alle Kernkraftwerke schließen und sie durch saubere Energiequellen ersetzen. Was hältst du davon? Gibt es in Irland bestimmte Umweltprobleme und was wird gemacht um sie zu bewältigen?

Haben Jugendliche in Irland ein starkes Bewusstsein für Umweltprobleme? Wie findest du das? Wie kann man Leute darauf aufmerksam machen, deiner Meinung nach?

Eine Welt ohne Müll wäre wunderschön, aber unmöglich, glaube ich. Was meinst du dazu? Nenn' drei Gründe für deine Antwort.

Jetzt muss ich Schluss machen. Dein(e) Karl(a)

Nützliche Sätze

Übersetzen Sie folgende Sätze ins Englische.

1. Überschwemmungen und Unwetter kommen immer häufiger vor.
2. Das Klima hat sich in den letzten Jahren deutlich verändert.
3. Windkraft ist eine tolle, saubere Energiequelle, die man nutzen sollte.
4. Immer mehr Leute nehmen an Umweltinitiativen teil.
5. Man muss zugeben, dass einige Leute immer noch nachlässig sind, wenn es um Müll geht.
6. Umweltschutz beugt Naturkatastrophen vor.
7. Ganz bestimmt braucht man mehr Aufklärung.

Übung Macht den Meister!

A Negation

1. Insert **nicht** or the correct form of **kein** where appropriate.

a) Ich habe ___ Schwester.	**e)** Ich kann ___ genau sagen, warum.
b) Wir essen ___ gern Fleisch.	**f)** Das spielt ___ große Rolle.
c) Er hat ___ Interesse an Geschichte.	**g)** Wir fahren ___ in die Berge.
d) Man trinkt ___ viel.	**h)** Ich treibe ___ gern Sport.

2. Translate the following sentences into German.

a) I don't go out at the weekend.	**e)** I did not do any homework.
b) I have no interest in sport.	**f)** We don't go out during the week.
c) I don't like listening to rock music.	**g)** We don't have a sportsground here.
d) We are not allowed to smoke in school.	**h)** There also isn't a canteen.

3. Turn the following **nicht** sentences into **kein** sentences. The sentences have been started for you.

a) Ich sehe den Mann nicht.	Ich habe keinen Mann gesehen.
b) Siehst du das Schloss nicht?	Du siehst kein Schloss.
c) Ich habe den Apfel nicht gegessen.	Ich habe ...
d) Ich habe den Aufsatz nicht geschrieben.	Ich habe ...
e) Ich habe das Buch nicht gelesen.	Ich habe ...
f) Ich habe den Pullover nicht gekauft.	Ich habe ...
g) Ich kaufe mir das Eis nicht.	Ich kaufe ...
h) Ich sehe mir den Film nicht an.	Ich sehe ...

4. Translate these sentences into German, using alternative negative expressions to **nicht** and **kein**.

a) I never watch documentaries.	**e)** Nobody will support this.
b) I eat neither fish nor meat.	**f)** I did not see a red but a green car.
c) It never rains in the summer.	**g)** I have not finished my exams yet.
d) They cannot find the dog anywhere.	**h)** I haven't made a decision yet.

B Difficult Words

1. Translate the following sentences into German. Be careful of the difficult words.

a) Do you know my neighbour?	**i)** I only paid 10 euros for it.
b) I don't know the answer.	**j)** It's only 11 o'clock.
c) We're going home after the film.	**k)** I saw a documentary about the environment.
d) I will be living at home next year.	**l)** My pen pal is staying about ten days.
e) When are you coming to visit me?	**m)** It happened about midnight.
f) I play computer games when it rains.	**n)** I was about to study grammar.
g) I was pleased when your letter arrived.	**o)** What did the teacher talk about?
h) I spend a lot of time practising German.	**p)** I think that we should behave responsibly.

2. Translate the following sentences into German. Be careful of the **Falsche Freunde**!

a) Actually I'm doing the Leaving Cert this year.	**e)** I want to go to college next year.
b) That is a new type of music.	**f)** I hope to become a teacher.
c) I always take notes in class.	**g)** I will receive a good salary.
d) My little sister is very well behaved.	**h)** We'll have holidays soon.

Für die Prüfung

1. Was passt zusammen?

1. Wir müssen alle zusammenarbeiten,	**A** soll man auf wenig Verpackung achten.
2. Während die Müllberge ständig wachsen,	**B** desto besser für die Umwelt.
3. Wenn man Produkte kauft,	**C** um die Umwelt zu schützen.
4. Je weniger Energie man verbraucht,	**D** benutzen wir die Biotonne.
5. Um die Umwelt zu schonen,	**E** wird die reine Natur zerstört.

2. Was passt zusammen?

1. Es wird gesagt,	**A** sollte man alle elektrischen Geräte ausschalten.
2. Um zum Klimaschutz beizutragen,	**B** bevorzuge ich natürliche Materialien.
3. Wenn man Produkte mit Umwelt-Gütesiegeln kauft,	**C** dass Bio-Lebensmittel immer beliebter werden.
4. Wenn ich es kann,	**D** trägt man positiv zur Umwelt bei!
5. Ich finde es toll,	**E** dass nachhaltige Energie die beste Lösung ist.

3. Select the correct prepositions for the following sentences.

a) Ich engagiere mich seit Jahren **(in/für/mit/auf)** die Umwelt.

b) Wir nehmen oft **(an/auf/in/für)** Umweltinitiativen teil.

c) **(In/An/Zu/Auf)** den letzten Jahren hat sich das Klima deutlich geändert.

d) Saubere Energiequellen sind der Weg **(zum/für/gegen/zur)** Lösung vieler Umweltprobleme.

e) Es gibt ständig Umweltberichte **(von/über/zu/an)** Abfall und Waldsterben in den Medien.

f) Wir müssen so viel wie möglich recyceln, **(für/um/an/in)** die riesigen Müllberge zu reduzieren.

4. What words make up the following compound words, and what do they mean in English?

a) Umweltschutz = ___ + ___ = ___

b) Klimawandel = ___ + ___ = ___

c) Wildtiere = ___ + ___ = ___

d) Müllberg = ___ + ___ = ___

e) Tierarten = ___ + ___ = ___

f) Müllvermeidung = ___ + ___ = ___

5. Translate the following sentences into German, using **nicht** or **kein**.

a) I don't believe we can do nothing.

b) I don't go to school by car.

c) I don't use any drinking straws.

d) I don't take a bath in the bathtub.

e) I don't want to buy an expensive car.

f) There are no countries unaffected by pollution.

6. Indicate whether the underlined nouns are singular or plural, their gender and their case.

a) Das Klima auf der Erde wird wärmer.

b) Was ist dein persönlicher Beitrag?

c) Strikte Gesetze sollten eingeführt werden.

d) Die Natur stirbt langsam.

e) Wir verpesten die Luft.

f) Wir müssen jeden Tag nachhaltig leben.

7. Lückentext: Fill in the blanks with the correct missing words from the box.

wenn   sparen   Müll   schalte   zur

Ich gehe unter die Dusche, um Wasser zu **1** ___ . Ich **2** ___ so oft wie möglich das Licht aus. Ich gehe zu Fuß **3** ___ Schule, um Benzin zu sparen. Wir trennen den **4** ___ und bringen Glasflaschen zur Sammelstelle. Ich benutze eine Stofftasche, statt einer Plastiktüte, **5** ___ ich einkaufen gehe.

Selbstbewertung: Ordinary Level

OL

Vocabulary

1. If I can translate theses sentences, I can talk about the environment. (1 mark each)

a) Wir müssen die Umwelt schützen.	**f)** Ich kaufe immer recyceltes Papier.
b) Ich spare so viel Wasser wie möglich.	**g)** Ich schalte den Computer aus.
c) Zu Hause trennen wir den Müll.	**h)** Natürlich müssen wir Energie sparen.
d) Ich benutze eine Stofftasche.	**i)** Man soll Elektrogeräte ausschalten.
e) Wir brauchen saubere Energiequellen.	**j)** Wir müssen den Müllberg reduzieren.

Your score: ___ / 10

2. If I can translate these nouns into English, I understand the main nouns needed to describe the environment. (1 mark each)

a) Umweltschutz	**c)** Müll	**e)** Regenwald	**g)** Orkane	**i)** Unwetter
b) Verschmutzung	**d)** Klimawandel	**f)** Waldsterben	**h)** Waldbrände	**j)** Hitzewelle

Your score: ___ / 10

Grammar

3. If I can conjugate these verbs in the 'I' form in the present and perfect tenses, I can talk about the environment. (1 mark for each tense)

a) schützen: I protect ___ I protected ___

b) sparen: I save ___ I saved ___

c) benutzen: I use ___ I used ___

d) trennen: I separate ___ I separated ___

e) sich engagieren: I'm involved ___ I was involved ___

Your score: ___ / 10

4. If I can choose the correct conjunction, I can use complex sentences. (2 marks each)

a) Ich trenne den Müll, **(denn/weil)** ich den Müllberg reduzieren will.

b) Ich schalte den Computer aus, **(um/also)** Strom zu sparen.

c) Wir brauchen saubere Energiequellen, **(denn/weil)** Verschmutzung ist ein Problem.

d) Heutzutage gibt es Hitzewellen, **(um/also)** müssen wir Wasser sparen.

e) Ich bringe Glasflaschen zur Sammelstelle, **(um/also)** Müll zu reduzieren.

Your score: ___ / 10

5. If I can choose the correct preposition, I understand the prepositions needed to describe the environment. (1 mark each)

a) Ich habe mich **(um/in/an/für)** die Umwelt engagiert.

b) Ich gehe **(in/unter/an/für)** die Dusche.

c) Wir nehmen oft **(an/in/um/für)** Umweltinitiativen teil.

d) Wir sparen **(am/im/um/zum)** Haushalt viel Energie.

e) Ich gehe **(mit/zu/an/für)** Fuß in die Schule.

f) Man sollte **(zu/ab/an/auf)** erneuerbare Energie umsteigen.

g) Verschmutzung hat ernste Folgen **(in/für/an/mit)** unsere Welt.

h) Viele Tierarten sind **(vom/beim/am/im)** Aussterben bedroht.

i) Treibhausgase führen **(an/zu/durch/für)** Luftverschmutzung.

j) Ich möchte positiv **(für/an/zur/in)** Umwelt beitragen.

Your score: ___ / 10

What have I learned?	
What must I improve?	
What do I want to revise?	

Your total score: ___ / 50

Selbstbewertung: Higher Level

HL

1. If I can translate these sentences, I can discuss environmental issues. (2 marks each)

a) Nowadays pollution is a growing problem.
b) Climate change has upset the balance of nature.
c) Climate catastrophes are occurring more and more frequently.
d) Sustainable energy is the best solution.
e) We must always behave in an environmentally friendly way.

Your score: ___ / 10

2. If I can make these sentences negative using **nicht**, I can use negatives. (1 mark each)

a) Umweltsünder werden bestraft.	**f)** Wir engagieren uns für den Umweltschutz.
b) Die Bevölkerung wird aufgeklärt.	**g)** Wir können die Umweltprobleme lösen.
c) Wir legen Komposthaufen an.	**h)** Ohne Zweifel schmelzen die Eisberge.
d) Wir tun genug für die Umwelt.	**i)** Es gibt Müll, der recycelt werden kann.
e) Abwässer werden in Flüsse geleitet.	**j)** Der Müll wird jetzt getrennt.

Your score: ___ / 10

3. If I can translate these sentences, I understand negatives and positives. (1 mark each)

a) Everyone is responsible for it.	**f)** Nowhere is safe from climate change.
b) We never drive a car.	**g)** I never use plastic bags.
c) We always recycle paper.	**h)** I always switch off the lights.
d) No one can ignore pollution.	**i)** One can't deny that climate change is real.
e) The consequences are everywhere.	**j)** Someone must find solutions.

Your score: ___ / 10

4. If I can translate these sentences, I understand German false friends. (2 marks each)

a) The environment is a topical issue.
b) Many types of animals are threatened with extinction.
c) Pollution causes billions of euros in damages.
d) We must behave sensibly to reduce environmental damage.
e) I'm interested in the environment, therefore I recycle as much as possible.

Your score: ___ / 10

5. If I can correctly fill in the gaps below, I understand word functions. (1 mark each)

der bin uns vermeide müssen Klimaschutz trenne aktuelles umweltbewusster zu

In Irland werden wir allmählich ein bisschen **1** ___ und wir machen **2** ___ Sorgen um den **3** ___ . Ich bin fest davon überzeugt, dass wir alle zusammen arbeiten **4** ___ , um die Klimakatastrophen **5** ___ verhindern. Natürlich **6** ___ ich den Müll und ich gehe zu Fuß zur Schule. Ich **7** ___ unnötige Verpackungen. Ich **8** ___ Mitglied der „Grüne Schule" Gruppe. Wir fördern das Umweltbewusstsein in **9** ___ Schule und zu Hause. Der Klimaschutz ist bestimmt ein äußerst **10** ___ Thema.

Your score: ___ / 10

What have I learned?	
What must I improve?	
What do I want to revise?	

Your total score: ___ / 50

Verb tables

Irregular Verbs

Infinitive	English Meaning	Present Tense (er/sie/es/man)	Imperfect Tense (ich & er/sie/es/man)	Past Participle (for perfect & pluperfect, formed with **haben** unless indicated, & passive)
backen	*to bake*	backt	backte	gebacken
befehlen	*to command*	befiehlt	befahl	befohlen
beginnen	*to begin*	beginnt	begann	begonnen
beißen	*to bite*	beißt	biss	gebissen
betrügen	*to deceive*	betrügt	betrog	betrogen
bewegen	*to move*	bewegt	bewegte	bewegt
biegen	*to bend, turn*	biegt	bog	gebogen
bieten	*to offer*	bietet	bot	geboten
binden	*to tie*	bindet	band	gebunden
bitten	*to ask*	bittet	bat	gebeten
blasen	*to blow*	bläst	blies	geblasen
bleiben	*to stay*	bleibt	blieb	**(bin, bist, ...)** geblieben
braten	*to roast*	brät	briet	gebraten
brechen	*to break*	bricht	brach	gebrochen
brennen	*to burn*	brennt	brannte	gebrannt
bringen	*to bring*	bringt	brachte	gebracht
denken	*to think*	denkt	dachte	gedacht
dürfen	*to be allowed*	darf	durfte	gedurft
empfehlen	*to recommend*	empfiehlt	empfahl	empfohlen
erschrecken	*to be frightened*	erschrickt	erschrak	**(bin, bist, ...)** erschrocken
essen	*to eat*	isst	aß	gegessen
fallen	*to fall*	fällt	fiel	**(bin, bist, ...)** gefallen
fangen	*to catch*	fängt	fing	gefangen
finden	*to find*	findet	fand	gefunden
fliegen	*to fly*	fliegt	flog	**(bin, bist, ...)** geflogen
fliehen	*to flee*	flieht	floh	**(bin, bist, ...)** geflohen
fließen	*to flow*	fließt	floss	geflossen
fressen	*to eat (for animals)*	frisst	fraß	gefressen
frieren	*to freeze*	friert	fror	**(bin, bist, ...)** gefroren
geben	*to give*	gibt	gab	gegeben
gedeihen	*to flourish*	gedeiht	gedieh	**(bin, bist, ...)** gediehen
gehen	*to go, walk*	geht	ging	**(bin, bist, ...)** gegangen
gelingen	*to succeed*	gelingt	gelang	**(bin, bist, ...)** gelungen
gelten	*to be valid*	gilt	galt	gegolten
genießen	*to enjoy*	genießt	genoss	genossen
geraten	*to get into*	gerät	geriet	**(bin, bist, ...)** geraten
geschehen	*to happen*	geschieht	geschah	**(bin, bist, ...)** geschehen
gewinnen	*to win, gain*	gewinnt	gewann	gewonnen
gießen	*to pour*	gießt	goss	gegossen
gleichen	*to resemble*	gleicht	glich	geglichen
gleiten	*to glide*	gleitet	glitt	**(bin, bist, ...)** geglitten

greifen	*to grab*	greift	griff	gegriffen
haben	*to have*	hat	hatte	gehabt
halten	*to hold*	hält	hielt	gehalten
hängen	*to be hanging*	hängt	hing	gehangen
hängen	*to hang*	hängt	hängte	gehängt
heben	*to lift*	hebt	hob	gehoben
heißen	*to be called*	heißt	hieß	geheißen
helfen	*to help*	hilft	half	geholfen
kennen	*to know*	kennt	kannte	gekannt
klingen	*to sound*	klingt	klang	geklungen
kommen	*to come*	kommt	kam	**(bin, bist, ...)** gekommen
können	*to be able to*	kann	konnte	gekonnt
kriechen	*to crawl*	kriecht	kroch	**(bin, bist, ...)** gekrochen
laden	*to load*	lädt	lud	geladen
lassen	*to let*	lässt	ließ	gelassen
laufen	*to walk, run*	läuft	lief	**(bin, bist, ...)** gelaufen
leiden	*to suffer*	leidet	litt	gelitten
leihen	*to lend*	leiht	lieh	geliehen
lesen	*to read*	liest	las	gelesen
liegen	*to lie*	liegt	lag	gelegen
lügen	*to tell lies*	lügt	log	gelogen
messen	*to measure*	misst	maß	gemessen
mögen	*to like*	mag	mochte	gemocht
müssen	*to have to*	muss	musste	gemusst
nehmen	*to take*	nimmt	nahm	genommen
nennen	*to name*	nennt	nannte	genannt
pfeifen	*to whistle*	pfeift	pfiff	gepfiffen
raten	*to advise, guess*	rät	riet	geraten
reiben	*to rub*	reibt	rieb	gerieben
reißen	*to tear, rip*	reißt	riss	gerissen
reiten	*to ride (a horse)*	reitet	ritt	geritten
rennen	*to run*	rennt	rannte	**(bin, bist, ...)** gerannt
riechen	*to smell*	riecht	roch	gerochen
rufen	*to call, shout*	ruft	rief	gerufen
scheiden	*to separate*	scheidet	schied	**(bin, bist, ...)** geschieden
scheinen	*to seem, shine*	scheint	schien	geschienen
schieben	*to shove*	schiebt	schob	geschoben
schießen	*to shoot*	schießt	schoss	geschossen
schlafen	*to sleep*	schläft	schlief	geschlafen
schlagen	*to hit*	schlägt	schlug	geschlagen
schließen	*to shut, finish*	schließt	schloss	geschlossen
schneiden	*to cut*	schneidet	schnitt	geschnitten
schreiben	*to write*	schreibt	schrieb	geschrieben
schreien	*to shout, yell*	schreit	schrie	geschrie(e)n
schweigen	*to be silent*	schweigt	schwieg	geschwiegen

schwellen	*to swell*	schwillt	schwoll	**(bin, bist, ...)** geschwollen
schwimmen	*to swim*	schwimmt	schwamm	**(bin, bist, ...)** geschwommen
schwingen	*to swing*	schwingt	schwang	geschwungen
schwören	*to swear*	schwört	schwor	geschworen
sehen	*to see*	sieht	sah	gesehen
sein	*to be*	ist	war	**(bin, bist, ...)** gewesen
senden	*to send*	sendet	sandte	gesandt
singen	*to sing*	singt	sang	gesungen
sinken	*to sink*	sinkt	sank	**(bin, bist, ...)** gesunken
sitzen	*to sit*	sitzt	saß	gesessen
sollen	*to ought to*	soll	sollte	gesollt
sprechen	*to speak*	spricht	sprach	gesprochen
springen	*to jump*	springt	sprang	gesprungen
stechen	*to sting*	sticht	stach	gestochen
stehen	*to stand*	steht	stand	gestanden
stehlen	*to steal*	stiehlt	stahl	gestohlen
steigen	*to rise*	steigt	stieg	**(bin, bist, ...)** gestiegen
sterben	*to die*	stirbt	starb	**(bin, bist, ...)** gestorben
stinken	*to stink*	stinkt	stank	gestunken
stoßen	*to push, bump*	stößt	stieß	gestoßen
streiten	*to quarrel*	streitet	stritt	gestritten
tragen	*to carry, wear*	trägt	trug	getragen
treffen	*to meet, hit*	trifft	traf	getroffen
treiben	*to force, drive*	treibt	trieb	getrieben
treten	*to step*	tritt	trat	**(bin, bist, ...)** getreten
trinken	*to drink*	trinkt	trank	getrunken
tun	*to do*	tut	tat	getan
verbergen	*to hide*	verbirgt	verbarg	verborgen
verderben	*to spoil*	verdirbt	verdarb	verdorben
vergessen	*to forget*	vergisst	vergaß	vergessen
verlassen	*to leave*	verlässt	verließ	verlassen
verlieren	*to lose*	verliert	verlor	verloren
verschwinden	*to disappear*	verschwindet	verschwand	**(bin, bist ...)** verschwunden
verzeihen	*to excuse*	verzeiht	verzieh	verziehen
wachsen	*to grow*	wächst	wuchs	**(bin, bist, ...)** gewachsen
waschen	*to wash*	wäscht	wusch	gewaschen
wechseln	*to change*	wechselt	wechselte	gewechselt
werben	*to advertise*	wirbt	warb	geworben
werden	*to become*	wird	wurde	**(bin, bist, ...)** geworden
werfen	*to throw*	wirft	warf	geworfen
wiegen	*to weigh*	wiegt	wog	gewogen
wissen	*to know*	weiß	wusste	gewusst
wollen	*to want*	will	wollte	gewollt
ziehen	*to pull, move*	zieht	zog	gezogen
zwingen	*to force*	zwingt	zwang	gezwungen

Modal Verbs

dürfen	*to be allowed to*	darf	durfte	gedurft
können	*to be able to*	kann	konnte	gekonnt
mögen	*to like*	mag	mochte	gemocht
müssen	*to have to*	muss	musste	gemusst
sollen	*to ought to*	soll	sollte	gesollt
wollen	*to want*	will	wollte	gewollt

Mixed Verbs

brennen	*to burn*	brennt	brannte	gebrannt
bringen	*to bring*	bringt	brachte	gebracht
denken	*to think*	denkt	dachte	gedacht
kennen	*to know*	kennt	kannte	gekannt
nennen	*to name*	nennt	nannte	genannt
rennen	*to walk, run*	rennt	rannte	**(bin, bist, ...)** gerannt
senden	*to send*	sendet	sandte	gesandt
wenden	*to turn*	wendet	wandte	gewandt
wissen	*to know*	weiß	wusste	gewusst

a > ä > ie > a

blasen	*to blow*	bläst	blies	geblasen
braten	*to roast*	brät	briet	gebraten
fallen	*to fall*	fällt	fiel	**(bin, bist, ...)** gefallen
fangen	*to catch*	fängt	fing	gefangen
in etw. geraten	*to get into*	gerät	geriet	**(bin, bist, ...)** geraten
halten	*to hold*	hält	hielt	gehalten
lassen	*to let*	lässt	ließ	gelassen
laufen	*to walk, run*	läuft	lief	**(bin, bist, ...)** gelaufen
raten	*to advise, guess*	rät	riet	geraten
schlafen	*to sleep*	schläft	schlief	geschlafen
verlassen	*to leave*	verlässt	verließ	verlassen

a > ä > u > a

fahren	*to go, drive*	fährt	fuhr	**(bin, bist, ...)** gefahren
graben	*to dig*	gräbt	grub	gegraben
laden	*to load*	lädt	lud	geladen
schlagen	*to hit*	schlägt	schlug	geschlagen
tragen	*to carry, wear*	trägt	trug	getragen
wachsen	*to grow*	wächst	wuchs	**(bin, bist, ...)** gewachsen
waschen	*to wash*	wäscht	wusch	gewaschen

e > i > a > e

essen	*to eat*	isst	aß	gegessen
fressen	*to eat (for animals)*	frisst	fraß	gefressen
geben	*to give*	gibt	gab	gegeben
messen	*to measure*	misst	maß	gemessen
treten	*to step*	tritt	trat	**(bin, bist, ...)** getreten
vergessen	*to forget*	vergisst	vergaß	vergessen

e > i > a > o

brechen	*to break*	bricht	brach	gebrochen
erschrecken	*to be frightened*	erschrickt	erschrak	**(bin, bist, ...)** erschrocken
gelten	*to be valid*	gilt	galt	gegolten
helfen	*to help*	hilft	half	geholfen
nehmen	*to take*	nimmt	nahm	genommen
sprechen	*to speak*	spricht	sprach	gesprochen
stechen	*to sting*	sticht	stach	gestochen
sterben	*to die*	stirbt	starb	**(bin, bist, ...)** gestorben
treffen	*to meet, hit*	trifft	traf	getroffen
verbergen	*to hide*	verbirgt	verbarg	verborgen
verderben	*to spoil*	verdirbt	verdarb	verdorben
werben	*to advertise*	wirbt	warb	geworben
werfen	*to throw*	wirft	warf	geworfen

e > i > u > o

werden	*to become*	wird	wurde	**(bin, bist, ...)** geworden

e > ie > a > e

geschehen	*to happen*	geschieht	geschah	**(bin, bist, ...)** geschehen
lesen	*to read*	liest	las	gelesen
sehen	*to see*	sieht	sah	gesehen

e > ie > a > o

befehlen	*to command*	befiehlt	befahl	befohlen
empfehlen	*to recommend*	empfiehlt	empfahl	empfohlen
stehlen	*to steal*	stiehlt	stahl	gestohlen

Regular Separable Verbs

abholen	*to collect*	holt ... ab	holte ... ab	ab**ge**holt
aufmachen	*to open*	macht ... auf	machte ... auf	auf**ge**macht
aufräumen	*to tidy up*	räumt ... auf	räumte ... auf	auf**ge**räumt
anblicken	*to look at*	blickt ... an	blickte ... an	an**ge**blickt
anflehen	*to implore*	fleht ... an	flehte ... an	an**ge**fleht

auswählen	*to select*	wählt ... aus	wählte ... aus	aus**ge**wählt
einkaufen	*to shop*	kauft ... ein	kaufte ... ein	ein**ge**kauft
fortsetzen	*to continue*	setzt ... fort	setzte ... fort	fort**ge**setzt
herstellen	*to produce*	stellt ... her	stellte ... her	her**ge**stellt
mitmachen	*to participate*	macht ... mit	machte ... mit	mit**ge**macht
nachahmen	*to imitate*	ahmt ... nach	ahmte ... nach	nach**ge**ahmt
umdrehen	*to turn around*	dreht ... um	drehte ... um	um**ge**dreht
vorstellen	*to introduce*	stellt ... vor	stellte ... vor	vor**ge**stellt

Regular Inseparable Verbs

behandeln	*to treat*	behandelt	behandelte	behandelt
entdecken	*to discover*	entdeckt	entdeckte	entdeckt
erleben	*to experience*	erlebt	erlebte	erlebt
erwarten	*to expect*	erwartet	erwartete	erwartet
gehören	*to belong to*	gehört	gehörte	gehört
misstrauen	*to mistrust*	misstraut	misstraute	misstraut
unterrichten	*to teach*	unterrichtet	unterrichtete	unterrichtet
übersetzen	*to translate*	übersetzt	übersetzte	übersetzt
verletzen	*to injure*	verletzt	verletzte	verletzt
zerstören	*to destroy*	zerstört	zerstörte	zerstört

Irregular Separable Verbs

anfangen	*to start*	fängt ... an	fing ... an	an**ge**fangen
aufstehen	*to get up*	steht ... auf	stand ... auf	**(bin, bist, ...)** auf**ge**standen
aussehen	*to look like*	sieht ... aus	sah ... aus	aus**ge**sehen
niederlassen	*to settle*	lässt ... nieder	ließ ... nieder	nieder**ge**lassen
rausbringen	*to bring out*	bringt ... raus	brachte ... raus	raus**ge**bracht
rumhängen	*to hang out*	hängt ... rum	hing ... rum	rum**ge**hängt
teilnehmen	*to take part*	nimmt ... teil	nahm ... teil	teil**ge**nommen
umziehen	*to move house*	zieht ... um	zog ... um	**(bin, bist, ...)** um**ge**zogen
vorkommen	*to occur*	kommt ... vor	kam ... vor	**(bin, bist, ...)** vor**ge**kommen
weiterfahren	*to drive on*	fährt ... weiter	fuhr ... weiter	**(bin, bist, ...)** weiter**ge**fahren

Irregular Inseparable Verbs

bekommen	*to receive*	bekommt	bekam	bekommen
besprechen	*to discuss*	bespricht	besprach	besprochen
empfehlen	*to recommend*	empfiehlt	empfahl	empfohlen
entscheiden	*to decide*	entscheidet	entschied	entschieden
erhalten	*to receive*	erhält	erhielt	erhalten
geschehen	*to happen*	geschieht	geschah	**(bin, bist, ...)** geschehen
übernehmen	*to take over*	übernimmt	übernahm	übernommen
unterbrechen	*to interrupt*	unterbricht	unterbrach	unterbrochen
vergessen	*to forget*	vergisst	vergaß	vergessen
verschwinden	*to disappear*	verschwindet	verschwand	**(bin, bist, ...)** verschwunden

	Grammatische Terminologie	Grammatical Terminology
p. 6	**Das Präsens**: *ich gehe* Ich gehe jeden Tag zur Schule.	**Present tense**: Example: *I go; I am going* Example sentence: I go to school every day.
p. 17	**Das Imperfekt/Präteritum**: *ich ging* Ich ging ins Kino.	**Imperfect tense**: *I went; I was going* I was going to the cinema.
p. 35	**Das Perfekt**: *ich bin gegangen* Ich bin ins Kino gegangen.	**Perfect tense**: *I went; I have gone* I have gone to the cinema.
p. 50	**Das Plusquamperfekt**: *ich hatte gesehen* Ich hatte den Film schon gesehen.	**Pluperfect tense**: *I had seen* I had already seen the movie.
p. 58	**Das Futur/die Zukunft**: *ich werde sehen* Ich werde morgen den Film sehen.	**Future tense**: *I will see* I will see the film tomorrow.
p 78	**Das Konditional**: *ich würde machen* Ich würde bestimmt dahin gehen.	**The conditional**: *I would do* I would definitely go there.
p. 95	**Koordinierende Konjunktionen/ Bindewörter**: *und; aber; oder; denn; sondern* Ich mag Mathe, denn es ist praktisch. Ich mag Deutsch, aber die Grammatik ist kompliziert.	**Co-ordinating conjunctions**: *and; but; or; because; but rather* I like Maths because it is practical. I like German but the grammar is complicated.
p. 70	**Modalverben**: *dürfen; können; mögen; müssen; sollen; wollen* Ich will nach dem Abitur auf die Universität gehen. Ich muss viel lernen, um gut abzuschneiden.	**Modal verbs**: *to be allowed; to be able; to like; to have to; to ought to; to want to* I want to go to university after the Leaving Certificate. I have to study a lot to get high grades.
p. 95	**Unterordnende Konjunktionen/ Bindewörter**: *als; weil; seit(dem); wenn; während ...* Ich gehe spazieren, wenn es sonnig ist. Ich lerne nicht gern Mathe, weil das Fach kompliziert ist.	**Subordinating conjunctions**: *as; because; since; if; while ...* I go for a walk when it is sunny. I don't like learning Maths because the subject is difficult.
p. 98	**Adverbiale Konjunktionen**: *dann; dennoch; darum; (je)doch ...* Ich dusche mich, dann ziehe ich mich an.	**Adverbial conjunctions**: *then; yet; therefore; however ...* I shower (myself) and then I dress myself.
p. 110	**Nomen/Substantive**: **Geschlecht und Zahl** Hund (m), Kuh (f), Pferd (n), Kühe (pl.)	**Nouns**: **gender and number** dog, cow, horse, cows
p. 130	**Bestimmte Artikel**: *der (m); die (f); das (n); die (pl.)* der Hund, die Kuh, das Pferd, die Kühe	**Definite article**: *the* the dog, the cow, the horse, the cows
p. 115	**Unbestimmte Artikel**: *ein (m); eine (f); ein (n)* ein Mann, eine Frau, ein Kind	**Indefinite articles**: *a; an* a man, a woman, a child
p. 130	**Demonstrative Artikel:** *dies-; jen-; jeder; welcher* Dieser Mann und jene Frau	**Demonstratives:** *this; that; those; each; which* This man and that woman
p. 190	**Adjektive**: *groß; klein; grün; interessant* Sie ist groß.	**Adjectives**: *tall; small; green; interesting* She is tall.
p. 118	**Possessive Adjektive**: *mein; dein; sein; ihr ...* Das ist mein Buch.	**Possessive adjectives**: *my; your; his; her ...* That is my book.

p. 150	**Personalpronomen**: *ich; mich; du; er; ihn; sie ...* Er hat mich gesehen. Ich habe ihn gesehen.	**Personal pronouns**: *I; me; you; he; him; she ...* He saw me. I saw him.
p. 155	**Reflexivpronomen**: *mich; dich; sich; uns; euch ...* Ich wasche mich. Er zieht sich an.	**Reflexive pronouns**: *myself; yourself; himself/herself/itself; ourselves; yourselves ...* I wash myself. He dresses himself.
p. 158	**Relativpronomen**: *der; die; das; die* Die Frau, die das Auto gestohlen hatte, wurde verhaftet. Der Mann, den die Polizei gesucht hat, wurde gestern heil gefunden.	**Relative pronouns**: *who; which* The woman who had stolen the car was arrested. The man whom the police were looking for was found yesterday, safe and sound.
	Possessive Pronomen: *meiner, meine, meins, meine; deiner, deine, deins, deine; seiner, seine, seins, seine; ihrer, ihre, ihres, ihre, ...* Das ist meiner (m) / meine (f) / meins (n). Das ist seiner (m) / seine (f) / seins (n).	**Possessive pronouns**: *mine; yours; his; hers ...* That's mine. That's his.
p. 115	**Nominativ, Akkusativ, Dativ, Genitiv**: Die Polizei (nom.) verhaftet die Frau (acc.). Der Junge (nom.) ist mit seinem Freund (dat.) ins Kino (acc.) gegangen.	**Nominative, accusative, dative, genitive**: The police arrest the woman. The boy went to the cinema with his friend.
p. 244	**Das Passiv**: *es wird gesagt; sie wird untersucht* Die Person wurde verhaftet. Die Menschen wurden an der Grenze gestoppt.	**Passive**: *it is said; she is being examined* The person was arrested. The people were stopped at the border.
p. 208	**Fragewörter**: *Wer? Was? Wann? Wo? Wie? Wieso? Warum? Für wen? Mit wem?* Wer ist das? Was macht sie?	**Interrogatives**: *Who? What? When? Where? How? Why? Why? For whom? With whom?* Who is that? What is she doing?
p. 6	**Trennbare Verben**: *ausgehen; fernsehen; wegfahren; abholen; anrufen; aussehen* Ich hole dich vom Flughafen ab. Ich rufe dich heute Abend an. Er sieht toll aus.	**Separable verbs**: *to go out; to watch TV; to go away; to collect; to telephone; to look* I will collect you from the airport. I will call you tonight. He looks great.
p. 7	**Untrennbare Verben**: *verlieren; besuchen; besichtigen; bekommen; erhalten; erfahren* Ich habe meine Tante besucht.	**Inseparable verbs**: *to lose; to visit; to go and see; to receive; to receive; to experience* I visited my aunt.
p. 231	**Konjunktiv II**: *wenn ich reich wäre; wenn ich das Geld hätte* Wenn ich reich wäre, würde ich die Welt bereisen.	**Subjunctive 2**: *If I were rich; if I had the money* If I were rich, I would travel the world.

Prüfungstipp

Now create your own table of grammar terms! As you make your way through this book, try and add to your table by finding one or two example sentences for each grammar point. This will strengthen your reading comprehension skills!

Klassenarbeit: 01 Meine Familie und ich

1. Füllen Sie mit den Adjektiven und Adverbien unten die Lücken aus.

ältere frech stressig manchmal gern

Ich sage Ihnen ___ etwas über mich und meine Familie. Meine Mutter hat einen Putzfimmel, der mir ___ auf den Keks geht. Mein Bruder ist ___und unartig. Meine ___ Schwester redet wie ein Wasserfall. Das Familienleben kann manchmal ___ sein!

___ 5

2. Finden Sie die passenden Satzhälften.

a) Meine Eltern schimpfen mit mir,

b) Da meine Eltern beide arbeiten,

c) Ich spüle regelmäßig ab

d) Ich muss viel mithelfen,

e) Wenn ich nicht zu Hause mithelfe,

i) helfe ich gerne bei der Hausarbeit mit.

ii) also habe ich wenig Freizeit.

iii) wenn ich schlechte Noten bekomme.

iv) gehen meine Eltern in die Luft.

v) und ich mähe den Rasen.

___ 5

3. Schreiben Sie die Verben im Präsens.

Mein Freund war so alt wie ich. Wir waren eng miteinander befreundet. Wir verstanden uns gut, denn wir hatten die gleichen Interessen und unternahmen viel zusammen. Wenn ich ein Problem hatte, konnte ich mit ihm darüber reden. Unsere Freundschaft war mir sehr wichtig. Wir trafen uns jeden Tag, was viel Spaß machte.

___ 10

4. Geben Sie das Antonym für die unterstrichenen Wörter.

Ich würde sagen, dass ich geduldig, tolerant und gutmütig sein kann. Meine Freunde sagen, dass ich auch zuverlässig und treu bin. Ich muss zugeben, dass ich faul sein kann. Ich denke, ich bin sympathisch und verständnisvoll. Auch bin ich ruhig und glücklich.

___ 10

5. Woraus bestehen diese Wörter?

a) auskommen **b)** hilfsbereit
c) Hausarbeit **d)** Ausgehen
e) zusammenarbeiten

___ 5

6. Ersetzen Sie die unterstrichenen Wörter mit ihrem entsprechenden Synonym.

köstliches Feier erhalten Kumpel fand ... statt

Ich gab letzte Woche eine Party. Die Party war bei mir zu Hause. Wir haben bis in die Nacht gefeiert. Alle meine Freunde sind zur Party gekommen. Es gab ganz leckeres Essen. Ich habe viele schöne Geschenke bekommen.

___ 5

7. Finden Sie die Antworten auf die Fragen.

a) Wann und wohin fährst du in Urlaub?

b) Wo wirst du übernachten?

c) Freust du dich darauf?

d) Wollen wir uns treffen, wenn du hier bist?

e) Was willst du machen, wenn du hier bist?

i) Ich werde in einer Jugendherberge wohnen.

ii) Ja, treffen wir uns am 3. Mai in der Stadt.

iii) Ich fahre im Mai für eine Woche nach Berlin.

iv) Ich freue mich sehr auf meine Reise.

v) Ich möchte die Berliner Mauer besichtigen.

___ 5

8. Übersetzen Sie diese Meinungen.

a) Ich liebe meine Familie, aber ich denke, Freunde sind auch Familie.

b) Ich glaube, dass Freunde die Familie sind, die man sich aussuchen kann.

c) Es ist leichter mit einem Freund ein Problem zu besprechen. Geteiltes Leid ist halbes Leid, wie man so sagt.

d) Auf gute Freunde kann man bauen und ihnen alles anvertrauen.

e) Meine Schwester und ich sind ein Herz und eine Seele, denn wir verstehen uns super gut und streiten uns nie.

___ 5

Klassenarbeit: 02 Mein Wohnort

1. Füllen Sie mit den Adjektiven und Adverbien unten die Lücken aus.

kleinen junge nett nicht freundlich

Ich wohne in einem relativ ____ Dorf auf dem Land. Außer Sportaktivitäten gibt es ____ viel für ____ Leute zu tun. Die Nachbarn sind ____ und ____.

__ / 5

2. Finden Sie die passenden Satzhälften.

a) Ich mag hier wohnen,

b) Leider gibt es weder ein Kino

c) Also muss man ins nächste Dorf fahren,

d) Die öffentlichen Verkehrsmittel

e) Ich würde lieber in der Stadt wohnen,

i) um ins Kino oder ins Hallenbad zu gehen.

ii) sind nicht so gut, da wo ich wohne.

iii) noch ein Schwimmbad.

iv) weil es dort viel mehr zu tun gibt.

v) weil es hier ruhig ist.

__ / 5

3. Schreiben Sie die Verben im Imperfekt.

Mein Wohnort liegt nicht so weit von hier entfernt. Ich fahre jeden Tag mit dem Bus zur Schule. Meine Freunde wohnen auch hier. Wir haben viel Spaß im Park, wo wir gälischen Fußball spielen. Wenn ich schwimmen gehen will, muss ich zum nächsten Dorf fahren. Oft treffe ich mich mit meinen Freunden im Dorf, und wir gehen spazieren oder wir trinken einen Kaffee im Café.

__ / 10

4. Geben Sie das Antonym für die unterstrichenen Wörter.

Mein Wohnort ist sehr ruhig, denn es gibt keinen Straßenverkehr. Die Nachbarn sind glücklicherweise auch sehr zuverlässig und freundlich. Sie sind sehr nett. Ich denke, ich werde hier bleiben, da die Stimmung so gut ist. Auch ist es billig hier zu wohnen.

__ / 10

5. Woraus bestehen diese Wörter?

a) Reihenhaus **b)** Nordirland
c) Nachtclubs **d)** Wohngemeinschaft
e) Dorfbewohner

__ / 5

6. Ersetzen Sie die unterstrichenen Wörter mit ihrem entsprechenden Synonym.

drinnen schlecht Grillfete köstliches Kumpel

Es gab in den Sommerferien eine Grillparty in meiner Nachbarschaft. Das Wetter war schlimm, also fand es in einem Zelt statt. Alle meine Freunde sind gekommen. Ich habe viel leckeres Essen gegessen.

__ / 5

7. Finden Sie die Antworten auf die Fragen.

a) Wo wohnen Sie genau?

b) Was gibt es hier zu tun?

c) Wohnen Sie gern hier?

d) Wie kommen Sie zur Schule?

e) Werden Sie hier wohnen, wenn Sie erwachsen sind?

i) Ich fahre mit dem Bus zur Schule.

ii) Hier kann man im Park spazierengehen.

iii) Ich wohne in einem Wohnblock in einer Wohnung am Stadtrand.

iv) Ich werde mich hier bestimmt niederlassen.

v) Ich mag hier wohnen, denn es gibt viel zu tun.

__ / 5

8. Übersetzen Sie diese Meinungen.

a) Ich wohne gern hier, denn meine Freunde wohnen alle in der Nähe.

b) Ich wohne nicht gern hier, denn es gibt nichts zu tun.

c) Es ist schön auf dem Land zu wohnen.

d) Ich wohne lieber in der Stadt als auf dem Land.

e) Ich werde von zu Hause wegziehen, wenn ich mit der Schule fertig bin.

__ / 5

Klassenarbeit: 03 In meiner Freizeit

1. Füllen Sie mit den Adjektiven und Adverbien unten die Lücken aus.

Sport gern wenn manchmal unternehmungslustig

In meiner Freizeit gehe ich ____ im Park spazieren. Ich bin sehr ____ . Ich treibe aber nicht viel ____. Ich gehe gern ins Kino, ____ ich Geld habe. ____ gehe ich mit meinen Freunden einkaufen.

___ / 5

2. Finden Sie die passenden Satzhälften.

a) Ich mag Hockey spielen,
b) Wenn das Wetter schlecht ist,
c) Ich gehe auch gern einkaufen,
d) Ich bin eine Leseratte
e) Mein Lieblingsfilm ist „Michael Collins",
i) mag ich zu Hause bleiben und auf soziale Netzwerke gehen.
ii) wenn das Wetter gut ist.
iii) und lese am allerliebsten Krimis.
iv) denn er ist sehr spannend.
v) wenn es Sonderangebote in den Geschäften gibt.

___ / 5

3. Schreiben Sie die Verben im Plusquamperfekt.

Ich bin mit meinen Freunden in die Disco gegangen. Wir sind mit dem Bus gefahren. Wir haben viel Spaß gehabt. Wir haben viel getanzt und gesungen. Dort haben wir auch noch andere Kumpel getroffen und wir haben mit ihnen gesprochen. Nach der Disco sind wir zum Schnellimbiss gegangen, wo wir Hamburger mit Pommes gegessen haben und Cola getrunken haben.

___ / 10

4. Geben Sie das Antonym für die unterstrichenen Wörter.

Ich bin sehr unternehmungslustig und mache viel um fit zu bleiben. Ich bin kein Faulpelz! Ich bin immer aktiv. Ich sehe gern fern. Ich finde es entspannend. Es macht mir Spaß Bücher zu lesen. Ich finde das sehr interessant. Ich gehe nicht gern auf soziale Medien, denn ich finde sie sehr langweilig.

___ / 10

5. Woraus bestehen diese Wörter?

a) Freizeit **b)** Freundeskreis
c) Computerspiele **d)** fernsehen
e) ausgehen

___ / 5

6. Ersetzen Sie die unterstrichenen Wörter mit ihrem entsprechenden Synonym.

prima fängt ... an Band den Pub begabt

Ich werde am Wochenende mit meinen Freunden in die Kneipe gehen. Wir werden die Musikgruppe namens The Half Landing hören. Das Musikspielen beginnt um acht Uhr. Es wird toll sein, denn diese Gruppe ist sehr talentiert.

___ / 5

7. Finden Sie die Antworten auf die Fragen.

a) Was machen Sie in Ihrer Freizeit?
b) Was lesen Sie gerne?
c) Sind Sie sportlich?
d) Spielen Sie ein Instrument?
e) Was machen Sie, wenn das Wetter schlecht ist?
i) Ich lese gern Zeitschriften aber ich lese lieber Krimis.
ii) Wenn es regnet, sehe ich gern fern oder ich sehe mir einen guten Film auf Netflix an.
iii) Ich spiele leider kein Instrument aber ich höre sehr gern Musik auf meinem Handy.
iv) Ich sehe gern fern und lese Krimis, wenn ich Zeit habe.
v) Ja, ich mag zum Fitnessstudio gehen und Sport treiben.

___ / 5

8. Übersetzen Sie diese Meinungen.

a) Um mich fit zu halten, gehe ich regelmäßig zum Fitnessstudio.
b) Der Mensch muss sich entspannen.
c) Ich schwärme für soziale Medien.
d) Wenn ich Geld habe, mag ich einkaufen gehen.
e) Ich mag Sachen online kaufen, denn sie sind billiger.

___ / 5

Klassenarbeit: 04 Schule

1. Füllen Sie mit den Adjektiven und Adverbien unten die Lücken aus.

schnell lokalen längere morgens erste gerne kurze normalerweise den bevor

____ stehe ich um 7 Uhr auf. Ich ziehe mich ____ an und frühstücke ____ mit meiner Familie, ____ ich mit dem Bus zur Schule fahre. Die ____ Stunde beginnt um 9 Uhr und die letzte endet um 4 Uhr. Jede Stunde dauert vierzig Minuten. Es gibt eine ____ Pause um 11 Uhr und eine ____ Pause um 1 Uhr. In ____ Pausen esse ich ____ in der Schulkantine oder im ____ Schnellimbiss.

___ / 10

2. Finden Sie die passenden Satzhälften.

a) Sobald ich aufgestanden bin,

b) Bevor ich das Haus verlasse,

c) Wenn das Wetter gut ist,

d) Ich gehe immer zu Fuß zur Schule,

e) In den Pausen hole ich meine Bücher

i) esse ich Toast mit Butter und trinke eine Tasse Tee.

ii) gehe ich zu Fuß zur Schule.

iii) denn die Schule ist ein Katzensprung von hier entfernt.

iv) und ich habe Spaß mit meinen Freunden.

v) dusche ich mich und ziehe mich danach an.

___ / 5

3. Verwandeln Sie die Verben unten in Modalverben.

Ich gehe gern mit meinen Freunden zum lokalen Schnellimbiss. Wir haben auch immer Lust auf ein Eis oder eine heiße Schokolade. Es wird nicht erlaubt, in den Klassenzimmern zu essen. Es ist auch Pflicht, eine Schuluniform zu tragen. Es ist sehr wichtig höflich und pünktlich zu sein.

___ / 5

4. Geben Sie das Antonym für die unterstrichenen Wörter.

Im großen und ganzen herrscht eine gute Stimmung in meiner Schule. Ich finde die Schulvorschriften fair und praktisch und die Lehrer sind nett und freundlich.

___ / 5

5. Woraus bestehen diese Wörter?

a) Klassenarbeit **b)** Stundenplan
c) Mathearbeit **d)** Hausaufgaben
e) Deutschstunde **f)** Mittagessen
g) Halbtagsschule **h)** Schuldirektor
i) Schulbücher **j)** Klassenzimmer

___ / 10

6. Ersetzen Sie die unterstrichenen Wörter mit ihrem entsprechenden Synonym.

sprechen
machen wir Hörverständnisse
notieren Sachen Tests

Im Unterricht hören wir uns CDs an. Wir reden über interessante Themen. Wir schreiben Vokabeln auf und schreiben oft Klassenarbeiten.

___ / 5

7. Finden Sie die Antworten auf die Fragen.

a) Wann stehen Sie morgens auf?

b) Wie kommen Sie zur Schule?

c) Wie sieht ein typischer Schultag aus?

d) Was machen Sie in den Pausen?

e) Wie gefällt Ihnen diese Schule?

i) Ich fahre jeden Tag mit dem Auto zur Schule.

ii) Normalerweise esse ich eine Kleinigkeit und rede mit meinen Klassenkameraden.

iii) Ich mag gern in diese Schule gehen, denn die Stimmung ist gut.

iv) Der Unterricht fängt um 9 Uhr an und ist um 4 Uhr zu Ende.

v) Ich stehe normalerweise um 8 Uhr auf.

___ / 5

8. Übersetzen Sie diese Meinungen.

a) Ich möchte jeden Tag Halbtagsschule haben.

b) Die Sommerferien in Irland sind viel länger als die in Deutschland.

c) Ich finde den Schultag in Irland viel zu lang.

d) Ich würde lieber in Deutschland in die Schule gehen.

e) Ich denke, gemischte Schulen sind besser als Jungen- und Mädchenschulen.

___ / 5

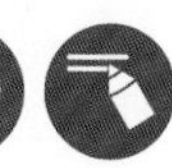

Klassenarbeit: 05 Sprachenlernen

1. Füllen Sie mit den Adjektiven und Adverbien unten die Lücken aus.

deutlich siebten wichtig heutigen sehr

An meiner Schule wählt man am Ende der ____ Klasse zwischen Deutsch und Spanisch. Ich denke, Fremdsprachen sind in der ____ Welt ____ ____. Man lernt auch dabei sich ____ zu verständigen.

__ / 5

2. Finden Sie die passenden Satzhälften.

a) Ich habe Deutsch gewählt,

b) Ich mag auch über die deutsche Kultur lernen,

c) Ich denke, der beste Weg eine Fremdsprache zu lernen

d) Fremdsprachenlernen erweitert nicht nur den Horizont,

e) Wenn man seine Deutschkenntnisse verbessern will,

i) ist einen Schüleraustausch zu machen.

ii) sollte man eine Zeitlang in einem deutschsprachigen Land verbringen.

iii) sondern ermöglicht es auch, in der Arbeitswelt weiter voranzukommen

iv) besonders über ihre tollen Bier- und Weinfeste.

v) denn ich finde die deutsche Aussprache leichter als die französische.

__ / 5

3. Ersetzen Sie die Konjunktionen unten mit einer passenden Konjunktion. Achten Sie auf die Wortstellung.

denn da deshalb jedoch weil

a) Ich lerne gern Deutsch, weil es einfach ist.

b) Ich lerne nicht gern Französisch, da die Aussprache zu kompliziert ist.

c) Ich lerne gern Vokabeln aber ich finde die Grammatik sehr schwierig.

d) Ich mag Deutsch sprechen, denn ich finde die Aussprache leicht.

e) Deutsch ist anspruchsvoll, darum lerne ich es fleißig.

__ / 10

4. Geben Sie das Antonym für die Wörter.

a) Fremdsprache **b)** interessant
c) nützlich **d)** praktisch **e)** wichtig

__ / 5

5. Woraus bestehen diese Wörter?

a) Deutscharbeit **b)** Sprachenlernen
c) Fremdsprache **d)** Muttersprache
e) Hörverständnisse **f)** Leseverständnisse
g) Grammatikübung **h)** Aussprache
i) Sprachkenntnisse **j)** Deutschkenntnisse

__ / 10

6. Geben Sie das Synonym für die Wörter.

a) lernen **b)** sprechen
c) Deutschunterricht **d)** Klassenarbeit
e) wohnen

__ / 5

7. Finden Sie die Antworten auf die Fragen.

a) Seit wann lernen Sie Deutsch?

b) Wie finden Sie es Deutsch zu lernen?

c) Was ist der beste Weg eine Fremdsprache zu lernen?

d) Wie bereiten Sie sich auf einen Vokabeltest vor?

e) Was gefällt Ihnen am wenigsten?

i) Ehrlich gesagt finde ich die Grammatik sehr kompliziert.

ii) Normalerweise pauke ich die Wörter jeden Tag für zwanzig Minuten.

iii) Ich lerne seit sechs Jahren Deutsch.

iv) Die beste Methode eine Fremdsprache zu lernen ist einen Schüleraustausch zu machen.

v) Im großen und ganzen finde ich es leicht Deutsch zu lernen.

__ / 5

8. Übersetzen Sie diese Meinungen.

a) Fremdsprachen sind sehr wichtig im heutigen Leben.

b) Ich finde die deutsche Grammatik einfacher als die irische.

c) Deutsche Wörter können sehr lang sein.

d) Viele deutsche Wörter klingen genau wie englische Wörter.

e) Wenn man Deutsch kann, hat man bessere Berufschancen.

__ / 5

  Klassenarbeit: 06 Im Ausland

1. Füllen Sie mit den Adjektiven unten die Lücken aus.

schönen eigenen interessierte guten tolle

An meiner ____ Schule wird jedes Jahr ein Schüleraustausch mit einem ____ Gymnasium in der ____ Stadt München organisiert. Viele ____ Schüler nehmen daran teil. Ohne Zweifel ist es eine ____ Gelegenheit, seine Deutschkenntnisse zu verbessern.

___ / 5

2. Finden Sie die passenden Satzhälften.

a) Ich bin letzten Sommer mit meiner Familie nach Frankreich in Urlaub gefahren,

b) Wenn man ins Ausland fährt,

c) Wenn ich die Wahl hätte,

d) Ich will unbedingt die Welt bereisen,

e) Spanien ist natürlich ein beliebtes Urlaubsziel,

i) lernt man viel über eine neue Kultur.

ii) weil das Wetter dort immer schön ist.

iii) würde ich gerne nach dem Abitur nach Australien fahren, um Arbeitserfahrung zu sammeln.

iv) denn das französische Essen schmeckt sehr gut.

v) bevor ich heiraten werde oder mich niederlassen werde.

___ / 5

3. Sind die folgenden Nomen Maskulinum, Femininum oder Neutrum?

a) Fremdsprache
b) Fremdsprachenlernen
c) Auslandsaufenthalt **d)** Berufschance
e) Urlaub **f)** Kurs **g)** Sprachschule
h) Arbeitserfahrung **i)** Entscheidung
j) Abflug

___ / 10

4. Geben Sie das Antonym für die Wörter.

a) Vorteile **b)** nötig **c)** Ankunft
d) schönes Wetter **e)** billige Unterkunft

___ / 5

5. Woraus bestehen diese Wörter?

a) Ausland **b)** Deutschland
c) Austauschpartner **d)** Gastfamilie
e) Umgangssprache **f)** Arbeitserfahrung
g) Reisebüro **h)** Auslandsaufenthalt
i) Reiseland **j)** Reiseagentur

___ / 10

6. Geben Sie das Synonym.

a) Berufschancen **b)** Stellenangebot
c) Austauschschüler **d)** Arbeit **e)** Urlaub

___ / 5

7. Finden Sie die Antworten auf die Fragen.

a) Waren Sie schon im Ausland?

b) Wo waren Sie genau?

c) Wie lange sind Sie dort geblieben?

d) Haben Sie die Muttersprache dieses Landes gesprochen?

e) Wie hat es Ihnen gefallen, dort Urlaub zu machen?

i) Es hat mir so gut gefallen, weil das Wetter herrlich war.

ii) Leider habe ich die Muttersprache des Landes nicht gesprochen.

iii) Wir haben in einem Hotel direkt am Strand gewohnt.

iv) Ja, bestimmt. Ich bin mehrmals mit meiner Familie nach Spanien geflogen.

v) Wir haben dort zwei Wochen verbracht.

___ / 5

8. Übersetzen Sie diese Meinungen.

a) Wenn man eine Zeitlang im Ausland verbringt, wird der Horizont dadurch erweitert.

b) Niemand kann leugnen, dass ein Auslandsaufenthalt das Leben bereichern kann.

c) Im Ausland kann man neue Erfahrungen sammeln.

d) Ich fahre unheimlich gern ins Ausland.

e) Es ist eine gute Idee eine Zeitlang im Ausland zu verbringen.

___ / 5

Klassenarbeit: 07 Zukunftspläne

1. Füllen Sie mit den Adjektiven und Adverbien unten die Lücken aus.

verständnisvoll gerne glücklicherweise guten wichtigen

_____ haben wir an meiner Schule einen ____ Berufsberater, der uns ____ bei der Karrieresuche hilft. Er ist ____ und sympathisch. Bei einer ___ Entscheidung braucht jeder Rat.

__/5

2. Finden Sie die passenden Satzhälften.

a) Ich weiß noch nicht genau
b) Ich will unbedingt auf die Uni gehen,
c) Man sollte den Berufsberater in der Schule um Hilfe bitten,
d) Ich will seit meiner Jugend Arzt werden,
e) Ich hoffe, ich kriege genug Punkte,
i) wenn man keine Ahnung hat, was man beruflich machen will.
ii) um meinen Kurs zu bekommen.
iii) um Fremdsprachen zu studieren.
iv) also werde ich Medizin an der Uni studieren.
v) was ich studieren werde.

__/5

3. Identifizieren Sie den Fall und das Geschlecht der folgenden Nomen und ihrer definitiven oder demonstrativen Artikel.

a) wegen dieser schlechten Erfahrung **b)** mit den besten Freunden **c)** aus dieser Sicht **d)** aus diesem Grund **e)** nach dem Abitur **f)** für den Kurs **g)** auf die Uni **h)** auf der Uni **i)** in dieser Schule **j)** nach der Schulzeit

__/10

4. Geben Sie das Antonym für die Wörter.

a) geplant **b)** Nachteile **c)** Entspannung **d)** teure Lebenskosten **e)** ein Fach bestehen

__/5

5. Woraus bestehen diese Wörter?

a) Ausland **b)** Deutschland **c)** Austauschpartner **d)** Geschäftsmann **e)** Zahnarzt **f)** wegziehen **g)** Punktezahl **h)** Prüfungsstress **i)** Eigeninitiative **j)** umziehen

__/10

6. Geben Sie das Synonym.

a) Beruf **b)** Schulabschluss **c)** Schulstress **d)** Hochschule **e)** Resultate

__/5

7. Finden Sie die Antworten auf die Fragen.

a) Was haben Sie nach dem Abitur vor?
b) Wollen Sie studieren oder sofort einen Beruf ergreifen?
c) Wie lange wird die Ausbildung dauern?
d) Werden Sie von hier wegziehen, wenn Sie mit der Schule fertig sind?
e) Wo werden Sie wohnen?
i) Ich werde bestimmt mit meinen Freunden eine Unterkunft mieten.
ii) Ich will unbedingt die Welt bereisen, bevor ich auf die Uni gehe.
iii) Ich werde zu Hause bleiben, um die Kosten an der Uni zu reduzieren.
iv) Ich denke, es wäre eine gute Idee, zuerst eine Ausbildung zu machen.
v) Der Kurs wird vier Jahre dauern.

__/5

8. Übersetzen Sie diese Meinungen.

a) Wenn ich im Abitur gut abschneide, werde ich auf die Uni gehen.
b) Eine gute Bezahlung ist mir sehr wichtig bei der Berufswahl.
c) Ich will Lehrer werden, denn ich denke, ich würde gerne mit Kindern arbeiten.
d) Man sollte einen Persönlichkeitstest machen, um die Berufswahl zu vereinfachern.
e) Es ist eine gute Idee Arbeitserfahrung zu sammeln.

__/5

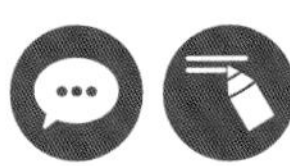

Klassenarbeit: 08 Feiern und Feste

1. Identifizieren Sie den Fall dieser Pronomen.

a) Du hast es mir gegeben.

b) Er spielte mit ihm.

c) Sie ging zu ihr hinüber.

d) Ich habe lange nichts mehr von ihnen gehört.

e) Er fuhr mit ihr zur Schule.

___ 5

2. Finden Sie die passenden Satzhälften.

a) Weihnachten ist mein Lieblingsfest,

b) In der Schule lernen wir viel über deutsche Feste,

c) Ich möchte gern am Karneval teilnehmen,

d) Weil sie so viele Süßigkeiten kriegen,

e) Meine Freunde und ich gehen gern in die Disco,

i) lieben Kinder Halloween.

ii) wenn einer von uns Geburtstag hat.

iii) aber nicht so viel über die schweizerischen oder österreichischen Feste.

iv) denn ich liebe den Weihnachtsschmuck.

v) weil es so spannend klingt.

___ 5

3. Schreiben Sie die Verben im Futur.

a) Ich feiere mit meinen Freunden.

b) Ich mache eine Abifahrt mit meiner Klasse.

c) Ich gehe im Sommer auf ein Konzert.

d) Nach dem Abitur fahre ich zum Musikfest namens Electric Picnic.

e) Ich nehme am Umzug teil.

___ 5

4. Schreiben Sie die Verben im Perfekt.

a) Wir feiern den Nationalfeiertag am 17. März.

b) Jeder geht zum Umzug.

c) Zum Festessen essen wir Lammfleisch mit Minzsoße.

d) Natürlich gibt es viele Ostereier.

e) Wir haben viel Spaß.

___ 5

5. Woraus bestehen diese Wörter?

a) Kleeblatt **b)** Dudelsackspieler
c) Lebensmittel **d)** Schutzpatron
e) Nationalfarbe

___ 5

6. Wählen Sie die richtige Präposition.

a) (in/mit/auf) dem Fest *at the festival*

b) (vor/zwischen/nach) dem Fest *after the festival*

c) (in/mit/auf) der Party *at the party*

d) (auf/um/durch) ein Konzert *to a concert*

e) (hinter/vor/auf) einem Konzert *at a concert*

___ 5

7. Finden Sie die Antworten auf die Fragen.

a) Wie feiern Sie Weihnachten?

b) Was isst man zum Festessen?

c) Besuchen Sie Verwandte?

d) Wie lange dauern die Ferien?

e) Wann fangen die Ferien an?

i) Zum Festessen isst man Putenfleisch mit Kartoffeln.

ii) Die Weihnachtsferien dauern zwei Wochen.

iii) Wir feiern mit einem großen Festessen.

iv) Ja, wir besuchen meine Großeltern.

v) Die Ferien fangen am 22. Dezember an.

___ 5

8. Übersetzen Sie diese Redewendungen ins Englische.

a) Da steppt der Bär!

b) Man hat Tomaten auf den Augen.

c) Du hast Schwein gehabt.

d) Übung macht den Meister.

e) Ich verstehe nur Bahnhof!

___ 5

9. Übersetzen Sie die Reflexivverben im Akkusativ ins Englische.

a) Ich ziehe mich an.

b) Ich wasche mich.

c) Er hat sich angezogen.

d) Sie bewirbt sich um die Stelle.

e) Meine Mutter erinnert sich daran.

___ 5

10. Übersetzen Sie die Reflexivverben im Dativ ins Englische.

a) Ich ziehe mir meine Jacke an.

b) Er zog sich seinen Mantel aus.

c) Wir haben uns die Zähne geputzt.

d) Ihr werdet euch die Zähne putzen.

e) Sie waschen sich die Haare.

___ 5

  Klassenarbeit: 09 Die große Arbeitswelt

1. Identifizieren Sie den Fall und das Geschlecht der Nomen:
a) mit dem Bus **b)** in die Schule
c) in der Schule **d)** in der Deutschstunde **e)** von der Mutter

__/5

2. Finden Sie die passenden Satzhälften.

a) Wenn man neue Erfahrungen macht,
b) Ich suche nicht nur ein gutes Arbeitsklima,
c) Nach dem Abitur will ich freiwillig arbeiten,
d) Ich habe keinen Nebenjob,
e) Ich bin zur Ausbildungsmesse gegangen,
i) um mich über Berufsmöglichkeiten zu informieren.
ii) weil ich so viel für die Schule lernen muss.
iii) sondern auch ein gutes Gehalt.
iv) wird man reifer.
v) denn es ist wichtig, anderen zu helfen.

__/5

3. Schreiben Sie die Verben im Perfekt.

a) Ich arbeite in einem Laden.
b) Er verdient acht Euro pro Stunde.
c) Wir sparen für die Uni.
d) Sie fahren mit dem Bus zum Arbeitsplatz.
e) Ich bediene die Kunden.

__/5

4. Schreiben Sie die Verben im Konditional.

a) Wir werden nach dem Abitur eine Abifahrt machen.
b) Ich werde auf die Uni gehen.
c) Er wird Arbeitserfahrung sammeln.
d) Natürlich wird es viel Geld kosten.
e) Wir werden viel Spaß haben.

__/5

5. Woraus bestehen diese Wörter?
a) Arbeitserfahrung
b) Bewerbungsformular **c)** Nebenjobs
d) Hausarbeit **e)** Nachhilfe

__/5

6. Wählen Sie die richtige Präposition und geben Sie den Fall und das Geschlecht der Nomen an.

a) (für/um/durch) die Zukunft *for the future*
b) (vor/zwischen/nach) dem Abitur *after the Leaving Certificate*
c) (in/mit/auf) einem Hotel *in a hotel*
d) (auf/um/durch) die Uni *to university*
e) (an/vor/auf) der Uni *at university*

__/5

7. Finden Sie die Antworten auf die Fragen.

a) Was wollen Sie nach dem Abitur unternehmen?
b) Welchen Beruf wollen Sie ergreifen?
c) Wo werden Sie studieren?
d) Wie lange wird der Kurs dauern?
e) Wo werden Sie wohnen?
i) Ich will Ingenieur werden.
ii) Ich habe vor, an der Uni in Galway zu studieren.
iii) Der Kurs wird vier Jahre dauern.
iv) Ich werde in einem Studentenwohnheim wohnen.
v) Ich will unbedingt eine Lehre machen.

__/5

8. Übersetzen Sie die Redewendungen ins Englische.

a) Ohne Fleiß kein Preis.
b) Ich habe keinen Bock mehr auf die Schule.
c) Ende gut, alles gut.
d) Vorbeugen ist besser als heilen.
e) Ich drücke dir die Daumen.

__/5

9. Identifizieren Sie den Fall und das Geschlecht der Nomen.

a) Der Rock steht dem Mädchen.
b) Er gratuliert dem Kind.
c) Wir verzeihen den Kindern.
d) Der Lehrer rät dem Jungen, zum Berufsberater zu gehen.
e) Der Berufsberater hilft dem Mann.

__/5

10. Übersetzen Sie diese Ausdrücke im Dativ ins Englische.
a) Es tut mir leid. **b)** Mir ist warm.
c) Das gefällt ihm. **d)** Es geht ihm gut.
e) Es ist mir bekannt.

__/5

Klassenarbeit: 10 Jugendthemen

1. Identifizieren Sie den Fall und das Geschlecht der Adjektive und der Nomen, die sie beschreiben.

a) unter den meisten Jugendlichen

b) auf den beliebten Webseiten

c) in den coolen Nachtclubs

d) in dem neusten Konzert

e) auf dem sozialen Netzwerk

___ / 5

2. Finden Sie die passenden Satzhälften.

a) Viele Jugendliche wollen mit ihren Freunden ausgehen,

b) Einige greifen zu Alkohol,

c) Viele Studenten machen freiwillige Arbeit,

d) Die Studenten arbeiten,

e) Manche Jugendliche stehen unter Druck,

i) um vom Schulstress abzuschalten.

ii) im Abitur gut abzuschneiden.

iii) um Geld zu verdienen.

iv) um Arbeitserfahrung zu sammeln.

v) obwohl das gefährlich ist.

___ / 5

3. Schreiben Sie die Verben im Präsens.

a) Er arbeitete in der Dritten Welt.

b) Wir halfen gern mit.

c) Wir gaben viel Geld für Unterkunft aus.

d) Sie fuhr mit dem Zug zur Uni.

e) Ich ging sofort dahin.

___ / 5

4. Schreiben Sie die Verben im Imperfekt.

a) Sie werden nach dem Abitur einen Kurs machen.

b) Du wirst auf die Uni gehen.

c) Sie wird im Ausland arbeiten.

d) Natürlich werde ich viel Geld verdienen.

e) Ihr werdet Arbeitserfahrung sammeln.

___ / 5

5. Woraus bestehen diese Wörter?

a) freiwillig **b)** Fremdenführer
c) Altersgenossen **d)** Erfolgsergebnisse
e) Bekanntenkreis

___ / 5

6. Wählen Sie die richtige Präposition.

a) (für/um/durch) einen neuen Laptop *for a new laptop*

b) (vor/zwischen/nach) einem langen Schultag *after a long school day*

c) (aus/mit/auf) guten Noten *with good marks*

d) (über/um/durch) die Zukunft *about the future*

e) Angst (an/vor/auf) der Zukunft *fear of the future*

___ / 5

7. Finden Sie die Antworten auf die Fragen.

a) Worüber machen sich die Jugendlichen Sorgen?

b) Machen junge Leute gerne ein Gap Year?

c) Würden Sie gerne ein Gap Year machen?

d) Wie bauen Sie den Schulstress ab?

e) Wo würden Sie freiwillige Arbeit machen?

i) Manche Jugendliche machen gerne ein Gap Year, um Erfahrungen zu sammeln.

ii) Ich lese ein Buch, um den Stress zu reduzieren.

iii) Ich würde lieber sofort auf die Uni gehen.

iv) Ich würde in einem Altersheim freiwillige Arbeit machen.

v) Sie machen sich Sorgen über ihre Zukunft.

___ / 5

8. Geben Sie den Komparativ und den Superlativ für die folgenden Adjektive.

a) Sie fuhr mit dem schnellen Zug.

b) Wir bekommen gute Noten.

c) Ihr seid sehr kluge Kinder.

d) Sie ist in gutem Zustand.

e) Der Chef spricht über die alte Technologie.

___ / 10

9. Geben Sie den Komparativ und Superlativ der folgenden Adverbien:

a) schnell **b)** gern **c)** oft **d)** gut **e)** viel

___ / 5

Klassenarbeit: 11 Die großen Ansprüche unserer Zeit

1. Identifizieren Sie den Fall der Fragewörter.

a) Auf wen wartet er?
b) Mit wem sprichst du?
c) Von wem hast du es bekommen?
d) Wer klopft an der Tür?
e) Wessen Laptop ist das?

__ / 5

2. Finden Sie die passenden Satzhälften.

a) Man muss eine Lösung finden,
b) Seit Jahren wandern Migranten ein,
c) Wenn man sich nicht integriert,
d) Niemand kann leugnen,
e) Ohne Zweifel sind Rauchen und Alkohol trinken heiße Themen,
i) dass viele Flüchtlinge und Migranten nach Europa ziehen.
ii) bevor die Situation noch schlimmer wird.
iii) und sie haben Aspekte ihrer Kultur mitgebracht.
iv) die man immer wieder bespricht.
v) kann es zu Problemen führen.

__ / 5

3. Schreiben Sie die Verben im Perfekt.
a) Er rauchte viel. **b)** Wir tranken Bier.
c) Wir nahmen das Leben ernst.
d) Sie entflohen dem Krieg.
e) Wir sprachen darüber im Unterricht.

__ / 5

4. Was bedeuten die Fragen auf Englisch?

a) Worüber spricht er?
b) Wovon reden sie?
c) Wovor hatte er Angst?
d) Worauf hat er sich gefreut?
e) Woraus besteht es?

__ / 5

5. Übersetzen Sie ins Englische.

a) Ich spreche darüber.
b) Wir haben Angst davor.
c) Ich bin damit zufrieden.
d) Er wartete darauf.
e) Ich brauche Geld dafür.

__ / 5

6. Was bedeuten die Fragen auf Englisch?

a) Welche Interessen haben Sie?
b) An welchem Tag hat es stattgefunden?
c) Welche Bücher hat er gemeint?
d) Welche Jahreszeit haben Sie am liebsten?
e) Welche Frau haben Sie gesehen?

__ / 5

7. Woraus bestehen die folgenden Wörter?
a) Wirtschaftspolitik **b)** auswandern
c) einwandern **d)** Bombenanschlag
e) Nahosten

__ / 5

8. Was bedeuten diese Sätze auf Englisch?

a) Gewalt erzeugt Gewalt.
b) Man sollte keine Verallgemeinerungen machen.
c) Ich bin Feuer und Flamme dafür.
d) Das bringt mich auf die Palme!
e) Alles hat sein Ende, nur die Wurst hat zwei!

__ / 5

9. Was passt zusammen?
a) vertreiben **b)** protestieren
c) Hintergrund **d)** Gewalt **e)** Rassismus
i) racism **ii)** to expel **iii)** to protest
iv) background **v)** violence

__ / 5

10. Was sind die Antworten auf die Fragen?

a) Warum ist Übergewicht ein wachsendes Problem?
b) Wie werden Falschinformationen heutzutage verbreitet?
c) Warum spielen die Medien eine wichtige Rolle im Leben der Jugendlichen?
d) Ist Rauchen immer noch ein großes Problem unter Jugendlichen?
e) Wie kann man Cybermobbing verhindern?
i) Man braucht Aufklärung, damit jeder versteht, wie gefährlich Cybermobbing ist.
ii) Falschinformationen werden im Internet sehr leicht verbreitet.
iii) Viele essen ungesund und halten sich nicht fit.
iv) Nein, die meisten Jugendlichen hassen das Rauchen.
v) Jugendliche verbringen viel Zeit online und deshalb spielen die Medien eine wichtige Rolle.

__ / 5

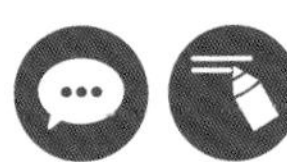

Klassenarbeit: 12 Die Medien

1. Geben Sie den Imperativ für die folgenden Verben.

a) Ihr wartet auf mich.

b) Du hörst gut zu.

c) Wir schreiben das auf.

d) Ihr schaut euch den Film an.

e) Sie geben mir das Geld.

__ 5

2. Finden Sie den Konjunktiv II für die folgenden Verben.

a) Man mag soziale Medien nutzen.

b) Man soll auf die Gefahren achten.

c) Man muss vorsichtig sein.

d) Junge Leute dürfen auf viel mehr Webseiten gehen.

e) Wir können viel tun, um uns zu schützen.

__ 5

3. Schreiben Sie die Verben im Präsens.

a) Er nutzte das Internet.

b) Sie verbrachte viel Zeit beim Computer spielen.

c) Ihr saht euch viele Filme an.

d) Sie spielte jeden Tag Computerspiele.

e) Wir sprachen online.

__ 5

4. Übersetzen Sie die folgenden Ausdrücke im Konjunktiv ins Englische.

a) Das wäre super.

b) Wenn ich nur das Geld dafür hätte!

c) Es gäbe viel zu tun.

d) Wenn das Wetter nur besser wäre!

e) Ich wäre sehr enttäuscht.

__ 5

5. Übersetzen Sie ins Englische.

a) Es ist eine schlechte Gewohnheit.

b) Ich bin computersüchtig.

c) Ich bin eine Leseratte.

d) Das geht mir auf die Nerven.

e) Ich bin daran sehr interessiert.

__ 5

6. Was bedeuten die Fragen auf Englisch?

a) Welche sozialen Medien nutzen Sie?

b) Wie viel Zeit verbringen Sie auf sozialen Netzwerken?

c) Wie oft nutzen Sie soziale Medien?

d) Welche sozialen Medien haben Sie am liebsten?

e) Wofür nutzen Sie das Internet?

__ 5

7. Woraus bestehen die folgenden Wörter?

a) Computersucht **b)** Medienkonsum **c)** Therapiezentrum **d)** Technologiewelle **e)** Bildschirm

__ 5

8. Übersetzen Sie die Redewendungen ins Englische.

a) Das ist das Modewort der Saison.

b) Du Glückspilz!

c) Jedem Tierchen sein Pläsierchen.

d) Andere Länder, andere Sitten.

e) Das dicke Ende kommt noch.

__ 5

9. Was passt zusammen?

a) wäre **b)** hätte **c)** ginge **d)** gäbe **e)** möchte

i) würde ... gehen **ii)** würde ... sein **iii)** würde ... geben **iv)** würde ... mögen **v)** würde ... haben

__ 5

10. Was sind die Antworten auf die Fragen?

a) Wofür benutzen Sie ein Handy?

b) Wofür benutzen Sie das Internet?

c) Verbringen Sie viel Zeit im Internet?

d) Welche Apps finden Sie vorteilhaft?

e) Was sind die Nachteile des Internets?

i) Ich benutze das Internet um für die Schule zu recherchieren, Kleidung zu kaufen und mir Filme anzugucken.

ii) Ich sehe gern Filme auf Netflix, also verbringe ich meistens zwei bis drei Stunden täglich im Internet.

iii) Ohne Zweifel finde ich WhatsApp fantastisch, denn ich kann darüber kostenlos telefonieren.

iv) Im Internet muss man vorsichtig sein, denn es gibt viele Betrüger und man kann sich nicht auf die Informationen verlassen.

v) Ich benutze mein Handy, um meinen Freunden Nachrichten zu schicken und um Musik runterzuladen.

__ 5

Klassenarbeit: 13 Die Gesundheit

1. Geben Sie das Passiv für die folgenden Verben.

a) Sie haben den Mann verhaftet.

b) Sie hat das Geld gestohlen.

c) Die Polizei hat 20 Kilogramm Kokain beschlagnahmt.

d) Die Polizei hat das Auto gestoppt.

e) Die Frau hat das Kind gekidnappt.

__ / 5

2. Übersetzen Sie die Passivsätze ins Englische.

a) Viele Autos wurden gestohlen.

b) Die Täter wurden gefunden.

c) Die Leute werden gestoppt.

d) Sie wurden sofort aufgegessen.

e) Wir wurden fotografiert.

__ / 5

3. Geben Sie die entsprechenden Sprachen.

a) Frankreich **b)** Deutschland **c)** China **d)** Irland **e)** Spanien

__ / 5

4. Übersetzen Sie die folgenden Ausdrücke im Passiv ins Englische.

a) Es wird gesagt, dass ...

b) Es wird behauptet, dass ...

c) Es wird richtig gefeiert.

d) Leider wird das noch toleriert.

e) Es wird leider verbreitet, dass ...

__ / 5

5. Woraus bestehen folgende Wörter?

a) Kühlschrank **b)** Lieferservice **c)** Kohlenhydrate **d)** Kochsendung **e)** Fitnessstudio

__ / 5

6. Was bedeuten die Fragen auf Englisch?

a) Wie sehen Sie aus?

b) Wie halten Sie sich fit?

c) Welche Sportmöglichkeiten gibt es in Ihrem Wohnort?

d) Welche Esstrends gibt es heutzutage?

e) Was isst du zum Frühstück?

__ / 5

7. Finden Sie die passenden Satzhälften.

a) Manche gehen zum Fitnessstudio,

b) Ich esse viel Obst und Gemüse,

c) Weil Diätpillen gefährlich sind,

d) Wir essen vegetarische Gerichte,

e) Jugendliche brauchen gute Essgewohnheiten,

i) weil wir Fleisch vermeiden wollen.

ii) denn ich will gesund sein.

iii) um in der Schule gut voranzukommen.

iv) um Muskeln aufzubauen.

v) würde ich nie so was probieren.

__ / 5

8. Wählen Sie die richtige Präposition.

a) Immer mehr Jugendliche legen Wert **(an/auf/in/für)** gesundes Essen.

b) Krafttraining ist **(an/zu/für/auf)** einem Lebensstil geworden.

c) Fitness **(zum/für/an/auf)** gutes Aussehen ist auch Identitätsarbeit.

d) Fast jeder leidet **(an/von/unter/durch)** Zeitdruck.

e) Ich trainiere täglich **(an/in/für/auf)** 30 Minuten.

__ / 5

9. Geben Sie das Antonym für die folgenden Wörter.

a) fettarm **b)** dick **c)** süß **d)** salzig **e)** voll

i) dünn **ii)** fettig **iii)** ungesalzen **iv)** leer **v)** sauer

__ / 5

10. Was sind die Antworten auf die Fragen?

a) Wie halten Sie sich fit?

b) Wie oft gehen Sie zum Fitnessstudio?

c) Essen Sie gesund oder ungesund?

d) Was bedeutet gesundes Essen?

e) Was soll man tun, wenn man gestresst ist?

i) Wenn ich gestresst bin, atme ich tief durch.

ii) Ich gehe täglich zum Fitnessstudio.

iii) Ich esse lieber gesundes Essen, denn es schmeckt halt besser.

iv) Ich trainiere ein paarmal pro Woche um mich fit zu halten.

v) Gesundes Essen bedeutet möglichst viel Obst und Gemüse zu essen.

__ / 5

Klassenarbeit: 14 Umwelt

1. Geben Sie das Negativ für die folgenden Verben.

a) Ich habe eine Stofftasche.

b) Sie verschmutzt die Umwelt.

c) Wir schützen die Umwelt.

d) Es gibt viele Windturbinen.

e) Ich sehe viel Müll auf der Straße.

__ 5

2. Geben Sie das entsprechende Antonym.

a) Wir kaufen wenige Plastiktüten.

b) Ich kaufe immer wieder aufladbare Batterien.

c) Ich recycle alle Verpackungen.

d) Ich werde umweltbewusster.

e) Wir sparen nie Energie.

__ 5

3. Finden Sie die passenden Satzhälften.

a) Weil die Gletscher schmelzen,

b) Die reine Natur wird zerstört

c) Klimakatastrophen, wie Überflutung, Orkane und Dürren,

d) Weniger Verpackung heißt,

e) Ich finde es toll,

i) und viele Tierarten sind vom Aussterben bedroht.

ii) steigt der Meeresspiegel.

iii) dass weniger Kohlendioxid produziert wird.

iv) dass Bio-Lebensmittel immer beliebter werden.

v) kommen immer häufiger vor.

__ 5

4. Übersetzen Sie die folgenden Ausdrücke im Negativ ins Englische.

a) Niemand hat ein Wort gesagt.

b) Wir haben weder Essen noch Getränke.

c) Sie hat nichts gesehen.

d) So was hätte er nie getan.

e) Nein, ich stimme damit nicht überein.

__ 5

5. Finden Sie die Antworten auf die Fragen.

a) Was machen Sie persönlich, um die Umwelt zu schützen?

b) Wie kann man Wasser sparen?

c) Wie kann man Strom sparen?

d) Wie kann man Plastik vermeiden?

e) Wie kann man nachhaltig leben?

i) Man soll immer Stofftaschen, statt Plastiktüten, benutzen, wenn man einkauft.

ii) Man soll Lichter ausschalten, wenn man sie nicht braucht.

iii) Ich gehe zu Fuß zur Schule, um Benzin zu sparen.

iv) Man soll Lebensmittel kaufen, die im eigenen Land produziert werden.

v) Wenn man die Zähne putzt, soll man den Hahn abdrehen.

__ 5

6. Woraus bestehen die folgenden Wörter?
a) Naturschutz **b)** Weltnaturerbe
c) Klimakatastrophe
d) Luftverschmutzung **e)** Treibhausgase

__ 5

7. Was passt zusammen?

a) Wenn die Katze aus dem Haus ist, tanzen die Mäuse auf dem Tisch.

b) Man hat schon Pferde kotzen sehen.

c) Der Fisch stinkt vom Kopf her.

d) Ich bin fleißig wie eine Biene.

e) Du bist ein Spaßvogel.

i) I'm as hard-working as a bee.

ii) The problems start at the top.

iii) You're a funny guy.

iv) When the cat's away, the mice will play.

v) When pigs will fly.

__ 10

8. Finden Sie das Synonym für die folgenden Wörter.
a) Desaster **b)** Aktivist
c) wiederverwerten **d)** schonen
e) Unternehmen

i) Firma **ii)** Protestierer **iii)** schützen
iv) recyceln **v)** Katastrophe

__ 5

9. Was passt zusammen?
a) nachhaltig **b)** katastrophal **c)** giftig
d) schädlich **e)** positiv

i) catastrophic **ii)** poisonous
iii) harmful **iv)** positive **v)** sustainable

__ 5

Listening and Reading Comprehension: Tips and Practice

Language of emotion & expressions showing the relationship between speakers

The expressions below have been taken from *Deutsch Komplett* listening exercises. Copy the table below and place the expressions from Groups A to D in the appropriate category. Note that on some occasions, an expression may fall under both categories.

Language of emotion	Expressions showing the relationship between speakers
Ich bin ganz empört! *I am very angry!*	Ja, aber mein Sohn ist so gestresst. *Yes, but my son is so stressed.*

Group A

1. Ich bin ganz empört!
2. ... die schlechte Note, die mein Kind von einem Ihrer Lehrer bekommen hat!
3. Bitte beruhigen Sie sich, Herr Beck.
4. Ja, aber mein Sohn ist so gestresst.
5. Könnten wir ... für eine Stunde mit unseren Freunden herumhängen?
6. Julia, hast du heute nach der Schule frei?
7. Spinnst du?
8. ..., wenn wir auf dem Weg zur Schule sind.
9. Ja, also, wir haben jetzt Mathe.
10. Ich will nicht mehr in die Schule gehen.

Group B

1. Ich habe so viel Angst, dass die Tasche nicht gefunden wird!
2. Wenn ich meine Tasche nicht wiederkriege, werde ich heulen!
3. Beruhigen Sie sich!
4. Ich habe die Nase voll.
5. Ja, ich schaffe es einfach nicht, genug für all die Klassenarbeiten zu lernen.
6. ... bin ich ja auch schlechter Laune.
7. Dann brauchst du nicht mehr wegen der Klassenarbeiten genervt zu sein!
8. Wir können zu zweit lernen, wenn du möchtest.
9. Wollen wir uns heute nach der Schule treffen?
10. Ich helfe dir beim Mathe lernen und du hilfst mir beim Geschichte lernen.

Group C

1. Ja, wir freuen uns riesig darauf.
2. Ein Austausch ist ja eine fantastische Gelegenheit die Kultur kennenzulernen!
3. Aber keine Sorge!
4. Es freut mich, so was für Sie zu organisieren.
5. Ich stehe wirklich unter zu viel Stress.
6. Ich schaffe kaum, was von mir verlangt wird.
7. Es ist mir viel zu viel!
8. Das ist ja ganz schön stressig, du!
9. Ja, schon! Wie geht es dir eigentlich?
10. Das hört sich toll an!

Group D

1. Hallo, Schatz.
2. So schlimm ist es doch nicht.
3. Mach dir keine Sorgen!
4. Du bist so lieb!
5. Ich freue mich auf heute Abend.
6. Es wird so viel Spaß machen!
7. Denk doch an das schöne Feuerwerk und an das Tanzen und Singen!
8. Für mich ist es die beste Zeit des Jahres.
9. ... aber für mich ist es deprimierend.
10. Du übertreibst da ein bisschen, Karla!

Prüfungstipp

As you make your way through the listening exercises and reading comprehensions in this book, find other examples of language that shows emotion.

Expressions which convey emotion, personal relationships and a change in behaviour by a character

The sentences below have been taken from some of the literary reading comprehensions found in four chapters of *Deutsch Komplett*. Copy the table below and place the expressions under the appropriate category. Give reasons for your choices. Some expressions may fall under two or more categories.

Emotion	Language showing the relationship between characters	Change in behaviour/relationship

Chapter 1, p.14, *Meine Familie und ich*: Which relationships and emotions are expressed in the story?

1. Bei Lauras neuer Patchwork-Familie gibt es viel Freude, aber auch manchmal Ärger.
2. Das Leben war ruhig und Mutti hatte immer Zeit für Laura und Franz.
3. Letztes Jahr hat Mutti ... geheiratet. // Jetzt hat Laura eine große Familie.
4. Laura kommt gut mit Magda aus, denn Magda ist ... ganz freundlich . // Aber Laura würde lieber ihr eigenes Zimmer haben.
5. Meistens verstehen sich Laura und Franz. // Aber Franz ist sehr unordentlich und will nie bei der Hausarbeit mithelfen.

Chapter 2, p. 36, *Mein Wohnort*: Discuss how the relationship develops.

1. „Ich wollte Sie zu einer Tasse Kaffee einladen." // „Gerne nehme ich Ihre Einladung an."
2. „Kann ich hierbleiben?" fragt Merle. // „Klar kannst du hierbleiben und ich glaube, wir sollten uns alle duzen", lacht Franziska.
3. Sie freut sich, dass jetzt ein Kind im Haus wohnt. // Die eigenen Kinder und Enkel vermisst sie sehr.
4. „Und wie kommt ihr zurecht?"// „Es geht wunderbar."
5. „Mama, es ist ganz prima bei Franziska und Björn. // Du kannst in aller Ruhe wieder gesund werden."

Chapter 3, p. 56, *In meiner Freizeit*: Which emotions/relationships are mentioned? Is there a change in the relationship?

1. Während die Mitschüler alle auf dem ... Eis Schlittschuh laufen und lachen, ist Julchen nicht froh.
2. „Blödes Eislaufen", denkt sie sich!
3. „Ich langweile mich hier..."
4. „Ich will nach Hause!"
5. Er versteht, dass Julchen Eislaufen nicht gernhat. // Er hat Mitleid mit ihr.
6. „Ich mag Eislaufen gehen, aber wenn Julchen es nicht mag, finde ich es unfair, dass wir das jedes Jahr machen."
7. Sie hat sich daran gewöhnt immer wieder enttäuscht zu sein.
8. Das ist immerhin ein Anfang, denkt Julchen und muss grinsen.

Chapter 4, p. 76, *Schule*: Which emotions/relationships are revealed in the story? Is there a change in Roswita's emotions?

1. Ihre Augen füllten sich mit Tränen.
2. Roswita erschrak, als sie die Stimme der Schulleiterin hörte.
3. „Ich hatte Angst, meinen Eltern das Zeugnis mit der Fünf zu zeigen, Mater Maria."
4. Sie hatte so viel Angst, dass er wieder denken würde, dass seine Tochter nicht erfolgreich genug gewesen war.
5. Sie fühlte sich wieder zufrieden.

Lexikon

A

ab und zu *now and again*
abbauen *to reduce*
abbrechen *to break off*
Abendessen (n) *dinner*
Abenteuer (n) – *adventure*
Abfahrtszeit (f) -en *departure time*
Abfall (m) Abfälle *waste; rubbish*
Abgase, pl. *exhaust fumes*
abgeben *to hand in*
abhängen von *to depend on*
Abitur (n) *Leaving Certificate*
ablaufen *to proceed; to expire*
ablehnen *to turn down*
Ablenkung (f) -en *distraction*
abmachen *to agree*
abnehmen *to lose weight*
abrutschen *to slide*
absagen *to cancel*
Absatz (m) Absätze *paragraph*
abschaffen *to get rid of*
abschalten *to switch off*
abscheulich *repulsive*
gut abschneiden *to score well*
absehbar *foreseeable*
abstellen *to turn off*
Abwasser (n) Abwässer *sewage*
Abwechslung (f) *variety*
Agentur (f) -en *agency; company*
ähnlich *similar*
Akku (m) -s *battery*
Albatros (m) -se *albatross*
Alkohol (m) *alcohol*
allein *alone*
Alltag (m) *daily routine*
Alptraum (m) -träume *nightmare*
Alter (n) – *age*
Alternative (f) -n *alternative***Altersgenosse (m) -n** *contemporary*
altbacken *stale*
(sich) amüsieren *to amuse oneself*
anbieten *to offer*
(sich) ändern *to change*
anders *different*
anerkannt *recognised*
Anerkennung (f) -en *recognition*
Anfang (m) Anfänge *beginning*
anfangen *to begin*
Anforderung (f) -en *requirement*
angeblich *alleged*
angehen *to concern; to involve*
angenehm *pleasant*
Angestellte (m/f) -n *employee*
Angriff (m) -e *attack*
Angst (f) Ängste *fear*
ängstlich *fearful*
angucken *to look at*
anhören *to listen*
Anker (f) – *anchor*
Anker lichten *to lift anchor*
ankommen *to arrive*
annehmen *to accept*
Anruf (m) -e *phone call*
anrufen *to call*
Anschluss (m) Anschlüsse *connection*
anspruchsvoll *challenging*
anständig *decent(ly), honest(ly)*
anstellen *to employ*
(sich) anstellen *to queue*
(sich) anstrengen *to make an effort*
anstrengend *strenuous*
antreten *to line up*
Antwort (f) -en *answer*
antworten *to answer*
(sich) anziehen *to get dressed*
Applaus (m) *applause*
Arbeit (f) *work*
arbeiten *to work*
Arbeitnehmer (m) – *employee*
Arbeitserfahrung (f) -en *work experience*
Ärger (m) *trouble*
(sich) ärgern *to get annoyed*
Arme (m/f) -n *poor person*
Armut (f) *poverty*
Arsen (n) *arsenic*
Art (f) -en *type*
Arzt (m) Ärzte *doctor*
Asylantenheim (n) -e *refugee shelter*
Asylbewerber (m) – *asylum seeker*
Ausdauer (f) *endurance*
aufbauen *to build up*
aufbessern *to improve*
Aufenthalt (m) *stay*
auffallen *to notice*
Aufgabe (f) -n *task*
aufgeben *to give up*
aufklären *to educate*
aufmachen *to open*
aufnehmen *to record; to absorb; to accept*
aufpassen *to mind*
aufräumen *to tidy up*
aufsagen *to recite*
Aufsatz (m) -sätze *essay*
aufschlagen *to set up; to open (book)*
aufstehen *to get up*
aufsteigen *to rise*
Auftrag (m) Aufträge *task*
aufwachen *to wake up*
aufwachsen *to grow up*
Aufwand (m) *effort*
Auge (n) -n *eye*
ausbilden *to train*
Ausbildung (f) -en *training*
ausdrucken *to print*
Ausflug (m) Ausflüge *excursion*
ausgebildet *educated*
ausgedient *worn out*
ausgehen *to go out*
ausgewählt *chosen*
ausgrenzen *to exclude*
aushalten *to endure*
auskommen *to get on*

Ausland (n) *abroad*
Ausländer (m) – *foreigner*
ausleihen *to borrow*
auslösen *to trigger*
Ausnahme (f) -n *exception*
ausnutzen *to take advantage of*
ausprobieren *to try out*
ausräumen *to empty*
ausreißen *to tear out*
ausrichten *to align*
ausrotten *to exterminate*
(sich) ausruhen *to relax*
ausschalten *to switch off*
Ausschlag (m) *rash*
aussehen *to look (like)*
Aussehen (n) *appearance*
außer *unless*
außerhalb *outside of*
Aussicht (f) -en *view*
Aussprache (f) -n *pronunciation*
ausspucken *to spit out*
ausstatten *to equip*
Austausch (m) *exchange*
austauschen *to exchange*
austragen *to deliver*
ausüben *to practise*
Auswanderer (m) – *emigrant*
auswandern *to emigrate*
Auswirkung (f) -en *effect*
ausziehen *to move out*
Autokennzeichen (n) – *car registration number*

bald *soon*
Bart (m) Bärte *beard*
bauen *to build*
Bauernhof (m) -höfe *farm*
Baum (m) Bäume *tree*
beabsichtigen *to intend*
beantworten *to respond*
bedeuten *to mean*
Bedeutung (f) -en *meaning*
bedrohen *to threaten*
bedrohlich *threatening(ly)*
(sich) beeilen *to hurry*
beeinflussen *to influence*
beenden *to finish*
befassen *to deal with*
Befehl (m) -e *command*
befehlen *to command*
(sich) befinden *to find oneself*
befragen *to question*
begabt *talented*
begeistert *excited*
beginnen *to begin*
begleiten *to accompany*
Begleiter (m) – *companion*
begreifen *to understand*
Begriff (m) -e *concept*
begründen *to justify*
begrüßen *to greet*
Behälter (m) – *container*
behandeln *to treat*
behaupten *to claim*
beherrschen *to master*
behilflich *helpful*
behindert *disabled*
beide *both*
beinahe *nearly*
Beispiel (n) -e *example*
Beitrag (m) Beiträge *contribution*
beitragen *to contribute*
bekannt *known*
Bekanntenkreis (m) -e *circle of acquaintances*
bekleidet *dressed*
bekommen *to receive*
Belastung (f) -en *burden; pollution*
beleidigt *insulted*
beleuchtet *lit*
beliebt *popular*
belohnen *to reward*
Belohnung (f) -en *reward*
bemerken *to notice*
(sich) bemühen *to make an effort*
benachteiligt *disadvantaged*
Benehmen (n) *behaviour*
(sich) benehmen *to behave*
benennen *to name*
benötigen *to need*
benutzen *to use*
beobachten *to watch*
Berater (m) – *advisor*
Beratung (f) -en *advice*
bereisen *to travel*
bereits *already*
Berg (m) -e *mountain*
Bergwerk (n) -e *mine*
berichten *to report*
Beruf (m) -e *profession*
beruflich *professional(ly)*
Berufsberater (m) – *guidance counsellor*
beruhigen *to calm*
berühmt *famous*
Besatzung (f) -en *crew*
(sich) beschäftigen *to be busy*
beschäftigt *busy*
beschlagnahmen *to confiscate*
beschließen *to decide*
frühstücken *to breakfast*
beschränken *to limit*
beschreiben *to describe*
Beschwerdebrief (m) -e *letter of complaint*
(sich) beschweren *to complain*
beseitigen *to redress; to remove*
besichtigen *to view*
besitzen *to own*
Besitzer (m) – *owner*
besorgen *to look after; to get*
besorgt *worried*
besprechen *to discuss*
bestehen auf *to insist on*
bestehen *to pass (exam)*
bestimmt *certain*
bestrafen *to punish*
besuchen *to visit; to attend*
beten *to pray*
betrachten *to view*
betragen *to amount to*
betreten *to enter*
betreuen *to look after*
betrügerisch *fraudulent*
Beurteilung (f) -en *assessment*
Beute (f) *loot*
Bevölkerung (f) -en *population*
bevorzugen *to prefer*
bewältigen *to overcome*

Bewegung (f) -en *exercise*
Beweis (m) -e *proof*
(sich) bewerben *to apply*
bewusst *aware*
bezahlen *to pay*
Bezahlung (f) -en *payment*
(sich) beziehen *to relate to*
Beziehung (f) -en *relationship*
Bibliothek (f) -en *library*
Bier (n) -e *beer*
bieten *to offer*
Bild (n) -er *picture*
Bildung (f) -en *education*
billig *cheap*
Bio- *organic*
Birne (f) -n *pear*
Bitte (f) -n *request*
bitten *to ask*
blass *pale*
bleiben *to stay*
Bleistift (m) -e *pencil*
blicken *to look*
blitzschnell *lightning-quick*
Blume (f) -n *flower*
Boden (m) Böden *floor; ground*
Bombenanschlag (m) -anschläge *bomb attack*
bösartig *malicious*
böse auf *angry at*
böse *bad*
Braten (m) *roast*
Brauch (m) Bräuche *custom*
brauchen *to need*
braungebrannt *tanned*
brav *well behaved*
brechen *to break*
Briefkasten (m) -kästen *letter box*
Brötchen (n) – *bread roll*
Brücke (f) -n *bridge*
buchen *to book*
Bücherregal (n) -e *bookshelf*
Bucht (f) -en *bay*
büffeln *to swot*
Bühne (f) -n *stage*
bunt *bright; colourful*
Büro (n) -s *office*

C

Chef (m) -s *boss*
Christentum (n) *Christianity*
circa *about*

Dachboden (m) -böden *attic*
Dame (f) -n *lady*
Damm (m) Dämme *dam*
Dampfer (m) – *steamboat*
danach *after that*
Dankbarkeit (f) *gratitude*
danken *to thank*
darstellen *to pose; to depict*
dauern *to last*
dauernd *continuously*
Decke (f) -n *blanket*
denken *to think*
Denken (n) *thinking*
deprimiert *depressed*
Desaster (n) – *disaster*
deswegen *therefore*
dicht *thick*
dick *fat; thick*
Dieb (m) -e *thief*
Ding (n) -e *thing*
dominieren *to dominate*
donnernd *thundering*
doppelt *doubled*
drastisch *drastic*
draußen *outside*
dringend *urgent; urgently*
Drogen, pl. *drugs*
Druck (m) -e *pressure*
drücken *to press*
dumm *stupid*
Dunkelheit (f) *dark*
durchfallen *to fail*
durchlesen *to read through*
durchschnittlich *average*
(sich) duschen *to shower*

ebenfalls *equally*
echt *real; genuine*
Ecke (f) -n *corner*
Ehre (f) *honour*
ehrlich *honest*
Ehrlichkeit (f) *honesty*
eigen- *own*
(sich) eignen *to be suited*
einfach *simple; simply*
Einfluss (m) Einflüsse *influence*
Eingabe (f) -n *entry*
eingreifen *to intervene*
Einheimische, pl. *local people*
Einheit (f) *unity*
Einkauf (m) Einkäufe *shopping*
einladen *to invite*
Einladung (f) -en *invitation*
Einrichtung (f) -en *facility*
Einsatz (m) Einsätze *commitment*
einschalten *to switch on*
einschlafen *to fall asleep*
einschränken *to limit*
einschüchtern *to intimidate*
einseifen *to lather*
einsetzen *to introduce; to insert*
einteilen *to divide*
Eintopf (m) Eintöpfe *stew*
eintreten *to enter*
einwandern *to immigrate*
Einwohner, pl. *inhabitants*
Einzelhandel (m) *retail*
einzeln- *individual*
einziehen *to move in*
einzig- *only*
Eis (n) *ice cream; ice*
Eisbahn (f) -en *ice rink*
Eisberg (m) -e *iceberg*
eislaufen *to ice-skate*
Eiweiß (n) *protein*
Eltern, pl. *parents*
empfangen *to receive*
empfehlen *to recommend*
empfinden *to experience*
empfindlich *sensitive*

eng *narrow*
Enkelkind (n) -er *grandchild*
entdecken *to discover*
entfernen *to remove*
entfliehen *to escape*
Entschädigung (f) -en *compensation*
(sich) entscheiden *to decide*
Entscheidung (f) -en *decision*
(sich) entschuldigen *to apologise*
Entschuldigung (f) -en *apology*
entsetzt *horrified*
entsorgen *to dispose of*
(sich) entspannen *to relax*
Entspannung (f) *relaxation*
entsprechend *accordingly*
enttäuscht *disappointed*
entwickeln *to develop*
Entwicklung (f) -en *development*
Entwicklungsland (n) -länder *developing country*
entwurzeln *to uproot*
Erdbeben (n) – *earthquake*
Erde (f) *earth*
erfahren *experienced*
erfahren *to discover*
Erfahrung (f) -en *experience*
erfinden *to invent*
Erfindung (f) -en *invention*
Erfolg (m) -e *success*
erfolgreich *successful*
erfordern *to require*
erfüllen *to fulfill*
Ergänzung (f) -en *addition*
Ergebnis (n) -se *result*
erhalten *to receive*
(sich) erholen *to recover*
(sich) erinnern an *to remember*
erkennen *to recognise*
erklären *to explain*
(sich) erkundigen *to enquire*
erlangen *to attain*
erlauben *to allow*
Erlaubnis (f) -se *permission*
erleben *to experience*
Erlebnis (n) -se *experience*
erledigen *to do*
erleichtern *to ease*
erleichtert *relieved*
ermöglichen *to enable*
ermutigen *to encourage*
Ernährung (f) *nutrition*
erneuerbar *renewable*
ernst *serious*
erreichen *to reach*
erschießen *to shoot*
erschöpft *exhausted*
erschrecken *to frighten*
erschrocken *terrified*
ersetzen *to replace*
erstaunen *to amaze*
erstklassig *first class*
erwähnen *to mention*
erwarten *to expect*
erweitern *to broaden*
erwidern *to reply*
erwünscht *desired*
Erzieher (m) – *childminder*
essen *to eat*
ewig *forever*

Fach (n) Fächer *subject*
fähig *capable*
Fähigkeit (f) -en *skill; function*
Fall (m) Fälle *case*
fallen *to fall*
fälschen *to forge; to falsify*
Familie (f) -n *family*
Farbe (f) -n *colour*
färben *to dye*
fassen *to grab*
fast *nearly*
faul *lazy*
fehlen *to be missing*
fehlend *lacking*
Fehler (m) – *mistake*
feiern *to celebrate*
Fensterscheibe (f) -n *window pane*
Ferien, pl. *holidays*
fertig *finished*
fest *solid*
Fest (n) -e *celebration*
feststellen *to assess*
fettig *greasy*
Fettleibigkeit (f) *obesity*
Feuerwerk (n) -e *firework*
fieberhaft *feverish(ly)*
finanzieren *to finance*
Firma (f) Firmen *firm*
Fischbestände, pl. *fish stocks*
Flasche (f) -n *bottle*
Fleisch (n) *meat*
fleißig *hardworking*
flexibel *flexible*
fliegen *to fly*
fließen *to flow*
fließend *fluent; fluently*
fluchen *to curse*
Flucht (f) -en *flight*
flüchten *to flee*
Flüchtling (m) -e *refugee*
Fluss (m) Flüsse *river*
Folge (f) -n *consequence*
folgen *to follow*
förderlich *useful*
fördern *to encourage; to promote*
forschen *to research*
fortsetzen *to continue*
Frage (f) -n *question*
fragen *to ask*
Freiheit (f) -en *freedom*
freiwillig *voluntary*
Freizeit (f) *freetime*
fremd *strange; foreign*
Fremdsprache (f) -n *foreign language*
(sich) freuen *to be pleased*
Freude (f) *fun*
Freundschaft (f) -en *friendship*
Frieden (m) *peace*
froh *happy*
(sich) fühlen *to feel*
führen *to lead*
Führerschein (m) -e *driver's licence*
funktionieren *to work*
fürchten *to fear*
füttern *to feed*

Gast (m) Gäste *guest*
Gebäude (n) – *building*
Gebiet (n) -e *area*
Gedächtnis (n) -se *memory*
Gedanke (m) -n *thought*
Geduld (f) *patience*
geduldig *patiently*
Gefahr (f) -en *danger*
gefährlich *dangerous*
gefallen *to like*
Gefallen (m) – *favour*
gefälscht *falsified*
Gefühl (n) -e *feeling*
gefüllt *stuffed*
Gegner (m) – *opponent*
Gehalt (m) *salary*
Geheimnis (n) -se *secret*
gehören *to belong*
Geisteswissenschaften, pl. *Arts*
Gelände (n) – *grounds*
gelassen *laid back*
Geldbeutel (m) – *purse*
Gelegenheitsjob (m) -s *odd job*
gelernt *qualified*
gelingen *to succeed*
gelten *to count as*
gemeinsam *together*
Gemüse (n) – *vegetable*
gemütlich *cosy*
genial *brilliant*
genießen *to enjoy*
genug *enough*
Gepäck (n) *luggage*
Gerät (n) -e *device*
Geräusch (n) -e *sound*
Gericht (n) -e *dish*
Gerücht (n) -e *rumour*
Geschäft (n) -e *shop; business*
geschehen *to happen*
Geschenk (n) -e *present*
Geschichte (f) -n *story*
geschmacklos *tasteless*
Geschmacksfrage (f) -n *question of taste*
geschmückt *decorated*
gesellig *sociable*
Gesellschaft (f) -en *society*
gesellschaftlich *social*
Gesetz (n) -e *law*
Gesicht (n) -er *face*
Gespräch (n) -e *conversation*
Gestalt (f) -en *figure*
gestern *yesterday*
gestresst *stressed*
Gesundheit (f) *health*
Getränk (n) -e *drink*
Gewalt (f) *violence*
Gewässer (n) – *body of water*
gewinnen *to win*
gewiss *certain*
Gewitter (n) – *thunderstorm*
(sich) an etw. gewöhnen *to get used to sth.*
Gewohnheit (f) -en *habit*
Gewöhnung (f) -en *adjustment*
giftig *poisonous*
Giftstoff (m) -e *toxin*
glatt *smooth*
glauben *to believe*
gleich- *same*
gleichaltrig *same age*
gleichgültig *indifferent*
gleichzeitig *at the same time*
Glück (n) *luck*
glücklich *happy*
Gottesdienst (m) -e *church service*
Gebrauch (m) Gebräuche *use*
greifen *to reach for*
Grenze (f) -n *border*
Grill (m) -s *barbecue*
grinsen *to grin*
Grippe (f) -n *flu*
Großeltern, pl. *grandparents*
großzügig *generous*
gründen *to establish*
gründlich *thorough*
gucken *to look*
günstig *favourable*
gütig *kind-hearted*
Gymnasium (n) Gymnasien *academic secondary school*

Hafen (m) Häfen *harbour*
halten *to consider; to hold*
handeln *to treat*
(sich) handeln um *to be about*
Handy (n) -s *mobile phone*
hänseln *to tease*
hassen *to hate*
hässlich *ugly*
häufig *frequently*
Hausarbeit (f) -en *housework*
Hausarrest (m) *to be grounded*
Haushalt (m) -e *household*
Heft (n) -e *copy*
heftig *fierce*
heil *safe*
heilig *holy*
Heimat (f) *homeland*
heimisch *domestic*
Heimweh (n) *homesickness*
heiraten *to marry*
heiß *hot*
Heizkosten, pl. *heating costs*
Held (m) -en *hero*
helfen *to help*
hell *bright*
herausfinden *to find out*
herausfordern *to challenge*
Herausforderung (f) -en *challenge*
Herd (m) -e *stove*
herumrennen *to run around*
herunterdrehen *to turn down*
herunterladen *to download*
Herz (n) -en *heart*
herzlich *warmly*
heute *today*
heutzutage *nowadays*
Hexe (f) -n *witch*
Hilfe (f) -n *help*
hilfsbereit *helpful*
hinter *behind*
Hitze (f) *heat*
hitzig *heated; heatedly*
hochgiftig *highly poisonous*

hochladen *to upload*
Hochschule (f) -n *college*
hoffen *to hope*
Hoffnung (f) -en *hope*
Hoffnungslosigkeit (f) – *hopelessness*
höflich *polite*
holen *to fetch*
Hölle (f) *hell*
hören *to hear*
Horizont (m) -e *horizon*
Hörsaal (m) -säle *lecture hall*
Hörverständnis (n) -se *listening comprehension*
hübsch *pretty*
Hunger (m) *hunger*
Husten (n) – *cough*

Idee (f) -n *idea*
Identität (f) -en *identity*
immer *always*
infiziert *infected*
informieren *to inform*
(sich) informieren *to inform oneself*
Initiative (f) -n *initiative*
inklusive *including*
Insel (f) -n *island*
insgesamt *altogether*
Instabilität (f) -en *instability*
installieren *to install*
(sich) integrieren *to integrate*
Interesse (n) -n *interest*
Interview (n) -s *interview*
irgendwann *sometime*
irgendwie *somehow*
irgendwo *somewhere*
Irrtum (m) -tümer *mistake*

Jahr (n) -e *year*
Jahreszeit (f) -en *season*
jährlich *annual*
jetzt *now*
jubeln *to cheer*
Jugendamt (n) -ämter *youth welfare office*
Jugendherberge (f) -en *youth hostel*

Kälte (f) *cold*
Kamin (m) -e *chimney*
Kämpfer (m) – *fighter*
Kanal (m) Kanäle *channel*
Kantine (f) -n *canteen*
Kapitän (m) -e *captain*
Karpfen (m) – *carp*
Karrieremesse (f) -n *careers fair*
Kasse (f) -n *till*
Katastrophe (f) -n *catastrophe*
Kaugummi (m) -s *chewing gum*
kennenlernen *to get to know*
kennen *to know*
Kenntnisse, pl. *knowledge*
Kernkraft (f) – *nuclear power*
Kind (n) -er *child*
Kinderkrippe (f) -n *creche*
kindisch *childish*
Kino (n) -s *cinema*
Kirche (f) -n *church*
klagen *to complain*
Klamotten, pl. *clothes (colloq.)*
klappen *to work out*
klar *clear*
klären *to resolve*
Klassenarbeit (f) -en *class test*
Klassenkamerad (m) – *classmate*
Kleeblatt (n) -blätter *shamrock*
Kleid (n) -er *dress*
Kleidung (f) – *clothing*
klettern *to climb*
Klima (n) *climate*
Klimawandel (m) *climate change*
Klingel (f) -n *bell*
klingeln *to ring*
klopfen *to knock*
klug *clever*
Kneipe (f) -n *pub*
Kobold (m) -e *leprechaun*
Koch (m) Köche *chef*
kochen *to cook*
Kochnische (f) -n *kitchenette*
Kofferraum (m) -räume *car boot*
Kohlenhydrat (n) -e *carbohydrate*
komisch *strange*
Kommode (f) -n *dresser*
kompliziert *complicated*
König (m) -e *king*
Konsum (m) *consumption*
konsumieren *to consume*
Kontinent (m) -e *continent*
kontrollieren *to check*
(sich) konzentrieren *to concentrate*
Kopf (m) Köpfe *head*
Kopfhörer (m) – *headphones*
Kopfschmerzen, pl. *headache*
Körper (m) – *body*
Körperkunst (f) *body art*
körperlich *physical*
kosten *to cost*
kostenlos *free*
Krach (m) *crash; trouble*
Kraft (f) Kräfte *strength*
krank *sick*
Kreis (m) -e *circle*
Krieg (m) -e *war*
kriegen *to get*
kritisch *critical*
Kugelschreiber (m) – *biro*
Kühlschrank (m) -schränke *fridge*
Kultur (f) -en *culture*
(sich) kümmern um *to look after*
Kunde (m) -n *customer*
kündigen *to resign*
künstlich *artificial*
kurios *strange*
Kurs (m) -e *course*
kürzlich *recently*
Küste (f) -n *coast*

Labor (n) -s *laboratory*
lächeln *to smile*

Lächeln (n) – *smile*
lachen *to laugh*
Laden (m) Läden *shop*
Lage (f) -n *situation*
lagern *to store*
Land (n) Länder *country*
Landschaft (f) -en *landscape*
Landwirtschaft (f) *agriculture*
langfristig *long term*
langsam *slow; slowly*
Langeweile (f) *boredom*
(sich) langweilen *to be bored*
Lärm (m) *noise*
lassen *to let*
Lastwagen (m) – *truck*
laufen *to run*
Laune (f) -n *mood*
launisch *moody*
laut *according to; loud*
leben *to live*
Leben (n) – *life*
Lebenskosten, pl. *living expenses*
Lebenslauf (m) -läufe *CV*
Lebensmittel (n) – *food*
Lebensraum (m) -räume *habitat*
Lebensstandard (m) -s *living standard*
Lebensstil (m) -e *lifestyle*
Lebensumstände, pl. *personal circumstances*
Lebensweise (f) -n *lifestyle*
lecken *to lick*
lecker *tasty*
Leckerbissen (m) – *delicacy*
Leder (n) – *leather*
legen *to place*
Lehre (f) -n *apprenticeship*
leicht *easy*
Leid (n) *sorrow*
leiden *to suffer*
leidenschaftlich *passionate; passionately*
leider *unfortunately*
leisten *to achieve*
(sich) leisten *to afford*
Leiter (f) -n *ladder*
Lernen (n) *learning*
lesen *to read*
leugnen *to deny*
Licht (n) -er *light*
lieb *sweet*
lieben *to love*
Lied (n) -er *song*
liefern *to deliver*
liegen *to be situated*
Liga (f) Ligen *league*
loben *to praise*
Locke (f) -n *curl*
locker *relaxed*
(sich) lohnen *to be worthwhile*
löschen *to erase*
lösen *to solve*
losfahren *to drive off*
Lösung (f) -en *solution*
Luft (f) Lüfte *air*
lüften *to air*
lügen *to tell a lie*
Lust (f) Lüste *interest; craving*
lustig *funny*
Luxus (m) – *luxury*

machen *to do; to make*
Machthaber (m) – *those in power*
Mädchen (n) – *girl*
Magersucht (f) *anorexia*
mähen *to mow*
malen *to paint*
manchmal *sometimes*
Mannschaft (f) -en *team*
Matrose (m) -n *sailor*
Mauer (f) -n *wall*
Medien, pl. *media*
Medikament (n) -e *medication*
Meer (n) -e *ocean*
Mehrheit (f) *majority*
meinen *to think*
Meinung (f) -en *opinion*
meistern *to master*
Meisterschaft (f) -en *championship*
(sich) melden *to get in touch*
Menge (f) -n *large amount*
merken *to remember*
merkwürdig *strange*
Messe (f) -n *exhibition*
Methode (f) -n *method*
Miete (f) -n *rent*
Migrant (m) -en *migrant*
minderjährig *underage*
Mindestvoraussetzung (f) -en *minimum requirement*
missachten *to disobey*
Missbrauch (m) -bräuche *abuse*
mitgestalten *to help create*
Mitglied (n) -er *member*
mithelfen *to help out*
Mitleid (n) – *sympathy*
mitmachen *to participate*
mitstimmen *to vote*
Mitteilung (f) -en *message*
mittlerweile *meanwhile*
Mobbing (n) *bullying*
Mode (f) -n *fashion*
möglich *possible*
Möglichkeit (f) -en *possibility*
momentan *at the moment*
morgen *tomorrow*
motivieren *to motivate*
müde *tired*
Müll (m) *rubbish*
mündlich *oral*
Muskel (m) -n *muscle*
Mütze (f) -n *cap*

nachahmen *to imitate*
Nachbar (m) -n *neighbour*
Nachbarschaft (f) -en *neighbourhood*
nachdenken *to think about*
Nachfrage (f) -n *follow-up question*
nachhaltig *sustainable*
Nachhilfestunde (f) -n *grinds*
Nachricht (f) -en *news*
Nachteil (m) -e *disadvantage*
Nachtisch (m) -e *dessert*
Nahost (m) *Middle East*

Natur (f) -en *nature*
Naturhaushalt (m) -e *ecosystem*
natürlich *of course*
Nebel (m) – *fog*
nebenbei *on the side*
nehmen *to take*
nennen *to call; to be called*
nerven *to annoy*
nervös *nervous*
nett *nice*
Netz (n) -e *net*
Neuerung (f) -en *innovation*
Neugier (f) *curiosity*
neugierig *curious*
neulich *recent; recently*
nicken *to nod*
nie *never*
(sich) niederlassen *to settle*
niemand *no one*
Niveau (n) -s *level*
Nonne (f) -n *nun*
normalerweise *normally*
Not (f) **Nöte** *trouble; emergency*
Note (f) -n *grade*
Notfall (m) -fälle *emergency*
nötig *necessary*
Notiz (f) -en *note*
notwendig *necessary*
Nutzerverhalten (n) – *user behaviour*
nützlich *useful*

Obdachlose (m/f) -n *homeless person*
oben *above*
Oberstufe (f) -n *senior cycle*
offenhalten *to keep open*
offensichtlich *obviously*
öffentlich *public*
öffnen *to open*
ohne *without*
opfern *to sacrifice*
organisieren *to organise*
Ort (m) -e *place*
örtlich *local*

Parade (f) -n *parade*
Parfümerie (f) -n *perfumery*
Pass (m) **Pässe** *passport*
passen *to fit*
passend *suitable*
passieren *to happen*
pauken *to study*
Pause (f) -n *break*
Pechvogel (m) -vögel *unlucky person*
pendeln *to swing*
Pendelzeit (f) -en *commute*
Pflicht (f) -en *obligation*
Pfote (f) -n *paw*
platzieren *to place*
plötzlich *suddenly*
Polizeiwache (f) -n *police station*
Portemonnaie (n) -s *purse*
Potenzial (n) -e *potential*
Praktikant (m) -en *trainee*
Praktikum (n) **Praktika** *work experience*
praktisch *practical*
prallen *to crash*
Preis (m) -e *price*
Priorität (f) -en *priority*
Prüfung (f) -en *exam*
Pulver (n) – *powder*
putzen *to clean*

Qualität (f) -en *quality*
Quelle (f) -en *source*

Rabatt (m) -e *discount*
rasen *to race*
Rasen (m) – *lawn*
(sich) rasieren *to shave*
Rassismus (m) *racism*
Rathaus (n) -häuser *town hall*
Ratschlag (m) -schläge *advice*
rauchen *to smoke*
Raum (m) **Räume** *room*
raus *out*
reagieren *to react*
recherchieren *to research*
Rechnung (f) -en *bill*
Recht (n) *right*
recht haben *to be right*
rechtzeitig *on time*
recyceln *to recycle*
reden *to talk*
Redewendung (f) -en *expression*
reduzieren *to reduce*
Referat (n) -e *presentation*
Regal (n) -e *shelf*
Regel (f) -n *rule*
regelmäßig *regularly*
regeln *to regulate*
Regenwald (m) -wälder *rainforest*
Regierung (f) -en *government*
regnen *to rain*
regnerisch *rainy*
reiben *to rub*
reichen *to be enough; to pass*
Reichtum (m) -tümer *wealth*
reif *mature*
reifen *to mature*
Reihe (f) -n *row*
reisen *to travel*
reizen *to attract*
rennen *to run*
Rente (f) -n *retirement*
retten *to rescue*
Rezession (f) -en *recession*
richtig *right; proper*
Richtung (f) -en *direction*
riechen *to smell*
riesig *huge*
Risiko (n) **Risiken** *risk*
Rolle (f) -n *role*
Rollenvorbild (n) -er *role model*
Roman (m) -e *novel*
Rückruf (m) -e *call back*
Ruf (m) -e *reputation*
rufen *to call*
Ruhe (f) *peace*
ruhig *quiet*

Sache (f) -n *thing*
sammeln *to collect*
Sammelunterkunft (f) -künfte *communal accommodation*
Sandkasten (m) – *sandbox*
satt *well fed*
Satz (m) Sätze *sentence*
sauber *clean*
saubermachen *to clean*
sauer *cross*
schaden *to damage*
schaffen *to manage*
Schalter (m) – *counter; switch*
Schande (f) *disgrace*
schätzen *to estimate; to value*
schauen *to look*
Schaufenster (n) – *shop window*
Schauspieler (m) – *actor*
Scheck (m) -s *cheque*
Scheibe (f) -n *slice*
Schein (m) -e *banknote*
scheinbar *apparently*
scheinen *to appear*
schenken *to give*
schicken *to send*
Schicksal (n) -e *fate*
schief *off-kilter*
schießen *to shoot*
Schiff (n) -e *ship*
Schild (n) -er *sign*
schildern *to portray*
Schimmel (m) – *mould*
schlafen *to sleep*
Schlafsack (m) -säcke *sleeping bag*
schlagen *to hit; to beat*
Schlagzeug (n) – *drum*
Schlange (f) -n *queue*
schließen *to close*
schließlich *after all*
Schlittschuh (m) -e *ice skate*
Schluss (m) Schlüsse *end*
schmecken *to taste*
schmelzen *to melt*
Schminke (f) -n *make-up*
schmücken *to decorate*
Schmuckstück (n) -e *piece of jewellery*
schmutzig *dirty*
Schnee (m) *snow*
schneien *to snow*
schön *lovely*
schonen *to protect*
Schranke (f) -n *barrier*
Schreck (m) -e *fright*
schrecklich *dreadful*
schreiben *to write*
Schreibtisch (m) -e *desk*
schreien *to scream*
Schritt (m) -e *step*
schubsen *to push*
Schulabschluss (m) -schlüsse *high school certificate*
Schuld (f) – *fault*
Schuldruck (m) – *school pressure*
Schule (f) -n *school*
Schulgebühren, pl. *school fees*
Schulgelände (n) – *school grounds*
schütteln *to shake*
Schutz (m) *protection*
schützen *to protect*
schwänzen *to skip school*
schwärmen für *to be crazy about*
schweigen *to keep silent*
schwer *difficult; heavy*
schwerfallen *to be difficult*
schwierig *difficult*
schwitzen *to sweat*
schwül *humid*
Seefahrer (m) – *sailor*
Sehenswürdigkeiten, pl. *sights*
(sich) sehnen *to long*
Sehnsucht (f) -süchte *longing*
seitdem *since then*
selbstbewusst *self-confident*
selbstgemacht *home-made*
selbstständig *independent*
Selbstständigkeit (f) *independence*
Sendung (f) -en *programme*
senken *to lower*
seufzen *to sigh*
sichtbar *visible*
Sinn (m) -e *sense*
sinnlos *pointless*
sinnvoll *sensible; sensibly*
Sitz (m) -e *headquarters*
Sklave (m) -n *slave*
SMS (f) – *text message*
sobald *as soon as*
sofort *immediately*
sogenannt *so-called*
Sohn (m) Söhne *son*
Sonne (m) -n *sun*
sonnig *sunny*
Sorge (f) -n *worry*
sorgen *to provide*
sowieso *anyway*
spannend *exciting*
Spannung (f) -en *tension*
sparen *to save*
sparsam *thrifty*
Spaß (m) *fun*
spät *late*
später *later*
Spaziergang (m) -gänge *walk*
speichern *to save (information)*
Spiegel (m) – *mirror*
Spiel (n) -e *game*
Spielplatz (m) -plätze *playground*
Spinne (f) -n *spider*
Sprache (f) -n *language*
sprechen *to speak*
springen *to jump*
Sprit (m) -e *fuel*
Spruchwort (n) -wörter *saying*
Spülmaschine (f) -n *dishwasher*
spüren *to feel*
Staat (m) -en *state*
Stabilität (f) *stability*
Stadt (f) Städte *town*
stammen *to originate*
Stand (m) Stände *stand*
ständig *constantly*
Standort (m) -e *location*
stark *strong*
starren *to stare*

stattfinden *to take place*
Stau (m) -s *traffic jam*
staunend *marvelling*
Steg (m) -e *jetty*
stehlen *to steal*
steigen *to rise; to increase*
Stelle (f) -n *job*
stellen *to place*
sterben *to die*
Stern (m) -e *star*
stets *always*
Stiefel (m) – *boot*
Stimme (f) -n *voice*
Stimmung (f) -en *atmosphere*
Stock (m) Stöcke *stick*
Stoff (m) -e *stuff; material*
Stofftasche (f) -n *cloth bag*
stolz *proud*
stören *to disturb*
Strand (m) Strände *beach*
streben *to strive*
Streit (m) -e *quarrel*
(sich) streiten *to fight*
streng *strict*
Stress (m) -e *stress*
Strom (m) *electricity*
strömen *to stream*
Studiengang (m) -gänge *course of studies*
studieren *to study*
Studium (n) Studien *studies*
Stunde (f) -n *hour; class*
Stundenlohn (n) -löhne *hourly pay*
Stundenplan (m) -pläne *timetable*
Stürmer (m) – *forward; striker*
Suche (f) -n *search*
suchen *to look for*
Sucht (f) Süchte *addiction*
süß *sweet*

Tageslicht (n) *daylight*
täglich *daily*
tanzen *to dance*
Taschengeld (n) -er *pocket money*
tätig *active*
Tätigkeit (f) -en *work*
Tätowierung (f) -en *tattoo*
Tatsache (f) -n *fact*
tatsächlich *in fact*
Technik (f) -en *technology*
teilen *to share*
Teilnahme (f) -n *participation*
teilnehmen *to participate*
Teilnehmer (m) – *participant*
Teller (m) – *plate*
Termin (m) -e *appointment*
Terror (m) *terror*
teuer *expensive*
Theke (f) -n *counter*
Thema (n) Themen *topic*
Therapie (f) -n *therapy*
tief *deep; deeply*
Tipp (m) -s *tip*
Tochter (f) Töchter *daughter*
Tod (m) -e *death*
tolerieren *to tolerate*
Tor (n) -e *goal*
tot *dead*
Tourist (m) -en *tourist*
Tracht (f) -en *traditional costume*
tragen *to wear; to carry*
Träne (f) -n *tear*
(sich) trauen *to trust (oneself)*
Traum (m) Träume *dream*
träumen *to dream*
traurig *sad*
(sich) treffen *to meet*
Trinkgeld (n) -er *tip*
Tropen, pl. *tropics*
Trophäe (f) -n *trophy*
trotzdem *nevertheless*
tüchtig *industrious*
tun *to do*
Tür (f) -en *door*
Tüte (f) -n *bag*

üben *to practise*
überall *everywhere*
übereinstimmen *to agree*
Überflutung (f) -en *flood*
überfordert *overwhelmed*
Überforderung (f) -en *overload*
Übergang (m) -gänge *crossing*
Übergangsjahr (n) -jahre *Transition Year*
überhaupt *at all*
überleben *to survive*
überlegen *to consider*
Übernachtung (f) -en *overnight stay*
überqueren *to cross (road)*
Überraschung (f) -en *surprise*
Überschwemmung (f) -en *flood*
übersetzen *to translate*
Übersetzung (f) -en *translation*
überstehen *to get through*
übertreffen *to outweigh*
übertreiben *to exaggerate*
überzeugen *to convince*
Übung (f) -en *practice; exercise*
umarmen *to hug*
(sich) umdrehen *to turn around*
Umfrage (f) -n *questionnaire*
Umgang (m) -gänge *use; handling*
Umgangssprache (f) -n *colloquial language*
Umgebung (f) -en *surroundings*
umrechnen *to convert*
umschauen *to look around*
umsteigen *to switch to*
Umwelt (f) *environment*
Umweltsünder (m) – *environmental offender*
umziehen *to move house*
Umzug (m) -züge *parade*
undenkbar *unthinkable*
Unfall (m) -fälle *accident*
ungerecht *unfair*
Unglück (n) -e *misfortune*
unglücklich *unhappy*
unheimlich *incredible; uncanny*
Universität (f) -en *university*
unordentlich *untidy*
unsicher *uncertain*
Unsinn (m) – *nonsense*
unterbrechen *to interrupt*

(sich) unterhalten *to talk*
unterhaltsam *entertaining*
Unterhaltung (f) -en *entertainment*
unternehmen *to do*
Unternehmen (n) – *business venture*
Unterricht (m) – *lesson*
unterrichten *to teach*
Unterschied (m) -e *difference*
unterschreiben *to sign*
Unterschrift (f) -en *signature*
unterstützen *to support*
Unterstützung (f) -en *support*
unterwegs *out and about*
Unwetter (n) – *storm*
unzufrieden *dissatisfied*
Urlaub (m) -e *holiday*

vegan *vegan*
(sich) verabschieden *to say goodbye*
(sich) verändern *to change*
veranstalten *to organise*
Veranstalter (m) – *organiser*
verantwortlich *responsible*
Verantwortung (f) -en *responsibility*
verbessern *to improve*
verbieten *to forbid*
verbinden *to connect*
Verbot (n) -e *ban*
verbrauchen *to expend*
(sich) verbreiten *to spread*
Verbreitung (f) -en *spread*
verbringen *to spend time*
verdammen *to condemn*
verdienen *to earn*
Verein (m) -e *club*
Verfügung (f) -en *disposal*
Vergangenheit (f) -en *past*
vergeben *to forgive*
vergessen *to forget*
vergleichbar *comparable*
verhaften *to arrest*
Verhalten (n) – *behaviour*
Verhältnis (n) -se *relationship*
verhindern *to prevent*
verjagen *to chase away*
Verkauf (m) -käufe *sale*
(sich) verkleiden *to dress up*
Verkehrsmittel (n) – *transport*
verknüpfen *to link*
verlangen *to demand*
verlassen *to leave*
(sich) verlaufen *to lose one's way*
verletzen *to injure*
verletzlich *vulnerable*
verlieren *to lose*
vermissen *to miss*
vermisst *missing*
vermitteln *to liaise*
vernachlässigen *to neglect*
Verpackung (f) -en *packaging*
verpassen *to miss (something)*
verpesten *to poison*
verrückt *crazy*
(sich) versammeln *to gather*
verschieden *different*
Verschmutzung (f) -en *pollution*
verschwinden *to disappear*
Versehen (n) – *by accident*
versenden *to send*
verseuchen *to contaminate*
Verseuchung (f) -en *contamination*
versichern *to assure*
Versicherung (f) -en *insurance*
versorgen *to provide*
versprechen *to promise*
verständnisvoll *understanding*
verstärkern *to strengthen*
(sich) verstecken *to hide (oneself)*
verstehen *to understand*
(sich) verstehen *to get on*
versuchen *to try*
verteilen *to distribute*
vertiefen *to deepen*
Vertrag (m) -träge *contract*
vertrauen *to trust*
Vertrauen (n) *trust*
Vertreter (m) – *representative*
verursachen *to cause*
verwandeln *to transform*
Verwandte (m/f) -n *relative*
verweigern *to refuse*
Verweis (m) -e *official warning*
verwenden *to use*
verwirklichen *to achieve*
verwirrt *confused*
Verwirrung (f) -en *confusion*
verwöhnen *to spoil*
verwöhnt *spoiled*
verzichten auf *to do without*
verzichten *to abstain*
verzweifeln *to despair*
verzweifelt *despairing*
Vielfalt (f) – *variety*
Viertel (n) – *quarter*
Visum (n) Visa *visa*
Vokabeln, pl. *vocabulary*
volljährig *of legal age*
vorbei *over*
(sich) vorbereiten *to prepare oneself*
Vorbereitung (f) -en *preparation*
vorgestern *day before yesterday*
vorhaben *to intend*
vorhanden *available*
vorher *earlier*
vorkommen *to occur*
vorlesen *to read out*
vorn *in front*
vorschlagen *to suggest*
vorsichtig *careful; carefully*
(sich) vorstellen *to imagine*
Vorstellungsgespräch (n) -e *interview*
Vorteil (m) -e *advantage*
vorteilhaft *advantageous*
Vortrag (m) -träge *lecture; talk*
vorwärts *forwards*

wachsend *growing*
wagen *to dare*
Wahl (f) -en *choice*
wählen *to choose*
wahr *true*

während *during*
Wald (m) Wälder *wood*
Waldbrand (m) -brände *forest fire*
Waldsterben (n) *forest decline*
Wand (f) Wände *wall*
Wandel (m) *change*
Wange (f) -n *cheek*
Wärmedämmung (f) -en *insulation*
warten *to wait*
Wechsel (m) – *change*
wecken *to wake*
Wecker (m) – *alarm clock*
Weg (m) -e *way; path*
wegspülen *to wash away*
wegwerfen *to throw away*
wegziehen *to move away*
wehtun *to hurt*
weinen *to cry*
Weinlese (f) -n *grape harvest*
weiterbilden *to update skills*
weitergehen *to continue walking*
weitermachen *to continue*
Welle (f) -n *wave*
Welt (f) -en *world*
wenig *less*
Werbebotschaft (f) -en *advertising message*
Werbeprospekt (m) -e *advertising brochure*
Werbungsbranche (f) -n *advertising industry*
werfen *to throw*
Wert (m) -e *value*
wertvoll *valuable*
Wesentliche (n) *essentials*
Westler (m) – *westerner*
Wettbewerb (m) -e *competition*
Wetter (n) – *weather*
wichtig *important*
wieder *again*
wiederholen *to repeat*
wiederverwenden *to reuse*
wiederverwertbar *reuseable*
Willen (m) – *will*
willkommen heißen *to welcome*
wirken *to act*
wirklich *really*
Wirklichkeit (f) -en *reality*
Wirtschaft (f) -en *economy*
wissen *to know*
Wissen (n) *knowledge*
Wissenschaft (f) -en *science*
Woche (f) -n *week*
Wochenende (n) -n *weekend*
wöchentlich *weekly*
wohl *well*
wohnen *to live*
Wohngemeinschaft (f) -en *flat sharing*
Wohnung (f) -en *apartment*
Wort (n) -e *word*
Wortstellung (f) -en *word order*
wunderschön *beautiful*
Wunsch (m) Wünsche *wish*
(sich) wünschen *to wish*
Wurst (f) Würste *sausage*
Wut (f) *rage*
wütend *furious*

Z

Zahl (f) -en *number*
zählen *to count*
Zahn (m) Zähne *tooth*
zeigen *to show*
Zeit (f) -en *time*
zeitgemäß *timely*
Zeitschrift (f) -en *magazine*
zelten *to camp*
Zerrbild (n) -er *caricature*
zerreißen *to rip apart*
Zettel (m) – *note*
Zeugnis (n) -se *report card*
Ziel (n) -e *goal*
Zielgruppe (f) -n *target group*
Zimmer (n) – *room*
zittern *to shiver*
zocken *to gamble*
Zollbeamte (m/f) -n *customs official*
zubereiten *to prepare*
zuerst *at first*
zufrieden *satisfied*
Zugang (m) -gänge *access*
zugeben *to admit*
Zuhause (n) *home*
Zukunft (f) *future*
zumindest *at least*
Zunahme (f) -n *increase*
zunehmen *to increase; to put on weight*
zurück *back*
zurückkehren *to return*
zusammen *together*
Zusammenfassung (f) -en *summary*
Zusatz (m) -sätze *supplement*
zusätzlich *additional*
Zuschauer (m) – *onlooker*
Zutat (f) -en *ingredient*
zuverlässig *reliable*
Zweck (m) -e *purpose*
Zweifel (m) – *doubt*
zwingen *to force*
zwischen *between*
zwischendurch *occasional*

Test Tracker

There are 28 tests in ***Komplett*** – one Ordinary Level and one Higher Level test at the end of each chapter.

When you have completed a test, enter your total mark (out of 50) on this page.

As you proceed through the tests, draw the graph on the next page. This will help you to monitor your progress.

Viel Glück!

	Mark out of 50	
	OL	**HL**
Kapitel 01: Meine Familie und ich		
Kapitel 02: Mein Wohnort		
Kapitel 03: In meiner Freizeit		
Kapitel 04: Schule		
Kapitel 05: Sprachenlernen		
Kapitel 06: Im Ausland		
Kapitel 07: Zukunftspläne		
Kapitel 08: Feiern und Feste		
Kapitel 09: Die große Arbeitswelt		
Kapitel 10: Jugendthemen		
Kapitel 11: Die großen Ansprüche unserer Zeit		
Kapitel 12: Die Medien		
Kapitel 13: Die Gesundheit		
Kapitel 14: Umwelt		
Total mark		

Ergebnisse der Selbstbewertungen

There are 28 tests in ***Komplett*** – two at the end of each chapter.

When you have completed a test, enter your total mark (out of 50) on this page. If you try both the Ordinary and Higher Level tests, you can use a different colour for each result.

As you proceed through the tests, draw the graph. This will help you to monitor your progress.

Viel Glück!

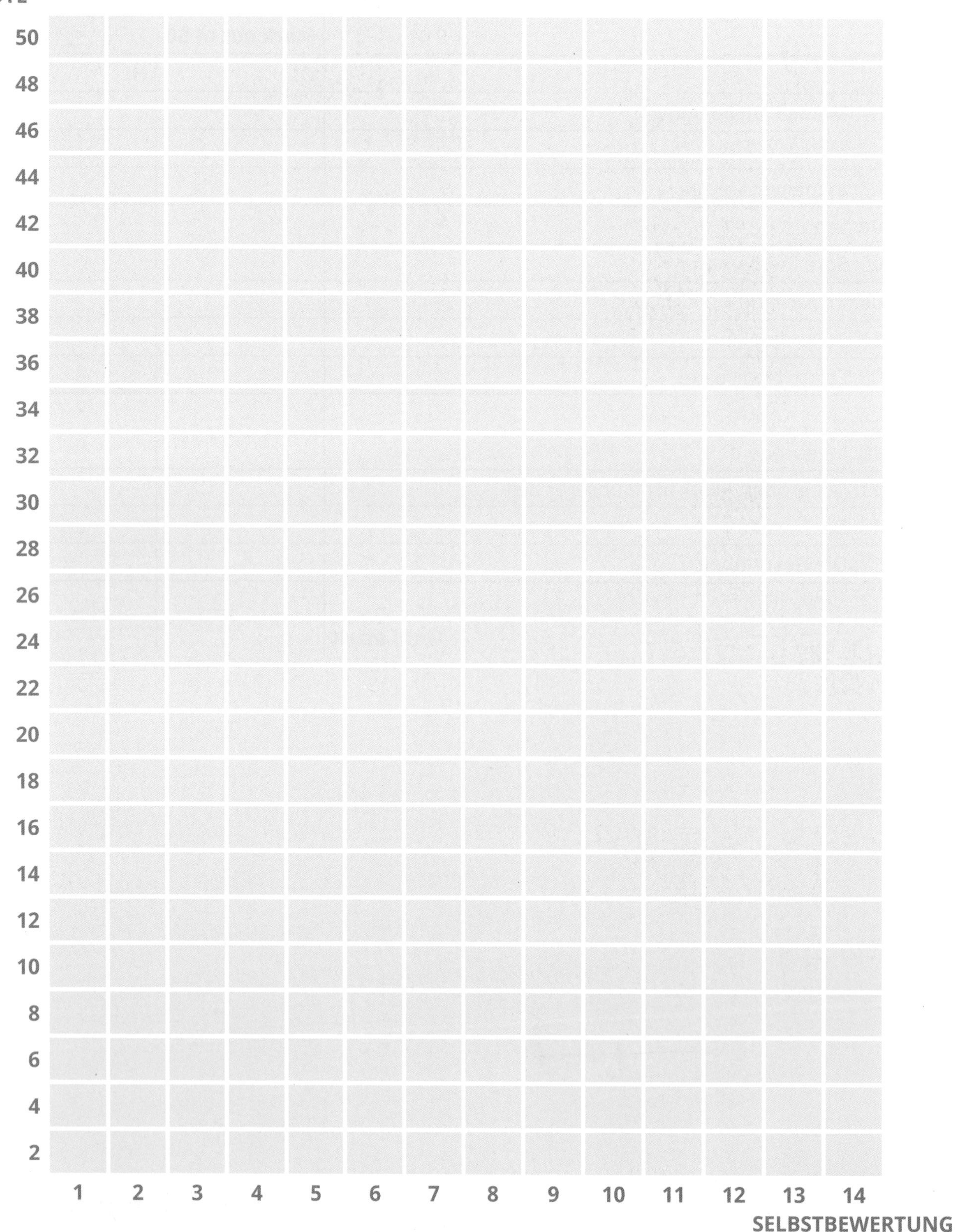